PANZERS EAST AND WEST

PANZERS EAST AND WEST

THE GERMAN 10TH SS PANZER DIVISION FROM THE EASTERN FRONT TO NORMANDY

Dieter Stenger

STACKPOLE
BOOKS

GUILFORD, CT

Published by Stackpole Books
An imprint of Globe Pequot

Distributed by NATIONAL BOOK NETWORK
800-462-6420

British Library Cataloguing in Publication Information available
Library of Congress Cataloging-in-Publication Data available

ISBN 978-0-8117-1627-7 (hardcover)
ISBN 978-0-8117-6590-9 (e-book)

∞™ The paper used in this publication meets the minimum requirements of American National Standard for Information Sciences—Permanence of Paper for Printed Library Materials, ANSI/NISO Z39.48-1992.

Printed in the United States of America

Contents

Foreword

THE *SCHUTZSTAFFEL* (SS) was the most bizarre political and military organization in German history. During the period of the Third Reich it was a state-within-a-state, and its military arm, the *Waffen-SS*, was an army-within-an-army. The *Waffen-SS* started out as the Nazi Party's armed and uniformed paramilitary force. As that force evolved from Hitler's bodyguard detachment, the *Wehrmacht* derisively called the *Waffen-SS Asphaltsoldaten* (Asphalt Soldiers), in reference to the fact that in their early years they spent most of their time performing ceremonial duties on the parade ground square. As the *Waffen-SS* grew into divisional-sized units, it theoretically remained completely separate from the *Wehrmacht*, a rival army. From 1939 on it came increasingly under the operational control of the German Army (*Heer*) for combat operations; yet, it was administratively independent. Personnel management, assignments, officer commissions, and promotions were controlled ultimately by Heinrich Himmler, the *Reichsführer-SS*. The *Wehrmacht*, on the other hand, had to equip, transport, supply, and to a certain extent train the *Waffen-SS*. Thus the *Waffen-SS* evolved into an army-within-an-army. The lines between the two organizations were never quite clearly drawn, and the friction between the two lasted throughout the war, and well beyond.

In May 1945, as the Germans were surrounded by the ruins of their devastated country, they faced history's harsh judgment for the brutal and barbaric policies and actions of the Third Reich. At the time, many Germans claimed to the Allied occupation authorities that they had known nothing about the attempted extermination of the Jews, or the widespread enslavement and mass murder of civilians in Poland and Russia. As early as the Nuremberg Trials, starting in November 1945, a sharp line of distinction was drawn between the "evil SS," the perpetrators of those crimes, and the "honorable Wehrmacht." Along with twenty-two top-ranking individuals of the Third Reich, six of its organizations were tried before the International Military Tribunal. Former *Wehrmacht* officers, led by Field Marshal Erich von Manstein, successfully argued for the acquittal of the German General Staff and the *Wehrmacht* High Command. And although the *Waffen-SS* was on trial as a component of the larger SS, former *Waffen-SS* officers led by *SS-Oberstgruppenführer* Paul Hausser pursued the argument that the Asphalt Soldiers had been "Soldiers like any other." Nonetheless, the SS including the *Waffen-SS* was convicted of being a criminal organization, and the SS became the "Alibi of the Nation."

Without a strong postwar belief in the idea of the "clean Wehrmacht," Germany and the NATO allies just might never have been able to establish the *Bundeswehr* in 1955. But only the Nuremberg Trials seemed to draw a sharp line between the *Wehrmacht* and the *Waffen-SS*. The reality was somewhat more nuanced, as reality always is. The "Good Germans vs. Evil Nazis" dichotomy held up quite well for some twenty years, until the follow-on German generation in the mid-1960s started questioning their parents' accounts of life during the war. And although the immediate postwar rationalization continued to hold up after a fashion for another twenty years, it came increasingly under challenge. The tipping point finally came in 1985 when German president Richard von Weizsäcker, himself a former *Wehrmacht* officer, delivered a speech to the *Bundestag* proclaiming that 8 May 1945 had been the day of Germany's liberation, rather than the date of its surrender and occupation. From that point on, all the old social and political taboos about the Third Reich period started to crumble, and critical enquiry expanded. In 1996 Daniel Goldhagen's controversial book, *Hitler's Willing Executioners: Ordinary Germans and the Holocaust*, seriously challenged the assertion that most Germans had not known about the Holocaust. Between 2001 and 2004 the *Wehrmachtsausstellung* traveling exhibition in Germany examined the German military's complicity in the crimes of the Third Reich, and helped pretty well demolish the myth of the "clean Wehrmacht."

The assessment of World War II Germany is a process that still continues more than seventy years after the Third Reich's final surrender. Despite all of the Nazi obsession with "racial purity," more than half of the eventual 900,000 troops who served in the *Waffen-SS* over the six-year period of war came from outside the original borders of pre-1939 Germany, and a great many were not even remotely ethnic Germans. Among the total of forty-two *Waffen-SS* divisions raised during the war, the 14th Waffen Grenadier Division of the SS consisted largely of Ukrainians; the 20th Waffen Grenadier Division consisted of Estonians; the 21st Waffen Mountain Division consisted of Albanian Muslims; the 29th Waffen Grenadier Division consisted of Italians; and the 30th Waffen Grenadier Division consisted of Belarussians. Even so, having been a member of the *Waffen-SS* was enough of a stigma in the postwar era that many Germans concealed their past membership. Nobel Prize–winning author Günter Grass, who built his literary reputation as a rather smug moral critic of the Third Reich, concealed his service in the *Waffen-SS* for more than sixty years. Trained as a tank gunner in 1944, he then served with the 10th SS Panzer Division (the subject of this book) until it surrendered to American forces at Marienbad in 1945.

Numerous *Wehrmacht* officers questioned the professional competence of their *Waffen-SS* counterparts. Many of the relatively apolitical regular officers remained skeptical of the large numbers of ideologically strident officers within the *Waffen-SS*, although the *Wehrmacht* itself also had no shortage of such. Many of the higher-numbered *Waffen-SS* divisions established late in the war were little more than armed mobs, but most of the lower-numbered and older Panzer and *Panzergrenadier Waffen-SS* divisions acquired justified reputations as skillful and tenacious combatants, every bit the equals of their *Wehrmacht* counterparts. A fair number of *Wehrmacht* officers were cross-posted to *Waffen-SS* units at various times, and a small handful of very senior *Waffen-SS* commanders, such as Hausser, held major *Wehrmacht* commands. Some *Waffen-SS* officers, including Hausser and *SS-Obergruppenführer* Wilhelm Bittrich, emerged from the war with reputations as generally competent and honorable officers. Others are remembered today as incompetent bunglers, whose only claim to senior-level command was their political connections and reliability. Among the most prominent of that group was *SS-Oberstgruppenführer* Josef 'Sepp" Dietrich, whose main qualification for senior command was the fact that in the earliest days of the Nazi Party he had been Hitler's bodyguard and chauffeur. Other *Waffen-SS* officers are remembered today as some of the worst butchers of the war, including *SS-Standartenführer* Joachim Pieper, whose troops committed the Malmedy Massacre; *SS-Gruppenführer* Jürgen Stroop, who destroyed the Warsaw Ghetto in 1943; and *SS-Obergruppenführer* Erich von dem Bach-Zelewski, who crushed the Warsaw Rising and leveled the entire city in 1944.

To this day, then, the SS remains something of an enigma, and the *Waffen-SS* remains an enigma within that enigma. Much has been written about the *Waffen-SS*, but relatively few operational histories of specific *Waffen-SS* units have appeared in English. The key questions include: How were they organized? How were they equipped? When and where did they fight? How did they fight? How were they commanded and led? How did they coordinate with the *Wehrmacht*? And very importantly, how did their peculiar political and ideological linkages with the Nazi Party affect any of the foregoing? In the case of the 10th SS Panzer Division, which bore the honorific title of "Frundsberg," Dieter Stenger addresses those very questions. Combining information from archival records with selected anecdotal evidence from some of the division's veterans, Stenger weaves together an impressive and richly detailed account. More than seventy years on, the operational military history of World War II is hardly a closed book. This account offers another page.

David T. Zabecki
Freiburg, Germany
January 2016

Acknowledgments

I RECEIVED A GREAT deal of support in researching this book. Without the assistance and encouragement of the people listed below, the book would never have been written. I extend my most sincere appreciation and gratitude to each of them. Any errors, omissions, faulty conclusions, however, are solely my own.

Individuals:

David T. Zabecki
Maik Sieberhagen
Alfred M. Beck
Prof. Dr. Bernd Wegner
Bernhardt Westerhoff
Willi Weber
Klaus Ewald
Werner Pietzka
Max Gerhard (Fransky)
Alexander Grenda
Otto Jacob
Hubert Meyer

Richard Hedrick
Kenneth L. Smith-Christmas
Cornelius Abelsma
Charles D. Melson
Dr. Timothy Mulligan
Don Troiani
Gunnery Sergeant Keith Alexander, USMC, Ret.
Colonel Douglas E. Nash, US Army, Ret.
Colonel Grant A. Knight, US Army, Ret.
Colonel Michael D. Krause, US Army, Ret.
Colonel Jon T. Hoffman, USMC, Ret.

Introduction

THIS BOOK IS A combat chronology of the 10th SS Panzer Division "Frundsberg" that blends the anecdotal accounts of its members with the recorded tactical and operational history of an SS panzer division continuously committed to battle from March 1944 until the division's final battles around May 1945. From its inception on paper in December 1942 until the bitter end on the last day of the war, the 10th SS Panzer Division "Frundsberg" fought the war almost without pause but generally without its full complement of personnel or equipment at any given time, with the exception of a brief period before and after the Ardennes Offensive. Though it never achieved great notoriety, the 10th SS Panzer Division participated in almost every key battle of the period, in both the East and West, influencing the outcome of the war throughout its brief existence.

This book's primary purpose is to fill a gap in the analysis of SS panzer divisions. Although several contemporary German-language books are available, this is the first book in English solely devoted to the 10th SS Panzer Division. *Panzers East and West* highlights the division's tactical skill and success throughout its operational history, but also analyzes its defeats on the battlefield. The book also incorporates a wealth of information concerning neighboring *Waffen-SS* and other supporting units, such as the 506th Heavy Panzer Battalion, which supported the division and helped to achieve German victory during the tank battle at Hill 112 near Caen. The major battles fought by the Frundsberg Division include Buczacz, during the

relief of the First Panzer Army in the east, Caen and Hill 112, Falaise, Arnhem, Nijmegen, Linnich in the Roer, the Ardennes, Operation Northwind, and finally Spremberg.

This book relies predominantly on primary sources, such as the official divisional records or war diaries and SS personnel records, located at the National Archives at College Park, Maryland. These records are contained in the Berlin Document Collection, Record Group 242. The war diaries become rather sparse after the Normandy Invasion, when the effort associated with documenting operational unit activity and reporting it back to Berlin became more difficult, but they are augmented by unpublished unit war diaries obtained from German veterans and unit associations, as well as published and unpublished memoirs of veterans, postwar eyewitness or anecdotal veteran accounts published in the division's association newsletters, and correspondence between veterans and the author in response to questionnaires. Though anecdotal accounts vary from one person to another, they are all part of the historical record, and they were included to preserve the experiences of as many individuals as possible. Significant disparities, mistakes that over the years have taken on reality, and far-fetched propaganda are mentioned briefly within the text and further diagnosed in the endnotes.

The primary sources were blended with secondary contemporary histories in both German and English. Also considered were a wide range of both primary and secondary Allied sources that offer a far greater perspective on theater strategy and fighting, although they were by no means used as part of in-depth investigations to challenge or confirm German reports. Primary Allied anecdotal sources were used as well with the understanding they presented the identical dilemma as the German examples. Although the book addresses topics such as SS ideology, which was documented as a concern by the commanding general in 1943 during the organization and training of the division, a comprehensive analysis of SS ideologies and their implementation related to all the divisions falls outside the scope of this work. Moreover, this book does not defend or condone the SS and its ideologies. While this book presents documented operational and combat achievements by individuals who may or may not have believed in the Nazi regime or an SS ideology, the author does not support or endorse Nazism.

The Frundsberg Division officially organized in December 1942 as a direct result of the threat of landings by Allied forces somewhere in Western Europe. By the end of 1943, the division numbered approximately 20,000 men and incorporated a cadre consisting of German commissioned and noncommissioned officers who made up the heart and soul of the division. Their extensive operational experience and battlefield prowess transformed the entire division into an elite fighting formation. SS men as well as service members from the Army, *Luftwaffe*, and *Kriegsmarine* consistently transferred in and out of the division until it reached full strength. The majority of the conscripted rank and file came from outside the German borders and were not considered ethnic Germans. The division trained in 1943 extensively throughout France for the purpose of repelling the anticipated Allied air and sea landings. The men prepared both physically and mentally for combat, focusing on strengthening morale and building esprit de corps, the foundation to combat effectiveness and survival.

In the first half of 1944, the 10th SS Panzer Division gained confidence after its combat debut on the Eastern Front during the successful relief-operation of the encircled First Panzer Army at Buczacz. In the East, the men of the division became well familiarized with the term "outnumbered [by the enemy] in great proportions." During the assault against Buczacz, the Germans successfully bypassed the Soviet first and second echelon defensive belts, usually manned by rifle regiments. German tanks directly struck antitank lines. Unprotected by infantry, the concentration of Soviet antitank guns easily succumbed to German spotters calling fire missions for self-propelled artillery and divebombers. Notable were the German uses of combined arms tactics reminiscent of early-war German operations, which relied heavily on close air support. The use of Stuka divebombers in April 1944, a scene of the past in other theaters, thrived on the Eastern Front.

In the West, the division lacked experience in fighting an enemy who enjoyed an unrestricted supply of materiel and complete air supremacy. By August 1944, well after the Allied breakout from Normandy and after leaving the combat area south of Caen, the weakened divisional strength became acute. From one action to another, the division suffered heavy losses without replacements and could not reassign personnel within the divisions to fill the gaps. Around Aunay-sur-Odon, the divisional operational readiness reached half its normal complement of tanks and infantry and only three-quarters of its artillery. At Barenton, only slightly more than a quarter of its tanks were available, 30 percent of the infantry, and half its artillery. According to the war diary of OB West, the 10th SS Panzer Division left the Falaise pocket with only "weak elements on foot, without tanks and artillery." The total strength of the division numbered to 3,000 men.

In Holland, the artillery regiment of the 10th SS assumed the formidable task of providing support across a front that exceeded 20 kilometers and additional fire support requirements for nearby weak Army units. To better cope with and meet the requirements, the commander of the artillery regiment, *SS-Obersturmbannführer* Hans-Georg Sonnenstuhl, strung together a seamless chain of artillery-blocking fire segments between the areas west of Arnhem and the Waal River at Nijmegen. Fire missions were easily called using field phones or radios, based on the number or name of the segment. Indeed, the entire regiment could place fire quickly on any designated segment. Sonnenstuhl's successful counter-battery tactics and the combined fire of several missions, from various German guns totaling up to 260 projectiles per mission, destroyed Allied gun positions and prevented the speedy collapse of the German lines in many areas. After the front lines in Holland stabilized and the fighting abated, the division relocated in November 1944 to Germany.

Fighting on German soil throughout the fall and beginning of winter in 1944, the 10th SS Panzer Division sustained heavy casualties during the battle for the Roer River, on either side of Linnich. When the division reached its lowest level of men and materiel but higher orders committed it to battle, their combat capability remained questionable without the possibility for reinforcement. Nevertheless, the division fought both offensively and defensively for twenty-two days in the Roer River area. The continued use and coordination of combined artillery, from a variety of units, enabled the division to continue to resist Allied pressure.

On 6 December 1944, amidst refitting, the division relocated yet again into the area of Blatzheim-Kerpen-Euskirchen where the division finally obtained its Panther tanks from Grafenwöhr, Germany, which formed the 1st Battalion of the tank regiment. While serving as a reserve component during the failed Ardennes counteroffensive, the division received orders in January 1945 for a new offensive, also known as Northwind, in the Alsace. Several attacks failed in the face of American defensive fire until February when the division relocated back to the east around Stettin. The Germans desperately tried to follow their strategy of fighting a two-front war and redeploying units from one hotspot to another.

Participating in Operation Solstice in February 1945, the division fought as part of the Eleventh SS Panzer Army. Heavy German losses forced the cancellation of the operation within only a few days, while the larger Soviet offensive to capture Berlin began on 16 March 1945 and pushed the division to the Oder River during a fighting withdrawal and into the areas west of Stettin. On 25 March 1945 the divisional strength totaled 14,967 men along with a number of heavy weapons. Forming an operational reserve the division redeployed to the area east of Görlitz and finally south of Lauban. Lacking fuel, only the combat portions of the division reached Spremberg, while the rear-echelon troops remained stuck in Bautzen. During heavy defensive fighting the division was encircled at Spremberg on 20 April but managed to break out. After its final engagements at Moritzburg on 3 May 1945, the remainder of the division marched toward Teplitz-Schönau until the final day of the war.

This book should help readers of military history to gain a better appreciation of how the *Waffen-SS* operated in the field. At the same time, the exploits of career SS soldiers and eyewitness accounts from all ranks show why the *Waffen-SS* earned a reputation for combat competence. Notwithstanding the numerical superiority of Allied materiel and men, Allied strategy and individual Allied soldiers ultimately defeated possibly the most effective combat organization of the twentieth century. This book is dedicated to the veterans of World War II, from all nations, who served honorably for their country, but particularly for those who did not return home to their families.

Dieter Stenger
Stafford, Virginia 2016

CHAPTER 1

Organization and Training of the 10th SS Panzer Division

Dec 1942–March 1944

ON 19 DECEMBER 1942, Adolf Hitler directed the organization of two new SS divisions, the 9th and 10th *SS-Panzergrenadier* Divisions, to form a new reserve for Panzer Group West in the area of *Oberbefehlshaber* (OB) or Commander in Chief West. The directive provided a replacement for the SS Panzer Corps, consisting of the 1st, 2nd, and 3rd SS Panzer Divisions, scheduled to depart to the East in February 1943. The *Oberkommando der Wehrmacht* (OKW) or High Command of the Armed Forces ordered the expansion of the *Waffen-SS*, which brought an end to recruitment into the combat formations of the SS. But recruitment of service-eligible men to the *Waffen-SS* had been in full swing since the spring of 1942. On 5 January 1943, OKW ordered that replacements for the new divisions be allocated no later than 1 February. OKW estimated raising 27,000 men from the birth-year 1925 in the *Reichsarbeitsdienst* (RAD) or compulsory labor service, 10,000 men from *Aktion Rü 43 Tausch* or Operation Armament 43 Exchange, and 5,000 ethnic Germans or ethnic Germans living outside Germany. In the event the latter 15,000 men could not be raised, OKW advocated extracting a higher yield from the birth-year 1925, despite their desire to forgo weakening the next generation of officers and noncommissioned officers (NCOs) of the armed forces. Even so, the SS could not guarantee mustering the personnel requirements. The predictable manpower shortages required that the chief of replacements, General Friedrich Fromm, challenge members from the birth-years 1923 and 1924 to volunteer for the *Waffen-SS*. *SS-Gruppenführer* Gottlob Berger, chief of the SS Replacement Bureau, spoke personally at various RAD camps to enlist men. According to Berger, involuntary methods for enlistment were not uncommon in the Hessian region. In order to stave off shortages, OKW directed the SS to lower recruitment standards and admit men who were previously considered unacceptable. Finally, 800 men from the protective border police also became available for service in the SS. Despite a lackluster beginning with 10,000 applications by 26 January 1943, OKW remained optimistic the number of recruits would double.[1]

The 10th *SS-Panzergrenadier* Division organized alongside its sister division the 9th *SS-Panzergrenadier* Division "Hohenstaufen" on 31 December 1942. Command of the Hohenstaufen Division fell to *SS-Brigadeführer* Wilhelm "Willi" Bittrich on 15 February 1943. *SS-Standartenführer*

Lothar Debes, the first commander of the Frundsberg Division, was a well-educated Prussian officer, career soldier, veteran captain of World War I, and ardent national socialist. In May 1919, Debes resigned his commission out of opposition to the Treaty of Versailles stating, "At the time, I sacrificed my commission based on my honest conviction that soldiers should not make their services available to any regime that they themselves opposed." Simply stated, Debes was unwilling to serve as a soldier in the new Weimar Republic. Instead, Debes joined the *Nationalsozialistische Deutsche Arbeiterpartei* (NSDAP or Nazi Party) on 1 May 1930 and the SS seven years later. His longest posting in the SS was a five-year assignment at the officers' school in Braunschweig. Between 1 January 1942 and 15 June 1944, Debes received seven different assignments and by early 1943 rated as "incapacitated by war." Having sustained four injuries that included two on a single day, Debes was best suited for administrative positions. SS officers who were especially talented but unable to meet the physical requirements for combat commands were not discharged but rather retained for administrative assignments. The practice had great long-term benefits.[2]

The majority of the enlisted personnel were either conscripted or volunteered for the division. The remainder of its strength consisted of men transferred from other units. The men were both *Reichsdeutsche* or German born and *Volksdeutsche* or ethnic Germans, between the ages of seventeen to twenty years from the inflationary period. The nucleus of the division consisted of a 30 percent cadre of older, seasoned soldiers of all ranks who gained combat experience in both the East and West. The cadre knew what to expect and offered the younger men a solid foundation of knowledge that surpassed basic military soldiering. Many of the older cadres passed through the *Jungvolk*, *Hitler Jugend*, and some even through the *Sturmabteilung* (SA or Storm Troops) or the *Allgemeine SS* (General SS). In the end, the men of the division received a comprehensive military training program that was, in many cases, almost a year long. The organization of units took place in various geographic areas that both required a certain degree of soldierly adaptation and achievement and also offered specific advantages for teaching self-reliance and sustainability. The strict and very challenging training was made easier by high-quality food, supplies, and quarters. At the onset of their training, many had already experienced three years of war within Germany that required their services in various places for labor or in the air defense zones. Indeed, at the end of their training in early 1944 the war was in its fifth year. Familiar with the reality and hardship of war, the young men and experienced officers and NCOs forged the steel mettle of the division.[3]

In January 1943, OKW emphasized to OB West the need to accelerate the organization and training of the 9th and 10th SS Divisions until May. After the transfer of three SS divisions to the East, German capabilities along the Atlantic coast were reduced to nothing more than operational security, altogether insufficient for large-scale defensive operations. Moreover, the prospects of imminent Allied landings along the Atlantic coast were taken very seriously and expected at any given time, which, for example, resulted in the planned countermeasure code-named Operation Gisela.[4]

The major organization, training, and replacement units were established at the following locations:

10th SS-*Panzergrenadier* Battalion	Brünn
SS Armored Half-Track Battalion	Keinsschlag/ Böhmen
1st SS Tank Destroyer Battalion	Rastenburg
1st SS Infantry Support Artillery	Breslau/Lissa
SS Antiaircraft Regiment	München
SS Signals Replacement Regiment	Nürnberg
SS Artillery Replacement Regiment	Prague
SS Tank Battalion	Bitsch/(Elsass)
SS Assault Gun (SP) Artillery	Heidelager
SS Pioneer Replacement Battalion	Dresden
7th SS Mountain Battalion	Werschatz[5]

A detachment for organizing the division began at Buchenwald in Weimar. *SS-Obersturmführer* (Dr.) H. Kube was assigned as adjutant to the infant SS Panzer Organizing Battalion. Their task was to register all the motorized vehicles for the division. The first commander of the 10th SS Panzer Organizing Battalion was Ullrich Besch, who later became the divisional engineer. After the *Waffen-Werkstattkompanie* or Weapons Repair Company was formed as the 4th Company, the battalion was renamed officially as "*Instandsetzungsabteilung* 10." The battalion consisted of four companies and one replacement troop. The staff and one company of the 10th Organizing Battalion deployed in the general vicinity of the divisional staff, whereas the remaining companies and replacement troop were located in the rear areas.[6]

The 10th SS Panzer Regiment began organizing on the last day of the year in 1942. The training of the regiment took place at the training facility near Bitsch in the Elsass (Alsace), France. Among eight companies in the area, the 6th Company, 10th SS Panzer Regiment quartered to the west in Rohrbach. The nuclei of the 6th Company came from the Panzer Replacement Battalion Weimar that included antitank hunters or tank destroyers, members from the 5th SS Panzer Division, and the other four older and more experienced divisions. Members arriving later were predominately NCOs from the SS *Polizei* Division or SS Police Division.[7]

The company commander of the 6th Company, 10th SS Panzer Regiment, *SS-Obersturmführer* Leo Franke, arrived at Bitsch in February 1943 to join other officers and NCOs to organize the company. At thirty-one years of age, Franke brought a wealth of experience to the division. As an enlisted man, he served four years in the *Reichsheer* and latter *Wehrmacht* (September 1933–October 1937) and two years with the *Polizei*. On 12 October 1939, Franke entered an SS policc unit and transferred to the *Waffen-SS* on 28 March 1940. Franke enrolled in the third wartime class at the SS officer candidates' schools at Bad Tölz and was nominated as an officer candidate. By 5 July 1940, Franke had joined the 14th SS Antitank Company in the 2nd Regiment "Der Führer" of the 2nd SS Panzer Division. In February 1941, Franke's reviewing officer noted gaps in his tactical knowledge but considered him honest, clean cut, disciplined, a man who loved organization, and considered him perfectly suited as an instructor with an excellent command voice. Franke participated in the campaign in southeast France and, on 21 June 1941, headed eastward against Soviet Russia during Operation Barbarossa.

Before arriving at Bitsch, Franke earned the Iron Cross 1st and 2nd Class, the Infantry Assault Badge, the War Merit Cross 2nd Class, and the Wound Badge in Black.[8]

The rank and file that consisted of ethnic Germans came from a variety of occupied nations and countries friendly to Germany, including Poland, Rumania, and Czechoslovakia, to name only a few. Alexander Grenda, a member of the enlisted ranks, was born on 6 February 1921 in Surpal, northeast Poland. As an ethnic German, life in Poland remained progressive until 1926 when Josef Pilsudski consolidated power. When Edward Rydz-Smigly assumed power as the successor to Pilsudski in 1935, life for ethnic Germans living in Poland changed dramatically for the worse. Germans were relieved of their positions throughout various industries and the free press was abolished. However, Alexander Grenda had a secure future as a baker and confectioner. Many ethnic Germans living outside the borders of the German Reich admired Adolf Hitler and greeted his prospects with open arms; Germany held the key to a prosperous future. Almost immediately following the admittance of ethnic Germans as citizens into the Greater German Reich, draft notices were distributed. Grenda attended the RAD in Liegnitz-Neustadt and volunteered for the *Waffen-SS*. He attended basic training in Debica-Polen where he learned to fire the 7.92×57mm bolt-action M1898 Mauser rifle and the 9×25mm *Maschinenpistole* (MP) 38. He received instruction in close combat drills using shape charges, mines, and bayonet training. He also learned how to drive a truck and went on to Bitsch-Westmark for tank drivers' training. The men became proficient in the disassembly and reassembly of different types of motors. After completing his examinations, Grenda received orders to the *Panzerjägers* or antitank units at Angoulême near Bordeaux in France.[9]

Werner Pietzka, a recruit at the age of seventeen, arrived at the barracks of the 6th Company, 10th SS Panzer Regiment, where he met the decorated and smiling *SS-Hauptsturmführer* Edmund Erhard. On the most anticipated day of all, when the men took the oath and were sworn in, Pietzka was so excited over the affair that he became sick to his stomach. Within the formation and ready to take the oath,

Pietzka broke rank and approached the regimental commander.

"*Panzerschütze* [tank gunner] Pietzka requests permission to step out!"

Upon his return to the formation, the festivities resumed and the men declared their oath with a consecrated flag and became genuine soldiers.[10]

In 1943, Niko Getsch was a 20-year-old *SS-Unterscharführer* in the 1st Company, 10th SS Tank Destroyer Battalion. Getsch arrived in Germany in May 1940, among thousands of other young ethnic Germans, from the Kingdom of Rumania. For many, arriving in Germany meant new opportunities for education and work. A number of the boys graduated from high school and looked forward to studying at one of the many prestigious universities within the German Reich. The steamship *Uranus* crossed the Donau to Wien where the boys were greeted by military music and *SS-Gruppenführer* Gottlob Berger. Their plans for further education and work were suddenly postponed when they were notified that their military service was required first. Some were dumbstruck and some immediately questioned the legitimacy of the requirement. Notwithstanding, the boys found themselves on a train traveling from Wien to Prag-Rusin, where they were to receive their uniforms. Niko Getsch was assigned to a sizeable room where he quartered with three other boys for several delightful days. Instructors were not present and the boys did as they pleased. Two of the boys were matriculation candidates and the others, including Niko, were farmers. Niko knew nothing about military life. The training in the *SS-Verfügungstruppe*[11] or dispositional troops began suddenly without warning. On the fourth evening of their stay in the barracks, a "room return" was scheduled. When the *Unterführer vom Dienst* (UvD) or duty NCO or drill instructor arrived, the boys did not greet him with proper military decorum. He became very angry and began shouting. His voice grew louder when he noticed trash in the wastebasket. He proceeded to empty the contents of the basket throughout the room and intentionally knocked their clothes out of the lockers. Shouting at the top of his lungs, while the boys stood thunderstruck at attention, the UvD stormed out the door and entered the next room yelling and

screaming. Barely seventeen years of age, Niko had never experienced such a theatrical fit of rage. He did everything he could to refrain from bursting into tears. Comrade Karras took Niko to the side and comforted him, explaining, "Hey, don't worry about him. From the way he was acting, he's just a farm boy!"

Growing up, Niko was reminded repeatedly by his elders never to act like a farm boy.[12]

The barracks in Prag-Rusin were situated next to an airfield. Niko had never before seen aircraft, so the constant takeoffs and landings were especially exciting. However, as soon as basic recruit training began, there was no time for watching aircraft. Niko recalled:

We were first taught how to stand up straight and in a row, which was referred to as a "rank." Our boots were to be placed next to one another, together in the back and open in the front. They expected us to understand in a short period the concept of "right face" and "left face," without having to ask which way was which. When the *SS-Unterscharführer* whacked his heels together, for everyone that meant "Attention!" But not for myself, because I did not feel that it was that important. As we stood in three rather wobbly and crooked ranks, an aircraft flew low over our heads. At the very same moment, while I was watching the multiple propeller aircraft, the senior NCO whacked his heels together. For all the recruits that meant "Attention," except for me. I was more interested in the aircraft landing. From that point forward I became our senior NCO's "favorite." First I was told to lay down, then get up, lay back down, and so on. After this drill became monotonous, I was then directed to run around the riding stable ten times.[13]

Otto Jacob was German-born in 1925 and reported to the Wanzleben county culture house for a required military medical examination in the spring of 1941. The attendees were examined from head to toe and a determination made for Otto Jacob: "KV" or "*Kriegsverwendungsfähig*" (war service capable). On 19 December 1942, Jacob began his compulsory service with the RAD. Several days after the new year, the newest members of the RAD unit, all of whom were born in 1925, were called to formation. A number of SS soldiers were present to examine the young men. A loud command abruptly broke the silence.

"Attention! First rank, five steps forward! Second rank, three steps forward!"

Quickly and efficiently, two SS men looked over every man in each rank and questioned him about his schooling, medical history, ailments, etc.

"Left, face! About, face!"

The men were either told to stand fast or summoned out: "Left, out! Attention!"

At the conclusion, the senior SS officer addressed the group of men standing to the left and out. Jacob was among them.

"Attention! As of this moment, you are candidates for the *Waffen-SS*! The Fatherland requires your services for the defense of our home!"

Jacob reported for duty on 13 January 1943 at the SS-barracks München-Freimann.[14]

The 1st SS Pioneer (combat engineers) Training and Replacement Battalion organized in early January 1943 at the pioneer school at Hradischko, Czechoslovakia. The organizational staff included *SS-Obersturmführer* Erich Adelmeier and *SS-Untersturmführer* Kurt Imhoff. The troops came from the RAD, which many joined only several weeks prior, before they arrived at the pioneer school. The NCO ranks included men from the 3rd SS Death's Head Division and graduates from the second NCO course held at the pioneer school. The graduates were not yet promoted to NCO.[15]

Around the middle of January, *SS-Hauptsturmführer* Wendler assumed command of the battalion and formed the companies. The 1st Company quartered in barracks whereas the 2nd Company occupied a school. The training for weapons, motor transport, and other disciplines began. In April, *SS-Hauptsturmführer* Benz, from the SS *Polizei* Pioneer Battalion, replaced Wendler. Basic training concluded without significant problems; however, pioneer training was more challenging. The lack of fully trained pioneers meant that each platoon received only one trained pioneer. Indeed,

throughout the period between January and March 1943, men shuffled back and forth from one unit to form another. For example, the 3rd Company from Pikowitz formed two pioneer platoons for the 10th Motorcycle Infantry Regiment. Later, the regiment converted to a reconnaissance battalion and the two pioneer platoons were consolidated. The single pioneer platoon then attached to the 5th Heavy Reconnaissance Company, and the remaining troops and NCOs transferred to the 10th Pioneer Battalion.[16]

The number of recruits joining the Frundsberg Division directly from the RAD gave a good indication of the success of the recruitment drives. RAD members also fleshed out the ranks of the pioneers. After three unsuccessful attempts to join the *Waffen-SS*, Helmut Vogelmann entered the RAD on 10 January 1943. Three weeks after joining the RAD, Vogelmann volunteered again for the *Waffen-SS* and arrived at the SS Pioneer School in Dresden on 28 January. The pioneer battalion staff was based in Stichowitz, whereas one of the companies trained in Dawle. Vogelmann particularly enjoyed the training for building bridges, firing machine guns, and the use of flamethrowers. Eventually, Vogelmann joined the 16th Pioneer Platoon, 21st *SS-Panzergrenadier* Regiment.

Similarly, Erich Werkmeister came from the RAD barracks at Budweis (unit K/1/384) and volunteered for the *Waffen-SS* in the summer of 1942. He joined the 29th Panzer Pioneer Training and Replacement Battalion in late fall where he completed his pioneer training for water service and bridge building. On 19 January 1943, Werkmeister received orders for basic training at the SS Training Regiment in Prag, where he remained for four weeks. In February, he transferred to Pikowitz and reported to the 8th Replacement Company. The men of the 3rd Replacement Company at Hradischko were almost all German-born from the birth-year 1925 and a few from 1926. Three companies made up the pioneer school, with the first company consisting of four platoons that were mechanized and equipped with armored half-tracks.[17]

A hardened member of the cadre and former member of the *Leibstandarte*, *SS-Hauptsturmführer* Karl Keck, the company commander of the 16th

Pioneer Platoon, 21st *SS-Panzergrenadier* Regiment, was born on 20 January 1914 in Zürich, Switzerland. He joined the SS on 28 May 1933 and received assignment to the SS Regiment "Deutschland." After his reassignment on 1 April 1935 to the regiment "Germania," he attended the SS Officer Candidates' School in Braunschweig from 4 April 1935 to 31 January 1936, and subsequently attended a platoon leaders' course. As a lieutenant in the constabulary or municipal police, Keck transferred to a police company from 1 May 1937 to 1 April 1938. Shortly thereafter, he joined the 1st SS *Leibstandarte* "Adolf Hitler" and participated in the campaign in the West against France. Keck received the Iron Cross Second Class for bravery in battle and then the Iron Cross First Class as a pioneer company commander in the East. His other decorations included the Infantry Assault Badge and the Bulgarian King's Medal for Bravery. As a company commander, Keck transferred to the Frundsberg Division on 5 February 1943.[18]

The commander of 1st Battalion, 21st *SS-Panzergrenadier* Regiment, *SS-Hauptsturmführer* Heinz Laubscheer, arrived for duty on 15 February 1943, in the French village of Saintes, along with 760 recruits. The troops were immediately assigned quarters in a school and cavalry barracks in Saintes Jean de Angley. The following day, work details organized to clean the barracks at Mazeray and a command center was established in Saintes Jean de Angley. The battalion did not have a single vehicle at its disposal and acquired local French wood-gas-propelled trucks that allowed them to transport supplies. *SS-Obersturmführers* Willi Lösken and Max Krauss arrived on 17 February and were assigned as commanders for each living quarter. During the organization of the battalion staff and various companies, the absence of a working rank structure among the enlisted men presented significant problems. At the time, the selection of acting-NCOs proved inappropriate as the men lacked the necessary training, especially in the replacement battalion. On 18 February, *SS-Untersturmführer* Siegfried Stadler reported for duty and assumed managerial control over the officer corps, general billeting assignments, and the battalion supply. Sixty-two rifles and bayonets arrived that same day.

The next day, *SS-Hauptsturmführers* Karl Dietrich and Kurt Gropp arrived and reported for duty. The officers assumed command of the individual companies, and a skeletal framework of the battalion staff (headquarters and service company) included 1st Company *SS-Obersturmführer* Lösken, 2nd Company *SS-Obersturmführer* Krauss, 3rd Company *SS-Hauptsturmführer* Dietrich, and 4th Company *SS-Hauptsturmführer* Gropp.[19]

Training began on 22 February, and it became readily apparent that the inexperience of the men required training from the ground up. The preparation and distribution of new divisional guidelines and orders required intensive work. *SS-Obersturmführer* Roland Vogl reported for duty as the battalion adjutant. The next day, the officer corps was introduced to the *Luftwaffe* major Hermann Graf, a recipient of Oak Leaves with Swords and Diamonds to the Knight's Cross to the Iron Cross. In addition, the regimental commander, *SS-Standartenführer* Martin Kohlroser, visited the battalion and ordered an exchange of members between the 1st Battalion and the 3rd Battalion, to provide stronger and RAD-experienced men for the armored half-track battalion. As noted, the number of NCOs and the level of training remained unsatisfactory. Despite the daily training of the NCOs, the number of occupied NCO billets remained at a mere 26 percent.[20]

The Replacement Bureau of the *Waffen-SS* and the General Office of the Armed Forces reviewed the progress of recruiting on 24 February for the still infant 9th and 10th SS Panzer Divisions. While the birth-year 1925 could yield more, OKW set the limit of volunteer replacements from the birth-year 1925 to 60,000 men. Indeed, the headquarters staff, OKW, the Replacement Bureau of the *Waffen-SS*, and RAD reviewed violations of recruiting for the *Waffen-SS*. Objections raised by the chief of the RAD to further recruiting from the RAD uncovered the stark reality that not enough volunteer replacements could be mustered for the *Waffen-SS*.[21]

Meanwhile, in a celebratory atmosphere on 28 February 1943, the regimental commander swore-in the recruits of the 1st Battalion, 21st *SS-Panzergrenadier* Regiment, who gave their oath of allegiance. The following day, Debes attended and reviewed the battalion training and inspected the billeting quarters. He gave a positive evaluation of the battalion and stated the existence of an organization in good order.

Debes expected the same level of discipline when the men were not in the field but out in town among French civilians. In the divisional special order No. 4, he specifically forbade all SS men of the division to discuss with civilians any matter concerning the unit. He pointed out that within the region of the division, the "enemy listening service" employed the French public to fraternize with the troops to extract information. The order emphasized that passing information equated to treason and was therefore punishable by death, and gave notice that all inbound and outbound correspondence from the junior enlisted ranks was to be reviewed until a more favorable outlook was represented.

Throughout March, the battalion also established special duty assignments for scouting parties within each company. Scouting parties provided early warning of Allied airborne combat troops and airborne agents, and prevented sabotage. The scouting parties were comprised of one officer, three NCOs, and thirty men. Each company was responsible for establishing a scouting party, equipped with three light machine guns and rifles.

Intensive drivers' training began as well within the respective battalions. None of the recruits were licensed due to their young ages. Basic training was concluded on 20 March 1943, which marked the beginning of group-level training. The training levels of the NCOs, especially those that arrived from the *Polizei*, continued to remain poor. Before 9 March, the battalion had only one single light machine gun available for training. By 23 March, the battalion reported eleven officers, sixty-one NCOs, and 763 men.[22]

Between 6 March and 25 March, the 1st SS Assault Gun Battalion received basic infantry, specialized, and gun battery training.

During the month of March, both pioneer platoons, attached to the motorcycle regiment, disbanded and converted to a single platoon. The consolidated platoon attached to the reconnaissance battalion. The pioneer battalion relocated to Angoulême and quartered on either side of the Charente River, and *SS-Untersturmführer* Gerd

Schättiger replaced the commander of the 1st Company, *SS-Untersturmführer* Günther Ostermann. The pioneer company attached to the 10th SS Panzer Regiment and relocated to Luxe along the Charente River.

According to Werkmeister, of the regimental tank pioneer company, the company commander, *SS-Obersturmführer* Albert Brandt, was a hardened soldier. The punitive actions Brandt administered for infractions of soldiering were especially severe, though he fostered a friendly and fatherly relationship with the men. Werkmeister recalled: "After a young pioneer soldier was caught stealing a rabbit, Brandt sentenced him to six months to the '*Verlorener Haufen*' (VH) [or 'lost bunch'.] The soldier was never seen again."[23]

In the German armed forces, the punishments for acts of insubordination were harsh and reflected the brutality of war. Given the warring nature of the Nazi regime and the ideological indoctrination of soldiers and strict discipline, inhumane and brutal acts against captured enemy soldiers or civilians were often overlooked and even encouraged in the case of "racial inferiors." The death sentence for German soldiers was reserved for the most heinous offenses, such as desertion. Extreme punishments for lesser offenses are documented within Army panzer units operating on the Russian front where, for example, eight soldiers were tried for negligence or dereliction of duty while on guard. Three were sentenced to imprisonment for three to four years and five for longer terms. One soldier received a sentence of five years in jail for sleeping in his position. In contrast to the Army, men of the 10th SS Tank Destroyer Battalion who were found guilty of infractions received more fair sentences. For example, *SS-Schütze* Preuss received a strong warning for smoking while on duty; *SS-Schütze* M. Schneider received three days arrest for negligence while on guard duty; *SS-Schütze* Myslinski received ten days arrest for stealing from a French vendor; and *SS-Schütze* H. Rausch received three days arrest for smoking while cleaning his weapon.[24]

For all infractions involving officers, the *Reichsführer SS* or General of the SS Heinrich Himmler had the final word. In cases involving behavior unbecoming of an SS officer, they lost their commissions and were expelled from the SS altogether. However, the option of retaining their rank and stature carried the price of serving, in many cases, at a concentration camp.[25]

On 3 April 1943, group-level training concluded for the 1st Battalion, 21st *SS-Panzergrenadier* Regiment, and was followed by a surprise inspection by Himmler, who viewed the training and inspected the barracks. During the month of April, the 13th Company arrived in the battalion billeting area and was attached to the battalion. The organization of the Battalion Signal Section was highlighted on 20 April 1943 by a one-hour-long battalion celebration, commemorating Adolf Hitler's birthday.

A thirty-eight-day regimental NCO training cycle began on 23 April 1943, for which the battalion selected thirteen individuals. Laubscheer was the NCO training supervisor and Krüger the training officer.[26]

Forming part of the cadre of the 1st Battalion, *SS-Hauptsturmführer* Karl Bastian joined the Frundsberg Division in early 1943 as the company commander of the 7th Company, 21st *Panzergrenadier* Regiment. Bastian entered the Hitler Youth in 1932 and completed his labor service voluntarily between 1933 and 1935. Shortly thereafter, Bastian enlisted in the SS and was assigned to the 2nd SS Death's Head Regiment "Ostfriesland." A little over one year later, Bastian was promoted to *SS-Unterscharführer*. He was reassigned to the Army from 1 November 1936 to 1 October 1938, where he served with the 5th Company, 61st Infantry Regiment and participated in the occupation of the Ostmark and Sudetenland. After his release from the Army, he joined the 3rd SS Death's Head Regiment "Brandenburg." In January 1939, while serving as a platoon commander, Bastian participated in the occupation of Bohemia and Moravia. During the same year, Bastian transferred to the newly organized SS Death's Head Division and received assignment to the 5th Company, 2nd SS Death's Head Infantry Regiment. One month later, he attended the Platoon Leaders Course at the Light Infantry Battalion in Kassel. In the campaign against the Low Countries in Holland, Belgium, and France, Bastian participated as a platoon commander. Decorated during the campaign in 1940 with both the Iron Cross

2nd and 1st Classes, the Tank Assault Badge, and the Wound Badge, Bastian then obtained orders to the officer candidates' school at Bad Tölz. After his successful completion of the officer course, he remained at Bad Tölz until 8 January 1943, until his assignment as a company commander to the Frundsberg Division.[27]

The 10th SS Panzer Pioneer Battalion continued to flesh out its billets in April and organized into three companies. Two basic pioneer companies were assembled for each of the two infantry regiments, each consisting of three platoons, one panzer pioneer company (disbanded in October 1943), and one pioneer platoon attached to the divisional reconnaissance battalion. Storm trooper training and intensive company-level combat training fostered confidence among the officers and men. However, according to the commander of the 3rd Company, *SS-Obersturmführer* Hugo Benger, the battalion commander made critical remarks during the gathering of an entire company. This led to resentment among the men. Additional but unqualified comments were made at the officers' mess during lunch that led to a written complaint. As a result, the commander of the 2nd Company, *SS-Obersturmführer* Hermann, was relieved and transferred.[28]

By the end of April 1943, the 6th Company, 10th SS Panzer Regiment transferred from Rohrbach to the division's organizational area at Angoulême and was assigned quarters in the small village of Vars sur Charente.

Bernhard Westerhoff, a cadre member from the 2nd SS Panzer Division, described the relationship between the Germans and the French civilians of Vars as good. The favorable relationship was a direct result of the strict leadership of Leo Franke and a handful of French-speaking soldiers. Field trips into the immediate French countryside were commonplace and treasured by the men, especially into the city of Angoulême. The most frequented attraction for the young tank men was the cathedral of St. Pierre.[29]

The combat baggage-train of the 6th Company, 10th SS Panzer Regiment, was responsible for the supply of the fighting units and consisted of seventeen NCOs and men including *SS-Unterführer* Stief, Supply Issue Chief Kaluza, Radio Chiefs

Blata and Dennerlein, Weapons NCO Bartsch, Equipment NCO Nitsch, Mess NCO Reisenberger, Medic Utsch, Bauer (typist), Mahler (truck driver), Kaucher, Sprössig (company clerk or writer), Cieslack (field cook), and Leister (stretcher bearer). The equipment or baggage-train consisted of a paymaster NCO as the responsible officer, the company cobbler, *SS-Oberschütze* Inneraski, and the company tailor *SS-Sturmmann* Aicher.[30]

On 3 May 1943, the 1st Battalion, 21st *SS-Panzergrenadier* Regiment conducted group combat field exercises. The officers studied the tactical war-game scenario "attacking from a forced march" and "assembly and attack up to the breakthrough."

Two light armored half-tracks arrived on 9 May, and the 2nd Company conducted combat field exercises near St. Julien, reinforced by one infantry howitzer platoon, an antitank platoon from the 4th Company, and one heavy infantry howitzer platoon from the 13th Company. The divisional and regimental commanders attended the exercise and afterward *SS-Standartenführer* Debes determined the training to be acceptable. Until the end of May, the battalion continued combat field exercises that focused on the attack after assembling. On 27 May, such an event was attended by *SS-Obergruppenführer* Maximilian von Herff, the chief of the SS Personnel Office, along with Debes and other commanders of the division. The training was approved and rated as exceptional. Herff addressed the men of the battalion, spoke to their loyal fulfillment of duties, and noted their exceptional progress.[31]

In the classroom, the men were indoctrinated by an ideological curriculum that emphasized German history in a global context, the obligations of SS men, and the elite status of the SS within German society. The indoctrination or grooming of SS men, known as *Weltanschauung* or *Weltanschauliche Erziehung*, in the broadest sense referred to a global perspective and responsibility as it related to their position and mission in German society, Europe, and on Earth. The literature of pure propaganda aimed to establish an army of political soldiers. Himmler cleverly amalgamated SS objectives and regulations with basic moral principles and responsibilities of honor. Peppered with nationalistic slogans and terminology, the SS dogma evoked romantic ideals of Teutonic chivalry, courage on the battlefield, honor, duty, and ultimately the *Heldentod* or Hero's death. The SS produced soldiers that contemporary historians have referred to as fanatical in spirit.[32] It should be noted that teaching men how to fire a rifle or march in formation are routine military activities that are easily mastered. On the other hand, expectations of soldiers that are based on political and or ideological theories are complex and require a great deal of understanding. The divisional commander's memo dated 12 May 1943, regarding the progress of the global training, showed signs of discontent. Himself a proponent of indoctrination training, Debes actually aided in the failure of the training by formally recognizing the shortcomings of the Nazi ideology. For example, men with pure Aryan attributes were not among those in the division. For the instruction topic, "The SS-Man and the Question of Blood," dealing with race and racial differences, Debes recommended that company commanders not emphasize Nordic racial features of the SS man, but rather inner character and achievement.[33]

In early June 1943, the 1st Battalion, 21st *SS-Panzergrenadier* Regiment conducted more field exercises that continued to focus on the unit "assembly and attack." The commanding general of the First Army in southwest France, General Johannes Blaskowitz, and divisional and regimental commanders attended the training. By 17 June 1943, the divisional and regimental commanders had also supervised exercises conducted by the Army 708th Infantry Division. In turn, the pioneer platoon, attached to the 10th SS Panzer Reconnaissance Battalion, received their first half-tracks around the end of June. *SS-Untersturmführer* Fritz Kögel and five NCOs attended the *Panzergrenadier* course in Prosetschnitz on 7 July 1943, and *SS-Obersturmführer* Georg Siebert transferred to the self-propelled training and replacement section in Heidelager. Three days later, the battalion transferred into the area of Heugas.[34]

On 16 July 1943, the 6th Company, 10th SS Panzer Regiment, loaded onto a train in Angoulême and traveled through Bordeaux to the railroad station at Dax. An advance party proceeded onto Souprosse, whereby the company made a brief stop in Mugron and occupied the former barracks of French soldiers. Training continued, and security precautions were adopted as a result of partisan activity.[35]

During the same period, the pioneer platoon attached to the heavy 5th Company, 10th SS Panzer Reconnaissance Battalion. At the onset they received French trucks for the training of various groups, whereas the first half-tracks arrived around the end of June. Early in July, the pioneer platoon relocated to the area Bayonne-Dax, and field exercises were held in the Bay of Biscay. At the end of the month, the 1st Battalion, 21st *SS-Panzergrenadier* Regiment acquired eight Volkswagens.[36]

For the men of the 6th Company, 10th SS Panzer Regiment, southern France excited the senses. Many saw lemon trees blooming for the first time. On a clear day, the Pyrenees Mountains were visible far off in the distance. Attending a bullfight in Mont de Marsan was a first-time experience for many.

In Souprosse, a crippled Allied bomber tried to make it back to England but the crew bailed out before the English Channel. A search party was quickly organized to find the crew, but no one was found. However, men from the 6th Company, 10th SS Panzer Regiment did discover a smoke house and returned with a ham. The discovery resulted in a ten-hour punishment drill.[37]

After the division transferred from control of the First Army to the Fifteenth Army, the pioneer battalion relocated to the vicinity of Nimes, north of Aix near the Mediterranean Sea. For the men from the divisional *Feldgendarmerie* or field police, as well as the Administrative Supply Battalion, the pioneers provided instruction and training in the use of explosives and how to set fuses.

Indoctrination training resumed during the month of August and focused on German history and enemies of the state. The divisional commander personally oversaw the progress of the training and assisted in those areas where he felt it necessary. In a memorandum to the company commanders dated 27 July, Debes emphasized the importance and urgency of teaching German history and identified the readily apparent need for such training throughout the majority of the units in the division. To transform historical facts into political thought, Debes

recommended abandoning the study of dates, names, and specific historic events. Instead, he advocated focusing on SS ideology or the natural philosophy that determined the course of German history: the forces that determined the fate of the Germans in both the past and future. These forces were identified by Debes as race and space, which connected the various details and transformed the historical into political thought. Invariably, when company commanders selected instructional material, they were directed to ask themselves if the historical events enabled SS men to learn something applicable to the past and future, to foster enthusiasm, pride, and a willingness to fight. However, due to time constraints, Debes required that only three training hours be allocated per month. The entire training phase involved twelve hours of instruction. For the topic "Our Enemies," Debes emphasized the objective of the instruction to foster "hatred and abhorrence against the brutal and criminal intent of the enemy" and "eagerness for combat and enthusiasm to destroy the enemy where he is encountered." His closing remarks reaffirm the nature of the training as pure indoctrination stating, "The lecture will require an intense degree of propaganda."[38]

In the beginning of August, the pioneers relocated to an airfield in the area around Marseilles. Near Istres, the reconnaissance battalion and other units received their baptism of fire during an Allied bombing attack. A machine gunner from the 3rd Company was killed and buried alongside members of the *Luftwaffe* and female signal auxiliaries.[39]

Following the Sunday-morning "pre-alert" on 7 August 1943, members of the 5th Company, 10th SS Panzer Regiment, still wearing their service uniforms from a previous inspection, loaded their equipment and trucks onto railcars. The day passed and various work details were sent in all directions. The company held a formation at 1900 hours and departed the station at 1945 hours. Rumors about their destination were settled when the company found itself traveling along the foothills of the Pyrenees Mountains. The train passed through the village of Lourdes, and the hot temperatures caused the men to sweat. Nevertheless, snow and glaciers covered the high Spanish alpine range as the train clattered past the never-ending rows of vineyards. The train made longer stops at various stations that allowed for the replenishment of supplies, such as water for large containers for cooking. By 10 August, the 5th Company, 10th SS Panzer Regiment arrived at Toulouse and continued toward Narbonne. The company arrived at Beziers around 1815 hours and continued along the coast toward the Mediterranean. Upon arriving at their final destination the next morning, the early cry of the duty NCO ordered the unloading of the train. Not knowing their exact location, the men were greeted by a dry and rocky arid desert with sparse vegetation.[40]

On 7 August 1943, the 1st Battalion, 21st *SS-Panzergrenadier* Regiment boarded trains at Dax for shipment and relocation. The following day the battalion arrived in Rognac, 20 km north of Aix. The battalion staff situated itself in St. Cannat. For the battalion, *SS-Untersturmführer* Walter Pfeil assumed the duties as adjutant. On 15 August 1943, the regiment was placed on "alert level II." Throughout the night, the battalion moved to a new location in anticipation of Allied airborne troops. The battalion was on full alert. Two days later, British and American aircraft attacked an airfield near the battalion staff.[41]

Meanwhile, on 20 August 1943, the 6th Company, 10th SS Panzer Regiment traveled from Souprosse along the Spanish border and Mediterranean coast to the Etang de Berre, a large body of water northwest of Marseilles. The charm of the region, with high temperatures and never before seen vegetation, required a new service uniform. The men were issued green shirts in place of the black tank jacket, and the sleeve rank insignia was introduced. Here, the men were quartered in sheep barns and received their first vehicle for training, an obsolete Pz.Kpfw.III.[42] Lacking additional vehicles, the two battalions shared the vehicle for technical and practical training applications, whereby basic infantry training continued. Radio operators also joined the company, arriving from radio training companies stationed in the alpine village of Cornillon, in close proximity to St. Chamas-Miramas.[43]

For many of the men of the 6th Company, 10th SS Panzer Regiment, the local melons were unfamiliar nutrition. The plentiful fruit, supplemented with grapes, was a novelty, but it caused acute diarrhea among the entire company. "Latrine commandos"—individuals who were caught stealing extra rations—dug new latrines almost daily for sanitary purposes. The 2nd Platoon under the leadership of *SS-Untersturmführer* Rudolf Henn attached to the 2nd Battalion, and the chief radio operator for the 6th Company was A. Wieser.

The pioneer company, 10th SS Panzer Regiment, relocated to the area around Pau and subsequently moved to Miramas, near St. Chamas, where the company quartered in former Army barracks. Chamas was located on the Etang de Berre, the center of the French petroleum industry. The training emphasized field maneuvers and building secondary bridges. The bridges were later turned over to the villagers, who showed their gratitude by serving food and wine in the village square. The German soldiers established a good relationship with the French civilians.[44]

On 22 August, the 1st Battalion, 21st *SS-Panzergrenadier* Regiment received a warning order for the relocation of the regiment. The battalion arrived in its new area for billeting after a forced march without a single casualty in personnel or equipment. One week later the battalion went on alert due to the imminent deployment and engagement of the battalion in the area of Marseilles and Toulon. A motorized column was organized.[45]

From the end of August until the latter part of September, the pioneer platoon of the 5th Company, 10th SS Reconnaissance Battalion bivouacked in tents in Merle. During this period, Italy capitulated and joined the Allies. On 24 September, the entire reconnaissance battalion was transferred to an area northeast of Marseilles. The 5th Company resided in Aubagne and received its full complement of half-tracks.[46]

On 1 September 1943, the 1st Battalion, 21st *SS-Panzergrenadier* Regiment awarded the War Merit Cross 2nd Class with Swords to *SS-Scharführer* Schreiter, *SS-Scharführer* Tanner, *SS-Unterführer* Kiefer, *SS-Unterführer* Rid, and *SS-Unterführer* Jäckel.

The War Merit Cross with Swords recognized service members for non-combat meritorious service.[47]

The battalion left their quarters around Mas de Payan and relocated, on 8 September, into their old quarters around St. Cannat. This relocation provided an excellent opportunity for training. The first three companies marched to their objective, whereas the 4th Company and the staff were mechanized. No casualties were reported. Four battalion NCOs received orders to the 5th Special Inter-Service Course at the SS Pioneer School at Hradischko from 13 September to 10 October 1943.

Around 17 September, due to inclement weather, the companies moved from the outside into quarters indoors. The 1st and 3rd Companies occupied Lambesc, the 2nd Company moved into Eguilles, and the 4th Company billeted in St. Cannat. After a long period on the alert, the battalion conducted field exercises on 23 September. Participants and observers included the commander of southern France, General of the Infantry Georg von Sodenstern, Debes, Lieutenant Colonel von Jansen, as well as the regimental and individual battalion commanders. The scenario for the training exercise was to "attack after preparatory positions." In support of the exercise, the 1st Battalion of the artillery regiment, the 2nd Company of the assault gun artillery battalion, and an attack squadron from the 2nd Aviation Division were attached to the battalion. At the conclusion of the exercise, General Sodenstern addressed the battalion and spoke highly of Laubscheer. Rounding out the remainder of the month, Gropp led the battalion for a night exercise around Lambesc. The exercise scenario was "entering the assembly area."

According to *SS-Untersturmführer* Hans-Dieter Sauter, the battery commander for the 1st Battery, 10th SS Panzer Artillery Regiment, the regimental commander, *SS-Standartenführer* Hans Sander, was a failure. After gunnery training near St. Cannat, there emerged an incident between officers. In front of the entire battery, Sander discredited Sauter and the battery. However, an army general officer was present as well, patted Sander on the shoulder and said, "Colonel, the Lieutenant is right. His decision prevented a greater catastrophe. I wish I had enough such Lieutenants in my Division." The following day, Sauter was summoned to the regimental command post. First, the regimental adjutant, *SS-Hauptsturmführer* Ruprecht Heinzelmann, admonished Sauter, and then Sander took his turn. However, Sauter remained calm. As a reservist he

did not have the pressure of adding a star (pip) to his collar tabs every year.

Several days later, the alarm sounded. The OKW feared imminent American landing operations along the coast around Marseilles and orders arrived directing the regiment to the coast. At the time, the ranking officer at the regimental staff quarters, in Pelisanne, was the 1st ordnance officer, *SS-Obersturmführer* Dr. Josef Sumper.[48] Sander and his adjutant were purportedly in Nizza, visiting members of the regiment at the field hospital. According to *SS-Sturmbannführer* Hans Lingner, the division 1st General Staff officer, Sander never went to the hospital.[49]

For most of October, the battalion continued intensive combat training. In the afternoon on 1 October, *SS-Obersturmführer* Krauss conducted a class in the field for all platoon commanders and NCOs on the "counterattack of a battalion in reserve to re-establish a critical situation." Several days later, the 1st Battalion assigned umpires for the 2nd Battalion field exercise that took place in Lambesc. The battalion staff, company, and platoon commanders received training on the use of command radios and signals for the scenario, "attack after assembly phase." *SS-Untersturmführer* Pfeil led the training that took place within the battalion. The 3rd Company, 10th SS Assault Gun Battalion, attached to the battalion for instructional purposes between 8 October and 10 October. This aspect of cross training was carried out with the greatest interest and enthusiasm. However, *SS-Grenadier* Haueis died a day after his foot was squashed between the tracks while mounting a vehicle.[50]

Before the end of the first week in October, the 10th SS Panzer Reconnaissance Battalion, commanded by *SS-Sturmbannführer* Heinz Brinkmann, received its remaining vehicles, placing the battalion at full strength.[51]

From 9 October to 15 October, the 1st Battalion, 21st *SS-Panzergrenadier* Regiment sent a number of individuals to a variety of training classes, including twenty-five students and four instructors to the NCO class at the 21st *SS-Panzergrenadier* Regiment in le Puy; *SS-Obersturmführer* Krauss attended a field exercise with the 2nd Battalion, 10th SS Panzer Regiment; *SS-Obersturmführer* Lösken attended training classes at the reserve 181st

Grenadier Regiment in Orleans; and ten NCOs and forty-three men attended classes for combating tanks in close combat, flamethrowers, mines, and building emplacements at the Army pioneer school in Cosne/Nievre.

At 0030 hours on 23 October, the regiment telephoned the battalion with the following message:

> The division is being moved into a new area. The battalion shall depart as the first transport. Embarkation time 0930–1730 hours. Time of departure, 1800 hours. Embarkation railroad station—Aix.

The relocation of the battalion was executed using two transports over Lyon, Versailles, and to Montfort (debarkation railroad station for the first transport) and Bernay (second transport). No casualties or losses of equipment were reported.[52]

Major changes transformed the *Panzergrenadier* Division when it reorganized into a regular SS panzer division. The daily order, number 1632/43, dated 26 October 1943, stipulated that the pioneer and construction companies of the 10th SS Panzer Regiment organize pioneer platoons for the 1st Battalion. Excess pioneers were to be absorbed into the 10th SS Pioneer Battalion. A flamethrower platoon was authorized to organize for the headquarters company, 21st *SS-Panzergrenadier* Regiment. Both motorcycle companies from the grenadier regiments, including all their equipment, weapons, and ammunition, were to transfer to the 17th SS Panzer Reconnaissance Battalion of the 17th *SS-Panzergrenadier* Division "Götz von Berlichingen." However, the company commanders were to remain with the 10th SS. The 4th Company of the reconnaissance battalion was to equip with *Schwimmwagen*, an amphibious version of the *Kübelwagen* or German Jeep. The equipping of the 10th SS Assault Gun Battalion depended on a special order, after a review by the inspector general of the tank troops. The 3rd Battalion, 10th SS Panzer Artillery Regiment, and all their equipment, weapons, and ammunition, also transferred to the 17th *SS-Panzergrenadier* Division, whereas shortages in personnel for the self-propelled battalion were to be made up through the SS main office.

The divisional observer battery remained under tactical control of the division until the General Staff of the VII SS Panzer Corps was organized. At such time, the battery transferred to the corps. A light detachment of the 10th SS Antiaircraft Battalion was ordered organized after completion of the reorganization of the division. In terms of engineer equipment, bridge columns were organic components of engineer battalions. Bridging equipment types B and K supported normal traffic of 24 tons. Type B was a pontoon trestle bridge, whereas type K was a box girder bridge supported on pontoons and trestles. Bridging equipment J was for supporting tanks. The Frundsberg Division received Bridging Column B that reorganized to Bridging Column K, and the delivery of equipment for the general organization of Bridging Column J was authorized. The supply units were expected to reorganize on their own, whereby the theoretical strength of the entire division was to near 90 percent. Excess personnel were to be reported to the SS main office for further use and the reorganization of the division was expected to be completed by 20 November 1943.[53]

On 24 September 1943, the OKH or Army High Command directed that all panzer divisions convert to the new table of organization "PzDiv43." The 10th *SS-Panzergrenadier* Division reorganized to a panzer division that followed the format outlined by the Army on 4 October 1943. In theory, the organization of an SS division resembled that of an army panzer division, with the exception of two reinforced panzer grenadier regiments. A panzer regiment, a single artillery regiment, a reconnaissance, antitank, pioneer, antiaircraft, signals, and replacement battalion, and supply and medical units made up the remainder of the division.[54]

The number of authorized tanks for a German SS panzer division mirrored an army division. The 1943-pattern division, established on 4 October 1943, provided for a margin of flexibility that prescribed three to four companies of seventeen to twenty-two tanks each. The published total numbers of tanks, in October 1943, reflect calculations based on seventeen tanks, in each of the three companies, in the 1st Panther Battalion. The total number equals fifty-one tanks in the 1st Battalion. The published figures for the 2nd Battalion, equipped with

17 Pz.Kpfw.IV in each of the four companies, to-taled sixty-eight tanks. The numbers accurately reflect the equipment totals for a 1943-pattern panzer division, as specified by the General Staff of the Army in the General Order 4500 dated 4 October 1943. Nevertheless, the actual number of companies in the 1st Battalion was four, and the authorized strength was actually twenty-two tanks per company. In 1943, the 1st Battalion did not receive any Panther tanks. Theoretically, seven flame-thrower tanks were allotted to the 2nd Battalion. When the Army High Command outlined the 1944-pattern panzer division on 15 August 1944, the regimental staff and both the battalions' staff companies received additional tanks. The regimental staff received three command Panther tanks and five additional Panthers. The Panther Battalion headquarters and staff company consisted of eight additional Panthers, and the same applied to the 2nd Battalion Staff Company, which received eight additional Pz.Kpfw.IV. Therefore, the 10th SS Panzer Division received twenty-two Pz.Kpfw.IV tanks for both the 5th and 6th Companies. Due to a shortage of tanks, both the 7th and 8th Companies received twenty-two assault guns. These numbers, however, differ from the theoretical numbers. After mid-August 1944, each of the four companies had twenty-two tanks for a total of eighty-eight tanks. When adding the tanks of the Command and Staff Company, an SS division was authorized 104 Panthers and ninety-six Pz.Kpfw.IV.[55]

The *Panzerkampfwagen* IV Ausf H (SdKfz 161/2) or medium tank IV Model H, evolved from a Krupp design 20-ton class support tank. First produced in 1937, the Pz.Kpfw.IV underwent seven revisions by April 1943. Produced by Krupp-Gruson, Vomag, and Nibelungwerke, the five-man crew H-model tank weighed 25 tons and was powered by the Maybach HL 120 TRM engine. The V-12 engine produced 300 horsepower at 3,000 rpm. The H-variant tank also featured the SSG77 transmission and reached speeds of 38 km/h with a range of 210 kilometers. Communications were made possible with the FuG5 radio set, a 10-watt transmitter c, and the USW receiver c1, which operated in the frequency ranges of 27,200–33,300 Kc/s and a maximum range of 4 kilometers. The front hull

was protected by 80mm of steel, whereas the sides consisted of 30mm, the rear of 20mm, and top of 10mm. The turret was manufactured with 50mm in the front, 30mm on the sides, 30mm in the rear, and 15mm on the top. The superstructure was fitted with 80mm in the front, 30mm on the sides, 20mm in the rear, and 12mm on the top. For added protection, the sides of the hull and turret carried supplementary steel plates of 5mm and 8mm, respectively. The main gun, a *Kampfwagen Kanone* KwK40L/48, the second longest 75mm gun of 48 calibers, was intended as an antitank gun and to fire armor piercing ammunition. The muzzle velocity of the gun reached 790 meters per second and could penetrate 64mm of homogeneous armor plate at 2,000 meters. The hull ball-mounted machine gun MG-34 was equipped with a *KugelZielfernrohr* 2 (ZgZF2) telescope that used a monocular magnification of 1.75 for a range of 200 meters. The main gun used a turret sighting telescope or *TurmZielfernrohr* 5f/1 (TZF5f/1) using a monocular magnification of 2.4 for a range of 1,200 meters for the coaxial machine gun MG-34. The vehicle carried eighty-seven rounds of armor-piercing, high explosive, and smoke ammunition. German ammunition was highly developed as well. The armor-piercing projectile was capped to improve performance against face-hardened armor, and capped again with a ballistic cap to improve long-range performance.[56]

At each level of command, whether for the division, regiment, battalion, or company, the individual staff functioned as an apparatus of the commander who made all the decisions and took full responsibility for the unit. As the commander's representative, the 1st General Staff officer led the staff in general. The commander of the 10th SS Panzer Regiment, *SS-Obersturmbannführer* Otto Paetsch, theorized that simple and tight leadership with a rigid scope of work for each department and close working relationships were fundamental to a cohesive staff. Moreover, taking personal pride in their work, a sense of responsibility, planning, and independency allowed a staff to perform their work most efficiently. The primary responsibility of each member of the staff contributed to the welfare of the troops.

At the division level or above, the command staff was organized into six sections, denoted by a sequential roman numbering system, and each department had several areas of responsibility. The division staff billets included three General Staff qualified officers, and another nineteen billets that were held by both officers and NCOs, depending on available personnel. The Ia, or 1st General Staff officer, was employed to effect the will of the commander. During combat, the commander and the 1st General Staff officer could not be away from their posts at the same time. The responsibilities of the 1st General Staff officer included informing the commander of all matters concerning the division, and the commander was obligated to inform the 1st General Staff officer of all directives. General Staff officers were usually qualified as such after attending the General Staff Academy.

SS-Sturmbannführer Hans Lingner joined the division on 20 February 1943 and became the divisional 1st General Staff officer. Lingner received a commission as *SS-Untersturmführer* in 1935 after attending officer candidates' school in Braunschweig and posted on 20 April 1936 as a platoon commander with the 1st Battalion, 2nd SS Regiment. After attending a parachute training course at the 2nd Airdrome Stendal, Lingner was assigned in January 1938 as 3rd Battalion adjutant, SS Regiment "Der Führer" (DF). Promoted one year later to *SS-Obersturmführer*, he was reassigned in April 1940 as the commander, 7th Company, 2nd Battalion, SS Regiment "DF," SS Division "Das Reich." After his promotion to *SS-Hauptsturmführer* in May he participated in the French campaign and was decorated with the Iron Cross 2nd Class on 30 May and the Iron Cross 1st Class on 6 June. He became the regimental adjutant and held the billet as 1st ordnance officer with the 2nd SS Division until March 1942, only two months after he received the German Cross in Gold. In September 1942 Lingner received orders to the SS Panzer Corps and by November to the Army General Staff Academy.[57]

For the division, the staff sections included:

Division Staff

Division Commander

Command Staff Section (Ia)
1st General Staff Officer

1st Ordnance Officer (O1)
3rd General Staff Officer (Ic)
3rd Ordnance Officer (O3)
Division Maps
Chief of Intelligence
Division Escort Company
Military Police Company

Adjutant:
Section IIa   Division Adjutant
Section IIb   Personnel Chief for NCO and Troops

Section III   Division Courts (Legal)
                      Defense Council
                      Judges
Commandant's Staff Quarters
Graves Registration

Logistics Section (Ib)
2nd General Staff Officer
2nd Ordnance Officer (O2)
Ammunition

Section IVa   Division Director
Section IVb   Division Doctor
                      Division Dentist

Section V   Division Engineer
Section VI   Propaganda and Troop Welfare

At the division level, the 1st General Staff officer answered any questions regarding tactical operations and ensured that all orders of the day were carried out while marching, in combat, or in bivouac. Correspondence as a whole, with the exception of secret mail and that of the general commands, was opened by the combat correspondent and provided to the adjutant for delivery to the individual battalions. Only the commander signed correspondence for the division as well as other units. All other reports and orders were to be routed and signed via the adjutant and prepared to the commander by 0800 hours the next day.

The Ib was responsible for the overall supply of the unit, whereas the Ic oversaw intelligence. The adjutant or operations officer was to be apprised of all matters concerning intelligence. The IIa and

IIb were responsible for all matters concerning the officer corps, promotions, transfers, replacements, and assignments. The III section concerned itself with legal affairs. The IVa section made recommendations to the commander concerning administrative matters. The IVb, or unit doctor, concerned itself with the medical well-being of the troops. The V section was responsible for the repair and equipping of items from the motor vehicular maintenance workshop. The last section, VI, oversaw unit training and propaganda, troop welfare, and officer burials. The following table of organization identifies the individual billets for the tank regiment:

Command Section:
Regimental Commander
Adjutant
Ordnance Officer
Intelligence Officer
Administrative Officer
Regimental Doctor
Technical Officer for Vehicles
Technical Officer for Weapons
Commander, Headquarters Staff
Commander, Supply Company

1st Battalion:
Battalion Commander
Adjutant
Ordnance Officer
Intelligence Officer
Administrative Officer
Regimental Doctor
Technical Officer for Vehicles
Technical Officer for Weapons
Commander, Headquarters Staff
Commander, 1st Company
Commander, 2nd Company
Commander, 3rd Company
Commander, 4th Company
Commander, Supply Detachment

2nd Battalion:
Battalion Commander
Adjutant
Ordnance Officer
Intelligence Officer

Administrative Officer
Regimental Doctor
Technical Officer for Vehicles
Technical Officer for Weapons
Commander, Headquarters Staff
Commander, 1st Company
Commander, 2nd Company
Commander, 3rd Company
Commander, 4th Company
Commander, Supply Detachment

In combat, the tank command vehicles provided the following functions:

Regimental Commander's Tank
  Leading the Troops
  Tactical Orders
  Tactical Directives
  Communication with Superior and Subordinate
    Commands

Regimental Adjutant's Tank
  The same responsibilities as the commander's
    but also:
  Supply of Ammunition and Fuel
  Repair Service

Ordnance Officer's Tank
  Supply of Ammunition and Fuel
  Repair Service
  Air Liaison[58]

The seven-day training schedule for the staff company of the assault gun battalion, from 4 October to 11 October 1943, allotted more than three and a quarter hours of maintenance or vehicle training per day for five days (Monday through Friday), totaling 16.25 hours a week. Training for drill received 45 minutes per day for four days (Monday through Thursday), while some form of combat training was conducted for two to two and a half hours, six days a week (Monday through Saturday), totaling approximately fourteen hours. Evenings were reserved for special projects that included singing. At 1800 hours on Saturday, an inspection concluded the training week, and Sunday was a day of rest. However, the same was not true for the 2nd Company, 10th SS

Assault Gun Battalion in November 1943, when training continued right through Sunday, although beginning somewhat later in the morning from 0830 hours until noon, consisting of forty-five minutes indoctrination training (see Appendix E for an overview of the training plans).[59]

On 28 October, the 10th SS Panzer Division relocated to Normandy and the association to the historical figure, Georg von Frundsberg, was forever cemented on 4 November 1943.[60]

Meanwhile, when the pioneer battalion relocated to Normandy by rail, disaster struck during the night when the advance party passed through Dijon. Hugo Benger, of the 3rd Company, 10th SS Panzer Pioneer Battalion, was playing a card game or hand of *Skat* as the railcars hurtled through the night, rocking softly back and forth. Suddenly, the screeching sound of steel pierced the night as the wheels of the train locked and braked. Benger recalls, "As if by the hand of ghosts, the doors tore wide open, luggage spilled from stowage compartments, and bodies flew through the air." The train then lunged forward but braked again, screeching until it stopped. Outside, whistling steam and mounting chaos filled the night. After warning-troops were sent to the back to stop other trains that followed, Benger made his way forward where the mangled bodies of men from the 2nd Company were brought out on shelter halves. An enraged company commander held two elderly Frenchmen at gunpoint who were later determined to be railroad shift workers. The locomotive lay halfway on its side and dug itself between the rails into the ground, up to the midsection of the boiler. Steam spewed from torn pipes and hot coal was strewn from the open fire pit. The first few railcars were piled on top of one another and formed a steeple-like wreck. Within the twisted steel, the misfortunate and dead were easily recognizable by their camouflage jackets. Some seriously injured men were found in other cars, but nothing could be done to help those in and among the wreck. Afterwards, Benger surveyed the railroad line and discovered where railroad tracks were loosened on a bridge. The fact that saboteurs moved the rails to the outside prevented an even greater catastrophe. Once a recovery train arrived in the early morning

on the neighboring track, the men boarded the transport train and continued their journey toward Normandy. The battalion unloaded south of Dieppe at Pont Audemer, and occupied quarters to the west and southwest of the village.[61]

An armored half-track training staff, comprised of an Army officer and five Army NCOs, arrived on 4 November at the 1st Battalion, 21st *SS-Panzergrenadier* Regiment. On 6 November the divisional Abt. VI (indoctrination branch) released the historical background on Georg von Frundsberg. The following day, the battalion hosted an hour of celebration in observance of 9 November 1923, the day Hitler's putsch failed. The regimental music platoon attended the event, which concluded with a commander's review of the battalion.

Throughout the next several days the battalion continued cross training and sent men to various different units. Six NCOs attended training at the reconnaissance battalion. The commander of the 3rd Company, *SS-Obersturmführer* Vogl, transferred to the SS-Pz.Gren.Rgt.22 and *SS-Untersturmführer* Krüger assumed the command. On 10 November, the battalion commander accompanied the divisional commander for training with Panther and Tiger tank units in Mailly-le-Camp.

An escort detail dispatched to Berlin on 14 November to pick up thirty-three armored half-tracks. The commanding general, LXXXI Army Corps, General of Panzer Troops Adolf Kuntzen, and General of Panzer Troops Leo Freiherr Geyr von Schweppenburg, commander of Panzer Group West, made a surprise visit to the battalion on 16 November. The following day, the battalion commander accompanied the regimental and division commanders for training for the 9th SS Panzer Division, and *SS-Unterführer* Teschow attended a short photo training session with the *Luftwaffe* in Brussels, Belgium.

Twenty-five additional armored half-tracks, along with instructors, arrived at the 1st Battalion and were distributed to the 1st and 3rd Companies. Driving school began on 22 November. Two days later, Debes accompanied the Army lieutenant general Josef Reichert, commander of the 711th Infantry Division, for a group field exercise of the 1st Company.[62]

Another detail of men dispatched to Elbing and Spandau to pick up additional armored half-tracks. On 30 November, Debes ordered 1st Battalion to conduct a demonstration for General Geyr and other tank officers from surrounding units. Among others, the topics included "combat over terrain with and without observation." The 2nd Company, 10th SS Panzer Artillery Regiment, reinforced by elements of the 1st and 4th Companies, carried out the "attack of a reinforced company." Despite poor weather, the exercise proceeded well.

On 14 December, the battalion received a total of forty-seven armored half-tracks (delivered to Lisieux) and thirty captured Italian trucks. Two additional combat training scenarios were conducted including "weaving into formation and march" and "attack of a reinforced company while underway." Under the direction of First Lieutenant Sievers, two courses for driving, one issue and supply training course, and one tank recovery class concluded.[63]

During November and December, the pioneer battalion buried Dutch trip-wire landmines along the Normandy coast and built beach obstacles, also known as "*Rommelspargel.*" "Rommel asparagus" referred to any standing obstacles, metal or wood beams, not only confined to the beaches, which were fitted with *Teller* or plate mines on the protruding end. Prospective glider and paratroop landing areas farther inland were also fitted with the Rommel asparagus. In conversation with Army soldiers stationed in the coastal area, the SS Pioneers learned of negative remarks about the asparagus suggesting that the SS wanted to prevent a withdrawal and to drag out the war.

Additional NCO training emphasized command terminology and using the radio to distribute assignments. Moreover, areas of terrain ideal for airborne landings were reconnoitered and dominating terrain features were incorporated into a fortified rearward defensive system. Protective trenches were dug around the billeting areas and ramparts for vehicles.[64]

Shortly before the divisional commander received his new assignment in Finland to command the 6th SS Mountain Division "Nord," Debes prepared a second detailed memo that quantified the fruits of his labor, or lack thereof. His hopes of creating a division of political soldiers were dashed, an aspect of training in which the company grade officers clearly failed him. To this end, Debes emphatically ordered two series of lectures that covered "German history" and "Our Enemies," the same classes he specifically addressed earlier in his memo from July. As before, he outlined the goal of each lecture—all the lectures were pure propaganda—but this time identified Germany's enemies, which included the British, Americans, Jews, and Bolsheviks. Finally, Debes skillfully placed the onus on every officer to ensure the political indoctrination of every SS man. Directives from the chief of the indoctrination office (Abt. VI) that followed on the heels of the Debes memos ordered a repeat of the basic classes, indicating the indoctrination program was a complete failure. Indeed, the 7 December memo from the Propaganda Branch VI reported that the companies were not teaching the prescribed topics that were ordered by the division.[65]

Interestingly, Bernhard Westerhoff, an enlisted member of the 6th Company, 10th SS Panzer Regiment, confirmed the absence of indoctrination training. When asked about the training, Westerhoff denied ever receiving such training and considered himself "a soldier just like others too" (referring to the army). He added, "The important aspect of the training revolved around learning how to fight and stay alive." In comparison, Pietzka touched on every key aspect of the training, as it related to the instruction for "Our Enemies," stating it was the same material taught while in the Hitler Youth. Otto Jacob, a member of a self-propelled 105mm *Wespe* battery of the artillery regiment, clearly recalls significant amounts of instruction that primarily focused on the reasons for the war, such as the Treaty of Versailles and the Allied bombing of German cities. Jacob remarked:

> The more complex issues went in one ear and out the other. No one ever questioned anything out of fear of embarrassment. We were so young. The fact that the Allies were bombing Germany and killing innocent civilians enraged us.[66]

The headquarters of the SS Panzer Corps that deployed to the East in February 1943 returned to

France in December of the same year and organized as the Headquarters II SS Panzer Corps, under the command of *SS-Obergruppenführer* Paul "Papa" Hausser.[67]

Lothar Debes commanded the division for less than one year, from 15 February until 15 November 1943, when he relinquished command to *SS-Obergruppenführer* Karl von Treuenfeld. Treuenfeld was a veteran officer from World War I with exceptional experience that included a close relationship with General Erich Ludendorff and a posting as the Army confidant during the secret armaments programs in April 1939. Treuenfeld entered the SS on 1 May 1939 as an *SS-Oberführer*. For a brief period of twenty days, he assumed the post as chief of staff of the Death's Head Formations, which at the time were not yet part of the *Waffen-SS*. From 1 July 1939 until 31 May 1940, Treuenfeld took an assignment as the inspector of the SS Officer Candidates' School. He transferred to the staff of the 2nd SS Panzer Division where, in June, he earned the clasp to the Iron Cross Second Class during the campaign in the West. On 9 November 1940, Treuenfeld was promoted to *SS-Obergruppenführer* and became the department chief for officer training at the main SS office in Berlin. One month after his return to a combat unit on 5 April 1941, as the commander of the 2nd SS Infantry Brigade (motorized), Treuenfeld was involved in an automotive accident that crushed his chest cavity and pinched the nerves along his neck at the fourth and sixth vertebrae. Treuenfeld returned to duty in January 1942 as commander of the *Waffen-SS* in the Sudetenland. The Sudetenland, a Reich territory, incorporated the Protectorate of Bohemia and Moravia. On 5 July 1942, Treuenfeld assumed command of the 1st SS Infantry Brigade (motorized) and posted lastly as the *Höhere SS- u. Polizeiführer Rußland Süd* or Higher SS and Police Commander Southern Russia before he joined the Frundsberg Division.[68]

Meanwhile in December 1943, the 1st Pioneer Company received their armored half-tracks. Shortly thereafter, the entire company began training in the mounting and dismounting of vehicles and the operational deployment of troops in the field. A fatal accident occurred during hand grenade training when a platoon commander inadvertently dropped a grenade in a vehicle and threw the pin. In an effort to shield others from the blast, the commander threw himself on the grenade.[69]

Hermann Max Gerhard, an SS volunteer, was born on 10 May 1925 in Paunsdorf, a suburb of Leipzig in the region of Saxony. In 1938, at the impressionable young age of fourteen and a member of the Hitler Youth, Gerhard experienced, firsthand, the first official visit by Adolf Hitler to the city of Leipzig. Among the thousands of cheering people and waving flags, the smart-looking, black-uniformed regiment of the *SS-Leibstandarte*, leading the motorcade through the streets, inspired Gerhard. He hoped that some day he could be one of them. At seventeen years of age, but against the will of his father, Gerhard volunteered for the *Waffen-SS* and joined the 4th SS *Polizei-Panzergrenadier* Division. Despite volunteering, Gerhard joined with mixed emotions. Foremost, he wanted to make a personal contribution to the war. On the other hand, he wanted the war to end as soon as possible in order to prevent people from suffering. On 9 November 1942, in the Polish village of Dubica, at the foot of the Carpathian Mountains, Gerhard swore allegiance to Hitler.

At the conclusion of his training in 1943 as an MG-42 gunner, Gerhard transferred with his machine-gun team to the 2nd Regiment of the 4th SS *Polizie-Panzergrenadier* Division. After experiencing their first combat and Russian winter around Wolgorod, the team transferred to Berlin where they joined *SS-Haupsturmführer* Otto Skorzeny in the *Sonderverband* or Special Formation Friedenthal. After six months of service, Gerhard was promoted to *SS-Mann*. In May 1943, Gerhard participated in Operation Schwarz or Black, the unsuccessful search in Yugoslavia for the Balkan guerrilla chief Josip Broz, or "Marshal Tito." Wounded in the leg, Gerhard was reassigned to an escort command for a Red Cross train until he arrived at a hospital. After his medical release, Gerhard reported to the SS signal barracks at Nürnberg in July 1943, and subsequently received orders to a small *Sicherheitsdienst* (SD) or security service detachment in southern France at St. Palais. Upon his arrival, Gerhard was promoted to the NCO rank of *SS-Unterscharführer*. After the death of his commanding officer, killed by a roadside car bomb, Gerhard transferred to the 2nd Battalion, 22nd *SS-Panzergrenadier* Regiment, located in Gardanne. He was in charge of the radio section of the 2nd Battalion and, before the year's end, transferred to the *SS-Nachrichtenführerschule* or Signal Officer School in Metz.[70]

In the meantime, infantry and tank training continued for the 6th Company, 10th SS Panzer Regiment, once they occupied quarters in the monastery Le Bec-Hellion. The single Pz.Kpfw.III tank was replaced with a *Sturmgeschütz* (StuG.III) or assault gun. Sometime between Christmas and the new year, *SS-Schütze* Schneider was ordered to take twelve men to Magdeburg-Königsborn and accept delivery of new tanks. Schneider recalled:

> Our *Spiess* or company *SS-Hauptscharführer* made sure we had ample supplies so that we could spend several pleasurable days in Magdeburg. Considering that the delivery of our tanks would take some time, our section transport chief, decided to go home for several days. Much to our surprise, twenty-two tanks were already waiting for us to take delivery! The first and most important task was to acquire a transportation number; it was also required to report the foreseen route over which the tanks would travel. The drivers, radio operators, and gunners all took their positions as young women from the factory drove the tanks over the ramps onto railcars. Once everything was loaded and tied down, the trip back to France began. Despite the efforts of French railroad personnel who tried to unhook one of the tanks, all twenty-two tanks were delivered to the company. A big reception and celebration ensued.[71]

The "*Spiess*" served as the proverbial mother of the company. His responsibilities included the everyday administration, order, and welfare of the unit. As a senior enlisted man, the Spiess usually bore the rank of Army First Sergeant or *SS-Hauptscharführer*. The *Spiess* was easily recognized by the thick notebook attached between the front tunic buttons, and the "piston rings" or "tress" (silver bullion fabric) around the tunic sleeve-cuffs.

The *Technischer Führer Kraftfahrzeugwesen* (TFK) or technical motor vehicle officer generally was a vehicle engineer responsible for the vehicles of a larger unit, such as a battalion or regiment. TFKs were usually captains or first lieutenants. The rank and billet of the *Schirrmeister* or supply chief originates from the period when horses and horse-drawn vehicles were used in the military. "*Geschirr*" referred to the leather used to hitch the vehicles to the horses. The term, however, evolved to incorporate additional technical aspects of soldiering. The *Schirrmeister*, usually a staff NCO, was responsible for the technical matters of a unit.[72]

Individual as well as "man and tank" training concluded before the new year. This phase taught the men, for example, how to escape or exit from inside a tank in the case of an emergency. A small hatch in the floor of the vehicle provided the exit. For this exercise, the instructors often selected areas where the ground was soft and the actual ground clearance very low.[73]

In order to enhance morale and marksmanship interest within the division, Treuenfeld established the Frundsberg sniper badge, which could be awarded and worn by NCOs and troops. Represented by a white whistle cord, instead of the standard black color, the cord attached from the second front tunic button from the top to the right breast pocket. A certificate accompanied the cord when the prescribed six marksmanship sniper requisites were successfully completed, in the field, within a period of one month. The requirements for the award included three hits out of five shots at 200 meters against a cranium target visible for five seconds; four hits out of five shots at 200 meters against a cranium target wearing a gas mask; three hits out of five shots at 300 meters against a moving (from left to right or vice versa) side-view motorcycle messenger target; two hits out of three shots at 100 meters against a kneeling rifleman target at night using white illumination flares; three hits out of five shots at 150 meters against a machine gun target at dawn; and three hits out of five shots at 100 meters against a moving aerial target visible for two minutes.[74]

During the first several days in January 1944, the 10th SS Assault Gun Battalion disbanded. In accordance with the special regimental order 1/44, ten self-propelled assault guns (Sd.Kfz.142) from the respective 1st, 2nd, and 3rd Batteries transferred to the 2nd Battalion to form the 7th and 8th Companies. An assortment of trucks was distributed to the regimental and battalion staffs, whereby each assault gun company was left with eight light and seven medium trucks. A number of trucks and equipment transferred to the 1st (Panther) Battalion as well.[75]

Unit drama and politics were commonplace in every larger group of individuals. On two separate occasions, Hans-Dieter Sauter, the adjutant of the 1st Self-Propelled Artillery Battalion, requested leave to get married. Sander, the regimental officer, declined the approval on both occasions, stating that no more than three officers were permitted absent at one time. The rejections came despite the fact that Sauter had already received permission to marry in January 1944, when the 1st Self-Propelled Battalion attached to the tank regiment and trained at Mailly-le-Camp. Seeking advice from a fellow colleague, the battalion commander (Jobst) spoke with Franz Kleffner, the regimental tank commander. Jobst explained Sauter's situation to Kleffner who granted permission immediately. Shortly thereafter, Jobst in turn relieved Sauter as battery commander.

When the regimental adjutant Heinzelmann aspired to become a General Staff officer, Sander requested a replacement through the SS main office. *SS-Obersturmführer* Walter Behrens from the 5th SS Panzer Division arrived as a replacement. When Heinzelmann was unable to pass the entrance examination and returned to the artillery regiment, he assumed his old duties and Behrens became the commander of the 1st Battery. In April 1944, Sauter assumed temporary command of the 3rd Battery when the eastbound train that carried the battery commander, *SS-Obersturmführer* Genz, and a number of NCOs, inadvertently was hitched to the wrong train heading in the wrong direction.[76]

After the 6th Company, 10th SS Panzer Regiment, received its full complement of men, the company relocated to Le Neubourg and continued combat training. Vehicle numbers were applied to the tank turrets. During the end of January, the 6th Company relocated southwest of Paris to the troop training facility in Mailly-le-Camp where larger formation training began. A group comprised two tanks. A platoon consisted of two groups of four tanks plus the platoon commander's vehicle. Finally, a company comprised four platoons and company troops.

The prerequisite for effective training was a comprehensive understanding of the use of the radio. Bernhard Westerhoff recalls this evolution of the training to have been a jovial experience that brought out the best in the men. Tank training rounded out with loading and gunnery training. Target locations were given based on their position on a clock: "Three o'clock—solitary oak—three mils right—enemy antitank!" Half of the division's success would depend on teamwork and well-defined and speedy target acquisition. Later, the lives of the men would depend on it.[77]

During an exercise in the loading and reloading of armor-piercing ammunition, the tank commander Schneider gave perfect target coordinates. Using the electronic firing device, one armor-piercing round fired from the barrel with a sharp bang. Despite thorough training, the recoil of the main gun caused Westerhoff to be thrown completely from the turret. As a result, Schneider was severely reprimanded.[78]

Larger battalion and regimental-sized training exercises were completed that focused on tank operations coordinated with the *Luftwaffe* and other supporting units. For the week around 8 February 1944, the II SS Panzer Corps, consisting of the 9th SS and 10th SS Panzer Divisions, conducted a large-scale training exercise with the *Luftwaffe*. *SS-Obergruppenführer* Paul Hausser led the exercise, whereas General of Panzer Troops Guderian, *SS-Standartenführer* Kurt Meyer, as well as other Army officers attended from nearby units. The exercise served to gauge the combat readiness of both divisions; it received high praise from General Guderian.[79]

The nearly complete training of the division gave tribute to the achievements of the officers and NCOs of the cadre. However, the training phases lacked essential equipment. Supply shortages and the effects of war forced units to rely on a mixed bag of vehicles for transportation. In turn, the training for mechanics became more complex and time consuming. The repair of a variety of vehicles required a larger stock and source of spare parts. For example, the company inventory of vehicles prepared by *SS-Scharführer* Kautz, 5th Company, 10th SS Panzer Regiment, exemplifies the dilemma with four British Triumph motorcycles, of which one had gear problems; four light Volkswagen (VW) and one Opel-Kadett cars, of which three VWs were unserviceable; one heavy Army Steyr-made automobile; one light French-made Citroen truck with engine damage; six American Ford V-8 medium trucks, three of which were unserviceable; one unserviceable Czechoslovakian Skoda-manufactured truck with steering problems; one unserviceable Opel-Blitz truck with a bad cylinder block; two Army Maultier (half-track trucks); one light Saurer-produced prime mover; nine Steyr Pz.Kpfw.IV, of which two were being serviced; and 11 Allkett-produced Pz.Kpfw.IV, of which six had replacement engines.[80]

On 22 February 1944, the 6th Company, 10th SS Panzer Regiment, left Mailly-le-Camp and returned to Normandy where they quartered in a castle in Pont Authou. At the end of March, the men of the pioneer company, 10th SS Panzer Regiment, returned to their quarters at Berville after laying mines and building obstacles at Dieppe. Protective vehicle ramparts were dug for the Ford trucks and armored half-tracks, and rocket launchers were distributed to the men. The end of March signaled the completion of the training. The strength of the division included 487 officers, 2,722 NCOs, and 16,104 men totaling 19,313 soldiers. For the men of the 6th Company, 10th SS Panzer Regiment, the distribution of large quantities of ammunition generated rumors of a deployment to the east, a movement confirmed on 30 March 1944. The division loaded onto trains in the area of Lisieux-Bernay and arrived in Lemberg on 2 April.[81]

Franz Holtrichter was a Radio Troop officer assigned to the staff of the 2nd Battalion, 22nd *SS-Panzergrenadier* Regiment. On 29 March, the battalion vehicles were staged at the railroad station in Mecidon, France. The driver of Holtrichter's vehicle, de Paris, hailed from the Elsass and asked for permission to see his French friends and bid them farewell. Holtrichter referred him to the transport officer. Around the same time the vehicles were being loaded onto the train, de Paris managed to disappear. Without his driver, Holtrichter drove the VW *Kübelwagen* onto the train himself. As the time of departure neared with no sign of de Paris, Holtrichter reported the matter to the transport officer, who held the train for an additional thirty minutes. In accordance with regulations, drivers were required to remain with their vehicles at all times. Since de Paris was absent without authorization, Holtrichter remained with the vehicle. Most everyone else was required to ride in the closed cars, which were modified to accommodate troops. After an Allied bombing attack that killed all the men in the railcars, Holtrichter and other drivers managed to crawl under their vehicles during a second attack. Other vehicles were driven away from the railroad station and parked in a nearby open field in order to avoid additional aerial attacks.

Holtrichter and the 2nd Battalion briefly attached to an antiaircraft unit, whereby the drivers received marching orders to the Training and Replacement Battalion "Brünn." Upon arrival, the drivers were issued new clothing and ten days special furlough, which allowed Holtrichter to spend Easter Sunday at home. After time with the family, approximately twenty-five men from the original 180 men that survived the bombing attack met back at Brünn.[82]

In conclusion, the division officially organized on paper in December 1942 as a direct result of the threat and anticipated landings by Allied forces somewhere in Western Europe. By the time 1943 ended, the 1943-pattern panzer division consisted of nearly 20,000 men. The cadre consisted of German officers and NCOs who made up the heart and soul of the division. These men were combat veterans with extensive operational experience. Their battlefield competence transformed the entire division into an elite formation ready for action. Men from the first five SS panzer divisions, as well as members from the Army, *Luftwaffe*, and *Kriegsmarine* consistently transferred in and out of the division until it reached full strength. The majority of the rank and file was conscripted and came from outside the German borders. Despite high morale, the division continued to lack adequate equipment and did not receive their full complement of vehicles until 1945. Nevertheless the division trained extensively throughout France for the purpose of repelling the anticipated Allied air and sea landings. The men prepared both physically and mentally for combat, but often the training did not include required curriculum, such as SS ideology. In many cases, the cadre ignored ideological training requirements that focused on Germanic ideals and concepts. Instead they focused on strengthening morale and building esprit de corps, the foundation to combat effectiveness and survival.

SS-Brigadeführer Lothar Debes hosting a field exercise for an army commander. Source: Gemeinschaftsarbeit des SS-Kriegsberichter-Zuges der 10.SS-Panzer-Div. "Frundsberg," *Dran Drauf und Durch! Buczacz-Caen-Nimwegen*, 1944.

Commander of the 10th SS Panzer Regiment, *SS-Obersturmbannführer* Otto Paetsch. Source: Gemeinschaftsarbeit des SS-Kriegsberichter-Zuges der 10.SS-Panzer-Div. "Frundsberg," *Dran Drauf und Durch! Buczacz-Caen-Nimwegen*, 1944.

Alexander Grenda, following his training
at Bitsch-Westmark, as a radio operator
and tank driver, and then assigned to
the Antitank Battalion at Angoulême.
Source: Alexander Grenda Archive.

SS Barracks München-Freimann. Departing for training, 1943.
Source: Jacob Archive.

SS officers at the training facility
München-Freimann, 1943. Source:
Jacob Archive.

The oath of enlistment
ceremony, SS Barracks
München-Freimann, 1943.
Source: Jacob Archive.

Formation of troops in preparation
for the oath of enlistment ceremony,
SS Barracks München-Freimann,
1943. Source: Jacob Archive.

New recruits stating the oath
of enlistment. SS Barracks
München-Freimann, 1943.
Source: Jacob Archive.

Pass and review of the troops, oath of enlistment ceremony, SS Barracks München-Freimann, 1943. Source: Jacob Archive.

Pass and review of new recruits, oath of enlistment ceremony, SS Barracks München-Freimann, 1943. Source: Jacob Archive.

New recruits stating the oath of enlistment. SS Barracks München-Freimann, 10 February 1943. Source: Jacob Archive.

Bivouac or tent camp in Senas, southern France, 1943. Source: Jacob Archive.

SS-Sturmmann Otto Jacob posing during a training exercise in the Pyrenees, France, 1943. Source: Jacob Archive.

SS-Sturmmann Otto Jacob (center) during time off in town, Auxerre, France, 1943. Source: Jacob Archive.

Group photo at the bivouac or tent camp in Senas, southern France, 1943. Source: Jacob Archive.

SS-Cannonier Otto Jacob (2nd from left) and his fellow soldiers posing during time off during the SS Artillery School, 1943. Source: Jacob Archive.

SS-Cannonier Schuster, SS Artillery School, 1943. Source: Jacob Archive.

SS-Cannonier Wallenhels, eight days after becoming an SS-Recruit, 1943. Source: Jacob Archive.

SS-Cannonier Otto Jacob, eight days after becoming an SS-Recruit, 1943. Source: Jacob Archive.

Bivouac or tent camp in Senas, southern France, 1943. Source: Jacob Archive.

An *SS-Unterscharführer* posing in front of the barracks; their first assigned billeting in France, near Angoulême, March 1943. Source: Jacob Archive.

SS-Cannonier Otto Six, in his walking out uniform, 10th SS Artillery Regiment, 1943. Source: Jacob Archive.

Heinz Martin posing in front of a larger *Zelt* tent, consisting of sixteen individual tents joined together. Bivouac or tent (*Zelt*) camp in Senas, southern France, 1943. Source: Jacob Archive.

SS-Mann Otto Jacob, 1943.
Source: Jacob Archive.

SS-Mann Otto Jacob, 1943.
Source: Jacob Archive.

Officers of the II SS Panzer Corps, including Heinz Harmel, *SS-Gruppenführer* Lothar Debes, and *SS-Obersturmbannführer* Sylvester Stadler, of the 9th SS Panzer Division "Hohenstaufen." Source: Sieberhagen Archive.

a.

a. Noncommissioned officers sit at the center table during summer festivities in Angoulême, France, 1943. Source: Sieberhagen Archive.
b–c. Burial of the fellow soldier Ternik in the city of Cognac, France. Source: Sieberhagen Archive.

b.

c.

Officers of the 2nd Company, 10th SS Panzer Signals Battalion. From left to right: An unidentified NCO, *SS-Untersturmführer* Friedhelm Lohbeck, company commander, *SS-Untersturmführer* Hans-Otto Pollähne, *SS-Untersturmführer* Jost von Brandis (profile), and *SS-Untersturmführer* Hans-Georg Wegner. *SS-Untersturmführer* Lohbeck was killed in action in April 1945, approximately 30 km from the village of Seessel. Source: Sieberhagen Archive.

Officers and NCOs of the 6th Company, 2nd Battalion, 10th SS Panzer Regiment. From left *SS-Hauptscharführer* Fritz Stief (*Spiess*), *SS-Untersturmführer* Rudi Schwemmlein, *SS-Hauptsturmführer* Leo Franke, *SS-Untersturmführer* Hans Quandel, and *SS-Hauptsturmführer* Helmut Stratman (possibly). Source: Sieberhagen Archive.

Recruit training. Source: Sieberhagen Archive.

SS-Unterscharführer Hanke.
Source: Sieberhagen Archive.

SS-Schütze Karl Heinz Schmidtz, 10th
SS Panzer Reconnaissance Battalion.
Source: Sieberhagen Archive.

2. Batterie der I. Abteilung, Artillerie-Regiment 10
10. SS-Panzer-Division "Frundsberg"

Sd Kfz 124 "Wespe"
10,5cm Leichte Feldhaubitze 18/2
auf Fahrgestell PzKpfw II (Sf)

SS-*Sturmbannführer* Paetsch (center),
commander of the 10th SS Panzer Regiment,
flanked by his adjutant and ordnance officer.
Source: Westerhoff Archive.

SS-*Sturmbannführer* Reinhold (left), commander of the 2nd Battalion, 10th SS Panzer Regiment with adjutant. Source: Westerhoff Archive.

Drivers' training on a Pz.Kpfw. IV Ausf. H, 6th Company, 2nd Battalion, 10th SS Panzer Regiment. Mailly-le-Camp, France, 1944. Source: Westerhoff Archive.

Two fellow soldiers posing in front of a Pz.Kpfw.IV Ausf. H; notice the missing right side skirts. Source: Westerhoff Archive.

Bernhard Westerhoff posing with a
fellow soldier cleaning the barrel of the
main gun. Source: Westerhoff Archive.

An inoperable Pz.Kpfw.IV broken down
due to engine problems in France,
1944. Source: Westerhoff Archive.

An inoperable Pz.Kpfw.IV broken down
due to engine problems in France,
1944. Source: Westerhoff Archive.

SS-Unterscharführer Karl Schneider, 6th Company, 2nd Battalion, 10th SS Panzer Regiment. Source: Westerhoff Archive.

SS-Oberscharführer Bernhard Westerhoff, 6th Company, 2nd Battalion, 10th SS Panzer Regiment. Source: Westerhoff Archive.

SS-Oberscharführer Erich Erhard, 3rd Platoon, 6th Company, 2nd Battalion, 10th SS Panzer Regiment, at the Panzer Replacement Battalion in Weimar, 1943. Source: Westerhoff Archive.

SS-Hauptsturmführer Leo Franke, commander of the 6th Company, 2nd Battalion, 10th SS Panzer Regiment, standing in front of the barracks in Rohrbach, France, in April 1943. Source: Westerhoff Archive.

Recruits standing on line outside the barracks at Rohrback, 1943. Source: Westerhoff Archive.

The comfortable relocation of the division from Rohrbach to Angoulême, France, 1943, occurred only once. Source: Westerhoff Archive.

Roll call in Vars, France, 1943.
Source: Westerhoff Archive.

Men of the 6th Company in
Angoulême, France, 1943.
Source: Westerhoff Archive.

SS panzer troops were trained at the
Army Tank School in Paderborn. Men
from the 6th Company included Hans
Ohlmeyer (far left) and Werner Pietzka
(far right). Source: Westerhoff Archive.

Members of the 2nd Battalion training course in Beneschau, a *Waffen-SS* training area in the territory of the Protectorate of Bohemia and Moravia. Source: Westerhoff Archive.

W. Helm, 6th Company, Vars, France, 1943. Source: Westerhoff Archive.

Men of the 6th Company at the marketplace in Angoulême. Source: Westerhoff Archive.

Two fellow soldiers from the 6th Company that grew to know each other very well. The 1st Battalion NCO and a tank driver. Source: Westerhoff Archive.

The cook was easily recognized by his white shirt and apron. Source: Westerhoff Archive.

Senior member of the combat baggage train depicted as a Private and a member of the Death's Head Regiments. Source: Westerhoff Archive.

The supply chief, an *SS-Oberscharführer*, of the
Supply Battalion. Source: Westerhoff Archive.

Members of a tank drivers' training course outside a cafe in Angoulême, France,
1943. Source: Westerhoff Archive.

Group photograph of an
assault gun company,
on top of an assault gun.
Source: Westerhoff Archive.

A company of the 2nd Battalion,
10th SS Panzer Regiment,
on a conditioning march near
Souprosse, France, 1943.
Source: Westerhoff Archive.

Members of the 6th Company,
2nd Battalion, 10th SS Panzer
Regiment, on the first day of
Easter in Angoulême, France,
1943. Source: Westerhoff Archive.

The 6th Company on their way to a
bullfight in Mont de Marsan, France, 1943.
Source: Westerhoff Archive.

One of the few Pz.Kpfw.III vehicles used during their training. Source: Westerhoff Archive.

Men taking a break after concluding a combat scenario. Notice the stack of arms in the background. Source: Westerhoff Archive.

SS-Oberschütze Werner Pietzka. Source: Westerhoff Archive.

Frundsberg-Lied

Trom meln dröh nen durch das Land, Krieg brennt al ler we gen

Him mel, Höl le, Mord und Brand, hell blinkt un ser De gen,

Frunds berg - Gre na die re, Ker le kühn und stolz,

ha ben hei ße Her zen, sind aus har tem Holz.

Dran, Drauf und Durch!

2. Furchtlos ziehn wir durch die Nacht,
   rauh sind unfre Lieder,
   blutig war so manche Schlacht,
   doch wir blieben Sieger.
   Frundsberg-Grenadiere......

3. Würfelspiel und Becherklang,
   dazu Zechkumpanen
   und ein rechter Landsknechtsang
   unter schwarzen Fahnen.
   Frundsberg-Grenadiere......

4. Mädel in dem roten Mohn
   laß das lange Zieren,
   hörst du den Fanfarenton,
   bald muß ich marschieren.
   Frundsberg-Grenadiere......

5. Frundsberg - Du bist unser Mann,
   Deine Schlacht wir schlagen,
   Nichts von Dir uns trennen kann,
   für Dich wir alles wagen!
   Frundsberg-Grenadiere......

The Frundsberg Song. Source: Westerhoff Archive.

Quarters of the 6th Company, 2nd Battalion, 10th SS Panzer Regiment, in the monastery building on the left. Le Bec-Hellouin, France, November 1943. Source: Westerhoff Archive.

A StuG III training vehicle of the 6th Company, received in exchange for the Pz.Kpfw III. France, 1943. Source: Westerhoff Archive.

The parade grounds at Le Bec-Hellouin on 9 November 1943, France. The formation depicts the 2nd Battalion, 10th SS Panzer Regiment. Source: Westerhoff Archive.

Recruit photograph of tank radio operator. Source: Westerhoff Archive.

Officers and noncommissioned officers of the 6th Company, 2nd Battalion, 10th SS Panzer Regiment. Source: Westerhoff Archive.

Tanks of the 6th Company moving to the railhead for the transportation from Le Bec-Hellouin to Le Neubourg, 1944. Source: Westerhoff Archive.

Ready for departure by rail during the relocation from Le Neubourg to the troop training facility at Mailly-le-Camp, southwest of Paris, January 1944. Source: Westerhoff Archive.

Tank commanders training. France, 1944. Source: Westerhoff Archive.

Drivers' training on a Pz.Kpfw. IV Ausf. H, 6th Company, 2nd Battalion, 10th SS Panzer Regiment. Mailly-le-Camp, France, 1944. Source: Westerhoff Archive.

Tank recovery training, Mailly-le-Camp, France, 1944. Source: Westerhoff Archive.

Tank target training. Mailly-le-Camp, France, 1944. Source: Westerhoff Archive.

Three fellow soldiers during tank target training, Mailly-le-Camp, France, 1944. Source: Westerhoff Archive.

The face of an *SS-Oberschütze*. Source: Westerhoff Archive.

The face of an *SS-Oberschütze.*
Source: Westerhoff Archive.

The face of an *SS-Oberschütze.*
Source: Westerhoff Archive.

The face of an *SS-Oberschütze.*
Source: Westerhoff Archive.

On 22 February 1944, the 6th Company relocated from Mailly-le-Camp to the castle at Pont Authou. Source: Westerhoff Archive.

A picture of circumstance: the tank driver Woita with his father on a transport train. Source: Westerhoff Archive.

CHAPTER 2

Commitment of the 10th SS Panzer Division in the East

March–June 1944

AT THE END OF MARCH 1944, snow and cold greeted the 10th SS Panzer Division in the northern Ukraine. In stark contrast to France, where the first blossoms had already sprouted, traces of spring had not yet emerged. The men of the division arrived in the devastated streets of Lemberg and awaited further orders after the long railroad journey. After the divisional convoys formed, one unit after another rolled out of Lemberg.

Galicia centered itself between the cities of the Austrian capital of Vienna in the east, Polish Warsaw in the north, the Russian city of Kiev in the west, and the Rumanian capital of Budapest in the south. The Carpathian Mountains arch from the southwestern base of the Weichsel River southeast to the mouth of the Donau south of Odessa. Galicia formed within the Polish Republic but was acquired in 1772 by Austria during the first partition of Poland. After World War I, Galicia returned to the Poles and formed in 1944 the district of the General Government of Poland. A neglected region of 4.5 million people, Lemberg numbered the third largest city with 350,000 poor inhabitants. The majority of the people were Ukrainians, and after the war in 1918, ethnic tension with the Poles lasted until the Soviets occupied the region in 1939. Once the Soviets entered the region, forced deportations began and a three-year reign of terror ensued. The Soviet People's Commissariat for Internal Affairs (NKVD) murdered many Ukrainians and Poles. To help fight Bolshevism, thousands of men from the region volunteered in April 1943 to form the 14th SS Volunteer Division "Galezien."

In the wake of the Soviet encirclement of Kamenez-Polodsk and Tarnopol, Russian forces penetrated farther west across the Strypa River and onto Buczacz. The II SS Panzer Corps faced the difficult task of safeguarding the General Government against the Soviets and relieving German forces trapped between the Dnjestr, Zbrutsch, and Strypa Rivers.[1]

The battles of Stalingrad, Tscherkassy, and Uman weakened German troops in the East. Although many units managed to break out of numerous encirclements and reach friendly lines, the lack of fuel resulted in the loss of large quantities of tanks and artillery. By mid-February 1944, the German situation along the Ukrainian front became precarious. Most of the reserve forces were exhausted and they found themselves in a situation that resembled that of the First Panzer Army, commanded by General

Hans-Valentin Hube. Continuous fighting placed light divisions near collapse and the front lines, held by infantry, were dangerously thin. The overextended front of the First Panzer Army reached from the western Ukraine along a general line north of Winniza and Schepetowka, northeast of Tarnopol. The only area along the front that resembled German containment stretched between the Dnjepr River delta and Schepetowka. From Schepetowka to the Pripjet Marshes, General Arthur Hauffe's Nürnberger 13th Infantry Division held an 80 km gap and protected an entire Army Corps.[2]

General Hauffe assumed the sole responsibility of safeguarding the strategic and decisive corridor south of the Pripjet Marshes and the task of preventing the Russians from closing the gap. The perilous situation became more acute after the Soviet Thirteenth Army crossed the strategic Dnjepr-Pripjet triangle. Despite the efficiency of General Hauffe in delaying the Soviet advance, he was unable to stop it altogether. Thus, six Soviet armies stood at the corridor along the old Polish border near Rowno. The Russians reorganized in order to launch a new and decisive attack with strong tank concentrations, hoping to force a decision and cause a general collapse across the German southern front. The main goal was the isolation and destruction of Army Group South, after splitting it away from Army Group Center and pushing it against the Black Sea or Carpathian Mountains.

In the west, the Russians threatened the important western railhead at Kowel, bordering the Pripjet area, and concentrated a large force to attack Field Marshal Erich von Manstein's northern flank. Based on personal visits to the sector of the LXIV Army Corps, Manstein repeatedly warned Hitler's Headquarters about a potential general collapse and requested additional forces for the formation of an army behind the threatened area of Rowno.

The Soviet armies of the 2nd Ukrainian Front, which Marshal Ivan Stephanovich Konev formed for earlier operations against the encirclement around Korsun, opposed the German Eighth Army. After a brief respite, Soviet forces waited to resume the attack against weak German positions with limited armor. Moreover, the Germans lacked the forces that fought at the encirclement of Tscherkassy. Indeed,

Marshal Konev stood a good chance of reaching his goal: Belorussia-Rumania.[3]

Throughout the latter portion of 1943, considered a transitional year, the Soviet Stavka made good use of refinements to the operational art of war. The Soviets improved their tactical command and control through greater use of radios, vehicles, aircraft, and command points. Tactical defenses evolved from non-continuous to deep and dense trench systems, supported by increased fire support, which provided for greater security. Theoretically, the compression of the defense in width and supplementation of artillery in depth provided for a concentration of force. This approach proved ideal and effective against German armored counterattacks. Soviet defensive belts usually deployed a rifle corps, consisting of two rifle divisions, within the first belt, and one rifle division in the second. Each rifle division manned the defenses in one or two echelons, while rifle regiments deployed in two echelons. Group artillery, antitank regions comprised of fortified points, artillery antitank reserves, and mobile obstacle detachments provided support for each rifle regiment. The antitank defenses became more durable by deploying stronger belts throughout the depth of the defense. First echelon counterattacks and reinforcements by mobile tank brigades or regiments, or self-propelled gun regiments of the rifle division reserve, were designed to restore any breaches within the defensive lines.[4]

Zhukov ordered the Soviet First Tank Army to strike against the Dnjestr in the direction of Tschernowitz. The Soviet Fourth Tank Army was to regroup and consolidate until its infantry divisions caught up. To the listening Germans, it was clear that weak forces of the Soviet Fourth Tank Army held the northern reaches of the Dnjestr, but only as long as its infantry divisions remained far behind. Additional radio intercepts indicated that Zhukov anticipated a German breakout to the south across the only remaining escape route at the Hotin bridgehead.

Soviet forces managed to gain control of all the major escape routes, four major tributaries to the west, and penetrate deep along the northern front of the pocket. While visiting Hitler at the Adlerhorst, Manstein received permission to break out to the west. At the same time, Hitler attached the II SS Panzer Corps to the Fourth Panzer Army, in order for General Hube to attack out of the southwest region of Tarnopol. The SS corps consisted of the 9th and 10th SS Panzer Divisions from France, as well as the 100th *Jäger* Division from Hungary and the 367th Infantry Division.[5]

In order to rescue the twenty-two divisions, the First Panzer Army and the reinforced Fourth Panzer Army had to stabilize the front between the Carpathians and the Pripjet Marshes. The Eighth Army, next to the Sixth Army of Army Group A, provided security in Rumania while the Hungarian Army held the mountain passes through the Carpathians.

The pocket closed on 25 March 1944, trapping the First Panzer Army north of the Dnjestr. Once General Hube detected the Soviet center of gravity concentrating in the east and north, he shortened the front along a more defendable perimeter around Kamenez-Podolsk. Primarily, the reduced front allowed for a greater concentration of forces to defend against Soviet attacks. Second, it provided for a more efficient means to distribute the limited supplies along interior lines of communications. However, the Soviets assumed the Germans were in a headlong retreat and gave the First Panzer Army time to seal off any penetrations along the northeastern portion of the salient.

The Soviet advance in the south, referred by David M. Glantz and Jonathan House, the authors of *When Titans Clash: How the Red Army Stopped Hitler*, as "freeing the Ukraine virtually without a halt," was rapid but not without pause. Marshal Zhukov planned to catch any German forces attempting to escape the encirclement with strong Soviet forces located along the Dnjestr south of Kamenez-Podolsk. Confident, Zhukov committed his entire 1st Tank Army and fast corps onto the southern bank of the Dnjestr and attacked Tschernowitz, Kolomea, and Stanislau. To that end, Zhukov removed his forces from the forward positions of the encirclement, a significant mistake in operational planning. He was thereafter unable to use his strength at the crucial moment in the north.[6]

Early German reports indicated that *Gruppe Mauss*, with its three divisions, almost linked with the Fourth Panzer Army, and the 1st Panzer Division continued to hold the Eckpfeiler Gorodok. The LXIV Corps successfully captured the area around Frampol-Jarmolinzy and, while air support remained consistent, the 17th Panzer Division stood ready for an attack at Kamenez-Podolsk.

On the evening of 28 March, the First Panzer Army formed two groups to achieve their objective. In the north, Corps Group Chevallerie received the objectives of covering the northern flank and, in conjunction with other forces, to establish a bridgehead across the Zbrucz to capture and hold open the larger crossings of the Seret. Corps Group Breith, forming a wedge in the south, received the task of destroying the enemy in the area of Kamenez-Podolsk and breaking out across the Zbrucz at Okopy.

The next day, forward elements of the northern wedge broke across the Zbrucz River while elements of the 16th Panzer Division from Westphalia and the 17th Panzer Divisions from Thüringen rolled up enemy resistance. The now free 1st Panzer Division that followed took over positions of the XXIV Panzer Corps. Attacks by the southern group struck in full swing to the southwest. With help from elements of the 2nd SS Panzer Division "Das Reich," the East Prussian 1st Infantry Division and 101st *Jäger* Division from Baden-Württemberg continued to hold their positions against Konev's 2nd Ukrainian Front. Corps Group Chevallerie secured bridgeheads across the Zbrucz and a bridge that remained intact at the Skala River. The first phase of the German relief succeeded by surprising the Soviets. Moreover, once Zhukov discovered his mistake, only a single Soviet tank corps employed into the decisive northern battle against the flank of the First Panzer Army, from the southern banks of the Dnjestr.[7]

General Hausser's staff of the II SS Panzer Corps arrived in Lemberg on 1 April. The corps also incorporated the 506th Heavy Panzer Battalion and the 2nd Battalion of the 23rd Panzer Regiment. The same day, warning orders alerted the individual units of their responsibilities, based on the 2 April Panzer Army Order Nr. 63, by the Fourth Panzer Army.

The II SS Panzer Corps received orders to surprise the enemy and drive it out of the line

Rohatyn-Brzezany and to the southeast, destroy the enemy south of Podhajce and attack onto Buczacz, via Monasterzyska. The 367nd Infantry Division, arriving from the area Burcztyn-Rohatyn, was to join the SS Panzer Corps and capture the area of Wolczkow (7 km east of Jezupol-Horozanka-Huilcze-Bolczowce). The secondary objective of the 367nd Infantry Division included supporting the eastward leading operations and providing security in the south along the Dnjster River. A panzer division was to attack forward via Brezezany and Podhajce and onto Monasterzyska, turning east to capture the sector along the Strypa River by Buczacz. The objective of the XLVIII Panzer Corps was to support and protect eastward-moving tank operations in the north, draw Russian forces away from the southern enemy wing, and block the enemy moving southward from the east. In order for the corps to establish bridgeheads on either side of Zlotniki in the sector of the Strypa, the corps was to attack against the center of gravity on both sides of Podhajce. The 100th *Jäger* Division and the 506th Heavy Panzer Battalion were to support the attack. Due to very small amounts of organic army pioneer equipment, all pioneers were directed to participate only in pioneer work. Once the breakout was underway, the II SS Panzer Corps would receive snow plows to clear the roads. The supply of the First Panzer Army consolidated in the area of Chodorow. Once contact was re-established between the spearheads of the relief force and the First Panzer Army, all supply units would assist to resupply the units under close coordination with the II SS Panzer Corps.[8]

Among the transport trains that carried the units of the 10th SS Panzer Division to their destination between 1 and 5 April, the 6th Company, 10th SS Panzer Regiment, arrived in the vicinity of Zloczow, east of Lemberg, in the afternoon on 2 April. The village lay along the rail line Lemberg-Tarnopol. Lacking an off-ramp, the company was detrained using bails of hay brought from France. The commander of the 3rd Platoon, Edmund Erhard recalled:

The platoon commanders were called to the company commanders and briefed on the situation. The Russians were marching on Lemberg and our own forces already made enemy contact. Chances were very good that we would be committed to combat before the day was over. With the use of maps, the situation was reviewed one more time and the order of march was determined in the assembly area.[9]

The company order of march was led by the 1st Platoon, under the command of *SS-Obersturmführer* Hans Quandel, followed by the 3rd Platoon, commanded by Erhard. The company details followed, commanded by Bernhard Westerhoff, and finally, the 2nd Platoon under *SS-Untersturmführer* Rudolf Schwemmlein. Wherever a problem arose, Leo Franke, the company commander, surfaced in his Volkswagen accompanied by two motorcycle messengers. The company reached the bivouac area of Slowita by way of the villages Jasionowce, Lackie, and Nowosiolki.[10]

The supply units of the 10th SS Panzer Division detrained in Lemberg and established supply points in the surrounding metropolitan area. Following the arrival of the 10th SS Administrative Supply Battalion, *SS-Sturmbannführer* Gerhard Schill immediately began baking operations. The bakers of the 1st Company, 10th SS Administrative Supply Battalion, were tasked on the first day with the preparation of 12,000 loaves of bread to feed 18,000 hungry men. The production of such quantities required 20,000 liters of water and 10 tons of flour. Meanwhile, *SS-Obersturmführer* Böhler arrived at the Army Supply Depot in Winnki, 6 kilometers southeast of Lemberg, in order to acquire fresh meat for the division. This amounted to 147 cattle, 120 pigs, or 240 sheep per day.[11]

The advance of Hausser's II SS Panzer Corps over two roads placed the 10th SS Division on the left side of Hohenstaufen. The 100th *Jäger* Division protected the flank on the left wing whereas the 367th Infantry Division secured the right. The replacement battalions from both SS divisions attached to the Köruck 585, in Zolkiew, and were assigned the task of protecting the northern flank of the Fourth Panzer Army.[12]

The approach march of the division proved especially difficult. For vehicle drivers in particular, the blowing snow and ice made the roads a great challenge and nearly impassable. On 3 April, tanks and vehicles proceeded through the villages of Przemyslany and Brzezany. The reality of war struck home when a vehicle became stuck along a ridgeline behind Lemberg. While the crew waited for the vehicle to be freed, Russian fighter aircraft appeared in the sky. A voice cried out, "Look out! Fighter aircraft!" The aircraft approached at low level, and the men tried vehemently to distance themselves from their vehicles through the knee-deep snow. Machine-gun fire danced across the road as the fighter planes roared off. Over the next few days, Russian aircraft attacked more frequently with machine guns, cannon, and bombs. The men of the division quickly understood the necessity of distancing themselves from their vehicles and finding cover. Some were not as fortunate and the first graves appeared along the side of the road.[13]

Meanwhile, the 367th Infantry Division and 100th *Jäger* Division began their attacks on 3 April. The 367th Division successfully established a bridgehead across the Narajowka, southeast of Rohatyn, whereas the 100th *Jägers* established bridgeheads across the Zlota Lipa at Litwinow, 10 km northwest of Podhajce, and at Litiatyn, southeast of Brzezany. Despite delays due to intolerable road conditions, the 974th Grenadier Regiment, of the 367th Division, captured Meducha, the western city heights, and managed to reach Horozanka. The 100th *Jäger* Division also managed to reach the eastern rim of the woods outside Podhajce. The attacking spearheads occupied northwestern Podhajce and the village of Bekersdorf to the northeast.[14]

A snowstorm between the Dnjestr and the Seret Rivers offered the Germans a brief respite from Soviet aircraft and, more importantly, the opportunity for the *Luftwaffe* to deliver supplies. Unfortunately, of the ninety-four supply containers dropped amidst the fighting by air, only six were recovered. On 4 April, the ground froze overnight and movement continued as rear-echelon troops of Corps Group Breith reached the Zbrucz River. The 1st Panzer Division made good progress on the attack and the 7th Panzer Division attacked against the important Chertkov-Buczacz road. Corps Group Chevallerie covered the northern flank west of the

Seret and prevented Soviet access to the river as units of the Fourth Panzer Army counterattacked along the Strypa toward Buczacz. While strong German forward elements seized the Czortkow-Buczacz road, Corps Group Breith seized crossings over the Strypa and opened crossings at Buczacz from the south. Destroying the bridges over the Dnjestr provided protection along the southern flank. With only 50 kilometers remaining before the breakout, the corps experienced bridging problems. At the same time, Zhukov tried to out-flank Corps Group Breith with the redirected 11th Guard Tank Corps across the Dnjestr and to the north. Even so, Corps Group Breith destroyed thirty-five Soviet tanks of the 11th Guard and fought it back across the Dnjestr.[15]

The objective of the II SS Panzer Corps was to attack to the southeast along the line Rohatyn-Brzezany, and then strike the Russians south of Podhajce and push through Monasterzyska to Buczacz. Advancing toward Podhajce, the most noticeable adversary remained below freezing temperatures, blowing snow, ice, and mud. Entire convoys stopped for hours to assist a single vehicle. Digging, pushing, and pulling reopened the roadway for about an hour, until the next vehicle became stuck. The 6th Company, 10th SS Panzer Regiment reached Brzezany around 0500 hours on 4 April. Tanks belonging to the 2nd Platoon, many of which became stuck or slid off the road, closed with the main formation throughout the day. By the evening of 4 April, 57 trains arrived carrying units of the 10th SS Panzer Division. Twenty-four hours later, the division was at full strength, minus the 10th SS Tank Destroyer Battalion and the 1st Battalion, 10th SS Panzer Regiment. As such, with several vehicles needing repair, the division reported thirty-two Pz.Kpfw.IV and thirty-eight StuG IIIs ready for combat.[16]

In the morning hours on 5 April, the 100th *Jäger* Division succeeded in pushing the Soviets out of portions of Podhajce and secured a crossing over the Koropiec stream. The 10th SS Panzer Reconnaissance Battalion received orders to reconnoiter the approach to Buczacz and protect a weak spot on the left flank of the division, in the sector north of Buczacz-Wisnioczyk, and establish a bridgehead over the Strypa. Around 1300 hours, armored half-tracks from scout detachments managed to reach the southern banks of the stream after crossing over a ford. A 12-ton auxiliary bridge was built across the Koropiec stream by the afternoon. While the 100th *Jäger* Division continued to advance in a southerly direction, the 10th SS Panzer Division began its attack at 1215 hours. The 10th SS Panzer Reconnaissance Battalion attacked directly to the south and southeast, down the middle of the funnel-shaped front of the 100th *Jäger* Division.

Of the three scout detachments, the 1st and 2nd Scouting Troops radioed the presence of a defensive blocking position, consisting of a Soviet antitank line, at the fork in the road southeast of Podhajce. In order to envelop the defenses, the 1st Scout Troop bypassed the line 1 km to the north until two vehicles became mired in the mud. Around 1700 hours, the 3rd Company, 10th SS Panzer Reconnaissance Battalion, commanded by *SS-Obersturmführer* Gerhard Hinze, was reinforced with two cannon platoons and one antitank platoon, the Scout Troop Hofmann, and the bulk of the reconnaissance battalion that bypassed the antitank line and captured Madzelowka. Although the bulk of the Russians managed to escape across the Strypa at Osowce, the reinforced 3rd Company, 10th SS Panzer Reconnaissance Battalion, continued the attack and captured Kurdwanowka. By 2100 hours, the village of Osowce and the intact bridge across the Strypa were in German hands. Scout Troop Küffner relentlessly pursued fleeing Russians back across the Strypa until ordered to reinforce the bridgehead. The remainder of the reconnaissance battalion closed with the bridgehead as far as Kurdwanowka, and the divisional tank companies took their turn crossing the ford at Podhajce.[17]

The Soviets were mindful of the strategic importance of Podhajce, which served as a stepping-stone to all future operations. Russian aircraft bombed and strafed the city to stop the German advance. However, on the ground Treuenfeld himself vehemently directed the flow of traffic.

The German armored attack began between 1700 and 1800 hours. Cautiously, the 6th Company, 10th SS Panzer Regiment approached the Russian antitank (AT) line. When the Russians opened fire

on the lead tank, ten Russian AT guns, emplaced along the road, were destroyed or overrun during the attack. Bernhard Westerhoff referred to it as a "real night-time battle." The Germans suffered no casualties; however Russian infantry persistently attacked individual tanks from positions on either side of the road. In this regard, *SS-Obersturmführer* Stock, of the 8th Assault Gun Company reported:

> Company received orders from Brigadeführer v. Treuenfeld to cross through the pocket in the most direct line and reach Buczacz. He anticipated the relief of the 6th Company, 2nd Battalion, which remained on the road and locked in combat.[18]

SS-Untersturmführer Hans-Dietrich Sauter, the adjutant of the 1st Battalion, 10th SS Panzer Artillery Regiment, and temporary 150mm "Hummel" battery commander brought his self-propelled battery into position at Podhajce to support the attack against Monasterzyska. The men prepared their battery positions by the book. Every artilleryman was required to dig a hole deep enough to accommodate one man. To his bewilderment, Sauter observed how German soldiers were reluctant to dig holes deep enough. On the other hand, Russian fighting holes encountered within captured positions were the absolute finest examples.[19]

After Hitler awarded Manstein the Swords to the Knight's Cross to the Iron Cross on 30 March, Field Marshal Walter Model took command of Army Group South on 2 April. Renamed to Army Group Northern Ukraine, Model ordered a change for the relief of the encircled army. Somewhat behind schedule, Model ordered the II SS Panzer Corps to form at Podhajce and attack to the southeast.[20]

The commander of 1st Battalion, 21st *SS-Panzergrenadier* Regiment, *SS-Sturmbannführer* Heinz Laubscheer, received orders to attack the village of Kowalowka. Heinz Laubscheer was born on 23 February 1913 in Marburg. After receiving a commission on 20 April 1936, from the officers' school at Braunschweig, Laubscheer attended a platoon commanders' course at Dachau before he posted as the adjutant, *SS-Oberabschnitt* "Elbe." He served for one year at the SS main office and first assumed command of a combat formation in 1 May 1938. As a company commander in the regiment "Germania," he participated in the campaign against Poland and France. After being wounded in the left shoulder on 24 May 1940, he posted as a tactics instructor to the officers' school at Bad Tölz. Returning to a combat unit, he commanded the SS Guard Battalion "Berlin" of the *Leibstandarte* SS "Adolf Hitler," as part of Battle Group Schuldt on the Eastern Front. By the time he arrived to command the 1st Battalion, 21st *SS-Panzergrenadier* Regiment, his decorations included the Iron Cross 2nd and 1st Class, the Infantry Assault Badge, the War Merit Badge 2nd Class, and the Wound Badge in Black.

On 19 December 1942, Laubscheer distinguished himself leading the remnants of "Battalion Laubscheer" (SS Guard Battalion LSSAH) when a portion of the Italian Army, situated along the Don River, was overrun by Russian troops. Battle Group Schuldt counterattacked east of Meschkoff to regain the dominating heights. In close combat, Laubscheer's battalion led the fight and defeated a Russian regiment. They held the heights until their last cartridge was expended and long enough to allow both the German and Italian troops to withdraw in good order. The next day, after fourteen days of fighting and breaking out of the encirclement, Laubscheer discovered that approximately a hundred men from his battalion had been left behind. With three junior lieutenants and ten men, Laubscheer drove 60 km back behind enemy lines to find the men. When Laubscheer arrived at the abandoned German positions, they discovered the men had withdrawn on their own accord. On 31 December, Laubscheer personally led a scouting party 15 km ahead of his own forces and made contact with the 11th Panzer Division. Thus, he established the prerequisite for the Battle Group to disengage from the pocket. For the achievements of Laubscheer, the commander of the Battle Group Schuldt, *SS-Standartenführer* Hinrich Schuldt, was awarded the Oak Leaves to the Knight's Cross to the Iron Cross on 2 April 1942.[21]

Meanwhile, Leo Franke, the commander of 6th Company, 10th SS Panzer Regiment, was wounded during the night on 5 April 1944 and

SS-Untersturmführer Quandel assumed command of the company. *SS-Rottenführer* Werner Pietzka was the driver of Franke's tank and assumed command of the vehicle. That evening between 5 and 6 April, both the 1st and 2nd battalions of the 21st *SS-Panzergrenadier* Regiment joined the 2nd Battalion, 10th SS Panzer Regiment to resume the attack. Erhard's 3rd Platoon of the 6th Company took the lead. Schneider's tank followed the lead tank that belonged to *SS-Sturmmann* Wennig. Half an hour later, Wennig's tank struck a mine with the right track. The radio operator was severely wounded on both legs and pulled out from the tank. A medic administered a tetanus shot and the wounded soldier was brought to an aid station. In order to assume the lead, Schneider's tank attempted to pass the immobilized tank when Quandel ordered him to stop. Fearing for the safety of his comrade and considerate of his marital status, he shouted, "Schneider! You are married!"

Erhard assumed the lead himself as they bypassed the heavily fortified village of Przeloka and passed through two blocking positions. In the open terrain they received enemy fire. From the right, a medium Russian T-34 tank opened fire. However, the lead 3rd Platoon destroyed the T-34, as well as several antitank guns and machine-gun nests. The attack pressed forward under constant supporting fire from the other tanks. During this phase, Russian trucks and several retreating prime movers, with their guns in tow, were also destroyed. Erhard described the Russians' withdrawal:

> As the road softly declined, we suddenly received fire from an antitank gun that had not been identified. The antitank gun was emplaced along the back slope in defilade. After three shots, I had not managed to destroy the gun. The AT gun fired at our tank when the fourth shot hit the left side of the track. The driver and radio operator were slightly wounded but we all managed to escape. Behind me, another tank quickly recognized the situation. Arcing around my tank to pass, the tank engaged the enemy AT gun. I stopped the next vehicle, climbed aboard, and continued to lead the assault. On the left, our own infantry joined in the assault when

a tank from our platoon destroyed the AT gun. This evolution took place in the village of Kowalowka. The Russians withdrew onto Buczacz. Under constant harassing fire that destroyed several of our vehicles, we arrived at Buczacz around 1700 hours and pushed forward to the village center. Here we dug in immediately and secured the position in all directions. Individual Russian infantry fired upon our tanks from surrounding houses, but thanks to our alertness, their attempts to close with our tanks failed. By radio we were instructed to hold the position.[22]

For a short period, the Russians managed to occupy the road behind Kowalowka. While the 6th Company, 10th SS Panzer Regiment deployed and successfully cleared the road, the company did not reach its objective around Buczacz to provide the support planned for the 3rd Platoon. At first light, however, the remaining combat formations engaged the objective at Buczacz.[23]

During the assault on Buczacz, Werner Pietzka's tank became immobile in the deep mud. The tank hull touched bottom and sat directly on the ground as the tracks churned freely. One by one, the other tanks disappeared out of sight as they pressed on the attack. The crew of the stranded tank remained patiently inside the vehicle. Pietzka scanned the surroundings with binoculars and spotted a nearby farmhouse. With the gunner and a submachine gun, they set off to the farmhouse. In the adjacent barn, the men discovered two young girls grinding wheat. As soon as they saw the soldiers, the girls ran into the farmhouse. Inside, the men found the mother as well. After removing the two machine guns from the tank, packing ammunition and rations, the crew of four returned to the warm farmhouse and bedded down for the night. During the night, Pietzka awoke and found the wide-awake mother, sitting upright in bed, arms clutching her two girls. The next day, recovery troops arrived and attached steel cables to pull the tank out of the mud with two 18-ton prime movers (SdKfz.9).[24]

During the fighting around Monasterzyska, *SS-Untersturmführer* Sauter and other forward observers from the 150mm "Hummel" batteries rode along in a communications half-track from the 1st Battalion, 21st *SS-Panzergrenadier* Regiment or "Laubscheer Battalion." Initial contact suggested the Russians outnumbered the grenadiers as additional Russian reinforcements arrived to bolster the defenses. When the attack across a field began to bog down due to well-camouflaged Russian positions, the forward observers radioed coordinates from the half-track "Laubscheer" with deadly accuracy. Even so, the grenadiers sustained numerous casualties from heavy Russian mortar fire between Oswolka and Monasterzyska. *SS-Sturmbannführer* Carl-Günther Molt, the commander of the 3rd Battalion, 21st *SS-Panzergrenadier* Regiment, was among the wounded. *SS-Standartenführer* Eduard Deisenhofer, the regimental commander, took command of the reinforced company and managed to capture the village that evening with supporting attacks by Stuka divebombers from the 77th Stuka Squadron.[25]

Dr. Eduard Deisenhofer was born on 27 June 1909 in Freising, Upper Bavaria. As a junior court barrister, he joined the Nazi Party on 1 September 1930 and, one month later, the SS. While a student, he established the 8th SS *Sturm* (company) and volunteered in 1934 for service with the *Leibstandarte* SS "Adolf Hitler" in Berlin. After receiving a commission, Deisenhofer led the 2nd Company of the "Deutschland" regiment in Munich and later the 2nd *Sturmbann* (battalion) of the 1st SS Death's Head Regiment "Oberbayern." He participated in both the occupations of the Sudetenland in 1938, and Bohemia and Moravia in 1939. Once the war broke out, the 2nd Battalion "Oberbayern" migrated to the 1st SS Death's Head Infantry Regiment as part of the new 3rd SS Death's Head Division. During the campaign in the West, when German troops broke through French lines and headed for the coast, Deisenhofer was shot through his knee. After his recovery and during the winter 1940/1941, he attended the University of Göttingen where he received a doctorate in legal science. He returned to his unit but did not disclose his academic achievements. Instead, he wanted to preserve the close relationship with his men and remain known as "Eddie." Deisenhofer was not a party apostle of SS global perspectives, nor a theorist of morality, but a cheerful officer who placed comradery and sol-diering before everything else. Deisenhofer was a married Catholic with three children.

Following his combat service in Norway and during his time in Russia in late 1941, Deisenhofer was wounded a second time. Before his full re-covery he returned to the SS Death's Head Division and assumed command of the 1st Battalion, 1st SS Death's Head Infantry Regiment. In February 1942, along with five Army divisions, Deisenhofer led his battalion for three months in the encircled fortress of Demjansk. Over a period of seventeen days, Deisenhofer and his men defended against twenty-three Russian attacks and launched counter-attacks that left as many as 1,088 Russians dead. Once German forces gained the upper hand and offensive operations resumed, Deisenhofer led two Death's Head companies against the village of Nowosselje on 30 April and routed a Russian battalion. However, subsequent Russian attacks of numerical superiority, supported by heavy tanks, managed to regain portions of the village in the late afternoon. Deisenhofer counterattacked immedi-ately and, after close combat, ejected the Russians indefinitely. Wounded a third time, Deisenhofer not only received the shield of Demjansk, but also the Knight's Cross to the Iron Cross for bravery and steadfast leadership.[26]

Meanwhile, the bodies of twenty German sol-diers were found in a mill outside Buczacz, shot in the back of the head, while their hands and arms displayed signs of being tied and beaten. Similar discoveries were made in the woods surrounding the city. According to eyewitness accounts by local city dwellers, Bolshevik troops handed captured German soldiers over to armed Jews. The dwellers brought food for the captured Germans but the guards threatened the dwellers and turned them away. When it became obvious the Russians could not hold Buczacz, the guards shot the prisoners and fled. Discussions between the author and Bernhard Westerhoff confirmed the murders. However, none of the eyewitness accounts or reports that identified the guards as being Jewish are considered reliable. Veterans of the division interviewed by the author consider the accounts contained and described within the wartime memorial publication, written by the divisional war correspondence platoon in 1944, as nothing more than pure propaganda. Despite the fact that the memorial chronicle, *Dran, Drauf, Durch! (Up To, On To, and Through!),* is bi-ased literature, it does contain valuable material for the reconstruction of the divisional history.[27]

Around 1700 hours on 6 April, with cold tempera-tures and falling snow, grenadiers of the Rhineisch-Westfälischen 6th Panzer Division fought their way through to Buczacz and linked with grenadiers from the 1st Battalion, 21st *SS-Panzergrenadier* Regiment, as the last remnants of Soviet resistance were elim-inated. Many Army and SS troops that fought their way out of the pocket around Kamenez-Podolsk were absorbed into the 10th SS Panzer Division. The appearance of the withdrawing troops markedly contradicted the expectations of the young SS vol-unteers. The experiences of their first engagement did not prepare them for the reality of the situation in the East. German propaganda of victory on the bat-tlefield quickly dissipated at the sight of their beaten comrades. According to *SS-Untersturmführer* Hans-Dietrich Sauter, the adjutant of the 1st Battalion, 10th SS Panzer Artillery Regiment, "The bewildered look of disbelief was expressed on every young sol-dier's face."

Bewilderment grew when a daily order of Field Marshal Walter Model was read before a man-datory troop formation. Model directed that any member of the German armed forces moving in a rearward direction without a map and marching or-ders from a superior officer, along a specific route, would be considered a deserter and shot immedi-ately. Numerous war-weary soldiers passed by the Frundsbergers and attempted to reach rearward areas, primarily at night, and rendezvous points for stragglers. Some, according to Sauter, even reached areas around Krakau. Draconian orders, such as the Model order, were uncommon at the onset of the war.[28]

In all, 200,000 men were saved from destruction after losing contact for fourteen days. Sauter, the ad-jutant for the 1st Battalion, 10th SS Panzer Artillery Regiment, whose mission it was to establish con-tact with the tank regiment, attached himself to the 21st *SS-Panzergrenadier* Regiment heading from Monasterzyska to Buczacz. In a half-track, Sauter encountered the first German soldiers coming out of the pocket. Battered, the men stumbled past the half-track, many supported by their comrades. It was a pitiful scene; the majority were wounded and every other man carried a weapon. A soldier from the *Leibstandarte*, passing by, among a group of men, yelled, "We knew you would come and get us out!" In sharp contrast, an Army officer without a weapon yelled, "Why are you idiots prolonging the war?"[29]

Sauter arrived at the combat command post of the 10th SS Panzer Regiment, situated in a farmhouse in Buczacz, where he found the regimental commander, *SS-Hauptsturmführer* Franz Kleffner, intoxicated. The adjutant whispered to Sauter that the divisional commander had relieved Kleffner for insubordination.[30]

Franz Kleffner was born on 2 June 1907 in Altena, Westphalia. He joined the NSDAP on 1 December 1930 and received his commission as an *SS-Untersturmführer* in the *Waffen-SS* on 20 April 1935. Serving almost three years at the SS Officer Candidates' School in Braunschweig, *SS-Hauptsturmführer* Kleffner transferred on 31 January 1938 to the 10th SS Death's Head Regiment "Oberbayern," and participated in the annexation of Austria on 13 March 1938. As a company commander, he transferred to the Regiment "Ostmark" and by 1 September 1939 became the 2nd Battalion commander. In this capacity, Kleffner participated on 1 October 1938 in the annexation of the Sudetenland. Throughout 1939, Kleffner attended formal SS schools for officer training, such as the one-month company commanders' course at the Infantry School at Döberitz and the two-week staff officers' course, held in Erfurt with the 29th Infantry Division. As the commander of the 13th Company, 2nd SS Death's Head *Jäger* Regiment, he participated in the campaign against France in the West and was decorated on 22 June 1940 with the Iron Cross Second Class. On 13 July 1941, during the campaign in the East, Kleffner received the Iron Cross First Class. On 25 October 1941 he assumed command of a motorcycle battalion in the 3rd SS Death's Head Division. At the rank of *SS-Sturmbannführer,* he commanded a mixed but weak Battle Group, which held a key position for two weeks against numerous Russian attacks. Decorated for his leadership, Kleffner received the Knight's Cross to the Iron Cross on 19 February 1942. Thereafter from 28 December 1942 until 21 March 1943, Kleffner attended four additional training courses almost without interruption, to include the one-month battalion commanders' course for tanks at Wünsdorf, the battalion commanders' course for tank gunnery at Pütlos, the battalion commanders' course for fast troops in Paris, and a basic course for the Pz.Kpfw.IV in Vienna.[31]

Officially assigned as the commander of the 1st Battalion, 10th SS Panzer Regiment on 1 February 1943, Kleffner brought considerable training and combat experience to the division. Debes described Kleffner as a large and broad-shouldered man who led an orderly and thrifty life. Debes also measured Kleffner as an average officer with basic military skills, but nevertheless considered Kleffner a mature old Nazi and convinced SS man, and loved by the troops.[32]

As late as 23 May 1944, Himmler ordered Kleffner arrested and tried by court-martial for intoxication in the line of duty. The arrest came in response to allegations by the divisional commander that Kleffner exhibited negligence during the assault on Buczacz. After Treuenfeld disregarded Kleffner's recommendations to bypass a village, only seventeen of sixty tanks reached the objective. For Kleffner's part in the assault, Field Marshal Model recommended Kleffner decorated; however, Treuenfeld blocked the award. A second allegation involved lying about the capture of a tactical landmark. Treuenfeld also alleged that Kleffner malingered in carrying out an order to cross a river with tanks. Despite terrain reconnaissance that suggested the ground was too soft to support an auxiliary bridge and the weight of tanks, Treuenfeld insisted on using the bridge. Five tanks got across when the bridge sunk into the ground. The remaining tanks could not cross until the next day, after Army pioneers built a secondary bridge. Moreover, Treuenfeld accused Kleffner of being under the influence of alcohol during each allegation. In the end and after a long investigation, Kleffner was acquitted of the charges and returned to duty on 7 September 1944 to the 5th SS Panzer Regiment "Wiking."[33]

Offsetting Model's earlier and unpopular order of the day, General Hube, commander of the First Panzer Army, wrote on 6 April, Easter Sunday, jubilantly acknowledging the successful breakout of German forces from the encirclement. He compared the action to the great battles of Cannae, Sedan, and Tannenberg. The achievement of the officers, NCOs, and troops was unique, he said. The combined breakout and breakthrough of the relief force accounted for the destruction or capture of 358 enemy tanks, 190 artillery pieces, twenty-nine assault guns, four self-propelled guns, two half-tracks, fifty-seven antitank guns, 174 machine guns, and numerous handguns. More importantly, all the wounded were rescued from the pocket.[34]

Model's influence continued in various forms. One such episode occurred when several tracked vehicles were missing. Every day, a motorcycle messenger delivered a folder full of orders to the adjutant, 1st Battalion, 10th SS Panzer Artillery Regiment. One such order gave notice of a special commission, ordered by Field Marshal Model and led by an army major, to inspect all the half-tracks belonging to artillery units. All the battalion vehicle mechanics were to be present, as well as all the appropriate paperwork for each vehicle. Similar surprise orders by Model were commonplace and arrived on a daily basis. Once the snow melted, one such order required the digging of fighting holes 50 meters apart, along the side of the road, and each hole marked with scraps of straw attached to a stake. However, the purpose of the half-track inspection remained a mystery until the *Spiess* of the Staff Battery requested the adjutant's presence for a confidential discussion. The senior enlisted man took responsibility for acquiring two "*Maultier*" half-tracks from an Army vehicle depot near Brzezany. The vehicles, and others, were designated for the anticipated Army infantry division scheduled to relieve the Frundsberg Division. The *Spiess* explained how he and two of his men acquired the vehicles. Sauter could only admonish the soldier forthwith. The *Spiess* was "deep in ink" as the highest ranks now demanded the return of both *Maultiers* and were looking for the culprits. As a twenty-two-year-old *SS-Untersturmführer*, and the battalion adjutant, Sauter considered the matter above his grade. Sauter brought the *Spiess* to the battalion commander, *SS-Sturmbannführer* Harry Jobst. Sauter presented the facts to his superior officer who broke out in a cold sweat. Jobst was a combat-hardened officer, and no one had ever seen him sweat before. Emphatically he exclaimed, "It had to be with Model!"

Immediately, Jobst summoned a "war council" with the vehicle specialist (TFK) to "avoid the irreplaceable *Spiess* from getting the ax." The solution to this potentially volatile situation, even for Jobst, came when the commander sent the *Schirrmeister* and the two implicated men with two bottles of cognac to Lemberg, in order to acquire scrap *Maultier* half-track truck parts. The *Schirrmeister* returned with two older, combat-damaged *Maultier* cabins and, after a special twenty-four-hour work detail, the vehicles were unrecognizable and complete with the appropriate paperwork.

The special commission arrived in "stage production uniforms," under the leadership of a very well dressed major. The terminology for the rank of an engineer, in all logistical units, was *SS-Schraubenführer*; a silver, screw head wheel or cog was incorporated on the officer's shoulder boards. Luckily, for the *Spiess*, nothing but beat-up equipment was found and the commission moved onto the next unit.[35]

Despite the success of the German breakout, Russian infantry companies, supported by tanks, counterattacked from the north and east against the 3rd Company of the reconnaissance battalion, occupying the bridgeheads at Osowce. Around 1900 hours, as the Russians threatened to envelop the bridgehead, the 3rd Company, 10th SS Panzer Reconnaissance Battalion, withdrew to Kurdwanowka. The Soviets intended on re-establishing a strong defensive line along the Strypa.[36]

No area was safe from potential Soviet detection. *SS-Unterscharführer* Werner Ohlig belonged to the 2nd Battalion of the artillery regiment that consisted of three batteries of six towed 105mm artillery pieces. Underway in a rearward area as a messenger from the command post of the 2nd Battalion, Ohlig hastily bounded across a major intersection. Halfway across the intersection he heard the whistle of an incoming projectile. Two steps further, a large fountain of earth sprang up to his right that catapulted him head over heels onto the ground. Severely wounded and covered in dirt, he sat up and looked around. He was in the middle of the intersection and before him lay two Russian soldiers, completely flattened into the ground. As the pain in his body began to build, he cried out for a medic. Shortly thereafter, Ohlig heard noises and detected two comrades, low-crawling toward him through the mud. The whistle of more incoming projectiles indicated that the Russians had observation onto the crossroads. Even so, the two SS men risked their lives and dragged Ohlig to safety. Overwhelmed with gratitude, Ohlig lost consciousness and awoke later in a small chapel where a doctor applied the first bandages to fourteen shrapnel wounds.[37]

On 7 April, the II SS Panzer Corps resumed its attack to the south and southeast. Forming the right wing, the 367th Infantry Division attacked toward the merge between the Strypa and Dnjestr Rivers. On the left, contact was established with the 21st *SS-Panzergrenadier* Regiment, situated at Monasterzyska. The bulk of the division closed on Monasterzyska while the divisional tanks secured Hill 379 northeast of Buczacz. The 100th *Jäger* Division and attached 506th Heavy Panzer Battalion fought a successful defense that cost the Russians twenty-five T-34 tanks. However, the Russians hoped to encircle the First Panzer Army west of the Strypa by funneling additional forces into a 15 km gap that formed between the 100th *Jäger* Division at Zlotniki and the 10th SS Panzer Division at Buczacz.[38]

The 6th Company, 10th SS Panzer Regiment, led by Wrobel and his crew, embarked on a special mission through the village of Pyskowce. After clearing the village outskirts, AT fire hit Wrobel's tank on the left side between the two middle return rollers. A second shot struck the left side of the superstructure above the damaged rollers, penetrating cleanly through the left-side wall and peppering the gunner (Scheele) with sixteen fragments. A third armor-piercing shot sliced off the ventilator, hit the turret, and deflected away after leaving a deep gorge across the turret. After recovering the vehicle and during cleanup, the crew found an unexploded armor-piercing projectile lying inside the tank.

From a house across a small stream, Russian small arms fire harassed the crew as they collected their tank track that lay scattered in front of their vehicle. Later, the tank crew determined that the Army, responsible for providing security, had departed the area earlier that morning and allowed Russians to infiltrate and reoccupy the village. The German tank crew conducted a fighting withdrawal and pulled its battered tank back to the company command post.[39]

Russian aircraft attacked the supply section of the 5th Company, 10th SS Panzer Regiment on numerous occasions and caused the loss of two trucks and wounding of four men. *SS-Unterscharführer* Gerhard received three fragments in his back, while *SS-Rottenführer* Fandrey lost two fingers from his right hand and shrapnel hit Krüger in his right ribs. *SS-Mann* Herbstreit was hit in his testicles, upper arm, and head. The poor road conditions, due primarily to mud, made forward progress for the supply convoys very difficult. Moreover, a lack of traffic control and discipline led to unnecessary delays and constant stopping. This placed a greater demand on the vehicles and increased vehicle fuel consumption.[40]

From his command post in Monasterzyska, Treuenfeld hoped to avoid encirclement and ordered the reserve 22nd *SS-Panzergrenadier* Regiment brought forward to strengthen the German position at Buczacz. Protection of the sector north of the Strypa fell to the mobile 10th SS Panzer Reconnaissance Battalion, which prevented several Russian attempts at crossing the river. Moreover, the battalion shot up a grounded Russian Type R 5 reconnaissance bi-plane. *SS-Obersturmführer* Rudolf Harmstorf, commander of the 2nd Company, 10th SS Panzer Reconnaissance Battalion, managed to infiltrate a Soviet position where he captured key documents that provided intelligence for the division. The 2nd Company supported several attacks by the reconnaissance battalion across the Strypa that ultimately assisted attacks by the grenadiers.[41]

The presence of a Russian tank corps in the vicinity of Trembowla prompted new orders from the Fourth Panzer Army. The mission of the II SS Panzer Corps was to attack to the northeast from Buczacz. A precursor to the threat at Trembowla, *SS-Sturmbannführer* Alois Wild attacked Dzinograd on 8 April with his 1st Battalion, 22nd *SS-Panzergrenadier* Regiment, and overran another antitank defensive line. Fourteen Russian antitank guns and one self-propelled gun were destroyed. The 2nd Battalion, 22nd *SS-Panzergrenadier* Regiment attacked northeast from Jezierzany and pursued the escaping Soviets from Przewloka and broke into Zielona. Eight tanks of the 5th Company, 10th SS Panzer Regiment, led an assault over soft terrain against the Russian main line of resistance to capture Zielona. The Soviet defenses included mined terrain, heavy artillery, approximately twenty AT guns along the main line, and ten AT guns on the right flank. The Frundsberger tank number 84765 followed the company commander's vehicle through a minefield but struck a mine after deviating slightly from the path. The left track assembly was damaged and the tank's hull pushed in. Vehicle number 84761 also struck a mine that damaged the left track assembly and steering. Moreover, artillery fire hit and severely damaged the turret. Both tanks were recovered.[42]

On 8 and 9 April, the Soviets launched multiple attacks against positions of the 22nd *SS-Panzergrenadier* Regiment, located on Hill 392 and in the forest of Petlikowce Stary. The Soviets subjected German positions to rocket and high-caliber artillery fire, and continuous attacks by fighter aircraft. Aerial bombardments struck the 13th and 14th Companies and aircraft cannon fire damaged several vehicles. A radio truck took a hit, burned out, and *SS-Obersturmbannführer* Ernst Schützeck's command half-track was damaged but remained operational.

Dangerous Soviet snipers caused numerous casualties. During a situation briefing outside the regimental command post with officers from the regimental staff and the 13th, 14th, and 16th Companies, the chief of the command staff, *SS-Obersturmführer* Gerhard Kalusche, was severely wounded when shot in the head. Kurt Tews and *SS-Rottenführer* Georg Vollmer attempted to escort their wounded commander back to an aid station. However, Kalusche insisted they remain at the front where they were needed most.[43]

At one location behind the front lines along the road from Buczacz to Medwedowce, a partisan

sniper harassed members of the 2nd Battalion, 22nd *SS-Panzergrenadier* Regiment. The battalion commander, *SS-Sturmbannführer* Hans Löffler, ordered a search party that resulted in the capture of a sniper in civilian clothing, with rifle and ammunition, in the attic of an abandoned house. The partisan was not shot immediately, but rather turned over to the divisional staff for interrogations.[44]

The Soviet threat gained momentum as it passed through Trembowla, into the area of Darawchow, and consisted of a tank corps, two motorized corps, and four to six rifle divisions. Moreover, aerial reconnaissance along the Strypa detected two Russian rifle divisions in a defensive line to the north of the II SS Panzer Corps. Considering the poor weather and road conditions that seriously hampered the movement of the 9th SS Panzer Division, and given the overall situation of the First Panzer Army that conducted a fighting withdrawal back to the Seret, Field Marshal Model detached the 9th SS from the II SS Panzer Corps. The new objective of the II SS Corps, consisting of the 10th SS and 100th *Jäger*, was to attack the Soviets northeast of Buczacz and establish a line north of the city reaching the Fourth Panzer Army. A major concern involved the Russian bridgehead at Bobulince, in the gap between the 100th *Jägers* and 10th SS Divisions. Potentially, the Soviets were positioned to launch a pincer movement to the southwest and encircle the First Panzer Army once again. Only the lighter reconnaissance battalion oversaw the gap from their positions at Kurdwanowka.[45]

On 10 April 1944, the II SS Panzer Corps attacked north and northeast of Buczacz to destroy Soviet troop concentrations and eliminate the gap at Bobulince. The 22nd *SS-Panzergrenadier* Regiment held positions to the left of the 21st *SS-Panzergrenadier* Regiment, the latter supported by units of the LIX Army Corps. The regimental objective on the left was to form a line from Biclawince to Hill 392 and to the northern portion of the lake at Medwedowce. On the right, the 6th Company, 10th SS Panzer Regiment supported attacks against Medwedowce where heavy Soviet tanks were reported on the battlefield. However, the destroyed bridge before Medwedowce prevented German tanks from supporting the grenadiers. As soon as possible, pioneers arrived to restore the bridge under harassing fire from Russian fighter aircraft.

On the left, the 2nd Battalion, 22nd *SS-Panzergrenadier* Regiment and the attached 3rd Company, 10th SS Panzer Reconnaissance Battalion attacked a defensive wooded area east of Petlikowce Stary. Heavily fortified, the Russians thwarted the German attack into the woods and then subjected the 1st Battalion, 22nd *SS-Panzergrenadier* Regiment to flanking fire, thereby foiling the attack against Hill 392.[46]

Around Hill 392, the 2nd Battalion, 22nd *SS-Panzergrenadier* Regiment secured the right flank of the regiment. With scouting troops, the 2nd Battalion, 22nd *SS-Panzergrenadier* Regiment guarded the sector eastward near Nowostawce where the 3rd Battalion, 21st *SS-Panzergrenadier* Regiment was located. The heavy 8th Company, 22nd *SS-Panzergrenadier* Regiment, comprising four platoons equipped with three 75mm antitank guns, three antitank rifles, four 75mm light infantry guns, and six 8cm mortars, held positions south of Zielona and west of the road leading to Buczacz. During the emplacement of the infantry guns, both the company commander and one battery commander were killed.

SS-Oberschütze Erwin Hörmann, a messenger for the 8th Company, 22nd *SS-Panzergrenadier* Regiment, neared a friendly infantry gun position when he heard the scream of Russian Katyusha rockets that began hitting the position. The rockets impacted around Hörmann as he took cover, and he witnessed the severe wounding of the crew chief of an infantry field gun. Several days later, while defending against a Russian night attack, Hörmann himself was wounded after a bullet hit his upper thigh.[47]

Meanwhile, Deisenhofer waited for the completion of the bridge before Medwedowce. Nevertheless, he ordered the attack to resume without armored support against Hill 366, northeast of Medwedowce. The 2nd Battalion, 21st *SS-Panzergrenadier* Regiment, commanded by *SS-Hauptsturmführer* Fritz Mauer, attacked against a fortified Russian antitank line. Deisenhofer, an advocate of the combined arms doctrine who managed to dislodge the enemy with close-air support at Monasterzyska, presumably called for aerial support a second time. Unfortunately, the air-liaison party officer was situated in the wrong position and directed Stukas against Mauer and his grenadiers. To no avail, Mauer tried waving off the Stukas with his cap in hand, as the grenadiers were in the midst of an attack. Once the Germans hit the defensive line, hand-to-hand combat ensued on Hill 366. One after another, the Russian positions were defeated and by 1800 hours the hill was in German hands. After Russian counterattacks failed to regain control of Hill 366, German tanks and armored half-tracks crossed the rebuilt bridge at Medwedowce and arrived to secure Hill 366. North of Hill 366, the attack continued as elements of the 21st *SS-Panzergrenadier* Regiment captured Pilawa.[48]

A member of the division cadre, *SS-Hauptsturmführer* Hermann Friedrichs, the company commander of the 8th Company, 21st *SS-Panzergrenadier* Regiment, was killed in action 2.5 km east of Medwedowce. Friedrichs transferred in and out of both the *Waffen-SS* and Death's Head formations, gaining training and experience. Born on 2 November 1914 in Niendorf, near Hannover, he attended the public high school for eight years and three subsequent years at an advanced salesman school. He worked as a sales clerk until his nineteenth birthday in 1933, when he joined the 17th SS Regiment of the *Allgemeine* SS. On 10 April 1935, he transferred to the *Waffen-SS* and took assignment as an *SS-Mann* in the 10th SS Regiment "Germania." Promoted to *SS-Rottenführer* by 1 September 1936, he then attended the officer candidates' course in Arolsen, from 1 May to 30 September 1937. For the next eleven months, he attended the SS Officer Candidates' School in Bad Tölz, south of Munich. As an *SS-Standartenjunker*, his final rating was "limited in appearance and average without a personal note." His composite evaluation and score of 197 points, consisting of various disciplines, was deemed "sufficient." In sequential order of precedence, the evaluation tested his knowledge of global perspective, tactics, field operations, the Nazi Party and Army, weapons, pioneers, maps, signals, motor vehicles, aircraft, general soldiering and infantry combat service, athletics, and horseback riding. Friedrichs excelled in map reading, but scored lowest in general soldiering and infantry combat service. Nevertheless, he was promoted to *SS-Standartenoberjunker* shortly before graduating and continued his training until 30 September 1938, at the Platoon Leaders' Course at Dachau. Assigned thereafter as the commander, 1st Platoon, 3rd SS Death's Head Regiment "Thüringen" (Buchenwald) from 1 October 1938 to 11 August 1939, he also completed the month-long company commanders' course held at the Infantry Training Regiment in Döberitz. While assigned to the 3rd SS Death's Head Regiment, Friedrichs showed considerable improvement as an officer and received an excellent evaluation from his reviewing senior. Friedrichs not only developed into a role model as a leader, with a flawless persona, but one whose national socialist global perspectives were anchored firmly. During this period, he was promoted to *SS-Untersturmführer* and assigned on 9 November command of the 4th Machine Gun Platoon, 7th SS Regiment. On 12 December 1939, Friedrichs transferred to the capital city of Vienna, Austria, where he commanded the 8th Machine Gun Company, 13th SS Death's Head Regiment. During this time, he married Lisa Schulz-Echmann and lived in the SS barracks in Schönbrunn.[49]

The 2nd Battalion commander, of the 13th SS Death's Head Regiment, considered Friedrichs to be a young and developing soldier. Despite receiving generally favorable remarks, Friedrichs lacked experience, firmness, and energy. Benevolence and his good temperament were signs of weakness, which his reviewing officer considered to have a negative impact on the company. Friedrichs was deemed better suited as a rifle company commander.[50]

On 30 January, Friedrichs was promoted to *SS-Obersturmführer*. Shortly thereafter, from 26 February to 20 March 1940, he attended the Infantry Gun Company course at Oranienburg. Returning to Vienna, a reorganization took place in August and he was reassigned in September to the 12th Company, 4th SS Death's Head Regiment. Friedrichs deployed to Holland for "security" from 10 September 1940 to 24 April 1941, during which time his first child was born on 5 December 1940. He received the Mar Merit Cross 2nd Class with Swords for his service in occupied Holland. He also attended from February to March 1941 a Technical Motor Vehicle Training course for company commanders

in Berlin-Lichterfeld. On 1 June 1941, Friedrichs received assignment to the "*Leibstandarte* Adolf Hitler" and in July to the staff of the 2nd SS Brigade. Returning to command a company in November 1941, he joined the 13th Company, 4th SS Infantry Regiment. The regiment participated in the deployment to Russia. On 3 January 1942, Friedrichs was decorated with the Iron Cross II Class, and three days later, the Iron Cross I Class. He transferred as the commander of the 4th Company, SS Infantry Replacement Battalion "Ost" in March, and was promoted to *SS-Hauptsturmführer* in November. On 9 November, he attended a two-week, first-level Army gas warfare training course in Celle, Hannover, and finally joined the Frundsberg Division on 15 February 1943.[51]

At the home front in Germany, the general population received news of the German successes on the battlefield through the Armed Forces Report. For 8 April 1944, the report specified:

> Despite difficult terrain, the attacks by Army and Waffen-SS units made good progress, as well as yesterday, between Tschernowitz and Tarnopol. During the previous night, the defenders at Tarnopol repulsed repetitive Soviet attacks.

For 9 April 1944, the report stated:

> In the area of Kamenez-Podolsk, the encirclement of a strong German force, consisting of Army and Waffen-SS units, under the command of General of Panzer Troops Hube, was prevented after fourteen days of fighting against an enemy of vast numerical superiority. After bitter fighting, the resolute enemy units were overrun and contact reestablished with the relieving Army and Waffen-SS units attacking from the west. German tank and infantry units fought off continuous Soviet attacks from the east, north and south, during a bitter defensive withdrawal. Suffering high and bloody casualties, the enemy lost 352 tanks and assault guns, 190 artillery pieces, as well as significant amounts of war materiel.[52]

On 11 April, the 22nd *SS-Panzergrenadier* Regiment attacked on the left flank to the east of the Strypa and the 100th *Jäger* pushed southward to capture Bobulince. The lead company for the attack against Bobulince was provided by Hinze and the 3rd reconnaissance company. The 3rd Company, 10th SS Panzer Reconnaissance Battalion, also captured the dominating Hill 180.

The 506th Heavy Panzer Battalion, commanded by Hauptmann Lange, received special recognition in the official Armed Forces Report for their contributions and successes during the fighting.[53]

During the fighting around Hill 392, Kleffner, the regimental tank commander, assumed command of the 22nd *SS-Panzergrenadier* Regiment when the commander Schützeck was wounded. The battalion command post of the 2nd Battalion, 22nd *SS-Panzergrenadier* Regiment, located in a "white house," lay approximately 800 meters from the Russian main line of battle. At that range, no great precautions were taken and Löffler summoned the company commanders to a briefing. The command post, an ancient farmhouse, had a straw roof. The adjacent smaller and numerous livestock barns had small basements under the main floor; however they were mostly flooded with winter ground water and mud. Halfway through the briefing, a single projectile penetrated the middle of the outside wall and exploded inside, against a steel oven located in the center of the house. The blast and concussion brought brick, mortar, and hot steel flying through the air, and the corps of officers were thrown to the ground. Still deafened as the last bricks fell and the dust settled, the men picked themselves up, each checking after another. Once they were all standing and accounted for, they discovered a miracle. The shrapnel pattern had wiped out the surrounding rooms, while the massive steel oven shielded the one room they occupied. Taking care of their minor scratches, they continued their briefing in one of the adjacent stalls.[54]

On the right flank, the 2nd Battalion, 10th SS Panzer Regiment, and 1st Battalion, 21st *SS-Panzergrenadier* Regiment, attacked in broad daylight over light terrain against Kosow. The 7th Company, 10th SS Panzer Regiment, and three tanks from 5th Company, 10th SS Panzer Regiment, supported the attack and provided preparatory and direct fire support 1.5 km west of Kosow. A projectile that hit vehicle number 84747, belonging to the 5th Company, penetrated the hull near the driver. Immediately, the tank caught fire and the ammunition ignited destroying the tank. Vehicle number 86727, also from the 5th Company, provided security and protection along the right flank, 1 km east of Zielona. An antitank projectile struck the vehicle turret below the cannon telescopic sight. The vehicle was salvaged, but the projectile caused considerable damage inside the turret to the gun traverse and elevation mechanism, as well as the turret traverse mechanism. Quandel, the commander of the 6th Company, 10th SS Panzer Regiment, was wounded during the tank battles when his tank was hit and set ablaze. The casualties for the 6th Company included two wounded and two killed. One additional tank was damaged as a result of AT fire. Two tanks were blown up in place.[55]

SS-Sturmbannführer Harry Jobst, the commander of the self-propelled 1st Artillery Battalion, personally provided observation in support of the armored attack on Kosow. As soon as the attack ran aground in front of the Russian antitank line, Jobst dismounted from a half-track and established a forward observation post with two messengers. The men laid approximately 200 meters of wire leading from the commanding height. Under heavy artillery and antitank fire, Jobst personally repaired the line on several occasions. The forward position allowed Jobst to call for accurate fire against the Soviet positions that, in turn, resulted in no armored losses.[56]

Tactically speaking, the term *Kampfsatz*, or "battle rate," described the amount of ammunition that one gun battery could fire within one minute. For example, when enemy artillery positions or tank concentrations were detected, the regimental commander ordered their destruction with the command, "Engage by destructive fire!" The commander determined the number of batteries, the type of ammunition, and the time. Counter-battery or tank assembly fire covered one hectare or 2.2 acres, on a quadrant, 100 × 100 meters. The minimum amount of ammunition used for counter-battery and tank assembly fire for light field howitzer (lFH) was 240 rounds, heavy field howitzers (sFH) 160 rounds, and 100mm field guns 200 rounds. The command for *Feuerüberfall* or "ambush" used approximately half the amount of ammunition and was based on greater degrees, beginning with individual, group, or sustained fire. The commander gave a variety of commands depending on the situation.

When engaging enemy artillery batteries or tank assembly areas, twelve batteries first fired three combat units of six rounds each ($12 \times 3 \times 6 = 216$ rounds), followed by four batteries with one combat unit ($4 \times 6 = 24$) termed *Nachnähren* or "follow feeder."

The effective range for the lFH was approximately 12,000 meters, the sFH 15,000 meters, and the 100mm field gun 18,000 meters. An additional increment increased the range by about 2,000 meters for each gun.

A full field combat complement of ammunition for a light howitzer battery included:

240 howitzer projectiles with
point detonating fuse 23

20 howitzer projectiles with double detonator S 60

88 howitzer projectiles with distant
concussion detonator (AZ F)

40 howitzer projectiles 100mm
red armor piercing (HL)

116 howitzer projectiles smoke (NL)
with a small concussion detonator

504 total projectiles for a full field combat
complement of ammunition

72 rounds were carried on the prime movers

240 rounds were carried by the
1st Ammunition Section

192 rounds were carried by the
2nd Ammunition Section

396 rounds were carried in the
divisional supply trains

900 rounds total made up one single
complement of gun ammunition that
included both field and supply numbers.

The full field combat complement of ammunition for a heavy howitzer battery included:

240 total projectiles for a full field combat
complement of ammunition

360 rounds were carried in the
divisional supply trains

600 rounds total made up one single
complement of gun ammunition that included
both field and supply numbers.[57]

When Russian tanks were detected inside the village at Pilawa, the heavy pioneer company moved forward with antitank weapons. Separated only by a house, the pioneer *SS-Oberschütze* Jesusmann closed with a Russian tank. Failing to hit the tank with a *Panzerfaust* or rocket launcher, the pioneer jumped onto the tank with a grenade and dropped it into the turret. Pioneers Jesusmann, *SS-Rottenführer* Schmidt, and *SS-Oberschütze* Poltzin, armed with a shaped charge, hunted down and destroyed a second T-34 tank. Leaving the motor running, the three commandeered the vehicle when a third T-34 appeared near the village church. With only a single grenade at their disposal, the three pioneers gambled. By extending one arm out of the tank and waving to the approaching Russian tank, as if they had engine trouble, they enticed a third T-34 pulled up next to the captured one. They watched in surprise as the Russian tank's hatch opened and a Russian crewman dismounted and began retrieving the tow cable when a pioneer dropped the grenade into the open tank. Finally, a fourth T-34 was knocked out by *SS-Oberschütze* Weida, from Leipzig, with the use of hand grenades. Four pioneers received the Iron Cross 2nd Class for their achievements.[58]

During the night on 11–12 April, after Kleffner assumed command of the 22nd Regiment, motorcycle messengers Tews and Vollmer drove to the divisional staff to pick up messages. During the night, a Soviet reconnaissance plane or "lame duck" circled above. They turned off their vehicle headlights and continued when the observation aircraft fired green illumination flares. Shortly before Zielona, the two messengers encountered more green illumination flares. They reported the sightings to the regimental staff command post, and shortly thereafter, a battalion of Soviet infantry infiltrated along the seam of two units to envelope Medwedowce. *SS-Obersturmführer* Gottlob Ellwanger, the battery commander of the medium 37mm antiaircraft guns, 10th SS Antiaircraft Battalion, engaged the Soviets with their battery in close combat leaving eighty Soviets dead. The Soviets attacked the 14th Antiaircraft Company and captured two antiaircraft guns before the German counterattack reclaimed the guns. The twenty-eight-year-old *SS-Obersturmführer* Alois Pühringer, second battery chief of a heavy 88mm antiaircraft gun, also participated in close combat in the same fighting at Medwedowce.[59]

Pühringer was born on 31 December 1916 in Innsbruck, Austria, and fought on the Russian front after completion of regular and reserve officer training in October 1941. During his assignment around Leningrad as a range officer for a light 20mm antiaircraft battery and a forward observer for a heavy 88mm antiaircraft battery, he earned the Iron Cross 2nd Class on 8 December 1941. In the Wolchow region near Leningrad, Pühringer distinguished himself again and earned the Iron Cross 1st Class on 12 March 1942 as a forward observer for an 88mm battery in the Antiaircraft Battalion "Ost." The recipient of the Assault Badge for heavy weapons, Pühringer was wounded on 6 April 1942. After his recovery, he received special leave to attend school and joined the Frundsberg Division on 2 April 1943.[60]

East of the street leading to Zielona, the 5th Company, 22nd *SS-Panzergrenadier* Regiment, under *SS-Hauptsturmführer* Richard Heidrich, occupied positions along the backside of an extended elevation between Zielona and Medwedowce. The 6th Company, under *SS-Obersturmführer* Albrecht Staas, held positions on the left, and the 7th Company held the right.

From Pilawa, the Russians had observation onto the dominating terrain feature, whose unique shape was spotted by outposts belonging to the 5th Company. However, the positions were withdrawn after the slightest movement brought artillery fire to bear against the positions. During the middle of the night, Soviet-raiding parties made silent and successful excursions into the German lines and brought back prisoners. During one such incident, the older and experienced *SS-Unterscharführer* Koelzer, and two other comrades, disappeared without a trace. On another occasion, a wild exchange of small arms fire erupted to the right above the company combat command post. A Soviet officer with the rank of major and 200 men infiltrated the German lines, silenced a machine gun and crew, and then attacked down the Zielona-Buczacz road. The neighboring machine gun fired in the direction where the breach in the line occurred, and thereby closed the gap. While there were no additional signs of the Soviet infiltration, the rearward areas were secured and both the battalion and regiment were informed of the breakthrough. In the morning, reserves from the rear, supported by an assault gun, neutralized the Soviet raiding-party that was equipped with mines and explosives. The Soviet mission to blow up the crossings over the Strypa River failed.

The command post of the 2nd Battalion lay in Medwedowce. During the night, the Soviets passed through the swamp and managed to occupy the northern-lying village of Nowoslawce that became a bridgehead for Soviet activity. The battalion commander, *SS-Sturmbannführer* Hans Löffler, received fire from Russians on straw roofs in Nowoslawce. Following a near miss, the village was eradicated, flattened by a self-propelled *Zwillingsflak* or double-barrel antiaircraft gun. However, the driver of the vehicle crossed the main German line and exposed the vehicle to Soviet fire. Immediately, the vehicle was destroyed.[61]

The fighting between 11 and 15 April, around Hill 392 and the woods east of Petlikowce Stary, involved four companies of the 22nd *SS-Panzergrenadier* Regiment. In order to utilize natural cover, attacks by the 1st and 3rd Battalions against Hill 392 were launched to the east and northeast. The Soviets adjusted their defenses on Hill 392 accordingly; however, they did not foresee a frontal attack up the southern slope, where no cover or concealment existed. In the evening on 12 April, on the advice and plan of the commander of the 2nd Battalion, 22nd *SS-Panzergrenadier* Regiment, Kleffner ordered the 1st and 3rd Battalions to attack in the early morning hours on 13 April, after preparatory fire by the 10th SS Panzer Artillery Regiment. *SS-Sturmbannführer* Laubscheer assumed command of the operation.

During the night, the 2nd Battalion, reinforced by a self-propelled assault gun and antitank platoon, was to occupy the southern slope of Hill 392. Following a Stuka attack and preparatory fire by the 10th SS Panzer Artillery Regiment, the 2nd Battalion was to attack the heights during the early morning hours on 14 April in a northerly direction.

SS-Hauptsturmführer Löffler led the attack with the 6th Company, 22nd *SS-Panzergrenadier* Regiment, on the left, supported by the heavy weapons 8th Company, 22nd *SS-Panzergrenadier* Regiment, and captured Hill 392. Immediately, Löffler transitioned to the defense and, in close combat, repelled numerous Russian counterattacks throughout the day. The 6th company, commanded by *SS-Obersturmführer* Staass, distinguished itself especially during the fighting.[62]

SS-Untersturmführer Hermann Baumeister, a platoon commander in the 6th Company, reached Hill 392 first with his platoon. After *SS-Obersturmführer* Wilhelm Willi was wounded, Baumeister assumed command of the 7th Company, which he led in the defense against a series of Russian counterattacks until he was wounded seriously a second time. Willi, who remained with his company and continued to fight despite his wounds, received additional injuries in the course of this action.

In the heat of battle and amidst the confusion, *SS-Unterscharführer* Georg Schreiber, leading a signal squadron from the battalion staff of the 22nd Regiment, ensured continual communications between the battalion and companies. His fearless and brave actions during numerous scouting and patrolling missions earned him the Iron Cross 2nd Class.

SS-Unterscharführer Siegfried Gerber distinguished himself while leading a heavy machine-gun crew that prevented a Russian counterattack against the flank of the 6th Company, 22nd *SS-Panzergrenadier* Regiment. Gerber engaged the enemy with a rifle and operated the machine gun until wounded.

SS-Rottenführer Rudolf Syrer, the crew chief of a mortar team in the 5th Company, 22nd *SS-Panzergrenadier* Regiment, operated a knocked out machine gun after his team expended their mortar ammunition in support of the attack by the 6th Company, and held the company position along the left wing until wounded.

While the 1st Battalion, 22nd *SS-Panzergrenadier* Regiment continued to fight around Petlikowce Stary and woods to the east, the 9th Company of the 3rd Battalion, 22nd *SS-Panzergrenadier* Regiment defended against Russian counterattacks on Hill 392.[63]

The 6th Company, 10th SS Panzer Regiment was relieved after the successful assault against Kosow and entered quarters at Buczacz in the early morning on 14 April. However, after loading ammunition, gassing up the vehicles, and a short break, the company was again placed on alert. *SS-Untersturmführer* Erich Stark led a small number of combat-ready tanks toward Pilawa to stabilize the situation. Schneider recalls the event:

> Reports indicated that Russian tanks and infantry were attacking Pilawa and Hill 366. The 5th company of 2nd Regiment engaged in bitter close combat as the small group of tanks counterattacked. Since my tank expended all its ammunition, I radioed Stark that I needed to reload. Our tank fell back to allow the ammunition half-track to approach our vehicle. *SS-Untersturmführer* Kulp, the company adjutant, suddenly appeared next to my tank and tried calling to me. Considering the noise of battle, and given the fact that I was wearing my headset, I could not hear a word he said. I climbed out of the tank and stood before him when a mortar hit us. A whistling crash of steel and flash hurled us wounded to the ground. Shortly after we received medical attention, a half-track brought us to the aid station. Unfortunately, I never found out what Kulp wanted to tell me.[64]

The counterattack against Pilawa was mounted by both the 5th and 6th Companies. During the counterattack, the 5th Company, 10th SS Panzer Regiment lost tank number 86209, 1 km southwest of Pilawa. Antitank fire struck the vehicle along the commander's cupola. The vehicle was recovered. In all, the company destroyed six antitank guns, two trucks, and one T-34 tank.[65]

Along the far left wing of the divisional line, the reconnaissance battalion at Kurdwanowka defended against several Soviet attacks from the bridgehead at Bobulince. On 14 April, a single T-34 managed to get within 30 meters of the main line of resistance when a *Panzerfaust* destroyed it and a heavy KV-1 tank became immobilized by a 75mm antitank gun. During the night of 14–15 April, *SS-Untersturmführer* Georg Siebenhüner set out to the north in half-tracks with two squads to determine the extent of the Russian presence. Chasing a group of Russians, the detachment ran headlong into an ambush and lost an entire squad. Siebenhüner was among the dead. In the morning, the Russians launched attacks against elements of the 3rd Company, 10th SS Panzer Reconnaissance Battalion, in the northern portions of Kurdwanowka, and killed the company commander, *SS-Untersturmführer* Rudolf Hofmann.[66]

The Germans detected Soviet pressure in several locations that included areas along the heights of Nowostawce, the northern rim of Nowostawce, east of the road Zielona and Hill 392, and the white house on Hill 392. In response to Soviet pressure, the 2nd Battalion, 22nd *SS-Panzergrenadier* Regiment, reinforced the defense along the right wing of the division. The Army's 7th Panzer Division held positions on the right. The 6th Company, 10th SS Panzer Regiment lay on the left, the 5th in the middle, and the 7th on the right. The entire sector of the 2nd Battalion spanned a line approximately 6.5 km. In areas where observation was not possible, such as the marsh on the right flank of the 5th Company, additional scout troops were employed.

On 15 April, the Soviets launched an attack with infantry and six T-34/85 tanks east of Nowostawce along the boundary between the right flank of the 2nd Battalion, 22nd *SS-Panzergrenadier* Regiment and the 7th Panzer Division. In order for the battalion commander to apprise himself of the situation, Löffler set out with his messenger to the command post of the 7th Company that was already under fire by heavy Russian artillery. Protected by a small ravine, Löffler made his way to the most forward positions. Looking back and up across the terrain occupied by his units, he detected a gap in the line. The 7th Panzer Division that relieved the 3rd Battalion, 21st *SS-Panzergrenadier* Regiment was in the process of entering their positions. The forward-lying positions along the main line of battle, which established the link to the 2nd Battalion, 22nd *SS-Panzergrenadier* Regiment, were unoccupied. Russian attack groups were leap-frogging forward and into the gap on the right flank.

Löffler responded instantaneously. With his messenger, they sprang up and dashed across the battlefield. A projectile impacted nearby and threw them back to the ground. Continuing down into the valley, they reached the first group of men situated along the seam of the neighboring units. The deep-echeloned Russian attack stalled at a ravine in the valley that ran along the main line of battle. Russian infantry that managed to cross the outer rim of the depression were repelled by combined fire from the 7th Company, 22nd *SS-Panzergrenadier* Regiment. Efficiently, Löffler gave orders to dig in for the impending Russian attack and then moved uphill to shore-up the next line of defense. Löffler detected anxiety in the faces of the youngest grenadiers as the turrets of the first Russian tanks approached their positions. Löffler yelled into his messenger's ear with orders to bring an antitank gun to the northern rim of the village (Nowostawce) and antitank equipment to the company combat command post. Tank machine-gun bullets zipped over their heads as the tanks approached slowly. The grenadiers remained calm as Russian infantry crossed the ravine and continued over the muddy paths. Well in advance of the tanks, Soviet infantry came within 30 meters when a hail of bullets stopped them. After a single soldier managed to escape, the first green tank closed within 40 meters of the grenadiers, spewing machine-gun fire. Löffler picked up a *Panzerfaust* and sought cover behind a wall. Ten meters before the wall, the tank stopped and traversed the turret outward and elevated the main gun. Slowly raising his head over the wall, Löffler discovered a clear shot into the tank's vulnerable side. The *Panzerfaust* hit the middle of the turret, causing it to collapse on one side and glow brightly on the other. Immediately, the front hatches clanked open. Two Soviets jumped out and took cover behind the burning tank. Löffler threw a hand grenade and killed one. The other Soviet fled but Löffler's well-aimed shots prevented his escape. The remaining five tanks withdrew into the valley and a second T-34 was knocked out by an 8th Company antitank gun, led by *SS-Oberschütze* Tapken. One of the remaining four tanks returned fire, killing Tapken as they fled back to the Russian lines.[67]

The situation in the north at Bobulince became acute. A nighttime reconnaissance determined that dug-in tanks, heavy weapons, and elements of the Russian 137th Rifle Division, consisting of approximately 600 men, were in Bobulince. To deal with the serious threat, two battalions of the 21st *SS-Panzergrenadier* Regiment moved up to Przewloka. Units from the 19th Panzer Division, elements of the 10th SS Panzer Reconnaissance Battalion, the 506th Heavy Panzer Battalion, Group Bock, and two battalions from the 21st *SS-Panzergrenadier* Regiment, and the entire 22nd Grenadier Regiment attacked on 16 April to eliminate the Russian threat.

A wild chase ensued by the armored group Bock that overran the Russian positions at Kurdwanowka and turned north toward Bobulince. From the north, the 54th *Jäger* Regiment attacked to the south while the 4th and 2nd Companies of the 10th SS Panzer Reconnaissance Battalion converged on Bobulince. Despite strong defensive fire, the momentum of the attack carried the Germans to the objective. By 2100 hours, Bobulince was firmly in German hands and the defensive phase began. *SS-Obersturmführer* Harmstorf and the 2nd Company, 10th SS Panzer Reconnaissance Battalion were instrumental in providing security for troop movements into new positions. Local Russian counterattacks were launched up and down the Strypa on 17 and 18 April; however the 10th SS Panzer Division "Frundsberg" remained in control.

Within Nowostawce, a company of Russians managed to infiltrate down the two main streets and reach the combat command post of the 2nd Battalion, 22nd *SS-Panzergrenadier* Regiment. Quickly, two ad hoc shock troops were formed from men of the battalion staff and the 8th Company and reinforced by a *Sturmgeschütz*. Moving to clear the western-leading road through Nowostawce,

the German troops encountered heavy small arms fire in the northern sector of the village. To avoid the deadly snipers, the shock troops moved down both sides of the road but behind the houses. But their precautions did not help *SS-Untersturmführer* Rolf Brodbeck, the adjutant of the 2nd Battalion, 22nd *SS-Panzergrenadier* Regiment. Brodbeck was following his messenger, *SS-Oberschütze* Wilhelm Balbach, down the road when a sniper bullet struck his helmet killing him instantly. As the assault troops closed with the enemy, the Russians fled across the stream to the north. Elements of the 5th Company, 22nd *SS-Panzergrenadier* Regiment, secured the area where the breakthrough occurred.[68]

The Soviets repeatedly exploited the weakness along the seam between the 7th Panzer Division and Löffler's 2nd Battalion and infiltrated the northern outskirts of Nowostawce. Löffler himself nearly became a victim of sniper fire when a round went through his pants on 17 April. In order to flush out the Russians on the same day, two regimental self-propelled 20mm antiaircraft guns (SdKfz.10/4) from the 14th Antiaircraft Company, 22nd *SS-Panzergrenadier* Regiment were attached to the 5th Company, 22nd *SS-Panzergrenadier* Regiment and conducted clearing operations. The following day, another clearing operation began after preparatory artillery fire by the II Battalion. Together with elements of the 7th Panzer Division, the 7th Company, 22nd *SS-Panzergrenadier* Regiment, supported by the heavy 8th Company and two assault guns, pushed the Russians back and recaptured the old German positions.[69]

During the more quiet days between 16 and 17 April, the 6th Company, 10th SS Panzer Regiment performed general day-to-day work that included inspecting, cleaning, and repairing both wheeled and tracked vehicles. To maintain morale, *SS-Untersturmführer* Quandel, the company commander, decorated crews with the *Panzerkampfabzeichen* or Tank Assault Badge, the first awards for combat action.[70]

The intelligence section of the division monitored the movement and buildup of Soviet forces. Russian tactics of deception were very effective in siphoning off valuable German resources to a specific area. By committing large numbers of men and materiel to a sector, the Russians gave the appearance of an impending attack. The German Enemy Intelligence Paper No. 2, dated 20 April 1944, outlined the situation. Soviet forces were pushed back east of the Strypa River and a bridgehead west of Osowce was destroyed on 16 April. Continuous Soviet attacks against the new main German line were repelled with high Russian casualties. The identified Soviet units included:

167th Rifle Division (520th and 615th Rifle Regiments)

8th Rifle Division (151st and 229th Rifle Regiments)

147th Rifle Division (600th and 640th Rifle Regiments)

155th Rifle Division (786th and 659th Rifle Regiments)

317th Rifle Division (606th and 761st Rifle Regiments)

276th Rifle Division (871st, 873rd, and 876th Rifle Regiments)

29th Mechanized Brigade

61st Guard Tank Brigade

63rd Guard Tank Brigade

2nd Airborne Division (4th Airborne Regiment)

The competency of the Soviet officers from the 167th Rifle Division was unknown. The division comprised the 520th and 615th Rifle Regiments. The 520th Rifle Regiment lost many of its infantry guns at Schepetowka. However, still available was the antitank battalion with eighteen 14.5mm antitank rifles. Each company was forty men strong, and the Ukrainian replacements underwent brief training.

The divisional commander of the 8th Rifle Division—consisting of the 151st and 229th Rifle Regiments—was unknown to German intelligence. The commander of the 229th Rifle Regiment was Lieutenant Colonel Alexandrow. While the company strength reached fifty to sixty men within the

divisional antitank regiment, the number of 76mm guns were not known. The division consisted mostly of Ukrainians, Caucasians, and Siberians, with very few Russians.

The 600th and 640th Rifle Regiments formed the 147th Rifle Division. The commanders were unknown and the company strengths reached between twenty and thirty men. The last group of replacements arrived on 7 April 1944; a group of 700 men from Schitomir consisted of untrained Ukrainians.

The 155th Rifle Division, comprising the 786th and 659th Rifle Regiments, arrived at the front on 15 April after a forced march out of the area of Tarnopol. The company strengths reached twenty to twenty-five men, of which 60 percent were Ukrainians, 20 percent Russians, and 20 percent Uzbeks.

The 317th Rifle Division incorporated the 606th and 761st Rifle Regiments with company strengths of twenty-five to thirty men. The division suffered extensive losses in the area around Kamenez-Podolsk. However, Ukrainian replacements received brief training.

The 871st, 873rd, and 876th Rifle Regiments formed the 276th Rifle Division. Each company consisted of approximately thirty men. For the most part, they were untrained Ukrainians. Each battalion was equipped with four antitank guns, as well as two to four heavy machine guns, and four to six medium mortars.

The 29th Mechanized Brigade, a component of the Tenth Guard Tank Corps, evolved with company strengths of 120 men. The brigade equipped with weapons similar to a basic rifle company.

On the other hand, the 61st Guard Tank Brigade, commanded by Colonel Zhukov, organized with six battalions each with twenty-five medium T-34 tanks. It suffered heavy losses and counted an armored strength of only eleven tanks in the entire brigade.

Colonel Vomischew commanded the 63rd Guard Tank Brigade. Prisoners from the brigade claimed it lost many tanks at Kamenez-Podolsk.

The 2nd Airborne Division consisted of only the single 4th Airborne Regiment, which was equipped with two tanks and fourteen artillery guns. Each company had twenty men, mostly untrained Ukrainians. The division's combat worthiness was rated very low.

Reliable sources reported the 49th Guard Mechanized Brigade, 28th Rifle Division, and 127th Rifle Division were within the area of the front. Moreover, prisoner interrogations revealed that tank assembly areas were located in the area of Mogielica-Romanowka, consisting of 130 to 150 medium T-34 tanks. Three heavy Joseph Stalin tanks were reported west of Mogielica, and a concentration of antiaircraft guns appeared in the area of Romanowka. Nevertheless, aerial reconnaissance did not report any unusual activity. Starting on 16 April, the Soviets conducted limited aerial operations. Heavy aerial attacks and the resumption of large-scale concentrated attacks were expected. The Soviets enjoyed tank superiority.

On 19 April, intelligence reported enemy losses of two self-propelled guns, twenty-six tanks, nine aircraft, one truck, 130 antitank guns, four heavy mortars, six medium mortars, eight antitank rifles, sixteen machine guns, ten submachine guns, fifty-two rifles, 144 prisoners, and 642 dead.[71]

On 21 April, the commanding general of the II SS Panzer Corps, *SS-Oberstgruppenführer* Hausser, accompanied by the divisional commander, *SS-Gruppenführer* Treuenfeld, visited the combat command post of the 2nd Battalion, 22nd *SS-Panzergrenadier* Regiment to congratulate Löffler on the achievements of his battalion and his personal exploits in the destruction of a Russian tank in close combat.[72]

After the Strypa-Pilawa front was extended, the Frundsberg Division was withdrawn on 25 April and, at long last, relieved by units of the LIX Army Corps. Several days later and in response to new Soviet developments near Stanislau, the division moved to areas along the Rohaytn-Halisz.[73]

SS-Standartenführer Heinz Harmel, a distinguished soldier with experience in several theaters, assumed command of the division on 27 April 1944. After Treuenfeld's departure, *SS-Oberstgruppenführer* Hausser recommended Treuenfeld receive the German Cross in Gold for his achievements as commander of the division in the East. However, Himmler did not approve the award of such high merit due to a lack of substance,

involving only four specific incidents within an eleven-day period.

But Harmel did not lack in bravery when he arrived directly from a training course for divisional commanders. The reviewing officer for the course evaluated Harmel as an impressive soldier with great initiative, temperament, and comradery. Moreover, Harmel was considered determined, energetic, and tough, smart, a clear thinker with an exceptional view for tactics based on impressive experience.[74]

Heinz Harmel belonged to a select number of men whose career in the German armed forces was not only exceptional but also virtuous. His commanding officers recognized early on and throughout his career the talent he possessed as a natural leader and a tactician. Harmel had the ability to evaluate a chaotic situation very quickly, make a good decision, and execute for a favorable outcome. Posted as a battalion commander before the attack against Soviet Russia in February 1941, he was described by his regimental commander as psychologically correct, standing well above average. *SS-Obersturmbannführer* Otto Kumm explained Harmel's success as a result of his constant personal leadership in battle. *SS-Oberstgruppenführer* Paul Hausser remarked of Harmel as an officer with an unnatural ability to lead men in battle. *SS-Obergruppenführer* Walter Krüger, the divisional commander of "Das Reich," considered his presence on the battlefield to work wonders.[75]

Harmel was born in Metz on 29 June 1906, as the oldest son of a physician. In 1912 he entered school in Metz. When his father received orders for a new assignment, Harmel transferred to the secondary school in Mecklenburg. As a student, he was a league youth member of the *Wandervögel* or Wandering Birds movement. With no prospects of completing his matriculation examination, Harmel left school at the age of twenty. From 1923 to 1926 Harmel was politically active, first in the youth group "Rossbach," a company of the *Freikorps* or Free Corps, and later as a town group commander in the *Frontbann*, a paramilitary branch or combat troops of the German People's Freedom Movement. By 1 May, Harmel had volunteered and joined the 15th Company, 6th Infantry Regiment out of Lübeck, in the 100,000-man *Reichswehr*, with a desire of becoming an officer. After six months, his hopes were dashed when problems with his eyes were discovered and he was released from service.

From the spring of 1926 to 1928, Harmel worked as an apprentice farmer and joined the non-Nazi veterans' organization *Stahlhelm* or Steel Helmet. Until December 1930, he worked as an agricultural civil servant in the regions of Schleswig-Holstein, Altmark, and Pommern. In December 1931, he completed his training at the agricultural seminar in Landsberg after passing the state examinations, but left the profession in early 1932 due to high unemployment and a lack of prospects. When Hitler eliminated the potential competitor organization *Stahlhelm* in 1933, by absorbing the ranks into the SA, Harmel served in the SA for seven months. At twenty-six years of age, Harmel became an officer in the volunteer labor service, exclusively working on coursework for the Reich's Board of Trustees for youth competency and as an instructor at a teaching facility until its dissolution in the summer 1935.[76]

In the summer and fall of 1935, Harmel joined the Army and took the first of two examinations for reserve officer training. In October, he entered active duty in Hamburg-Veddel as an *SS-Oberscharführer* in the SS-VT or disposal troops, SS Regiment "Deutschland." He transferred in September 1936 to the SS Regiment "Deutschland" in Munich as a platoon commander and officer candidate. On 30 January 1937, Harmel was commissioned an *SS-Untersturmführer* and was accepted into the officer corps.

In April 1937 in Landsberg, Heinz Harmel married Irmgard Müller, who bore a daughter on 6 June 1939.

As a participant in the annexation of Austria from 3 December 1937 to 19 March 1938, Harmel was promoted on 30 January 1938 to *SS-Obersturmführer* and transferred to Austria in Klagenfuhrt as the commander of the 9th Company, of the newly organized SS Regiment "Der Führer." Serving during the occupation of the Sudetenland in October 1938, he was promoted one year later to *SS-Hauptsturmführer* and participated in March 1939 in the occupation of Czechoslovakia. From June to July 1939, he attended the War College in Potsdam and applied his knowledge as a company commander during the campaign across the lower countries Holland and France. He displayed exceptional combat resolve and bravery during the assault on the Grebbe-Berges, the eastward Dutch fortified front strengthened by water barriers. On point at the head of the formation, Harmel led the charge against the Grebbe Line and hit the first bunkers. By December 1940, Harmel had earned the Iron Cross 2nd and 1st Class and the Infantry Assault Badge in Silver. During the operations in Yugoslavia, as the commander of the 2nd Battalion, Regiment "Der Führer," Harmel was promoted to *SS-Sturmbannführer*.

In the east, the 2nd Battalion, Regiment "Der Führer," aided in preparation for the 2nd SS Division "Das Reich" crossing of the Dnjepr River. West of Skloff along the Dnjepr, Harmel personally led his battalion to capture the Russian heavily fortified bridgehead at Hill 215. On 22 July 1941, the regiment attacked the heights east of Jelnja. Again, Harmel led by example at the front of his battalion and captured the dominating Russian position at Pronino. After improving his position and preparing for the defense, Harmel personally interjected himself at various locations to rally his men and launched successful counterattacks to repel every Russian attack. On 4 September, the battalion attacked and routed Russian forces in the village of Usiki, south of Awdejekwa. Harmel pursued the fleeing Russians with a single platoon and reached the Rudnja sector, capturing a river crossing intact, nineteen heavy guns, seventy-five trucks, and causing heavy casualties. Two weeks later, the regiment attacked again with the objective of capturing the city of Priluki. The 2nd Battalion led the charge and broke through the defensive position at Itschnja, entering the city in the early morning on the following day. Fierce fighting ensued when the Russians counterattacked with two armored platoons, supported by heavy artillery and machine-gun fire. A strong Russian force, which had been bypassed earlier, managed to flank and threaten the rear of the battalion in the northern section of Priluki. Hamel counterattacked immediately and captured seventeen heavy guns, eight antitank guns, one tank, forty trucks, and 140 horses. Russian casualties included approximately 150 men killed and 300 captured, including a colonel and several other officers. Preparing to counterattack together with the 1st Battalion on 20 September, out of the bridgehead of the 41st Infantry Regiment against Russian attacks on Romny, the Russians launched a spoiling attack against the 2nd Battalion with thirteen heavy tanks. The German attack was delayed significantly when several Russian tanks were destroyed with combined fire from antiaircraft and antitank guns. Orders for the reserve 2nd Battalion, located on the east bank of the Ssula River, included seizing the high ground at Pustowoitowka, the regiment's first objective, and conducting reconnaissance across the river into the village. The opposition in control of the village had an estimated strength of three squadrons with artillery, which remained completely quiet. After allowing the German scouts to enter the village, the Russians attempted to encircle and destroy the scouts. On his own accord, Harmel attacked immediately and destroyed the Russian force. The 1st Battalion, which infiltrated the village from the south, helped capture the remnants of the Russian defense. Altogether, the regiment captured over 200 horses, one field gun, and 150 Russians.

Continuing the attack on 23 September, both battalions attacked to capture the village of Ssakunowo. After reconnaissance reported only light enemy activity, the bulk of the two battalions encountered little resistance, passed through the village, and seized the heights to the south. Suddenly, rear elements of the 2nd Battalion received rifle and machine-gun fire when approximately three Russian companies attacked out from hemp and sunflower fields. Leaving a minimal line of security facing forward, Harmel counterattacked with the bulk of the 2nd Battalion. Meanwhile, the Russians were hiding in houses and barns in the village. Interrogations of Russian prisoners revealed that 3,000 men occupied the village. After hours of house-to-house fighting, Harmel claimed victory after routing the enemy, leaving approximately 700 dead and capturing 500. For his bravery in combat, he received on 26 November 1941 the German Cross in Gold.

At the beginning of December 1941, along the outskirts of Moscow, Harmel was appointed commander of the SS Infantry Regiment "Deutschland," when *SS-Gruppenführer* Wilhelm Bittrich replaced the seriously wounded *SS-Oberstgruppenführer* Paul Hausser as commander of the SS Division "Das Reich."

After the defeat of the Sixth Army at Stalingrad, the seemingly unstoppable Russian advance threatened to reach the Dnjepr River. On 19 February 1942, the SS Panzer Division "Das Reich" received orders to push south against Nowomoskowsk and relieve weak German units holding the line. The *SS-Panzergrenadier* Regiment "Deutschland" was ordered to attack from Otrada against Pereschtschepino and establish a bridgehead. The *SS-Panzergrenadier* Regiment "Der Führer" attacked from the bridgehead against Nowomoskowsk on the following day. Under the cover of darkness in order to exploit the element of surprise, Harmel personally led a reinforced tank battalion against Pereschtschepino, despite the successful infiltration of Russians on both sides of the main German route of march. German reconnaissance reported the village occupied by a single Soviet regiment. The bulk of the reinforced motorized battalion surprised and routed the enemy in its entirety. Approximately 1,500 Russians were killed. Exploiting the situation, Harmel immediately struck south to expand the bridgehead with the reinforced battalion. Despite enemy antitank fire, Harmel led the attack from inside an armored radio car (Sd.Kfz.232) and personally rallied a tank company to attack. Bitter combat ensued as the battalion succeeded in capturing Dimitrijewka-Golubowka. Harmel's immediate response to exploit the situation led to the complete rout of Soviet forces and expansion of the bridgehead, allowing for the division's speedy advance south.

Several weeks later, between Losowaja and Bereka, the regiment was in full pursuit of a fleeing Russian division. However, thawing weather usurped the movement of wheeled vehicles that became stuck in the deep mud. The reconnaissance battalion, commanded by *SS-Hauptsturmführer* Hans Weiss, somehow managed to cut off the retreating Russians. Harmel received the message and promptly mounted a command tank in order to form a battle group. Hastily, Harmel led an attack in tandem with the reconnaissance battalion and obliterated the enemy division. Despite being wounded, Harmel continued to command the regiment.

On 12 March, during the second German capture of the city of Charkov, Harmel fought his way through the city, despite stiff opposition. By reaching the railroad line south of Rogan, the regiment closed the escape route to strong withdrawing forces and caused its destruction. Linking with Battle Group Baum of the Death's Head Division, additional Russian forces were cut off escaping east and northeast from the area of Smijew. As a decisive commander who led by example at the very tip of the spear, Harmel was decorated on 31 March 1943 with the Knight's Cross to the Iron Cross and the Tank Destruction Badge for single-handedly destroying an enemy tank.[77]

On 30 July 1943, the reinforced *SS-Panzergrenadier* Regiment "Deutschland" employed on the left side of the divisional panzer grenadier group, during an attack against Soviet positions that breached the German line. Mission: Capture Hill 203.9, proceed 1 km north, and secure the western portion of Stepanowka to protect the main divisional thrust to the south in the northeast and east.

The attack against Hill 203.9 threatened to bog down early due to stiff enemy resistance in well-camouflaged and deep echelon positions along the heights, a thick minefield, and flanking artillery fire from the dominating heights of Hill 213. During this phase, the regiment employed sixteen assault guns and lost seven vehicles to damage by mines. Again, Harmel proved his worth at the front of his battalion, leading them into battle and capturing Hill 203.

Ignoring orders to allow the armored group and remainder of the regiment to close with Hill 203, Harmel used the brief confusion among the Russians to his advantage and launched an attack against Stepanowka. The Russians held the town in considerable strength, and Harmel's pursuit of abruptly fleeing Russians along the outskirts within the first series of houses paid off. Harmel's decision to continue the attack provided a breach in the defensive network, from where successive attacks could be launched. Harmel pushed farther

into the town when his command vehicle struck a mine. Under heavy fire, he dismounted and boarded a prime mover, which also became disabled after hitting a mine. He continued the attack by encouraging his troops forward, against a defensive system complete with interconnecting underground tunnels from one house to another. Each house was fortified and every Russian fought to the bitter end. The release of reinforcements from the *SS-Panzergrenadier* Regiment "Deutschland" could not help the plight of the beleaguered attackers after Russian counterattacks committed the remainder of the regiment along the entire line. However, Harmel never gave up, despite the horrendous loss of life, and led his men to victory after thirty hours of combat. During the night on 31 July and early morning on 1 August 1943, Stepanowka fell into German hands and the bulk of the Russian 24th Guard Rifle Division was either destroyed or captured. The tally of captured materiel included eighteen medium T-34 tanks, one German assault gun, two scout cars, three 150mm guns, one 280mm heavy howitzer (phosphor projectiles), eight 100mm and 75mm guns, three 37mm and 50mm antiaircraft guns, twelve 76mm antitank guns, seventeen 47mm and 37mm antitank guns, eight oversized mortars, forty-one heavy mortars, thirty-three light mortars, hundreds of machine guns, and well over a thousand rifles. Approximately 800 men were dead, and 400 men were captured. Harmel's leadership of the armored group fighting against Hill 203 led to the speedy return to the old main line of battle along the Mius River.

Heinz Harmel distinguished himself further during the summer battles against Beresoff in the north around Bjelgrod, where his regiment was the first to break into the deep-echeloned Russian defensive system. In the subsequent attack against Teterewino on 7 July, and the defensive tank battles at Kalinin on 8 and 14 July, Harmel provided the leadership and example to make a decisive difference on the battlefield. For the achievements at Stepanowka, Teterewino, and Kalinin, on 10 September 1943 he became the 296th recipient decorated with Oak Leaves to the Knight's Cross.[78]

Meanwhile, during a brief period throughout the early summer evenings in 1944, when the division became the Army reserve in the area around Pomorzany, Galicia, the 1st Battalion, 10th Panzer Artillery Regiment enjoyed time playing cards. Soldiers of the regiment earned the nickname "Self-Propelled Double-Header Battalion." Meanwhile, the battalion surgeon, *SS-Hauptsturmführer* Dr. Willi Dörr, kept busy assisting the local population. He offered medical consultations during the evening. According to Sauter, the visits began after several people asked for assistance. As soon as the word got out that a German doctor was seeing patients, the undertaking grew exponentially. People brought their sick on Panje-wagons (horse-drawn vehicles) from far away and the line outside the doctor's tent grew longer. Dr. Dörr knew that Sauter had studied medicine for several months before he entered the *Waffen-SS*. And so, Dörr summoned Sauter for a second opinion for more complicated cases. On one occasion, a young lady was delivered on a Panje-wagon who suffered from severe pain. For over a week, she was unable to release water and immediately Dr. Dörr admitted her. Kidney stone blockage! No one could believe the doctor removed over 4 liters of urine! The population was grateful for his services and brought food, such as eggs, as a token of their appreciation. The medical personnel of the Frundsberg Division used eggs and French cognac to obtain the required medicines and bandages, sometimes from the black market.[79]

For the entire month of May and first part of June, the division remained in reserve to Army Group Northern Ukraine as a part of the II SS Panzer Corps. The II SS Panzer Corps shadowed the ever-changing Soviet concentration of forces that posed an immediate threat at Stanislau, then Brody, then Luzk, and finally Lemberg. In fact, the Soviet attack did not materialize until late June and early July, but against Army Group Center. The Soviet deception strategy worked. Consequently, the very two German divisions that were specifically trained to combat Allied airborne and amphibious landing forces along the Atlantic coast were busy chasing a would-be army when American, Canadian, and British forces landed at Normandy on 6 June 1944.[80]

The inevitable redeployment and transportation of the division by rail back to France provoked the divisional 1st General Staff officer (Ia) to review

on 26 May the protective or defensive procedures when underway by rail. In general, discharging weapons while the train was underway was prohibited. However, in the case of an attack by aircraft, every rifle, carbine, and machine gun was to engage against enemy aircraft without any special order. During an aerial threat, the locomotives would provide an alert whistle signal using alternating long and short tones. If possible, the train would stop, at which time small arms fire could engage the aircraft.[81]

On 2 June, a flamethrower tank platoon was organized for the 2nd Battalion, 10th SS Panzer Regiment. At the same time, tank gunners, drivers, and radio operators were transferred from the 2nd Battalion, 10th SS Panzer Regiment, to the 10th SS Tank Destroyer Battalion and vice-versa. Those individuals transferring to the latter were directed to turn in their black tank uniforms in exchange for the gray *Jäger* wrap uniforms.[82]

On 9 June, the remaining armored portions arrived in Ostrow, to include the nine assault guns of the 8th Company, 10th SS Panzer Regiment, that were to remain in the old assembly area. Throughout the day, the tanks were camouflaged. By 0500 on 11 June, the wheeled vehicles, company supply units, and staff vehicles arrived in Ostrow. Immediately, all the vehicles were dug in and camouflaged.[83] During the night between 9 and 10 June, scouting troops from the 6th Company, 22nd *SS-Panzergrenadier* Regiment entered Russian trenches.

As late as 12 June, Pioneers participated in forced reconnaissance against Russian positions. However, after German preparatory artillery fire, aerial support bombardment, clearing mines, and assault, the Soviet positions were occupied by loudspeakers only. The sound of tanks fooled the division.[84]

As the divisions of the II SS Panzer Corps geared up to return to the West, Field Marshal Model provided his thanks and gratitude for the men of the corps. New orders arrived on the same day for the tank regiment's 2nd Battalion at 0300 hours on 12 June. The battalion was to entrain onto six transport trains from the stations Krystynopol and Sokal. Immediately, preparations for the departure were ordered and transport officers were selected.

Special detachments were designated to retrieve all the tanks, including Tigers and Panthers, which were under repair. The destination for the special commandos was Saarbrücken. Around 0700 hours, the battalion was fully prepared to march. The combat staff began loading the trains at 1100 hours. Once all the provisions for fourteen days were loaded, the first transport train, which also carried the battalion commander, departed at 1750 hours. The remaining trains followed throughout the night and consisted of:

1st Transport Nr. 612311 Departure Station: Krystynopol

Transport Officer: *SS-Untersturmführer* Rudolf Henn

2nd Transport Nr. 612329 Departure Station: Krystynopol

Transport Officer: *SS-Untersturmführer* Dr. Franz Riedel

3rd Transport Nr. 612319 Departure Station: Krystynopol

Transport Officer: *SS-Untersturmführer* Hans Quandel

4th Transport Nr. 612331 Departure Station: Sokal

Transport Officer: *SS-Obersturmführer* Alfred Alius

5th Transport Nr. 612315 Departure Station: Sokal

Transport Officer: *SS-Untersturmführer* Ludwig Schmidt

6th Transport Nr. 612323 Departure Station: Sokal

Transport Officer: *SS-Untersturmführer* Rolf Hilbertz

7th Transport Nr. 612335 Departure Station: Sokal

Transport Officer: *SS-Untersturmführer* Wilhelm Paschen.

The remaining vehicles were consolidated onto the final train. Over a four-day period, the trains passed quickly through Rawa-Rasca-Jaroslau and onto the main line. Via Debica-Tarkow and Krakau,

the well-guarded rail lines allowed for the quick ride through Opplen and by 0800 on 14 June, the trains passed Breslau, Sagan, Cottbus, and Halle. The next day, the division passed Fulda, Hanau, and Frankfurt. At Rüdesheim, the division reached the Rhine River and followed the Mosel from Koblenz to Trier. After the trains crossed the French border at Metz on 15 June, their speeds diminished considerably. In wide-open terrain, the train stopped for hours.[85]

In review, the combat debut of the 10th SS Panzer Division "Frundsberg" was noteworthy. From an operational standpoint, the entire division of nearly 20,000 men and their equipment traveled more than 2,500 kilometers or 1,600 miles within a five-day period. The average per day was 500 km or 300 miles. The successful move of the entire II SS Panzer Corps from central France to the area of the Dnjepr River in the Ukraine suggests a high level of operational competency.

In comparison to the fighting in the East during World War I, the defensive use of interior lines by way of railroad proved especially effective in supporting operations quickly and reinforcing specific areas with troops through rapid concentrations. Albeit piecemeal, the commitment of the II SS Panzer Corps, which excluded the 9th SS "Hohenstaufen," provides a good example of successful counterattacks and defensive concentrations against an enemy of considerable strength. Strategically the railroad provided offensive troops in the defense.[86]

In tactical terms, the predominant German use of the tank was comparable to the French campaign in 1940. Both the French in 1940 and the Russians in 1944 had sufficient antitank guns to withstand an infantry-supported tank assault across a broad front. However, the Russians placed troops and tanks poorly in the defense. A suitable comparative may be the employment of heavy cavalry against lines of light infantry. Even larger numbers of antitank guns in successive lines were no match for armor. The concentration of heavy mobile artillery and infantry, combined with the advance by heavy cavalry and precision divebombers, sufficed to dislodge the most stubborn entrenchment and overrun the defensive lines with ease.[87]

During the assault against Buczacz, the Germans omitted the Soviet first and second echelon defensive belts, usually manned by rifle regiments. German tanks struck antitank lines directly. Unprotected by infantry, the concentration of Soviet antitank guns fell easy prey to German spotters calling fire missions for self-propelled artillery and divebombers.

The theoretical doctrine of Soviet operations did not change between 1942 and the end of the war. The Marxist-Leninist foundation remained the political focus, and although military theorists examined and tested different operational theories, Stalin remained in firm control and made all the decisions on doctrine and high command strategy. His concept of "permanent operating factors," which reflected the Marxist-Leninist principles of war, included stability in the rear, morale of the army, quantity and quality of the divisions, armament of the army, and organizing ability of the command personnel.[88]

According to David Glantz, the Soviets perfected their combat force structure during the third and final period of war by adding logistical and combat support forces. However, the use of combined arms armies and rifle divisions, with aviation, tank, artillery, self-propelled artillery, and mechanized units did not become customary until the last year of the war.[89] Taking the strategic initiative, Soviet operations employed vast resources without interruption across a broad front. Glantz points out:

> While earlier Soviet operations occurred on separate strategic directions, by 1944 they took place along the entire strategic front, successively in 1944 and simultaneously in 1945. Each operation was conducted within the context of a deception plan coordinated by the Stavka which encompassed the entire campaign. These plans successfully concealed both the location and scale of the strategic offensives, and to some extent the timing as well.[90]

Successive Soviet strategic offensives conducted under the cloak of deception did not succeed following the Korsun-Shevchenkovskii operation, as noted by Glantz. Nevertheless, Soviet operational initiatives across a broad front, with sufficient resources, allowed the offensive center of gravity to shift without great effort from one spot to another. German areas of concentration were easily avoided until they dissipated; such was the case around Tarnopol. The Soviet offensive in the Ukraine succeeded after the II SS Panzer Corps withdrew to France. The multiple Soviet "front" operations, such as the drive on Kamenenz-Podolsk, failed due to poor tactical judgment, despite having all the strategic ingredients for victory. Soviet eagerness in pursuit of deep battle resulted in Russian tanks outrunning their own infantry and becoming isolated, which prevented the destruction of the First Panzer Army. Theoretically, Soviet fronts attacked at depths of 150 to 300 kilometers, whereas operational densities packed 200 to 250 guns and mortars and seventy to eighty-five tanks and self-propelled guns per kilometer. Superiorities were calculated for a ratio of 3-5:1 in man-power, 6-8:1 in tanks and artillery, and 3-5:1 in aircraft.[91]

In terms of the machinery itself, the T-34/85 medium tank was superior from a technical standpoint. From an operational standpoint, Werner Pietzka claimed well-trained German crews in the German medium Pz.Kpfw.IV tank easily knocked out the fast and more heavily gunned T-34/85.[92]

While a thorough examination of the 9th SS Panzer Division "Hohenstaufen" lies outside the scope of this study, the combat results of the divisions in the East differed significantly. Panzer Group Friebe, which incorporated elements of the 9th SS Panzer Division and the 10th SS Panzer Pioneer Battalion, failed in the attempt to relieve German forces encircled at Tarnopol. Of the approximately 4,600 men encircled, only fifty-five reached German lines. The high cost for the relief attempt by the XLVII Panzer Corps included 1,200 dead and wounded and eighteen tanks.[93]

Among the operational and strategic considerations that overshadowed the tactical success of the 10th SS Panzer Division were the close coordination and timing of attacks by the Soviets in the East and Anglo-American forces in the West. Stalin's greatest victory was won at the conference table, especially at Tehran in November 1943, where he backed the American strategy for

"Overlord," the Anglo-American and Canadian landings at Normandy, to coincide with his own spring offensive in the East. Thus, Germany was to be crushed between the coordinated attacks from the east and west. The timing of the Soviet offensive against Army Group South in early 1944 brought about the transfer of II SS Panzer Corps from OB West to the East. The two divisions specifically trained to counter airborne and amphibious landings were thus busy chasing a deceptive adversary and mock force concentrations in the Ukraine at the exact moment when Allied forces landed at Normandy.[94]

Estimated German losses on the Eastern Front from November 1943 to June 1944 were 1,500,000 men. Soviet losses for the Right Bank of Ukraine Offensive from 24 December 1943 to 17 April 1944 were 1,109,528. Materiel losses included 4,666 tanks or self-propelled guns, 7,532 artillery pieces, and 676 aircraft.[95]

SS-Obersturmbannführer Hans Lingner, the 1st General Staff officer, in conversation with officers of the 2nd SS Panzer Corps. Source: Gemeinschaftsarbeit des SS-Kriegsberichter-Zuges der 10.SS-Panzer-Div. "Frundsberg," *Dran Drauf und Durch! Buczacz-Caen-Nimwegen,* 1944.

The supply officer of the division, *SS-Sturmbannführer* Dr. Hans Klingsohr. Source: Gemeinschaftsarbeit des SS-Kriegsberichter-Zuges der 10.SS-Panzer-Div. "Frundsberg," *Dran Drauf und Durch! Buczacz-Caen-Nimwegen,* 1944.

The division adjutant, *SS-Hauptsturmführer* Rudolf Reinicke. Source: Gemeinschaftsarbeit des SS-Kriegsberichter-Zuges der 10.SS-Panzer-Div. "Frundsberg," *Dran Drauf und Durch! Buczacz-Caen-Nimwegen*, 1944.

An MG-42 in operation. Source: Gemeinschaftsarbeit des SS-Kriegsberichter-Zuges der 10.SS-Panzer-Div. "Frundsberg," *Dran Drauf und Durch! Buczacz-Caen-Nimwegen*, 1944.

The Baker Company provides fresh bread for many hungry men. Source: Gemeinschaftsarbeit des SS-Kriegsberichter-Zuges der 10.SS-Panzer-Div. "Frundsberg," *Dran Drauf und Durch! Buczacz-Caen-Nimwegen*, 1944.

Automotive mechanics keep the great variety of motor vehicles running. Source: Gemeinschaftsarbeit des SS-Kriegsberichter-Zuges der 10.SS-Panzer-Div. "Frundsberg," *Dran Drauf und Durch! Buczacz-Caen-Nimwegen*, 1944.

Supplies being loaded for delivery to the front lines. Source: Gemeinschaftsarbeit des SS-Kriegsberichter-Zuges der 10.SS-Panzer-Div. "Frundsberg," *Dran Drauf und Durch! Buczacz-Caen-Nimwegen*, 1944.

A heavy 150mm self-propelled battery in direct fire against Russians only 500 meters away. Source: Gemeinschaftsarbeit des SS-Kriegsberichter-Zuges der 10.SS-Panzer-Div. "Frundsberg," *Dran Drauf und Durch! Buczacz-Caen-Nimwegen*, 1944.

SS-Gruppenführer Karl von Treuenfeld shaking hands with recipients of awards in Russia, 1944. Source: Gemeinschaftsarbeit des SS-Kriegsberichter-Zuges der 10.SS-Panzer-Div. "Frundsberg," *Dran Drauf und Durch! Buczacz-Caen-Nimwegen*, 1944.

A telephone lineman passing by a knocked out Russian T-34 medium tank, Russia, 1944. Source: Gemeinschaftsarbeit des SS-Kriegsberichter-Zuges der 10.SS-Panzer-Div. "Frundsberg," *Dran Drauf und Durch! Buczacz-Caen-Nimwegen*, 1944.

A heavy 150mm self-propelled gun battery firing on the Eastern Front, 1944. Source: Gemeinschaftsarbeit des SS-Kriegsberichter-Zuges der 10.SS-Panzer-Div. "Frundsberg," *Dran Drauf und Durch! Buczacz-Caen-Nimwegen*, 1944.

Armored half-tracks (Sd.Kfz. 251/9) with 75mm KwK37 guns pass through a Russian village, Russia, 1944. Source: Gemeinschaftsarbeit des SS-Kriegsberichter-Zuges der 10.SS-Panzer-Div. "Frundsberg," *Dran Drauf und Durch! Buczacz-Caen-Nimwegen*, 1944.

A Russian bi-plane engulfed in flames, Russia, 1944. Source: Gemeinschaftsarbeit des SS-Kriegsberichter-Zuges der 10.SS-Panzer-Div. "Frundsberg," *Dran Drauf und Durch! Buczacz-Caen-Nimwegen*, 1944.

ICH SPRECHE DER
SS-PANZER-AUFKLÄRUNGS-
ABTEILUNG 10
FÜR DEN ABSCHUSS VON
DREI FEINDLICHEN FLUGZEUGEN
BEI KURDWANOWKA
AM 6. 4. 1944
MEINE
BESONDERE ANERKENNUNG AUS.

HAUPTQUARTIER·DEN 1. AUGUST 1944

DER FÜHRER

Citation for the achievement of three aircraft shot down by the 10th SS Panzer Antiaircraft Battalion, Russia, 6 April 1944. Source: Gemeinschaftsarbeit des SS-Kriegsberichter-Zuges der 10.SS-Panzer-Div. "Frundsberg," *Dran Drauf und Durch! Buczacz-Caen-Nimwegen*, 1944.

A medical orderly attends to a wounded soldier, Russia, 1944. Source: Gemeinschaftsarbeit des SS-Kriegsberichter-Zuges der 10.SS-Panzer-Div. "Frundsberg," *Dran Drauf und Durch! Buczacz-Caen-Nimwegen*, 1944.

The endless Russian expanses, 1944.
Source: Gemeinschaftsarbeit des SS-
Kriegsberichter-Zuges der 10.SS-Panzer-
Div. "Frundsberg," *Dran Drauf und Durch!
Buczacz-Caen-Nimwegen*, 1944.

Pioneers of the 10th SS Pioneer Battalion construct a bridge
despite the cold and wet. Source: Gemeinschaftsarbeit des SS-
Kriegsberichter-Zuges der 10.SS-Panzer-Div. "Frundsberg," *Dran
Drauf und Durch! Buczacz-Caen-Nimwegen*, 1944.

Infantry guns provided direct fire support
close to the forward-most positions. Source:
Gemeinschaftsarbeit des SS-Kriegsberichter-
Zuges der 10.SS-Panzer-Div. "Frundsberg,"
*Dran Drauf und Durch! Buczacz-Caen-
Nimwegen*, 1944.

Buczacz-Tarnopol, 1944. *SS-Oberführer* Heinz Harmel and *SS-Sturmbannführer* Willi Kruft at the combat command post. Source: Sieberhagen Archive.

Heinz Harmel on the far lower right, at the main line of battle in Russia. Source: Sieberhagen Archive.

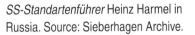

SS-Standartenführer Heinz Harmel in Russia. Source: Sieberhagen Archive.

Officers' meeting between the 10th SS Panzer Division and the Divebomber Squadron 77, after the relief of the First Panzer Army at Buczacz. *SS-Oberführer* Heinz Harmel in conversation with Lieutenant Colonel Helmut Bruch, the commander of the squadron. Source: Sieberhagen Archive.

SS-Oberführer Heinz Harmel in conversation with Lieutenant Johann Wallhauser of the Divebomber Squadron 77. Source: Sieberhagen Archive.

SS-Oberführer Heinz Harmel in conversation with Lieutenant Colonel Helmut Bruch, the commander of the Divebomber Squadron 77. Source: Sieberhagen Archive.

SS-Oberführer Heinz Harmel in conversation with Lieutenant Colonel Helmut Bruch, the commander of the Divebomber Squadron 77. Source: Sieberhagen Archive.

SS-Oberführer Heinz Harmel in conversation with Lieutenant Colonel Helmut Bruch, the commander of the Divebomber Squadron 77. Source: Sieberhagen Archive.

SS-Standartenführer Heinz Harmel and *SS-Sturmbannführer* Günther Wisliceny, a member of the 2nd SS Panzer Division. Source: Sieberhagen Archive.

Germanic runes on a Christian cross.
Source: Westerhoff Archive.

SS-Oberscharführer Bernhard Westerhoff, company troop NCO, 6th Company, 2nd Battalion, 10th SS Panzer Regiment, posing on a well-camouflaged personnel vehicle. Russia, 1944. Source: Westerhoff Archive.

SS-Oberscharführer Bernhard Westerhoff with his crew in tank number 622, shortly before departure. Russia, 1944. Source: Westerhoff Archive.

SS-Oberscharführer Bernhard
Westerhoff and crew in front of their
vehicle, Pz.Kpfw.IV Ausf. H, tank number
622, 6th Company, 2nd Battalion, 10th
SS Panzer Regiment. Russia, 1944.
Source: Westerhoff Archive.

The commander of the 2nd
Battalion, 10th SS Panzer Regiment,
and the company commander, 6th
Company, during a burial ceremony
of fellow soldiers in Russia. Source:
Westerhoff Archive.

Rifle salute of the Honor Company
during a burial ceremony. Source:
Westerhoff Archive.

Honor Company at attention at an open grave during a burial ceremony. Source: Westerhoff Archive.

Marching forward in Russia, Tarnopol-Brody, 1944. Source: Westerhoff Archive.

Officers and noncommissioned officers on 13 May 1944 in a bivouac site in a forest, Russia. Source: Westerhoff Archive.

Enlisted bivouac site in a forest outside Buczacz, Russia, 1944. Source: Westerhoff Archive.

Distributing market products at the forest bivouac site, Russia, 1944. Source: Westerhoff Archive.

Respite between the fighting, Russia, 1944. Source: Westerhoff Archive.

Decoration and awards ceremony, Russia, 1944. Source: Westerhoff Archive.

Enemy shell that hit the rear of the vehicle and blew off the idler wheel. The crew short-tracked the right side for continued temporary operations. Russia, 1944. Source: Westerhoff Archive.

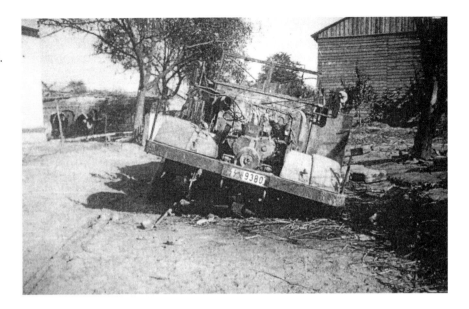

Supply trains ambushed by resistance fighters, Russia, 1944. Source: Westerhoff Archive.

The 6th Company, 2nd Battalion, 10th SS Panzer Regiment, posing with animals. Note the *Spiess* on the far left side, indicated by the double rings on his cuffs. Source: Westerhoff Archive.

The medical noncommissioned officer with his *Kübelwagen*. The lives of many fellow soldiers depended on both. Source: Westerhoff Archive.

Officers and men of the 6th Company in the rail transport cars on their way to Russia, Spring 1944. Source: Westerhoff Archive.

Two tank commanders of the 6th Company during a march halt in Russia, 1944. Source: Westerhoff Archive.

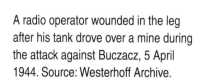

A radio operator wounded in the leg after his tank drove over a mine during the attack against Buczacz, 5 April 1944. Source: Westerhoff Archive.

The gunner and vehicle number 631 of *SS-Oberscharführer* Erhard, after being hit by four antitank projectiles. Source: Westerhoff Archive.

Crew Wrobel, Russia, 1944. Source: Westerhoff Archive.

Reloading 75mm ammunition. Russia, 1944. Source: Westerhoff Archive.

Moving forward in Russia, 1944. Source: Westerhoff Archive.

SS-Unterscharführer Karl Schneider, 14 April 1944. Source: Westerhoff Archive.

On 17 April 1944 the combat elements of the 10th SS Panzer Regiment bivouacked in a small forest near Buczacz, and remained in the same location until 24 April, before the attack on Buczacz. Depicted is the kitchen of the 6th Company. Source: Westerhoff Archive.

From left to right: The supply officer, *SS-Obersturmführer* Otto Kasten, IVa, 2nd Battalion, 10th SS Panzer Regiment, the *Spiess* Stief, and *SS-Oberscharführer* Bernhard Westerhoff, Russia, 1944. Source: Westerhoff Archive.

Men of the 6th Company, 2nd Battalion, 10th SS Panzer Regiment, enjoying the Easter sun, Russia 1944. Source: Westerhoff Archive.

Relaxing and passing around a bottle
in the forest bivouac site, Russia, 1944.
Source: Westerhoff Archive.

Crew Schneider, shortly before
departure, Russia, 1944.
Source: Westerhoff Archive.

A hit tore off the rear idler wheel.
Source: Westerhoff Archive.

The 6th Company *Spiess* Stief relaxing on a bench in the sun, Russia, 1944. Source: Westerhoff Archive.

The face of an *SS-Oberschütze*, after their first engagements. Source: Westerhoff Archive.

The face of an *SS-Oberschütze*, after their first engagements. Source: Westerhoff Archive.

The face of an *SS-Oberschütze*,
after their first engagements. Source:
Westerhoff Archive.

The face of an *SS-Oberschütze*, after their first
engagements. Source: Westerhoff Archive.

SS-Obersturmführer Gernot Traupel, the
adjutant, 2nd Battalion, 10th SS Panzer
Regiment. Source: Westerhoff Archive.

CHAPTER 3

Normandy

28 June–21 August 1944

IN THE FIRST QUARTER OF 1944, the 10th SS Panzer Division gained great confidence after its combat debut in East Galicia during the successful relief-operation of the encircled First Panzer Army at Buczacz. In the East, the men of the Frundsberg Division became well familiarized with the term "outnumbered [by the enemy] in great proportions." Comparatively the division lacked experience in fighting an enemy who enjoyed an unrestricted supply of materiel and complete air supremacy, which they would face in the West against Anglo-American forces.

Soon after the division's first combat in the East, command of the division transferred to *SS-Standartenführer* Heinz Harmel, who had recently graduated from the Divisional Command course. Despite his advanced training, he lacked the practical experience of commanding a panzer division. *SS-Sturmbannführer* Hans Lingner was the 1st General Staff officer. In June 1944, the regiments and independent battalions were led by:

SS-Sturmbannführer Paetsch
10th SS Panzer Regiment

SS-Standartenführer Deisenhofer
21st *SS-Panzergrenadier* Regiment

SS-Obersturmbannführer Schulze
22nd *SS-Panzergrenadier* Regiment

SS-Standartenführer Sander
10th SS Panzer Artillery Regiment

SS-Sturmbannführer Brinkmann
10th SS Panzer Reconnaissance Battalion

SS-Sturmbannführer Tröbinger
10th SS Panzer Pioneer Battalion

SS-Hauptsturmführer Schrembs
10th SS Panzer Anti-Aircraft Battalion

SS-Sturmbannführer Kruft
10th SS Signal Battalion

The individual staff billets naturally changed quite frequently during the post-deployment phase.

The 10th SS Panzer Division was nearly fully equipped with both personnel and equipment, minus the units yet to receive their vehicles, which included the 1st Battalion, 10th SS Panzer Regiment, and 10th SS Tank Destroyer Battalion. The division was trained well and ready for combat.[1]

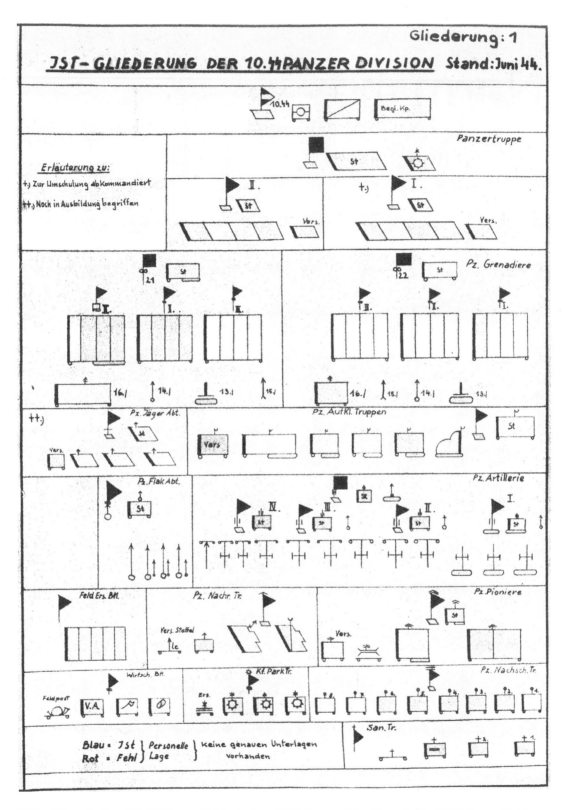

Table of Organization; 10th SS Panzer Division in June 1944. Source: Heinz Harmel, *Die 10.SS Panzer-Division "Frundsberg" im Einsatz vom Juni bis November 1944,* Foreign Military Studies, MS # P-163 , 1954.

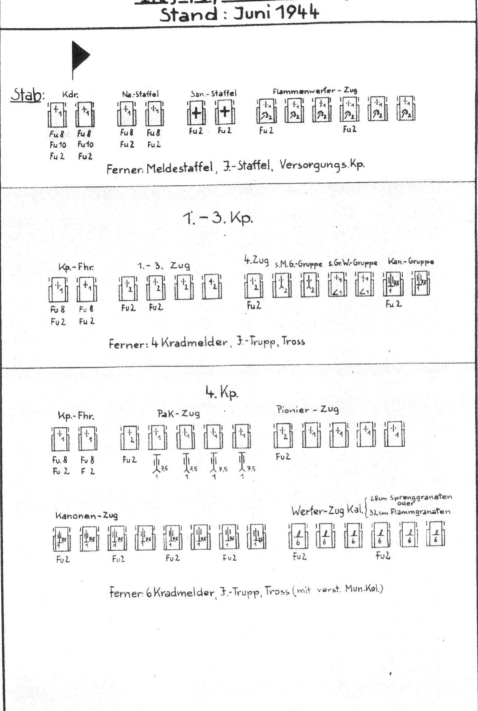

Table of Organization; 1st Battalion, 21st *SS-Panzergrenadier* Battalion in June 1944. Source: Heinz Harmel, *Die 10.SS Panzer-Division "Frundsberg" im Einsatz vom Juni bis November 1944,* Foreign Military Studies, MS # P-163, 1954.

At this stage, the individual units included reinforced panzer grenadier regiments, each comprised of three battalions, a single artillery regiment, consisting of four battalions with a total of twelve 105mm "Wespe" self-propelled guns divided among the 1st and 2nd batteries, six 150mm "Hummels" in the 3rd battery, twelve 105mm light field howitzers, and reinforced supply and logistics units. The tank regiment consisted of eight companies evenly divided into two battalions. Theoretically the 1st Battalion consisted of four companies of the new Pz.Kpfw.V "Panther" that by June 1944 did not have any vehicles but continued to train on the use of the tank. Of the four panzer companies that formed the 2nd Battalion, the 5th and 6th Companies consisted of the Pz.Kpfw.IV (Ausf H), with the long-barreled high velocity 75mm gun (KwK L42). The latter two companies were made up of *Sturmgeschütz* IIIs, or assault guns, armed with the 75mm StuK 40 main gun. The 1st Battalion, 10th SS Panzer Regiment, did not join the division until January 1945. The 10th SS Tank Destroyer Battalion continued to organize within Germany and did not join the division until September 1944.[2]

After its rail transportation and return to the West, the 10th SS Panzer Division faced difficulties similar to what they experienced in the East that prevented the division from achieving a successful breakthrough during their initial commitment into battle southwest of Caen.

At the onset of the Allied invasion at Normandy on 6 June 1944, the division remained part of the II SS Panzer Corps, commanded by *SS-Oberstgruppenführer* Paul Hausser. Still a reserve element of the Army Group Northern Ukraine, located 80 km southeast of Lemberg, the II SS Panzer Corps remained in the East. As late as 7 June, portions of the divisional reconnaissance, artillery, pioneer, and the reinforced 21st *SS-Panzergrenadier* Regiment were ordered 100 km south of divisional billeting in support of a separate attack against Soviet forces. These units were the last to arrive in the Normandy area and were committed piecemeal into battle without sufficient preparation.

Meanwhile, the division redeployed north of Lemberg but split in two and separated over 180 km. During the night of 12–13 June, the division received orders to entrain immediately. Together with the headquarters staff of the II SS Panzer Corps, the division received orders to prepare its troops, including those belonging to the 9th SS Panzer Division, for transfer to OB West as soon as possible. To expedite the process by rail, all tracked rolling stock was brought west of Paris. The wheeled rolling stock detrained around the areas of Metz-Bar le Duc and Saarbrücken-Nancy, from where they continued to march under their own power on a southerly route, bypassing Paris, in order to reach the assembly area.

The rail transport began on 12 June from the Lemberg area. Members of the pioneer battalion traveled in passenger cars. Destroyed rail lines and attacks by fighter aircraft delayed the movement by rail through the western regions and resulted in detours and extended periods of delay. For example, the train that carried Bernhard Westerhoff, of the 6th Company, 10th SS Panzer Regiment, suddenly stopped along a section of track. Partisans were reported in the vicinity. Nearby, a cow was spotted grazing. Before the train departed, the cow was loaded onto the train. The kitchen chef Reisenberger and his helpers slaughtered the cow underway. However, at the next train station, the *Feldgendarmerie* or military police boarded the train and conducted an inspection. Of course, no one knew anything about a cow.[3]

The first divisional order addressed Allied air supremacy and prescribed the method of march. All units were to expect Allied aerial reconnaissance and fighter aircraft as far inland as southeast of Paris. The march of units between 17 and 19 June was to occur during the night, beginning at 2200 hours and ending before first light at 0400 hours. The fueling points 79 and 80 in Nancy provided three and four units of fuel, respectively. However, units were directed to carry as much fuel as possible. The prescribed distance between vehicles when traveling was 150 meters, and the use of vehicle staff pennants and blackout lights was prohibited. The *Feldgendarmerie*, responsible for the flow and direction of traffic, was not available in the more remote areas and unable to assist until the division reached the assembly area. Until such time, unit officers were responsible for determining the correct route of march. Field hospitals were to establish locations in Bar le Duc, Toul (Army), Nancy (equipped with a variety of services including dental), Verdun, and Commercy (both Army). For the assembly phase, the divisional command post was located in Lonny.

The bivouac areas for the various units included:

10th SS Pioneer Battalion; Gace-Orgeres

21st *SS-Panzergrenadier* Regiment and 3rd Battalion, 10th SS Artillery Regiment; St. Sulpics, St. Evroult, St. Cauburgs-Moulings la Marchem, St. Martin

10th SS Panzer Reconnaissance Battalion; Foret de Leigle, Laigle, St. Quen

10th SS Panzer Antiaircraft Battalion; Vitrau, la Chapelle, Notre Dames

10th SS Panzer Regiment and 1st Battalion, 10th SS Artillery Regiment; La Senetes, St. Hileres, Authieul

10th SS Adminstrative Supply Battalion; Esseckes, St. Innges, Ewi Marde

22nd *SS-Panzergrenadier* Regiment and 2nd Battalion, 10th SS Artillery Regiment; Verneuil, Chaise Bieu, Sonnefei, Karah-Siexille

10th Medical Battalion; Morvilles, La Ferte Vidame, Sennonches

10th Replacement Battalion; Ardelles, La Villes sur Nonainz, St. Maurice

10th Organizational Battalion; Belhomert, Les Pas, Vaupillon

Commander, 10th SS Panzer Signal Troop between Medical Battalion, 22nd *SS-Panzergrenadier* Regiment and 10th Organizational Battalion

Divisional Staff and Signal Battalion; area north of Langny (Escort Company, and Military Police Company)[4]

According to Erich Werkmeister, of the 2nd Pioneer Company, elements of the pioneer battalion detrained at Bar le Duc. Their first priority was to camouflage the half-tracks and trucks, and build protective shrapnel crates. The camouflage was very effective against Allied aircraft. The men then dug protective fighting holes for themselves. In the evening, Allied aircraft dropped parachute illumination flares but the battalion went undetected. Due to the unreliability of road signs, messengers and company troops marked a new route for the westward advance.

SS-Obersturmführer Hugo Benger, the former 3rd Company commander who transferred as a reserve officer to the Field Replacement Battalion during the end of March, returned to the pioneer battalion and assumed command of the Staff Company. Southwest of Metz, the company detrained and proceeded into their assigned areas for assembly.[5]

On 18 June, the 6th Company, 10th SS Panzer Regiment, detrained in Haudan. Immediately, the vehicles were brought under cover and concealed. *SS-Untersturmführer* Quandel gave notice that the Allies controlled the skies. The operation of vehicles was to occur only at night. The following day, the 6th Company traveled through Chateauneuf-Digmy-Le Magne-Longny and into the bivouac area of Toret du Perche. On 20 June, the company entered their designated assembly area and lost one tank after an attack by fighter aircraft.[6]

The 1st "Panther" Battalion, 9th SS Panzer Regiment, training at Mailly-le-Camp since 1943, concluded its training around 18 June when the first Pz.Kpfw.V "Panthers" were allocated to the II SS Panzer Corps. However, only the Hohenstaufen Division received its full complement of Panther tanks. Technically, a Panther battalion numbered sixty-eight tanks divided evenly between four companies. The battalion staff received an additional eight tanks. Departing Mailly-le-Camp by railroad, the battalion suffered their first vehicle losses to Allied aerial attacks. Offloaded west of Paris, the battalion joined the corps on their way to the front.[7]

By the end of the morning on 20 June, fifty-one divisional trains had unloaded, of which thirteen unloaded west of Paris. Three days later, an additional twenty-one trains unloaded west of Paris.

Once the divisional units detrained in the same area, they faced a 150 to 200 km forced march into the assembly areas of Gacé-Falaise-Briouze. The route of march for the bulk of the division that detrained in eastern France was as much as 600 km. Because the Allies controlled the skies, the Germans conducted all movement under the cover of darkness, which caused additional delays.

Allied air supremacy and the impotent German *Luftwaffe*, which could not provide any degree of protection for German troops, contributed to low troop morale. A good example, which also speaks to the effectiveness of the Allied bombing campaign against logistical targets, occurred when twenty-five to thirty German Bf 109 fighter aircraft flew over the heads of divisional troops at low altitude. The troops cheered only to learn later that many aircraft crashed due to a lack of fuel.[8]

The French Resistance actively operated only on a limited basis with little effect on German operations, but their presence was felt when German troop movements were hampered and slowed by explosive devices strewn across the road that caused flat tires. Nevertheless, German losses in personnel and equipment during the movement forward and within the assembly areas were kept to a minimum. The last portions of the division arrived in the assembly area on 28 June.[9]

On 25 June 1944, the commander of the 10th SS Panzer Division hastily proceeded ahead of his division and reported to the commanding general of the II SS Panzer Corps. Harmel was briefed on the situation along the Normandy Front and the disposition of the corps and its intended use.

Allied forces managed to gain a foothold along the Normandy coast and establish bridgeheads north of Caen (British Second Army) and on the Cotentin-Peninsula (U.S. First Army). By 25 June, the two Allied armies reached the line north of Caen-Tilly's-Seulles-Caumont-St.Clair-s.l'Elle-Portbeil; the boundary of both armies lay near the Caumont-Bayeux line. However, the Allied gains in front of Caen were not proceeding as planned. General Sir Bernard L. Montgomery, commanding general of 21 Army Group, commanded all Allied ground forces in Western Europe. His goal to double-envelop Caen failed when the opportunity passed to exploit a gap on the western side between the German defenses. The operation was deemed disappointing and cancelled on 13 June. Five days later, Montgomery hoped to maintain the initiative by launching Operation Epsom, with the goal of capturing Caen and bridgeheads across the Orne River south of the city.[10]

Caen lay at the center of a convergent road network as the capital city of the northwestern French region of Calvados. North and south of Caen, the terrain featured gentle rolling meadows and wheat fields. Along the line Caen-Bayeaux-Falaise, small woods, orchards, and stone houses or farming hamlets characterized the countryside. West of Falaise, the *bocage* spread northwest, west, and southwest to form a tightly woven patchwork of small fields that were surrounded by thick earth embankments of high impenetrable thickets.[11]

To accomplish the objective, Montgomery planned to commit the full power of the Second Army. The attacking forces included three corps, including the 8 Corps, 30 Corps, and I Corps. Under the command of Lieutenant General Sir Richard O'Connor, 8 Corps spearheaded the attack with three divisions, including the 15th Scottish, 43rd Wessex, and 11th Armoured, augmented by the 4th Armoured Brigade, and a tank battalion. The total strength of 8 Corps reached 60,000 men and over 600 tanks. In addition, artillery support from the other two corps brought 700 guns to bear against the German defenses, plus naval firepower from three Royal Navy cruisers. The 2nd Tactical Air Force (TAF) provided fighter cover and fighter-bomber support.[12]

Originally planned to begin on 18 June, Epsom did not commence until 25 June. By the end of the first day, the 15th Division, considered the best infantry division in 21 Army Group, reached a line only several kilometers south of their start line. Thirty Corps, on the right, nearing Rauray, advanced but the skillful German defenses held despite Allied superiority in tank, artillery, and airpower.[13]

German planning aimed to launch a counterattack to the north from the area of Caumont with tanks from both the I and II SS Panzer Corps and the XLVII Panzer Corps. The objective was the destruction of the flank of the U.S. V Corps in the east around Balleroy, followed by a flanking attack against British landing forces.[14]

The commander of the 10th SS Panzer Division received orders to reconnoiter and evaluate the division's positions and disposition for an attack around Villers-Bocage-Caumont. On 26 June, after a two-day reconnaissance, Harmel established contact with elements of the 2nd Panzer Division, engaged in combat along the heights east of Caumont.

The following day, forward elements of the division located near Caumont were called back and redeployed north of Thury-Harcourt. Around Caen, a critical situation developed that forced German leadership to change the planned counterattack. Allied forces succeeded in penetrating the thin German defensive lines west and southwest of Caen. For a general southeasterly advance, the Allies also crossed the road Villers-Bocage-Caen and the Odon River. Under the control of Panzer Group West, the II SS Panzer Corps received new orders to attack from positions south of the line St. Honorine-du Fay-Tournay (2.5 km west of le Locheur), against both sides of the Odon River in order to sever the Allied spearhead and thereby eliminate the threat of an encirclement of German forces at Caen.[15]

Meanwhile, the 10th SS Panzer Division moved the bulk of its units into the assembly area. During the preceding night of 27–28 June, the division had hastily moved into the forward assembly areas south of the line St. Honorine-Neuilly. This movement occurred prior to obtaining the results of a previous reconnaissance. Despite unfavorable weather, Allied aerial reconnaissance remained active and the 10th SS Panzer Division suffered numerous losses due to Allied aircraft and artillery attacks. Allied naval gunfire was concentrated against the bridge at Thury-Harcourt, which represented the only crossing over the Orne River for the 10th SS Panzer Division.[16]

SS-Sturmmann Kurt Tews, a divisional staff courier for the messenger squadron, witnessed the Allied bombing of the bridge at Thury-Harcourt. When an estimated fifty aircraft bombed the bridge at low-level, Tews and *SS-Scharführer* Karl Schmid sought cover behind their motorcycle with sidecar. After the attack, the men approached the bridge and found unexploded ordnance scattered across the road. Medical vehicles coming from the front quickly jammed the road when they approached the unexploded ordnance. Tews and Schmid followed the slogan of elite soldiers, "*Waffen-SS* Forward!" Leaving their motorcycle in the middle of the road, the two men approached each of the 500-pound bombs and, after a loud "heave-ho," rolled each of the bombs off the road.[17]

Near the German lines around Longraye, the British major and chief staff medical officer, S. Darling and Kenneth Wilson, both from the British 6th Airborne Division, were captured in civilian clothing by a neighboring unit. Their interrogation revealed the two men were wounded and captured on 6 June, and brought to a German field hospital. After three days they transferred to a different hospital where they remained until 22 June. During their near two-week stay, the men were never searched and retained their personal effects that included a compass, map, knife, money, camouflage, and smock. The next day the men fled from the hospital and obtained civilian clothes in an effort to reach British lines.[18]

By the evening on 28 June, Allied forces captured the villages of Gavrus, Baron, and Pontaine-Etoupefour, as well as Hill 112 and Esquay.

Facing west, the 12th SS Panzer Division of the I SS Panzer Corps held the line Carpiquet-Bretteville-sur Odon-Eterville and a narrow bridgehead west of the Orne near Maltot, Feuguerolles, and Bully. The eastern flank of the Panzer Lehr Division engaged in heavy defensive fighting northeast of Villers-Bocage. Weak armored *Kampfgruppen* of the 2nd SS Panzer Division, detached from the main body of the division marching west, held the ground between the 10th SS and 12th SS Panzer Divisions. At this point, the *Kampfgruppen* of the 2nd SS could not have assembled a defense capable of stopping any serious Allied attempt at breakthrough. The 10th SS Panzer Reconnaissance Battalion provided additional security in the divisional assembly area.

On 28 June, *SS-Brigadeführer* Bittrich, commander of 9th SS Panzer Division, assumed command of the II SS Panzer Corps. The corps received the following order:

> Attack to the northeast astride the Odon and destroy the enemy who has penetrated to the southeast and free the road Villers-Bocage–Caen of Allied forces.

For the attack:

Echeloned on the right, the 10th SS Panzer Division is tasked with the objectives of capturing Gavrus and Baron and continuing the attack and capturing Hill 112 and establishing contact with the 12th SS Panzer Division at Verson on the right.

Echeloned on the left, the 9th SS Panzer Division is tasked with the objective to attack over Missy and Noyers against Mouen and Cheux and establishing contact with the Panzer Lehr Division on the left.

The divisional boundaries: the Odon River.

Commencement of attack: 29 June. 0600 hours.[19]

German commanders were anxious to begin the attack early. Until the evening of 28 June, the 10th SS Panzer Division prepared for combat operations under security and in positions along the line Maizet-Neuilly. The villages of Amayé, Avenay, and Hill 113 north of Evrecy were reconnoitered. The bulk of the artillery was also brought into position.

Records suggest the attack was delayed more than once. According to the commander of the 7th Assault Gun Company, *SS-Obersturmführer* Franz Riedel, orders were received at 0700 on the morning of the attack. His mission was to attack against Hill 113 and onto Gavrus. The 7th Assault Gun Company assembled in Evrecy. The plan of attack called for the 7th Company to lead the attack, while the 5th and 6th tank companies provided security on both the left and right flanks. However, due to the delayed arrival of a panzer grenadier regiment, the attack was postponed until 1000 hours. Moreover, Riedel was not notified of the change and began his attack at 0700. At the same time and shortly after the 7th Company traveled several hundred meters, Allied Sherman tanks crossed over Hill 113. Immediately, German self-propelled assault gun projectiles were fired resulting in eleven Sherman tanks burning. Riedel's vehicle, which led the company at point, knocked out five Allied tanks. The 7th Company

suffered only a single loss; the commander's vehicle of the 1st Platoon took a hit by which the commander, *SS-Untersturmführer* Erwin Hilpert, was wounded and the driver killed. As soon as the British tanks turned and fled, white Allied smoke prevented the Germans from pursuit. Then suddenly, a motorcycle with sidecar approached Riedel's vehicle at a dangerously high speed. To his surprise, it was Leo Reinhold, the commander of the 2nd Battalion, who furiously yelled and demanded to know what all the shooting was about. Somewhat perplexed, Reinhold looked at the burning Sherman tanks and asked, with a calmer voice, "What did you do with them?"

After Riedel explained the situation, Reinhold was very happy. Heinz Harmel, the divisional commander, expressed his satisfaction over the matter, calling it the best birthday present he received that day. Later, *SS-Unterscharführer* Ewald Menzel received one full day off and was awarded both the Iron Cross 2nd and 1st Class.[20]

In the meantime, the 10th SS Panzer Reconnaissance Battalion received orders for corps-level operational preparedness for employment south of St. Honorine. The divisional strategic combat command post was in Goupillières, whereas the forward tactical combat command post was in a forest 1.5 km southeast of St. Honorine. The bulk of the 21st *SS-Panzergrenadier* Regiment and portions of the artillery regiment and pioneer battalion did not arrive on the battlefield until early in the afternoon. Their delayed arrival, caused in part by Allied aerial activity, further postponed the attack on 29 June until 1430 hours.[21]

In lieu of the attack on 29 June 1944, German leadership recognized that ownership of the dominating Hill 112 would determine the outcome of the battle. The plan of attack for the II SS Panzer Corps emphasized terrain considerations and concentrated the center of gravity of the attack on the left flank of the 10th SS Panzer Division. The bulk of the fighting would fall to the grenadier regiments, whereby the 1st Battalion, 21st *SS-Panzergrenadier* Regiment was designated as a mobile reserve. This designation was effective only until pioneers succeeded in preparing a crossing over the eastward-flowing river from Evrecy and once avenues were blasted through the river's twisting bends. For the coming attack, the 1st and 3rd Company commanders of the pioneer battalion rolled the dice to lead their companies into battle. *SS-Obersturmführer* Horst Schneider, of the 3rd Company, would lead the attack with his men into the inferno.[22]

The objectives of the 22nd *SS-Panzergrenadier* Regiment, on the left, included the villages of Gavrus and Baron, while those of the 21st *SS-Panzergrenadier* Regiment, on the right, included Hill 113 and, following the capture of Esquay, Hill 112. The reinforced regiments incorporated elements of the pioneer battalion, equipped with flamethrowers and other close-quarter combat equipment, for the fighting along the unavoidable river basin and within the village.

The 2nd Battalion, 10th SS Panzer Regiment was to support the attack with the 21st *SS-Panzergrenadier* Regiment and engage any enemy armor that emerged on the battlefield. The 6th Company, 10th SS Panzer Regiment, crossed the riverbed between Avenay and Vieux and assembled along the road Avenay-Maltot. On certain occasions, as an act of gratitude for all their hard work, supply troops were able to replace tank crew members to experience an attack. One such attack was named "Operation Calvados."[23]

The divisional artillery and specific portions of the 8th Launcher Brigade or rocket launchers were tasked with combined fire missions against the attack objectives with emphasis on Hill 112.

Moreover, the II SS Panzer Corps arranged for supporting fire by the corps artillery, the 12th SS Panzer Division, and supporting attacks from any advances made by the neighboring unit.

Allied artillery fire and the employment of both reconnaissance and fighter aircraft increased throughout the late morning and caused numerous losses. However, at 1430 hours, the division was ready to attack.[24]

Franz Widmann, an *SS-Unterführer* and the Motorcycle Squadron leader of the 10th SS Panzer Reconnaissance Battalion, joined the Frundsberg Division after recuperating from wounds sustained in the East while serving with the Death's Head Division. In Normandy, the messenger squadron disbanded, but Widmann functioned as a divisional courier for orders or directives. He spent most of his time with the divisional command staff and had a *Schwimmwagen* with driver at his disposal. Widmann obtained missions or tasks for the delivery of orders to the reconnaissance battalion, or any other unit, by a messenger on foot who brought the assignment to Widmann at the divisional combat command post. Most missions involved the delivery of secret general command directives. The receipt of the directives usually required Widmann's signature. To avoid enemy aerial danger, most deliveries took place at night. In a personal letter written home, Widmann mentioned delivering directives throughout the entire night and falling over exhausted when returning to his quarters.[25]

Around 1600, despite the piecemeal commitment of troops as they arrived, Bittrich reported good progress by the 10th SS on the right, after eleven British tanks were reported destroyed in front of Gavrus. On the left, the 19th *SS-Panzergrenadier* Regiment engaged British forces and penetrated the enemy line. British artillery, fighter aircraft, and the 9th Royal Tanks contained the German advance. One hour later, the British regained their initial positions and captured a German officer and documents containing the plan of attack against Cheux.[26]

Accounts of the sequence of events and units involved during the fighting in the afternoon around 1800 vary. More than likely, the 1st Battalion and armored 3rd Battalion, 20th *SS-Panzergrenadier* Regiment of the 9th SS Panzer Division assembled around the Bas-de-Forges for the continued attack against Cheux. In addition, the captured documents placed all three battalions of the 19th *SS-Panzergrenadier* Regiment in the woods. The German historian for OKW, Percy E. Schramm, attributed the failure of the counterattack to Allied aerial operations; approximately one hundred Lancaster bombers appeared overhead and saturated the assembly area. With twenty dead, forty wounded, and a 20 percent reduction in half-tracks reported, the attack petered out and was called off.[27]

Initially, the reinforced 22nd *SS-Panzergrenadier* Regiment made a speedy advance through the river basin. The regiment encountered heavy defensive small arms fire along the outskirts of Gavrus but managed to infiltrate and capture the village by late afternoon, after bitter house-to-house fighting. Shortly thereafter, the Allies launched a counterattack. Supported by heavy Allied fire of all calibers during the evening hours, the 22nd *SS-Panzergrenadier* Regiment was pushed back, step by step, out of Gavrus.

The reinforced 21st *SS-Panzergrenadier* Regiment, of which elements were committed to battle immediately after their arrival, followed its left neighbor toward Hill 113. The lead battalion emerged onto the open terrain at Evrecy and ran into enemy artillery fire only minutes after it began the assault. Allied infantry, along with several tanks, managed to infiltrate the eastern portions of Gavrus and made a determined stand. Tanks from both the German and Allied units supported the bitter fighting for Evrecy and Hill 113. The attack of the 21st *SS-Panzergrenadier* Regiment was smashed by Allied flanking fire from Avenay, continuous fighter aircraft attacks, and artillery fire against the northern and southern portions of Hill 113. By nightfall the 2nd Battalion, 10th SS Panzer Regiment reported the destruction of twenty-eight Allied tanks at the cost of only two. The 6th Company, 10th SS Panzer Regiment, lost tank number 632, commandeered by *SS-Unterscharführer* Krölls, which caught fire. Two men were wounded. An antitank projectile hit tank number 602, commanded by *SS-Unterscharführer* Bernhard Westerhoff.[28]

SS-Hauptsturmführer Karl Keck, the pioneer company commander, 15th Company, 21st *SS-Panzergrenadier* Regiment (2nd Battalion), continued the counterattack. While the regiment instructed Keck to establish contact with the 9th SS Panzer Division with a scouting force, he discovered a gap between the left neighbor and the Odon River that threatened the left wing of the 2nd Battalion. Immediately, and on his own initiative, he rallied his men forward and routed approximately two Allied companies. Capturing a number of weapons and equipment, Keck provided the groundwork for holding the village of Gavrus and, indirectly, for holding Hill 112.[29]

The division did not foresee any success in continuing the attack against Hill 112 using the selected formation and direction. Effective Allied fire coming from Avenay-Vieux and Baron made that impossible. In the morning at 0130 hours on 30 June, the division resumed the attack after a change in formation.

The reinforced 21st *SS-Panzergrenadier* Regiment reached a new plateau for the attack against Hill 112 after the capture of Avenay and infiltrating Vieux, on the heels of negotiating a river that ran directly across all the avenues of attack. The 1st Battalion, 22nd *SS-Panzergrenadier* Regiment attacked from the southern area of Evrecy along the road toward Eterville. After reaching their first objective, the road fork at la Polka, the battalion moved up to the regimental boundary to the north, and established a security line. The reinforced 22nd *SS-Panzergrenadier* Regiment controlled Gavrus before first light when shock troops, equipped with flamethrowers, provided the necessary impetus for the tactical victory. However, the attempt to continue the attack forward against Baron ended with heavy casualties at the hands of Allied defensive fire. Consequently, the momentum of the attack shifted to the 21st *SS-Panzergrenadier* Regiment on the right.

At first light on 30 June, the 21st *SS-Panzergrenadier* Regiment launched a double envelopment attack around the southern and southeastern portions of Hill 112. The 2nd Battalion, 10th SS Panzer Regiment supported the attack and successfully crossed the river between Avenay and Vieux before nightfall without loss. In addition, elements from Hill 113 joined the attack against the southwestern slopes through the small patch of homes at la Polka. Elements of the Hitler Youth Division in Maltot supported the attack by fire. By midday, the division controlled Hill 112 and established communications with the neighboring division on the right. The forward edge of the battle line subsequently ran from Hill 112 to la Polka to the northern rim of Hill 113 and Gavrus.[30]

Pioneers from the 2nd Company were ordered to relieve grenadiers on Hill 112 on 1 July. The command post of Battalion Sattler, 21st *SS-Panzergrenadier* Regiment, was located under a knocked out Sherman tank. For the pioneers, and all the men of the division, Hill 112 became known as the "Woods of the Half-Trees." The 2nd Company's first casualty on 1 July was Anton Tenhumberg. Doors were attached to a

Schwimmwagen to transport the dead to the rear areas after provisions were delivered to the men. Most often, Erich Werkmeister and his comrades in the 2nd Pioneer Company received warm peach soup. The senior sergeant or first sergeant even managed to organize whipped cream. However, the sweet odor of decomposing bodies that swept across Hill 112 squelched their appetite. As a messenger, Werkmeister reported back to the battalion command post in Baron to deliver the daily situation report.[31]

Allied counterattacks against Hill 112, supported by tanks, ensued immediately but were repulsed. Allied defensive small arms fire, tank, artillery, fighter aircraft, and naval gunfire repulsed the southern and western attacks by the reinforced 22nd *SS-Panzergrenadier* Regiment against Baron. Even so, individual elements of the regimental spearheads managed to reach the village gardens along the southern outskirts of Baron and refugees fleeing north from the west. However, these elements could not hold their ground as a result of heavy casualties.[32]

SS-Obersturmführer Fritz Kirsten, of the staff 2nd Battalion, 22nd *SS-Panzergrenadier* Regiment, displayed exceptional leadership in fulfilling his duties and managed to maintain good order and morale by caring for the wounded. *SS-Sturmmann* Günter Heitepriem, a messenger for the 5th Company, delivered messages with resolution and bravery during the attack against Baron. The Austrian *SS-Sturmmann* Leopold Kimberger, of the 6th Company, also displayed exceptional bravery when his group, exposed to extended periods of Allied artillery and engaged in hand-to-hand combat, held the company left flank against Allied counterattacks. For their actions, the soldiers received the Iron Cross 2nd Class.[33]

Renewed attempts by the 21st *SS-Panzergrenadier* Regiment during the second part of the day to resume the attack were also fruitless, though they allowed for marginal improvement of their positions. Therefore, the corps ordered a halt to the attack and the consolidation of the newly gained forward line. *SS-Hauptsturmführer* Benger assumed command of the pioneer battalion when *SS-Hauptsturmführer* Leopold Tröbinger was wounded.

The staff and four companies of the 1st Battalion, 22nd *SS-Panzergrenadier* Regiment reported two NCOs and nine men wounded.

The overwhelming superiority of Allied combat materiel was responsible for the ineffectiveness of the German attack, which lasted one-and-a-half days. The Germans failed to reach their objectives between the Orne and the Odon bridges. Furthermore, the 10th SS Panzer Division had yet to experience the full wrath of Allied power. Nonetheless, a German operational plan to combat or even temporarily disable Allied artillery was not developed due to the German lack of aerial reconnaissance and observation, but also artillery ammunition shortages.

The movement of German supplies over rail and road was hampered severely by the Allied air forces. At times, the 10th SS Panzer Division utilized its own convoys to bring ammunition forward from locations west of Paris. According to the war diary of OB West, the II SS Panzer Corps reported at 1520 hours, on 2 July 1944, "The attacks against Baron and Cheux, ordered by the Corps headquarters for 28 June, the night on 30 June, and 1 July, failed in the face of 20-times stronger destructive Allied artillery and naval gunfire." The cumulative strength and actual employment of Allied artillery, from one day to the next, was not the decisive factor. More decisive was accurate aerial bombing, reflected in a report by the II SS Panzer Corps to *SS-Oberstgruppenführer* Hausser, which referred to the weight of British artillery and effects of British aerial bombing. The report confirmed that the British bombing of Panther tank assembly areas, those belonging to the 9th SS Panzer Division, contributed to the failure of the attack. Moreover, an officer of the 9th SS was captured along with the overall plan prior to the beginning of the counterattack. The divisional commander of the 10th SS Panzer Division reported that combined heavy Allied fire, consisting of at least four artillery regiments using the heaviest caliber guns, ploughed every meter of ground. The German *Luftwaffe* was also unable to relieve ground forces from enemy attacks by air. On 1 July, the 10th SS Panzer Division did not continue the attack, after the assembly point was demolished by Allied aircraft and artillery.[34]

The turning point of Epsom came when the commander of the British Second Army, General Sir Miles Christopher Dempsey, ordered O'Connor to withdraw the 11th Armoured behind the Odon River. In fact, the order to withdraw came as early as 28 June. Harmel's hunch that the Allies anticipated the attack was correct, considering the intelligence that fell into Allied hands. For the Allies, the operation concluded with serious losses. The 8 Corps suffered 4,020 casualties, of which 2,331 (over 58 percent) belonged to the 15th Division. The remainder or 25 percent, which was mostly infantry, of approximately 18,350 men belonged to a British infantry division. The actual number of men in rifle companies was no greater than 25 percent.[35]

By the end of the day, Dr. Horst Moeferdt, the 1st Battalion doctor, 22nd *SS-Panzergrenadier* Regiment, had provided medical attention for fifty-one wounded soldiers. Thirty men were killed and 110 went missing.[36]

An excellent example of the effectiveness of Allied artillery and aerial bombardment came at 0114 hours on 1 July. The 1st Battalion, 22nd *SS-Panzergrenadier* Regiment assembled along the road Evrecy-Eterville for a renewed attack against Baron. Prior to the attack, the battalion was subjected to a fifteen-minute barrage. Once the barrage lifted, the German companies assaulted across the bombarded terrain. The companies were ordered to proceed along prescribed azimuth compass bearings. After approximately twelve minutes, the battalion staff followed behind the 3rd Company. The road Evrecy-Eterville was subjected to heavy artillery fire. Telephone contact was lost after the first bombardment and then radio contact was lost to the companies. While communication to the 2nd and 3rd Companies was maintained with the use of star-cluster pyrotechnics, the only effective means of communication was by messenger. The 1st Company, designated as the battalion reserve, echeloned to the left and to the rear for the protection of the left flank, and made good progress for roughly 1 kilometer. At 0230 hours, the staff was within 200 meters of the objective at Baron. Messengers attempted continuously to establish contact with the companies. Since nothing other than artillery fire could be heard on the battlefield, the adjutant dispatched a reconnaissance party to Baron. The reconnaissance party encountered British defensive positions before Baron and triggered a firefight. After a British machine-gun nest was silenced with hand grenades, the reconnaissance party withdrew. Around the same time at 0300 hours, the Allies fired illumination flares that were followed by heavy defensive artillery fire. The battalion commander ordered the staff to withdraw and return to the earlier command post of the 3rd Company. Allied artillery continued during the withdrawal and shifted onto the road Evrecy-Eterville. The 2nd and 3rd Companies were trapped by heavy Allied artillery fire along a depression 100 meters southwest of Baron. Once Allied blocking fire ended and the companies defended against numerous Allied infantry counterattacks that resulted in close combat, the companies disengaged and withdrew. The companies returned to their original positions around 0845 hours with their lightly wounded. The 1st Company, which made considerable progress up to 1,000 meters, remained trapped under heavy artillery fire. The company commander ordered to dig in; however, the ground was too hard so the company withdrew. The battalion suffered extensive losses to include four NCOs and thirty-six men killed; two officers, six NCOs, and thirty-five men wounded; and one officer and fifty-five men missing. The 1st Company suffered the most casualties. On the other hand, the 12th SS Panzer Division succeeded in capturing Fontaine.[37]

Combined and concentrated heavy Allied fire on various small sectors preceded a number of energetic, tank-supported, battalion-strength attacks in support of Allied penetrations against Baron, Esquay, and Hill 112. Despite the devastation, German morale maintained a certain degree of integrity through sound leadership among the junior officers. *SS-Obersturmführer* Fritz Meissen, of the battalion staff, 22nd *SS-Panzergrenadier* Regiment, aided and cared for the wounded in the face of heavy artillery fire. For his bravery he received the Iron Cross 2nd Class. The Austrian *SS-Unterscharführer* Franz-Xavier Bindl took no regard for his own safety during heavy mortar fire and earned the Iron Cross 2nd Class for aiding and evacuating the seriously wounded during the Allied attack on Baron.

His fearless bravery in the face of horrific Allied artillery fire allowed every seriously wounded soldier to reach the aid station.[38]

During the evening on 2 July, the 277th Infantry Division began the relief of the entire 9th SS and 10th SS Panzer Divisions, with the exception of elements belonging to the 22nd *SS-Panzergrenadier* Regiment that remained engaged in order to close the encirclement around Gavrus. The 9th SS Panzer Division was placed at the disposal of Panzer Group West behind the front of the II SS Panzer Corps, between the Orne and Odon Rivers. The movement was completed early on 3 July. Portions of 22nd *SS-Panzergrenadier* Regiment became the divisional reserve. The day as a whole passed without any significant developments. German fighting positions were improved during the lull in the fighting, although the task proved very difficult on Hill 112. Beams or tree trunks covered by a layer of earth were used to protect the overhead in artillery protective holes. Over that, a strong 1-meter layer of branches was covered with a second layer of beams that was topped with an additional layer of earth. The coverings proved especially effective and could withstand a direct hit from a medium-caliber projectile. The slightest movement drew heavy small arms and artillery fire. Entrenching tools were useless, as they could not penetrate the rocky ground. Knocked out Allied tanks that littered the battlefield offered the only form of cover and protection. For the day, the 1st Battalion, 22nd *SS-Panzergrenadier* Regiment suffered casualties consisting of only a single NCO and six men wounded.[39]

The enlisted regimental staff messenger, Gerhard Brunn, 10th SS Panzer Regiment, from the city of Prenzlau in Brandenburg north of Berlin, stood over 6 feet at nineteen years of age and received double rations. When his BMW motorcycle needed servicing, Brunn received a *Schwimmwagen* to perform his duties and the additional task of delivering rations to the regimental supply. Several hours later, the regiment reported no receipt of rations. The first sergeant became angry and, as soon as Brunn returned, told him what to expect if he did not find the containers. When darkness fell, Brunn disappeared to find the rations. The following evening, after the company commander considered reporting Brunn

as missing, a forward observation post reported an approaching Allied vehicle. From the vehicle a voice called, "Frundsberger! Don't shoot!"

Brunn feared the wrath of the first sergeant, and therefore conducted a one-man reconnaissance and single-handedly captured an Allied vehicle, its crew, important documents, and a trailer with provisions. The half-ton of provisions, which included whiskey, cigarettes, and delicacies, earned him the Iron Cross 1st Class.[40]

On 2 July, Panzer Group West, formerly part of Army Command (AOK) 7, was reassigned to Army Group B. The same day, Hitler assigned Field Marshal Günther Hans von Kluge to replace the pessimistic OB West, Field Marshal von Rundstedt, and General Eberbach replaced General von Geyr as commander, Panzer Group West. The actual change of command took place in the field on 3 July, at the same time Hitler gave his final directive concerning an elastic defense. Due to the German inability to even the odds in the air, there would be no elastic defense.[41]

Elements of 22nd *SS-Panzergrenadier* Regiment, relieved twenty-four hours earlier at Gavrus, were embroiled in battle north of Esquay on 1 July. Throughout the night on 3 July, the regiment relieved troops belonging to the 19th *SS-Panzergrenadier* Regiment of the 9th SS Panzer Division "Hohenstaufen." Other portions of the 22nd *SS-Panzergrenadier* Regiment were committed along the main line of combat to expand the divisional sector on the right, along the northeast face of Hill 112, and to establish contact with the 12th SS Panzer Division. The regiment lost two men killed in action and two men wounded, all from the 3rd Company.[42]

Strong Allied attacks, extensively supported by artillery and aircraft, resumed on 3 July against Hill 112 and along the extended front of the 12th SS Panzer Division on the right. Allied pressure was also heavy along the boundaries of the two divisions in the direction of Eterville and Maltot. Around 0900 hours, the Allies captured Eterville, and Maltot fell around 1300 hours. At Hill 112, the Germans repulsed the Allied attacks. The previously alerted 9th SS Panzer Division counterattacked against Maltot at 1300 hours and managed to clear the village two hours later, despite strong Allied resistance. At 1400 hours, amidst the German counterattack, the Allies launched a new and concerted attack against Hill 112 to relieve the Allied troops already fighting at Maltot. Allied artillery fire and the employment of fighter aircraft increased with unprecedented effectiveness. The last reserves of the 10th SS Panzer Division, comprised of the 1st Battalion, 21st *SS-Panzergrenadier* Regiment, and elements of 10th SS Panzer Regiment, were committed to the battle and effectively supported by the divisional artillery regiment and antiaircraft battalion, the Rocket Launcher Brigade 8, and portions of the heavy Tigers from the 502nd SS Heavy Panzer Battalion.[43]

The 502nd SS Heavy Panzer Battalion organized in early 1944. Forty-five Tiger I Ausf.E were transported on eight trains between 21 April and 29 May 1944 to Wezep. Several other Tiger groups were also established in Bordeaux, Argentan, and Paderborn. *SS-Sturmbannführer* Lackmann commanded the 502nd during the initial phase of organization. In Argentan, *SS-Hauptsturmführer* Fischer assumed command of the battalion.

After a short but rigorous training phase, fourteen brand new Tigers were transferred to the 2nd Company, commanded by *SS-Hauptsturmführer* Willy Endemann, the day of the Allied invasion along the French coast. On 13 June the 502nd Heavy Panzer Battalion loaded onto railcars south of Calais to St. Pol. Two days later, the battalion entrained again and proceeded west of Paris. The battalion obtained orders to the front on 2 July. Eight Tiger tanks, vehicle numbers 211, 212, 213, 214, 224, 231, 233, and 221 of the 2nd Company rolled from Paris toward the front.[44]

Meanwhile, the scanty portions of the 21st *SS-Panzergrenadier* Regiment that remained capable of fighting could not hold Hill 112. After a four-hour battle, leading Allied attack elements reached the plateau where individual German fighting positions continued to control the western slope.

The summit and demolished woods on the eastern slope of Hill 112 offered the Allies good observation and placement of fire against units of the 9th SS Panzer Division that managed to infiltrate Maltot. As a result, the German attack came to a halt at 1400 hours along the northern outskirts of Maltot. The continued German attack in the direction of Eterville depended on recapturing Hill 112 and neutralizing Allied flanking fire. At a minimum, the effectiveness of the Allied fire had to be reduced after nightfall.

Once reinforcements were brought forward, the attack by the 9th SS Panzer Division did not resume against Eterville and Hill 112 until darkness. The 10th SS Panzer Division and portions of the 12th SS Panzer Division supported the attack from locations east of Verson and within the village.

While the attack on Eterville gained ground, the attack on Hill 112 floundered at the foot of the small woods on the eastern slope.

On 4 July, at 0100 hours, elements of the 9th SS Panzer Division captured Eterville. Subsequently, the attack from the southeast against Hill 112 gained momentum. By 0430 hours, the 9th SS secured the woods on the southern slope. Step by step the Allies withdrew to the north, forgoing the opportunity to launch counterattacks, as they relinquished control of Hill 112. However, in the early morning, the Allies launched a tank-supported counterattack against Eterville that again placed the Allies in control of the village. The battle for Eterville lasted the entire day with varying degrees of success until evening, when the village remained in the firm hands of the Hohenstaufen Division.

German forces deflected weak Allied advances against la Polka and the westerly retreating Allied forces from Hill 112. In the evening on 4 July, the main line of battle ran from the western outskirts of Eterville over Maltot (both villages controlled by 9th SS) over Hill 112 (controlled by the 9th and 10th SS), la Polka to Hill 113 (both 10th SS) and onto Gavrus (277th Infantry Division).

In order to re-establish the 9th SS Panzer Division as an operational reserve in the area of St. Honorine, elements of the 22nd *SS-Panzergrenadier* Regiment relieved groups of the 9th SS on Hill 112. The 12th SS Panzer Division assumed control of the sectors of the 9th SS around Eterville and Maltot. Losses for the 1st Battalion, 22nd *SS-Panzergrenadier* Regiment included one officer and one SS-man killed, and two officers, two NCOs, and five men wounded.

The 10th SS Panzer Reconnaissance Battalion, previously designated as the reserve of the II SS Panzer Corps, transferred to Army Group B during the night of 3–4 July at Bonnoeil, halfway between Thury-Harcourt and Falaise. En route, the 10th SS Panzer Reconnaissance Battalion sustained losses from attacks by Allied fighter aircraft.[45]

The Allied outlook around Caen remained bleak. Montgomery's first attempt to seize the city failed. The Second Army outnumbered the Germans two to one in infantry and four to one in tanks. Unable to provide a firm bridgehead across the Allied front, to capture additional logistical ports in Brittany, Montgomery directed the second attack against Caen. The first phase of Operation Charnwood opened on 4 July with preliminary attacks by the 3rd Canadian Division, in the northwest, to capture the airfield and seal the western exits of the city.[46]

The significant number of captured Allied prisoners of war (POWs) resulted in a special divisional order from the 1st General Staff officer (Ia), outlining the standards and responsibilities for the men of the division. SS men were to search prisoners immediately and turn the prisoner and his belongings over to the staff intelligence officer (Ic). Casual conversations outside the line of duty were strictly forbidden and "detrimental to the image of the German Army." The order notified every SS soldier of their direct responsibility for guarding British prisoners, whose duty it was to escape. Allowing POWs to escape was a punishable offense by a military court. Most importantly, the order emphasized that POWs were governed by international conventions. However, special accommodations were not to be provided for British soldiers, such as unnecessary friendliness or brutality.[47]

Over and above the numerous Allied reconnaissance probes repelled by the 10th SS Panzer Division, the days between 5 and 7 July remained relatively quiet. The divisional troops utilized the short respite to improve their positions, organize and consolidate their forces, and perform weapons and equipment maintenance. Once the 10th SS Panzer Reconnaissance Battalion reverted back under the control of the division, it received orders to establish observation posts at specific locations along the divisional boundaries and make radio

contact with the division. This measure proved to be of great value during the coming period of operations.[48]

On 5 July, the boundaries of the 10th SS Panzer Division slightly shifted to the right; the new boundaries joined the 12th SS Panzer Division (I SS Panzer Corps), Eterville-Verson (villages occupied by the 10th SS); and the 277th Infantry Division Grimbosq-Evrecy (villages occupied by the 10th SS) to Mondrainville (277th). The command post of the 10th SS Panzer Division relocated from Goupillières to Grimbosq.

On the same day the Allies redeployed away from the right flank of the 10th SS Panzer Division toward Fontaine. Units of the 22nd *SS-Panzergrenadier* Regiment holding the main line of battle pursued the Allies and occupied the Chateau de Fontaine (1.5 km west and northwest of Maltot) without a fight.

Both the neighboring divisions of the 10th SS Panzer Division reported increased enemy activity on 6 July; a new attack seemed imminent. That same day the Allies wrestled control of Noyers from the 277th Infantry Division. The 9th SS Panzer Division launched a necessary counterattack on 7 July, after the additional losses of Gavrus and Bougy. While both villages were recaptured, Gavrus was lost yet again around 1900 hours. Under the command of the 10th SS Panzer Division, the 9th SS Panzer Division remained locked in battle on the left flank of the 10th and absorbed the remaining combat-worthy units of the 277th Infantry Division. The boundary of the 10th SS Panzer Division remained unchanged.[49]

General Eisenhower's concern regarding the over-cautious progress within the British sector had merit; one of the invasion beaches remained under German fire. In a letter dated 7 July 1944, he urged General Montgomery to expand the bridgehead with "all possible energy in a determined effort." In the wake of a previously unsuccessful British attempt to capture the city of Caen, purportedly due to insufficient artillery to smash the German defenses, Montgomery replied, "I am, myself, quite happy about the situation."

Indeed, Montgomery's plans officer, Brigadier Charles Richardson, rejected a stationary strategy reminiscent of trench warfare. Richardson advocated the use of tanks and their numerical superiority as absolutely essential.[50]

Heavy bombers proceeded the second phase of Charnwood to saturate an area on the northern outskirts. The British hoped to destroy German infantry and artillery, isolate the front line, demoralize German troops, and raise the morale of their own troops. On 7 July, the RAF Bomber Command flew unopposed missions beginning at 2150 hours dropping 2,300 tons of high explosive bombs from 460 planes. The bombing raid destroyed a large portion of the city. The full force hit the 16th *Luftwaffe* Field Division, which, for the most part, ceased to exist, and portions of the 12th SS Panzer Division. Rommel estimated a total loss of approximately four infantry battalions.

Before dawn on 8 July, five additional groups of American aircraft from IX Bomber Command softened the defenses when the Allies launched their anticipated large-scale concentrated attack against Caen. Bitter fighting and costly casualties ensued for both sides, and by the next morning, British and Canadian troops advanced up to the Orne River. Destroyed bridges and rubble brought the Allies standing to end operations. The 1st Battalion, 22nd *SS-Panzergrenadier* Regiment suffered one man KIA and three men wounded. While Rommel and Eberbach formulated plans to evacuate the city, Hitler yielded no ground.[51]

In a bizarre circumstance in the midst of battle, Max Gerhard, a radio operator in the 10th SS Panzer Signals Battalion, was confronted by his girlfriend who was visiting her relatives in Caen. Gerhard left his post without permission in a *Kübelwagen* with his girlfriend stowed away in the back under a shelter half. They drove away from the fighting with no real destination. Strafing American P-38 "Lightning" fighter aircraft hit their vehicle and killed his girlfriend.[52]

Meanwhile, the fighting spilled into the right sector of the 10th SS Panzer Division. The division managed to repel the Allied attempts to break through the lines around Maltot and Hill 112, thanks to elements of the 502nd Heavy Panzer Battalion that provided support after they arrived at St. Honorine. On 9 July, the timely detection of an Allied assembly area within the Odon Bridge valley, subjected to well-placed German fire, relegated the Allies to nothing more than reconnaissance probes from Fontain to Verson, and from Baron to Chateau de Fontaine; the attacks were repulsed.

During the night of 9–10 July, *SS-Scharführer* Kurt Leven (vehicle 531), a platoon leader in the 5th Company, 10th SS Panzer Regiment, deployed with three tanks forming a security platoon on Hill 112. Around 0300 hours, *SS-Hauptscharführer* Mathias Borrekott (vehicle 524), deployed in the same area leading tanks of the alarm platoon. The mission of both platoons was to stop Allied attacks and counterattack, and provide enough time for the remaining company to engage the enemy. At 0500 hours, after unrelenting Allied artillery fire, the Allies attacked with approximately twenty-five tanks, supported by infantry and antitank guns, against the alarm and security platoons of Borrekott and Leven. As soon as Borrekott sounded the alarm, Leven attacked with three tanks. The Allied attack was ensnarled long enough to allow the remainder of the 5th Company to counterattack and repel the Allied attack. While Leven and Borrekott were each credited with the destruction of one Sherman on 10 July, both were killed in action along with nine others from the 5th Company.[53]

Nothing, however, could prevent the town of Caen from being lost. On 10 July, the Allies sought the decisive battle and launched their attack against the 10th SS Panzer Division. Based on the direction of the attack, the division predicted Allied intentions to drive deep into the flank of the I SS Panzer Corps, whose center of gravity was concentrated along the east bank of the Orne River, and capture the crossing over the Orne River at Thury-Harcourt. However, the prerequisite for Allied success was control of Hill 112.

From within the Odon valley moving out from Verson and Baron, the Allies launched a two-pronged tank attack, which was preceded by an unprecedented artillery barrage that struck against the German main line and rear areas. Between Eterville and Hill 112, the Allies achieved a 5 to 6 km wide penetration using smoke and special new ordnance or non-exploding shells. Allied half-tracks stormed forward in support of the tank assault and ground to bits German defenders by driving on top of fighting positions and then quickly traversing. Concurrently, Allied flamethrowers and close-quarter combat weapons pinned down neighboring German defensive positions. This combat method came as a surprise to the defenders, who sustained costly losses.[54]

After the loss of Eterville and Maltot, the 10th SS Panzer Division counterattacked without delay. Meanwhile, the 10th SS Panzer Artillery Battalion, together with batteries from the corps and 8th Launcher Brigade, sealed off the Allied attack from Baron and prevented the reinforcement of penetrations by spearheads on Hill 112. The divisional reserve, consisting of the 10th SS Panzer Reconnaissance Battalion and 1st Battalion, 21st *SS-Panzergrenadier* Regiment, supported by Tigers of the 502nd Heavy Panzer Battalion, drove against Allied tanks that had broken into Maltot. Like a tidal wave, the division reserve picked up every straggler from shattered units and reached the village of Verein before the British consolidated their new positions. The 6th Company, 10th SS Panzer Regiment accounted for the destruction of three British tanks and six tracked vehicles.[55]

SS-Hauptsturmführer Hans Günther Handrick, the battalion doctor, 2nd Battalion, 10th SS Panzer Regiment, provided first aid to over seventy wounded men along the front line. Amidst heavy artillery fire, Handrick's resolve and calm demeanor allowed him to carry out his life-saving responsibility.[56]

At 0530 hours on 10 July, *SS-Hauptsturmführer* Endemann gave verbal orders for the attack for the heavy 102nd Panzer Battlaion, from positions north of St. Martin, after his radio became inoperable. On the right, the 1st Platoon of *SS-Unterscharführer* Schroif rolled forward and the 3rd Platoon of *SS-Unterscharführer* Rathsack followed on their left. Allied fighter aircraft attacked the 1st Platoon, which occupied a hedge in front of a partial slope. As the 1st Platoon provided suppressing fire from the hedge, the 3rd Platoon rolled past the hedge on the left and established suppressing fire 200 meters in front of the square of woods. In the next move, 1st Platoon bounded forward and past the forest on the left. Several grenadiers huddled behind the Tigers as they moved forward. The 3rd Platoon,

moving between the forest and the 1st Platoon, received antitank fire from the depression that lay ahead. Vehicle 213, of *SS-Unterscharführer* Piller, took an antitank hit and became disabled. Tigers of the platoon withdrew in reverse gear and then continued forward but the next time on the right. Vehicle 231, of *SS-Unterscharführer* Rathsack of 3rd Platoon, knocked out one Allied tank that lay in the depression whereas *SS-Unterscharführer* Schroif of 1st Platoon knocked out two Allied tanks and one antitank gun. The line right of the depression was secured. Combined Allied aircraft and artillery fire forced the Tigers to abort their mission. The Allied method of firing smoke projectiles between the German tanks created confusion for the Tiger crews. As a result of intolerable visibility around 1100 hours, orders arrived for the Tiger battalion to clear the plateau.[57]

In Eterville, near a chateau near the command post of the 1st Battalion, 22nd *SS-Panzergrenadier* Regiment, the battalion doctor remained busy attending to the many wounded. Dr. Moeferdt worked with two enlisted assistants at his side. The wounded included the commander of the 3rd Battalion, *SS-Sturmbannführer* Bünning, who reported the British had succeeded in breaking through his lines. *SS-Hauptsturmführer* Friedrich W. Richter, the commander of the 1st Battalion, 22nd *SS-Panzergrenadier* Regiment, arrived at the aid station with news that the battalion was relocating. However, Moeferdt received orders to remain and care for the wounded. Around 0700 hours, British soldiers stormed into the aid station with blackened faces and rifles at the ready. The Allied soldiers ordered "hands up" and the slightly wounded were told to remove their helmets and bayonets. Despite Moeferdt's demands to remain with the wounded, everyone that could walk was ordered out of the aid station and brought to a command post of the Dorset Regiment. After a British interpreter arrived, Moeferdt spoke of international treaties, medical responsibilities, and his rights as a doctor, and demanded that he and his helpers be returned to Eterville to care for the wounded. The doctor's wishes were granted, whereby the three German medical personnel remained with the seriously wounded Germans until they were evacuated. Upon completion, Moeferdt was brought to an intermediate collection point for prisoners of war. Behind a double row of barbed wire, the Allies treated Moeferdt with dignity and respect as he emptied his pockets of his belongings. The prisoners were able to retain only a comb and handkerchief. However, the small pocket calendar that Moeferdt kept in his back pocket was not confiscated.[58]

The successful defense of the 10th SS Panzer Division on 10 July must partially be attributed to elements of the artillery that set aside ammunition during the more quiet days, ensuring that larger quantities of ammunition were available. However, division losses were exceptionally high and it became more and more questionable as to how long the division could hold out against Allied superiority of troops and materiel.

At the end of the day on 10 July, the tank crews of the 5th and 6th Companies, 10th SS Panzer Regiment tabulated the success of the fighting:[59]

Tank Commander	Tank No.	KO	Type	AT gun	Misc
SS-Haustürmführer Hauser	525	1	Sherman	1	
SS-Unterscharführer Kellermann	502	-	-	2	
SS-Unterscharführer Hinze	535	3	Sherman		-
SS-Unterscharführer Dröge	534	3	Sherman		-
SS-Hauptscharführer Borrekott	524	1	Sherman		-
SS-Unterscharführer Stelzer	521	1	Sherman		-
SS-Oberscharführer Leven	531	1	Sherman		-
SS-Obersturmführer Heggemann	602	1	Sherman		-
Feldwebel Seifert	611	1	Sherman	3	
SS-Oberscharführer Westerhoff	622	1	SP		-
SS-Unterscharführer Krölls	633	4	half-track	1	
SS-Unterscharführer Schwemmlein	624			2	
SS-Unterscharführer Franke	621	1	Sherman		-

In the morning on 11 June, the German Tiger attack resumed. Vehicle 212, of *SS-Untersturmführer* Schroif of 1st Platoon, destroyed the first two Allied tanks it encountered. Meanwhile, vehicle 232, of *SS-Unterscharführer* Winter, was hit by antitank fire. On the Aunay-side of Hill 112, heading north, the 1st Platoon, commanded by *SS-Hauptsturmführer* Alois Kalls, moved forward utilizing a covered path in defilade. Allied spotter planes that circled above brought artillery to bear against the Tigers of the 1st Platoon. Additional smoke subjected the Tigers to almost no visibility when projectiles hit Kalls' vehicle turret and hull. Kalls ordered his tank forward to clear the smoke. "Panzer halt!" Before them at 100 meters, the British were clearing their positions. Kalls ordered the turret machine gun into

action and loading of the main gun. Two Churchill tanks providing security were knocked out immediately. When the Germans reached the heights, a total of three tanks, eight antitank guns, and fifteen Allied armored vehicles were destroyed. With Hill 112 back in German hands, the former main line of battle was re-established. However, surprise Allied artillery attacks against the heights demanded the withdrawal of the Tiger company.[60]

Together with small pockets of resistance that managed to hold out, the village was cleared of all British forces. In complete disarray, the British withdrew onto Eterville with the 2nd Company of 1st Battalion, 21st *SS-Panzergrenadier* Regiment and portions of 22nd *SS-Panzergrenadier* Regiment in close pursuit.

Tanks of the 5th Company, 10th SS Panzer Regiment reported the destruction of five Sherman tanks, four antitank guns, and the capture of four POWs. *SS-Sturmmann* Bernhard Flenker, the driver of an assault gun in the 7th Company, 10th SS Panzer Regiment, was in his vehicle when Allied artillery hit and set his vehicle ablaze. Despite heavy artillery fire, Flenker jumped out of his vehicle and successfully smothered the fire with the vehicle fire extinguisher. The vehicle was not lost.[61]

The fighting on Hill 112 teetered back and forth and continued for hours. The single battalion of 22nd *SS-Panzergrenadier* Regiment committed to action at Chateau de Fontaine made a valiant stand despite the fact that it had been bypassed on either flank. Once British infantry, tanks, and half-tracks breeched the defensive line, close combat ensued whereby the high numbers of German casualties proved a continued defense untenable. After the battalion doctor and the severely wounded were brought into the castle cellar where they were later captured, the surviving elements of the battalion withdrew to a prepared position along the road Caen-Evrecy. The battalion was directly responsible for the success of the defense.[62]

Throughout the night of 11 July, elements of the 21st and 22nd *SS-Panzergrenadier* Regiment infiltrated Eterville and established contact with the battalion group that had previously withdrawn from the Chateau de Fontaine. The main line of battle was re-established on Hill 112. *SS-Hauptsturmführer* Karl Keck, the commander of the 16th Company, 21st *SS-Panzergrenadier* Regiment, was severely wounded during the fighting and evacuated on a *Schwimmwagen*. Passing the pioneer battalion combat command post, Hugo Benger consoled the wounded Keck, and stroked his face lightly. There was nothing that could be done to save Keck and he died soon thereafter. *SS-Hauptsturmführer* Willi Markus assumed command of the 16th Pioneer Company.

Markus had a stately figure, weighing approximately 220 pounds. In Evrecy, the 16th Company, 21st *SS-Panzergrenadier* Regiment, and the command post dug in behind a 1-meter-high wall that surrounded a castle with outer-lying terraced gardens. A radio communications position for a *Nebelwerfer* or rocket projector was established within the castle. The first radio test caused heavy Allied artillery fire to descend on the position. The first round hit the upper level and wounded Markus. *SS-Obersturmführer* Oskar Munsky, the commander of the 16th Company, 22nd *SS-Panzergrenadier* Regiment, assumed command of the company when the two regimental pioneer companies were combined as the 19th Company.[63]

The Allied failure to capture certain objectives following the Normandy landings led directly to the massive Anglo-American Operations Cobra and Goodwood. General Omar Bradley planned for the American thrust to strike down the road St. Lô-Périers, preceded by saturation bombing along a narrow sector and followed immediately by a ground attack. The road itself provided a distinctive marker and guide for the most accurate and effective bombing possible. On the other hand, General Dempsey's plan also began with saturation bombing and was followed by four corps with over 750 tanks to rip the German defenses open and outflank the city of Caen from the east. Additional fire support from naval ships and 700 artillery guns, tactical aircraft, and strategic bombers made the aerial operation the largest air-support ground operation in history.[64]

After midnight on 11 July, Allied artillery fire suddenly intensified against Eterville. As the fire shifted against Chateau de Fontaine and in the area around Maltot, Allied tanks, half-tracks, and infantry broke through German positions on both sides of Eterville and into the village itself. This marked the first occasion when Allied forces launched a large-scale nighttime attack within the sector of the 10th SS Panzer Division. Spotlights, located well behind the Allied front line, illuminated the cloud cover and provided a limited source of light across the battlefield.

After Eterville was temporarily lost on 11 July, panzer grenadiers of the 10th SS recaptured the village early that day. Shortly thereafter, the Allies launched a counterattack with sixty tanks after heavy preparatory fire. The German defenders could no longer hold. Badly mauled and severely weakened from the high number of casualties, and considering that a reserve was no longer available,

Eterville was lost to the Allies yet again. Although the path to the mere 2.5 km distant Orne River Bridge near St. André remained open, the Allies did not attempt to exploit the opportunity.

Commanders of the I and II SS Panzer Corps conferred with one another in the afternoon on 11 July, and the II SS Panzer Corps ordered a combined counterattack against Eterville. The 10th SS Panzer Division was tasked with the rescue of the remaining units that were consolidated in Eterville. While the attack lasted until dark, it was unable to break through. The Allies complicated matters when they launched diversionary attacks from Baron against Hill 112. While the defenders repulsed the secondary attacks, Eterville remained permanently lost. During the night on 12 July, the Frundsberger divisional artillery effectively targeted Allied armored staging areas in Baron.[65]

Outside of a small number of Allied reconnaissance probes that resulted in the German capture of Allied prisoners on 12 July, Allied infantry remained relatively quiet. The capture of Allied prisoners brought in extensive cartographic material. Daily updated maps indicated German firing positions, observation posts, locations of engagements, and even movements along hedges. The maps revealed the effectiveness of Allied ground and aerial reconnaissance and observation. During the following night, divisional artillery fired against Allied movement detected across the Odon River around Baron and Gavrus. On the same day, Allied artillery concentrations centered against Hill 112, Evrecy, and Gavrus.[66]

The next day also passed relatively quietly. On 13 July, the 6th Company, 10th SS Panzer Regiment assumed positions on the reverse slope of Hill 113. Early in the morning, General of Panzer Troops Heinrich Eberbach, OB West, visited the regimental command post in the sector of the 22nd *SS-Panzergrenadier* Regiment. After a brief stop at Hill 112, he arrived at the command post of the 10th SS Panzer Division, in a forest south of Grimbosq. Eberbach outlined the future intentions of the German leadership and ordered the continued defense of the main line of battle. In addition, he instructed the 10th SS Panzer Division to prepare for movement in lieu of a new assignment, as soon

as the 271st Infantry Division relieved the division. The 271st Infantry Division marched en route near the area around Lisieux-Orbec-Bernay. Truck convoys of the 10th SS were dispatched to hasten their arrival.[67]

The reduced strength of the 10th SS Panzer Division raised great concerns. On 13 July, the 22nd *SS-Panzergrenadier* Regiment reported a combat strength of only 400 men. In order to maintain its fighting capabilities, the division needed 1,000 replacements every ten days, of which 90 percent were needed for the grenadier regiments. In reality, only 120 to 150 men arrived for both regiments from the field replacement battalions. Out of necessity, the 22nd *SS-Panzergrenadier* Regiment disbanded one of three battalions due to the high losses of company, squad, and group commanders.

Before the reorganization could be completed, British troops launched a large-scale attack on 14 July against the sector of the 10th SS Panzer Division. The main objective of the attack was Hill 112. A thick smoke screen and heavy artillery fire preceded the attack. While lacking a divisional reserve, the 10th SS Panzer Division successfully defended and repelled every attack with the support of artillery that made good use of large stores of ammunition at its disposal.[68]

The 502nd Heavy Panzer Battalion assisted in reclaiming Hill 112. *SS-Scharführer* Paul Egger, a squad leader in the 1st Company, took matters into his own hands and led a counterattack through the thick smoke with four Tigers into the Allied flank. Egger's Tigers knocked out fourteen tanks and seven antitank guns. After pursuing the retreating Allies, German infantry reclaimed lost ground. Egger personally destroyed seven Allied tanks raising his career total to sixty-eight. For this action, Paul Egger received on 30 April 1945 the decoration of the Knight's Cross to the Iron Cross.[69] Meanwhile, immediate German counterattacks also repelled other smaller Allied penetrations.

Despite the high number of casualties sustained on 15 July from uninterrupted artillery and tank fire, the division remained in control of Hill 112, known to most as the "woods of the half-trees."

For several days, the Germans observed a new Allied attack tactic. While a rolling artillery barrage stalked back and forth across the main line of battle, heavy tanks and armored tracked vehicles (scouts) with mounted infantry closed with the main line of battle, under the cover of heavy smoke. Suddenly, the scouts darted out and far forward at very high speeds. After establishing good fields of fire, the scouts stopped in a fan formation and fired rockets at the German positions and tanks. Just as quickly, the scouts then disappeared back into the smoke screen while tanks and infantry attempted to break into the lines under the cover of dummy mortar fire. The new tactic was successful as long as it remained an anomaly.[70]

The divisional operational reserve consisted of the 1st Battalion, 21st *SS-Panzergrenadier* Regiment at St. Honorine, 10th SS Panzer Reconnaissance Battalion at Hamars (5 km northwest of Thury-Harcourt), and the 2nd Battalion, 980th Infantry Regiment, on the right of the 10th SS Panzer Division.[71]

Throughout the night of 15–16 July, *SS-Mann* Arwed-Viktor Pusch, of the 6th Company, 10th SS Panzer Regiment, served as a company messenger at the forward-most warning post. From 2145 hours until 0510, under heavy Allied artillery fire and despite being wounded just below his right eye by shrapnel, Pusch reported four separate nearing tank formations. After he lost excessive amounts of blood and his body weakened, the company commander ordered him to the aid station.

Allied artillery fire that impacted around the positions of the 6th Company, 10th SS Panzer Regiment shook the ground to such a degree that it caused the brakes to release on vehicle number 621, commandeered by *SS-Scharführer* Klein. The vehicle rolled backwards down Hill 113 and into the stream basin.[72]

Another example of the fighting involved the 3rd Platoon, 6th Company, 10th SS Panzer Regiment, commanded by *SS-Hauptsturmführer* Edmund Erhard. The mission was to intercept an Allied attack on Hill 133. At 0400 hours, Erhard entered his positions and camouflaged the platoon of tanks. The tanks were made invisible. They resembled large mounds of hay. Approximately 100 meters in front of the position, a tree-lined road ran 150 meters and turned left for another 500 meters and into a village. Around 0730 hours, Allied tanks appeared on the road coming out of the village. The commanders were visible in each of the turrets, and the tanks proceeded forward casually without significant spacing between them. They moved forward as if during peacetime. Erhard counted twenty-four tanks and instructed his commanders to hold their fire. Infantry accompanied the tanks at the very rear of the formation on either side. Once the lead Allied tank entered the curve at a distance of 150 meters, the German tanks opened fire against pre-registered firing points. Twelve Allied tanks were destroyed.[73]

During the morning on 16 July, after heavy preparatory artillery fire, the Allies launched another attack. Under the cover of smoke and supported by flamethrowers, the Allied forces succeeded in breaching the German line. *SS-Untersturmführer* Hans Reiter, commander of the Staff Company, 21st *SS-Panzergrenadier* Regiment, who had already distinguished himself during the previous night, was in the defense during the early morning fighting on Hill 112. In fact, the divisional commander requested Reiter be mentioned in the official Armed Forces report for his achievements.

Reiter was born on 20 April 1920 in Feldkirchen and entered service on 1 September 1939. Before joining the Frundsberg Division, Reiter held a post as a member of the 14th Company, 1st SS Death's Head Infantry Regiment. His awards included the Iron Cross 2nd Class on 1 July 1941, the Wound Badge in black on 11 October 1941, the Iron Cross 1st Class on 1 November 1941, the Infantry Assault Badge in bronze on 5 January 1942, the Infantry Assault Badge in silver on 17 March 1942, the German Cross in Gold on 1 May 1942, the Wound Badge in gold on 23 June 1942, the Eastern Medal 1941–42 on 6 September 1942, and the Demjansk Shield on 19 June 1944.

As Reiter held his own position while the lines of the neighboring company were breached, he gathered up nearby stragglers and formed a circular position. On his own initiative during the afternoon hours on 16 July, Reiter broke out of the encirclement and re-established contact with friendly forces. During the fighting with his company, Reiter destroyed one Churchill and two Sherman tanks, two armored artillery prime movers, seven ammunition trailers, two trucks, and two anti-guns. Moreover, forward-moving Allied infantry of approximately three companies, supported by flanking fire, were engaged with combined fragmentation shell and machine-gun fire that demolished the majority of the Allied force and caused the remainder to flee. Reiter's courage, skill, and personal leadership made no longer necessary a planned regimental counter-attack for the relief of Company Reiter. Instead, the already prepared forces re-established the main line of battle in the eastern sector of Battalion Bastian. Directly and indirectly, Reiter helped both the regiment and the division retain Hill 112, for which on 23 August 1944 he was awarded the Knight's Cross to the Iron Cross.[74]

During the night of 16 July, the Allies shifted their main attack from Hill 112 to the area of Maltot. The attack against the village commenced in the dark at 0200 hours under field illumination and was supported by Crocodile flamethrower tanks. Close combat ensued. Battalion Schulz of the 22nd *SS-Panzergrenadier* Regiment, temporarily encircled east of Maltot, broke free after a counterattack by the 10th SS Panzer Reconnaissance Battalion. Chateau de Fontaine, occupied by the division several days earlier during a shift in the main line of battle, was permanently lost.

The progression of the entire day was characterized by continuous Allied artillery fire that increased and decreased in volume across the entire divisional battlefield, and by the unprecedented lack of German operational control. The chaotic situation was partly due to the Allies' use of smoke (artillery). The commander of the 10th SS, in and among the troops to better grasp the situation and make immediate decisions, committed the 1st Battalion, 21st *SS-Panzergrenadier* Regiment, from the division reserve to bolster the defenses along Hill 112. Soon thereafter, a crisis developed along the left flank of the division. For 16 July, the Armed Forces report reported:

In the fighting around Caen, the 9th SS Panzer Division "Hohenstaufen," commanded by *SS-Standartenführer* Stadler, and the 10th SS Panzer Division "Frundsberg," commanded by *SS-Oberführer* Harmel,

distinguished themselves together with Army units with exceptional bravery. In the attack and defense, both divisions caused significant losses to enemy personnel and materiel. The divisions accounted for the destruction of 140 tanks. . . .

During the evening around 2100 hours, fifty Allied tanks attacked Hill 113 and the main eastward-lying line. The armored force tore a 400- to 500-meter-wide opening into the German position east of the height. However, despite Allied success, Hill 113 was not occupied. German forces on the left also reported an Allied penetration near Gavrus. An armored *Kampfgruppe* of the 9th SS Panzer Division, comprised primarily of assault guns from the 7th and 8th Companies, 2nd Battalion, 9th SS Panzer Regiment, portions of the 19th *SS-Panzergrenadier* Regiment, and the 277th Fusilier Battalion, counterattacked immediately against the Allies east of Hill 113. At the same location, between la Polka and Hill 113, the grenadiers of the 15th Company, 21st *SS-Panzergrenadier* Regiment were encircled. The grenadiers warded off Allied tanks until relief arrived from the *Kampfgruppe* of the 9th SS. Consequently, the estates Maison Blanche and la Polka were lost to the Allies; however, the arrival and determined defense of the lead company of the 1st Battalion, 21st *SS-Panzergrenadier* Regiment, prevented a deeper penetration. Extending on the right, the 3rd Battalion, 21st *SS-Panzergrenadier* Regiment, repelled an assault against the northern slope of Hill 112. Both towns of Maison Blanche and la Polka were permanently lost to the Allies while the remaining line of battle was re-established. The Allies then moved in the direction of Gavrus. The fighting along the front of the II SS Panzer Corps lasted from 17 to 18 July. Despite a decrease in Allied intensity, Allied attacks on 17 July that began late in the afternoon against the entire sector of the division and its left neighboring division were repulsed.[75]

On 18 July the Allies looked for a decisive engagement east of the Orne, after weeks of unsuccessfully attempting to move forward west of the Orne in the direction of Thury-Harcourt. After an unprecedented artillery barrage that lasted several hours, supported by approximately 1,000 RAF heavy bomber aircraft, followed by 751 heavy bombers from the U.S. Eighth Air Force, and eleven groups of approximately 350 medium B-26 Marauders from the IX Bomber Command, Allied tanks and infantry launched Operation Goodwood and broke through positions of the I SS Panzer Corps across a 10 km front. In comparison, the Allied attacks against the front of the II SS Panzer Corps were more characteristic of a holding action.

The combat strength of the 10th SS Panzer Division decreased, once again, from losses suffered during several days of battle. As the division's strength no longer sufficed to defend its previously assigned sector, the corps reduced the sector boundaries. The new divisional boundaries bordering the 272nd Infantry Division on the right were: Pont du Condray (1 km east of Amaye)(10th SS)-Vieux (10th SS)-Maltot (272nd) to the 277th Infantry Division on the left: Maizet-la Polka-Baron (villages of the 10th SS).[76]

During the same time, the first elements of the 271st Infantry Division, including the 1st Battalion, 979th Infantry Regiment and 2nd Battalion, 978th Infantry Regiment, portions of the artillery, the pioneer battalion, and signal troops arrived. The plan called for the 1st Battalion, 979th Infantry Regiment to relieve the 2nd Battalion, 980th Infantry Regiment, west of Maltot. During the night on 18 July, amidst relief operations, the Allies launched an attack that both battalions repelled. The 2nd Battalion, 978th Infantry Regiment moved into the front lines during the night on 19 July, along the divisional left wing, and relieved portions of the 22nd *SS-Panzergrenadier* Regiment. Under the cover of darkness the divisional command post relocated from Grimbosq to a patch of forest 1 km west of Ouffières.[77]

East of the Orne River on 18 July, the Allies declined the opportunity to exploit their gains for a decisive breakthrough to the south. Indeed, the Allies did not renew their attack until the afternoon on the following day. The failure to eradicate defensive artillery along the Bourguébus Ridge was key to the "German genius for defense," according to author Carlos D'Este. D'Este went on to say:

Despite the heaviest tactical bombardment of the war and open countryside which was not particularly suited for defensive operations against a powerful enemy who controlled the air, Panzer Group West had not only prevented a British breakthrough but had turned the battlefield into a massive scrapyard of broken and burnt-out British armour.[78]

As a result, the I SS Panzer Corps organized a new defensive line. German leadership, ever mindful of establishing a command reserve, accurately calculated that the Allied attack would continue east of the Orne River.[79]

On 19 July, the 10th SS Panzer Division received an urgent directive to hasten the process of their relief by the 271st Infantry Division. Nevertheless, the 10th SS Panzer Division fully intended on preserving German control of Hill 112, for as long as possible, through an armor-supported defense by panzer grenadiers.

The Allies attacked within the sector of the 272nd Infantry Division (I SS Panzer Corps) along the road Caen-Thury-Harcourt, capturing St. André-sur Orne, and threatened May-sur Orne. As of 19 July, the 10th SS Panzer Reconnaissance Battalion, designated as the reserve of the II SS Panzer Corps, attached to the I SS Panzer Corps around the area of Grainville (15 km east-northeast of Thury-Harcourt) and arrived early on 20 July as a stopgap measure.

In the morning on 20 July, once the II SS Panzer Corps received higher orders that transferred the 9th SS to the I SS Panzer Corps, the 9th SS Panzer Division established command between Esquay and the Odon and began disengaging. In this respect, the reduction of the sector of the 10th SS Panzer Division that occurred during the night of 18–19 July was counterproductive. Once the 10th SS Panzer Division obtained orders to relieve the engaged elements of the 9th SS Panzer Division with the 21st *SS-Panzergrenadier* Regiment, it became the heir to a sector that reached as far as Bouchy. Therefore, the 277th Infantry Division formulated the neighboring left wing. The relief concluded without incident. Thus, all the panzer grenadier battalions of the 10th SS Panzer Division found themselves back in the main line.

Considering the poor weather conditions and Allied attacks from Baron against Hill 112 that proved unsuccessful, the following days leading up to 21 July remained relatively quiet.[80]

Excessive losses sustained by the division during the fighting prior to 21 July, with no replacements in sight, required that drastic changes to the order of battle were necessary. In accordance with the daily order number 1715, the II SS Panzer Corps ordered the consolidation of the two grenadier regiments into a single regiment. The reorganization provided a regimental staff, a staff company, four grenadier battalions, of which one was armored, and a separate heavy infantry gun, flamethrower, and pioneer company. Any remaining grenadiers formed the replacement personnel. Crews and personnel for heavy equipment and materiel were limited to that which could be carried, and remaining personnel formulated the supply reserve. The divisional signals troops were consolidated within the regimental staff, 3rd Truck Company and Supply Company. However, the companies were ordered fully equipped. Unassigned personnel were instructed to report to the 1st Field Replacement Battalion for grenadier training.

More specifically, the reorganization of the 21st *SS-Panzergrenadier* Regiment absorbed the former *Kampfgruppe* Bünning as the fourth battalion. The 13th, 14th, and 15th Companies of the 22nd *SS-Panzergrenadier* Regiment that formed part of *Kampfgruppe* Bünning were redesignated as the 17th, 18th, and 19th Companies, 21st *SS-Panzergrenadier* Regiment. Any remaining elements from the 13th and 14th Companies that exceeded the theoretical organization of the company were directed to form two additional platoons. NCOs and troops from the 22nd *SS-Panzergrenadier* Regiment were to fulfill the table of organization requirements of the regimental 4th Battalion first.

While the 22nd *SS-Panzergrenadier* Regiment disbanded, an organizational staff organized in the event the regiment became reactivated. The commander of the former regiment led the staff.[81]

Erich Werkmeister and Bernd Risch delivered the 2nd Company commander of the pioneer battalion, *SS-Obersturmführer* Albert Brandt, to the aid station after he broke his legs. That same day, Werkmeister received the Iron Cross 2nd Class, and news of the failed attempt to assassinate Hitler.[82]

During a German nighttime artillery barrage, an NCO of the Frundsberg Division who entered British captivity on 16 July escaped from his captors. Upon his return to friendly lines, the NCO reported numerous changes in unit positions and ammunition transports from Caen heading west. The observations pointed to a potential reinforcement, accurately confirmed late in July. The 6th Company, 10th SS Panzer Regiment reported the destruction of five Allied tanks, two antitank guns, and one heavy machine gun.[83]

SS-Hauptsturmführer Karl Bastian, commander of the 2nd Battalion, 21st *SS-Panzergrenadier* Regiment, refused to remain static and took advantage of the situation. In the evening on 21 July 1944, Bastian was situated along the main line of battle and across from a British stronghold. The Allied force consisted of a company of approximately 120 men and occupied improved positions within basements and bunkers. On his own initiative, Bastian organized a small group of men from the 6th Company, supported by a detachment of StuG assault guns, and personally led an attack that made use of the terrain to infiltrate and destroy the Allied position. Bastian confidently led by example with a grenade in hand. The successful envelopment ensured that none of the 120 British could escape. Sixty-eight men and one officer were captured during the raid. The capture of the Allied stronghold reinforced the German defenses on Hill 112.

However, once the Allies made successful gains east of the Orne on 20 and 21 July, Allied attention diverted to the west bank of the river. Moreover, Allied intentions were uncovered based on captured documents, the number of POWs, weapons, and equipment. Bastian's exploits positively raised the morale and self-confidence of the troops in the defense. On 23 August 1944, *SS-Hauptsturmführer* Karl Bastian received the decoration of the Knight's Cross to the Iron Cross.[84]

At the end of the day on 21 July, the tank crews of the 6th Company, 10th SS Panzer Regiment tabulated their successes:

Tank Chief	Tank No.	Hit	Type	AT gun	Misc
SS-Obersturmführer Quandel	601	1	Sherman	-	-
SS-Oberscharführer Westerhoff	622	1	Sherman	-	1 MG
SS-Junker Bier	634	1	Sherman	-	-
SS-Untersturmführer Schwemmlein	624	2	Sherman	2	-[85]

On 22 July, the commander of the 10th SS Panzer Division ordered the improvement of positions in the sector around Esquay by way of recapturing the estate of la Polka and then Maison Blanche. In the afternoon, the Allies responded to the German operation against la Polka with intense artillery fire against the main battlefields stretching from Hill 112 to Maltot. By 1700 hours, the remaining German elements had reached the objective with the extensive use of smoke. Shortly thereafter, the Allies launched an armor-supported attack against Hill 112 and Maltot. While the defense at Hill 112 managed to hold, Allied forces broke through the lines both at Maltot and east thereof, capturing the village and castle. The engaged elements of the 272nd and 271st Infantry Division conducted a fighting withdrawal in the direction of Feuquerolles while sustaining heavy losses. The interdiction of the 10th SS Panzer Division established a new defensive line 500 meters south along the castle and village heights.[86]

The attack by the 1st Battalion, 21st *SS-Panzergrenadier* Regiment against Maison Blanche allowed for the recapture of la Polka by the 2nd Battalion, 21st *SS-Panzergrenadier* Regiment during the night of 22–23 July. The 1st and 3rd Companies of the 1st Battalion, 21st *SS-Panzergrenadier* Regiment were tasked with capturing the group of houses at Maison Blanche where an Allied machine gun was positioned, along with two heavy mortars and two antitank guns. According to the plan, the advance of the 1st Company was supported by fire from 3rd Company from positions along the western slope of Hill 112. Once the group of houses were in German hands, the 3rd Company swung east of the houses across the road Caen-Evrecy and occupied positions. Without a single casualty, the 1st Company surprised the Allies and occupied the group of houses. Both companies captured thirty POWs, four antitank guns, and three heavy mortars. During the operation against la Polka by the 2nd Battalion, 21st *SS-Panzergrenadier* Regiment, sixty-seven POWs were taken from the Welsh Regiment. That same day, an Allied battalion of ten to twelve tanks counterattacked along the road Gavrus-Esquay after preparatory artillery fire. Despite a temporary breech at la Polka, the Germans repelled the Allied attack. For the success of the operation, *SS-Brigadeführer* Bittrich recognized *SS-Standartenführer* Deisenhofer. The totals included fifty Allies killed, one officer and eighty-six men captured, two tanks and three antitank guns destroyed, and one antitank gun captured.[87]

In the evening on 22 July, the Orne valley railroad line was designated as the new boundary between the I and II SS Panzer Corps (between the 272nd Infantry Division and 10th SS Panzer Division). A ramification of the new boundary included the enlargement of the sector of the 10th SS Panzer Division.

The 10th SS Panzer Reconnaissance Battalion, attached to an armored *Kampfgruppe* of the I SS Panzer Corps from 21 to 22 July, participated in a counterattack, east of the Orne River, against Allied tanks that broke into May-sur Orne from St. André on 21 July. The battalion suffered serious losses and was subsequently attached to the 9th SS Panzer Division that arrived on the east bank of the Orne River.

The armored *Kampfgruppe* Koch, comprised of Panthers from the 1st Battalion, 12th SS Panzer Regiment, and panzer grenadier units of the 12th SS and the 10th SS Panzer Reconnaissance Battalion, assembled 2 km south of May-sur Orne in the Laize Valley on 21 July. The following night, *Kampfgruppe* Koch advanced to the southern rim of the Allied occupied village. At 0600 on 22 July, two companies began to assault the village. The supporting battalion of Panthers did not arrive until midday; the Panthers attacked without prior reconnaissance or coordination. Eleven tanks fell prey to strong defensive fire from the northeastern heights of May-sur Orne. After the gain of ground at the onset, the right company of 10th SS Panzer Reconnaissance Battalion remained caught under heavy flanking fire from the east. The left company pushed forward to the village center. By the afternoon on 27 July, Allied artillery and heavy mortars were concentrated against May-sur Orne, which forced the 10th SS Panzer Reconnaissance Battalion to be withdrawn.[88]

The British attacked Hill 112 again on 21 July, and the village of Maltot with flamethrower tanks. Edmund Erhard and Bernhard Westerhoff of the 6th Company, 10th SS Panzer Regiment were credited with the destruction of four and two Allied tanks, respectively.[89]

On 25 July, the 10th SS Panzer Division, minus the 10th SS Panzer Reconnaissance Battalion, was reinforced by elements of the 271st Infantry Division and the 9th SS Panzer Reconnaissance Battalion. In the evening on 25 July, additional infantry and artillery elements of the 271st Infantry Division arrived. The divisional staff (Second Lieutenant Danhauser) established a fighting command post at Grimbosq, however with no operational orders to engage. Meanwhile, the 10th SS Panzer Reconnaissance Battalion engaged alongside the 272nd Infantry Division east of the Orne River.

The Allies achieved a new breakthrough on 25 July against the 272nd Infantry Division between Bourguebus and the Orne. A counterattack by the 9th SS Panzer Division that lasted until evening reduced the Allied penetration to 5 km wide and 3 km deep. The division subsequently captured May-sur Orne.

The Allies increased their pressure in the sector of the 10th SS Panzer Division. The continual aerial reconnaissance, combined fire missions, and attacks by fighter aircraft made the relief of units very difficult. Nonetheless, the division repelled advances by battalion-strength Allied reconnaissance probes against Hill 112 and 113.[90]

Arriving in the area of operations of the II SS Panzer Corps on 26 July, *SS-Sturmbannführer* des Coudres, of the 102nd SS Rocket Launcher Battalion, accompanied by his adjutant and ordnance officer, reported to the 1st General Staff officer (Ia), II SS Panzer Corps and 102nd Artillery Commander (ARKO), around midday. In theory, rocket launcher battalions were comprised of a headquarters battery and three launcher batteries, each equipped with six 210mm *Nebelwerfer* 42 (Nb.Wf.42) for a total of eighteen launchers. Each launcher had five tubes in a circular arrangement, mounted on a towed wheel carriage. Tactically, the rocker launcher battalion attached to the 8th Launcher Brigade that in turn attached to the 10th SS Panzer Division Frundsberg.

The same day, de Coudres reported to Colonel Leis, the commander of the 8th Launcher Brigade, and they deployed into their operational positions south and southeast of St. Honorine. In the process, the adjutant, *SS-Obersturmführer* Boden, was wounded and delivered to an aid station. The commander of the 3rd Battery, *SS-Obersturmführer* Knischek, was also wounded. Knischek did not recover from his wounds and died on 16 August 1944. The following day, de Coudres reported to the commanding general of the II SS Panzer Corps. *SS-Brigadeführer* Bittrich placed the rocket launcher battalion tactically in the center of the corps' sector to function within the center of gravity. On 29 July, the rocket battalion was assigned back to the 10th SS Panzer Division Frundsberg. Among other things, the rocket launcher battalion established contact with First Lieutenant Wiseomiersky, the commander of the 2nd Heavy Rocket Launcher Regiment. The next day, the 3rd Battery lost two launchers when Allied artillery caused damage to one tube on each projector. The rocket launcher battalion was reassigned to the 3rd Battalion, 1st Launcher (Training) Regiment, when the Allies broke through the lines on the left side. Once darkness set in, the 102nd SS Launcher Battalion assumed prepared positions east of Landes, vacated by the 3rd Battalion, 1st Launcher (Training) Regiment.[91]

Apart from the usual German and Allied reconnaissance activity west of the Orne, from 26 to 30 July, the infantry remain relatively quiet. The

Germans observed increased Allied movement toward the front as German relief operations along the line came to an end. However, relieved units that remained behind the sector formulated the operational reserve. Artillery batteries were brought into position. The staff of the 10th SS Panzer Division remained in command; following the relief of the 272nd Infantry Division, the 9th SS Panzer Division formed the division's (10th SS) right neighbor.

The division anticipated impending action in the west. In this regard, the division learned that the Allies would launch a decisive attack on 29 July, combined with the breakthrough on either side of St. Lô (German Seventh Army), against the west wing of Panzer Group West. The main weight of the attack toward the south would fall on Chaumont.

Allied infantry remained quiet on 31 July in the sector of the 10th SS Panzer Division. Divisional artillery detected and fired upon the assembly of Allied units around Baron. Subsequently, the infantry of the 271st Infantry Division occupied the main battlefield. The main body of the 10th SS Panzer Division was located behind the sector and designated as the operational reserve, despite the fact that the majority of the division's artillery remained actively engaged. Overall command remained with the 10th SS Panzer Division.[92]

Though both the near full-strength divisions of the II SS Panzer Corps specifically trained for the fighting against Allied landings at Normandy, ultimately good Allied strategy caused both divisions to arrive late along the Normandy Front. This was particularly true once the Allies consolidated their material superiority and German leadership could no longer combine a superior armored force and launch a decisive counter-operation.

The divisions of the II SS Panzer Corps were committed to battle without sufficient intelligence and probable operational success. After the first few days, the divisions were forced into a defense, whereby the strength of the 10th SS Panzer Division artillery proved to be the most effective weapon against the Allied forces. The division sustained severe losses of personnel during the defensive battles in the month of July, including a high number of weapons, vehicles, and other equipment.

Nonetheless, the 10th SS Panzer Division, together with the 9th SS Panzer Division, supported by Army troops and antiaircraft artillery, dominated the four-week-long fighting that seesawed back and forth between the Orne and Odon Rivers.[93]

On 1 August, the situation along the west wing of the Fifth Panzer Army (LXXIV Army Corp) and Seventh Panzer Army developed into a precarious situation. Early in the morning, uninterrupted and increased Allied artillery was reported along the left side of Maisonelles Courqueret, the battalion command post of the 102nd SS Rocket Launcher Battalion.[94]

Despite the ability of the 276th Infantry Division, forming the eastern wing of the LXXIV Army Corps, to repel attacks from the north on either side of Villers-Bocage, the 326th Infantry Division was badly battered by units of the 2nd British Army that broke through west of Caumont. On 31 July, the Allies managed to gain ground along the heights on the road Villers-Bocage-St. Martin des Besaces between Cahagne and La Ferrière-au-Doyen. The following day, the attack continued against Amaye sur Seulle-Coulvain-Jurgues. Allied forces crossed the defensive line La Ferrière-au-Doyen-Guilberville on either side of the Seventh Army's dividing boundary toward Le Mesnil-Anzouf, Beny-Bocage in the direction of Vire.

The counterattack by the 21st Panzer Division to the west did not succeed, after marching east of the Orne River toward Aunay-sur-Odon and crossing the line Coulvain-Jurques for an attack.

Surprisingly, three American armies reached Avranches along the west wing of the Seventh Army and threatened an operational breakthrough into Brittany.

It is unknown to what degree the 10th SS Panzer Division was informed of this development on 1 August, as their attention focused on the unstable situation in the sector of the Orne/Odon Rivers, the area between Hill 112 and Evrecy, where the bulk of the divisional artillery and panzer grenadier battalions were locked in combat. During the afternoon on 1 August, the division received the following orders from the II SS Panzer Corps:

> The II SS Panzer Corps, with the attached 9th and 10th SS Panzer Divisions, to include

the 21st Panzer Division, shall clear the enemy breakthrough at Coulvain by closing the gap between the LXXIV Army Corps and the east wing of the Seventh Army (II Fallschirm Army Corps) with the 21st Panzer Division and 9th SS Panzer Division by way of a counterattack by the 10th SS Panzer Division. Contact with the corps (II Fallschirm) shall be established at Hill 205, in close proximity west of Beny-Bocage.

Following reconnaissance, the 10th SS Panzer Division shall immediately advance on Aunay sur Odon-Ondefontaine with available units. Reconnaissance shall be conducted to the west and southwest. Contact shall be established with LXXIV Army Corps. All divisional troops that remain engaged shall be relieved to follow on. The division sector in the east shall be assumed by the 271st Infantry Division and in the west by the 277th Infantry Division.

The 9th SS Panzer Division, supported by the 502nd Heavy Panzer Battalion, shall be committed south of the 10th SS Panzer Division from Vassey toward Beny-Bocage.

Without delay, the 10th SS Panzer Division placed the 10th SS Panzer Reconnaissance Battalion (minus 5th Company), the 2nd Battalion, 10th SS Panzer Regiment, and *SS-Obersturmbannführer* Paetsch in march toward Aunay-sur-Odon. *Kampfgruppe* Paetsch, consisting of the 2nd Battalion, 10th SS Panzer Regiment, elements of the 1st Battalion, 21st *SS-Panzergrenadier* Regiment, 1st Battalion, 10th SS Panzer Artillery Regiment and 1st Company, 10th SS Panzer Pioneer Battalion, operated under the direct command of II SS Panzer Corps. This began the relief of the remaining units still engaged.

SS-Obersturmbannführer Otto Paetsch was born on 3 August 1909 in Rhinehausen along the lower Rhine. His father was an x-ray assistant who placed Otto into public school from 1915 to 1919. After nine years he completed high school but was rejected as a seaman's officer candidate in the navy in the spring 1920 due to a lack of funding. Instead, Otto Paetsch studied protestant theology in Marburg, Tübingen, and Bonn from 1921 to 1928.

On 1 April 1930, Otto joined the Nazi Party. An *SS-Mann* after 1 February 1931, Paetsch discontinued his studies due to his increased involvement and work in the party. In May 1933, he volunteered for the SS Special Commandos, which eventually converted into the 1st SS Panzer Division "SS Adolf Hitler" in September of that year. On 1 October, Paetsch received a commission as a *SS-Untersturmführer* and was assigned as adjutant at the SS Officer Candidates' School at Bad Tölz from March 1934 to August 1935. A staff officer in the SS Sector XXI Görlitz, he transferred as a company commander to the newly organized SS battalion, SS-"N," Dachau, where he commanded billets for infantry, motorcycle, and antitank companies until 1 September 1939.

During the war, Paetsch commanded the Motorcycle Replacement Battalion Ellwangen. After attending a battalion commanders' course, he transferred in November 1940 to the SS Division "Wiking" and assumed post as the intelligence officer (Ic). From 1 January 1942 until 1 April 1943, Paetsch commanded the reconnaissance battalion and participated in the campaign into Russia. After a reschooling course in Paris for tank battalion commanders, he received orders with the organization of the 2nd Battalion, 11th Panzer Regiment. After completion, he transformed the tank battalion into the 103rd SS Heavy Panzer Battalion and deployed to the Balkans, to fight Partisans, from August 1943 until January 1944. On 10 March 1944, Paetsch commanded the Panther battalion of the 5th SS Panzer Regiment and led the battalion into action at Kowel in the spring 1944. As of 12 June 1944, he assumed command of the 10th SS Panzer Regiment "Frundsberg." His decorations included the Iron Cross 1st and 2nd Class, the German Cross in Gold, and the Tank Assault Badge in bronze.[95]

Meanwhile, the 102nd SS Rocket Launcher Battalion received its first fire mission at 2100 hours against Allied assembly areas northwest of Gavrus, to which German infantry reported observing well-paced fire. Around 2200 hours on 1 August, *Kampfgruppe* Paetsch reached Aunay-sur-Odon and began reconnaissance to the west and southwest. The advance through the destroyed village of Aunay was delayed due to debris, so the

10th SS Panzer Pioneer Battalion was dispatched for cleanup work. Once a link had been established with LXXIV Army Corps (command post located at the Chateau de Courvadon, 5 kilometers east of Aunay), Paetsch received a situation report advising the corps' right wing to hold the line Tournay-Vollers-Bocage-Tracy-Bocage. The enemy advance from Cahagnes to the south was sealed off by the 21st Panzer Division along the line Amaye sur Suelles-Graham east of Coulvain-La Bigne. Further south, portions of the 21st Panzer Division made contact with the enemy between the southern outskirts of the Bois de Homme, Le Tourner, and north of Montchamps. Advancing southeast, the enemy captured Beny-Bocage and reached Montchamp with forward armored elements.

Accordingly, Paetsch made reconnaissance to the north, west, and southwest, to occupy the area around Ondefontaine, as a security precaution for the division that followed. In the process of carrying out the objective, several contacts were made with Allied forces during the night on 2 August on the northern outskirts of Bois de Buron and Hill 301, about 2 km southwest of La Bigne.

The reconnaissance that concluded at 0400 hours on 2 August revealed that an undetermined Allied force had infiltrated and prepared positions in the villages of Pitot, Saugues, and La Bigne on Hill 188, 1 km east of Saugues.

Kampfgruppe Paetsch secured the line Pied du Bois—south of La Bigne on Hill 301 along the northern edge and south of the Bois de Buron, meeting with portions of the 2nd Battalion, 10th SS Panzer Regiment. Sporadic Allied movements to the west, which included tanks, were detected in the area where a breach occurred. The *Kampfgruppe* fought off continuous attacks against their own line of security throughout the day until La Bigne was lost. Exceptionally hard defensive fighting developed on Hill 301 where the Allies, supported by artillery, attacked from the north and south. At the cost of twenty Allied tanks, the height was not lost.

Extending to the south, elements of the 21st Panzer Division formed a defensive flank from Hill 321, just west of Hill 301, over Bremoy to Hill 209, 2 km southwest of Le Mesnil-Anzouf; Hill 321 and the village of Bremoy were lost to Allied attacks.

The Allies reinforced themselves steadily around the Allied breakthrough area of St. Georges d'Aunay-Hill 188-La Bigne. Nevertheless, the German command felt the Allies were not strong enough to continue the attack. On 2 August, from a command post in the vicinity of St. Jean le Blanc, the II SS Panzer Corps ordered the 10th SS Panzer Division, marching toward Aunay, to attack the enemy in the breakthrough area and push them back to the west. Furthermore, the strongest possible portions of the division were to be held southwest of Aunay and prepared for a continued advance to the southwest. *Kampfgruppe* Paetsch subsequently re-attached to the division.[96]

The attack by the 10th SS Panzer Division did not materialize on 2 August. Accordingly, the divisional commander postponed the attack until 3 August, until all portions of the division arrived. The attack, whose center of gravity focused on the Allied positions on Hill 188, was scheduled to commence early from an assembly area between Aunay and Ondefontaine. However, Harmel considered an Allied attack to the east imminent and predicted the most success through an immediate spoiling attack by the 10th SS into the Allied southern wing and flank.

Kampfgruppe Paetsch received orders to secure the division assembly area and to increase reconnaissance against the area of the Allied breakthrough.

In the afternoon on 2 August, forward elements of the 9th SS Panzer Division crossed the line Montchauvet-Estry and continued forward to the southwest and captured Montchamp. Allied activity was detected in Beny-Bocage moving toward Vire.[97]

On the morning of 3 August, the 21st *SS-Panzergrenadier* Regiment, supported by a concentration of the divisional artillery and elements of the 2nd Battalion, 10th SS Panzer Regiment and the *Jagdpanther* battalion of the LXXIV Army Corps, attacked Allied positions on Hill 188. *Kampfgruppe* Paetsch managed to prevent an Allied spoiling attack against the reinforced 21st *SS-Panzergrenadier* Regiment after attacking against La Bigne. At 1300 hours, *Kampfgruppe* Paetsch attacked with thirty tanks and destroyed seven Allied tanks and seven antitank guns. One hundred thirty prisoners were captured along with maps and materiel.[98]

The reinforced 21st *SS-Panzergrenadier* Regiment struck against an Allied force of approximately eighty tanks coming from St. Georges d'Aunay. Weak German forces of the 326th Infantry Division from La Vallée and Courcelles were committed against the Allies. A seesaw battle developed and a large quantity of Allied artillery intervened. The reinforced 21st *SS-Panzergrenadier* Regiment captured Hill 118 by late afternoon and dominated the heights against Allied counterattacks that were launched during the night from the north and west. *Kampfgruppe* Paetsch continued the attack with a company of tanks and mounted pioneers against Allied tank spearheads. In close combat, the *Kampfgruppe* destroyed three additional tanks. The tactical victory secured the left sector of the 326th Infantry Division and prevented the loss of Aunay. It also provided the necessary security to execute the relief of the division. For the achievements of *Kampfgruppe* Paetsch, *SS-Obersturmbannführer* Otto Paetsch was awarded the Knight's Cross to the Iron Cross.[99]

On 3 August, *Kampfgruppe* Paetsch did not occupy La Bigne. Instead, the *Kampfgruppe* continued to hold Hill 301 against Allied attacks and sealed off penetrations moving east and south from La Bigne.

On the same day, the 21st Panzer Division and 9th SS Panzer Division were embroiled in combat against the eastern flank of the Allied spearhead moving on Vire. The 21st Panzer Division, supported by the 503rd Heavy Panzer Battalion and the 8th Rocket Launcher Brigade, was positioned along the line Bremoy-St. Pierre-Tarentante. The boundary to the 10th SS Panzer Division ran along the line Hill 295, 1.5 km northeast of Le Mesnil-Anzouf, and Hill 321, with both points belonging to the 21st Panzer Division. The 10th SS recaptured Hill 321 during a counterattack.

The bulk of the 9th SS Panzer Division, supported by 502nd Heavy Panzer Battalion, reached the area around Montchauvet-Montchamp-Presles on 2 and 3 August. During the evening hours around La Bistiére, some 6 km southwest of Montchamp, the division re-established contact with the 3rd *Fallschirmjäger* Division of the Seventh Army.

The 10th SS Panzer Reconnaissance Battalion reconnoitered with a reinforced scouting troop at the main line of battle south of Caumont along the line Culvain-Jurques, to establish the depth of the Allied penetration. Heavy Allied pressure pushed the main line of battle back along the line St. Georges to La Bigne to Hill 302 to Hill 301. Additional withdrawals were planned during the night however; preparations for the defense of the new main line were not completed. A temporary containment line stretching from the church Ondefontaine to Point 297 and Point 259 was occupied. *SS-Scharführer* Erich Rech, commander of the Scout Troop Platoon, 2nd Company, 10th SS Panzer Reconnaissance Battalion, received the mission to secure Point 297 with a reinforced troop, report the withdrawing friendly elements, and return with the last returning units.

At the age of twenty-two, Erich Rech belonged to the cadre of the division. He gained his combat experience on the Eastern Front as a member of the 15th Company, *SS-Panzergrenadier* Regiment "Westland," 5th *SS-Panzergrenadier* Division "Wiking." By the time Rech was wounded on 26 September 1942, he had already received the Infantry Assault Badge and the Iron Cross 2nd Class. In May 1944 he received the Close Combat Clasp and on 12 June the Iron Cross 1st Class, and a promotion to *SS-Scharführer*. On 25 March 1943 he left the Replacement Battalion in Ellwangen to join the Reconnaissance Battalion, 10th SS Panzer Division.

Meanwhile, as the last man passed the security outpost of the reinforced scout troop, Rech took it upon himself, along with one additional trooper, to ascertain the location of the enemy about 3 kilometers through the woods at Bois du Min Ronceux. They withdrew when enemy scouts detected them. Along the way, under constant small arms fire, Rech observed enemy infantry on either side of the road. Once Rech reached his platoon, he discovered his communications were cut and enemy tanks with infantry were in his rear. The platoon fell back along a southerly route until they encountered men from the Divisional Escort Company, who indicated that wounded men remained behind at Point 297. Immediately, Rech took his vehicle to extract the wounded men. He fought past the enemy until he reached the wounded and returned to his company.

However, enemy tanks and infantry cut their escape route. To prevent the loss of his vehicles, Rech decided to surprise the enemy along the road and charge through the enemy lines. With all guns blazing, Rech and his men managed to surprise the enemy and break through their lines without a single casualty. In an effort to reach the command post of *Kampfgruppe* Bünning and report his findings, he learned the command post had fallen into Allied hands. Driving farther he came upon the adjutant of *Kampfgruppe* Bünning, who asked that Rech acquire reinforcements after the men abandoned the containment line in a disorganized headlong retreat. Rech drove his vehicle back and collected the stragglers to form a new containment line. His energetic intervention re-established the containment line and blocked the advancing enemy. Rech remained engaged with the enemy until the defensive preparations along the new main line of battle were completed. For his bravery against a numerically superior enemy, to evacuate wounded and re-establish the containment line, which significantly delayed their advance, Rech received the Knight's Cross to the Iron Cross.[100]

The 3rd Company, 10th SS Panzer Reconnaissance Battalion, commanded by *SS-Obersturmführer* Hinze, had secured the left flank of the division along the road Villers Bocage-Vire on 2 August. Two days later, Hinze received orders to relocate his position 1.5 km east of Ondefontaine and provide security for the withdrawal of the 21st *SS-Panzergrenadier* Regiment and *Kampfgruppe* Paetsch. However, the enemy managed earlier to seize the crossroads east of Ondefontaine that threatened their withdrawal. Hinze attacked the crossroads as well as Ondefontaine. Over the course of one and a half hours the enemy counterattacked repeatedly and attempted to infiltrate the village but to no avail. By 2200 hours, Hinze received new orders from the battalion, but remained committed to the protection of his left neighbor. Once the last elements were withdrawn, Hinze then departed the village. In the process of his action, the 3rd Company, 10th SS Panzer Reconnaissance Battalion took in ten POWs and captured one heavy antitank gun, one antitank rocket launcher, four machine guns, three light mortars, five half-tracks, and numerous

handguns. Fifty Englishmen were counted dead. While providing security on the right flank of the division, Hinze and the 3rd Company, 10th SS Panzer Reconnaissance Battalion prevented the encirclement of the *Kampfgruppe* Paetsch and the 21st *SS-Panzergrenadier* Regiment, for which Hinze received the German Cross in Gold.[101] On 20 August, Hinze went missing in action around Trun.

On 4 August, the Allies broke off additional attempts to regain control of Hill 188. Under the protection of heavy artillery fire at Hill 188 and holding attacks against La Bigne and Hill 301, the Allies pressed against the Odon River in areas north of St. Georges-d'Aunay. However, combined artillery fire of the 10th SS Panzer Division brought the attacks to a halt.

With the availability of a division reserve southwest of Aunay and based on the success of the interdiction fire, the 10th SS Panzer Division notified the II SS Panzer Corps of their immediate intentions: continue the attack against the line Coulvain-Jurques. The Corps rejected the plan and ordered the division to disengage from the enemy and prepare for its relief, after the onset of darkness, by the 326th Infantry Division. A second order followed that placed the 10th SS Panzer Division under the command of Army Group B and instructed the division to assemble in the area of Vassey, some 20 km southwest of Aunay. A corps-level situation report revealed the division was earmarked for a planned counterattack by the Seventh Army in the direction of Avranches.

Meanwhile, the situation of the 21st Panzer Division on 4 August remained unchanged. The 9th SS Panzer Division threw the Allies out of Presles and Chenedolle and permanently closed the gap on the eastern wing of the Seventh Army, by the 3rd *Fallschirmjäger* Division of the II *Fallschirm* Army Corps, on Hill 119 near La Bistiére.

Considering the inability of the 326nd Infantry Division to relieve the division on Hill 188, the 10th SS Panzer Division disengaged from the enemy under the cover of a rear guard, comprised of an armored *Kampfgruppe* with artillery, which followed suit.[102]

The relief of the 10th SS Panzer Division during the night of 4–5 August from positions on Hill 188 and near La Bigne was complicated by Allied pressure. The rear guard was forced into costly fighting on Hill 188 in order to reduce the pressure on portions of the 326nd Infantry Division, the right neighbor. Subsequently, after the Allies occupied Ondefontaine, the rear guard fought its way back to the division. The renewed night attack against La Bigne on 4 August, led by the 10th SS Panzer Reconnaissance Battalion, was successful.

Despite heightened Allied aerial harassment during the division's march on 5 August to the area of Vassey, the 10th SS Panzer Division stood ready for action with portions that arrived eastward of Chenedolle, including the 22nd *SS-Panzergrenadier* Regiment, the 2nd Battalion, 10th SS Panzer Artillery Regiment, 10th SS Panzer Antiaircraft Battalion, and portions of the 10th SS Panzer Pioneer Battalion.

The west wing of the Fifth Panzer Army, joined during the night on 5 August with the east wing of the Seventh Army, detached from weak Allied pressure along the line Estry-Presles-Burcy. In the afternoon on 5 August, the Allies broke into the German defensive lines of the 9th SS Panzer Division on either side of Presles. A 4-km-wide and 3-km-deep penetration allowed the Allies to establish a foothold south of the river basin on Hills 224 near Sourdeval and 242 north of Chenedolle, running the length of the boundary between the Fifth Panzer Army and Seventh Army. Portions of the 9th SS Panzer Division that counterattacked with combined artillery support from every available battery were unable to eradicate the Allied penetration.

Again, the situation required the commitment of the 10th SS Panzer Division to prevent a tactical crisis. On 6 August, the 10th SS Panzer Division, reinforced by portions of the Panzer Lehr Division and under the command of the II SS Panzer Corps, attacked the Allies that had pushed nearly as far forward as Chenedolle. To the west, security was provided by the 10th SS Panzer Reconnaissance Battalion that reconnoitered and blocked the large road by Viessoix leading to Vire. The attack forced the Allies to withdraw to the north where Hill 224 was contested bitterly. After the 10th SS Panzer Division captured Hills 242 and 224, the attack was broken off. Allied aerial activity proved so effective

that the strength of the division no longer sufficed to clear the entire penetration.

In the early morning on 7 August, the Seventh Army launched a decisive attack against Avranches to force a deciding outcome. At the highest level, and after considering all the risks involved, the 10th SS Panzer Division would follow up the attack. The Frundsberg Division was placed under the control of the Seventh Army and received orders to assemble around the area of St. Clement-Ger-Yvrandes-Tinchebray-St. Jean de Bois-Le Fresne Poret, once it was relieved by the 3rd *Fallschirmjäger* Division around Presles-Burcy.[103]

In the early afternoon on 7 August, the village of Vire fell into Allied hands, which resulted in the further loss of German ground east of the city as far as a line 3 km east of Presles-Chenedolle-Roullons. In the process, the 10th SS Panzer Division broke contact with the Allies and marched to their designated area. During the march, the divisional command post relocated near St. Quentin in Le Coudray, 8 km south of Chenedolle.

Later in the day, Heinz Harmel established contact with the 2nd SS Panzer Division that assembled in the area of Ger-St. Clement-Mortain. He was advised that Allied tanks and motorized units were advancing east and southeast out of the bridgehead area. On his own accord, Harmel dispatched the 10th SS Panzer Reconnaissance Battalion across the line Mortain-Domfront, the area of the 275th Infantry Division responsible for providing security, and ordered reconnaissance to the south. Reports that arrived throughout the night on 8 August indicated that Allied forces had also seized Barenton during the night on 7 August and were nearing the road east of the village that headed toward Domfront. The 10th SS Panzer Reconnaissance Battalion provided security by occupying several key positions.

During the same night, the 10th SS Panzer Division was attached to the LVIII Panzer Corps and ordered to relieve engaged elements of the 275th Infantry Division in Barenton. At the same time, the 10th SS Panzer Division was reminded of the planned coming operation toward Avranches and to make the bulk of its forces available in the assembly areas. In fulfilling their mission, the 10th SS Panzer Reconnaissance Battalion and 1st Battalion,

21st *SS-Panzergrenadier* Regiment assumed the task of providing security along the road that led north, from the northwestern, northern, and northeastern heights of Barenton. They also made reconnaissance to the south. The 10th SS Panzer Artillery Regiment was ordered to deploy its batteries for security and overwatch to the south.[104]

On 8 August, a threat emerged from the south. Allied motorized and armored units were marching eastward just south of the divisional security lines. Allied armored reconnaissance vehicles suddenly appeared south of Ger. The 10th SS Panzer Division feared high numbers of casualties among the weaker units that were assigned to security, stretching over 20 kilometers.

The division requested operational independence of the corps to forgo a critical situation. However, the corps responded by ordering the division to attack and occupy Barenton and block the main road against a further Allied advance. The Allied crossing of the high ground at Foret de Mortain and de Lande Pourrie was to be avoided.

The 10th SS Panzer Division planned to attack with the center of gravity over Hill 266, just 2 km southeast of Rancoudray, along the road leading to Barenton. The 22nd *SS-Panzergrenadier* Regiment was assigned to lead the attack, reinforced with the 2nd Battalion, 21st *SS-Panzergrenadier* Regiment, and ten to fifteen tanks of the 2nd Battalion, 10th SS Panzer Regiment, and supported by the 10th SS Panzer Artillery Regiment. Due to a shortage of ammunition, the artillery regiment was directed to work with the 10th SS Panzer Antiaircraft Battalion.

Moving on Bousentier, the objective for the 10th SS Panzer Pioneer Battalion was to occupy Hill 263, due northeast of the village. The 1st Battalion, 10th SS Panzer Pioneer Battalion was to be made available to the division 2 km north of Hill 263.

The rearward assembly of the 21st *SS-Panzergrenadier* Regiment, minus the 2nd Battalion, was made available to the division around the area south of Ger. The regiment was to prepare for an Allied attack moving north from St. Georges de Rouelle.

The 10th SS Panzer Reconnaissance Battalion received orders to conduct reconnaissance to the south over the road Mortain-St. Georges. In addition, the battalion was to establish contact with the *Kampfkommandanten* or local town or district commander in the Domfront.[105]

On 9 August, the necessary regrouping of the 10th SS Panzer Division was carried out. In the morning, a regimental-strength Allied armor attack encircled portions of the 10th SS Panzer Reconnaissance Battalion, which was providing security 3 km north of Barenton at Hill 266. Pushing forward from Barenton in battalion-strength, the Allies closed on the height southwest of Bousentier. Up to sixty Allied tanks were identified around Barenton.

The attack of the reinforced 22nd *SS-Panzergrenadier* Regiment, in the early morning hours of 10 August, met an armored enemy at Hill 266 moving forward to the north. At the onset, the attack gained ground and the German tanks succeeded in destroying Allied self-propelled artillery located within the forward-most line. In heavy fighting, in some cases man-against-man, the regiment reached the line 161-Bousentier, which lay 3 km north of Barenton. However, casualties were high as a result of heavy Allied fighter aircraft and artillery activity. The 10th SS Panzer Pioneer Battalion established contact with the east wing of the regiment. The high number of German casualties did not allow a continuation of the attack. The reinforced 22nd *SS-Panzergrenadier* Regiment assumed the defense along the line 161-Bousentier, and the Allies emerged with tanks out of St. Georges from the north, supported by artillery and fighter aircraft. After crossing the river roughly 2 km north of St. Georges, the Allies struck the 21st *SS-Panzergrenadier* Regiment that dominated positions astride the road north of the river.[106]

On 11 August, the Frundsberg Division defended their positions, which consisted of a string of numerous emplacements, against repeated Allied attacks. The Allied attacks were not considered as "preparatory attacks" for a greater thrust to the north, but rather holding attacks to ensnarl the opposing German forces and provide cover along the northern flank for the Allied forces moving east. The 10th SS Panzer Division considered the possibility that the Allies would make use of the

Egrenne valley through Lonlay-l'Abbaye and move forward against the division's eastern wing. As a result, the 10th SS Panzer Artillery Regiment received orders to register specific terrain features in the threatened area. A weak reserve, comprised of the 1st Company, 10th SS Panzer Pioneer Battalion, portions of the 10th SS Panzer Reconnaissance Battalion, and supply troops converted to alarm units, was situated behind the division eastern wing. However, the regrouping could not take place until the evening hours.

After establishing contact with the Combat Command Domfront, it was determined that the village had been defensively prepared by the alarm-units and portions of the 708th Infantry Division that stood prepared for a defense, northwest of the Domfront along the heights between the valleys of Varenne and Egrenne.

Keeping in mind the overall situation and the increased importance of maintaining the defensive front in the sector Mortain-Domfront, the LVIII Panzer Corps ordered the positions to be held to the last.[107]

On 12 August at 0730 hours, an unexpected broad Allied attack launched to the north from Barenton and St. Georges. Heavy-caliber artillery fire preceded and then supported the Allied attack that struck primarily German artillery positions. The German defense required the commitment of the last reserves, whereby the 10th SS Panzer Division successfully defended against a predictable systematic Allied attack.

The main line of battle of the 10th SS Panzer Division, following the engagement, ran from Rancoudray and passed north of Bousentier along the heights north of the river basin 3 km north of St. Georges.

In the evening on 12 August, the 10th SS Panzer Division reported a combat strength of:

10th SS Panzer Regiment (minus the 1st Battalion)	5–10 Pz.Kpfw.IV
21st *SS-Panzergrenadier* Regiment	500 men
22nd *SS-Panzergrenadier* Regiment	250 men
10th SS Panzer Artillery Regiment	23–29 guns, of which 5–8 were self-propelled
10th SS Panzer Reconnaissance Battalion	350 men
10th SS Panzer Pioneer Battalion	150 men
10th SS Panzer Antiaircraft Battalion	9 88mm guns and several 37mm and 20mm guns.

As a result of the depleted units, the divisional command ordered a significant reassignment of personnel, which included the Escort Company, portions of the Field Police, and personnel from the cartography or map unit. All personnel were made available to the grenadier regiments.

In the afternoon on 12 August, the division received orders to disengage Allied forces after dark and return to the line Hill 307 (1 km southeast of Placitre)-La Buisonnière and the eastern bank of the river flowing in the direction of Rouelle, and establish contact with the right neighboring *Kampfgruppe* 17th SS Panzer Division, while maintaining contact with the Combat Command Domfront. The movement was executed according to plan in the right sector of the divisional boundaries. However, an Allied attack forced the 21st *SS-Panzergrenadier* Regiment into defensive positions along the line Le Buisonnière-Lonlay-l'Abbaye.

The 10th SS Panzer Division estimated the Allies would strike en masse on 13 August against Lonlay and the Egrenne valley. Based on this assumption, the division concentrated their defenses in the same locations while exposing the remaining divisional sectors. The bulk of the divisional artillery moved into positions southwest of Larchamp and one battalion of the 21st *SS-Panzergrenadier* Regiment employed southeast of Lonlay to secure the road coming from the Domfront. The flak troops of the 10th SS Panzer Antiaircraft Battalion, temporarily converted to infantry, protected the divisional front from an Allied thrust into the area north and northeast of Barenton.[108]

On 13 August, the Allies remained relatively quiet across the entire sector of the 10th SS Panzer

Division. The 10th SS Panzer Artillery Regiment, whose ammunition supply situation improved significantly, persistently fired on Allied movement and newly detected assembly points south of Lonlay-l'Abbaye. During the night on 14 August, the division withdrew behind the Ergenne-sector on either side of Lonlay.

Observed Allied activity, moving from the south toward the Domfront and from the west of the village to the north, revealed that the Domfront had fallen into Allied hands on 14 August. Moreover, approximately thirty Allied tanks penetrated forward onto the heights just north and northwest of the Domfront. After considering the threat of an exposed southern wing and flank, the 10th SS Panzer Division committed the only remaining eight tanks, including a few panzer grenadier units, along the higher terrain 5 km north of the Domfront. Combined with the previously committed battalion of the 21st *SS-Panzergrenadier* Regiment, which assumed their positions on 12 August, an attack with limited objectives could be launched against the Domfront. The 10th SS Panzer Artillery Regiment, weakened by a reduced fire capability, was assigned the difficult task of placing fire on the open divisional wing in the northwest, to repel Allied attacks at Lonlay and, additionally, support divisional attacks and defenses along the southern wing and flank. The amount of available ammunition would determine the combat employment of the artillery; the right neighbor that consisted of *Kampfgruppen* of the 17th and 2nd SS Panzer Divisions provided assistance.

Shortly after 1400 hours, the 10th SS Panzer Division fought off Allied forces in the area of the Domfront with renewed levels of ammunition. Enough time was available to hastily prepare jump-off positions for the attacking groups. Moreover, the Allies were pushed back in the direction of the Domfront. The successful German defense and counterattack resulted from the effective employment of the artillery and the remaining eight tanks of the 2nd Battalion, 10th SS Panzer Regiment. However, the division did not possess enough strength to sustain the attack and capture the village. By 14 August, the remainder of the divisional front was no longer in jeopardy.

Strong Allied attacks were then anticipated based on the observation of Allied movement that originated from the area of the Domfront. Observed movement was fired upon, whereas during the evening and night hours, the Domfront and the road leading to the north received harassing fire. At this juncture, the 10th SS Panzer Division could not effectively defend its position.[109]

During the night on 15 August, after a renewed penetration toward the Domfront, the 10th SS Panzer Division withdrew on orders from the LVIII Panzer Corps into a new defensive line, close-in northeast of St. Bomer-les-Forges. Weak reinforcements remained within the Ergenne sector until morning. During the withdrawal on 15 August, Allied armor moving northeast from the Domfront struck against the division during the late morning hours. The terrain that offered little to no observation resulted in fighting at the closest proximity. As a result, the coordination of combat elements of Allied and German troops proved extremely difficult. For a considerable time, Allied artillery fire hit against their own tanks. Troops of the 10th SS Panzer Division, along with elements of the Army Antitank Cannon Battalion, which used motorized 88mm antitank guns, destroyed Allied tanks and prevented a more serious crisis.

Soon thereafter, the 10th SS Panzer Division received orders to be relieved by other units nearby and to then assemble east of Saire-la-Verrerie by daybreak on 16 August.[110]

The relief of the 10th SS Panzer Division on 16 August proved difficult. Poor terrain compounded the situation and delayed the movement. Elements of the division did not arrive within the new ordered area until the early morning hours, and the Allies managed to infiltrate Bellou-en-Houlmes from the south. Allied armored spearheads were reported southeast of the village that attacked against the village of Briouze. The LVIII Panzer Corps ordered an attack from the west with the objective of pushing the Allies back to the south. Repeatedly, the LVIII Panzer Corps indicated the importance of a successful outcome.

The fact that some Panzer grenadier units were unavailable for the attack influenced the operational plan. While the 10th SS Panzer Artillery Regiment was available, the 10th SS Panzer Pioneer Battalion was just arriving. The broad and extremely high hedge-works or *bocage* almost reduced observation to nothing. Under the circumstances, the division ordered moving troops to attack against Bellou; the center of gravity emerged within the terrain north of the road leading to the east from Saires. Individual artillery batteries supported the infantry, a measure that accordingly proved itself very effective.

According to Harmel, the attack of the 10th SS Panzer Division was a complete success. Bellou was captured, the Allies were thrown back to the south, and la Ferminiere was cleared. Following the success, the division converted to the defense and adopted a southerly-facing front line that utilized a series of strongpoints. The threat of encirclement of the division and the Seventh Army, west of the Orne River, abated. Losses were expectantly low, considering the the almost nonexistent number of divisional troops.[111]

In the morning on 17 August, *SS-Grenadier* Josef Robertz, of the 3rd Company, 1st Battalion, 21st *SS-Panzergrenadier* Regiment, entered the village of Fromentel in a half-track. Army Sergeant Becker, the replacement group commander, had transferred to their unit several days earlier, and was nicknamed *Kommisskopf* or bread head. When the grenadiers hoped to get sleep in the attic of a barn, Sergeant Becker ordered weapons cleaning.

In the afternoon, the units continued in the direction of the Orne River crossing at Ecouche. Along the way, four American P-38 Lightning fighter aircraft attacked Robertz's platoon. After spotting the aircraft well in advance, the men were able to reach the trenches along the side of the road. One comrade was hit in the shoulder with a projectile and severely wounded. The half-track rear machine gun was shot up, the only loss of equipment. Unable to cross the river, the company found lodging.[112]

That night, the 10th SS Panzer Division subordinated under the command of the LXXXIV Army Corps and marched over two roads via St. André-de-Briouze and Briouze-Fromentel to the area southwest of Putanges. The headquarters of the LVIII Panzer Corps deployed to control the movement over the Orne River. However, the situation in the south, of which little was known, forced the

protective flank southeastward toward Briouze, south toward St. Hilaire-de-Briouze, and south of Fromentel, whereby the 10th SS Panzer Pioneer Battalion and the only remaining company with eight tanks of the 2nd Battalion, 10th SS Panzer Regiment were committed to action. After managing to destroy several Allied tanks in the evening on 17 August, Allied armored reconnaissance probes were repelled. Concurrently, the division absorbed the 9th SS Panzer Reconnaissance Battalion that operated in the same area; however, this measure did nothing to increase the overall strength of the division.

Before the end of the day on 17 August, the 10th SS Panzer Division fulfilled its mission by breaking enemy contact in its entirety, crossing the Orne River at Putanges, and assembling the division in the area around Habloville-Norville-Monceaux-Giel. Here, the division attached to the Fifth Panzer Army. However, portions of the 10th SS Panzer Reconnaissance Battalion were dispatched to a position just west of Putanges.

The withdrawal of the division experienced delays when non-divisional troops intermingled southwest of Putanges and caused serious traffic congestion. The division did not cross the Orne River until 0400 hours on 18 August. The crossing itself was well executed without any major incidents, though two Allied artillery batteries placed harassing fire on the bridgehead for a considerable time. Once the 10th SS Panzer Reconnaissance Battalion crossed the river, it provided security on the east bank on either side of Putanges. Heavy Allied aerial units overhead made movement in the area difficult for the division. Regardless, by the afternoon on 18 August, all the divisional elements had arrived between Habloville and Putanges.[113]

During the night on 17–18 August, Hugo Benger, the pioneer battalion commander, on his motorcycle became hopelessly entangled in a withdrawing convoy. Moving cautiously forward, he tried linking with elements of the 1st SS Panzer Division. However, the Allies were closing on a parallel road from the opposite direction with tanks and mounted infantry. Turning off the road, Benger received fire at close range from an Allied scouting unit. Wounded, he arrived at a *Luftwaffe* aid station later that night. In the early morning, a medical NCO woke Benger and said, "If it is important that you are not captured, you will have to continue on your own. We are under orders to surrender the wounded and medical personnel to the enemy."

To avoid captivity, Benger sought refuge in a slit trench that belonged to a small *Organization Todt* (OT) unit. Eventually, Benger managed to link up with 105mm self-propelled *Wespe* batteries of the 1st SS Panzer Division and made his way to the command post of that division. By the evening hours, a significant surge and flow of withdrawing units and vehicles began yet again. A staff officer ensured for Benger's safety with pistol drawn, in a staff vehicle of the *Feldgendarmerie*. During Benger's flight to safety that continued into the following day, he recalled the event: "I can barely describe what I experienced during that night. Insanity, hysteria, and violence gripped the snaking convoy. The uninterrupted aerial attacks and artillery fire created the greatest sacrifices."

Within the vehicle, the driver and Benger came to a halt at the end of a small convoy for no apparent reason. A higher elevation climbed high before them when tank projectiles sailed over their heads. On Benger's command and with the greatest speed, the vehicle sped over the height and disappeared into a nearby forest for safety.[114]

Confusion prevailed during a change of assignment or command subordination, throughout which the division directly attached to Panzer Group Eberbach. All attempts by the division to establish contact with Panzer Group Eberbach proved unsuccessful. Later, it was determined that the LXXXIV Army Corps, operating and in command in the area of Tru Ronai, received orders on 18 August to attack with the 10th SS Panzer Division to restore the situation at Necy (sector south of Falaise). Despite the corps' orders, only a small number of tanks from the 10th SS Panzer Division were committed in the area of Ronai. During this period, the division was unaware of the overall situation.[115]

In the afternoon on 18 August, the LXXXIV Army Corps directed the 10th SS Panzer Division to march eastward and proceed to the area around Villedieu-les-Bailleul. The concentration of vehicles on all the roads and throughout the villages, and

the continual harassment by Allied aircraft, delayed their progress. The 10th SS Panzer Antiaircraft Battalion provided security approximately 2 km east of Commeaux for the crossing of the greater road Falaise-Argentan, and later followed on to Tournai-sur-Dives where it was emplaced again. Movement of the division over Habloville-Pommainville-Vorche and onto Villedieu did not conclude until noon on 19 August.[116]

Earlier that morning, around 0700 hours, the men of the 3rd Company, 1st Battalion, 21st *SS-Panzergrenadier* Regiment, exited their vehicles with orders to capture the village of Ri and protect the withdrawal of troops from the Orne bridge moving toward Putanges. Only a few homes populated the very small village; a knocked out Tiger tank sat beside a house. Tactically, groups traveled in firing lines at intervals of 40 to 50 meters. While crossing a large cow pasture, Allied machine-gun fire engaged the 3rd Company. The high rate of fire suggested a heavy machine gun; Robertz found cover behind a watering trough. The group maneuvered to the right and proceeded forward through a line of shrubbery. After 200 meters, the group ran into a gravel pit and could not move further. The number two gunner from the number one MG reported being fired upon by a machine gun. He was alarmed when he could not see the number one gunner. Before they set out, the number one machine gunner of the 3rd Company, *SS-Mann* Loisl Sturz, asked Robertz to wait a moment; Sturz commented he needed a bolt from a machine gun. With Sturz missing, the four men decided to search for Loisl. Walter Lämmerhirt, the number one gunner from the second MG, provided cover with a machine pistol. Robertz, Stark, and Döbber removed their gear and began searching, low-crawling forward. After 30 meters, Loisl was found dead lying behind his MG. A bullet had hit Loisl in the middle of his forehead. While trying to place Loisl onto a *Zeltbahn* or rectangular segments of a tent, to evacuate him, Lämmerhirt suddenly motioned quietly to take cover. He pointed toward the shrubbery, where a British soldier stood on top of a well-camouflaged tank, with his back to the three men, looking down the road with binoculars. The three Germans grabbed each corner of the shelter and ran. As soon as they reached a barbed-wire pasture fence after about 30 to 40 meters, an Allied MG fired at them. In the prone position and still under fire, the men tried to slide the body of Loisl under the wires. Unfortunately, Loisl's chin caught on the lower wire. Each time, when they tried maneuvering the body, the Allied MG sprang to life. Unable to free the body of their comrade, they left Loisl behind and low-crawled back to the gravel pit where they found members of the 17th SS Panzer Division "Götz von Berlichingen." *SS-Scharführer* Becker was among the group and requested a full report. The men reported the presence of a well-camouflaged tank about 50 meters away, and a heavy machine gun in a field. Robertz, the ninth man of the group, carried a rocket launcher. Becker asked if Robertz could destroy the tank. Robertz, confident he could succeed, received orders to destroy the tank with heavy grenades. Robertz flanked the tank from the right but could not actually see it. Carefully, he fired two shots but missed when the British tank fired its cannon. The tank projectile hit along the edge of the gravel pit and killed Becker instantly as well as severely wounding several soldiers from the 17th *SS-Panzergrenadier* Division.[117]

After completing reconnaissance missions and general orientations on 19 August, the 10th SS Panzer Division provided an assessment in the following situation report:

Allied pressure was weak against the western facing defensive line of the Seventh Army along the Orne River. In the north, the Allies advanced across a broad front and pushed the remaining German units back west of the line Merri-Brieux-Necy. In the east, Allied tank units advanced along the Dives River over Trun to the southeast; the situation in that area remained unclear. Precise information remained lacking concerning the situation along the southern front line Ecouché-Argentan. The deepest concerns were of the pocket closing between Trun and le Bourg-St. Leonard. Various units were pressed together within the pocket; Allied artillery and aerial attacks had devastating effects.[118]

At 1430 hours on 19 August, the commander of the 10th SS Panzer Division was briefed by the headquarters, Seventh Army, on the situation and intent along the eastern fringe of Villedieu-les-Bailleul. The breakout of the pocket was planned for the evening of 19–20 August, along the weakest points of the Allied encirclement on either side of the villages Chambois and St. Lambert-sur-Dives, southeast of Trun. The division was to receive detailed orders from the LXXXIV Army Corps. However, because of a complete loss of all communications, the division could not locate the command group in the field. After establishing contact with the 12th and 1st SS Panzer Divisions, the 10th SS issued the following orders for the breakout of the pocket:

1. Strong Allied armored forces have encircled German troops in the area south of Trun. It is anticipated that the encirclement will be strengthened during the night of 20 August, especially in the vicinity of southeast Trun.

2. At 0400 hours on 20 August, the 10th SS Panzer Division shall attack from the area of Villiedieu-Tournia toward the north and south against the enemy located on either side and east of St. Lambert-sur-Dives, and breakthrough to Coudehard-Mont-Ormel. Two *Kampfgruppen* shall be formed for the attack; *Kampfgruppe* 21 (21st *SS-Panzergrenadier* Regiment and 10th SS Panzer Pioneer Battalion) and *Kampfgruppe* 22 (22nd *SS-Panzergrenadier* Regiment with the remaining elements of the division).

3. The 10th SS Panzer Reconnaissance Battalion (advanced verbal order) shall reconnoiter the enemy situation and the far side of the road Chambois-Trun and reconnoiter suitable bridges (for use by armored vehicles) and other available crossing over the Dives River. Reinforced by elements (armored reconnaissance vehicles) of the 1st Battalion, 21st *SS-Panzergrenadier* Regiment and proceeding forward at 0300 hours and capture bridgeheads at Chambois and St. Lambert and provide security for the divisional crossing of the river.

4. Artillery support and Flak-security.

5. The division staff shall accompany *Kampfgruppe* 21; establish the divisional command post at St. Lambert and later at Coudehard.[119]

Lacking communication, close coordination and oversight could not be provided for the task at hand. Moreover, it was doubtful that the various divisional troop elements could form combat-ready formations.

Among other assignments for the various task forces, the 10th SS Panzer Regiment was ordered to form an armored mobile defensive reserve. Included in the reserve formation were elements from the 2nd Battalion, 10th SS Panzer Regiment, 1st Battalion, 21st *SS-Panzergrenadier* Regiment, the Army 9th Panzer Reconnaissance Battalion, and portions of the 10th SS Panzer Pioneer Battalion that formed *Kampfgruppe* Paetsch. On 19 August, the *Kampfgruppe* entered the line Ronai-Neuvy au Houlme, to provide a defense against Allied attacks. The company commander, 6th Company, 10th SS Panzer Regiment, *SS-Obersturmführer* Heggemann, was killed in action during the crossing over the Orne River.[120]

In the early morning hours on 20 August, the remaining units of the division arrived in the area of Villedeu-Bailleul. At 0300 hours, the 10th SS Panzer Reconnaissance Battalion proceeded forward and secured the Dives River crossing at Chambois and St. Lambert. Unfortunately, high-ranking officers of various commands gave orders that subordinated elements of the 10th SS Panzer Reconnaissance Battalion to other units, insofar as the only remaining combat-worthy units of the 10th SS Panzer Division were at different locations and carrying out different objectives. Around 0500 hours, Heinz Harmel and his 1st General Staff officer (Ia), *SS-Obersturmbannführer* Lingner, arrived at the command post of *Kampfgruppe* Paetsch. Harmel discussed the situation:

> The enemy reinforced the encirclement and the encirclement has tightened. No [own] corps or division is in the picture. Clear information can no longer be obtained. It [survival] will depend on the current darkness to breakout expeditiously.
>
> The foreseen breakout is to occur at Chambois-St.Lambert. The surrounded elements are to break out in two groups, one in the south and the other in the north. The II SS

Panzer Corps shall open the encirclement by way of an attack from the east in a northeasterly direction against Mont Ormel. The divisional 21st *SS-Panzergrenadier* Regiment and 10th SS Panzer Reconnaissance Battalion shall assemble in the forest west of Aubry en Exmes and attack through the village in the direction of Chambois-Moissy toward Mont Ormel. *Kampfgruppe* Paetsch shall provide security for the first sector of the attack, west of Bailleul and along the northern rim of the woods south of Bailleul, as well as along both sides of the road Trun-Argentan, in order to follow up the breakthrough and attack later to the east.

The divisional command post was located in the small woods west of Aubry. The few remaining vehicles from *Kampfgruppe* Paetsch that were not already executing new orders formed Panzer Group Groth, consisting of three assault guns and the armored half-track Battalion Wolter. Paetsch deployed the group of tanks of Bailleul and portions of Army Major Bockhoff's reconnaissance battalion, 9th Panzer Division, in the sector southwest of Bailleul. The bulk of the remaining vehicles, five Pz.Kpfw.IV and assault guns, were distributed individually in the high terrain between Aubry and Bailleul. This security measure was to combat any Allied tanks that appeared along the southern divisional flank as the division attacked south to break out of the encirclement.[121]

The assaults by the *Kampfgruppen* 21 and 22 were delayed until 0900 hours on the morning of 20 August due to heavy Allied artillery fire. The divisional artillery took direct fire and was knocked out after Allied self-propelled batteries appeared on the high ground southeast of Bailleul, despite the efforts of the 10th SS Panzer Antiaircraft Battalion to eliminate portions of the Allied SP-artillery.

When Paetsch did not receive any reports or orders by 0900 hours, he set out alone on a *Kettenkrad* or tracked motorcycle to find the divisional command post. After a prolonged period of driving back and forth while subjected to heavy artillery fire within the small Allied encirclement, Paetsch found the command post along a height about 3 km east of Bailleul. Assembled at the command post were the commanders of the artillery regiment, *SS-Sturmbannführer* Sonnenstuhl, the signals battalion, *SS-Sturmbannführer* Kruft, and the antiaircraft battalion, *SS-Hauptsturmführer* Schrembs. For quite some time, the divisional commander and his 1st General Staff officer were in the field personally conducting reconnaissance and observing the fluid breakout operation. Upon the return of Heinz Harmel, the second phase of the attack was ordered to begin around 1200 hours. *Kampfgruppe* Paetsch planned to attack over Moissy and break through toward Mont-Ormel.

Amidst beautiful summer weather, the 3rd Company, 1st Battalion, 21st *SS-Panzergrenadier* Regiment, mounted their half-tracks for the coming operation. Their objective was the village of St. Lambert, approximately 3 to 4 kilometers away. At significant intervals, the half-tracks proceeded through wheat fields. Each vehicle (SdKfz.251) carried a driver, assistant driver, and twelve grenadiers, and each vehicle was equipped with two machine guns. The front gun was fitted with a splinter shield, and the rear gun, on a swinging arm, was designed to combat aircraft. Hans Vordermeier, from Bayern, drove the vehicle to which Robertz was assigned.

Meanwhile, the Allies had occupied the heights east of St. Lambert with tanks and infantry. By 1700 hours, the continuous Allied use of five spotter planes, known to the Germans as "lame ducks," enabled the placement of concentrated fire on the bridge by St. Lambert. A bottleneck effect developed and the massing of vehicles blocked the crossing and the attack petered out. While the crossing at Chambois was destroyed, the *Kampfgruppen* of the 10th SS Panzer Division that crossed the river on foot secured the east bank of the river and established a bridgehead. Henceforth, small groups carried the attack forward in an eastward direction. Hereafter, there could be no mention of a coordinated plan of attack.

Josef Robertz and his comrades dismounted from their vehicles 1 km south of St. Lambert, and proceeded further on foot. Allied defensive fire intensified as they neared St. Lambert. Machine-gun fire from the west of the city forced the men to low-crawl over 200 meters through a storm water runoff gutter, running parallel to the Dives River. However, the slightest exposure placed the men in a dangerous situation. Döbber, who crawled over a dead fellow comrade, was also killed. Eventually, the gutter came to an end and merged into the river, where the men found safety. The men gathered in the village church, but only six men were left. Robertz dispatched to find water and upon his return found the church empty. Behind the church an Allied antitank gun remained in action against targets around the Dives bridge. Making his way to locate his comrades, an SS officer crossed the path of Robertz when the antitank gun fired and hit the officer's upper body. The officer's belt and pistol flew against Robertz's legs, and the officer's entire chest cavity disappeared. While his head, shoulders, arms, and lower body were still joined together, the officer could not be saved. Along the village outskirts, Robertz found shelter behind an abandoned tank. Eventually, other comrades joined him. Despite continued Allied fire against their position, the men waited until darkness and then made their escape out of the pocket.

Despite increased Allied fighter aircraft activity throughout the day, the Germans secured the bridge at St. Lambert. Elements from the 10th SS Panzer Division, the Army reconnaissance battalion 9th Panzer Division, and the 12th SS Panzer Division crossed the bridge. German tanks were committed to action against Allied tanks northwest of St. Lambert on Hill 117. Utilizing cover fire of the aforementioned units, any vehicles of the 10th SS Panzer Division that remained operational, especially flak and signal vehicles, managed to cross the bridge.[122]

SS-Unterscharführer Leopold F. M. Knebelsberger, a member of the 3rd Battery, 10th SS Panzer Antiaircraft Battalion, rejoined his battery when it became stuck in traffic heading toward St. Lambert. He noticed several batteries were missing. They were either lost during the chaotic withdrawal or destroyed when their prime movers broke down. The remaining prime movers, 18-ton half-tracks, carried all the gear and supplies from the abandoned vehicle; they were overloaded with ammunition and men. The flak battalion formed part of a never-ending convoy and the prime movers clung to the high hedgerows and stopped often, for hours at a time. In the late afternoon, the battery arrived at the destroyed wooden bridge across the Dives. Next to the wrecked bridge, unattended wounded soldiers lay next to the dying or already dead in a farmhouse ruin. While St. Lambert took heavy Allied fire, the battalion experienced great difficulty getting the prime movers and batteries across the remains of the bridge. Tree trunks and planks that were placed into the riverbed could not support all the equipment. As a result, many items were left on either side of the route of withdrawal.[123]

The seventeen-year-old *SS-Grenadier* Hans Reimers, of the 10th Company, 3rd Battalion, 21st *SS-Panzergrenadier* Regiment, woke up alone in a barn on 20 August, Sunday morning. His fellow comrades departed without him. Outside, stragglers from other units moved throughout the area. Reimers learned that he was in the encirclement. After catching several horses, Reimers and two other soldiers of the *Waffen-SS* rode around the area with no real destination. At the onset of darkness, an Army officer requested their assistance as mounted scouts, to lead a company out of the pocket. Somewhat apprehensive about their situation, the three SS soldiers led about 150 men out of the pocket. Before darkness, the group came upon security outposts for a *Kampfgruppe* of approximately 100 *Fallschirmjägers* and members from the *Waffen-SS*. The *Kampfgruppe*, led by *SS-Untersturmführer* Werner Reimers, intended breaking out of the pocket at nightfall. Along the way, two Army officers without rank insignia asked to join the group. Reimers granted them permission but immediately informed them that he was in command. During the night, the *Kampfgruppe* unintentionally separated itself while crossing a river. Reimers and their group of fifty men continued to march.[124]

The remainder of the 10th SS Panzer Division, which arrived during the evening hours on 20 August in the area of Coudehard-Mont-Ormel, quickly organized individual breakout-groups and attacked in an east-northeasterly direction. *SS-Obersturmführer* Harmstorf, commander of the reinforced 2nd Company, 10th SS Panzer Reconnaissance Battalion, provided security for rearward moving forces and received for his actions, in conjunction with several earlier acts of selflessness and bravery, the German Cross in Gold.[125]

By nightfall, the gun batteries of 10th SS Panzer Antiaircraft Battalion made their way through St. Lambert toward Mont Ormel, but at an excessively slow pace and eventually halted for several hours. The troops had not received any organized provisions for several days. Knebelsberger had not eaten for days, except for a single piece of bread he found in a bread bag belonging to a dead comrade. Over-tired and weary, Knebelsberger gave instructions to the driver not to drive any farther without notifying him first, as he and a comrade laid down to rest under the gun. In the middle of the night, movement suddenly resumed. The two men under the carriage managed to escape being crushed, but it was evident that no one was concerned about the other man. Everyone wanted to get out of the pocket alive. As dawn broke on Sunday morning, the withdrawal of the battered army progressed slowly. The road, which ran through a depression flanked by high hedges on either side, became steeper and stops were more frequent. Knebelsberger's battery stopped next to a destroyed building where more wounded German soldiers gathered, crying for help and begging to be taken out of the pocket. A scouting vehicle passed by that carried nothing but wounded soldiers who lay across the vertical surfaces.

To determine the reason for their stop, Knebelsberger dismounted from the 18-ton half-track and moved forward about 100 meters, squeezing past a number of vehicles. Ahead, a Pz.Kpfw.IV engaged an Allied heavy machine gun hidden among some trees. Knebelsberger then heard the faint sound of distant artillery battery fire. Immediately, he recognized the deep sound of incoming projectiles that were targeting the convoy. Unrelenting, projectiles struck along the sunken road. The devastation and carnage was awesome. Knebelsberger witnessed a direct hit to his battery half-track that demolished the vehicle and disintegrated the entire crew. Not a single man from his battery survived as yet additional projectiles rained down on the convoy. Dead bodies and wounded soldiers littered the road as the convoy began moving again. However, no one pulled them to the side; no one was responsible.

The individual soldier was concerned only about himself, and leaving the area as quickly as possible with the notion that the next projectile might very well hit him.[126]

In the meantime, Harmel and his wounded adjutant relocated the divisional command post to the church at St. Lambert. In the altar choir booths, Harmel briefed the entire staff and commander of the 2nd Panzer Division, General of Panzer Troops Heinrich Freiherr von Lüttwitz. The church was completely filled with commanders, NCOs, and men of the Army, *Luftwaffe*, and *Waffen-SS*. Harmel took matters into his own hands and challenged everyone to continue to fight the battle.

"Everybody listen! All the remaining Frundsberger and anyone else who is here from the Waffen-SS who has the will, to fight on, should come here immediately!"

The commanders and officers in attendance responded to the challenge immediately. In order to devise a plan for the stalled attack, Harmel, Major Bockhoff, and the officers entered a small attic adjacent to the church. However, General von Lüttwitz and his staff of the 2nd Panzer Division did not attend.[127]

The first phase of the renewed attack to break out included reoccupying and holding Moissy. A report arrived from the II SS Panzer Corps that it managed to close within 4 to 5 km of St. Lambert, from Mont-Ormel and Coudehard. Major Bockhoff received orders to secure St. Lambert, especially the northwestern portions of the town facing Trun, with his reconnaissance battalion and ad-hoc combat elements. *SS-Obersturmbannführer* Paetsch received orders to consolidate any straggler Army and *Waffen-SS* armored elements with the remainder of his tank regiment, link with the half-track Battalion Wolter during the night in Moissy, and launch the final phase of the attack. Under heavy Allied artillery, tank, and small arms fire, the plan was executed.

At the command post Battalion Wolter in Moissy, the plan for the attack involved the half-track battalion; the tank regiment was earmarked to attack the next night. The attack was scheduled to begin at 0300 hours. The order of march included the 10th SS Panzer Pioneer Battalion, 21st *SS-Panzergrenadier* Regiment, and armored spearheads comprised of Army and Frundsberger tanks. The severely wounded *SS-Obersturmbannführer* Lingner was scheduled to be evacuated during the attack.

At 0300 hours on 21 August, it was determined the armored group no longer existed. Commanders had previously siphoned off individual tanks here and there for various emergencies. Nevertheless, the breakthrough succeeded in gaining ground as far as Sourdeval without any significant Allied interference. *Kampfgruppe* Paetsch established contact and linked with the command group at Sourdeval where Paetsch met both Harmel and Lüttwitz. Despite the efforts of Lüttwitz to hamper the continued breakout, Harmel led the breakout from the front of the formation and managed to link up with the II SS Panzer Corps. Among the elements that escaped the Allied encirclement were the severely wounded commander of the Seventh Army, *SS-Oberstgruppenführer* Hausser, as well as the severely wounded divisional commander of the 1st SS Panzer Division, *SS-Gruppenführer* Theodor Wisch. For his leadership, Harmel received on 15 December 1944 the Swords to the Knight's Cross.[128]

In the early morning on 21 August, Reimers and a group of fifty men crossed through forested terrain when the group spotted Allied soldiers. Hoping to remain undetected, the Allied group discovered the German group and promptly attacked. Outnumbered, Reimers recommended the group destroy their weapons and surrender. However, Reimers detached himself from the group and disappeared into the forest. Reimers crawled into a large growth of shrubbery and remained there until dark. At nightfall, Reimers made his way to a nearby village and hid in an abandoned chicken stall. Tuesday morning, 22 August, Reimers discovered that British soldiers occupied the village. However, these soldiers departed around noon, and Reimers left his hideout and encountered a French civilian. With his last cigarettes, Reimers convinced the civilian that he meant no harm and merely sought to return to his unit. The Frenchman provided the general direction and Reimers departed, crossing through a vegetable garden. While climbing over a fence and briefly looking back, he recognized the Frenchman as well as Allied soldiers in close pursuit. Seeing no possibilities for a defense, Reimers surrendered to the Canadians.[129]

The small remaining contingency of men from the 3rd Company, 1st Battalion, 21st *SS-Panzergrenadier* Regiment, reached Mont Ormel at first light. Horse-drawn carts clogged the road that led down into the valley. In a farmhouse, the group of men discovered two Polish soldiers in British uniforms who willingly surrendered and joined their party. Once it began to rain, Robertz discovered his *Zeltbahn* missing but found bedding to cover his head and shoulders. Moving down a narrow forest road, *SS-Obersturmbannführer* Schultze, the commander of the 22nd *SS-Panzergrenadier* Regiment, came running up behind them. He called out, "Frundsbergers follow me!"

Immediately, Robertz was designated as the regimental staff. Along the way, Schultze sighted a thermos container, lying at the side of the road in an embankment, and ordered Robertz to carry it. As if he did not trust him, the officer was very careful not to lose sight of Robertz. At the end of the road, where a Tiger tank of the 502nd SS Heavy Panzer Battalion stood positioned, the group turned north. The group rested in Vimoutiers where Schultze assigned Robertz the responsibility of guarding prisoners for the night. Schultze added two additional prisoners to the group and pressed a British Sten submachine gun into Robertz's hands. Robertz remained awake while both the prisoners and his fellow comrades snored throughout the night. To ease the pain, Robertz opened the thermos container and found a full portion of green pea soup. After waking a comrade to share the contents, the alarm was sounded when vehicles approached their position. The vehicles were actually German half-tracks, and everyone returned to bed. However, Robertz caught a glimpse of the vehicle numbers and recognized a "3." He moved in front of one vehicle, causing it to stop, and boarded the vehicle. After handing his comrade the half container of soup, Robertz reunited with his unit and escaped the clutches of *SS-Obersturmführer* Schultze.[130]

SS-Unterscharführer Knebelsberger managed to escape the deadly pocket and arrived at a large estate in Cambrai, with other members of the *Waffen-SS*. A large sign was posted with large letters that read "Straggler Collection Point." Inside the estate courtyard, Knebelsberger found parked vehicles from units that had arrived earlier. The men learned that stragglers were to report to the collection point for further assignments. For the Frundsberg Division, the collection point became an official reporting station. Supplies arrived by truck that included canned goods, vegetables, and various other types of provisions. Heinz Harmel visited the supply point and after lunch, plum dumplings were served for dessert. The divisional commander also enjoyed the sweet delicacy.[131]

In the morning on 21 August, the Frundsberg Division contacted the eastward-moving 2nd SS Panzer Division 2 km east of Mont-Ormel. The II SS Panzer Corps, along with the 9th and 2nd SS Panzer Divisions, advanced out of the area of Vimoutiers toward Trun-Coudehard for the relief of the encircled Seventh Army. The disabled tank number 601, 6th Company, 10th SS Panzer Regiment, was blown up on or around 29 August to prevent capture.[132] At the time, the actual amount of German materiel and men lost in the pocket could not be determined. The Seventh Army could not produce an accurate strength report, and the I SS Panzer Corps reported the 10th SS Panzer Division consisted of only a weak infantry battalion numbering approximately 300 men, no tanks, and no artillery guns; the Hitler Youth Division had 300 men, ten tanks, and no artillery; the 1st SS Panzer Division could not provide any numbers. The II SS Panzer Corps reported the 2nd SS Panzer Division consisted of 450 men, fifteen tanks, and six guns; the 9th SS Panzer Division had 460 men, twenty to twenty-five tanks, and twenty guns; the 116th Panzer Division had one battalion of infantry consisting of 500 to 600 men, twelve tanks, and no artillery.[133]

By the end of the month, Allied tank forces of the U.S. Third Army captured Avranches. It was the eve of an Allied operational breakthrough. The German High Command ordered a counterattack with all available armored forces that were to be removed from their operational commitments without replacements, and reach Avranches to cut off and destroy the Allied breakthrough.

At approximately the same time, the 10th SS Panzer Division was withdrawn and relieved from action between the Orne and Odon Rivers. Originally earmarked to participate in the counterattack at the beginning of August, the 10th SS Panzer Division was employed repeatedly at various other locations to stabilize critical situations. From 1 to 4 August they were called to Aunay, from 5 to 7 August to Chenedolle, and after 8 August they provided security for the new southern flank of the Seventh Army. For this reason, the division did not participate in the battle west of Mortain.

In conclusion, an evaluation of the divisional lower-level leadership and fighting capabilities in August 1944 must consider the weakened strength of the division after leaving the combat area south of Caen. From one action to another, the division suffered heavy losses without replacements and could not, without impact, reassign personnel within the divisions to fill the gaps. The divisional level of operational readiness at Aunay-sur-Odon remained severely compromised where it arrived with 50 percent of its normal complement of tanks and infantry and 75 percent artillery. At Barenton, only slightly more than a quarter of the tanks were available, 30 percent of the infantry, and 50 percent of the artillery.

According to the war diary of OB West, the 10th SS Panzer Division left the Falaise pocket with only "weak elements on foot, without tanks and artillery." The total strength of the division came to 3,000 men.[134]

A Panther Pz.Kpfw.V Ausf.G in Normandy. Source: Gemeinschaftsarbeit des SS-Kriegsberichter-Zuges der 10.SS-Panzer-Div. "Frundsberg," *Dran Drauf und Durch! Buczacz-Caen-Nimwegen*, 1944.

SS-Obergruppenführer Wilhelm Bittrich (left) and *SS-Oberstgruppenführer* Paul Hausser, observing the action in Normandy from a fighting hole. Source: Gemeinschaftsarbeit des SS-Kriegsberichter-Zuges der 10.SS-Panzer-Div. "Frundsberg," *Dran Drauf und Durch! Buczacz-Caen-Nimwegen*, 1944.

SS-Standartenführer Eduard Deisenhofer inspects a rifle for good maintenance, Normandy, France, 1944. Source: Gemeinschaftsarbeit des SS-Kriegsberichter-Zuges der 10.SS-Panzer-Div. "Frundsberg," *Dran Drauf und Durch! Buczacz-Caen-Nimwegen*, 1944.

Wounded soldiers being carried out of the line in Normandy, France, 1944. Source: Gemeinschaftsarbeit des SS-Kriegsberichter-Zuges der 10.SS-Panzer-Div. "Frundsberg," *Dran Drauf und Durch! Buczacz-Caen-Nimwegen*, 1944.

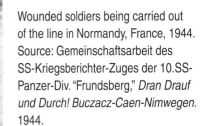

An expedient combat command post situated under a knocked out Sherman tank. Source: Gemeinschaftsarbeit des SS-Kriegsberichter-Zuges der 10.SS-Panzer-Div. "Frundsberg," *Dran Drauf und Durch! Buczacz-Caen-Nimwegen*, 1944.

Awards for personal bravery given in the field. Source: Gemeinschaftsarbeit des SS-Kriegsberichter-Zuges der 10.SS-Panzer-Div. "Frundsberg," *Dran Drauf und Durch! Buczacz-Caen-Nimwegen*, 1944.

SS-Oberführer Heinz Harmel and *SS-Sturmbannführer* Willi Kruft, commander of the 10th SS Panzer Signals Battalion, outside the church at St. Lambert, August 1944. Source: Sieberhagen Archive.

SS-Oberführer Heinz Harmel shaking hands with an *SS-Untersturmführer* during a field expedient award ceremony. *SS-Standartenführer* Hans Sanders, commander of the 10th SS Panzer Artillery Battalion, wearing an assault gunner's tunic, looks on. Source: Sieberhagen Archive.

Divisional staff in St. Lambert, 1944.
Source: Sieberhagen Archive.

Divisional staff in Normandy, 1944.
SS-Oberführer Heinz Harmel at a
table with *SS-Hauptsturmführer* Rudolf
Reinicke, on a field telephone. Source:
Sieberhagen Archive.

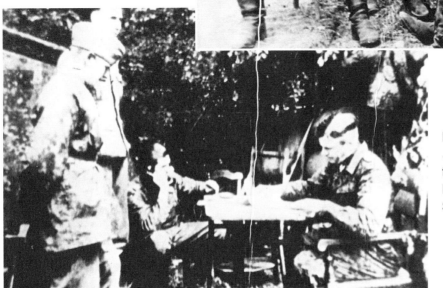

Officers' meeting in Normandy, 1944.
From left to right: Heinz Harmel, at the
center *SS-Oberstgruppenführer* Paul
Hausser, and *SS-Standartenführer*
Sylvester Stadler on the right. Source:
Sieberhagen Archive.

SS-Oberführer Heinz Harmel underway in the command half-track, 2nd Company, 10th SS Panzer Signals Battalion, in Normandy, 1944. Source: Sieberhagen Archive.

SS-Oberführer Heinz Harmel with fellow officers sitting on a command half-track, 2nd Company, 10th SS Panzer Signals Battalion, in Normandy, 1944. Source: Sieberhagen Archive.

SS-Oberführer Heinz Harmel in a camouflaged *Schwimmwagen*, in Normandy, 1944. Source: Sieberhagen Archive.

Combat command post, division
staff, 10th SS Panzer Division,
Normandy, 1944. Harmel depicted
as a *SS-Standartenführer.* Source:
Sieberhagen Archive.

SS-Brigadeführer Heinz Harmel in his official
BMW staff car. Source: Sieberhagen Archive.

SS-Brigadeführer Heinz Harmel
outside his staff car with *SS-
Hauptsturmführer* Rudolf
Reinicke, in Normandy, 1944.
Source: Sieberhagen Archive.

Heinz Harmel firing the StG44. Normandy, 1944. Source: Sieberhagen Archive.

Heinz Harmel firing the K98 Rifle. Source: Sieberhagen Archive.

The wounded *SS-Oberstgruppenführer* Paul Hausser being evacuated from the front, Normandy, 1944. Source: Sieberhagen Archive.

Heinz Harmel awarding the Knight's Cross to the Iron Cross to *SS-Sturmbannführer* Friedrich Richter, commander, 3rd Battalion, 21st *SS-Panzergrenadier* Regiment. Source: Sieberhagen Archive.

An optimistic *SS-Oberführer* Heinz Harmel outside the church at St. Lambert, August 1944. Source: Sieberhagen Archive.

SS-Oberführer Heinz Harmel and *SS-Sturmbannführer* Willi Kruft, commander of the 10th SS Panzer Signals Battalion, outside the church at St. Lambert, August 1944. Source: Sieberhagen Archive.

SS-Oberführer Heinz Harmel underway in the command half-track, 2nd Company, 10th SS Panzer Signals Battalion, Normandy, 1944. Source: Sieberhagen Archive.

SS-Oberführer Heinz Harmel underway in the command half-track, 2nd Company, 10th SS Panzer Signals Battalion, Normandy, 1944. Source: Sieberhagen Archive.

Heinz Harmel depicted as an *SS-Standartenführer*. Source: Stenger Archive.

SS-Hauptscharführer Hermann Max Gerhard. Source: Stenger Archive.

A British Alligator at the memorial site, Hill 112, Normandy, France, 2016. Source: Stenger Archive.

Looking up at Hill 112 from the south, Normandy, France, 2016. Source: Stenger Archive.

On the far right, a farming road leading up to Hill 112, Normandy, France, 2016. Source: Stenger Archive.

At the top of Hill 112, looking eastward, Normandy, France, 2016. Source: Stenger Archive.

The trees of Hill 112, also known as the "woods of the half-trees," Normandy, France, 2016. Source: Stenger Archive.

Looking westward from Hill 112, Normandy, France, 2016. Source: Stenger Archive.

The view from Hill 112 to the south, which overlooks the nearby village. Hill 112 was fiercely contested because it provided excellent observation of the surrounding area. Normandy, France, 2016. Source: Stenger Archive.

The view from Hill 112 looking back down the farming road to the main highway. Normandy, France, 2016. Source: Stenger Archive.

Taking a break behind a Tiger I or Pz.Kpwf.VI Ausf. E. Source: Westerhoff Archive.

An assault gun (StuG III) of the 8th Company, 2nd Battalion, 10th SS Panzer Regiment, parked concealed along a tree line in France. Source: Westerhoff Archive.

The highly decorated *SS-Hauptscharführer*
Edmund Erhard commanded tank no. 613
and was credited with the destruction of four
Sherman tanks. Source: Westerhoff Archive.

The view from Westerhoff's tank on Hill 112, Normandy, France,
July 1944. Source: Westerhoff Archive.

Army Staff Sergeant Seifert commanded tank
no. 611. Source: Westerhoff Archive.

The youngest NCO of the division, tank driver Mehlan, who was promoted from *SS-Schütze* to *SS-Unterscharführer.* Source: Westerhoff Archive.

The tank gunner/layer A. Scheele. Source: Westerhoff Archive.

K. Thomas was a supply truck driver who was brought into the line as a replacement. Source: Westerhoff Archive.

SS-Unterscharführer Johann Schleghuber was the gas training NCO. Source: Westerhoff Archive.

One of the youngest NCOs of the 6th Company, *SS-Unterscharführer* Fritz. Source: Westerhoff Archive.

SS-Unterscharführer Fritz overseeing rifle cleaning, even between fuel barrels. Source: Westerhoff Archive.

A Pz.Kpfw.IV Ausf. E in support of the division. Source: Westerhoff Archive.

SS-Obersturmbannführer Otto Paetsch, commander of the 10th SS Panzer Regiment. Source: Westerhoff Archive.

Withdrawal of the 10th SS Panzer Division through Northern France and Belgium to the Meuse River

21 August–5 September 1944

THE CONTINUED ALLIED pressure and their successful advance against German forces in northern France ultimately led to a major victory for the Allies around Falaise. The Allies encircled and captured an estimated 75,000 German prisoners, and found about 10,000 men dead within the pocket, as well as over 8,000 combat and supply vehicles. Couched by American historians as symbolizing another Stalingrad, the victory fell short of capturing the German higher headquarters, which could quickly rebound and re-establish viable combat formations.[1] The battered German forces that managed to escape the pocket around Falaise, east of the Seine, numbered about 1,500 to 2,000 men per infantry division, and about 3,000 men per armored division. The total number of men that escaped the pocket numbered approximately 20,000 to 40,000; however, almost no heavy equipment survived. From the German perspective the Allied victory was incomplete, due to the seam between the American and British forces that delayed the quick and full encirclement of the thrust by the American XV and XIX Corps west of the Seine to the north.[2] Moreover, the Germans touted the incomplete Allied victory as a greater German achievement. According to the official war diary of the OKW:

> A large portion of the heavy equipment belonging to the combat forces within the pocket was already destroyed during the previous days; additional equipment was lost during the breakout. The combat troops also suffered significant losses and additional casualties occurred during the extraction, however about half still managed to escape. Therefore, the breakout from Falaise shall remain . . . one of the greatest armed achievements of the campaign.[3]

Nevertheless, despite the tremendous losses, around midday on 21 August the shattered *Kampfgruppen* of the 10th SS Panzer Division began reorganizing. A number of troops from fragmented Army, *Fallschirmjäger*, and *Waffen-SS* units were attached to the breakout groups of the 10th SS Panzer Division. The estimated cumulative strength totaled 6,000 to 7,000 men. Most of the combat vehicles were destroyed either in the pocket or during the breakout. Allied pressure continued after the breakout and little control existed over the mass of personnel. After a concerted German effort to distance them from the Allies, individual stragglers were sorted and reunited with their respective units. The wounded were transported out of the pocket and to the rear on the few remaining trucks of the division.

Meanwhile, the 10th SS Panzer Division established contact with the command element of the II SS Panzer Corps, located in Vimoutiers. The division learned that Allied forces had advanced between Dreux and Paris to encompass and reach both Mantes sur Seine and Vernon. The Allied advance revealed the forming of a new pocket that aimed to encircle German troops still west of the Seine River. However, the Anglo-American forces did not pursue their greatest opportunity by driving hard against the northern banks of the river and cutting off both the Fifth Panzer Army and Seventh Army.

Under the circumstances, all subsequent German developments occurred with a great sense of urgency. Harmel said of his men, "Only self-discipline and a strong will to reorganize allowed individual units to work together; extensive orders did not exist."[4]

At the command post of the II SS Panzer Corps in Vimoutiers, the 10th SS Panzer Division learned that it would form part of a new defensive front south of St. Pierre sur Dives, together with the 9th SS Panzer Division and elements of the 12th SS Panzer Division. Effective immediately, the new front was subordinated to the I SS Panzer Corps, belonging to *SS-Oberstgruppenführer* Sepp Dietrich, in order to protect the Vie-sector south of Livarot.

However, the 10th SS Panzer Division experienced paralysis. Their objective could not be fulfilled within the expected time period. The replacement of weapons, equipment, and ammunition had not been taken into consideration. German combat vehicles, damaged by Allied aircraft, which littered the roads, were salvaged to restore the fighting ability of the division. Badly needed personnel and materiel were absorbed from supply troops streaming to the east. The II SS Panzer Corps assisted the effort by providing the necessary vehicles; however, it did not prove effective until twenty-four hours later. The bulk of the 10th SS Panzer Division reached the Vie-sector on foot, in order to carry out its objective to provide security south of Livarot.

In the evening on 21 August, the 10th SS Panzer Reconnaissance Battalion secured both sides of the village of Orbec, the same location where the battalion found refuge once it broke out from the encirclement from Falaise. The 1st Battalion of the 10th SS Panzer Artillery Regiment, forced northeast during the breakout and located due east of St. Pierre sur Dives on 21 August, returned to the division with an entire complement of guns and vehicles.[5]

During the night on 22 August, the 10th SS Panzer Division crossed through the Vie-sector at Vimoutiers when a message arrived from the I SS Panzer Corps that cancelled the mission for security south of Livarot and the immediate reattachment to the II SS Panzer Corps. Shortly thereafter, the 10th SS Panzer Division received confirmation of the message from the II SS Panzer Corps, and orders to proceed by rail through Orbec-Bernay onto Brionne and establish a new line of security behind the Risle-sector. The withdrawal of the division continued during the night on 22 August.

A general directive required that all serviceable tanks, self-propelled and other vehicles, and excess supply troops proceed to Elbeuf on the east bank of the Seine River. There, they were to be made operational with all available resources. Concurrently, contact was to be established with the service and supply units of the 10th SS Panzer Division that were already underway. Furthermore, all armored elements, to include stragglers, that crossed the Seine River were to assemble around Beauvais and be made available to the LVIII Panzer Corps.

In order for the division to provide security for the route of withdrawal over Orbec-Bernay on 22 August, despite the fact that the II SS Panzer Corps committed a rear guard of the 9th SS at Orbec, the

10th SS released combat-capable portions of the 10th SS Panzer Reconnaissance Battalion to Bernay and its surroundings, reinforced by the remainder of the Army 9th Panzer Reconnaissance Battalion. Harmel justified the precautionary measures as a result of increased Allied pressure, especially in the area around Orbec, and armored penetrations against the German flanks. Other elements of the 10th SS Panzer Reconnaissance Battalion dispatched to Elbeuf to reconnoiter a suitable crossing over the Seine River. The measure proved especially valuable, several days later, when the division experienced a shortage of bridging equipment and known crossing points, many of which were blocked by vehicles. The 10th SS Panzer Reconnaissance Battalion crossed the Seine River on 23 August, while the remainder of the battalion followed the next day.[6]

On 23 August, strong Allied pressure that had begun the previous day forced the embattled elements of the II SS Panzer Corps to give ground. The corps successfully disengaged and moved over Bernay out of the Risle-sector. During the night of 23–24 August, rear-guard troops of the 10th SS Panzer Division at Bernay reported Allied armored spearheads west of the city. The same rear guard succeeded, under the cover of darkness, in breaking contact with the Allies and crossing the Risle River. Throughout the day on 24 August, the railroad brought the rear guard back to the Seine River where it also crossed.

In the morning on 24 August, the day Allied forces liberated Paris, Allied armored spearheads continued to apply pressure from the west. The Allies faced a wide defensive line of the II SS Panzer Corps on either side of Brionne. Both the 9th SS Panzer Division, situated north of Brionne, and the 10th SS Panzer Division, located south of the city, engaged in bitter fighting throughout the day but retained their positions. To the south and southwest of Brionne, Allied armored assembly areas were reported. Around midday on 24 August, the corps' left flank became critical when Allied armored units captured Le Neubourg, surprised the 17th *Luftwaffe* Field Division at Louviers, and smashed through a gap in the line. By evening, Allied armored spearheads entered Elbeuf.

Kampfgruppe Schwerin, formed during the night of 23–24 August from elements of the 1st SS Panzer Division and the Army 2nd Panzer and 116th Panzer Divisions "Windhund," counterattacked to restore the situation until elements of the 2nd SS Panzer Division, also part of the II SS Panzer Corps, ejected the Allies from Elbeuf on 25 August.

The fighting on the right flank involving the 9th SS Panzer Division east of St. Georges-du-Vièvre became especially bitter. The situation remained critical as strong Allied armored forces managed to cross into the Risle-sector, in the northern neighboring sector of the LXXXVI Army Corps at Montfort. The Allies captured additional ground to the east. The II SS Panzer Corps dispatched elements of the 9th SS Panzer Division against the threat, however with no results. Allied armored thrusts against the sector of the 10th SS Panzer Division prevented the II SS Panzer Corps from assisting the threatened neighbor. As the 9th SS Panzer Division remained embroiled in the fighting east of Brionne, the 10th SS Panzer Division received an order to disengage cautiously after darkness and form a new defensive line from the left flank to the heights south of Bourgtheroulde. The 9th SS Panzer Division was to conduct a fighting withdrawal and extend the line to the north.[7]

After the 9th and 10th SS Panzer Divisions prepared defensively early on 25 August on either side of Bourgtheroulde, both divisions were ordered across the Seine River en masse. Once a strong rear guard was positioned, which fought throughout the entire day and into 26 August against the steadily advancing Allies, the 10th SS Panzer Division proceeded east to begin the ordered crossing over the Seine River north of Elbeuf. In the meantime, the 9th SS Panzer Division proceeded back to the north, in order to cross the Seine River at Duclair. By sheer happenstance, as the result of reconnaissance, the 10th SS Panzer Division located a secondary bridge next to a destroyed railroad bridge. Despite the damage from daily Allied aerial activity, the bridge was repaired and pressed back into service. Moreover, the 10th SS Panzer Antiaircraft Battalion was emplaced for security.

After the breakout from the pocket at Falaise, the 4th Battery (37mm), 10th SS Panzer Antiaircraft

Battalion was the only battery that remained fully operational. The remaining batteries of the battalion, including the staff battery, consisted only of remnants after the batteries lost most of their equipment and vehicles during the breakout of the pocket. During the breakout at Falaise, the 4th Battery lost Erwin Brichl, Hans Heimann, and Emil Spedl, whereas Fritz Gebhard, Günter Gossen, and Ewald Leypold were wounded.

SS-Obersturmführer Gottlob Ellwanger, commander of the 4th Battery, set the wagon train in march heading west. At the same time, the *Spiess*, *SS-Stabsscharführer* Theodor Gran, the senior NCO of the unit by appointment rather than rank, denoted by two braided rings on the lower portion of his tunic sleeve, of the maintenance detachment, along with the TFK-I, *SS-Hauptscharführer* Alfred Wölfe, were set in march. Both men led the wagon train back, which suffered no setbacks. They were directly responsible for the security and safety of the supply train, and managed to elude Allied aircraft altogether. The *Spiess* was especially astounded when he learned the 4th Battery, as the only battery of the battalion that remained complete, had depleted its entire uniform and clothing supply after distributing clothing allowances to all the other batteries.

During the continued withdrawal of remnants of the division, the battery reached the Seine at Rouen. Heinz Harmel personally oversaw the crossing of units over the Seine and greeted Ellwanger when the 4th Battery arrived. Harmel congratulated Ellwanger and praised the members of the battery for successfully securing the breakout point at St. Lambert. Harmel immediately ordered the fully operational battery across the Seine to provide protection against aerial attack.

Crossing the Seine over the most poorly constructed bridge imaginable was challenging. The bridge consisted of railroad tracks and beams, and was held together by various types of building material. The vehicle drivers were especially challenged, but the TFK-I, Alfred Wölfe, brought each and every vehicle safely across the bridge with only centimeters to spare.[8]

The Foret de la Londe nearly reached the riverbanks, whose hilly typographical features provided the German troops waiting to cross good camouflage, cover, and concealment. Allied aviators did not detect the bridge until later. However, once Allied aviators detected activity on the bridge, artillery fire followed an intensive bombardment by fighter aircraft. No casualties were sustained during the crossing.

The divisional commander and other officers provided the inspiration to hold the crossing point until the evening on 27 August. Amidst the crossing of the rear guard, shock troops repeatedly engaged Allied forces that harassed German units that were preparing to cross and assembled along the southern rim and southern portions of the Foret de la Londe. All the elements of the 10th SS Panzer Division, including the heavy artillery section, reached the far side of the Seine River by utilizing their remaining vehicles. Surprisingly, the number of casualties during the crossing remained minimal. Considered by the divisional commander an exceptional achievement, the discipline, self-constraint, and overall willingness to assist others, led to the crossing of all participating units within a forty-eight-hour period.[9]

By the time the Allies prepared for a renewed assault on 28 August, striking northward against Rouen from the bridgehead at Pont de l'Arche, east of Elbeuf, the 10th SS Panzer Division was already marching east of the Allied line of assault and into the assembly area around Beauvais.[10]

Meanwhile, German leadership decided to occupy the position at the Somme after weak German forces made it apparent that an effective defensive line could not be formed along the Seine River. The units withdrawn on 28 August across the Seine to the northern banks were directed to proceed to the assembly area, one sector at a time.

The 10th SS Panzer Division attached to the LVIII Panzer Corps, commanded by General of the Panzer Troops Walther Krüger, as soon as the remaining elements of the division crossed the Seine at Elbeuf, in the evening on 27 August. The division reached the assigned assembly area of Beauvais with minimal Allied pressure. Individual units managed to acquire abandoned vehicles, which other units were forced to leave behind at the crossing.

A sense of urgency and caution prevailed throughout the division, based on the premonition that the Allies had already established bridgeheads on the northern banks of the Seine River. As late as 27 August, larger portions of the division arrived unexpectedly at an established divisional supply depot, belonging to the Quartermasters Battalion in the Foret Domaniale, 12 km west of Gournay-en-Bray. Numerous stragglers and smaller units crossed the Seine at other locations but were later reunited with the division.[11]

After the 10th SS Panzer Division arrived in the area around Beauvais on 28 August, the division attached to the LXXXI Army Corps, commanded by General of the Infantry Straube. At the same time, the strongest combat elements of the division formed a *Kampfgruppe* and moved through the sector at Montdidier, in order to occupy and hold the Somme-sector at Corbie-Bray sur Seine-Peronne. Supply and rear-echelon troops that could be spared, as well as other fillers and materiel, were to transfer into an area 30 km southeast of Brussels, via the Albert-Mons. According to Heinz Harmel, the reception centers became the primary consideration for the eventual rest and refitting of the division in Holland.[12]

The combined strength of the *Kampfgruppe* 10th SS numbered approximately 3,000 men and organized into command and supply echelons including a diminished divisional staff, the Divisional Escort Company, Military Police Platoon, and elements of the Divisional Signals Battalion of the *Kampfverband* or Task Force Schultz (commander of the 22nd *SS-Panzergrenadier* Regiment). The combat formation equipped with the following units: one single battalion from the remaining 21st *SS-Panzergrenadier* Regiment and the 22nd *SS-Panzergrenadier* Regiment; one light battalion, 10th SS Panzer Artillery Regiment; and elements of the 10th SS Panzer Reconnaissance Battalion.

Kampfverband Paetsch, led by the commander of the 10th SS Panzer Regiment, equipped with: two tank companies (twelve to fifteen tanks), the remainder of the 1st Battalion, 21st *SS-Panzergrenadier* Regiment, elements of the 10th SS Panzer Reconnaissance Battalion, elements of the 10th SS Panzer Antiaircraft Battalion, and the remainder of the 10th SS Panzer Pioneer Battalion.[13]

By 30 August, the *Kampfgruppe* had arrived in the area of Montdidier-Fescamps, whereas the *Führungsstaffel* or command squadron was at Montdidier. *SS-Hauptsturmführer* Wilhelm Büthe replaced the divisional 1st General Staff officer (Ia), *SS-Sturmbannführer* Lingner, who sustained wounds in the pocket at Falaise.

After the divisional staff crossed the Seine River and established the divisional command post in Montdidier, Colonel Heimedinger, of the air facility command, reported to the divisional staff. Heimedinger recommended the transfer of 15,000 liters of fuel and stores of ammunition from the abandoned and closed airport. The offer came as a complete surprise, considering that not a single drop of fuel or ammunition was available to the division when it arrived. *SS-Hauptsturmführer* Ewald Klapdor, of the divisional staff, traveled to the airport where he found bunkers full of aircraft bombs, thousands of pounds of explosives, comfortable barracks, tool rooms, and heavy equipment, such as cranes that were stored in concrete revetments. When the order arrived to abandon the air facility at the last minute, transportation vehicles were not available to relocate the assets. The 88mm flak guns also remained behind as no prime movers were available. In an ammunition storage facility, Klapdor acquired, among other items, 200,000 rounds of 20mm and 400,000 rounds of 7.92 × 57mm rifle ammunition. Later in the afternoon, the highway was destroyed and replacement troop facilities set fire.

The divisional commander, the Ib for supply, *SS-Hauptsturmführer* Rösch, and Klapdor drove to the train station at Montdidier, in an effort to save the ammunition. French rail yard workers explained that the last German trains had departed earlier in the morning. While empty railcars stood on the tracks, a locomotive was not available. Hopes of utilizing a nearby Rangier locomotive were dashed when the Frenchmen called ahead to the next station at Moreuil, to determine if the rail line was clear for passage. The response, "O non, a Moreuil sont deja des panzers anglaises," clearly indicated that Montdidier awaited liberation and the time had come for the staff to depart immediately.[14]

On 30 August, elements of the 10th SS Panzer Reconnaissance Battalion made reconnaissance to the northwest, west, and southwest, and managed to infiltrate well beyond Allied armored spearheads. The Allies captured Beauvais, but Amiens remained in German hands. Contact could not be established with the LXXXI Army Corps. Despite optimism that they could obtain an orientation and situation report at the command post of the II SS Panzer Corps, which was believed to be located in Roye, a meeting never took place. Over a period of several days, the divisional command group felt more and more isolated. Lacking adequate communications with higher command staffs, the division more frequently made decisions on its own.

By way of a coincidental meeting on 30 August with the commander of the I SS Panzer Division, the long awaited link to a command post was restored. The *Kampfgruppe* of the 10th SS Panzer Division was subordinated to the I SS Panzer Corps. After receiving a situation report about developments in areas southwest of the Somme and the Oise-Serre-sector, the commander of the 10th SS Panzer Division became privy to the danger of a renewed encirclement.

The I SS Panzer Corps ordered the *Kampfgruppe* of the 10th SS Panzer Division to withdraw, by railroad, behind the Somme and seal off the river-sector along the line Corbie-Bray sur Seine-Peronne.[15]

By midday on 31 August, the *Kampfgruppe* 10th SS Panzer Division made the following progress: *Kampfverband* Schultz crossed the river at Bray sur Seine and began organizing itself for the defense in the sector of Corbei-Bray. Strong security units engaged in fighting on either side of Bray and along the line Baizieux-Bresle and south thereof, approximately 8 km southwest of Albert. The villages Corbie and Lahoussoye, 12 km northeast of Amiens, were occupied as forward outposts. Elements of the 10th SS Panzer Reconnaissance Battalion conducted reconnaissance at Amiens and in the direction of Doullens. Contact was to be restored after the German occupation of Amiens; however individual vehicles departing the city to the east reported Allied tanks approaching the city.

Kampfverband Paetsch first reached the Somme at Peronne. Around midday on 31 August, the *Kampfverband* entered positions along the Somme. The command and staff of the *Kampfgruppe* remained in Montdidier until noon and followed *Kampfverband* Paetsch, after renewed reconnaissance around Beauvais reported strong Allied armor approaching 5 km south of Montdidier. The command and staff departed for Peronne quickly, under the cover provided by scouting troops.

During the evening hours, the operational command of the *Kampfgruppe* received alarming messages from the *Kampfverband* Schultz that strong enemy armored units had captured Amiens, shattering and partially capturing the command and staff of the Seventh Army. While bitter street fighting continued in various portions of the city, Allied forces attacked in the direction of Albert. The forward security of *Kampfverband* Schultz, at Lahoussoye and Corbie, withdrew after brief fighting to the western outskirts of Albert. Before darkness set, *Kampfverband* Schultz made a concerted stand and fought off Allied armor in fast pursuit.

Smaller groups of German soldiers that either avoided the encirclement around Amiens or managed to break out were gathered together to reinforce the defense. The heavy Infantry Gun Platoon of the 21st *SS-Panzergrenadier* Regiment, missing since the crossing of the Seine River, was among the groups. With their 150mm guns, the platoon fired upon Allied tanks approaching the western rim of Albert. One tank was hit and caught fire while the remaining Allied tanks withdrew.

Reconnaissance troops of the 10th SS Panzer Reconnaissance Battalion, dispatched from Albert to the northwest, ran into Allied tanks southeast of Doullens. Shortly thereafter, a troop transport train from Germany carrying approximately 500 replacements for the 10th SS Panzer Division ran into Allied gunfire and was destroyed.

In the evening on 31 August, after the Allies attacked Montdidier and continued their march toward Peronne, the forward-most units reached the Somme River. The arrival of the Allies along the Somme was reported immediately to the I SS Panzer Corps, which ordered the Allied advance on Albert stopped and to clear the city. Troops of the *Kampfgruppe* on either side of Peronne were to hold the Somme-sector and then, depending on the situation, fall back to Cambrai.

The command and staff of the *Kampfgruppe* 10th SS spent the night of 31 August to 1 September at Bertincourt, 5 km east of Bapaume, under security watch along the western fringe of Bapaume. Less than a hundred remaining men of the 1st Battalion, 10th SS Panzer Artillery Regiment quartered around Cambrai. The artillery battalion possessed a few trucks and automobiles, but not a single gun, no prime movers, and had no form of communications. As luck would have it, men of the battalion discovered an abandoned train at the Cambrai rail yard, loaded with brand new Army light howitzers.[16]

SS-Hauptsturmführer Friedrich Richter, the commander of the 1st Battalion, 22nd *SS-Panzergrenadier* Regiment, received orders to establish a straggler collection point on the opposite side of the Orne River with the remainder of his battalion staff and the combat remnants of both grenadier battalions. *SS-Untersturmführer* Heinz Damaske, the 1st Battalion Adjutant and *Gefechtsschreiber* or combat diarist, accompanied Richter and three motorcycle messengers, the supply managerial officer and maintenance officer, along with twenty over-tired grenadiers. During the first several days, Richter collected an additional twelve to fifteen regimental grenadiers.

Richter's leadership maintained unit integrity and morale. Given the high number of casualties and the obvious superiority of Allied materiel and manpower, Richter pulled the men together at a crucial moment when resources were available. Good leadership shows cognizance of the importance of timing gestures of reward, even for basic subsistence. The positive effects on morale were immediate after distributing rations and other sundries.

After a fourteen-day period in August, when the staff lost communications with the divisional command and staff, the small combat contingency received an additional one hundred members of the division with the assistance of rearward-moving *Feldgendarmerie*.[17]

The *Feldgendarmerie*, most often referred to by the common soldier as *Kettenhunde* or chain dogs, so-called after the large chained luminous gorget worn on the front of their chest that read "*Feldgendarmerie*," administered collection points to catch and collect withdrawing or deserted German soldiers. The *Feldgendarmerie* established collection points primarily at crossroads or intersections but also camouflaged points in the center of a village. They were responsible for stopping all soldiers regardless of rank or unit. Soldiers were collected and placed into larger groups for new front-line combat assignments. The *Feldgendarmerie* took their task to reconstitute combat units very seriously. They were forthright and carried out their assignment rigorously. As a deterrence for desertion, collection points established summary courts-martial. Selected officers functioned as summary judges. Soldiers who were caught withdrawing or found away from their units without written orders were summarily sentenced to death, which was carried out by hanging at the nearest tree. These measures deterred soldiers from deserting their units. The individuals that were hung, in some cases, wore a sign around their neck that read, "I am a coward."

The measure by violence minimized desertion and tightened discipline. According to the Army pioneer Johannes Juhl:

> the consequences for the "little soldier" included that you would die no matter what direction you went. You were hanged if you went to the rear and you faced the enemy if you went forward. Death waited for you in both directions. Rearward movement was actually more dangerous considering the summary courts martials gave no pardons. Facing the enemy, you could always surrender and enter captivity, but with the risk of the enemy reacting indifferently and killing you.[18]

Less than half the stragglers assigned to the 10th SS Panzer Division were combat worthy. Despite the setback, the large number of wounded resulted in the assignment of two German Red Cross nurses to the unit. The arrangement allowed Richter to have a reinfected grazing gunshot wound he received on 10 July treated professionally.

At the end of August, the collection staff withdrew across the Seine in the general direction of the Somme to avoid being overrun by American armored spearheads.[19]

In the morning on 1 September 1944, Harmel and Ewald Klapdor departed for the command post of the Fifth Panzer Army headquarters, in Cambrai, where they experienced confusion and an agitated commanding general. Upon their arrival, the chief of the General Staff acted very nervous and asked if the men saw any pioneer activity during their trip. Neither man reported seeing any preparations for a blocking force, or the destruction of the Seine bridges. *SS-Oberstgruppenführer* Dietrich, the commanding general, reacted bitterly to the news and suggested their tone was disrespectful. During the discussion, Dietrich displayed frustration over an unresolved matter at Albert, when the boundaries between the Fifth and Fifteenth Armies changed by telephone. After the 1st General Staff officer made corrective annotations to the operational maps, the commanding general relinquished responsibility to the Fifteenth Army for the situation at St. Lambert.

Poor communications, the disorientation and location of various command posts, and the reckless standing order that sealed the fate of *Kampfgruppe* Schulze at St. Albert characterized the less than favorable atmosphere at the divisional command post at Bapaume. In the late afternoon, Harmel took the initiative and ordered the *Kampfgruppe* to break out of St. Albert. However, the order came too late.[20]

SS-Untersturmführer Rudolf Dannetschek had joined the Frundsberg Division earlier in the year on 17 August. Born on 28 August 1919, Dannetschek completed his four-month compulsory service with the RAD on 28 March 1939 and entered the SS on his twentieth birthday that same year. After a four-year enlistment, Dannetschek received a commission on 1 September 1943 and a posting to the SS Main Economic Administration Department for Economic Enterprises at the Bohemian Ceramic Works, a joint stock company. Exactly one year after he received his commission, Dannetschek went missing on 1 September 1944.[21]

Meanwhile, after the breakout from the pocket at Falaise, the command echelon of the divisional *Kampfgruppe* 10th SS lost all communications with units in Albert, including radio contact with the *Kampfvernband* Schultze. The regimental staff Radio Troop, of the 22nd *SS-Panzergrenadier* Regiment, crossed the Seine at Mantes on 30 August 1944, with orders to proceed to Albert.

The Radio Troop consisted of six men, including Gerhardt Franzky, Heinz Forkefeld, Hans-Peter Kähler, Kurt Möller, Willi Schneider, and one additional comrade (name unknown). They departed Mantes and detoured north around Paris, arrived in Peronne, crossed the Somme, and continued on to Albert. Troops from other units used the same road to withdraw eastward and clogged the road incessantly. The withdrawing troops considered the radiomen crazy, as they were heading in the wrong direction.

On the western fringe of the city, Allied armored spearheads engaged in heavy fighting. The Radio Troop was located near a church where they utilized the height of the church tower for their radio antenna. Immediately they established communications with the command group of the *Kampfgruppe* 10th SS. According to Gerhardt Franzky, a radio section leader with regimental staff Radio Troop, 22nd *SS-Panzergrenadier* Regiment, the regimental commander at Albert, *SS-Obersturmbannführer* Wilhelm Schultze, appeared distraught and nervous. Other soldiers told Franzky the Old Man was going crazy and took pills incessantly. After street fighting that took place throughout the night on 1 September, the Allies managed to encircle and overwhelm the remaining contingent of the *Kampfverband* inside Albert.[22]

On 1 September 1944, the Radio Troop received the last radio transmission from the divisional commander: "2200 hours attempt breakout to the east. Supplies, fuel, and ammunition at the collection center Mons."

Accordingly, the radiomen destroyed their documents and prepared for departure. Vehicles and combat teams capable of fighting assembled along the road to break out. Shortly thereafter, Allied artillery fire began to fall along the road and among the lines of German vehicles. Items that were being left behind, such as munitions or fuel, were destroyed.

The Radio Troop assumed responsibility for a British major, whom the regimental staff 22nd *SS-Panzergrenadier* Regiment took prisoner, and four Canadian prisoners. The captured officer contended emphatically, over and over, the hopelessness of the situation. Nevertheless, the Radio Troop did not share his opinion.

After some time, under the cover of darkness, the convoy departed Albert. The order of march began with two Sdkfz.251 armored half-tracks, followed by the commander Schultze, and the radio truck. After turning off the main road and nearing the end of a long depression, the leading half-track was hit and destroyed by artillery fire that stopped further progress. At 0130 hours on 2 September, the Radio Troop received orders from Schultze to establish radio contact with the *Kampfgruppe* 10th SS. However, communication could not be established.[23]

On the following morning the Germans found themselves surrounded by British units. With fuel supplies nearing depletion, the remaining fuel was made available to tracked vehicles and the wheeled vehicles were destroyed. The Radio Troop, now on foot, headed out across fields and pastures, while the prisoners carried boxes of ammunition. The British major refused to carry anything. Allied illumination flares slowed their progress and forced the men to seek cover on several occasions. The attempt by Franzky and others to break out floundered in the face of British 20mm cannon fire. Franzky and his men, along with the wounded, gathered in a barn. Despite the British officer having given his word that he would arrange for medical assistance for the wounded Germans, Franzky and the other men left him behind, along with four Canadians and their own wounded. Franzky could not care for their comrades or take them along. The small group of radio operators who belonged to the regimental staff, 22nd *SS-Panzergrenadier* Regiment, headed into the bushes and waited for darkness. It rained the entire day and once darkness set in, the men used a compass and headed toward Mons.[24]

The armored half-tracks of 1st Battalion, 21st *SS-Panzergrenadier* Regiment, also received orders to break out of the encirclement on 1 September 1944. Shortly before darkness at 2100 hours, orders arrived to begin a rearward march out of Albert heading to the north. After approximately 4 km, the battalion encountered Allied defensive small arms fire from a forested area. However, in the rear portion of the convoy, *SS-Rottenführer* Erwin

Markowski, the driver of the crewless radio half-track #302, which belonged to the 3rd Company, observed other half-tracks slowly passing him to the rear. In the dark, Markowski followed the shadows but remained completely unaware of the situation. The progress was very slow as the fields were tested to ensure they were suitable for armored half-tracks. After a half-hour wait, while scouting troops reconnoitered the area, the advance resumed. After driving nearly 1 km, a sudden detonation at the front stopped the convoy. Slowly, the convoy backed up 100 to 200 meters. The half-track engines were shut off and quiet prevailed. No one moved and only faint sound of distant combat could be heard. The convoy stopped in the middle of a field. Though everyone was over-tired, no one slept. Several hours later, day broke and first light from the east hit the skies. Suddenly, a messenger appeared. Markowski recognized the messenger who belonged to the 3rd Company. His name was Feldmann and came from Danzig. Feldmann stopped at vehicle #302, also known as the "final light" and the last vehicle along the messenger route. The two men engaged in conversation whereby Markowski learned the convoy consisted of fifteen half-tracks, of which all were full except #302. The order read, "Destroy all vehicles and head toward the homeland in small groups."

Slowly, morning broke and Markowitz began to recognize his surroundings. They were in the town of Pys and had driven into a dead end.[25] After carrying out their orders and blowing up the vehicles, Markowitz entered the tree line where he encountered his *Spiess* Deike and the journal writer *SS-Unterscharführer* Reissmueller. Both men held two American soldiers captive. Markowitz asked the *Spiess* what was next, whereby Deike turned his head and glanced to the south and replied, "American tanks are coming from there!"

Markowitz could neither see nor hear any tanks and continued toward home. Along the way he met his friend Achim Zerlett, the half-track driver of the other vehicle #301, and others from the 3rd Company, 21st *SS-Panzergrenadier* Regiment. Together they moved across various villages and joined a group of forty armed Army soldiers. The local population detected this rag-tag bunch immediately and the Marquis appeared close on their heels. After the group was reduced to approximately ten men, they were captured in Lille and the war came to an end for them.[26]

Meanwhile, the *Kampfverband* Paetsch successfully defended both sides of Peronne throughout the day. The *Kampfverband* received orders to withdraw after dark into Cambrai.

In most cases, Allied movements disrupted German directives or orders given to units by way of radio. Even verbal orders given personally at the command post were only partially carried out due to extenuating circumstances within fluid situations that constantly changed. The lack of sufficient ammunition and fuel restricted combat operations and movement. The momentum of Allied operations assumed such speed that German command posts were forced to move from one location to another. Allied armored forces in pursuit of withdrawing Germans often overran and neutralized command and control.

From his command post approximately 2 km south of Mons, *SS-Brigadeführer* Bittrich dispatched on 2 September 1944 the adjutant or Ic, *SS-Untersturmführer* Schöberle, in the direction of Valenciennes to establish contact with the 9th SS Panzer Division, which they suspected was nearby. Bittrich intended the 9th SS Panzer Division to halt the Allied advance north of Mons. Despite the capture of Schöberle in Valenciennes, the Ic managed to carry out his orders.

After the LVIII Panzer Corps provided a situational orientation and report in the afternoon on 2 September 1944, the Allies attacked eastward from Valenciennes against the line Maubeuge-Mons. Moreover, Allied forces attacked toward Mons from the south. Late in the afternoon the final radio message from *Kampfgruppe* Schwerin arrived at the II SS Panzer Corps: "Strong Allied armored forces broke through the Front Avesnes, now advancing on Maubeuge. Gruppe von Schwerin cut off in the Ardennes."

As the message arrived, the first American tanks drove past the command post of the II SS Panzer Corps. By evening, the Allies had subjected the command post to tank and machine-gun fire. The remaining elements of German infantry units in the area of Mons-Valenciennes-Cambrai-Maubeuge were cut off from the Canal Conde-Mons. According to Bittrich, worthwhile assets were unable to be rescued from the pocket forming around Mons. Only the most mobile elements were able to escape captivity during the night of 2–3 September. The escape routes were over side roads or directly through Allied gaps in the Allied order of march. From the west, and during the night on 2–3 September 1944, the staff of the II SS Panzer Corps broke through American armored convoys that were heading from Valenciennes toward Mons and on to Brussels. North of Mons, the staff of the II SS Panzer Corps met the 9th SS Panzer Reconnaissance Battalion and ordered the reconnaissance battalion to secure the sector of Senette, west of Nivelles.[27]

In the night on 2 September, the pursuing Allied armored spearheads suddenly appeared within the sector of the *Kampfgruppe* 10th SS Panzer Division, in the lightly held village of Bapaume. The *Kampfgruppe* committed the few forces that could be mustered to Bapaume. Notwithstanding the need to provide troops for security for the deployment of the *Kampfgruppe* itself, the operation ultimately aimed to provide time for the *Kampfgruppe*, 9th SS Panzer Division, moving from the Serre-sector over St. Quentin to Cambrai. After bitter but hopeless fighting, Bapuame was left to the Allies after midnight. The command and staff of the *Kampfgruppe* 10th SS broke contact under the cover of darkness and proceeded through Cambrai in the morning. Earlier, the Allies had subjected Cambrai to heavy bombing. *Kampfverband* Paetsch withdrew from Peronne over Cambrai and into Valenciennes.[28]

Allied strategy, at this point, directed by General Eisenhower, entered a new phase of operations that applied a broad-front strategy, as opposed to the previously favored narrow-front strategy. By mid-August, Field Marshal Sir Bernard L. Montgomery, commander of 21 Army Group, convinced Eisenhower to place the bulk of Allied forces north of the Ardennes, a concession to Montgomery's general plan that favored a narrow-front or single-thrust strategy. Montgomery's demands strained the Anglo-American coalition that rested on a proposal of concentrating all Allied divisions in the north to drive on the Ruhr, the hub of industrial Germany.

The secondary objective included clearing German V-1 rocket sites that launched attacks across the English Channel against targets in Britain. In fact, the OKW reported on 1 September the discontinuation of V-1 attacks on London from old V-1 bases and the delayed commencement of V-2 attacks, originally scheduled to begin on 5 September. Nevertheless, Eisenhower acquiesced despite several unproductive operations that Montgomery commanded, including the breakout of Caen in June and Operations Goodwood in July and Totalize in August. The broad-front strategy now placed continuous Allied pressure across the entire front in order to slowly wear down German defenses. Eisenhower's strategy spread Allied forces thin in certain areas and created a vulnerability that could allow the Germans to concentrate their forces and achieve deep penetrations. On 2 September, Eisenhower sent the U.S. Third and First Armies toward the Rhine and hoped to stretch German forces thin and preclude an effective defense at the West Wall. The objective of Patton's Third Army was Mannheim and Frankfurt, while Major General Courtney Hodges's First Army focused on Koblenz and Cologne. The resulting gap between the First and Third Armies was covered by a corps through the Ardennes.[29]

In the morning on 3 September, the staff of the II SS Panzer Corps reached the village of Ways, 15 km south of Wavre. In the area around Wavre, the staff met elements from the *Kampfgruppe* 10th SS, as well as the staff and portions of troops from the 9th SS Panzer Division. Harmel received orders to reach Maastricht and establish a bridgehead on the west bank of the river. Moreover, the 10th SS was to resupply itself with motorized vehicles and ammunition from withdrawing *Luftwaffe* units. The staff of the II SS Panzer Corps, and portions of the 9th SS Panzer Division, dispatched toward Hasselt. In search of the Army group command post, the commander of the II SS Panzer Corps found the command post of the Seventh Army, where he met the commanding general, General of the Panzer Troops Erich Brandenburger, as well as the commanding general of the LXXXI Army Corps, General of the Infantry Erich Straube. Unable to determine Allied intentions and movements, Bittrich ordered the staff

officers from the corps' troops to reconnoiter along the general line of Löwen-Gembloux.

Numerically superior Allied armored units attacked relentlessly from the Seine and crossed the Somme, across a broad front, within a few days. The German High Command, considerate of their own reduction in troop mobility, ordered the German armies to avoid encirclement and conduct a fighting withdrawal up to the line of the Schelde River delta-Antwerpen-Albert-Kanal-Maas and the western fringe of the Argonne. During the night on 2 September the *Kampfgruppe* 10th SS Panzer Division was ordered back through Mons to the area of Hasselt in the region of southern Belgium.[30]

The 2nd Battery, 1st Battalion, 10th SS Panzer Artillery Regiment, commanded by *SS-Hauptsturmführer* Karl Godau, retained approximately twelve trucks and automobiles, and one hundred men. Despite the setback, the morale of the men was good. On 1 September, the 2nd Battery prepared to depart at 1000 hours. The vehicles were packed with as many supplies as possible. A favorite item among the men was canned asparagus. Before the scheduled departure, the battalion commander arrived and gave specific orders to Godau: "Purportedly, there is a train at the station with unclaimed lFH 18 howitzers. Secure the guns for the 10th SS Panzer Artillery Regiment!"

Godau proceeded to the train station where he found thirty-one brand new light howitzers. Each gun was fully equipped with optics, firing tables, lanyard, bore brush, and shovel. Inside a small house on the ramp, Godau discovered a major of the *Feldgendarmerie* and two Army staff sergeants, all of whom awaited the arrival of a 1300-hour locomotive. Their purpose was to ensure the pickup of three railcars full of *Luftwaffe* telescopic devices. In response to Godau's inquiry regarding the artillery pieces, the major explained how the owning Army unit chose to abandon the guns. Godau was free to take them for any purpose he saw fit. The major agreed to ship the artillery guns with the special *Luftwaffe* equipment to Cambrai where the 9th SS offloaded the equipment.

Godau departed northward in the direction of Mons, Belgium. Shortly before the city, Godau spotted the train from Valenciennes, pulling the equipment and his thirty-one guns, when three Allied aircraft swooped down and attacked the train. Approaching from behind, they strafed the train, hit the locomotive and brought it standing, and banked away in a westerly direction. Luckily, the guns were not damaged.

Continuing through the city of Mons to locate his battery and the battalion, Godau spotted a number of *Luftwaffe* personnel whose faces looked familiar. They were men from his battery dressed in *Luftwaffe* uniforms! They found bundles of uniforms lying in the street and requested permission to wear them, since their own uniforms were tattered and worn. Godau gave permission with the caveat that they had to apply their collar insignia. Godau also discovered the battalion staff and immediately made a full report to Harry Jobst, the commander of the 22nd *SS-Panzergrenadier* Regiment. At once, the battalion began work to retrieve the guns. By the end of the night, the battalion consisted of a near full complement of guns, however without ammunition. On 2 September, the battalion continued their march toward Brussels and ultimately Holland.[31]

Concurrently, the battalion commander, 1st Battalion, 10th SS Panzer Artillery Regiment, sent Hans-Dietrich Sauter on a westward reconnaissance mission down various roads to determine the location of American forces. Sauter first entered the village of St. Quentin, which was free of enemy forces. Nevertheless, Sauter remained uneasy over the general situation. A German female signals auxiliary approached his motorcycle and demanded they take her along, since no other German troops were in the village. However, after delivering her to another unit, Sauter encountered German troops along the outskirts of the village. With information that the village of La Fere was also free of Allied forces, Sauter decided to reconnoiter yet another village. Upon reaching the outskirts, Sauter noticed a number of trucks and dismounted American soldiers. Turning the motorcycle around quickly, Sauter headed undetected back to Cambrai.

In the meantime, the battalion commander learned that a large quantity of *Luftwaffe* communications equipment was planned for destruction. When Sauter reported back to Jobst, he received a new mission to acquire as much equipment as possible. The regimental commander's main concern was to be combat ready. With a communications truck and *SS-Unterscharführer* Walter Weiglhofer, the driver, Sauter arrived in the village of Douai, east of Cambrai, around 2300 hours. After passing a singing Army march-column heading toward Cambrai, Sauter and his driver encountered what appeared to be a German tank, parked in the middle of the road. Sauter dismounted the truck to ask the tank driver to move the vehicle when they discovered the crew to be British. For Sauter and the driver, the war abruptly came to an end as they entered captivity.[32]

Around noon on 3 September, the command and staff of the *Kampfgruppe* 10th SS Panzer Division reached the city of Mons, free of Allied forces. Within the city they encountered a message center or bridgehead where individuals and fragmented straggler groups of the *Kampfgruppe* gathered. Moreover, the opportunity presented itself to acquire vehicles and weapons from other German units. Subsequently, the command and staff continued their withdrawal by way of Soignies-Nivelles into Wavre.[33]

Under the cover of a rear-guard defense provided by the *Kampfgruppe* 9th SS Panzer Division at Cambrai, the *Kampfgruppe* 10th SS Panzer Division arrived in the evening on 2 September at Valenciennes. However, the commander of the *Kampfgruppe* 10th SS Panzer Division decided to turn off the route of withdrawal and head north toward Tournai, as a result of congestion, increased Allied aerial attacks against the cramped convoy along the route of withdrawal to Mons, and an armored Allied spearhead that approached the city. During the night on 3 September, the *Kampfgruppe* 10th SS Panzer Division escaped a renewed encirclement. The German achievement came despite Allied success after reaching Mons by units from both Cambrai-Valenciennes and Avesnes-Maubeuge and cutting off German forces streaming back from the west and southwest. Passing through Tournai the *Kampfgruppe* 10th SS Panzer Division reunited with elements of the *Kampfgruppe* coming from Arras-Dounai.[34]

Before dawn on 4 September, the command and staff unexpectedly met the staff of the II SS

Panzer Corps in Wavre. Bittrich subordinated the *Kampfgruppe* 10th SS Panzer Division under his command and ordered the 10th SS to proceed immediately to Maastrich and defend the city. Heavy vehicle congestion between Wavre and Tirlemont, under constant attack by aircraft, caused the *Kampfgruppe* to redirect their march through the industrial region of Löwen. Active Belgian Partisans in the area harassed the individual German drivers.[35]

The commanding general of the II SS Panzer Corps arrived at the command post of the Army Group southeast of Lüttich. Bittrich received orders to assemble the remainder of the 9th and 10th SS Panzer Divisions in the area around Appeldoorn-Arnhem and prepare for their refreshment. Shortly before the departure of the commanding general of the II SS Panzer Corps, new orders were issued to "establish immediately *Kampfgruppen* from the remainder of both divisions and make them available to the Army Group as soon as possible."[36]

During the evening on 4 September, the *Kampfgruppe* 10th SS Panzer Division occupied a bridgehead due west of Maastricht. The following evening, additional elements of the *Kampfgruppe* 10th SS arrived and occupied the bridgehead. However, enough forces were not available to occupy the entire sector, which spanned 8 kilometers. Thus, individual or groups of stragglers that were fragmented from their units and found crossing the bridge were stopped and absorbed into the defenses. The *Kampfgruppe*'s complement of vehicles, weapons, and ammunition improved from numerous withdrawing units. The *Kampfgruppe* 10th SS Panzer Division was not involved in any significant fighting around the bridgehead. During the night on 6 September, the *Kampfgruppe* was ordered to march east of Arnhem for refitting.[37]

In conclusion, the continuous commitment of the 10th SS Panzer Division to major engagements and numerous subsequent hotspots, notwithstanding the near destruction of the division altogether within the encirclement at Falaise, underscores the breakdown of German logistics and their inability to sustain uninterrupted battle. Without sufficient forces to hold the lines, the remnants of shattered units were absorbed into the ranks of quasi-functional combat formations that conducted a fighting withdrawal. The rapid advance of the Allies with overwhelming superiority in manpower and materiel, on the ground and in the air, made evident the supremacy of Allied strategy. On 4 September, according to the war diary, OKW, Army Group B predicted facing no fewer than 2,500 Allied tanks and outlined requirements to hold the line from the Albert Canal to the Meuse and the West Wall, to include twenty-five fresh divisions and an armored reserve consisting of five or six divisions. Two tank brigades and several infantry divisions were needed immediately along the western wing. Moreover, more than ten infantry and five tank divisions were needed within the next ten days to guard the gateway to northern Germany. To meet these unrealistic demands, combat formations, such as the 10th SS Panzer Division, were rushed from one place to another. The series of German stopgap measures became emblematic of the fighting, and yet more typical were the expectations of units in the field to achieve the impossible. Despite the successful defensive outcome at Caen, and the continued commitment of the Frundsberg Division for the next two months until the beginning of September, while lacking significant replacements of men and materiel and having lost all of its heavy equipment at Falaise, the division arrived at the Meuse River numbering barely 3,000 men. Against all odds, the division continued to exist under steadfast and perhaps fanatical leadership. German command elements managed to escape to fight another day. Their escape, considered as their greatest tactical achievement, may also be considered as a key Allied blunder.

CHAPTER 5

Holland

6 September–18 November 1944

DESPITE THE SUCCESSFUL defensive outcome at Caen, the continued commitment of the 10th SS Panzer Division over two months almost destroyed the division entirely. Casualties among commanders, noncommissioned officers, and the experienced cadre of the troops were especially high. Consequently, when the division came off the line during the night of 6 September 1944, it experienced difficulties throughout the process of refitting due to a lack of experienced leadership.

Supply and service troops that could be spared from the divisional rear echelons, as well as all the repairable vehicles and equipment, were dispatched to an area between Iyssel and the German border. Units arrived during the first several days in September with minimal losses while the 2nd General Staff officer (Ib) and divisional adjutant (IIa) planned and prepared for refitting the division.[1]

The continued withdrawal of German forces in the direction of the German border remained hectic as the routes were completely blocked with vehicles. *SS-Obersturmführer* Gottlob Ellwanger, the commander of the 4th Battery (37mm), 10th SS Panzer Antiaircraft Battalion, directed traffic himself at road crossings to keep the battery together. For the most part, the battery arrived in the designated area east of Arnhem with no casualties in men or materiel. The 10th SS Panzer Antiaircraft Battalion began to refresh and reorganize the 88mm antiaircraft batteries. The 4th Battery established positions in Ede, and the heavy batteries were situated farther east in the area of Elten. Replacements for the 4th Battery included *SS-Obersturmführer* Wagner and *SS-Scharführer* Georg Pichler, as platoon leaders, as well as other NCOs and crews. A large portion of the NCOs came from the *Luftwaffe*.[2]

SS-Obersturmführer Karl Rüdele, the commander of the battery staff, assumed command of the newly organized 5th Battery, equipped with 20mm antiaircraft machine guns. The machine guns came from the 88mm batteries and the 14th Companies of the grenadier regiments. Many of the guns the division received came from the Hohenstaufen Division.

When the division reorganized to a tank brigade, a new *Kampfgruppe*, with a new tank battalion consisting of Panthers, was organized and led by *SS-Sturmbannführer* Adolf Weiss. For protection against aircraft, the 4th Battery provided a 20mm antiaircraft machine-gun battery and one platoon of 37mm antiaircraft cannon. *SS-Untersturmführer* Günter Schoknecht assumed command of the battery. Ellwanger personally organized the 37mm battery and assigned *SS-Scharführer* Georg Pichler as commander. *Kampfgruppe* Weiss was employed for a special assignment in Belgium along the Albert Canal. The mission of the *Kampfgruppe* was to establish a blocking position, for which the anti-aircraft battery provided defenses for a commando mission led by Skorzeny. After the battery depleted its ammunition, the crews were employed as infantrymen. The drivers returned in their vehicles to Ede in Holland, but without the guns or crews. On 20 September, the crews of the 37mm antiaircraft platoon entered British captivity. Subsequently, the 4th Battery listed the following men as missing: *SS-Scharführer* Pichler, and crewmembers Hans Ams, Hans Fuchs, Matthias Hutwenger, Walter Lemke, Josef Mueller, Georg Protzel, Johannes Ressler, Gerhard Schreiber, Schuldis, Josef Studener, and Alfred Wolter.[3]

On 6 September, the *Kampfgruppe* 10th SS Panzer Division was extracted from the Maastricht bridgehead during the first several hours without Allied interference and began marching north to the east of the Maas River. The division arrived the next day in the bivouac area at Zutphen-Doesburg-Didam-s'Heerenberg-border of Germany-Eibergen-Lochem. The area was extended somewhat to the north through the occupation of the area Deventer-Diepenveen. The divisional staff was situated and quartered in Ruurlo.

The General Staff of the II SS Panzer Corps occupied Doetinchem. Both the 9th and 10th SS Panzer Divisions were subordinated to the II SS Panzer Corps. The 9th SS had recently returned to the line and occupied the area north and northeast of Arnhem. The 10th SS Panzer Division consisted of two panzer grenadier regiments with a total of four battalions, each consisting of two rifle companies and one heavy company with motorized elements; one tank regiment staff and one tank battalion; one tank reconnaissance battalion, of which portions were motorized and some were equipped with bicycles; one armored artillery regiment consisting of two battalions, of which the command element was motorized; one armored antiaircraft battalion that was partially motorized; one armored pioneer battalion with motorized portions; and one armored

signals battalion with motorized portions. The personnel and materiel of various troop elements were especially weak.[4]

As a result of a threatening situation in the area around Aachen, Field Marshal Walther Model, the commander of Army Group B, directed the II SS Panzer Corps to organize mobile *Kampfgruppen* and alarm units from both divisions. However, a hasty march and preparations for combat were prerequisites, notwithstanding the accelerated efforts to refresh the division. To complicate matters, by the night on 8 September, the 10th SS Panzer Division received direction to set in march one *Kampfgruppe* subordinated to Major Heinke of the First Parachute Army headquarters,[5] located around Weert (20 km northwest of Roermond). The *Kampfgruppe* consisted of one battalion from the 21st *SS-Panzergrenadier* Regiment, one company equipped with bicycles from the 10th SS Panzer Reconnaissance Battalion, one battery from the 10th SS Panzer Artillery Regiment, and one company from the 10th SS Panzer Pioneer Battalion. The unit was later apportioned to the divisional *Kampfgruppe* Walther in the area of Neerspelt.[6]

In St. Lambert, *SS-Rottenführer* Edmund Zalewski of the signals company, 10th SS Panzer Signals Battalion, and three SS troopers rode in a workshop-truck loaded with radios. They crossed the Dives River amongst a continuous flow of soldiers and a melee of materiel that included trucks, artillery, and tanks. German units withdrawing from the Falaise pocket formed a long and slow-moving convoy. All the while, Allied small arms fire from every direction and Allied aircraft from above harassed the withdrawing army. By nightfall, the shop truck reached the other side of the Dives River.

Around 6 September, the small signals detachment expected to reach their company in the village of Rouen. Instead they crossed a wooden bridge over the Seine River and did not rejoin their parent company. Traveling in the direction of Hasselt, the vehicle broke down in the village of Orsmaal. Well camouflaged along the side of the road, the vehicle remained undetected as Allied units, followed by French Resistance fighters, passed by. After waiting twenty-four hours, the four soldiers wired the vehicle for demolition and blew it up. Immediately thereafter, the men set out in a northeasterly direction to reach friendly lines. However, they soon stumbled onto American troops and were promptly captured by four Americans in a Jeep. Moving quickly, Zalewski and his comrades ran ahead of the Jeep when artillery projectiles impacted around them. The Americans sped off in the Jeep. Free once again, the four signal troops quickly sought cover. As soon as darkness set in, the men slept in the open. However, their growling stomachs prevented them from achieving a deep sleep.

In the early morning, the small group descended upon a small cluster of homes where they hoped to find food. Presumably, the area was Flemish and pro-German. When they entered a house, the inhabitants were almost exclusively women and acted very suspiciously. The German men determined the women were not Flemish and searched the area. In a barn they encountered a gathering of men. As soon as the Germans entered, the group dispersed, leaving behind a submachine gun. The SS men quickly captured one of the men, confiscated the weapon, and departed from the unfriendly village on bicycles. At the outskirts, the Germans freed their Belgian captive and sought a safe haven. The four SS men did not realize they were actually in the middle of a partisan redoubt. As they traveled farther, rifle and submachine gun fire erupted on both sides of the road. Zalewski and his comrades rode straight into an ambush. The SS men were forced from their bicycles and one was wounded. Unable to drag their comrade to safety, due to increased small arms fire, the remaining three men managed to find cover. After approximately one hour, the men tried to retrieve their wounded comrade. However, the partisans were waiting and fired well-aimed shots to prevent their efforts. The submachine gun they captured earlier was out of ammunition, and despite their misgivings, they left their wounded comrade behind. They reached friendly forces in Hasselt, near the Albert Canal, where they were absorbed into a unit. The NCO of the group was assigned to lead a group of infantrymen and they joined a *Kampfgruppe* of approximately 150 men, led by the *Luftwaffe* Captain Ilsemann, which consisted of the remaining elements of the Regiment Riedel and Füsilier Battalion 275.[7]

In a similar situation, *SS-Unterscharführer* Matthias Hutwagner, of the 4th Battery (37mm), 10th SS Panzer Antiaircraft Battalion, was caught in the pocket at Falaise. In St. Lambert, Allied artillery subjected the 4th Battery to fire from every direction. However, Hutwagner and his comrades escaped the encirclement by exploiting the most opportune moment. They withdrew across France and Belgium and billeted for several days in a cafe named Kongo, which was attached to a farm.

The owner of the cafe had two beautiful, seventeen-year-old twin daughters. Hutwagner and his comrades gave their rations to the girls who, in turn, fed the rations to the farm pigs. However, the owner returned the favor and fed the men well.

Hutwagner stood guard three times a night. Over-tired, he tried staying awake by marching back and forth. Eventually, he fell asleep at his post, and awoke to someone frantically shaking his shoulders. Hutwagner jumped up and found the owner of the cafe standing before him. In a fatherly tone the owner said, "No sleeping on post!"

The 10th SS Panzer Antiaircraft Battalion reorganized in Arnhem. The 4th Battery, which consisted of three guns, was assigned to a *Kampfgruppe* that formed a blocking line in Belgium along the Albert Canal. The 4th Battery entered positions around Hasselt with self-propelled 37mm cannon.[8]

The self-propelled antiaircraft cannon, essentially a half-track or 5-ton prime mover Sd.Kfz.6/2, was manufactured by the firm Büssing-NAG from 1939 to 1943. It weighed 10.4 tons and reached a maximum speed of 50 km/h. The rear portion of the vehicle super-structure utilized fold-down gates or sides that allowed the antiaircraft gun to traverse 360 degrees. The ammunition was towed on a single-axle trailer. The antiaircraft cannon or Flak (*Flug-Abwehr-Kanone*) 36 L/98 cyclic rate of fire reached between 120 and 160 rounds per minute. High-explosive and armor-piercing ammunition had a maximum range of 6,500 meters and a maximum height of 4,800 meters.[9]

In a church tower, the men observed a window open and close at various intervals. Assuming it was an Allied artillery observation post, the battery placed fire on the tower and consumed their last ammunition. As a result, the three guns were sent back to Arnhem but the crews were retained and employed as infantry. According to Hutwagner, the men were not equipped sufficiently to fight as infantry. He received an MG-42 and held a position, together with a seventeen-year-old SS comrade, along a railroad line leading north. A railroad watchman's blockhouse was 10 meters to the right of the machine-gun position. Behind them on the left were three Army staff sergeants in a position. Twenty meters beyond them were their fellow troopers Hans Ams, Fritz Eckstein, and a soldier from the *Luftwaffe*.[10]

Hutwagner detected British troops moving cautiously forward. Aiming the MG-42, he pulled the trigger but nothing happened. Ams and Eckstein recognized the situation and opened fire. One British soldier was hit and fell to the ground while the remainder scampered into the railroad blockhouse and returned fire. With the enemy merely 10 meters away, Hutwagner and his comrade had no weapon other than the inoperative MG-42. They had no means of defending themselves. Hutwagner observed the British soldiers in the blockhouse as they spread out and studied a map. Shortly thereafter, British snipers reinforced the blockhouse and subjected the German positions to well-aimed rifle fire. Both Ams and Eckstein managed to withdraw to the north where an additional blockhouse stood along a tree line. Hutwagner and his comrade watched as the three German Army soldiers met their fates and the systematic Allied fire shifted onto their position. Suddenly, Hutwanger's seventeen-year-old comrade was severely wounded and a projectile grazed the left side of Hutwagner's head. He summoned his comrade to follow him, but the young wounded soldier explained he was unable to move and would stay behind. Alone, Hutwagner low-crawled back along the rail-line toward the woods. Crossing the railroad tracks brought well-aimed mortar fire down around him. The mortar fire disoriented him as he turned in every direction, hoping to stay alive. When a group of Germans approached him, a genuine feeling of relief overcame Hutwagner. However, the feeling dissipated quickly when he discovered they were a scouting team heading back toward Hutwagner's previous positions. Hutwanger promptly joined the team as they moved forward

until they encountered an Allied artillery position and a concentration of several armored vehicles. Without detection, the team crossed the road and hid in a thicket. When British motorcyclists passed by their hideout, one of the men could not control his anxiety, stood up, and fired on one of the motorcyclists. A good shot knocked the cyclist off his bike, which continued to roll into a wheat field and then fell over. Immediately, a large number of British attacked the position and fired indiscriminately into the thicket. Hutwagner watched as thirty fellow SS troopers were taken prisoner. Together with two *SS-Untersturmführer*, an *SS-Rottenführer*, and an Army staff sergeant, Hutwagner hoped to remain hidden in the thicket until darkness fell. However, around 1700 hours, Belgian resistance fighters discovered their positions and turned the men over to the British. They were led past the Allied artillery position which they had discovered earlier, and into an enclosed farm courtyard. There the men were able to sit down and received food and water. Later, the men were moved to a larger camp with many more prisoners of war. Along the way, French civilians spit on them and made throat-cutting gestures.[11]

Meanwhile, progress for the refreshing and refitting of the 10th SS Panzer Division was jeopardized already after the first day. The German High Command intended to fill the latest gaps in personnel with replacements.

On 7 September, *SS-Sturmbannführer* Gustav Krause, a member of the 9th SS Panzer Division, joined the 10th SS to organize an artillery group in Valkenburg. In addition, *SS-Obersturmführer* Horst König transferred from the Hohenstaufen to the Frundsberg Division. Battery König consisted of no fewer than fifty men and four heavy 100mm guns, towed by trucks instead of prime movers. They received the task of supporting operations with the Blocking Unit Roestel and Kerrut.

Battery Godau consisted of fifty-two men, four light 105mm howitzers, and three trucks of various manufacturers. Considering the batteries of the mechanized 1st Battalion maintained four to five trucks, and the 2nd and 3rd Battalions did not have a single gun, Battery Godau attached to Blocking Unit Heinke. The combat command post Krause of the artillery group situated itself on an east-west axis. Unobserved but registered fire missions were commonplace, as were those called by the artillery group. Commands, supply of gasoline, ammunition, and other sundries were provided solely by the Command Post Krause.[12]

At 1800 hours on 7 September 1944, Field Marshal Gerd von Rundstedt, OB West, released an urgent situation report to Hitler, after a personal discussion with Field Marshal Model. Rundstedt outlined the number of Anglo-American forces occupying Belgium and northern France, which neared fifty-four mechanized or motorized divisions. Supporting these forces from the British Isles were six airborne divisions and thirty divisions reported ready for action on the main land. Rundstedt announced the beginning of the concerted transfer of American forces from the United States. Moreover, he indicated that the British 21st Army Group planned to envelop the German Fifteenth Army between Boulogne and Antwerp with eight to ten divisions and over 600 tanks. A second group of five to six divisions with roughly 400 tanks was estimated ready between Antwerp and Diest, with the task of crossing the Albert Canal and attacking toward Rotterdam and Amsterdam. An additional six to eight divisions, with 400 tanks, were estimated in reserve that could be augmented to either prong of the attack leading into Holland. With the exception of the fortification at Le Havre, where two to three Allied divisions, with support from one hundred tanks, attacked the very important harbor, the fortifications Duenkirchen, Calais, and Boulogne continued to commit badly needed troops to their defense against the British Fifteenth Army. The U.S. Twelfth Army, with fifteen to eighteen divisions and approximately 1,000 tanks, stood across a broad front between Hasselt and Toul, for an attack east and across the Rhine. Rundstedt identified the previous center of gravities for Anglo-American forces in the area between Hasselt, leading east of Namur to the southern heights around the Maas, the area of Charleville-Sedan, and both sides south of Metz.[13]

In sharp contrast, Rundstedt reported that German forces consisted of various battered and partially burned-out combat formations. They lacked artillery and antitank weapons, and reserves were not available. The numerical superiority of Allied tanks was obvious. Army Group B accounted for approximately one hundred operational tanks. The Allied air forces claimed aerial supremacy and controlled the skies deep into the rear areas. Rundstedt pointed out that the Allied advance toward Lüttich, via Aachen, and into the industrial region of Westfallen, would develop into a dangerous situation. Moreover, he advocated stopping the advance immediately with strong forces, at least five or ten divisions with assault guns and sufficient antitank weapons, as well as a number of armored divisions. Rundstedt ordered all available units toward Aachen, including the weak 9th Panzer Division, one weak tank assault battalion, and two assault gun brigades with expected additional assault guns delivered along the way. While Allied airborne operations had not yet taken place, Rundstedt predicted the Allies would conduct airborne landings behind the West Wall and form bridgeheads on the east bank of the Rhine, along their route of advance. The German task, by using the available forces to gain time, was to prepare the western positions and West Wall for a defense. The number of personnel required for the preparation of the western positions, which Rundstedt reported at an earlier date, exceeded 135,000 men. According to the commander of Fortifications West, General of Pioneer Troops Walter Kuntze, the improvements required six weeks. Rundstedt recommended gaining the required time by committing the forces available for combat. To help ensure success, Rundstedt appealed to Hitler for the immediate transfer of available tanks and assault guns, as well as antitank weapons, to resist Allied pressure. Moreover, to carry out Hitler's order for a northwestern attack into the eastern American flank around the region of Epinal, the delivery of 10,000 units of fuel was required as a prerequisite.[14]

The hasty refreshment of both SS divisions progressed away from the fighting and suffered additional setbacks on 10 September. To the complete surprise of all the troops, the OKW directed that one division refit near the front lines while the other refit near the borders of the Reich. Bittrich elected to return the 9th SS Panzer Division to Germany. As soon as the 10th SS Panzer Division learned of the OKW-directive, the planned refitting of the division was no longer considered a realistic goal. Immediately thereafter, the division applied every possible means, through improvisation, to make the division combat ready.[15]

After the Frundsberg Division regrouped in Ruurlo, Harmel gave Richter orders on 8 September, to report to the divisional combat command of the Parachute Division *Kampfgruppe* Colonel Walther. The 1st Battalion, which Richter commanded, would follow after its reconstruction. Immediately, Richter departed in a vehicle with his combat journal writer, his personal messenger *SS-Unterscharführer* Schwingel, and an accompanying motorcycle messenger. Upon the arrival of Richter at the command post of the Parachute Division *Kampfgruppe*, Colonel Walther begged Richter to take command of a battalion that was overrun by British armored spearheads. According to Walther, the former commander lost his nerve and was admitted into a field hospital. Before dark, Richter and his messenger managed to reach the first elements of the unit and brought the situation under control. Before dawn, the reconstituted 2nd Battalion, 22nd *SS-Panzergrenadier* Regiment arrived, which consisted of the remainder of the 1st Battalion staff, a new medical officer, and three grenadier companies each of fifty to sixty men. Their weapons consisted of one carbine and one light machine gun; both were low on ammunition.[16]

On 8 September 1944, the division reorganized to a brigade. The 21st *SS-Panzergrenadier* Regiment was ordered to organize one Antitank Company with twelve antitank guns (75mm Pak) and one mechanized heavy Infantry Cannon Company with four guns. Throughout 9 September, all available heavy and medium antitank gun crews and prime movers transferred to the 21st Regiment. The artillery regiment was to make available three light field howitzers crews for the organization of the heavy Infantry Cannon Company. The location of the transfer was Terwolde. The artillery regiment also received orders on 9 September 1944 to transfer all available tank drivers and radio operators, and report to the combat command post of the tank regiment. The 21st *SS-Panzergrenadier* Regiment and Pioneer Battalion were ordered to relinquish all their half-tracks, both operational and non-operational, to the reconnaissance battalion. All antiaircraft guns, with the exception of Vierlings or quadruple guns, along with their crews and replacement parts but without prime movers, were to be transferred to the 10th SS Panzer Antiaircraft Battalion in Klaarenbeek.[17]

The 6th Company of the tank regiment lost all of its tanks and consisted only of the baggage train and about sixty to seventy men. Their withdrawal into Arnhem led them through Amiens-Albert-Cambrai-Mons-Maastrich. The company occupied civilian quarters in Zupften. The orderly room and company troop, as well as portions of the supply, quartered in the guest house "Graf." Security measures were established and activities focused on establishing an inventory: the amount of vehicles and equipment lost. Detailed reports concerning the loss of individual tanks were of great concern. While the exact dates were essential for keeping good records, Bernhard Westerhoff could not remember what transpired during the confusing withdrawal.

The men of the 6th Company, 10th SS Panzer Regiment enjoyed the life of staging and refitting. Everyone had money and could afford to buy items still available in Holland. Considering that very little could be acquired in Germany, most of the men bought items and sent them home. Larger items were shipped when under official travel orders, but very few enjoyed that privilege. The men did not have conveniences, such as cigarettes and schnapps, which helped soldiers overcome the stress of war.[18]

Comparatively, Westerhoff observed men wearing brown political uniforms and wide belt buckles who had an abundance of these conveniences. They referred to them as "golden peasants." They were the operations managers of the Dutch Front Workers.[19] To acquire the items needed, the men of the 6th Company, 10th SS Panzer Regiment offered the golden pheasants fuel, which was scarce and in high demand for the general public. Contact with the political officials resulted in a proposed trade of 200 liters of fuel for cigarettes, numerous bottles of schnapps, and liquors. The company commander was made aware of the situation. While he knew of such dealings, he also reminded everyone that such activity would be punished severely. In actuality, the men were not thinking of providing 200 liters, but rather 3 to 5 liters. The remainder would be water.

Westerhoff recalled how they filled barrels with water in the courtyard of the Graf. The first section commander then topped off the barrels with 3 liters fuel. The lighter properties of fuel, compared to water, allowed it to float on top. No matter how they turned the barrels, the fuel always floated at the top. The exchange took place without any problems. The tankers got their cigarettes and the political types got their water. While such dealings were highly illegal, the redistribution of comfort products was made more fair than before. The commander also knew of efforts to steal horses, but when he investigated he only heard "I know nothing!"[20]

Frontline Welfare, an effort to improve the morale of the troops, included artistic song and dance exhibitions. However, evenings of comradery were the favorites, even when they were intended mainly to improve a commander's popularity. Friendly relations existed between the German soldiers and the Dutch female population. The Dutch men, on the other hand, often caused trouble by throwing lit cigarettes into the boots of soldiers as a prank. While grenadiers wore their trousers inside their boots, tankers did not have such problems because they wore full-length trousers and quarter-ankle boots.

The enjoyable period did not last very long, and soon the 6th Company relocated to a senior citizens' home in Lochum. In a barracks-like setting, they began classroom instruction on formations of various types. The company relocated several times to various towns along the Dutch-German border, including Bocholt, Elten, Stokkum, Zeddam, Doetinchen, and Hengelo.[21]

Following the orders of Army Group B, the 9th SS Panzer Division made available to the Frundsberg Division combat units, weapons, and motorized vehicles. On 12 September, the 9th SS Panzer Division provided one battalion from the 19th *SS-Panzergrenadier* Regiment, led by *SS-Hauptsturmführer* Karl-Heinz Euling, which was located in Deventer, units from the 9th SS Panzer Artillery Regiment located in Dieren, as well as the weapons and equipment. With the additional units, the 10th SS Panzer Division consisted of two panzer grenadier regiments with a total of four battalions, each consisting of two rifle companies and one heavy company with motorized elements; the tank regiment staff and one tank battalion consisting of eight tanks; one tank reconnaissance battalion, of which portions were motorized and some were equipped with bicycles; the artillery regiment staff with one armored artillery regiment consisting of two battalions, of which the command element was motorized; one partially motorized armored antiaircraft battalion; one armored pioneer battalion with motorized portions; and one armored signals battalion with motorized portions. No tanks were transferred. The 9th SS Panzer Division returned to Germany where it began refitting as well.[22]

SS-Hauptsturmführer Euling, born on 16 August 1919 in Dorndorf, in the Thürischen region of Eisenach, was a good example of an officer with front-line experience. On 22 March 1932, he joined the Hitler Youth and earned the Hitler Youth Proficiency and Golden Honor Clasp. On 1 September 1937, Euling joined the NSDAP. After elementary school, Euling attended a high school and, in February 1938, passed his matriculation examination. On 1 April, he volunteered and joined the *Waffen-SS*. His basic training was completed with the 2nd Company, SS-Death's Head Regiment "Brandenburg," which later participated in the campaign against Poland. After successful completion of the SS Officer Candidates' School in Braunschweig from 1 February to 8 May 1940 and achievements during his service in the 10th SS Infantry Regiment, Euling was promoted on 1 August 1940 to *SS-Untersturmführer*. After being wounded, Euling transferred to the SS Infantry Replacement Battalion "Ost" and again on 1 August 1942, to the 1st SS Infantry Brigade. During his time as a platoon commander, ordnance officer, and regimental adjutant, Euling earned the War Merit Cross 2nd Class and 1st Class with swords, and the Iron Cross 2nd and 1st Class. On 9 November 1943, Euling was promoted to *SS-Hauptsturmführer*. He transferred to the Western Front and joined the staff of the II SS Panzer Corps. In early 1944, Euling headed east and returned to Normandy where he transferred to the 10th SS Panzer Division and assumed command of 1st Battalion, 21st *SS-Panzergrenadier* Regiment.[23]

Meanwhile, the resupply from Germany slowly resumed. Around the same time, the soldiers received confirmation of the long-awaited arrival of the 10th SS Tank Destroyer Battalion, organized and trained in East Prussia, consisting of twenty-seven *Jagdpanthers*. Every effort to find the still missing 1st Battalion (Panther), 10th SS Panzer Regiment remained unsuccessful.[24]

The *Jagdpanther* (SdKfz.173) or Hunting Panther, a heavy tank destroyer, utilized the long barreled 88mm Pak L/71 gun on a Panther chassis. Production by MIAG did not begin until January 1944 and the firm MNH began producing the vehicle in November 1944. The *Jagdpanther* had a crew of five men. It weighed 46 tons propelled by a Maybach HL230P30 engine that could reach a top speed of 46 km/hr. The armor plate thickness and slope at the front superstructure consisted of 80mm/50 degrees, the sides 50/30, and the back 40/35. The gun barrel was protected by a 100mm blended pig's head mantle.[25]

Late in the evening on 14 September, the OB Army Group B attended an operational meeting that took place at the corps' staff headquarters in Doetinchem. They learned the German front lines in the west had hardened significantly during the first half of September. However, German units remained considerably weak and the combat strength of individual units did not exceed 1,500 men. The OB showed particular interest in the speedy refitting of the 10th SS Panzer Division, especially since the 9th SS Panzer Division was on a train heading toward western Germany, as of 12 September. In light of the situation, the meeting adjourned with orders for the divisional commander of the 10th SS to report to the main SS office at Bad Saarow, where the 10th SS was refitting.[26]

As of 16 September, the 10th SS Panzer Division was organized with troops from the 9th SS Panzer Division in the following manner:

Ruurlo	Divisional Staff, elements of the Signals Battalion, Divisional Escort Company, *Feldgendarmerie* Platoon
Borculo-Eibergen	10th SS Panzer Reconnaissance Battalion
Vorden	Staff and 2nd Battalion, 10th SS Panzer Regiment
Deventer	21st *SS-Panzergrenadier* Regiment, Diepenven augmented by one battalion of the 19th *SS-Panzergrenadier* Regiment (9th SS)
Dieren	One battery of the 9th SS-Panzer Artillery Regiment (9th SS)
Rheden	Battalion Euling (of the 20th *SS-Panzergrenadier* Regiment)

The main SS Office in Bad Saarow, which was responsible for providing personnel and materiel for the *Waffen-SS*, had received prior guidance concerning the OKW directive. Replacement personnel for the 9th SS were placed en-route to the area of Siegen in Westfalia, as opposed to Holland.

The high-level command decision provides evidence that the OKW did not anticipate any large-scale Allied airborne operations in Holland. Army Group B approved a request by the II SS Panzer Corps for Heinz Harmel to travel to Bad Saarow one day before the Allied airborne operation began. Harmel personally met with the chief of the main SS office in order to speed the refreshment of the 10th SS. Referring to the orders that his division received from the OB of the Army Group and II SS Panzer Corps, he discussed the need for additional speedy replacements of personnel and materiel. In particular, the commander emphasized the speedy allocation of the 1st Battalion, 10th SS Panzer Regiment, to the division. The main SS office concurred with the extensive request for support and ordered the immediate activation of 1,500 replacements to the division. In the afternoon on 17 September, a telegraph arrived with orders for Harmel to return to his unit. It should be noted that the Germans received information about the impending airborne operations from the Dutch double-agent Christian Lindemans, also known as "King Kong."[27]

Meanwhile, the 2nd Battery, 10th SS Panzer Artillery Regiment attached to the *Kampfgruppe* Walther. The 2nd Battery consisted of only fifty-two men (they were ninety-four at full strength), and four towed 105mm howitzers lFH 18 that were recovered earlier at the rail yard at Cambrai. The battery prime movers, former field kitchen vehicles, were brought out of the encirclement of Falaise. The cook, when necessary, served as a cannonier or telephone operator, depending on the situation. The battery communications equipment consisted of two field telephones, no radios, and only a few rolls of wire. Approximately eighty rounds of ammunition were available. *Kampfgruppe* Walther, comprised of a *Fallschirmjäger* Regiment, covered the area south of the line Valkenswaard-Achel-Hamont-Bree. The 2nd Battery assumed positions along the Dutch and Belgian border, east of the small village of Schaft and about 5 km south of Valkenswaard. The terrain consisted primarily of fields, mixed with high broom and juniper. The limber position was about 400 meters to the west, and the vehicles were concealed in the village of Schaft.

The battery attempted to establish contact with an infantry unit, located 2 km south of the battery position along the northern bank of a canal near a secondary village. No activity suggested the infantry unit was not in position, although their task was to cover the southern road leading to Valkeswaard.[28]

On Sunday 17 September, after 1200 hours, men from the 2nd Battery prepared a birthday cake for the battery commander. As Godau marveled over the decorated cake, the sound of approaching aircraft engines broke up the party and forced them back to the battery positions. Overhead, dozens of Allied aircraft towed transport gliders to the north and low-altitude fighter aircraft fired into the village of Schaft. After two additional fighters flew over the battery without firing a shot, the commotion ended as fast as it began. However, after several minutes, activity on the road sprang to life. A Sherman tank appeared moving at high speed to the north. From the battery, a solitary cry gave coordinates: "Tank from the right! Eight hundred meters!"

The cannoniers lowered the barrels and traversed the guns, but only two batteries in the right-side platoon could engage. As additional tanks followed, Karl Godau withheld the order to open fire. Nine Sherman tanks had already passed by and none stopped to offer a good shot. With only two rounds of armor-piercing ammunition per gun, Godau counted a total of twenty-seven tanks moving in the direction of Valkenswaard. Godau reported the tanks to the battalion and received orders to fall back and change the position of the battery at the next best opportunity.

The battery rear guard, used to protect against pursuing Allied forces, recovered their vehicles. Allied aircraft managed to puncture several vehicle tires, but no losses to personnel were recorded. By 1600 hours, the battery had completed preparations and had begun movement toward the battalion area when darkness fell.[29]

British paratroopers also surprised *SS-Obersturmführer* Gottlob Ellwanger. At his battery command post in front of a guesthouse in Ede, Ellwanger observed a massive armada of C-27 transport aircraft, some towing gliders, flying in the direction of Arnhem, as paratroopers descended from the sky. The antiaircraft battalion commander, *SS-Sturmbannführer* Rudolf Schrembs, was not present, so command of the battalion fell to Ellwanger.

In accordance with orders received from *SS-Sturmbannführer* Otto Paetsch, the temporary commander, the battery conducted reconnaissance during the evening to determine the location of the enemy. In the process, the 1st Platoon gun crew chief *SS-Unterscharführer* van Duellen and Walter Bunzel were killed in action. The platoon leader *SS-Scharführer* Behm received head wounds. *SS-Obersturmführer* Karl Ruedele immediately went into action, providing air defense along the lower Rhine with 20mm machine-gun batteries of the 5th Battery, and shot down seven transport aircraft towing glider transport aircraft.

Ellwanger subordinated Ruedele under his command. The 4th Battery, reinforced by the 20mm antiaircraft machine guns from the grenadier regiments, as well as the 37mm antiaircraft guns on the Pz.Kpfw.IV chassis from the tank regiment, assumed the responsibility of air defense for the ferry service across the Pannerdens Canal. Moreover, the battery was responsible for defending against landed airborne troops in the greater area around Pannerden-Loo-Angeren. In the process, three British aircraft were shot down. The supply section, 4th Battery, was in the school at Didam, while the battery command post was situated in Zevenaar.

The battalion adjutant, during the middle of September, was *SS-Untersturmführer* Otto Stolzenburg. When Stolzenburg transferred to the 3rd Battery, *SS-Untersturmführer* Karl Funk filled the billet as the battalion adjutant.[30]

American and British airborne operations had begun over Holland. By mid-August, a new combined Allied airborne headquarters, the First Allied Airborne Army, planned for airborne operations deep behind enemy lines. The objective, by providing momentum to bring the Allies across the Rhine River, included avoiding potential logistical delays and denying the Germans time to fortify behind the Rhine. Field Marshal Montgomery's Operation Market Garden combined two plans. Operation Market employed three and a half airborne divisions to drop in the vicinity of Grave, Nijmegen, and Arnhem to seize bridges over several canals and the Meuse, Waal (Rhine), and Neder Rijn Rivers. Their objective included opening a corridor more than 50 miles long leading from Eindhoven northward. An air portable division was to be flown in as reinforcement. Operation Garden, using ground troops of the Second British Army, would push from the Dutch-Belgian border to the IJsselmeer (Zuider Zee), a total distance of 99 miles. XXX Corps provided the main effort of the ground attack from a bridgehead across the Meuse-Escaut Canal a few miles south of Eindhoven on the Dutch-Belgian frontier. On either flank the VII and XII Corps were to launch supporting attacks.[31]

The U.S. 101st Airborne Division landed in the area of Eindhoven-Veghel, the U.S. 82nd Airborne Division landed in the area of Grave-Nijmegen, and the British 1st Airborne Division landed at Arnhem. At approximately the same time, British armored forces attacked north from out of the bridgehead at Neerpelt. One of the greatest battles in history, around the area of Arnhem-Nijmegen, unfolded for the II SS Panzer Corps.

The story of Karl Schneider, who did not become a member of the division until 22 September 1944, is an excellent example of how the division acquired new personnel, in a less conventional manner. Karl Schneider was born on 19 July 1925 in Rhinebishofsheim. On 5 October 1942, at the age of seventeen, he entered the RAD. His basic army training was completed at the Lorette Barracks, in Karlsruhe, with the 4th Company, 111th Training and Replacement Grenadier Regiment. He received additional training in Rambervillers, France, before departing to the Eastern Front. After the middle of December 1943, Schneider joined the 4th Heavy Machine Gun Company, 1st Battalion, 111th Infantry Regiment, 35th Infantry Division, as part of Army Group Center. He held the rank of Private 1st Class.

Fragments from a hand grenade wounded his left leg and foot on 2 March 1944. Schneider arrived at the field hospital in Thorn, West Prussia, and later transferred to the Military Hospital in Brussels, Belgium. In the middle of June 1944, Schneider returned to duty with the Rehabilitation Company of the 111th Grenadier Replacement Battalion, stationed in Vlissingen, Walcheren. After the Allied landings at Normandy and breakout from the bridgehead into France, the Rehabilitation Company, commanded by 1st Lieutenant Gebauer, was called into action at the beginning of August with other Army units against British armored spearheads west of Antwerp. The Rehabilitation Company was almost completely annihilated during the fighting at Beveren and Antwerp. Wounded a second time by a fragment that stuck in his left knee, Schneider managed, with the help of his comrades, to fight his way to safety across the Schelde River. As a straggler crossing the Waal River aboard a ferry at Gorinchem, Holland, he was absorbed on 26 August 1944, along with others retreating out of France, into the 4th SS Police Training and Replacement Battalion. The *Auffangskommando* or Collections Detachment on the ferry wore the SS Police Division cuff bands. Schneider thought them to belong to the *Feldgendarmerie*. The battalion established a collection point in Gorinchem, and a command post in a nearby sugar factory.

An *SS-Scharführer* escorted Schneider and others from various service branches to the sugar factory to determine their unit origination. In the factory on 26 August 1944, the *Waffen-SS* absorbed Schneider into their ranks. He received a field gray uniform jacket with SS collar tabs and the rank of *SS-Rottenführer*. The entry in his service book read, "Collected on 26.08.1944 and issued to the 6th Company, 4th *SS-Panzergrenadier* Training and Replacement Battion (Police)." His Army rank as Private 1st Class was crossed out and replaced with *SS-Rottenfuehrer*. With the stroke of a pencil, he was made a member of the *Waffen-SS*. The tattoo commonly applied to all SS soldiers under the left arm, which indicated their blood type, was not administered to Schneider on that day since he was underway to Utrecht as the driver for the one-armed and one-eyed company commander, *SS-Untersturmführer* Puder. As a vehicle driver for the 4th SS Training and Replacement Battalion, Schneider was quartered at the sugar factory at Gorinchem.[32]

Around noon on Sunday 17 September 1944, Karl Schneider observed Allied fighters protecting hundreds of transport aircraft flying in the direction of Germany and towing airborne gliders. Everyone knew that something big was underway. By 1400 hours, the alarm sounded with reports of Allied airborne landings at Arnhem and Nijmegen. British paratroopers were reported to have established a toehold west of Arnhem.

Orders arrived in Gorinchem for all combat-capable troops to close with the enemy immediately in motorized march. The 6th Company, under the command of Puder, deployed as part of elements from the 4th SS Training and Replacement Battalion, under the command of *SS-Hauptsturmführer* Mattusch. All available vehicles were fueled and loaded with weapons and ammunition. By 1600 hours, units began departing. Schneider drove a Ford V-8 truck, loaded with two groups of men. Despite several attacks by Allied fighter aircraft, the convoy arrived at 1800 hours in Wageningen, where all units were directed further onto Rekumer-Heide.

Upon arrival, Schneider could hear clearly the sound of combat in the landing zone of the British 1st Airborne Division. The handicapped company commander issued orders to attack, and they encountered the enemy a few minutes north of Heelsum. The exchange of fire continued throughout the night. Bitter individual close combat developed using pistols, submachine guns, and hand grenades. The front lines were everywhere where there was gunfire. Flares continuously lit up the night, but it was impossible to determine friend or foe.

Under the cover of darkness, during a moonless night, British airborne forces opposing the 4th SS Police Training and Replacement Battalion withdrew in the direction of Wolfheze, where they regrouped with other airborne forces.[33]

The experience of Karl Schneider was very similar to that of Rudi Trapp and his comrades. Enjoying a bite to eat during a beautiful late summer afternoon, they observed an armada of aircraft passing overhead. Alarm!

Rudi Trapp was born on 27 July 1925 in Iserlohn. A member of the division since it organized in 1943, he was the *Schütze* 1 or first gunner, in the Machine Gun Platoon, 3rd Company, Half-track Battalion Laubscher, 1st Battalion, 21st *SS-Panzergrenadier* Regiment. *SS-Obersturmführer* Ernst Vogel, who left the battalion shortly after its organization in 1943, returned to command the battalion. Around the Dutch village of Deventer, the battalion assembled to reorganize with replacements that arrived from the 9th SS Panzer Division and the 10th SS Training and Replacement Battalion, from Brünn.

Trapp and his comrades Adolf Lochbrunner and Jupp Wagner, all of whom attended divisional combat school together, oversaw individual group combat training for the new replacements. Of the original 3rd Company, only twelve men survived along with few weapons, including several MG-42s.[34]

From the staff quarters in Doetinchem, the II SS Panzer Corps, after receiving the first reports of Allied airborne landings, alerted the 10th SS Panzer Division and remaining elements of the 9th SS Panzer Division. The commander of the 10th SS Panzer Division, located at the main SS office in Bad Saarow, was ordered by telegram to return to his troops. Around 1600 hours, the II SS Panzer Corps ordered the 10th SS Panzer Division to proceed immediately via Arnhem to Nijmegen, occupy both bridges over the Waal River, and establish and hold a bridgehead south of the city. All applicable German troops near Nijmegen were attached to the division.

The 9th SS Panzer Reconnaissance Battalion, commanded by *SS-Untersturmführer* Viktor-Eberhard Gräbner, consisting of approximately thirty armored half-tracks and scouting vehicles, attached to the 10th SS Panzer Division to reconnoiter from Arnhem to Nijmegen. In exchange, the 10th SS Panzer Division released their reconnaissance battalion, commanded by Brinkmann, to the *Kampfgruppe* 9th SS Panzer Division.[35]

Conflicting reports exist regarding the assignment of the 9th SS Panzer Reconnaissance Battalion on 17 September. According to Bittrich, the 9th SS Panzer Reconnaissance Battalion received orders to reconnoiter to the west over Arnhem to Nijmegen, and seize and hold open the bridges assigned to the 9th SS that lay closer to Allied drop zones. Later, when the 10th SS Panzer Division arrived at Nijmegen, the 10th SS was to attach itself to the reconnaissance battalion of the 9th SS already on location. On the other hand, Harmel maintained the 9th SS Panzer Reconnaissance Battalion was attached to the 10th SS from the very beginning, which accounted for the detachment of the 10th SS Panzer Reconnaissance Battalion.

Considering the circumstances and in order to save time, it was more practical to employ the 9th SS Panzer Reconnaissance Battalion instead of the 10th SS Panzer Reconnaissance Battalion, the latter of which was located 50 aerial kilometers from Nijmegen. The immediate subordination of the 9th SS Panzer Reconnaissance Battalion to the 10th SS is not plausible in light of the fact it reconnoitered to the west of Arnhem as well. Bittrich's version of events seems more credible. The fact that the 10th SS Panzer Reconnaissance Battalion went into action at the Arnhem bridge, as part of the 9th SS, was not foreseen when orders were issued in the afternoon on 17 September.[36]

At approximately 1800 hours, the 9th SS Panzer Reconnaissance Battalion arrived at the city of Arnhem, broke through weak defenses at the bridge crossing the lower Rhine, and continued in the direction of Nijmegen.

The 10th SS Panzer Reconnaissance Battalion reconnoitered toward Arnhem and continued over Emmerich against Nijmegen. Heading in the direction of Wesel, Allied airborne drops were reported.

Around 1900, the 1st Scout Company made reconnaissance toward Arnhem and reported the bridge at Arnhem, and reinforcement thereof, to be in Allied hands. The acting divisional commander Paetsch was en route from Ruurlo to Velp with elements of the command staff. The Allies controlled antiaircraft bunkers next to the bridge and gained considerable strength. Soon thereafter, additional elements of the 10th SS Panzer Reconnaissance Battalion arrived in Arnhem. Brinkmann, the commander of the reconnaissance battalion, received orders to attack with the attached *Kampfgruppe* 9th SS, commanded by *SS-Obersturmbannführer* Harzer, and destroy the enemy at the northern approach to the bridge with the objective to open the divisional route of advance on Nijmegen. In this respect, the section was placed under orders of *Kampfgruppe* Spindler, of the 9th SS Panzer Division.[37]

The 5th Battalion, SS Artillery Training and Replacement Regiment, commanded by the former member of the SS Polizei Division, *SS-Hauptsturmführer* Oskar Schwappacher, situated the staff, Staff Battery, and the 21st Heavy Howitzers Battery east of Oosterhout. The forward observers were on the northern banks of the Waal southwest of Oosterhout and 1 km west of Neerbosch. The 19th Light Howitzer Battery relocated from Zaltbommel to join the staff throughout 19 and 20 September. To improve observation on the bridge at Arnhem and within the center of the city, Schwappacher placed the forward observers of the 21st Battery southwest of Oosterhout. Both batteries provided effective rifle and cannon fire from four 20mm antiaircraft guns of the 21st Battery against low-flying aircraft. The staff and 21st Battery succeeded in shooting down two planes.[38]

By the evening on 17 September, Paetsch ordered the formation of *Kampfgruppe* Reinhold. Paetsch intended the task force to follow the 9th SS Panzer Reconnaissance Battalion into Nijmegen. The very able and experienced *SS-Sturmbannführer* Leo Reinhold, commander of the 2nd Battalion, 10th SS Panzer Regiment, commanded *Kampfgruppe* Reinhold.

Leo Reinhold was born on 22 February 1906 in the East Prussian capital city of Königsberg. In 1928, Reinhold joined the police as a candidate and transferred to the *Wehrmacht* in 1935. As a first lieutenant in the Army protective police, he returned to the municipal police force in January 1939, only to return to active military duty one month later, as an antitank company commander in the 4th SS Polizei Division. In June 1940, during the campaign in the west, Reinhold earned the Iron Cross 2nd Class. In the east, in September 1941, he received the Iron Cross 1st Class and qualified to wear the wound badge in silver. On 10 March 1943, Reinhold transferred to the Frundsberg Division as a battalion commander in the 10th SS Panzer Regiment. On 17 September, Reinhold was awarded the German Cross in Gold for his exploits in the east at Buczacz and Pilwa, in the west at Hill 112, Esquay, and Hill 188.[39]

The *Kampfgruppe* consisted of the *SS-Panzergrenadier* Battalion Euling, which was released several days earlier from the 9th SS, the 2nd Battalion, 10th SS Panzer Regiment, made up of sixteen to twenty Pz.Kpfw.IV, a light howitzer battalion of the 10th SS Panzer Artillery Regiment, and one company of the 10th SS Panzer Pioneer Battalion.

After Battalion Euling departed from Rheden in the late evening and arrived in the hard-fought section of the city, the armored scouting vehicles of the forward-most elements joined in the fight alongside the reconnaissance battalion. The bulk of Battalion Euling closed on Arnhem directly southeast of the city.

The 10th SS Panzer Reconnaissance Battalion and forward elements of Battalion Euling engaged together in fierce street and house-to-house fighting against a determined and experienced opponent. The German attack was broken off after only nominal gains. From positions around Oosterbeek along the northern banks of the lower Rhine, the Allies reinforced the bridge at Arnhem with heavy and antitank weapons. By midnight it was apparent that clearing the bridge of Allied forces would require a planned advance and more time. Portions of the 10th SS Panzer Division following the Battalion Euling were intercepted and brought to rest east of Velp.

After the first reports of Allied airborne landings in the southern sector of the city, Colonel Henke of the 1st Parachute Training Staff, located at the Nebo Monastery south of the city, sounded the alarm for all ground units quartered in Nijmegen. With men from the homeland defense units, permanent personnel of the training staff, men from the railroad security guard, and stragglers from fragmented units, Henke secured the southern rim of the city and occupied a bridgehead across the Waal. His mission was to keep open both bridges along the northern riverbanks to the north of the city, with his left and right flank leaned against the rim of the village of Lent.[40]

Allied parachute and airborne glider troops had already landed around Arnhem when orders arrived directing the 3rd Company, 1st Battalion, 21st *SS-Panzergrenadier* Regiment into action. The mission was to attack forward toward the Rhine and the bridge at Arnhem. Lacking vehicles, the men acquired bicycles from the general population. Trapp encountered several Army stragglers fleeing the city, many yelling, "Run away! The Tommies have landed!"

At the outskirts of the village, the men abandoned their bicycles and proceeded forward in a tactical column. Close to the front of the houses, the 3rd Company, 21st *SS-Panzergrenadier* Regiment, moved ever closer to the bridge. The civilian population was nowhere to be seen, and the homes seemed abandoned.

After crossing several streets, the machine-gun company approached individual British airborne supply canisters that littered the road. The search of nearby houses began immediately when small arms fire erupted from all sides. Lacking weapons, the Germans recovered weapons and ammunition from dead British soldiers. The process of ferreting out British paratroopers, hiding in the compartmentalized alleyways of the inner city, proved very difficult. House-to-house close combat became a necessity, and several entryways were found mined with improvised explosive devices. Slowly, the German perimeter around the paratroopers tightened. When German troops reached the Rhine River by the evening, the Arnhem Bridge was in view. British defensive fire intensified and the fighting continued throughout the night, from house to house. No soldier thought about sleep.

As the German troops pressed forward, Rudi Trapp emplaced his heavy machine gun tactically to provide covering fire at various street corners. British paratroopers tried evading the encirclement and ran from one house to another. Wounded British shared Trapp's position. One British soldier had been hit in the testicle and was in severe pain. Trapp and other SS men evacuated wounded British from the front lines and brought them to the rear for medical attention. The Germans recovered Dutch civilians, also wounded during the fighting. Among the Dutch was a severely injured woman. Civilians hiding in the cellars were forced out into the open when many homes caught fire during the fighting.

Supplies arrived during the night for Trapp and his comrades. They received *Panzerfausts*, ammunition, and assault rifles. However, basic food provisions were not included. The men looted food stocks from nearby abandoned cellars, which primarily consisted of pickled fruit. A chocolate warehouse was located along the Rhine River road, but no trace of chocolate was found. A three-wheel bicycle found in a warehouse was impounded and used to carry weapons, ammunition, and heavy guns to and from the front lines.

Luftwaffe forward observers arrived amidst the rubble and sketched out the terrain where Trapp and his company were located. These sketches were given to Stuka divebomber squadrons to guide them in precision bombing sorties. In the end the Stukas never came. Actually, Trapp was very happy the Stukas did not come, considering he was the recipient of the botched close air support during the fighting at Buczacz.

Instead, ground support arrived in the form of an Army field howitzer. The gun provided direct fire support, from the Rhine road, for the attacks. The gun effectively placed preparatory assault fire on several houses, which were later overrun by Trapp and his company. Many of the British defenders were killed in their fighting holes from falling debris.[41]

Kampfgruppe Henke was not equipped or trained well enough to engage in battle. The *Kampfgruppe* consisted of approximately 750 primarily older men, and a number of antiaircraft batteries to protect the bridge and provide antitank defenses. *Kampfgruppe* Henke was organized in the following manner:

HQ Henke Parachute Training Regiment

6 Replacement Battalions
(consisting of 3 companies)

Herman Göring Company Runge

NCO School Company

Railway Guards/Police Reservists
(consisting of 2 companies)

Antiaircraft Battery
(88mm & 20mm guns, dispersed)

Nijmegen remained free of Allied forces until dark. However, during the night on 18 September, the Allies managed to push German security forces back into the inner city.

In the evening on 17 September, forward scouts of the 9th SS Reconnaissance Battalion reported back to the battalion that Nijmegen and both bridges were in German hands. Moreover, no Allied attacks against the bridges were reported. The battalion commander Gräbner foresaw a threat by Allied forces and ordered it to return to Arnhem, rather than scouting against Nijmegen. South of Elst, Gräbner permitted scouts to contact the *Kampfgruppe* at Nijmegen. Portions of the 9th SS Panzer Reconnaissance Battalion returned to Arnhem during the night on 18 September. Heavy casualties were suffered on the Rhine Bridge. Burning armored half-tracks littered the entire width of the road. The residual elements remained on the southern banks and sealed off the bridge along a front, facing north, barring the Allies from advancing from the south. The small contingency prevented the Allies from capturing the southern approach to the bridge.[42]

Around midnight, the 10th SS Panzer Division received superseding orders from the II SS Panzer Corps that diverted the division from their original route of march over Arnhem. Instead, they were directed to travel southeast of Arnhem over the lower Rhine and utilize a ferry service. From there, the division was to capture Nijmegen and establish a bridgehead on the southern bank of the Waal; both bridges were to be prepared for demolition.

Immediately, the division placed the *Kampfgruppe* Reinhold in march over Zevenaar and then on to Pannerden. The 1st Company of the 10th Pioneer Battalion assumed the lead at the point. The objective was to propel the 1st Company, 10th SS Panzer Pioneer Battalion, forward against Nijmegen, after crossing the lower Rhine (Pannerdian Canal) at the ferry cross-over points with rubber assault boats and other acquired boats. Together with the 9th SS Panzer Reconnaissance Battalion, expected to arrive at any moment, the pioneer company was to be attached to the local unit and facilitate ejecting the Allies, who had infiltrated the city during the night. Moreover, the 1st Company, 10th SS Panzer Pioneer Battalion, was tasked with the preparation for the demolition of both Waal bridges. Army Group B reserved the right to rescind the order to blow up the bridges.

The decisive task around Nijmegen fell to the 10th SS Panzer Division: to prevent the American 82nd Airborne Division from making contact with the British 1st Airborne Division at Arnhem. Nonetheless, while the entire division knew of the objective, *Kampfgruppe* Reinhold was responsible for preventing a link before the bulk of the division arrived at the battlefield.

Considering the pioneer and antiaircraft battalions that were detached earlier but particularly needed at the crossing-points west of Pannerden, the bulk of the 10th SS Panzer Division redirected over Doesburg and Doetinchem.[43]

During the first morning hours on 18 September, the Allies attempted to expand their bridgehead north of the Arnhem Bridge. Battalion Euling engaged the attackers and thwarted the Allied attempt. Around 0400 hours, Battalion Knaust, a training and replacement battalion, arrived with four weak companies, consisting of wounded or disabled soldiers, and ten older tanks along the northeastern fringe of Arnhem. Bittrich ordered the Battalion Knaust attached to the *Kampfgruppe* Brinkmann. The battalion replaced Battalion Euling, squad for squad, to allow the latter to resume its mission as part of *Kampfgruppe* Reinhold. However, the relief took longer than expected as individual groups from the battalion engaged in close combat.

Around the same time, the commander of the division Heinz Harmel returned from Bad Saarow and arrived at the forward divisional combat command post at Velp. After a short orientation by the 1st General Staff officer, Harmel made his way to the entrenched *Kampfgruppe* Brinkmann, located near the bridge along the outskirts of the city. Every house and every floor was bitterly contested. Harmel ordered the employment of a divisional light howitzer battery in the gardens along the road approaching the bridge; the houses on the opposite side were taken under direct fire. Shortly thereafter, Harmel reported to the commanding general of the II SS Panzer Corps (within the immediate vicinity) and assumed command of the battle around the Arnhem Bridge.

In terms of additional armored assistance, only a single company of old Army Tigers were available to support combat operations of the 10th SS on 19 September. The veteran Army captain Hans Hummel commanded the company of Tigers, which gained experience during the fighting in Sicily, at which time Hummel was wounded when he commanded the 2nd Company, 504th Heavy Panzer Battalion. The company organized as an alarm unit in early July 1944, for which Hummel gathered members of his former company from the *Wehrkreiskommando* Münster, the *Wehrmacht* District IV. The company, christened Heavy Panzer Company Hummel, was specifically organized to support the coup d'état against Hitler on 20 July.

The Heavy Panzer Company Hummel received the alarm and activated on 18 September at Sennelager. The company unloaded at the train station at Bocholt. From the station, they traveled 80 km, but only two Tigers, those belonging to Lieutenant Knack and Sergeant Barneki, reached Arnhem. The remaining tanks suffered from mechanical failures but arrived in Arnhem shortly thereafter.[44]

Meanwhile, in accordance with the OKH directive of 15 August 1944, the 506th Heavy Panzer Battalion was refitted and freely organized in Ohrdruf with King Tigers or Tiger IIs. Under the new organization, the staff and tank companies reassigned the supply and service units into a supply company. The battalion staff and staff companies were amalgamated with the flak platoons. Under the command of Army Major Lange, forty-five King Tigers were allocated to the battalion between 20 August and 12 September. During the training that emphasized contending with aerial threats, several vehicles caught on fire. The fuel-line linkages on many tanks were not completely sealed and the fuel reservoir access ports were located too close to the very hot exhaust pipes. Despite inspections by members of the *Heereswaffenamtes* or Army Ordnance Department, the deficiencies were never adequately corrected.[45]

Upon the arrival of two Tigers from the Heavy Tank Company Hummel, *Kampfgruppe* Brinkmann and all its elements returned under the control of the 10th SS Panzer Division. According to Harmel, Field Marshal Model ordered the 10th SS Panzer Division to fight to open a line of communication to Nijmegen, and ensure for the speedy resupply of all German units in that area.

The commander of the 10th SS Panzer Division personally led the attack against the bridge throughout the entire day and night of 19 September. The divisional combat command post was moved throughout 18 September from Velp to Pannerden.[46]

Army Major Hans-Peter Knaust, commanding Battalion Bocholt, led by example and with a wooden prosthetic leg. The battalion displayed its worth during the attack against the bridge by ensnarling the enemy, from house to house, in close combat for hours. The defending soldiers of the British 1st Airborne Division fought courageously but at a great cost. According to Heinz Harmel, the fighting spirit and skill of the British airborne equaled his own division; Harmel considered them honorable and just in battle.[47]

On Monday morning, 18 September, additional Allied paratroopers landed on the opposite side of the river. Trapp and his few remaining comrades were surrounded. Trapp mounted the heavy machine gun on a tripod, for better targeting. However, he was out of ammunition.

A half-track arrived in order to recover the men killed in action from between the opposing two lines of battle.[48] Trapp manned the two vehicle machine guns and provided cover fire as the vehicle descended into the fight. One soldier was killed when

hit in the heart after a projectile traveled through his *Soldbuch* or soldier's pay book. He was barely nineteen years old.

The 3rd Machine Gun Company retained the half-track; it was the only vehicle in the sector between the church tower and the ramp to the river bridge. Using the half-track, Trapp and two other SS troopers were selected to establish contact with the adjacent *Kampfgruppe*, locked in combat beyond the ramp of the bridge. To achieve their objective, they had to pass under the ramp. The remaining company machine guns were to suppress the British antitank gun emplaced along the bridge, which had excellent observation across the roads along the riverbanks. Bernd Schulz, a farmer from Sendenhorst near Münster, was one of the last of the old fighters and was assigned as a driver. During the situation briefing, Schulz began to cry and had a bad feeling about the mission. Despite his misgivings, the men carefully stuffed their camouflage jacket pockets full of egg hand grenades and belts of ammunition for the MG-42.

No sooner had the half-track sped across the intersection when an antitank projectile hit the driver-side of the vehicle. The half-track lurched to a stop; Schulz was killed instantly when the projectile hit him. The two remaining men exited the vehicle and darted into a demolished house, which was between two Allied defensive positions. In order to escape their predicament, Trapp provided suppressing machine-gun fire as his comrade ran across the street. As Trapp prepared to cross, several British soldiers suddenly surrounded Trapp. Using hand grenades to keep the British at bay, Trapp escaped across the street and jumped over a river wall and into the Rhine. After removing his wet clothing on the back of a half-sunken dredge, he swam toward friendly lines in his undergarments, armed only with a pistol. Shortly thereafter, Trapp reached his unit and received replacement clothing and equipment from fallen comrades. For Trapp, the fighting continued until he was wounded in Elst, when a bullet hit his knee. He was evacuated to the rear in a half-track, along with the commander of the *Kampfgruppe* Knaust. The major showed Trapp his wooden leg and commented, "Don't worry. I was able to walk again."[49]

SS-Hauptsturmführer Schwappacher personally made several reconnaissance excursions into the area around Nijmegen earlier that morning to clarify the situation, which allowed him to place heavy artillery fire on Allied troop concentrations around Berg en Dal. Around 1000 hours Allied forces moving north toward the city were subjected to observed artillery, as well as on the main approaches east of the city. Around noon, Allied troops attacking northward that reached the road-triangle at the southern rim of the bridge were stopped by artillery fire from batteries of the 5th Company, SS Artillery Training and Replacement Regiment. Additional artillery fire allowed infantry from the Herman Göring Company Runge and the forward observers to relocate to the northeast along the railroad line. Schwappacher managed to gain considerable advantages with a single heavy artillery battery that gained fire control over the entire area of operations.[50]

The 1st Company, 10th SS Panzer Pioneer Battalion, crossed the lower Rhine at Pannerden first and reached the bridge at Nijmegen, on 18 September, in vehicles and bicycles. However, the 9th SS Panzer Reconnaissance Battalion had yet to arrive at their forward position at the Nijmegen Bridge. Both German and British forces engaged in costly street fighting in the center of the city. Members of the Dutch underground also participated in the fighting.

Around midday on 18 September, the commander of *Kampfgruppe* Reinhold arrived from Pannerden-Bemmel at the Waal River Bridge. Located south of Lent, Reinhold arrived with Battalion Euling, but missing those elements that could not be disengaged in time from the fighting at Arnhem. The timely arrival of Euling allowed nearby homeland defense units and the 2nd SS Pioneers to provide the additional energy needed to ward off several Allied attacks against the Waal bridges. Shortly thereafter, the half-track company and battalion staff of Battalion Euling rolled across the bridge at full speed. The bridge was under fire by Allied artillery. The remainder of the battalion arrived throughout the afternoon in trucks and on bicycles. However, due to the increase of artillery fire, only portions of the battalion managed to cross the bridge. Other portions of the battalion crossed the river upstream in rubber rafts. *SS-Hauptsturmführer*

Euling established his combat command post in the city citadel, between the two bridges of Nijmegen. Local troops fighting under the command of Major Ahlborn were subordinated to Battalion Euling. The 9th SS Panzer Reconnaissance Battalion reported the bulk of the battalion to be located at Elst and, according to rumor, designated as the division reserve. According to Harmel, the *Kampfgruppe* 9th SS Panzer Division requested the return of the 9th SS Panzer Reconnaissance Battalion to the II SS Panzer Corps. Sensing a certain lack of dependability, Harmel ordered the battalion to secure their lines south of Elst, launch an attack to stop an Allied advance from Nijmegen to the north, and reconnoiter points of opportunity against new airborne landings south of Arnhem.[51]

Around 2000 hours on 18 September, stray Allied machine-gun fire damaged the radio belonging to *SS-Cannonier* Albrecht, 21st Battery, 5th Company, SS Artillery Training and Replacement Regiment. Participating in an infantry counterattack, Albrecht managed to climb onto a Sherman tank and knocked out the vehicle by dropping a hand grenade into the open turret.[52]

Late in the morning on 19 September, Battery Godau, of the Blocking Unit Heinke, relocated from their positions west of Budel. The battery relocated south of Weert. Moreover, the bridge across the Zuid-Willemsvaart was prepared for demolition.[53]

Despite the lack of a German unit command structure west of Arnhem, the Allied landing zones at Oosterbeek were contained and Allied movement was constricted as *Kampfgruppe* Brinkmann slowly managed to gain ground. The road leading to the bridge lay only several hundred meters before the *Kampfgruppe*. The Allies formed a formidable and tough defensive group around the city church. The German center of gravity shifted for the attack to gain access to the defenders.

At Pannerden, the 10th SS Panzer Pioneer Battalion built a 70-ton pontoon ferry that enabled tanks from the 2nd Battalion, 10th SS Panzer Regiment to reinforce *Kampfgruppe* Reinhold. Wary of Allied aerial reconnaissance, the first tanks did not cross until after nightfall.

During the afternoon on 19 September, the Allies launched a concerted attack at Nijmegen and employed heavy tanks for the first time. This provided evidence that the Allied armored forces, the British Guards Armoured Division of XXX Corps, commanded by Lieutenant General B. G. Horrocks, which attacked on 17 September to the north out of the bridgehead at Neerpelt, had linked with the U.S. 82nd Airborne Division. Moreover, heavy artillery fire supported and preceded the attack. At the onset, heavy Allied flanking machine-gun fire was placed on the Waal bridges from the west that threatened German communications and resupply traffic. However, the Allied attack against the bridgehead was thwarted with the help of the timely arrival of elements of the 10th SS. Bitter street fighting caused fires to break out in the northern sectors of the city. The poor weather that had dominated the last several days prevented any additional airborne landings.[54]

Between 17 and 19 September, and in response to the Allied airborne operations, K. Mahler drove a small detachment of men from the 6th Company, 10th SS Panzer Regiment, into action at Arnhem. The majority of the 6th Company was either in Germany undergoing training or looking for tanks.[55]

Late in the morning on 19 September the main line of battle remained relatively quiet; however, the 5th Company, SS Artillery Training and Replacement Regiment, combated Allied assembly points at the southern rim of Nijmegen and tank concentrations along the road leading from Nijmegen to the southwest. *SS-Scharführer* Hotop of the 21st Battery placed well-observed fire against troops on the road and disabled two Sherman tanks operating near the railroad line. A second Allied attack against the bridge around 1400 hours also received well-observed artillery fire from the 21st Battery, called by the commander of the main forward observation post, *SS-Hauptsturmführer* Horst Krüger. One Allied tank was knocked out by an antitank gun, and projectiles from the 21st Battery landed 300 meters south of the bridge, forcing the remaining Allied tanks to break off the attack. Moreover, *SS-Scharführer* Hotop succeeded that evening in disrupting two tank assembly areas west of the railroad and, through the application of short combat fire sets, beat off a closed tank assault.[56]

After heavy night fighting at the Arnhem Bridge, *Kampfgruppe* Brinkmann, reinforced by the 10th SS Panzer Reconnaissance Battalion and Battalion Knaust, began operations on 20 September, in close combat with flamethrowers and *Panzerfausts*, to eliminate individual nests of resistance. A portion of the group of houses that lay near the church caught on fire, whereby plumes of smoke reduced Allied observation. As a result, the *Kampfgruppe* managed to shorten the distance to the bridge. In the process, a number of severely wounded Allied soldiers were taken prisoner. In the afternoon, an Allied prisoner divulged the fact that the Allied fighting spirit had wavered and the situation had become hopeless. Consequently, the Allied commander of the defensive bridgehead was asked to surrender. He did not concede and the fight for the bridge continued, without result, throughout the entire night.

West of Arnhem, *Kampfgruppe* Harzer of the 9th SS further compressed the Allies and eliminated any possibilities of relief or reinforcement in Arnhem.

On the same day in Nijmegen, the Allies renewed their attacks from the east against the northern sector of the city after additional forces, consisting of tanks, artillery, and engineers, were brought forward. Battalion Euling, reinforced by the 1st Company, 10th SS Panzer Pioneer Battalion, and other local ground units, mounted a bitter defense. Batteries from the 5th Company, SS Artillery Training and Replacement Regiment, placed well-observed artillery fire directed by *SS-Hauptsturmführer* Krüger onto the road, which slowed their advance. The German bridgehead reached 1 km in width but only 300 meters in depth. The right boundary ended along the railroad line whereas the left boundary ran approximately 100 meters east of the bridge road. German artillery repeatedly beat off Allied attempts to attack the position. Krüger's forward observation post brought artillery fire to bear against the Allies within 100 meters of the German position.

Allied Typhoons bombed and strafed the northern banks of the Waal while British preparatory artillery and tank fire, along with heavy white phosphorus smoke, allowed the first of two battalions from the 504th Parachute Infantry Regiment of Brigadier

General James M. Gavin's "All American" 82nd Airborne Division to conduct a diversionary assault across the Waal, west of the city, and secure a foothold on the northern bank.

The 21st Heavy Howitzer Battery of the 5th Company, SS Artillery Training and Replacement Regiment, fired against tank and troop assemblies without respite from its location in Nijmegen, but also provided effective blocking fire on the main roads. All available guns fired onto a main artery. The 19th Light Howitzer Battery fired against Allied landings on the northern and southern banks of the Waal. The 5th Company, SS Artillery Training and Replacement Regiment, provided observation and fire direction for the 19th Battery that subjected American troops crossing the Waal to 250 rounds of sustained destructive fire, as well as thirty minutes of slow harassing fire that hit several landing boats and caused high numbers of casualties. The Alarm Platoon, led by *SS-Untersturmführer* Friedrich Brandsch, dispatched to the area around Valburg to combat Allied paratroopers. However, Schwappacher recalled the Alarm Platoon in order to provide patrols and secure the area of operations of the 5th Battalion. *SS-Untersturmführer* Alfons Büttner received orders to defend against advancing Allied troops moving north and northwest. His mission was to hold the Damn Road south of Oosterhout. With vehicle drivers and members of the staff, they fought Allied troops with rifle and machine-gun fire. During the most critical period shortly after 1500 hours, many of the men that held the defensive line along the Damn Road, including *Fallschirmjägers*, members of the RAD, as well as antiaircraft batteries, suddenly withdrew in order to obtain ammunition. Schwappacher, who went to great effort to establish a defensive line during the night 19–20 September, was left only with fifteen men, including drivers and the battalion staff that held the line. Schwappacher ordered forming a defensive hedgehog position with the 21st and Staff Batteries.

Around 1700 hours, following the decoy crossing further upstream, Allied armored forces attacked both bridges at Nijmegen after artillery fire and smoke landed on both banks of the Waal River, northeast of Lent. Portions of the 1st Company,

10th SS Panzer Pioneer Battalion, which were engaged at the southern approaches to the bridge, immobilized several Allied tanks with close-quarter weapons. Nevertheless, large numbers of additional tanks at high speeds, supported by armored half-tracks, could not be prevented from crossing the bridge. While the Army Group B remained in control of the bridge, approval to blow up the bridge could not be obtained soon enough before the Allies rolled across and as far as Lent.[57]

One hour later the 5th Company, SS Artillery Training and Replacement Regiment formed a hedgehog position and continuously sent scouting patrols that maintained contact with the enemy with small arms fire. The small contingency of men holding the Damn Road were withdrawn to the northwestern portion of Oosterhout, after Schwappacher personally led a diversionary counterattack around 1900 hours with two assault groups against the road, south of Oosterhout. While the assault groups managed to take control of the center and southern exits of Oosterhout, they were unable to capture the Damn Road entirely. The cost of the counterattack included one dead and two wounded.[58]

Heinz Harmel was in Lent when he received the news of the Allied crossing and ordered the bridge blown up. However, the demolition failed. Apparently, shrapnel or small arms fire had damaged the detonation cable.

After a brief respite from Allied preparatory fire along the southern outskirts of Lent, Allied tanks infiltrated the village and broke the resistance of the poorly armed and trained Home Defense units and elements of the 1st Company, 10th SS Panzer Pioneer Battalion. The Allies pushed through Lent and north, but slowed and moved forward cautiously after sustaining losses from the effects of their own smoke. Harmel drove back from Lent to Bremmel to the combat command post of *Kampfgruppe* Reinhold, where he ordered portions of the 2nd Battalion, 10th SS Panzer Regiment, and one battalion of the 22nd *SS-Panzergrenadier* Regiment arriving from Pannerden, to counterattack immediately. Bringing forward the expected arriving elements of the 9th SS Reconnaissance Battalion, south of Elst, was stymied when only scouting teams of the battalion were available. Moreover, the counterattack lacked the necessary fire support. *Kampfgruppe* Reinhold lacked heavy weapons as a result of the limited ferry traffic, and the light field howitzer battalion had only a single battery that was moving into position east of Flieren.

On 20 September, the railroad bridge at Nijmegen fell into Allied hands. Despite being completely cut off and surrounded, *SS-Hauptsturmführer* Euling, with approximately sixty men from his battalion and Major Ahlborn, commanding a group of *Fallschirmjäger* from the 1st *Fallschirmjäger* Training Staff, continued to hold the citadel of the city. The stubborn defense of *Kampfgruppe* Euling and 1st *Fallschirmjäger* Training Staff accounted for one Sherman tank destroyed and approximately thirty British killed or wounded. The artillery battery firing positions of Blocking Unit Heinke, renamed to Blocking Unit Roestel, were positioned in the south near Weert, Heelen Meijel, and Helden.[59]

At dusk, approximately 1 km north of Lent, a small contingent of Horrocks' Guards tanks were stopped and they withdrew to the south. *Kampfgruppe* Reinhold occupied and secured a new defensive line during the counterattack. The renewed commitment of the *Landesschützen* or Local Security Forces of *Kampfgruppe* Hartung bolstered the new line developed on the morning of 21 September that ran from the crossroads 1.8 km west-southwest of Ressen (south of village) and passing south of Bemmel. When Allied tanks managed to cross the bridge at Lent around 1900 hours, contact between the 5th Company, SS Artillery Training and Replacement Regiment and Nijmegen was lost. Until 1930 hours, *SS-Hauptsturmführer* Krüger directed fire for the 21st Battery using signal flares. *SS-Scharführer* Meckler assumed fire direction from the intermediate post when SS Senior NCO Nowak received orders from *SS-Sturmbannführer* Reinhold to form a defensive line along the northern banks of the Waal, west of the bridge. The defensive line consisted of fragmented infantry and a construction company that inflicted casualties on the advancing Allies. *SS-Oberscharführer* Riese assumed command of the defensive line. When the radio of the forward observation post became inoperable from a direct hit, *SS-Unterscharführer* Hotop and his men joined in the hard fighting with Company Runge

in southwest Lent. Krüger and the main observation post remained completely cut off when it was overrun and they engaged in close combat with the enemy. According to the eyewitness accounts of two members of Krüger's main observation post, *SS-Rottenführer* Köhler and Private Burgstaller, *SS-Hauptsturmführer* Krüger personally rallied fragmented members from all service branches amidst the chaos to hold the defensive line:

> The trenches held in close combat until the last cartridge around 2030 hours. Previously wounded around 1800 hours, Krüger continued to direct fire for the batteries when he was wounded a second time in the back by three submachine gun rounds. He was evacuated to the first aid bunker only after being wounded a third time, when a tank projectile hit his thigh. Once the defenders in the trenches depleted their ammunition, the Allies fired smoke and phosphor projectiles into the trenches that forced roughly twelve surviving men out of the trenches.

When *SS-Rottenführer* Köhler and *SS-Mann* Burgstaller exited the trenches, they were immediately captured by American troops under the command of an American officer. However, they managed to escape and made their way to Battalion Euling. As they fled, *SS-Mann* Burgstaller witnessed the shooting of *SS-Unterscharführers* Lindenthaler and Beissmann, as well as an unknown *Fallschirmjäger*. *SS-Hauptsturmführer* Krüger, together with several severely wounded German soldiers, and two medical orderlies, were also captured in the first aid bunker.[60]

Southwest of Lent, around 1930 hours *SS-Cannonier* Albrecht and Army Staff Sergeant Piebeck knocked out a Sherman tank with a *Panzerfaust*. Shortly thereafter, Albrecht and an *SS-Unterscharführer* undertook a special scouting patrol into Nijmegen to rescue and extract Army Captain Runge. The two-man team made it across the Waal in a boat but the senior corporal was killed by rifle fire. Albrecht, joined by a *Fallschirmjäger*, made it to the command post of Company Runge, where they met Army Lieutenant Schulz, who guided them to the northern banks of the Waal. At the bridge, Albrecht and Schulz examined Germans who appeared to have been wounded earlier but were mutilated, displaying signs of stabbing wounds to the head, neck, and heart. A full report was filed with the nearest higher command post.

Around 2200 hours Schwappacher personally relocated the Staff and 21st Battery in the hedgehog position at Oosterhout into a defensive island that repulsed advancing Allied scouts. Around 2230 hours, an Army battery, commanded by First Lieutenant Bock, which operated some 400 meters north of the hedgehog position, relocated with a prime mover and the remainder of a RAD battalion into the hedgehog position. At midnight, General of Infantry Hans von Tettau, chief of the Command and Training Staff Netherlands, received a radio message that the position at Oosterhout would hold until the last man. At the same time, Army Captain Krüger, commanding an antiaircraft battalion, promised Schwappacher additional infantry reinforcements to Oosterhout. As the situation became more acute and the hedgehog position ran out of illumination flares to protect against attacks, five houses near the town exit were set on fire.[61]

Around 0400 hours, von Tettau radioed a message to withdraw to Elst. Schwappacher immediately dispatched a staff officer to reconnoiter positions at Elst. At 0500 hours Schwappacher directed the heavy artillery and prime mover to exit Oosterhout. The individual security groups—positioned in the south, southwest, and southeast—repeatedly parried Allied mortar-supported infantry attacks when *Kampfgruppe* Knaust arrived. Schwappacher quickly oriented Knaust and provided fire support for Knaust from the 21st Heavy Howitzer Battery, located in Huis Reed, some 2.5 km south of Elst. The continued fire direction for the battery was then provided by the forward observer *SS-Untersturmführer* Haase, from an armored scout car. For the combat achievements of the 5th Company, SS Training and Replacement Regiment, Schwappacher received the Knight's Cross of the Iron Cross.[62]

In the early morning on 21 September and in anticipation of a general Allied advance in the direction of Elst, the commanding general of the II SS Panzer Corps ordered the 10th SS Panzer Division to concentrate its strength, moving forward from Pannerden, and attack the southern flank of the Allied spearhead, thereby throwing the Allies back across the Waal. When the combat command post of the 10th SS, located in Pannerden, received heavy Allied artillery fire in the night on 21 September, it relocated to Didam. However, the forward command post remained in Doornenburg. The following units remained available for the attack on 21 September 1944:

22nd *SS-Panzergrenadier* Regiment (approx. 1-1/2 Btl.),

Kampfgruppe Hartung (Landesschützen),

2nd Battalion, 10th SS Panzer Regiment (approx. 16 Pz.Kpfw.IV),

1st Company, 10th SS Panzer Pioneer Battalion,

2nd Battalion, 10th SS Panzer Artillery Regiment in position east of Flieren, and two supporting battalions of the 10th SS Panzer Artillery Regiment (positioned on the east bank of the Pannerden'schen canal).[63]

On or about 21 September, *SS-Hauptsturmführer* Büthe relinquished the duties of the divisional 1st General Staff officer to *SS-Sturmbannführer* Hans Stolley, who came to the division from the II SS Panzer Corps and with ample experience. Born on 21 November 1914 in Kiel, Hans-Jochim Stolley first received a commission as an *SS-Untersturmführer* on 20 April 1937. Serving as a platoon commander in the 1st Battalion, SS Death's Head Regiment "Oberbayern," he participated in the French campaign and for heroism was awarded the Iron Cross 2nd and 1st Class simultaneously on 30 June 1940. Stolley served from 3 March 1941 until 1 June 1943 in the SS *Leibstandarte* Regiment "Adolf Hitler," the SS Mountain Division "Nord," as well as the 6th SS Mountain Infantry Replacement Regiment. Having distinguished himself while holding the billets of company commander, regimental adjutant, the divisional 1st ordnance officer (OI), and the quartermaster officer (Ib) while assigned to the SS Division "Nord," he received orders during the same period from 1 December 1942 to 1 June 1943 to attend the General Staff Academy. Graduating from the academy, he posted as the 1st General Staff officer (Ia) to the II SS Panzer Corps and was credited with refreshing the 3rd Panzer Division, overseeing the completion of the defenses surrounding Charkow, and working tirelessly during offensive and defensive operations in July 1943 between Bjelgorod and Obojan. In August 1943, after the corps relocated to northern Italy, Stolley was instrumental in foiling the Anglo-American landings along the coast after extensively reconnoitering and studying the terrain. Stolley made the greatest contributions in Russia as the aid to the commander of the General Staff, and planning for three major offensives in the areas of Göritz-Udine, Istrine and Fiume, and Slovenia, which brought about the capture of some 11,000 resistance fighters as well as weapons and supplies. Stolley also gained experience with the II SS Panzer Corps at Buczacz and around the end of July during the defensive battles in Normandy.[64]

Meanwhile, the 21st *SS-Panzergrenadier* Regiment, consisting of approximately one and a half battalions, did not arrive east of Haalderen until the afternoon due to poor ferry service. In the face of mounting Allied strength and artillery effectiveness north of the Waal, and without the presence of the regiment, the corps could not achieve a decisive success. Nevertheless, numerous Allied attacks to the north were repulsed and the advance of Battalion Knaust at Elst prevented a speedy Allied breakthrough. In the evening on 21 September, the line from the southern fringe of Elst to the western fringe of Bemmel Altwasser south of Bemmel lay firmly secured in the hands of the 10th SS Panzer Division. The 3rd Battalion of the regimental artillery, under the command of *SS-Sturmbannführer* Fritz Haas, was credited with a significant contribution to the division's success.[65]

As an *SS-Hauptsturmführer*, Fritz Haas assumed command of the 1st Battalion, 10th SS Panzer Artillery Regiment on 3 February 1943. As an *SS-Sturmbannführer* he then took command of the 3rd Battalion on 10 March 1944. Haas gained combat experience in the West, in the Balkans, and on the Eastern Front. His decorations included the Iron Cross 2nd and 1st Class, the Panzer Assault Badge, the Eastern Medal, and the Wound Badge in Black. He commanded the 3rd Battalion, 3rd SS Death's Head Artillery Regiment, until the end of 1943 when he transferred to the Training Group A of the 2nd Artillery School, at Beneschau, Bohemia. The commander of the Artillery School, *SS-Sturmbannführer* Karl Schlamelcher, considered Haas to be a well-read and widely knowledgeable commander, but criticized Haas as "later losing his way in the details that compromised the clear and continuous line of the officer training group."[66]

Based on the divisional commander's experience gained at Normandy, Harmel ensured the artillery regiment was refreshed and resupplied very carefully. Harmel's philosophy on artillery in the attack or defense was that enough artillery was never available. Panzer grenadier regiments supported the artillery as much as possible, which included providing the necessary vehicles to tow allocated artillery batteries. During the refreshing of the division, every effort was made to organize the artillery regiment in the following manner:

1st Battalion	two batteries with 6 guns lFH Pz.III (Wespen) one battery with 6 guns sFH Pz.IV (Hummel)
2nd Battalion	three batteries with 6 guns lFH
3rd Battalion	three batteries with 6 guns sFH
4th Battalion	three batteries with 6 guns 100mm cannon
	Total number of guns = 72

By September, the division had not achieved its desired goal. At Nijmegen, approximately thirty to forty guns were employed to support operations. To bolster support, the artillery was augmented by 320mm rocket launchers, of which six were attached to the outer hulls of the half-track (Sd. Kfz.251/1 Ausf.C), also known as *Stuka zu Fuss* or Walking Stuka. The 10th SS Panzer Reconnaissance Battalion and 10th SS Panzer Pioneer Battalion were each equipped with one platoon of three half-tracks for an additional thirty-six guns. In an emergency situation, the antiaircraft battalion could also employ their twelve 88mm guns.[67]

Meanwhile, at the citadel in Nijmegen, Battalion Euling and the Parachute Group Ahlborn defended the last remaining building complex still in German hands, until the roof caved in over their heads. Apparently, the Allies assumed the *Kampfgruppe* had been destroyed. However, around 2300 hours on the same day, *SS-Sturmbannführer* Euling and the defenders managed to break through Allied lines and crossed the Waal River in boats, several kilometers northeast of the bridge, and re-established contact with the 10th SS Panzer Division at Haalderen.

Support for *Kampfgruppe* Brinkmann during the concentrated attack of the II SS Panzer Corps against the British 1st Airborne Division in the center and west of Oosterbeek included a battalion of the 21st *SS-Panzergrenadier* Regiment, King-Tigers of the 504th Heavy Tank Battalion, and 88mm antiaircraft guns. Around 1100 hours, *Kampfgruppe* Brinkmann captured the bitterly contested bunker on the northern approach to the bridge. The task force took possession of the bridge and opened a single path after clearing the burned wreckage of the 9th SS Panzer Reconnaissance Battalion. Simultaneously, remaining Allied nests of resistance were neutralized in the vicinity of the bridge. At a minimum, Allied harassing fire against the bridge was brought to an end.[68]

Battalion Knaust, reinforced by eight vehicles including Panther tanks and assault guns, marched across the Arnhem Bridge shortly after midday on orders to proceed quickly onto Elst. The 10th SS Panzer Reconnaissance Battalion neutralized the remaining pocket of resistance near the bridge and gathered freely in the southern sector of the city of Arnhem. While Arnhem remained under continued Allied artillery fire and aerial attacks on 21 September, Field Marshal Model ordered the city cleared of civilians. Around the same time, the II SS Panzer Corps ordered the 10th SS Panzer Division to place all remaining elements of the 9th SS Panzer Reconnaissance Battalion, located on the southern bank of the Lower Rhine around Elst, in march toward Elden.

Amidst the reorganization on 21 September, an unexpected message arrived in the early afternoon that Allied airborne troops had parachuted and landed near Driel. The airborne forces in question were identified as the Polish 1st Airborne Brigade. The reinforced Battalion Knaust, whose lead elements were scheduled to arrive in Elst around 1600 hours, received new orders from the Corps to deploy immediately against the new threat. However, the situation south of Elst did not allow for a change. Allied pressure moving north developed substantially throughout the course of the late morning. The Allied airborne landings at Driel served to strengthen Allied pressure. The reinforced Battalion Knaust moved through Elst in order to stop the attacking Allied spearheads. Shortly thereafter, troops of the 10th SS Panzer Division assumed a loose defense south of Elst.

Notwithstanding the presence of Battalion Knaust, the 10th SS Panzer Reconnaissance Battalion, located in the southern portion of Arnhem, received orders from the II SS Panzer Corps, during the time of their attachment to *Kampfgruppe* Harzer (9th SS), to proceed forward over Elden and attack the new enemy around Driel.[69]

The batteries of the antiaircraft Brigade Swoboda and 191st Artillery Regiment, operating in the vicinity of the 9th SS Panzer Division, received orders to provide support and moved into position around Elden. The terrain offered little to no cover, and poor driving conditions forced the 10th SS Panzer Reconnaissance Battalion to move forward along a narrow path. Strung out over a considerable distance from north of Elst, the reconnaissance battalion moved into positions for an attack against Driel with unfavorable conditions. *Kampfgruppe* Harzer unexpectedly ran into flanking fire from forward elements of the British 43rd Division shortly before the Germans reached the village. However, under the cover of darkness, *Kampfgruppe* Harzer changed direction and headed southeast, and transitioned to the defense on 22 September along the railroad line Arnhem-Elst, as the southern flank lay north of Elst.[70]

The 10th SS artillery regiment's task of providing support across a front that exceeded 20 km was complicated further by additional fire support requirements for the neighboring weak Army 191st Artillery Regiment. To better cope and meet the requirements, the commander of the artillery regiment, *SS-Obersturmbannführer* Hans-Georg

Sonnenstuhl, strung together a seamless chain of artillery-blocking fire segments between the areas west of Arnhem and the Waal River at Nijmegen. Each segment, numbered 1 to 75, represented the effective area of fire for a single battery. A woman's name further identified each segment. Fire missions were easily called using field phones or radios, and based on the number or name of the segment. Indeed, the entire regiment could place fire very quickly on any designated segment. Each forward observer knew his segment number or name. Instead of calling coordinates, the forward observer simply identified the segments.

Sonnenstuhl's successful counter-battery tactics were based on calculations taken from Allied artillery muzzle flashes at night. The results provided the artillery regiment an accurate layout and the locations of Allied batteries. The combined fire from various German guns, each consisting of several fire sets, brought to bear as many as 260 projectiles per mission, which effectively destroyed Allied gun positions. Each fire set per gun consisted of six projectiles for light howitzers and five projectiles per heavy howitzer.[71]

Throughout the period from 18 to 21 September, *SS-Sturmbannführer* Leo Reinhold provided leadership for the three-day defense at the bridgehead at Nijmegen. Despite very high losses and the addition of unfamiliar ad hoc troop elements, Reinhold effectively rallied the defense against superior Allied armored forces and closed several critical gaps that developed during the fighting. Reinhold's men accounted for the close-quarter destruction of twenty-four Allied tanks. On orders to recapture the bridgehead, Reinhold contained the wavering defense and personally led a counterattack to establish a blocking line along the northern bank of the Waal. Not only did Reinhold prevent an Allied breakthrough from the bridgehead at Nijmegen to Arnhem, but he also provided the necessary time for the destruction of the Allied airborne forces at Arnhem. For his achievements, *SS-Sturmbannführer* Reinhold was decorated on 16 October 1944 with the Knight's Cross to the Iron Cross.[72]

Meanwhile, Battery Godau received orders to withdraw to the east and crossed the Wessem-Nederweert-Kanl at Kelpen. During the crossing,

Allied units were in such close pursuit that the battery employed two guns at point blank range. From 22 to 24 September, the battery assumed firing positions in Panningen.[73]

Throughout 22 September, Allied resistance from remnants of the British 1st Airborne Division sprang up, here and there, in sectors of the city to the west of the Arnhem Bridge. *Kampfgruppe* Harzer ordered portions of a battalion from the 21st *SS-Panzergrenadier* Regiment and the 1st Company, 10th SS Panzer Reconnaissance Battalion to mop up in the city sectors. However, Allied pockets of resistance were not eliminated or captured until the next day. Considering the outcome of the previous day, especially at Elst and Driel, the II SS Panzer Corps ordered the formation of a new boundary line between the 9th SS on the right and the 10th SS on the left; the mouth of the Jissel River in the Lower Rhine (2 km northeast of Huissen)–north Elst–south Valburg. Allied attacks in the sector of the 10th SS Panzer Division were thwarted throughout the day by German counterattacks south of Elst and west of Bemmel.[74]

Throughout the day on 23 September, portions of the 10th SS Panzer Reconnaissance Battalion and 21st *SS-Panzergrenadier* Regiment attached to the *Kampfgruppe* 9th SS and eliminated the last pockets of resistance in the southern sector of the city. In the process, communications were established with the left wing of the *Kampfgruppe* 9th SS. Heading west from the Arnhem Bridge, the 1st Company, 10th SS Panzer Reconnaissance Battalion, was ordered to push forward along the northern bank to points south of Oosterbeek. Their mission was to guard portions of the river on either side of Driel and report immediately any Allied movement to the *Kampfgruppe* 9th SS.

The bulk of the 10th SS Panzer Reconnaissance Battalion, supported by the Artillery Groupe Elden, defended the railroad line against repeated attacks by Polish paratroopers between Elst and Elden.

The II SS Panzer Corps ordered the 10th SS Panzer Division to occupy the defensive front south of Elst and west of Bemmel. To that end, the Corps provided artillery and antiaircraft reinforcements in the area of Huissen, and the Fortress Machine Gun Battalion 37 was attached to the 10th SS Battalion

Euling of the 21st *SS-Panzergrenadier* Regiment, which had recently managed to free itself in Arnhem, and traveled over Elden-Huissen to bolster the defensive front. The northern wing of the 10th SS Panzer Reconnaissance Battalion established contact with *Kampfgruppe* Gerhardt, of the 9th SS.

The consolidation of Allied bridging equipment west of Nijmegen indicated the reinforcement of Allied forces between the Waal and Lower Rhine. Sufficient stocks of ammunition allowed the artillery regiments to fire harassing fire missions from their 100mm cannon and, at times, the antiaircraft battalion. As a result, the 10th SS Panzer Division held the bridges of Nijmegen and ferry points west of the city.

In the night on 23 September, the forward-most elements of the British 43rd Division from Valburg bypassed Driel to the west and reached the southern banks of the Lower Rhine.[75]

On the following day, the 10th SS Panzer Division and right-neighboring 10th SS Panzer Reconnaissance Battalion managed to repel Allied attacks against the German defensive front. After the airborne landings by the Polish 1st Airborne Brigade at Driel, the 10th SS Panzer Reconnaissance Battalion was reinforced. As of 24 September, the reconnaissance battalion numbered nearly 500 men and consisted of three reconnaissance companies, of which one remained attached to the 10th SS divisional *Kampfgruppe* Walther, tank elements of the 2nd Battalion, 10th SS Panzer Regiment (Pz.Kpfw. IV), the 102st SS Antiaircraft Battery, and the 37th Fortress Machine Gun Battalion. The numerical strength of the reinforced reconnaissance battalion included:

Personnel: 13 OFC 39 NCO 415 men.
Weapons: 49 light MG   35 heavy MG
           15 medium mortars
           3 Antiaircraft Guns   37mm
           8 Antiaircraft Guns   20mm
           3 Tank Guns   20mm
           3 Tank Guns   88mm (Tiger)
           1 Antitank Gun   75mm[76]

Between 22 and 24 September, forty-five King Tigers from the 506th Heavy Panzer Battalion traveled over Köln and Wesel to directly support the 1st Parachute Army. Near Oosterbeek and west of Arnhem, the King Tigers were attached to the 10th SS Panzer Division. One company of King Tigers detrained in Zevenaar and Elten, 5 km northwest and 8 km southeast of Pannerden. Attached to the *Kampfgruppe* 9th SS, the company prepared for operations in a forest 3 km north of Elten. According to Harmel, the heavy tank battalion served as a replacement for the 1st Battalion, 10th SS Panzer Regiment.[77]

The King Tiger or Tiger II was manufactured by Henschel and weighed 68 tons. The vehicle crew numbered five and fired the awesome 88mm tank gun of 71 calibers. The main gun was sighted using the TZF9d telescopic sight, with a monocular magnification of 2.5 and a range of 3,000 meters for armor piercing and 5,000 meters for high explosive ammunition, and also fired two MG-34 machine guns. The muzzle velocity of the main gun, using armor-piercing ammunition, reached 1,130 meters per second and could penetrate 153mm of armor plate at a distance of 2,000 meters. The M4A3 Sherman tank, at its thickest point, had approximately 100mm of steel. The main guns of British Shermans, including the 76mm Firefly and 17-pounder MKs IV and VII, could penetrate 98mm and 111mm, respectively, at 2,000 meters. The King Tiger was least protected along the sides and rear with only 80mm of steel. Powered by the Maybach HL 230P30 engine, the Tiger II had eight forward and four reverse gears that gave it a maximum speed of 35 km/h and a range of 170 kilometers.[78]

Battalion Knaust suffered many losses on 23 September when it repelled an Allied armored attack at Lienden, west of Elst. Compounded by the lack of divisional reserves, the II SS Panzer Corps ordered the 10th SS Panzer Division on 25 September to evacuate the town of Elst. Throughout the day, the division provided security as Battalion Knaust withdrew into prepared positions south of Elden astride the two roads leading from Arnhem to Nijmegen. The Allies pursued the movement only cautiously.

While the remaining elements of the 10th SS Panzer Division held the defensive front on 25 September, strong Allied pressure continued to persist throughout the following day against the entire front of the II SS Panzer Corps, extending across a line from the railroad embankment 2 km west of Elden to approximately 1 km west and southwest of Rijkerswoerd-Vergert and to the western fringe of Bemmel-Ziegelei Groenendaal. On 26 September, the fighting of the II SS Panzer Corps against the British 1st Airborne Division was successfully brought to a close. During ten days of bitter fighting and numerous failed Allied attempts to rescue the encircled British airborne, a total of 6,450 prisoners were taken and many thousand reported dead. Thirty antitank guns, numerous weapons, and 250 vehicles were captured. Moreover, over 1,000 gliders were either destroyed or captured and over one hundred aircraft were shot down.[79]

Immediately after the destruction of the British 1st Airborne Division west of Arnhem, preparations began for an attack against Allied forces situated between Arnhem and Nijmegen. German leadership hoped to quickly resolve the situation north of the Waal.

Command of the anticipated attack rested with the II SS Panzer Corps. However, at 0000 hours on 27 September, command of the sector west of Arnhem transferred to the newly arrived XII SS Corps, commanded by the East Prussian veteran of World War I, *SS-Oberstgruppenführer* Curt von Gottberg. The Army's 9th (Austrian) and 116th Panzer Divisions, selected to execute the attack, were approaching Arnhem from the area east of Aachen. The task of providing adequate security for the assembly of both Army tank divisions fell to the II SS Panzer Corps. To that end, the Corps dominated and held the defensive front against renewed Allied attacks.[80]

On 27 September, the Allies concentrated their attacks against the main line of battle held by the 10th SS Panzer Division in the sectors of Vergert and Osten. Penetrating into the German line, the Allies captured Baal and Haalderen, although both towns were recaptured after German counterattacks.

After 27 September, Allied pressure relented notably, which offered the division the opportunity to reorganize various troops that arrived throughout the next several days. The replacements included Gruppe Hemsoth, commanded by a *Luftwaffe*

colonel from a *Luftwaffe* Ground Field Service Unit, which consisted of personnel from three individual Flight Commands. Made up primarily of *Luftwaffe* officers, the poorly equipped group had no front-line experience. Battalion Wesel consisted for the most part of poorly equipped older soldiers with medical problems. The ranks of the 251st Labor Service Battalion were filled with younger men who lacked weapons training and heavy weapons altogether. An additional Fortress Machine Gun Battalion augmented the previously attached 37th Fortress Machine Gun Battalion. The new battalion operated with vintage MG 08/15 machine guns. The remainder consisted of portions of alarm units from Nijmegen and Battalion Bruhns that contained better trained and experienced troops. Battalion Bruhns proved their worth during the fighting at Arnhem as part of *Kampfgruppe* 9th SS. However, on 29 September, Battalion Bruhns was detached and joined the 9th Panzer Division. Multiple efforts by the division to receive back their own units, such as the fresh 10th SS Tank Destroyer Battalion, with a full complement of *Jagdpanthers*, proved unsuccessful. Since 26 September, the 10th SS Tank Destroyer Battalion had continued to fight as part of *Kampfgruppe* Walther at Venlo.[81]

With the additional manpower, the 10th SS Panzer Division formed two reinforced regimental *Kampfgruppen*, whose nuclei and skeleton were formed around the remainder of the 21st and 22nd *SS-Panzergrenadier* Regiments. To compensate for the inexperience and lack of stamina of the new troops in general, the division exchanged the inexperienced personnel with previously wounded but experienced personnel from the divisional supply and service units. The division Field Replacement Battalion, consisting of 800 men, could not be employed during this period due to a complete lack of infantry weapons. The 506th Heavy Panzer Battalion as well as both the proven battalions Knaust and Bruhns were detached on 29 September and made available to the newly arriving 9th Panzer Division, a reduction in force for the 10th SS Panzer Division.[82]

The veteran 9th Panzer Division organized originally in 1938 after Austria entered into the greater German Reich. As the 4th Light Division, it participated in the occupation of Czechoslovakia in March 1939, fought in Poland in September, and reorganized, on 3 January 1940, to the 9th Panzer Division. The 33rd Panzer Regiment was raised from personnel from the Austrian tank troops, consisting of the staff from the Panzer Regiment Conze and the Tank Training Battalion. The 9th Panzer Division saw action in Holland, the Balkans, and entered Russia where it took such heavy losses during Operation Zitadel (Kursk) that it was withdrawn from the line. In March 1944, the division refitted in southern France and saw action again in Normandy and Falaise.

As a member of the 8th Panzer Company, Kurt Gätzschmann volunteered on 29 October 1935 for service in Dresden with the 12th Cavalry Regiment. At the age of eighteen, he was "interested in everything military." After escaping the pocket at Falaise, where the majority of the company entered American captivity, Gätzschmann relocated to Aachen on 9 September and then to Bergisch-Gladbach around 15 September, to obtain new Panther tanks. Once the tanks arrived, the vehicles were transported by rail to Arnhem and attached to the 1st Parachute Army. After the 8th Company personnel were distributed among the other three companies in the battalion, it was reorganized to the 2105th Panzer Battalion of the 105th Panzer Brigade. Gätzschmann, a staff sergeant, was assigned to the Staff Company, commanded by First Lieutenant Günther.[83]

Despite the commitment of two fresh Army divisions, the success of the operation remained questionable, considering the combat experience of replacement troops and the general weakness of units earmarked for the attack. The commanding general of the II SS Panzer Corps had similar reservations. Nevertheless, the commanders of the Army 9th and 116th Panzer Divisions and 10th SS Panzer Division received their orders during the operational situation brief, held on 28 September at the Corps' command post at Velp.

The attack was scheduled to begin on 29 September. As a result of insufficient fuel supplies and the presence of Allied aircraft, the attack was postponed to 1 October. The first objective of the attack was Elst. The 116th Panzer Division, on the right, and the left-side 9th Panzer Division, were to attack with the center of gravity along the interior line from the area of Elden-Huissen. The 10th SS Panzer Division had orders to support the attack of the 9th Panzer Division by launching a holding attack from the old line of battle and over the southern rim of Heuvel against Bemmel. In addition, the reinforced 10th SS Panzer Artillery Regiment supported the attack against targets south of Elst. Needless to say, the division could not provide full support due to limited ammunition stores, despite the resupply that was well underway.[84]

Around 29–30 September, a German Navy commando frogman arrived at the command post of the 10th SS Panzer Division. The commando mission was to destroy the bridge after the *Luftwaffe* II Pursuit Corps failed repeatedly to destroy the bridges over the Lower Rhine at Nijmegen and Oosterbeek. A single bomb blew a hole into the main bridge across the Waal, and the center span of the railroad fell. The frogmen floated explosives down the river in black rubber boats and succeeded in damaging the bridge, but ultimately failed. The Nijmegen Bridge remained serviceable.[85]

On 29 September, the regimental artillery attached to the Blocking Unit Heinke relocated south of Venray without any contact with the blocking force.[86]

At 0600 hours on 1 October, the 9th and 116th Panzer Divisions entered positions to launch their attack under the cover of darkness and foggy weather. The 10th SS Panzer Division supported the advance of its right neighbor, *Kampfgruppe* Volker of the 9th Panzer Division, with fire missions against strong Allied positions at Elst and the Aamsche Bridge. The German attacks struck a well-prepared defense and the Allies launched immediate counterattacks. The 9th Panzer Division made only minimal gains in the direction of Elst.

Meanwhile, on 1 October, Karl Schneider transferred from the 9th SS to the 10th SS as a half-track driver, 1st Company, Half-track Battalion Laubscheer, 21st *SS-Panzergrenadier* Regiment, and returned into the line between Arnhem and Nijmegen. The 1st Company, 1st Battalion, 21st *SS-Panzergrenadier* Regiment, under the command of *SS-Untersturmführer* Haase and *SS-Hauptsturmführer* Hans Lohr, engaged in bitter defensive fighting in the area around Huissen-Angeren, east of the Linge Canal. The division occupied positions at Haalderen and Elst, within a triangular front that included Arnhem-Nijmegen-Milligen, between the Lower Rhine and Waal Rivers, against British units belonging to XXX Corps. Shortly after Schneider's arrival to his new company, *SS-Untersturmführer* Haase prepared for an afternoon attack against Elst. However, the attack bogged down in the face of stiff British defensive fire. After the Germans recaptured small British gains made during a counterattack in the night in Heuvel, a second British assault launched on 2 October. Allied fighter aircraft supporting British infantry broke the German defense and the 1st Company abandoned their positions at the road fork, south of Heuvel. In the evening on 4 October, the 1st Company counterattacked and recaptured the intersection. Several British soldiers were taken prisoner in the process.[87]

Heavy Allied flanking fire from Vergert slowed the attacking troops from *Kampfgruppe* Volker between Vergert and Aam. Accordingly, the 10th SS Panzer Division moved across the southern rim of Heuvel against Vergert and assembled throughout the afternoon with elements of the reinforced 21st Regimental *Kampfgruppe*, supported by the divisional artillery from positions east of the Pannerdian Canal.[88]

The flooded terrain of numerous waterways and trenches made the attack very difficult. The terrain offered no cover or concealment, the ground water made entrenching practically impossible, and heavy casualties were sustained. After minimal gains, the attack ran aground along the southern rim of Heuvel in the face of concentrated fire from all calibers of Allied weapons. Even so, the forward thrust of the 10th SS Panzer Division provided relief for the right neighbor, *Kampfgruppe* Volker of the 9th Panzer Division, as the division drew Allied fire onto itself for the remaining day.

Elements of the 21st Regimental *Kampfgruppe* moved forward from Baal against Bemmel, pushed the front line up to the road north of Bemmel, and immediately rebuffed oncoming Allied counterattacks. The tank-supported attack led by the 22nd Regimental *Kampfgruppe* against Bemmel, from Klein Baal and the area 1 km west of Haalderen, could not penetrate through the strong Allied defense. Once the weather cleared during the evening on 1 October, numerous Allied fighter aircraft interdicted, especially against the artillery positions and ferry points at Pannerden that caused German casualties.

The attack throughout the course of the first day confirmed Bittrich's assessment of the situation on 28 September. Despite the greatest German effort by all the troops involved in the attack, a successful penetration was out of the question. Fragmented, smaller, and localized German attacks had varying degrees of success. The greater level of Allied strength caused the Germans to believe the German attack struck amidst Allied assemblies and preparations for an attack. Despite less than satisfactory results from the first day of the attack, and almost complete lack of a reserve to bolster the attack, German leadership clung to the idea of pressing on the attack.[89]

In the early morning on 2 October, during an Allied reconnaissance probe against the northern wing of the 10th SS Panzer Division, the Allies managed to infiltrate the village of Heuvel and wreaked havoc on portions of the German Fortress Machine Gun Battalion and the 251st Labor Service Battalion. By morning, however, panzer grenadiers from the 21st *SS-Panzergrenadier* Regiment restored the situation.

Around 1000 hours, along the boundary seam of the 9th Panzer Division, Allied tanks and infantry were observed assembling near the crossroads south of Vergert (road Bemmel-Vergert). The 10th SS Panzer Artillery Regiment dispersed the Allies with concentrated fire. While the Allied infantry moved in the direction of Merm, several heavy Allied tanks remained south of the crossroad.

The 10th SS Panzer Division and southern wing of the 9th Panzer Division could not achieve any territorial gains in the face of an exceptionally high volume of Allied artillery fire and aerial activity. The Germans were unable to employ comparable countermeasures and found it more difficult to defend against stronger Allied counterattacks. A local attack launched independently by *SS-Hauptsturmführer* Euling helped push forward the main line of battle.[90]

The 10th SS Panzer Reconnaissance Battalion, whose combat command post was in Huissen, served as the divisional reserve in the area of Huissen-Angeren. Previously assigned to the 9th SS, the battalion released back to the 10th SS.

Based on Allied radio messages, the German leadership anticipated additional Allied airborne landings in the areas of Nijmegen-Emmerich-Kleve. On orders from headquarters of the 1st Parachute Army, the II SS Panzer Corps directed the speedy formation of deployable alarm units from rear-echelon service and supply units. Every occupied village was to ready at least one alarm platoon.

To counter additional Allied airborne landings, the 10th SS Panzer Division reorganized the 10th Field Training Battalion, located in Didam and Doetinchem, to the reserved contingency. Moreover, the change allowed for the motorization of the battalion and issue of light and heavy weapons. A single artillery training battery, consisting of four light howitzers, reinforced the 10th SS Panzer Artillery Regiment. Replacements arriving from Germany were continuously allocated to the Field Replacement Battalion. The separation of the replacement and training battalions paid great dividends, as *Luftwaffe* personnel who joined the division required weapons training.

The 10th SS Panzer Division also assumed responsibility for defending against airborne landings in the rearward areas: the left boundary Rees-Ijsselburg and the right boundary Pannerden-Doetinchem.[91]

On 3 October, neither the 9th nor the 116th Panzer Divisions achieved success in the attack. The Allies counterattacked during the afternoon to the east, from the area of Driel, and pushed forward against the northern wing of the 116th Panzer Division and relentlessly thwarted the division's plan of attack. Moreover, the Allies managed to occupy the four-way intersection immediately south of Heuvel that lay along the seam of the 9th Panzer Division and the 10th SS. From this location, the Allies inflicted heavy flanking fire of all calibers against the southern wing of the 9th Panzer Division. To provide relief, the commander of the 10th SS Panzer Division requested from the 9th Panzer Division permission to attack the Allies at the four-way intersection,

to throw them back toward Bemmel. The 10th SS Panzer Reconnaissance Battalion, the last reserve, would attack from Huissen and Angeren over Huis de Karbrug. The 21st Regimental *Kampfgruppe*, supported by tanks from the 2nd Battalion, 10th SS Panzer Regiment coming from Baal and heading to the northwest, was ordered to support the attack. Moreover, the attack of the 10th SS Panzer Reconnaissance Battalion was augmented by elements of the 1st Battalion, 11th *Panzergrenadier* Regiment, of the 9th Panzer Division.[92]

Portions of the 10th SS Panzer Reconnaissance Battalion that led the attack over Heuvel achieved success in the early morning hours on 4 October. German attacks from Heuvel, Huis de Karbrug, and Baal caused the Allies to abandon the four-way intersection, though both sides suffered considerable losses and left behind equipment. The Germans destroyed several Allied tanks and both the 10th SS Panzer Reconnaissance Battalion and the 21st *SS-Panzergrenadier* Regiment brought in prisoners.

The continued attack after daybreak by elements of the 10th SS Panzer Reconnaissance Battalion against Bemmel, designed to provide protection against Vergert, ran into heavy Allied defensive fire 800 meters south of Heuvel. Using greater vehicle speeds, the 1st Company, 10th SS Panzer Reconnaissance Battalion, managed to gain ground in the direction of Bemmel. The forward elements of the company managed to infiltrate the northern portion of the village. However, it was entangled in bitter fighting and the 1st Company commander, *SS-Obersturmführer* Karl Ziebrecht, was severely wounded. The unit fought its way back to Klein Baal and Haalderen, whereas the bulk of the 10th SS Panzer Reconnaissance Battalion withdrew to Heuvel while sustaining additional casualties.

Around midday, defensive Allied artillery fire transitioned into fierce preparatory fire that shifted onto the main line of battle. Shortly thereafter, Allied infantry and armor counterattacked across a broad front, from the areas of Vergert and Bemmel, against the sector of the 10th SS Panzer Division and the left wing of the 9th Panzer Division. By 1400 hours, bitter combat raged within the village of Heuvel that was fought, for the most part, by elements of the 21st *SS-Panzergrenadier* Regiment.

Between the villages of Heuvel, Baal, Klein Baal, and Haalderen, the *SS-Panzergrenadiers*, Army soldiers, and young men of the Labor Service Battalion were committed to battle across open terrain. Subjected to incessant artillery bombardments, they sustained heavy casualties. The wet ground did not allow for entrenchment, whereas multi-layered piles of grass and sod created obstructions for observation rather than protection against incoming fire. Then, once lively Allied fighter aircraft engaged in the ground fighting with rockets and bombs, the poorly equipped and inexperienced alarm units succumbed, falling back to the east, seeking refuge behind the Linden Canal. Allied loudspeakers across from the sector of the 10th SS Panzer Division invited German troops to defect with their weapons. Several men from the Fortress Machine Gun Battalion answered the call and defected with their weapons and equipment. Heuvel and Baal were lost after continuous back and forth fighting for possession of the villages. Portions of the British 50th Division captured Haalderen. The Battalion Euling, supported by Pz.Kpfw.IV of the 2nd Battalion, 10th SS Panzer Regiment, and elements of the 10th SS Panzer Reconnaissance Battalion, counterattacked and recaptured the village before dark. The success of Battalion Euling came partially after Euling managed to catch battered and fragmented troops reeling from the Allied attack and then rallied them to join the counterattack. For his achievements, *SS-Hauptsturmführer* Euling received the Knight's Cross to the Iron Cross on 15 October 1944. Allied attempts to cross the Waal were repelled by the division from positions south of the brick factory at Haalderen.[93]

The divisional commander personally established a defensive line during the night and morning of 4–5 October, along the northern banks of the Linge Canal. Harmel summoned every available unit, which meant primarily alarm units that were brought forward as quickly as possible by bicycle.

Based on the past developments, the 9th Panzer Division also brought her left wing behind the Linge Canal during the night of 5 October and established contact with the 10th SS Panzer Division.

The most costly day since the 10th SS Panzer Division began fighting in Holland was 4 October.

The divisional losses were so high that they were incapable of mounting an attack for some time.

Harmel considered the mission of the German leadership completed: to contain the Allied advance. The unexpected shift of the Allied center of gravity after 4 October from the north to the east that struck against the sector of the 10th SS contained the Allied advance. Whether intentionally or not, the Allies struck against the Achilles' heel along the sector of the II SS Panzer Corps but did not exploit the opportunity.

As the northern portion of the German front solidified in depth with the introduction of the 9th and 116th Panzer Divisions between 1 and 3 October, the 10th SS Panzer Division launched isolated holding attacks with limited objectives to entangle Allied forces. As a result, the division suffered high numbers of casualties. The commitment of inexperienced alarm units, against enemy tanks with far superior numbers and fighting strength, would eventually backfire. A similar development was experienced on 4 October along the southern wing of the II SS Panzer Corps.[94]

Despite the adverse conditions, the division managed to halt superior Allied forces along the Linge Canal. Moreover, the 10th SS counterattacked into the Allied southern wing and recaptured the village of Haalderen, west of the canal. The southern wing of the 9th Panzer Division that bordered the 10th SS entered into the action as well. The Austrian division parried every Allied attack against its right wing. However, the division could not launch their own attack. The attack of the 116th Panzer Division on 4 October crossed the train embankment to the west.

On 5 October, several hours before daybreak, the 9th Panzer Division and 10th SS Panzer Division, at this stage referred to as *Kampfgruppe* Harmel, received orders from the II SS Panzer Corps to transition to the defense and hold the line Kanal de Linge–Wahlenburg–Steenfabrik south of Haalderen, with centers of gravity northeast of Heuvel and west of Haalderen. The divisional boundaries ran from the knee of the Merm Canal 500 meters southwest of Huis de Karburg–Kullenburg–Angeren.[95]

The following several days transpired without incident within the sector of the 10th SS Panzer

Division, despite lively German and Allied scouting activity measured in the smallest increments. Energetic Allied artillery and aircraft were the only noticeable activities. As such, the removal of the civilian population out of the danger zone was necessary, notwithstanding the possibility of counterespionage.

The new front line along the northern bank of the Linge Canal was subjected to Allied artillery and mortar fire for the entire day on 5 October.[96]

On 6 October, troops of the 22nd Regimental *Kampfgruppe* improved their positions during a lull in the fighting west of Haalderen.

Allied bombers targeted and severely damaged the bridge over the Lower Rhine, but during the evening the bridge returned to working order.

The intensified employment of Allied artillery and aircraft, especially against the German artillery positions east of the Pannerischen Canal, in the area around Huissen, and the crossing points east of Huissen and Doornenburg, gave the impression of a new and imminent large-scale Allied attack.[97]

Allied aircraft bombed and destroyed the Arnhem Bridge around midday on 7 October. Suddenly, the resupply of all German combat troops located west of the Lower Rhine was severely hampered and the resumption of German offensive operations was no longer possible.

However, the II SS Panzer Corps received a directive from Army Group B for the final transition for the defense between the Lower Rhine and Waal Rivers and the extraction of the 116th Panzer Division. The corresponding directive by the II SS Panzer Corps, issued around 2115 hours on 7 October, confirmed the earlier assignment for the 10th SS Panzer Division (also referred to as Blocking Unit Harmel) to defend the main line. The directive also established the relief of the 116th Panzer Division whose sector would be occupied by the Blocking Unit Harzer, commanded by *Oberst* Gerhardt and the 9th Panzer Division. It called for strengthening the defense by construction of a second position along the line of the bridgehead Elden–Rijkersvoord–het-Zand–Flieren (linking the Blocking Unit Harmel to the 9th Panzer Division at the road-fork of Kullenberg). Additional pillboxes were to be constructed in depth and the bridgeheads

of Elden and Doornenburg reinforced. Moreover, once the civilian population relocated to the river's east bank, the Lower Rhine position was completed.

To carry out the order of 8 October, the 10th SS Panzer Division employed the 10th Field Training Battalion to expand the position on Lower Rhine: the right boundary of the river confluence Rhine-Ijssel, the left boundary of the factory, on the east bank across from Millingen. The 10th SS Panzer Pioneer Battalion strengthened the bridgehead east of Huissen and at Doornenburg. A small pillbox was established east of Angeren. Furthermore, the bridgeheads were mined and observation positions, which could inevitably be used by the Allies, prepared for demolition. The 10th SS Panzer Reconnaissance Battalion and pioneer units of the grenadier regiment enlarged a second position in the line het-Zand–Kullenburg, the western rim to Flieren, and the western rim of Gent and the brick factory 1 km southeast of Gent. The day transpired without incident.[98]

During the night on 9 October, the 10th SS Panzer Division absorbed the remainder of Battalion Bruhns; in accordance with orders of the II SS Panzer Corps, one battalion was formed by combining the remnants of the severely battered Battalion Wesel and the remainder of Battalion Bruhns.

The men within the main line of battle of both the 9th Panzer Division and the 10th SS Panzer Division were uprooted and brought back into prepared secondary positions: a return to the line Elden–Rijkersvoord–het-Zand–Flieren–Gent. The movement took place under the cover of protective artillery fire that resulted in no Allied pressure. Elements of the 10th SS Panzer Reconnaissance Battalion moved into the bridgehead positions east of Huissen and Doornenburg. The remaining 2nd Battalion, 10th SS Panzer Regiment withdrew across the river and quartered in the area of s'Heerenberg-Zeddam in anticipation of additional airborne landings east of the Lower Rhine. The second tank battalion was ordered to service and repair the tanks.

The less glamorous job of herding cattle across the Lower Rhine on the ferry was assigned to special units of the 10th SS. The cattle were found grazing and standing unattended for days in stalls.[99]

The re-occupation of the Lower Rhine progressed one sector after another, by way of dominating the bridgeheads south of Arnhem and around Doornenburg, and thereby fulfilling the 10 October directive of Army Group B.[100]

The days that followed passed reasonably quietly. On 12 October, the 10th SS Panzer Division obtained 1,600 replacements that arrived from Germany. Thirty percent were non-commissioned officers and troops from the *Luftwaffe* (ground and antiaircraft personnel). The replacements required technical weapons training and combat skills training as it related to a tank division. For this task they were assigned to the 10th SS Field Replacement Battalion, which was first located at Doetinchem and later in Goor, 30 km northeast of Zutphen.

One interesting episode involved new recruit *SS-Unterscharführer* Heinz Winzbeck, who received his basic training at Brünn. In the middle of November 1943, he transferred to Berlin-Lichterfeld for training as a vehicle electrician. Only a few days after his arrival, the British bombing campaign began and Berlin was targeted between 20 and 22 November. Winzbeck was employed in a cleanup detail within the inner city. By the middle of December, Winzbeck transferred to the *Volkswagenwerk* (VW plant) in Wolfsburg, to undergo both theoretical and practical training for the VW. After completion, he transferred in February 1944 for advanced motor vehicle training to Vienna, Austria. Winzbeck successfully completed the approximately four-month training and then returned to Berlin-Lichterfeld, and joined the 2nd Tank Maintenance Company. Off and on, Winzbeck worked at the 1st Tank Maintenance Company, stationed at Oranienburg. The maintenance group, which consisted of both companies, was reassigned to the Driver's School at Weimar-Buchenwald. However, when the group arrived they discovered a Hitler Youth training sequence was underway, designed to provide various cities with fire truck drivers. Any other vehicles that were available were used exclusively to transport the NCO corps to the invasion front. In the interim, the maintenance group received additional but less welcomed basic training. When the group discovered a maintenance

workstation, the group was greeted with open arms and immediately reassigned to the maintenance station. Winzbeck was assigned to assist an *SS-Unterscharführer*, who converted vehicles from gasoline to wood-gas. Other men from the group repaired large numbers of motorcycles, of which all were destroyed during the Allied bombing of the Buchenwald concentration camp. Returning to Berlin-Lichterfeld in September 1944, after completing their driver's examinations of various levels, the group was sent back and forth, as experienced earlier in May: two days in Lichterfeld, two days at Oranienburg, and then back again.

In October, after the fighting at Arnhem and Nijmegen ended, the maintenance group returned to the division in Holland. Winzbeck rejoined his fellow soldiers from the 1st Company, with whom he completed basic training at Brünn. In groups, their job entailed delivering motor vehicles coming from the Reich to the troops at the front. They were constantly underway. For example, they picked up several vehicles in Viersen, and then several in Krefeld, or from the area around München-Gladbach.[101]

Meanwhile, in the evening of 13–14 October, troops of the II SS Panzer Corps abandoned the second position that they had occupied since 10 October, and returned to the positions at the Lower Rhine. The bridgeheads south of Arnhem, east of Huissen and Angeren, to include Doornenburg, remained occupied by German forces. As the changes took place, higher orders withdrew the 9th Panzer Division from the front line for use elsewhere. Generally speaking, the movements were executed without incident.[102]

By way of vigorous scouting activity and the unrestricted employment of the division artillery, the 10th SS Panzer Division aimed to recapture the front. The Allies cautiously felt their way forward up to the Lower Rhine and the German-occupied bridgeheads. According to Harmel, the prevailing German notion was that the Allies recognized German intentions. Captured Allied prisoners, brought in by the scouting troops, revealed that the Allied command decided to withdraw as soon as reinforced German artillery went into action. This tactic was consistent with basic operational movements experienced since the landings at Normandy. As a result, the division gained valuable time to regroup and reorganize. The division remained attached to the II SS Panzer Corps, and the latter assumed responsibility on 13 October for the sector of the XII Panzer Corps, held by the 363rd Volks Grenadier Division (VGD). The II SS Panzer Corps became the west wing of the 1st Parachute Army and the 10th SS Panzer Division became heir to the entire sector that extended west of Arnhem to the Waal. The right boundary of the 363rd VGD of the II SS Panzer Corps ran along the line Oosterbeek-Driel (villages occupied by the 10th SS). The left boundary, held by the 84th Infantry Division of the II Parachute Corps, ran along the line Didam-Babberik (both villages occupied by the 10th SS)-Millingen (occupied by 84th Infantry Division).[103]

On 14 October, the 10th SS Panzer Division entered a phase of positional warfare within the framework of a defensive front. German infantry scantily held the main line of battle along the Lower Rhine. Concentrated battle positions or strongpoints held the flooded terrain whereas minefields protected the bridgeheads along the western banks of the river. At the fork of the Lower Rhien and Waal Rivers, a well-camouflaged gun emplacement from the old Dutch bastion dominated the Rhine at Millingen. The emplacement also served as an excellent artillery observation post and was protected by mines and wire entanglements.

Blocking Unit Gebhardt, which consisted of one Fortress Machine Gun Battalion and alarm units, held the bridgehead at Elden, south of Arnhem. Since 22 October, Blocking Unit Gebhardt had employed first with *Kampfgruppe* Harzer, then the 116th Panzer Division, and later with the 9th Panzer Division. Portions of the 10th SS Panzer Reconnaissance Battalion held the bridgehead east of Huissen and Angeren, while the 10th SS Panzer Pioneer Battalion deployed around Doornenburg. Elements of a second Fortress Machine Gun Battalion reinforced the defenses of the eastern bridgehead.

The divisional artillery stood in positions east of the road Arnhem-Zevenaar-Babberik. Forward observers were positioned in each of the four bridgeheads. The 5th and 8th Tank Companies assembled approximately two companies of tanks from the 2nd

Battalion. Serving as a mobile reserve and operating from the village of s'Heerenberg, the tanks were attached to the reinforced *Kampfgruppe* along the eastern wing of the Fifteenth Army from 24 October until 10 November. The remaining personnel of the 2nd Panzer Battalion, primarily specialists, were employed as infantry at less dangerous positions along the western bank of the Lower Rhine.[104]

This phase of positional warfare included fighting based on probing and scouting operations that were launched by the division from the bridgeheads Huissen and Doornenburg. Every so often, the 10th SS Panzer Antiaircraft Battalion engaged Allied bombers that were returning home after daylight raiding missions into the Reich. A four-engine Allied bomber was shot down at Pannerden.

Otherwise the following days and weeks passed very quietly. The division utilized the time to improve their positions and to refresh its units. The most difficult task included the acquisition of weapons, equipment, and vehicles. Allied air attacks against the German armament industry could be felt. Special emphasis was placed on the training of the replacements.

In successive and good order, the 21st and 22nd *SS-Panzergrenadier* Regiments pulled out of the line one battalion at a time for a short period of refitting.[105]

On or near 14 October, *Kampfgruppe* Roestel (formerly Heinke) arrived at the division from the bridgehead at Venlo. Since the beginning of September, as part of the formation of the divisional commander Walther, *Kampfgruppe* Roestel had fought in the area of Neerpelt-Veghel and subsequently in the Maas-bridgehead at Venlo. After the *Kampfgruppe* was disbanded, the individual troop elements returned to their parent units.[106]

On 24 October, the daily routine was suddenly interrupted when a crisis developed along the eastern wing of the Fifteenth Army in the area of s'Hertogenbosch. Since 1 October, the British Second Army had been attacking to reduce the German bridgehead south of the Meuse between Turnhout and s'Hertogenbosch. The successful British penetration into s'Hertogenbosch and subsequent advance through the city on 24 October could not be contained. The Allied attack did not halt until 4 km farther west in the area of Vlijmen. The fighting in s'Hertogenbosch continued as the combat strength of the fighting units of the Fifteenth Army steadily declined.

To cope with the Fifteenth Army's crisis, the II SS Panzer Corps received orders to provide one reinforced regimental *Kampfgruppe* from both the 363rd VGD and the 10th SS Panzer Division, to the LXXXVIII Army Corps, in command along the east wing of the Fifteenth Army. The reduced strength of the II SS Panzer Corps was amendable since Allied forces were withdrawn in the area south of Arnhem.[107]

The 10th SS Panzer Division carried out their assignment by withdrawing one battalion of the 21st *SS-Panzergrenadier* Regiment out of the line along the Lower Rhine. However, this did not occur until the night of 25 October. The *Kampfgruppe*, consisting of two battalions of the 21st *SS-Panzergrenadier* Regiment that were commanded by Traupe, and two tank companies of the 2nd Battalion, 10th SS Panzer Regiment (including twenty-five to thirty Pz.Kpfw.IV), prepared its personnel and materiel for the forced march and coming engagement, while the Allies launched their attack against the eastern wing of the Fifteenth Army. Supported by tanks, flamethrower tanks, and Dutch resistance fighters, the Allies permanently captured s'Hertogenbosch when the last pockets of German resistance were flushed out. During the night of 26 October, the reinforced regimental *Kampfgruppe* 10th SS assembled to counterattack in the area of Duiven-Zevenaar-Didam.[108]

On 27 October, north of Elst, Karl Schneider observed unarmed British troops, carrying a Red Cross flag to evacuate their wounded from between the lines. During the evacuation, SS soldiers did not fire on the British and did not restrict their efforts.

In the morning on 28 October, the *Kampfgruppe* marched over Veenendaal-Doorn-Culenborg. After a 65 to 70 km forced march during the night of 27 October, it arrived in the area of s'Hertogenbosch. Without delay they immediately crossed the Meuse River and entered a northerly position to prevent an Allied advance farther north. However, the Allies made additional penetrations through the German lines on 26 October between Tilburg and

s'Hertogenbosch. Attempting to expand the Allied lines, a comprehensive British attack, presumably by the 7th Tank Division, was launched against Tilburg along with a simultaneous advance from s'Hertogenbosch to the north.[109]

A devastating preparatory artillery barrage preceded the Allied attack on 28 October, from Tilburg to the north and northwest astride the road Tilburg-Besoijen. The continued Allied attack on the following day required the commitment of the reinforced *Kampfgruppe* 10th SS, north of Tilburg. Elements of the *Kampfgruppe* broke out of their positions along the Meuse northwest of s'Hertogenbosch and arrived, via Heusden, at the bog north of Waalwijk in the early morning on 30 October. The bulk of the *Kampfgruppe* that remained north of s'Hertogenbosch defended their positions against Allied attacks.[110]

As of 26 October, the sector of the 10th SS Panzer Division, along the Lower Rhine, remained relatively quiet. Several Allied attacks during the beginning of November, against the bridgeheads south of Arnhem and at Doornenburg, were repelled effortlessly.[111]

Having participated in several combat reconnaissance missions within the front-line triangle Arnhem-Nijmegen-Millingen, Karl Schneider volunteered on 1 November 1944, for a scouting mission. West of the bridgehead at Doornenburg, intelligence was required in the direction of Haalderen. Seven men set out to determine the disposition and strength of British forces in front of Haalderen. The German positions, consisting of shallow trenches and fighting holes in the middle of a watery bog, were raked throughout the entire day with Allied artillery fire of all calibers. The scouting troop moved southward from Flieren, and unexpectedly ran into a British forward listening post, approximately 1 kilometer east of Haalderen. The British fired heavy machine guns and mortars that wounded one grenadier and forced the scouts to withdraw. The wounded SS man was left behind, approximately 200 meters from the others, but continued to cry for help. Schneider and three others decided to recover their wounded comrade, before he bled to death. Sometime between 1800 and 2000 hours, the men shed their weapons, belts, and helmets, and obtained a Red Cross flag and litter kit. Schneider carried the 1×1-meter Red Cross flag, which he waved in front of him as they approached the British position. Two men carried a stretcher, whereby an *SS-Rottenführer* in charge called out to the post in English, which was recognizable 50 meters ahead of them (there was a full moon overhead). As they were placing their wounded comrade onto the stretcher, the British opened fire again with the machine gun. Unable to evacuate the wounded Frundsberger, and after discovering the NCO was slightly wounded in the shoulder, the scouts withdrew all the way back to Doornenburg where they reported the incident immediately.[112]

Several days later, on 3 November, a 14×220mm "Red Cross" leaflet was fired from a German field howitzer into the British lines and titled, "British Troops in the Area of Nijmegen and Arnhem." The message contained the incidents of 27 October and 1 November and was signed by the commander of all German Armed Forces in the area of Arnhem-Nijmegen. The leaflet concluded with:

> From this day forward, if an incident similar to 1 November 1944 comes before me again, I shall give the order to fire upon unarmed medical personnel, even if they wave a Red Cross flag. I cannot believe that British officers are willing to ruin their good reputation as Gentlemen, by issuing orders to fire on unarmed medical personnel. Such an act is not considered by either side fair play.[113]

For personal bravery and special achievements, in the face of the enemy, during close combat attacks as well as numerous assault troop operations, Schneider was decorated during the middle of November with the Iron Cross 1st Class and the Close Combat Clasp in bronze. *SS-Brigadeführer* Wilhelm Bittrich, the commander of the II SS Panzer Corps, personally bestowed him with the decorations.[114]

The newly organized Army Group H assumed command over the Fifteenth Army and 1st Parachute Army on 11 October. Five days later, Army Group H released the 10th SS Panzer Division from the 1st Parachute Army and placed the entire division in march; the wheeled elements were to march over

land eastward to Venlo, while the tracked elements were to march over rail to Erkelenz. In accordance with a preliminary order by the II SS Panzer Corps, the division prepared for their relief and departure during the night on 17 October. Relief of the 10th SS by the 6th *Fallschirmjäger* Division, commanded by Lieutenant General Wolfgang Erdmann, proceeded without incident. Moreover, OB West attached a single company of Tigers from the 506th Heavy Panzer Battalion to the 10th SS Panzer Division. Despite the special ration of fuel made available to accelerate the transfer of the division, the additional allowance arrived late and delayed the departure of the wheeled elements of the division.

New orders arrived from OB West in the evening on 18 October. As quickly as possible, the 10th SS Panzer Division was to proceed and attach to Army Group B. At 0000 hours on 19 October, the 6th *Fallschirmjäger* Division assumed control of the former sector of the 10th SS, whereby the Frundsberg Division was removed from the operational control of the II SS Panzer Corps, and the higher command of the 1st Parachute Army headquarters.[115]

On 10 November, the OB West ordered the return of the reinforced regimental *Kampfgruppe* from the Fifteenth Army back to its parent division. The *Kampfgruppe* 10th SS departed the Arnhem area on the same day.

The daily order, dated 18 November 1944, from General Kurt Student, commander of the First Parachute Army, recognized Heinz Harmel and the Frundsberg Division for uninterrupted fighting from 21 September 1944. In the attack and defense, the division accomplished all its objectives in a brave and heroic manner. In particular, from 17 to 26 September, the division achieved the destruction of the British 1st Airborne Division.[116]

Highlighting the combat operations of the 10th SS Panzer Division during the period from 6 September to 18 November 1944 in Holland were defensive actions related to the artillery regiment. Much like all artillery units coming out of Normandy, the regiment lost almost all their guns. However, the regiment acquired sufficient Army artillery pieces abandoned at the Cambrai rail yard to make up two battalions, which allowed the regiment to assume the formidable task of providing support across a front that exceeded 20 kilometers and additional fire support requirements for nearby weak Army units. *SS-Obersturmbannführer* Hans-Georg Sonnenstuhl, the regimental commander, abandoned the old practice of establishing blocking fire segments as outlined in the *Herresdruck Vorschriften* or Armed Forces Printed Regulations. The procedures in the training regulations for artillery were simply too slow and cumbersome to quickly establish blocking fire segments. Instead, Sonnenstuhl strung together a seamless chain of seventy-five segments between the areas west of Arnhem and the Waal River at Nijmegen. Fire missions were easily called using field phones or radios, based on the number or name of the segment. Indeed, the entire regiment could place fire quickly on any designated segment. The best example came along the right bank of the Waal River west of Nijmegen, where large concentrations of Allied supplies were gathered. The 10th SS, as well as the 502nd SS Artillery Corps, and the army 191st Artillery Regiment fired on segments Dora a-f, Gerds, Inge, and Anita, which hit Allied ammunition and gasoline supplies. News of Sonnenstuhl's applications spread quickly and were adopted in the field by the higher artillery commander OB West, General of Artillery Heinrich Meyer-Buerdorf. In terms of artillery ammunition, the 10th SS received large quantities of ammunition for their guns, including 1,200 armor-piercing hollow projectiles in 105mm, several hundred 150mm projectiles, and 3,000 rounds for the 105mm light howitzers. The large quantity of 105mm ammunition became available because very few units used light howitzers. After the front lines in Holland stabilized and the fighting abated, the division relocated in November 1944 to Germany.[117]

A Panther Pz.Kpfw.V Ausf. G guarding a road in Holland, 1944. Source: Gemeinschaftsarbeit des SS-Kriegsberichter-Zuges der 10.SS-Panzer-Div. "Frundsberg," *Dran Drauf und Durch! Buczacz-Caen-Nimwegen*, 1944.

Members of a 20mm Flak gun, Holland, 1944. Source: Gemeinschaftsarbeit des SS-Kriegsberichter-Zuges der 10.SS-Panzer-Div. "Frundsberg," *Dran Drauf und Durch! Buczacz-Caen-Nimwegen*, 1944.

Captured wounded British airborne glider infantry being brought to aid stations, Arnhem, 1944. Source: Gemeinschaftsarbeit des SS-Kriegsberichter-Zuges der 10.SS-Panzer-Div. "Frundsberg," *Dran Drauf und Durch! Buczacz-Caen-Nimwegen*, 1944.

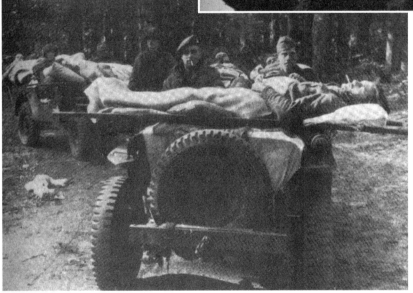

A scouting troop returning from reconnaissance along with a wounded fellow soldier, Holland, 1944. Source: Gemeinschaftsarbeit des SS-Kriegsberichter-Zuges der 10.SS-Panzer-Div. "Frundsberg," *Dran Drauf und Durch! Buczacz-Caen-Nimwegen*, 1944.

Patroling at night, Holland, 1944.
Source: Gemeinschaftsarbeit des SS-Kriegsberichter-Zuges der 10.SS-Panzer-Div. "Frundsberg," *Dran Drauf und Durch! Buczacz-Caen-Nimwegen*, 1944.

Fighting positions in the area around Nijmegen, Holland, 1944. Source: Gemeinschaftsarbeit des SS-Kriegsberichter-Zuges der 10.SS-Panzer-Div. "Frundsberg," *Dran Drauf und Durch! Buczacz-Caen-Nimwegen*, 1944.

Men of the 10th SS Escort Company crossing flooded areas using ladders in Holland, 1944. Source: Gemeinschaftsarbeit des SS-Kriegsberichter-Zuges der 10.SS-Panzer-Div. "Frundsberg," *Dran Drauf und Durch! Buczacz-Caen-Nimwegen*, 1944.

Captured British airborne glider and paratroopers around Holland, 1944. Source: Gemeinschaftsarbeit des SS-Kriegsberichter-Zuges der 10.SS-Panzer-Div. "Frundsberg," *Dran Drauf und Durch! Buczacz-Caen-Nimwegen*, 1944.

Handling ordnance on a bridge in Holland, 1944. Source: Gemeinschaftsarbeit des SS-Kriegsberichter-Zuges der 10.SS-Panzer-Div. "Frundsberg," *Dran Drauf und Durch! Buczacz-Caen-Nimwegen*, 1944.

Relieving the forward position in the early morning, Holland, 1944. Source: Gemeinschaftsarbeit des SS-Kriegsberichter-Zuges der 10.SS-Panzer-Div. "Frundsberg," *Dran Drauf und Durch! Buczacz-Caen-Nimwegen*, 1944.

A well-camouflaged antitank gun and crew around Aachen, Germany, 1944. Source: Gemeinschaftsarbeit des SS-Kriegsberichter-Zuges der 10.SS-Panzer-Div. "Frundsberg," *Dran Drauf und Durch! Buczacz-Caen-Nimwegen*, 1944.

A mortar crew operating around Nijmegen, Holland, 1944. Source: Gemeinschaftsarbeit des SS-Kriegsberichter-Zuges der 10.SS-Panzer-Div. "Frundsberg," *Dran Drauf und Durch! Buczacz-Caen-Nimwegen*, 1944.

The Flak Vielling or quadruple-barreled 20mm MG was effective against low-flying enemy aircraft. Source: Gemeinschaftsarbeit des SS-Kriegsberichter-Zuges der 10.SS-Panzer-Div. "Frundsberg," *Dran Drauf und Durch! Buczacz-Caen-Nimwegen*, 1944.

Allied prisoners guarded by two sentries in a church. Source: Gemeinschaftsarbeit des SS-Kriegsberichter-Zuges der 10.SS-Panzer-Div. "Frundsberg," *Dran Drauf und Durch! Buczacz-Caen-Nimwegen*, 1944.

SS-Brigadeführer Heinz Harmel, commander of the 10th SS Panzer Division. Source: Gemeinschaftsarbeit des SS-Kriegsberichter-Zuges der 10.SS-Panzer-Div. "Frundsberg," *Dran Drauf und Durch! Buczacz-Caen-Nimwegen*, 1944.

A well-camouflaged tank hunter with *Panzerfaust*, Holland, 1944. Source: Gemeinschaftsarbeit des SS-Kriegsberichter-Zuges der 10.SS-Panzer-Div. "Frundsberg," *Dran Drauf und Durch! Buczacz-Caen-Nimwegen*, 1944.

A portion of Allied supplies landed within the German lines. Holland, 1944. Source: Gemeinschaftsarbeit des SS-Kriegsberichter-Zuges der 10.SS-Panzer-Div. "Frundsberg," *Dran Drauf und Durch! Buczacz-Caen-Nimwegen*, 1944.

The evacuation of the Castle Doornenburg, from where Nijmegen was well observed. Source: Gemeinschaftsarbeit des SS-Kriegsberichter-Zuges der 10.SS-Panzer-Div. "Frundsberg," *Dran Drauf und Durch! Buczacz-Caen-Nimwegen*, 1944.

Officers of the 10th SS Panzer Division, including Harmel, during a field expedient meeting with Field Marshal Model. Source: Sieberhagen Archive.

Field Marshal Model and Harmel
reviewing a map, September 1944.
Source: Sieberhagen Archive.

Field Marshal Model and Harmel
reviewing a map, September 1944.
Source: Sieberhagen Archive.

Arrival or departure of Field Marshal Model,
September 1944. Source: Sieberhagen Archive.

SS-Hauptsturmführer Karl-Heinz Euling. Source: Stenger Archive.

Heinz Harmel and F.M. Model reviewing a map. Source: Stenger Archive.

In Holland, the men of the division found quarters among civilian homes, August to December 1944. Source: Westerhoff Archive.

The field kitchen operations. Source: Westerhoff Archive.

The field kitchen operations.
Source: Westerhoff Archive.

The distribution of food by the field kitchen. Source: Westerhoff Archive.

Cutting hair in the field. Source: Westerhoff Archive.

CHAPTER 6

Commitment of the 10th SS on German Soil

19 November–10 December 1944

WINTER WAS FAST APPROACHING, but it was out of the question for the Allies to hold their ground through the cold-weather months and wait until spring to launch an all-out offensive. Such a course of action and delay would provide the Germans time to train and equip new units, fortify their defenses, and potentially bring advanced weapons, such as jets and proximity fuses, to bear against the Allies. In keeping with General Eisenhower's broad-front strategy, unrelenting pressure was to be applied in early November by the U.S. First Army to gain a footing over the Rhine south of Cologne. The U.S. Ninth Army, which protected the left flank of the First Army, also planned to drive on the Rhine. Field Marshal Montgomery's 21 Army Group intended to begin operations around 10 November using the British Second Army to drive southeast from Nijmegen and link with the U.S. Ninth Army. On the right, the U.S. Third Army protected the First Army's right flank and the U.S. 6th Army Group in the south was to resume its advance to the Rhine at Strasbourg.

Strategically, Eisenhower could not see beyond the Rhine and the subsequent advance deep into Germany without improved logistical support. Capturing the Ruhr and ending the war before Christmas would have to wait until the Allied November offensive eliminated any remaining German units west of the Rhine. However, due to a last minute change by Montgomery, Patton's Third Army attacked first on 8 November.[1]

Despite the strategic withdrawal of the 10th SS from the line in Holland for the upcoming secret offensive in the Ardennes, the division responded on 18 November 1944 to the critical situation in the Ruhr around Aachen. The Frundsberg Division was relieved during the night from the sector along the Lower Rhine and Waal. The 10th SS arrived very slowly out of Holland and in battalion-size formations. On 20 November, the wheeled portions of the division were 20 to 25 km north of Erkelenz. The tracked portions of the division arrived by rail for offloading beginning in the evening on 21 November in the area Erkelenz-Titz-Iuchen. The 6th *Fallschirmjäger* Division replaced the weakened *Kampfgruppe* of the 10th SS from the bridgehead at Doornenburg. The tank division moved its tracked elements to the rail stations for transportation at Zevenaar and Elten. Railroad transport cars that arrived were loaded immediately.

The wheeled elements of the division prepared to march and waited for the distribution of fuel. The march was approximately 150 km. When, by midday on 19 October, the special ration of fuel from OB West had not arrived in its entirety, the division collected all available units of fuel and provided them to the combat elements of the *Panzergrenadier* Regiment, the divisional command squadron, and portions of the 10th SS Panzer Signals Battalion. The combat elements prepared to march in the afternoon on 19 November over Emmerich-Wesel-Jssum-Aldekerk in order to reach the area of Dülken-Erkelenz-Titz-Rheydt.

The troop elements received, at the most, a single unit of fuel that was consumed after one hour of travel. While the high command pushed for the speedy delivery of fuel to the 10th SS, the forward-most elements in the area of Dülken-Viersen, and the divisional command squadron in Grefrath, waited for two days for additional units of fuel.

In the night on 20 November, due to a lack of fuel, the last portions of the wheeled elements of the 10th SS continued to remain paralyzed in the area southeast of Arnhem, including the 13th Company, 21st *SS-Panzergrenadier* Regiment.

The transportation of the tracked elements by rail began as well. The first train, carrying elements of the 10th SS Panzer Regiment with a small ration of fuel, arrived at Erkelenz in the late evening hours on 21 November. Allied artillery fire against the city made the detraining of the regiment difficult. The train station and rail directional switches at Erkelenz were severely damaged by Allied air raids, so the majority of the transport trains that followed were unloaded at the smaller train stations to the east and southeast of Erkelenz at Juchen, Ötzenrath, and Titz. Here too, delays were experienced due to Allied aerial attacks. The last train (no. 13) of the railroad movement of the 10th SS Panzer Division was not unloaded until 28 November.[2]

West of the Pannerden Canal, Karl Schneider relinquished his position quietly and proceeded by ferry across the canal with all available vehicles. Wheeled vehicles brought Schneider to the new assembly area around Erkelenz. Due to shortages in fuel, the movement was delayed. All semi-tracked vehicles were loaded on railcars in Doetinchem and Emmerich, and transported by rail to Erkelenz. While the lack of fuel delayed the relief effort, it concluded the following night.

The *Kampfgruppe* 10th SS had an approximate strength of 150 men, after the 1st and 2nd Companies of the half-track battalion were consolidated. The remnants of the two companies were commanded by *SS-Untersturmführer* Oskar Hasse, and the half-track battalion was commanded by *SS-Hauptsturmführer* Hans Lohr. After requisitioning fuel and despite frequent attacks by Allied fighter aircraft, the vehicles got underway in the afternoon on 19 November. Schneider drove a 3-ton Opel Blitz truck, Type 3, 6-36S, with a full load of men and their equipment. The motorized march led through the towns of Elten-Emmerich-Rees-Wesel-Alpen-Aldekerk, and as far as St. Tönis, west of Krefeld. Here, the fuel ran dry, but on 20 November the vehicles were refueled during the night. The convoy proceeded on to Rhinedahlen and eventually arrived, at 0600 hours, at the western outskirts of Kückhoven, approximately 3 kilometers southeast of Erkelenz. The men dismounted the vehicles and concealed them in order to protect them, once daylight broke, from Allied aircraft under a boulevard of large trees along the eastern rim.[3]

Schneider and the company assembled in the village and waited for orders. With the arrival of the half-track battalion, the small group had a combat strength of approximately 300 men. Around noon, reports arrived that American paratroopers had landed to the south in Lövenich and Baal, and taken up positions in a creek bed.

German scouting troops confirmed the presence of American paratroopers on 21 November. However, the Americans had not only occupied a creek bed, but also the Haberger Estate and farm. The battalion-sized *Kampfgruppe*, 21st *SS-Panzergrenadier* Regiment, received orders to "clear the breech of all Americans." *SS-Hauptsturmführer* Lohr prepared for the attack and departed at noon, armed only with machine guns and infantry weapons.

The terrain was flat, clear, and provided for unobstructed observation. Several fields of sugar cane and various small concentrations of shrubs lay before the objective. Due to aggressive Allied aerial activity throughout the morning, which fired on anything that moved, the frontal attack against the American position between Lövenich and Baal was planned in deep echelon across a broad front. Around 1300 hours, when the *Kampfgruppe* reached the Lövenich Road, concentrated machine-gun and rifle fire erupted to repel the German attack. All at once, the *Kampfgruppe* dropped to the ground and sought cover in the sugar cane field. Movement forward was only possible using short bounding spurts. No sooner were the German machine guns able to change positions, they went into action and the German general assault began. Shortly thereafter, Schneider's machine-gun team leader, also the number 1 gunner, was hit by sniper fire in the head and killed instantly. Schneider, the number 2 gunner, pulled the machine gun out from under his dead comrade and low-crawled a few meters forward. Placing well-aimed bursts of machine-gun fire against the steeple of the estate building, Schneider was able to suppress the sniper as the German attack against the estate continued. Another nearby grenadier assisted Schneider and brought forward a box of ammunition. However, the two-man team attracted the attention of other American marksmen, and well-aimed rifle fire soon befell the two men. Acting quickly, Schneider and his loader sprang up to change positions when a single projectile struck Schneider, penetrating through his upper left arm, entering his left upper torso, and exiting the left side behind the breast after breaking a rib. Schneider went down unconscious.

The German assault succeeded in clearing the American paratroopers out of their positions. When the Germans searched the terrain for survivors, Schneider was found unconscious with a gaping hole in his back, having lost significant amounts of blood. He was evacuated to the main field medical station at Kückhoven, where he received medical attention in the basement of a schoolhouse.[4]

After the arrival of the 10th SS in the area of Erkelenz, OB West directed the division subordinated under the command of Army Group B. The division was attached to the Fifth Panzer Army headquarters and was under specific orders from OB West to be employed only as a closed unit in its entirety.[5]

In the afternoon on 21 November, the commander of the 10th SS received orders to provide a comprehensive report to the combat command post of Group Manteuffel at Königshoven, concerning the movement of the division. Once Harmel reported the lack of fuel for the division, he was assured speedy relief. Subsequently, Harmel was briefed on the situation in the combat area of Aachen, the most recent developments, and instructed on the intentions of the higher German leadership. With the intelligence brief along with additional information received since the withdrawal from the Lower Rhine Front on either side of Arnhem, Harmel formulated a clear picture of the circumstances.

On 16 November, after an exceptional and massive employment of Allied aircraft, the U.S. Ninth and First Army launched a large-scale attack in the area of Aachen, to gain control of the Roer sector for a subsequent offensive against, and across, the Rhine River. The center of gravity of the American attack was placed against the XII SS Corps, consisting of the 7th Panzer Division from Thüringen and the 548th Grenadier Division from Saxony, while the main attack was east of the Wurm Valley in the direction of Linnich, the sector of the 183rd VGD. Three days later, the attack continued over Aldenhoven onto Jülich against the north wing of the LXXXI Army Corps, consisting of the 116th Panzer Division, 49th Infantry Division, 275th Infantry Division, and the *Kampfgruppe* 10th SS, and against the same corps but over Eschweiler, astride the autobahn in the direction of Düren. The Allies succeeded in capturing the villages including Immendorf, Loverich, and Puffendorf. On 18 November, Prummern and Süggerath were lost, and Geilenkirchen was lost on the following day. The 9th Panzer Division counterattacked and subsequently assumed the overall responsibility for the defense of the sector where the 183rd VGD took a beating. The far-reaching front of the 176th Infantry Division (XII SS Corps) to the Meuse River, ahead of Heinsberg, was not attacked with great effort.[6]

After several hours of Allied aerial bombardment along the seam between the boundaries of the XII SS Corps and LXXXI Army Corps, the Allies began their attack against Gereonsweiler, held by the 9th Panzer Division, and the north wing of the LXXXI Army Corps at Ederen. After bitter fighting, both villages fell into Allied hands.

The 11th *Panzergrenadier* Regiment of the 9th Panzer Division, employed on either side of the road Linnich-Puffendorf, suffered heavy casualties. Nevertheless, the 9th Panzer Division managed to contain the Allied attack along the broad backside of the heights that ran south of Beeck, over Point 98 (3 km west of Linnich) up to Ederen, which was anchored at the West Wall. The containment of the front, however, in the area of the XII SS Corps, was severely jeopardized. While the XLVII Panzer Corps, which included the 15th Panzer Grenadier and 9th Panzer Divisions, were already attached to the XII SS Corps, additional fresh forces were necessary. Fresh forces did not exist for the 10th SS Panzer Division. The division had engaged in continuous combat since it arrived in the west at Normandy and suffered heavy casualties during the battles between the Lower Rhine and the Waal, in September and October.[7]

Due to the number of casualties, the Allies remained relatively quiet on 21 November along their newly established front line. Southwest of Beeck, the Allies marginally improved their positions.

The immediate concern was to strengthen the German main line of battle across the broad higher ground west of the Roer to dominate the heights in anticipation of a continued Allied attack. In the area where the main line of battle was pushed back and compressed too close to the Roer River, during the last days of fighting, counterattacks were necessary to expand and return the line forward. It was absolutely necessary, with every means possible, to prevent the Allies from reaching and breaching the Roer.

The 10th SS attached to the XII SS Corps and received orders to quickly come up behind the sector of the corps. The panzer grenadier regiments were to proceed along the shortest route to the west and up to Erkelenz while bypassing München-Gladbach. The regimental artillery along with any other remaining heavy weapons, including units previously withdrawn, were to be brought forward over Rheydt-Titz, to the area east of Linnich. During the night the divisional staff established its combat post in a farming estate 3 km west of Königshoven.[8]

In the early afternoon on 22 November, the commander of the 10th SS drove through Titz, Hottorf, Lövenich, and Baal to arrive at the combat command post of the XII SS Corps, located in a West Wall bunker within the lower reaches of the Roer, approximately 1 km southeast of Hückelhoven. En route, Harmel obtained his first impressions of the terrain on either side of the Roer and an appreciation for the Allied operational activity along the front. The terrain reminded Harmel of the fighting for Hill 112 near Caen.

The heights, immediately south of Kofferen, offered a broad panoramic view that overlooked the wild and overgrown Roer valley with its flooded marshes, and a view up to Hill 98 west of Linnich. From there, observation revealed shot-up tree crowns at Gereonsweiler, the long drawn out heights north of Ederen, and the subsequent protruding Hill 100 north of Merzhausen and up to the Hills 113 and 104 north and northeast of Dürboslar. Harmel observed everywhere the detonation of artillery fire that revealed the approximate location of the main line of battle.

From the heights east of Linnich, the commander of the 10th SS clearly recognized the Allied intention to force a decisive and timely decision around the reinforced sector of the Roer and to avoid a costly positional battle of attrition. A high volume of Allied artillery fire delayed Harmel at Hottorf, Lövenich, and Baal. The towns of Linnich, Körrenzig, and Rurich appeared to be the focal points for Allied artillery fire.

The road conditions were catastrophic as a result of bad weather; the streets were riddled with potholes and secondary field-roads were completely muddied. The Roer flooded.

The commander of the 10th SS arrived at the combat command post of the II SS Panzer Corps in the early afternoon on 22 November, where the first reports arrived concerning a renewed Allied attack. However, a clear picture of the magnitude of the Allied attack did not exist. Amidst the situation brief for the commander of the 10th SS, the Allies placed artillery fire in the sector of the corps on either side of the Wurm Valley while only a small number of Allied aircraft operated overhead due to the rainy and dismal weather.[9]

The 176th Infantry Division, under the command of General of Infantry Günther Blumentritt's

XII SS Corps, deployed exclusively on the right up to Waldenwarth about 6 km northwest of Geilenkirchen, and the XLVII Panzer Corps commanded by General Lüttwitz deployed on the left. The latter corps, whose combat command post was in Katzem, 5 km east of Aal, controlled the 15th Panzer Grenadier Division and 9th Panzer Division, west and east of the Wurm up to Ederen, respectively. The north wing of the LXXXI Army Corps linked at this point.

Alarming news arrived from the right wing of the XLVII Panzer Corps when the Allies captured Hoven and Müllendorf. However, German forces recaptured the latter village during a counterattack. In the sector of the 9th Panzer Division, West Wall positions to the west and south of Beeck and the surrounding heights west of Linnich were contested bitterly, not for the bunker complexes but rather the view offered by the heights into the Roer valley, from Linnich to Hückelhoven. It also included a direct view into the villages of Körrenzig and Glimbach, as well as the heights east of the Roer.

Around 1400 hours on 22 November, General Blumentritt personally and verbally ordered the commander of the 10th SS to assemble all his available divisional elements over Erkelenz at Linnich and intervene to assist the embattled 9th Panzer Division. The objective was to restore a bunker-line, the old main line of battle. After the 10th SS reestablished and strengthened the front, the severely battered and weakened 9th Panzer Division was to be withdrawn from the line.[10]

General Blumentritt knew well enough that in order for the 10th SS to carry out his order they needed sufficient fuel supplies. On 22 November, the 10th SS remained attached to the XII SS Corps. This command arrangement remained in place at the request of Harmel, who had a difference of opinion with General Lüttwitz, the commander of the XLVII Panzer Corps.

The difference of opinion between Harmel and Lüttwitz related to the operational situation in their sector, which Harmel believed required a quick response. Reporting the situation to the XLVII Panzer Corps, which was located in Katzem, before taking action would have cost valuable time. Moreover, Harmel believed he could not have received any additional useful information from Lüttwitz, considering Harmel was better oriented and informed. General Günther Blumentritt, commander of the XII SS Corps, acted quickly to stabilize the front lines of the 9th Panzer Division through intervention; the 10th SS reinforced the lines. Later, after the XII SS Corps communicated with Group Manteuffel, the 10th SS was subordinated to the XLVII Panzer Corps to consolidate three tank divisions under one command, which included the 10th SS, 9th Panzer, and 15th Panzer Grenadier Divisions. The directive was distributed during the night on 22 or early morning on 23 November, at the same time Harmel reacted on his own intuition, after receiving orders from Blumentritt. In the interim, the 10th SS remained attached to the XII SS Corps.[11]

The commander of the 10th SS remained aware of the critical situation in the sector of the 9th Panzer Division. The highest priority was to ensure that units could operate quickly and independently. Harmel was determined to bring all available divisional troops into action, based on his perception and evaluation of the front, by way of short verbal orders. This technique allowed noncommissioned officers to decide the best course of action for carrying out orders. During Harmel's return trip from the combat command post of the XII SS Corps, over Baal to Erkelenz, of which both villages and the crossroads at Granterath were subjected to artillery fire, the commander unexpectedly met Battalion Euling of the 22nd *SS-Panzergrenadier* Regiment, between 1500 and 1600 hours, during their drive through the burning village of Erkelenz. Immediately Harmel provided a situation brief and ordered Battalion Euling to proceed without hesitation onto Linnich, cut across the road at the positions of the 9th Panzer Division, attack the Allies at Hill 98 west of Linnich, and secure the heights.[12]

When Harmel departed from Erkelenz late in the afternoon on 22 November, he left behind the staff ordnance officer with the task of orienting the regimental staff and the battalions of the grenadier regiments that arrived later. *SS-Obersturmbannführer* Hans Lingner provided orders to proceed further into the area east of Linnich. Their arrival into the prescribed area was then reported to the divisional combat post at Hottdorf. The 1st General Staff officer placed in-march the grenadier regiments as soon as they received fuel. Portions of the grenadier regiments traveled over Dülken and past Waldniel to the southeast; Rickelrath to Wegberg until Örath (near north of Erkelenz); portions over Viersen-Hardt (west of München-Gladbach) to Rhinedahlen to Erkelen. At some point, the artillery received orders to move forward into the area of Hottorf. The lack of fuel delayed movement of the artillery until 22 November.[13]

When Battalion Euling departed from Erkelenz around 1630 hours, a battalion (2nd or 3rd) of the 21st *SS-Panzergrenadier* Regiment also arrived. The commander of the 10th SS ordered this unit into action as well. The 21st *SS-Panzergrenadier* Regiment was to follow Battalion Euling as far as Linnich and then, backwards staggered on the left, attack from the western rim of Linnich along both sides of the road leading to Gereonsweiler moving past pinned down elements of the 11th *Panzergrenadier* Regiment (9th Panzer Division) and against Allied positions along the heights.

SS-Hauptsturmführer Euling was well aware of the critical situation in the sector of the 9th Panzer Division and the need for timely action. Euling discovered intact remnants of units within the positions in front of Linnich who were not only happy eventually to be relieved but also familiar with the disposition of the enemy, which proved very helpful. Most importantly, Euling emphasized the need to camouflage their positions in preparation for the counterattack.

Battalion Euling managed to reach Linnich. The battalion began their assault at dusk, directly after concluding their movement on 22 November. The assault began without tank or artillery support, across the light rising slope of Hill 98, roughly 3 km west of Linnich. The attack allowed the capture of prisoners who were overrun and surprised in their bunkers.

The attack on 23 November of the additional battalion of the 21st *SS-Panzergrenadier* Regiment, which also proceeded without a preliminary assemblage or preparatory position, continued into the night. The battalion was stopped by Allied artillery fire at the crossroads and bridges west of Linnich, but Battalion Euling moved forward with a fast-paced, spirited attack that resulted in losing contact with the single battalion of the 21st *SS-Panzergrenadier* Regiment to their left and right. They faced the difficult task of orienting themselves in the pouring rain and dark, in unfamiliar hostile terrain.

The method of attack by the battalion of the 21st Regiment differed from that of Battalion Euling. In this case, within assault troop formations, the battalion commander utilized the companies, after closer orientation by elements of the 11th *Panzergrenadier* Regiment, against a West Wall bunker and the surrounding terrain located directly north of the road Linnich-Gereonsweiler (across from Point 95). The forward-most company moved to within 5 meters of the bunker under the cover of darkness; the bunker was overrun and captured before the Allies could mount a defense.

Both battalions fulfilled their missions. The Allies were ejected from Hill 98 and the old main line of battle was restored at the hotspot northeast of Gereonsweiler. The Allies no longer enjoyed a view into the Roer. After the onset of darkness, two additional SS battalions arrived, one from each of the 21st and 22nd *SS-Panzergrenadier* Regiments. Harmel deployed the two battalions against new points of danger and Allied penetrations in the sector of the 9th Panzer Division.[14]

Two battalions received the following orders:

One battalion of the 21st *SS-Panzergrenadier* Regiment was to push through Linnich and onto Wegespinne directly northwest of Welz. Here, under the cover of darkness, the Allies managed to infiltrate Welz, by way of a deep ravine, while fighting with weak elements of the 11th *Panzergrenadier* Regiment (9th Panzer Division).

Mission: Eject the enemy that penetrated the line and restore the old main line of battle, and turn right to establish contact with elements of the 21st *SS-Panzergrenadier* Regiment, engaged astride the road Linnich-Gereonsweiler.

For one battalion of the 22nd *SS-Panzergrenadier* Regiment; traveling over Rischmühle, 1.5 km west southwest of Körrenzig, and over the road Linnich-Lindern, attacked against the backside of the heights between the southeast corner of Beeck and Point 98, roughly 3 km west of Linnich.

Mission: Eject the enemy that penetrated the line and restore the old main line of battle; establish and maintain contact on the left with Battalion Euling on Hill 98; on the right, establish and maintain contact with elements of the 9th Panzer Division located in Beeck.[15]

The attack by the two battalions on 23 November did not materialize until the early morning hours.[16]

During the evening hours on 22 November, the 10th SS established a command post in Hottorf. Within the same night, a directive arrived from the XII SS Corps that subordinated the 10th SS to the XLVII Panzer Corps.

During the course of the evening, the individual staffs of both the 21st and 22nd regiments arrived within the area east and west of Linnich. Without delay, the two staffs were employed to assume command of their respective battalions deployed along the main line of battle. The staff of the 21st *SS-Panzergrenadier* Regiment occupied a command post in Linnich and positioned the 2nd Battalion, 21st *SS-Panzergrenadier* Regiment, at Point 95 and Welz. The staff of the 22nd *SS-Panzergrenadier* Regiment established a command post at the southeastern exit of Brachelen and positioned the 2nd Battalion, 22nd *SS-Panzergrenadier* Regiment, on Hill 98 and near Beeck.[17]

The operational employment of artillery west of the Roer, near Brachelen, was discontinued as a result of the delay from a detour movement over Baal-Doveren-Hückelhoven-Hilfarth, due to poor crossing points over the Roer, and the endangerment of the forward-most portions of the artillery. The Allies succeeded in destroying the few bridges that remained during a push toward the Roer. During the night, the 10th SS Panzer Artillery Regiment traveled over Titz and Gevelsdorf to occupy temporary firing positions on either side of Hottorf. The soft clay ground made moving the cannon very cumbersome.[18]

On 23 November 1944, the interdiction of the 10th SS from the evening on 22 November until the night on 23 November, provided significant relief for the crisis of the 9th Panzer Division. The battalions from the 21st and 22nd *SS-Panzergrenadier* Regiments, and elements of the 11th *Panzergrenadier* Regiment (9th Panzer Division), firmly held the dominating center of the sector, which consisted of the main line of battle, located west and southwest of Linnich, on the Hills 98 and 95. For the most part, the battalion of the 21st *SS-Panzergrenadier* Regiment fulfilled its mission along the network of paths west of Welz. Allied forces that penetrated through the weakened lines of the 11th *Panzergrenadier* Regiment and deep into German positions were pushed back to the original Allied line of departure northeast and east of Ederen.

The situation appeared less promising on the right wing of the 22nd *SS-Panzergrenadier* Regiment. During the night, one of the regimental battalions managed to work itself as far forward as the road Lindern-Gereonsweiler. At dawn however, effective Allied fire, from between the right wing of Battalion Euling and the village of Beeck, pinned down the battalion. The frontal attack petered out without the support of artillery or heavy weapons. The artillery of the 10th SS was not prepared to fire as communications with the forward observers of the 102nd Panzer Artillery Regiment (9th Panzer Division) had not been established. As a result, the battalion commander decided to lead the attack over Beeck with uncommitted front-line forces and supplementary elements of the 9th Panzer Division from the right. Coincidentally, troops of the 9th Panzer Division who were preparing to launch a counterattack against the village were captured by Allied forces that infiltrated the village during the night.

The battalion of the 22nd *SS-Panzergrenadier* Regiment, reinforced with portions of the 10th *SS-Panzergrenadier* Regiment (9th Panzer Division), joined on the left to exploit the advance on Beeck. Well supported by fire from the 102nd Panzer Artillery Regiment, the panzer grenadiers of both divisions pushed the Allies out of Beeck, after bitter fighting in the village. Following the German recapture of Beeck, units of the 9th Panzer Division defended against an Allied counterattack from Süggerath and Prummern, while the battalion from the 22nd *SS-Panzergrenadier* Regiment attacked the Allied flank and destroyed the formation southeast of Beeck. Consequently, contact with Battalion Euling on Hill 98 was re-established and the battalion of the 22nd *SS-Panzergrenadier* Regiment fulfilled its mission.

The next immediate task for both regiments of the 10th SS included establishing and separating local reserves and reinforcing the position. In Linnich, the arrival of the regimental staffs, their units, and the third battalion from each regiment were particularly advantageous. Supplementing the line of the 9th Panzer Division with units from the 10th SS made it necessary to develop a new command structure within the sector on either side of Linnich. At the Castle Rurich, Harmel made contact at the command post of the 9th Panzer Division with Lieutenant General Harald Freiherr von Elverfeldt, the commander of the 9th Panzer Division; they came to a mutual understanding in the early morning on 23 November. According to Heinz Harmel:

> Around midday, on 22 November 1944, after I first reported to the XII SS Corps, I first became aware the 9th Panzer Division would be relieved from out of the line around Linnich as soon as the front line was reinforced by the 10th SS. Reason: high casualties of the 9th Panzer Division. Considering the verbal intentions of the corps, the immediate measures taken by the 10th SS to employ the first four battalions ran its course. At the same time they were to be harmonized with the expressed directive from OB West to employ the 10th SS as a closed unit and the subjection to continual enemy alterations, such as shifting the center of gravity against Beeck, Linnich, and against the seam of the XLVII Panzer Corps and the LXXXI Army Corps. The 10th SS was very careful to bring its battalions into the line, one after the other, in order to later allow for a change of command; one sector at a time. Elverfeldt, an experienced tank commander, understood the practicality behind the wishes of OB West,

to operate the 10th SS as a closed unit. The 10th SS was of the same opinion; however, the piecemeal arrival of the division made it almost impossible to carry out the order.

Considering the change in the enemy's attack centers of gravity, and after Harmel met with Elverfeld early on 23 November, German defensive concentrations were formed without waiting for the arrival of orders from the Corps. The situation was far too precarious; both Harmel and Elverfeld quickly agreed how to work together. Both commanders trusted one another at a professional and personal level, which eased the relationship considerably.

> My meeting with Elverfeld on 23 November in the castle of Rurich was the first since my enrollment at the Divisional Commanders course in Hirschberg between March and April 1944. I was shocked over his poor state of health. At that point, my sympathy for his physical and mental condition wanted to help him. I was grateful for what he taught me as an instructor, and discovered that he was no different as a professional soldier and a human being. I offered to assume a portion of the responsibilities.[19]

The command structure and distribution of responsibilities in the sector of the 10th SS and 9th Panzer Division was irregular; both parties made the situation less complicated and more personal.

Both commanders agreed that spontaneity would achieve a speedy and successful breakthrough in the Roer. Their basic principles of experience took precedence over theoretical debates and rules in the art of war, which neither commander disputed. In this case, however, something out of the ordinary was required, whereby the decision for the command relationship and determining responsibility was not an obstacle for either commander. The boundaries and division of command and responsibilities formulated themselves naturally. To achieve an effective working relationship they reduced the areas of responsibility to acquire a better overall view of the sector of the 9th Panzer Division. They achieved better responsiveness within the sector of responsibility, secured the attack, and achieved success in the defense by better understanding the abilities of their own divisional troops.

After an unavoidable mixing of both units, troops were to be sorted one platoon at a time, once a general withdrawal took place. Later, an overall extraction of the 9th Panzer Division would take place, but without ignoring the combat requirements of the vacated areas. Achieving success depended on continuous contact and situational updates from both sides, on matters both friend and foe in the sub-sectors of the 9th Panzer Division and 10th SS.

The two commanders honored their agreed commitments and were busy in the main field of battle or busy with command situations at their respective command posts. The XLVII Panzer Corps did not receive a situational report until after the fact. The enemy attack was brought to a standstill and a breakthrough prevented.[20]

Units of the 9th Panzer Division that were relieved by elements of the 10th SS transferred to the combat area around Lindern. The remainder of the 11th *Panzergrenadier* Regiment, comprised of three men, held the outer left wing of the sector until relieved by the 10th SS Panzer Reconnaissance Battalion. A unit boundary between the 9th Panzer Division and 10th SS was recommended to the XLVII Panzer Corps based on the development of circumstances and included adopting the line Brachelen-Linden-Prummern (villages for the 9th Panzer Division). The left boundary of the 10th SS belonging to the 340th VGD of the LXXXI Army Corps ran from Roerdorf over Welz onto Puffendorf.

Around midday on 23 November, the 10th SS Panzer Artillery Regiment reported fire mission ready. The 10th SS Panzer Antiaircraft Battalion assumed positions east of the Roer and provided security for artillery positions as well as the Roer bridges at Linnich. Thus, the strength of the defensive artillery within the sector of the XLVII Panzer Corps was reinforced by approximately seventy-five guns. If necessary, twelve 88mm guns of the antiaircraft battalion were also available. The 10th SS Panzer Artillery Regiment registered blocking fire coordinates in front of the main line of battle around Linnich and deep within the threatened left wing south and southeast of Welz. Throughout

the afternoon, the regiment detected and harassed Allied tank concentrations and assembly areas around Gereonsweiler with observed success. The ammunition supply of the 10th SS was again uncommonly plentiful during its entire commitment in the Roer; every battery had a daily allowance of 400 rounds. Anticipating a stronger showing by Allied airpower as soon as the weather improved, the artillery regiment reconnoitered new positions in the area of Kofferen-Rurich-Gevenich.[21]

Throughout 23 November and the subsequent day, units arrived in the division combat area. The units detrained in Erkelenz, comprised of tanks from the 2nd Battalion, 10th SS Panzer Regiment, minus the 6th and 7th Companies, which had no tanks, one company of a 506th Heavy Panzer Battalion, and the 10th SS Tank Destroyer Battalion. The units assembled in a small, forested area around Rurich, while the staff of the 10th SS Panzer Regiment occupied an estate between Baal and Lövenich. Later the regiment moved to the castle Rurich.

The King Tigers from the 506th Heavy Panzer Battalion supported the 10th SS in Holland. In the beginning of October, the 506th Heavy Panzer Battalion withdrew and entrained to Apeldoorn, Zutphen, and later to Bocholt. Ten trains loaded the battalion on 3 October. Seven days later, five reached their objective, and four arrived the following day. On 13 October the last train arrived. During the journey, an antiaircraft railcar battery shot down an Allied aircraft, which crashed into the battery. The objective of the Tigers was to relieve the encirclement around Aachen. The battalion was subordinated to the Seventh Army. Between Geilenkirchen and Eschweiler, the King Tigers fought bitter battles until they relocated several kilometers west of the Roer along the defensive front Geilenkirchen-Freialdenhoven. Also operating in the same area was the Heavy Panzer Company Hummel, which on 20 November lost their commander, Captain Hummel. Army Lieutenant Flöhr assumed command of the company, which integrated as the 4th Company into the 506th Heavy Panzer Battalion.[22]

Company-sized armored units deployed to bolster the front according to their arrival on the battlefield; the 10th SS Tank Destroyer Battalion supported the 22nd *SS-Panzergrenadier* Regiment, and the 2nd Battalion, 10th SS Panzer Regiment, along with the attached company of heavy Tigers, supported the 21st *SS-Panzergrenadier* Regiment. Group Manteuffel directed the individual placement and digging-in of tanks in so-called tank entrenchments at key points and terrain features. Only the turrets remained exposed, which proved especially effective during the defensive battles around Linnich.

The eventful fighting on 23 November of the 9th Panzer Division around Beeck and the bunker position southwest of the village lasted the entire day. Beeck remained in German hands when the 22nd *SS-Panzergrenadier* Regiment blocked an Allied breakthrough along the seam of the 9th Panzer Division and 10th SS southeast of Beeck.

Until evening on the same day, the 10th SS managed to form a connected front of individual strongpoints that suited the terrain very well. The main field of battle consisted of blocking positions in depth. Allied tactical activity diminished on 23 November.[23]

During the night on 24 November, the Allies responded to German artillery fire with lively counterbattery fire onto the rear terrain and positions of the artillery regiment on either side of Hottorf. The division command post of the 10th SS relocated during the same night from Hottorf to Klein Bouslar. In the morning, the XLVII Panzer Corps objected to the location of the new command post and the excessive distance to the main line of battle. Therefore, the 10th SS moved its combat command post to Linnich and closer to the command post of the 21st *SS-Panzergrenadier* Regiment. The Corps accepted the change in location.

Heinz Harmel advocated providing combat leadership as close to the front line as possible. As the war continued, greater emergencies and more frequent setbacks required such measures. The Germans' experiences in the East and West justified such actions. For example, the division did not relocate its combat post forward to Linnich, contrary to the wishes of the XLVII Panzer Corps, as the conditions on the battlefield dictated the overall situation. The depth of the bridgehead at Linnich on 24 November was no more than 2 kilometers. The bridges at Linnich were the target of Allied artillery and aerial fighter

bombers. Relocating the leadership apparatus of a tank division into Linnich was, according to Harmel, irresponsible. The villages of Körrenzig, Glimbach, and Gevenich, east of the Roer, were located along the forward edge of the mountain range, which were observed by the enemy and constantly targeted by combined enemy fire. The smooth flow of message traffic and work performed by the command staff would not have been secure in those locations. Despite several requests to relocate the combat post to Linnich, the division remained at Klein Boslar. The relocation would have minimized Harmel's basic tenets of command and leadership by way of maintaining a constant communication link, layered with the 1st General Staff officer, as well as the division with the regimental combat posts, and the battalions and detachments.[24]

Before dawn, elements of the 10th SS Panzer Reconnaissance Battalion arrived at the battalion command post in Roerdorf. The battalion assumed the positions of the 11th *Panzergrenadier* Regiment (9th Panzer Division), from the boundary of the 340th VGD to the inverted front bending to the southern edge of Flossdorf. Any half-tracks or combat vehicles not needed on the east bank of the Roer were pushed into the river. The right wing of the 340th VGD lay approximately 1 km east of Ederen, visible along the cliffs of the ravines.[25]

In the early morning on 24 November, despite a low-lying cloud cover and pouring rain, the Allies placed especially heavy sustained destructive artillery fire on the German position and the Roer bridges in the sector of the XLVII Panzer Corps. The Allied fire was directed by an astonishingly plentiful number of aerial observers. The city bridge of Linnich received a direct hit by Allied artillery. Allied aerial activity was lively throughout the entire Roer sector, especially between Linnich and Jülich. Low-level flying aircraft constantly attacked the positions along the main line of battle and any movement detected on the battlefield. Another great defensive battle began.

The Allies launched numerous attacks against the main line of battle of the 10th SS. An Allied attack with sixteen tanks, from Gereonsweiler in the direction of Linnich, ran aground from defensive fire from dug-in German tanks and blocking artillery fire. In the afternoon, a second tank attack from Gereonsweiler astride the road leading to Linnich was also repelled and cost the Allies numerous casualties. Artillery from the 9th Panzer Division and 10th SS battered Allied infantry and tank assembly areas south of Beeck by way of concentrated fire. While sustaining high numbers of casualties, the 9th Panzer Division successfully defended against repeated tank-supported Allied attacks south of Beeck.

The bulk of the 10th SS engaged in combat for some time. Numerous German units continued to arrive east of Linnich but were delayed during their approach-march by Allied aircraft or disabled divisional vehicles. Various unit elements scheduled to arrive by rail transport were delayed; five out of eight transports that arrived in the area of Erkelenz were unloaded by evening on 24 November.

The sustained destruction of rail lines and railroad stations by Allied air forces made necessary lengthy detours and frequent stops on open stretches. Railroad stations for unloading, even at smaller stations, were constantly under surveillance of enemy reconnaissance aircraft. Enemy aircraft flew missions undisturbed without any risk.[26]

In the evening hours on 24 November, the XLVII Panzer Corps ordered the withdrawal of the 9th Panzer Division into the area of Hückelhoven-Baal, following its relief by the 10th SS. Unable to provide forces not already committed elsewhere and assuming the vacated positions of the 9th Panzer Division on either side of Weeck, the sectors of the Grenadier 21st and 22nd *SS-Panzergrenadier* Regiments were enlarged. Regrouping began during the night on 25 November.[27]

The new right divisional boundary, which bordered the 15th *Panzergrenadier* Division, consisted of the old line separating the 15th *Panzergrenadier* Division, the 9th Panzer Division, and the rail line Erkelenz-Geilenkirchen. The left divisional boundary, which bordered the 340th VGD, remained along the line Roerdorf-Welz. These villages were under control of the 10th SS.

On 25 November, the sector remained generally quiet. Despite an overall improvement in the weather, Allied artillery fire and the effectiveness of Allied air forces rescinded noticeably. The 15th *Panzergrenadier* Division on the right of the 10th

SS effortlessly deflected an Allied company-sized advance from Tripsrath to the north. Conversely, the Allies managed to break into the line of the 340th VGD on the left, south of Merzenhausen in the direction of Barmen, 2.5 km southeast of Roerdorf. Nevertheless, the break in the line was subsequently sealed off.

By the evening on 25 November, all portions of the 9th Panzer Division were extracted out of the front with the exception of the 102nd Panzer Artillery Regiment. Colonel Heyman, the artillery commander of the XII SS Panzer Corps, attached the 102nd Panzer Artillery Regiment to the 10th SS as combined reinforcing artillery between Brachelen and Lindern. Portions of the artillery arrived during the evening in Hückelhoven-Baal, traveling in very small groups over Lindern-Himmerich-Hilfarth, while some portions moved over Brachelen-Doveren and Brachelen-Körrenzig. The divisional staff of the 9th Panzer Division relocated to Klein Gladbach, 3 km north of Hückelhoven.

Within the greater framework of regrouping the 10th SS, the move on 25 November into new positions north of Körrenzig began for the 10th SS Panzer Artillery Regiment. In addition, the staff of the 10th SS Panzer Regiment under Paetsch was employed tactically to command all the divisional tank units. The number of tanks available to the division was insignificant, considering the tank regiment had not received any replacements since its withdrawal from Normandy. The 1st Battalion was still missing; only the 5th and 8th Companies existed from the 2nd Battalion. Each company contained twelve Pz.Kpfw.IV. The reinforcement of a single company of Tigers, presumably the 506th Heavy Panzer Battalion, was an indispensable measure. The 10th SS Panzer Regiment also incorporated the 10th SS Tank Destroyer Battalion, which remained underway from the detraining area to the battlefield. During the night on 26 November the staff of the 10th SS Tank Destroyer Battalion established quarters in the former command post of the 9th Panzer Division in the Castle Rurich.[28]

The exceptionally well-led artillery regiment was instrumental in the success of the defense of the 10th SS west of the Roer. Despite the total lack of German aerial observation to effectively combat

Allied artillery, German artillery efficiently aided panzer grenadiers along the forward line by battering detected Allied tank assembly areas. Often, well-coordinated and combined German artillery fire prevented Allied penetrations. American prisoners repeatedly stated that German artillery fire accounted for high numbers of casualties among American troops.

On 25 November, the Germans prepared in and around Gereonsweiler against Allied concentrated attacks. While no additional large-scale Allied attacks were launched against the main line of battle of the 10th SS, the objectives of the 10th SS Panzer Artillery Regiment and Army 102nd Panzer Artillery Regiment were divided. The defensive center of gravity for the 102nd Panzer Artillery Regiment lay in front of the right wing around Beeck and in front of the sector of the 22nd *SS-Panzergrenadier* Regiment. On the other hand, the 10th SS Panzer Artillery Regiment focused on the areas of Gereonsweiler and Ederen. In front of the northern, middle, and southern sectors of the division, the two regiments coordinated their fire. An artillery liaison officer from the 102nd Panzer Artillery Regiment was consistently attached to the divisional staff of the 10th SS. When necessary, the artillery commander of the XII SS Panzer Corps could draw on additional combined fire from artillery of the 183th VGD, elements of the 15th *Panzergrenadier* Division, and two Volks artillery corps to support the 10th SS. During the fighting around Linnich at the end of November, the 388th, 407th, and 410th Volks Artillerie Corps were attached to the XII SS Corps. The 408th and 766th Volks Artillery Corps were assigned to the LXXXI Army Corps. The 10th SS, subordinated to the XLVII Panzer Corps, employed only the 1st Battalion of the 388th Volks Artillery Corps, which attached directly to the 10th SS for a short period. The majority of the Volks Artillery Corps were equipped with the following guns:

18 × 75mm field cannon 40
18 × 105mm light howitzer 18/40
12 × 100mm cannon 18
12 × 122mm heavy howitzer 396 (r)
12 × 152mm howitzer 433 (r)

On 25 November in the sector of the XII SS Panzer Corps, the well-organized battlefield observers reported lively vehicular traffic between Sittard and Geilenkirchen. The Germans predicted the addition of fresh Allied troops within the line and a resumption of even stronger attacks.[29]

Allied aerial activity became more prevalent on 26 November as the weather continued to improve. While aerial bombing and strafing attacks were aimed at German traffic that flowed across the Roer bridges, sorties against the bridges proper were not flown that day. As soon as the weather cleared altogether, around noon, numerous Allied aerial observers joined the already active fighter aircraft. With considerable success, observers directed a steadily increasing volume and number of artillery attacks against villages and crossroads. New divisional casualties added to the high numbers already suffered days before; the main divisional aid station in Jackerath was well occupied as the combat strength of the battalions diminished significantly.

Several days of rain softened the clay ground that made entrenching very difficult for the panzer grenadiers. Valuable time passed amidst repeated Allied attacks, but German troops eventually managed to prepare rudimentary forms of cover.

In the afternoon on 26 November, previously identified Allied assembly points were engulfed with fog. The forward observers of both German artillery regiments immediately placed combined fire on the areas around Ederen and Gereonsweiler, although the effects could not be ascertained through the thick fog. The Allies did not launch their attack with the customary level of strength. The attacks, supported in some cases by tanks, were similar to insignificant reconnaissance probes. Close coordination between the German infantry and artillery brought the Allied attacks to a halt. Nonetheless, the fighting brought new casualties for the 10th SS within the main line of battle.

The adjacent unit on the right flank of the 10th SS achieved a similar and encompassing success during their defense on either side of Tripsrath. Two Allied battalions and approximately thirty tanks attacked to the north around 1600 hours from out of thick fog in the direction of Heinsberg.[30]

Throughout the entire day on 27 November, the Allies launched attacks across a broad front against the Roer and the northern and southern neighbors of the 10th SS. The division itself, however, experienced only limited Allied attacks that were preceded at 0645 hours by short rolling artillery barrages. The Allied attacks did not reach beyond that of local holding attacks. By 1015 hours, the Allies launched four battalion-sized assaults from Ederen and Gereonsweiler. While tanks supported the attacks, all four attacks were repelled.

Allied artillery machinations began to resemble those of the Normandy campaign. German troops again experienced the wrath of never-ending Allied materiel. During sunshine and limited cloud cover, single low-level fighter-bombers, or pairs of two or four aircraft swarmed overhead in the area of Heinsberg-Jülich-Erkelenz. Allied aircraft attacked German battery positions with rockets and other on-board weapons. The planes also dropped bombs on the villages within the battlefield. The main divisional first aid station in Jackerath was hit.

Extensive Allied movement and the assembly of infantry and tanks in the area of Gereonsweiler-Ederen was combated with fierce artillery fire. Several days of persistent Allied pressure pushed against the front of the LXXXI Army Corps, whose center of gravity lay between Merzenhausen and Koslar. Thus, the commander of the 10th SS predicted that a new large-scale attack could be expected to concentrate in front of the divisional left wing in the direction of Linnich. The commander's assumptions were validated when the Allies launched their attacks on 27 November against Kolar and Barmen. At the expense of increased personnel and materiel, Allied spearheads fought their way close to the Roer. While the right neighbor of the 10th SS also detected the assembly of infantry and tanks on either side of Tripsrath, the division was not threatened on the right wing. Indeed, the direction of the Allied assault by units around Tripsrath was to the north. Based on the success of earlier German defenses in that area, morale was high. The impending attacks raised no serious concerns.

Consequently the 10th SS focused its efforts on the left around the center of gravity of the defense. The strength of the division did not suffice to establish a second center of gravity. The only local reserve that remained under control of the division was the Division Escort Company, located south of Hubertuslinde along the road Linnich-Lindern, near the center of the divisional sector with opportunities to deploy on both sides.[31]

On 28 November, the Allies conducted reconnaissance probes against the 10th SS, which were repelled. For a period, however, Allied artillery was directed against the Frundsberg Division on the battlefield especially around Linnich, Welz, and the villages along the banks of the Roer. Despite renewed rain showers and poor visibility, Allied aerial activity increased considerably compared to the day before. Allied targets included the numerous bridges and smaller passages across the Roer River and its branches. Most of the bridges were constructed of wood with limited carrying capacities. The 10th SS Panzer Pioneer Battalion reinforced key bridges to meet divisional weight requirements.

Allied bombing attacks caused the first bridge to fall within the sector of Roerdorf, which brought an end to vehicular and pedestrian traffic across the bridge. Indeed, the identical circumstances two days later created a precarious situation for the 10th SS Panzer Reconnaissance Battalion. Sometime between 1230 and 1300 hours, Allied aircraft dropped eight to ten bombs before they scored a direct hit on the bridge across the Roer along the outer road north around Linnich. Thus, the main divisional routes of supply to the western banks of the Roer were temporarily severed. The reconstruction of the bridge was considered pointless, and would have caused unnecessary casualties. The wooden bridge between Brachelen and Körenzig was the only remaining crossing point. However, it was incapable of carrying more than 5 tons and too small to carry more than a small farming cart. The disruption of communications to the rear created psychological anxiety among the troops and also far-reaching operational consequences.

Soldiers with little combat experience who arrived as replacements invariably suffered from the psychological effects of the fighting. Subconsciously they looked for opportunities to cross the swelling Roer River, in the event they had to fall back against the river. On the other hand, the combat-experienced soldier did not allow such a situation to deter him. The experienced soldier was more concerned about the resupply of ammunition that ran out too quickly. The thought of being wounded without the possibility of being transported from the battlefield may also have weighed heavily on the minds of the *Landser*. A decisive factor that helped many replacements overcome their spiritual inhibitions were the role models or officers and NCOs of the division. Over the next few days, many successful local achievements in the face of the overwhelming superiority of enemy forces displayed the value of sound leadership. The leadership of the division balanced the conflict of conscience and common sense with the highest directives to hold every meter of ground and the responsibility toward the rank and file, in terms of weighing the life of individuals and maintaining the combat strength of the division.[32]

On 28 November, the regimental tank commander reported the unloading of the last transports in Erkelenz, consisting of portions of the 10th SS Tank Destroyer Battalion, which signaled the completion of the movement. The same day the division commander conducted a tour of various regimental and battalion command posts and experienced, firsthand, the affects of Allied air and artillery firepower. Harassing enemy artillery fire landed on Lövenich and Baal and fighter aircraft attacked and bombed the castle and Estate Rurich. Fire from heavy-caliber weapons with time-delayed detonations and bombing attacks on Linnich completely destroyed the city. The enemy enjoyed observation from Gereonsweiler into Roerdorf that permitted firing artillery on the village and coincidentally hit at the same time Harmel arrived in the village. The bridge across the Roer River due north of Linnich was destroyed moments before Harmel's vehicle arrived; a combat correspondent riding in the vehicle captured the attack on film, which was televised in December 1944 on the German *Wochenschau* or weekly news.[33]

When Harmel arrived in Roerdorf, occupied by the 10th SS Panzer Reconnaissance Battalion, the reconnaissance commander Brinkmann reported that portions of the battalion had received fire from the village of Welz. The situation in the village itself remained uncertain. With the last reserves of the battalion, Brinkmann established a rendezvous

position at the cliffs east of Welz. Harmel ordered the battalion to re-establish and hold the old main line of battle west of Welz. The divisional commander traveled back through Linnich and provided a situation report on the reconnaissance battalion to Laubscheer, the commander of the 21st *SS-Panzergrenadier* Regiment. The regimental tank commander, present at the time of the briefing, received instructions to support a counterattack by the 10th SS Panzer Reconnaissance Battalion.

A disrupted telephone line prevented a call for supporting artillery fire for the 10th SS Panzer Reconnaissance Battalion from the command post of the 21st *SS-Panzergrenadier* Regiment. As a result, Harmel attempted to reach a firing position in Körrenzig, which also failed when the bridge across the Roer blew up approximately twenty paces in front of the commander's half-track.[34]

Harmel passed through Rischmühle and arrived around 1300 hours, east of Brachelen, at the command post of the 22nd *SS-Panzergrenadier* Regiment. No new developments were reported from the main line of battle. By 1400 hours, he had traveled by way of the command post of the 10th SS Panzer Artillery Regiment at Kofferen past Hottorf, and arrived back at the divisional command post at Klein Bouslar. The 1st General Staff officer, *SS-Sturmbannführer* Stolley, reported that the offloading of the remainder of the division was complete and it had arrived in the area of Linnich. Moreover, he reported receiving a message from the 10th SS Panzer Reconnaissance Battalion, which confirmed the activities of the LXXXI Army Corps along the northern wing, based on the flanking orientation of the XLVII Panzer Corps.

Meanwhile, the 10th SS Panzer Reconnaissance Battalion re-established a firm grip on Welz, despite high numbers of casualties suffered from sustained Allied artillery fire along the main battlefield and main line of battle. For a period, neither the Germans nor the Allies occupied Welz. Allied artillery fire on Welz, Roerdorf, and Flossdorf intensified around 1300 hours. After firing smoke onto the terrain between Welz and Flossdorf, and thereby neutralizing German artillery observation posts, the Allies prepared to attack with tanks and infantry from the south and southwest against Flossdorf, as well as the front of the LXXXI Army Corps. The center of gravity for the concentrated attack struck against the Roer sector, which lay between Kolsar and Bramen, and the XLVII Army Corps. The Allies had previously succeeded in gaining ground in the sector, but only after costly fighting on both sides.[35]

The 10th SS responded to contain the expansion of the Allied breakthrough in the direction of Barmen, after the successful Allied attack against the 340th VGD in Flossdorf. At the same time, the 10th SS remained responsible for stemming the main Allied attack along the northern flank, where Allied smoke covered the terrain at Welz-Flossdorf. According to Harmel, the Allies may have expected a German counterattack into their left flank.

Additional Allied attacks were prepared north of Ederen; Harmel suspected these attacks would come as soon as German counterattacks were launched to the south from the areas of Welz-Roerdorf. Harmel also recognized the potential of an Allied strike utilizing the same forces, in echeloned formation along the seam of the XLVII Panzer Corps and the LXXXI Army Corps against Welz and Roerdorf. As a result, Heinz Harmel implemented protective measures against such a possibility and directed the reinforcement of the 10th SS Panzer Artillery Regiment with the 102nd Panzer Artillery Regiment. He also directed portions of the 10th SS Panzer Artillery Regiment to bolster the left neighbor's blocking fire, south of Flossdorf, in order to destroy Allied preparatory tank and infantry positions north and east of Ederen.

Portions of the reinforced 10th SS Panzer Reconnaissance Battalion, consisting of the 1st Company, 10th SS Panzer Pioneer Battalion, and elements of the 10th SS Tank Destroyer Battalion, were ordered to immediately establish a defensive blocking position south of Flossdorf. Reconnaissance troops were ordered forward in the direction of Flossdorf and to establish contact with the 340th VGD along the left wing.

Over the course of the afternoon, the 10th SS Panzer Reconnaissance Battalion reported the successful defense of the Allied attack against Flossdorf. Despite poor visibility, well-placed artillery fire from the 340th VGD and the 10th SS helped achieve success. Portions of the 10th SS

Tank Destroyer Battalion, within defensive positions south of Roerdorf, managed to knock out several Allied tanks. Moreover, Allied assembly areas north of Ederen were destroyed by way of combined artillery fire.[36]

In the ravine about 400 meters south of Welz, communications were established with the right wing of the 340th VGD. A scout radio half-track, of the 10th SS Panzer Reconnaissance Battalion, reported from Flossdorf contact with troops from the 340th VGD, along the west side of Flossdorf. However, infantry positions along the main line of battle between Welz and Flossdorf remained undetermined and the combat strength of those portions of the 340th VGD defending Flossdorf was only marginal.

The situation report was passed on to the XLVII Panzer Corps. In response, the Corps ordered the 10th SS to reinforce and hold, with reserves, the main line of battle between the southern rims of Welz and Flossdorf. The pioneer company attached to the 10th SS Panzer Reconnaissance Battalion, carrying out this measure along the general line and western fringe of the ravine, 400 meters south of Welz and the southern rim of Flossdorf, after suffering a weak indentation into the main line of battle east of Welz.

On 28 November, the XLVII Panzer Corps extended the area of responsibility of the 10th SS to the south, buttressing the line Bolsar-Flossdorf-Ederen. Despite the lack of resources, the increased responsibilities committed the local reserves along the divisional left wing. The order stripped the main line of battle of substance and removed the ability to oppose an Allied thrust. The commander's sentiments, on numerous occasions, were brought to the attention of the Corps; however, nothing could help the situation. Harmel was directed to use what resources he could to manage the situation. Once again, supply and rear-echelon troops provided extraneous personnel that were organized into small local reserves. Enough men were ordered out from the main line of battle so that each regiment had at least one reserve platoon. The remainder of the day and night on 29 November was used to improve existing positions along the newly assigned divisional left wing and, wherever possible, the defensive capabilities of the troops.[37]

Over several days the Allies had attacked against both the left and right neighbors of the 10th SS, but had not fully committed to the battle. However, in the morning of 29 November, a large-scale Allied attack struck against the 10th SS. Allied tanks and infantry massed their attack across a broad front, and the 10th SS fought the most severe and significant battle during its commitment in the Roer.

During the first phase of combat on 29 November, the American objective to expand their breakthrough was achieved to the north as far as the Roer against the LXXXXI Army Corps, following the same course of action as seen at Flossdorf. American tactics consisted of saturating villages and key points along and beyond the main line of battle with artillery fire before the first light at dawn. As before, the Allies increased artillery fire along the northern flank, this time on both sides of the village of Würm. According to Harmel, Allied artillery fire included the use of smoke fired continuously. The Allies were masters at placing smoke at a moment's notice over broad and deep areas of terrain consisting of several kilometers.[38]

Around 1105 hours, troops of the 10th SS repelled local Allied attacks. Casualties on both sides were high. The establishing and assembly of local reserves to counterattack paid off, despite the accepted weakening of the main line of battle. Within several hours, a single tank from a company of the Tigers destroyed fourteen Sherman tanks.

Several forward observers of the artillery battalion positioned themselves directly in the middle of the main line of battle. They were comfortable and familiar with the terrain, and accustomed to Allied tactics to such a degree that the forward observers could predict Allied movements. Observers of the Army 102nd Panzer Artillery Regiment coordinated quickly between the grenadiers and the artillery batteries of the 10th SS. The coordination effort had a profound impact on the success of the defense on 29 November in the early and late morning hours. In locations where the Allies engaged in close combat, such as the shallow breach along the southern portion at Beeck, the reserve panzer grenadiers of the 22nd *SS-Panzergrenadier* Regiment repelled the attack and pushed the Allies back to their positions of departure. Battalion Euling,

of the 22nd *SS-Panzergrenadier* Regiment, counterattacked across open terrain on both sides of the muddy auxiliary road of Gereonsweiler-Lindern, where the Americans succeeded in breaching the main line of battle of the 10th SS along the Hubertus Heights.[39]

At the same time, an Allied tank assembly point around Erderen was combated with combined German artillery fire. Further south, the artillery of the LXXXI Army Corps subjected Allied assembly areas to fire in the area of Barmen.

The threat along the left divisional flank remained a concern for the leadership of the division throughout the entire day. Similar concerns arose sporadically in other sectors of the division, such as the massive combined Allied attack at 1000 hours by fire with artillery and aircraft against the villages of Beeck, Lindern, Brachelen, Linnich, and Welz. The fire increased between the villages of Beeck (10th SS) and Würm (15th Panzer Grenadier), and at times resembled a barrage.

Allied fighter aircraft consistently attacked German field fortifications within the main battlefields and artillery battery positions with bombs and on-board rockets. German commanders considered the main area of Allied airpower operations to be the area of Würm-Linnich-Baal. Since German efforts to build and improve positions and fortifications progressed well over the course of the several days and nights, the Allied fire had more suppressive than destructive effects, relative to the massive amounts of materiel expended by the Allies, and the low number of German casualties. Many more German casualties were sustained during the counterattacks across open terrain.[40]

During the second phase of combat in the afternoon on 29 November, the Allies neared the smoke screen that had been placed between Beeck and Lindern earlier in the morning. As a result, the German panzer grenadiers that were positioned in the forward-most fighting holes, in a loose-knit fashion along the main line of battle, had little visibility. The companies that numbered fifty to sixty men covered areas as wide as 1,000 meters. Fighting positions lost visual contact between each other and the terrain went unchecked from the constant and skillful Allied use of smoke.

The Allies utilized the favorable situation from the effects of continuous artillery fire and smoke and began a concentrated attack between 1100 and 1200 hours against Beeck, and areas south thereof, from the areas west of Beeck. While every Allied attack against the village from the west was repelled at a high cost to the attackers, the Allies did manage to fight their way up to the Schlackenberg mountain range and break through at points south of Beeck. Allied tanks and infantry utilized smoke to gain ground at the Schlackenberg, a natural elevation in the terrain. German panzer grenadiers allowed the tanks to bypass their positions in order to engage the infantry that followed in close combat. Bitter and costly hand-to-hand combat ensued for both sides. Around 1400 hours, the Schlackenberg fell into Allied hands, and the Allies captured many German wounded. Immediately after the German loss of the Schlackenberg, combined German fire from every available weapon struck against the heights and surrounding terrain that caused additional Allied casualties and forced the eastward attack toward the Roer to be broken off. The Allies shifted to the north, with limited forces, in the direction of Beeck. Nevertheless, the same forces managed to infiltrate the eastern portion of the village and established a firm bridgehead. Immediately, the battered 22nd *SS-Panzergrenadier* Regiment counterattacked.

A small Allied force with tanks managed to penetrate undetected through the smoke and deep into the main line of battle, as far as the western fringe of Lindern. Moreover, the small force caused considerable confusion for the rear-echelon portions of the 22nd *SS-Panzergrenadier* Regiment and other straggler units. The brick factory and several groups of houses south of the rail line fell into Allied hands. Without reinforcements, the small Allied force with two to three tanks became isolated and halted its advance toward Lindern. Despite the advantage of the element of surprise, the Allied forces did not exploit the situation and formed a defensive position in the western portion of Lindern. Hastily, weak elements of the 22nd *SS-Panzergrenadier* Regiment and all available straggler units were consolidated to eject the Allied force. However, not a single German tank was available to support the attack and insufficient strength prevented success against a stubborn Allied defense.

The counterattacks by the 22nd *SS-Panzergrenadier* Regiment against a determined adversary in the eastern portions of Beeck did not establish German control of the village until after dark.[41]

The third phase of combat began in the afternoon on 29 November amidst efforts by the 22nd *SS-Panzergrenadier* Regiment to contend with the Allied breakthrough along the right divisional wing at Beeck and along the Schlackenberg. At 1400 hours, new Allied forces attacked from positions south of Gereonsweiler against the front of the 3rd Battalion, 21st *SS-Panzergrenadier* Regiment, between the road leading to Linnich and Welz. The still incomplete German antitank ditch before the main line of battle caused the attacking Allied tanks to separate from the infantry. Consequently, Tigers from the heavy tank battalion destroyed a number of Allied tanks.

Allied forces broke into the position of the 9th Company, 21st *SS-Panzergrenadier* Regiment around 1430 hours when the commander, *SS-Obersturmführer* Karl Eberts of the 9th Company, rallied his men and led a counterattack that repelled the assault. The Allies suffered both dead and wounded; twenty-four Allied prisoners were captured and brought in.

Before the fighting concluded around Beeck, on the Schlackenberg, and in northern Gereonsweiler, Allied tanks and infantry, supported by fighter aircraft, attacked out of Gereonsweiler along two auxiliary field paths leading toward Lindern. The attack received supporting flanking fire from the Allies on the heights of the Schlackenberg, which enabled the Allied breakthrough across the German main line of battle on both sides of the road Gereonsweiler-Lindern. Several Allied tanks were lost to defending *Panzerfausts*. In the open, after the smoke cleared, the Allies pushed forward some 800 meters. The threat of a breakthrough across Lindern-Brachelen toward the Roer became imminent.

Artillery fire from the 10th SS, which included that of the 10th SS Panzer Artillery Regiment and 102nd Panzer Artillery Regiment, was unavailable due to a variety of combat fire missions already underway. Nevertheless, artillery from the XLVII Panzer Corps responded to the call for defensive fire support and managed to stop a deeper threat.

Local reserves from the 21st *SS-Panzergrenadier* Regiment, supplemented by one flak platoon, an antitank platoon, and an infantry gun platoon of the nearby 10th SS Panzer Escort Company in the area around Point 87 (Hubertus-Linde), and tanks from the 2nd Battalion, 10th SS Panzer Regiment, counterattacked around 1800 hours. Paetsch led the counterattack. After seesaw fighting, the Germans succeeded in pushing the Allies back to their line of departure and re-established the original line of battle. Individual Allied groups diverted to the north and northwest where they reached the encircled Allied units at Lindern. The Allies mounted a second attack simultaneously from the area south of Gereonsweiler, against the 9th Company, 21st *SS-Panzergrenadier* Regiment; however, the same German reserves repelled the attack.[42]

At 2000 hours on 29 November, the tactical changes for the 10th SS included a shift of the main defensive effort from 28 November along the outer left wing to that of the right wing. Throughout the fighting, the division captured seven officers and 137 men.

Along the right wing, which neighbored the Army 15th *Panzergrenadier* Regiment, portions of the 22nd *SS-Panzergrenadier* Regiment cleared Beeck of enemy forces. Command of the Schlackenberg remained in Allied hands, which provided them complete observation into the village of Beeck. German counterattacks against the heights during the day were destined to fail, as preparations for an attack could not go undetected. The heights dominated the entire region and offered 360 degrees of good observation, to include the northern riverbeds of Apweiler and Gereonsweiler, which the Allies used as assembly areas. Therefore, the Schlackenberg represented a key position within the main line of battle of the 10th SS. The Schlackenberg had to be recaptured at all costs but that objective could only be achieved at night. The Americans did not exploit their success and push farther toward the Roer after capturing the heights. Instead, they allowed the 22nd *SS-Panzergrenadier* Regiment to build a thin security line facing to the west, south, and northeast, against Lindern. The artillery of the 10th SS and 102nd Panzer registered points along the line of security before darkness and then began containment or holding fire against the heights of the Schlackenberg.

Alarm messages from Lindern indicated the Allies had succeeded in reinforcing the small contingency at Lindern, which suggested the Americans planned to capture the remainder of the village.

In the middle sector, Group Paetsch continued to fight for control of the main line of battle. During the night, a gap developed between the road Lindern-Gereonsweiler and the northern slope of the Schlackenberg. The gap closed temporarily with provisional artillery fire, but infantry needed to occupy the gap. To make matters worse, the commander of the 10th SS could not spare any additional infantry.

On the left divisional wing, relative calm prevailed. German observation detected Allied troops assembling around Ederen and Barmen, but they were of no concern to the German leadership.

The situation for the 10th SS became critical when the entire local reserves were engaged along the main line of battle. Only portions of the 10th SS Divisional Escort Company—carefully organized and trained with select personnel and equipment—remained at the disposal of the division. Most of the NCOs were combat experienced. The unit had especially good morale and combat esprit de corps. In addition to its regular duties as an escort company, the unit undertook other difficult combat missions. The company was organized in the following manner:

Company Troop
1 Motorcycle Rifle Platoon
    3 Groups, partial on BMW 75
    partial in *Schwimmwagen* (VW)
1 Rifle Platoon
    approx 92 men,
    ea Group 2 MG42 with a total of 9 medium
      mortars
1 Pioneer Group
1 Antiaircraft Platoon
    six 20mm cannon (SP) (1 towed)
1 Antitank Platoon
    three 75mm cannon (SP) (1 towed)
1 Heavy Infantry Gun Platoon
    three 150mm cannon
Total strength: 225 men.

The XLVII Panzer Corps and the XII SS Corps were able to provide nothing more than artillery support. However, the XII SS Corps responded quickly to provide new infantry troops to the Group Manteuffel. In addition, the Army Group released elements of the 9th Panzer Division, withdrawn earlier for refitting.

The 10th SS expected the Allies to resume their attack on 30 November, in response to the German observation of continuous reinforcement of the American 9th Armored Division. If the 10th SS hoped to continue forestalling Allied pressure, the Schlackenberg had to be recaptured, the gap closed east of the heights, and the Allies destroyed in the German rear at Lindern.[43]

In the evening on 30 November, the divisional commander decided to recapture the Schlackenberg in order to retake Lindern from three sides. Before orders were distributed to the troops, higher orders arrived from the XLVII Panzer Corps to immediately attack the Allies at Lindern. By withdrawing newly organized local reserves from the left wing, the 10th SS led two attacks simultaneously.

An attack was launched against the Allies on the Schlackenberg with portions of the 22nd *SS-Panzergrenadier* Regiment, supported by elements of the Group Paetsch and artillery from the 10th SS and 102nd Panzer. The other attack was directed against Lindern with the 10th SS Divisional Escort Company, consisting of approximately one hundred men under the command of the company commander, *SS-Obersturmführer* Heinz Fischer. Before dawn, the commanding heights of the Schlackenberg were back in the hands of the division.

SS-Obersturmführer Fischer was born 25 June 1921 in Leipzig. In November 1941, Fischer attained the rank of *SS-Rottenführer* while serving with the 4th Company, 2nd SS Artillery Regiment. In July 1943, Fischer received a commission as a *SS-Untersturmführer* with a posting to the 4th Company of the 2nd Battalion, 14th SS Mountain Infantry Regiment. In November 1943, he was promoted to *SS-Obersturmführer* with the V SS Volunteer Corps, and transferred one year later to the 10th SS Divisional Escort Company.[44]

Between 29 and 30 November, shortly after midnight, Fischer and the 10th SS Panzer Escort Company attacked the village of Lindern from the south and east, and overran the enemy. Despite increasing enemy resistance they fought their way slowly forward to the railroad station at Lindern. The fighting was carried out primarily using hand grenades, *Panzerfausts*, and submachine guns. Seven enemy tanks were knocked out with *Panzerfausts*, of which three were destroyed by Fischer. The enemy counterattacked and inflicted heavy casualties, which forced the 10th SS Panzer Escort Company to withdraw. Utilizing a ravine, the 10th SS Panzer Escort Company assumed the defense in order to regroup. The company fought a withdrawal back to the edge of town. In the process the 10th SS Panzer Escort Company captured four officers and fifty-seven men. Contrary to German expectations, the Allies did not attack on 30 November from Lindern.[45]

After successfully regrouping, the 10th SS Panzer Escort Company resumed the attack in the early morning on 30 November. Moving toward Lindern from the northeast, support for the attack was assigned to the Group Paetsch, which became available after the recapture of the Schlackenberg. At the same time, the Allies launched attacks under the cover of thick smoke east of the Würm toward the north and northeast. The German units earmarked to support the attack against Lindern responded to the new threat against the Schlackenberg and around Beeck. The strength of the 10th SS Panzer Escort Company did not suffice to capture Lindern. Over the course of 30 November, control of the Schlackenberg and the villages Beeck and Lindern changed hands several times. By nightfall, ownership remained in Allied hands.

German defensive nests continued to hold on both sides of the road Linnich-Gereonsweiler, despite the Allies bypassing these positions. Allied tanks and infantry attacked the West Wall bunker several times, located along the road at Hill 95. The bunker and its ten-man crew remained operational until Allied flamethrower tanks and recovery vehicles finally knocked it out of commission.

On the left wing of the 10th SS, the Allies captured Welz. Weak German counterattacks proved unsuccessful, but portions of the 10th SS Panzer Reconnaissance Battalion successfully repelled an Allied attack between Ederen and Flossdorf.

At the onset of darkness, only weak German forces opposed deep Allied advances. The line of defense ran from Müllendorf in the north to the southern rim of the heights at Würm. It extended to the ravine north of the terrain at Beeck; south of the rail line up to west Lindern, north of the heights at Lindern and northwest of Lindern as far as Hill 87 at Hubertus-Linde and onto Welz in the north; as far as the cliffs east of Welz and west of Flossdorf; and finally to the south of Flossdorf.

Around 2000 hours, the Allies attacked from Lindern against Brachelen, and in a southeastern direction toward Hubertus-Linde. The attack was repelled. The 10th SS Panzer Escort Company managed to infiltrate back into the eastern sector of Lindern at the conclusion of the American attack. Under the command of Fischer, the company struck forward as far as the center of the village. However, after Fischer was killed in close combat, the company disengaged from the Allies and entered a position 400 meters northeast of Lindern. German artillery combated Allied assembly areas during the night of 1 December in the area Beeck-Lindern.

The 10th SS anticipated an Allied attack would hit against Brachelen and Linnich the following day. At the same time, an expansion to the north and northwest was expected in the direction of Heinsberg. A final and broad unstoppable Allied breakthrough occurred up to the Roer. For this reason, the division tasked the 10th SS Panzer Pioneer Battalion with the construction of a holding position on the east side of the Roer River.[46]

In the morning on 1 December 1944, a reinforced regimental group of the 9th Panzer Division, which hastily arrived from the area of Heinsberg-Orsbeck, was poised to attack in two groups west and northwest of Lindern. The 9th Panzer Division committed to battle as a closed unit between Würm and Roer. The left boundary adjoining the 10th SS ran in a line from Brachelen–Hill 87, roughly 1.6 km southeast of Lindern, to the location of the 9th Panzer. Allied reinforcements coming to Lindern were combated by artillery from the XII SS Corps.

The combat center of gravity lay in the area of Lindern. When the attack by the regimental group of the 9th Panzer Division finally got underway around midday, to recapture the village of Lindern,

SS panzer grenadiers of the 10th SS Panzer Escort Company joined the attack from positions northeast and southeast of Lindern. The four spearheads of the attack penetrated into the village. In close combat, troops of the 9th Panzer Division reached the rail crossing around the train station in the western portion of Lindern, while the 10th SS Panzer Escort Company reached the center of the village.

The battle over Lindern suddenly became a secondary priority when around 1440 hours, Allied tanks and infantry assembled out of Welz for an attack against Linnich. In misty weather, the Allies fired heavy smoke and preparatory artillery fire. Instantly, the defensive center of gravity for the 10th SS shifted back to the exposed left wing. The Allied smoke collected and settled for a considerable time in the numerous ground depressions and crevices in front of the sectors of the 3rd Battalion, 21st *SS-Panzergrenadier* Regiment, and 10th SS Panzer Reconnaissance Battalion. German forward observers carefully followed every Allied movement. Unable to control the situation, the Germans called for blocking fire onto pre-registered points. When Allied hand grenades landed in their positions, the forward observers engaged in hand-to-hand combat.

Meanwhile, the commander of the 10th SS was at the command post of the 22nd *SS-Panzergrenadier* Regiment in the southern portion of Brachelen. Harmel obtained an orientation message from the commander of the 21st *SS-Panzergrenadier* Regiment, which read, "Enemy broken through at Linnich with tanks and infantry. Strength still undetermined." Harmel gave orders to four to five nearby Tiger tanks of the 506th Heavy Panzer Battalion, and directed them to assist the 21st *SS-Panzergrenadier* Regiment, on either side of the road of Brachelen-Linnich.

The Tiger tanks advanced cautiously, bounding forward one in front of the other, up to a mill. Before Linnich, four Allied tanks suddenly appeared out of the smoke, also moving forward cautiously. The Tigers engaged the tanks and set all four ablaze. Shortly thereafter, it was determined the tanks were actually friendly from the 2nd Battalion, 10th SS Panzer Regiment. The unfortunate tanks lost their way in the smoke while carrying out orders to attack at Hubertus-Linde.[47]

The Allied breakthrough into Linnich on 1 December did not advance farther north. In accordance with higher orders not to give ground between Würm and the Roer, German troops managed to free Linnich of the U.S. 102nd Infantry Division and re-establish the western main line of battle. During a fierce exchange of small arms fire, the nucleus of enemy resistance broke when *SS-Obersturmführer* Karl Eberts, commander of the 9th Company, 21st *SS-Panzergrenadier* Regiment, fought his way forward through the gardens and up to the church and engaged the dug-in enemy.

Meanwhile, an unfavorable situation developed for the Germans in Lindern. A strong Allied counterattack pushed back elements of the 9th Panzer Division, which fought as far forward as the railroad station. The Allies now pushed the same elements against the brick factory west of the village. The 10th SS Panzer Escort Company conducted a withdrawal to the northeast portion of the village against the weight of the Allied force. Lindern was considered lost.

Casualties on 1 December were high for both the German and American sides. The 10th SS lost a total of twelve tanks, including four to friendly fire.[48]

The 10th SS anticipated the continuation of attacks of unabated strength on 2 December by the U.S. 9th Armored and 102nd Infantry Divisions against both sides of Linnich. The 10th SS was unable to organize a consolidated defense. Despite the German defense, which stood fast against alternating American attacks from the left and right, the 10th SS had insufficient manpower to hold even the most important defensive positions in the main line of battle.

U.S. forces that broke through the western rim of Linnich were pushed back along the outskirts of the city. German forces dominated the fighting that teetered back and forth on 2 December around Linnich. However, shortly after midday, strong and continuous American artillery fire began to fall on Linnich, Roerdorf, and Flossdorf. At the same time, heavy-caliber U.S. artillery pummeled villages east of the Roer. Despite rainy weather conditions, Allied fighter aircraft were also active. Within a period of fifteen to twenty minutes, the Americans completely covered with smoke an area of several square kilometers; the affected areas included Merzenhausen-Barmen-Hill 109, and some towns 3 kilometers northeast including Müntz-Ralshoven-Katzem-Baal-Rorich-Linnich-Welz.

On 2 December 1944, German leaders took matters into their own hands when command of the battlefield around Linnich was impossible with telephone or radio. They led by example carrying only a weapon in hand and issuing verbal orders. German soldiers developed instinctual leadership qualities and naturally banded together but also independently undertook missions and took responsibility for their actions. On 2 December the Germans managed to remain focused throughout the confusion around Linnich. Individual resistance groups of the 10th SS fought their way out of the rubble in Linnich in the morning on 3 December, and through enemy lines toward Brachelen. Deserving particular mention was the heavy mortar platoon, 3rd Battalion, 21st *SS-Panzergrenadier* Regiment, which held its position until noon on 3 December. The platoon evacuated its position, along with its weapons, and reported for duty in the area around Rischmühle.

Out of the smoke at Welz, American tanks and infantry from the U.S. 102nd Infantry Division broke through the main line of battle along the left wing of the 10th SS, and penetrated deep into the main field of battle. Street fighting in Linnich again teetered back and forth. Harmel found the situation very difficult to judge and control.[49]

The 10th SS Panzer Reconnaissance Battalion, with little experience in close combat, appeared unassertive and confused after enduring the American attacks. The battalion, surrounded on three sides, had no route of escape considering the small bridge to its back, leading over the Roer, could only carry emergency pedestrian traffic. Unable to parry the massive American superiority of force, which in many cases bypassed the German defensive positions west of Roerdorf and Flossdorf, the 10th SS engaged American infantry that followed the tanks. During the evening, surviving members of the reconnaissance battalion, still alive across the Roer, were systematically hunted down. Roerdorf and Flossdorf fell into Allied hands. The battalion gathered its stragglers in Hottorf and relocated to Juchen on orders from the division. The battalion could no longer function operationally.[50]

German units reported American forces occupied the greater part of Linnich. Nevertheless, in the evening on 2 December, fighting continued over several individual nests of German resistance. In these locations, the situation on 3 December changed during the evening almost hourly. *SS-Obersturmbannführer* Laubscheer, commander of the 21st *SS-Panzergrenadier* Regiment, sustained a serious leg wound but was able to be recovered.

To prepare and defend against an anticipated American attack across the Roer River, the 10th SS occupied random defensive nests along the east bank of the Roer, from the bridge at Koerrenzig to the Linnich railroad station, and up to the large Roer-River bend east of Flossdorf. However, the continuation of Allied attacks across the river did not materialize. The Americans missed the opportunity to gain a foothold on the east bank of the Roer, in the absence of a serious German defense.

American attacks from Lindern against Brachelen were repulsed on 2 December at other locations along the front of the 10th SS. Along the boundary seam of the 15th *Panzergrenadier* Division west of Lindern, American forces seized the village of Leiffarth after a hopeless attempt to resist by troops from the 9th Panzer Division. However, the Germans held the village of Würm. Despite pressure by American forces, elements of the 9th Panzer Division withdrew out of the line during the night on 3 December after reassignment as the army reserve behind the sector of the XII SS Corps.[51]

American pressure declined notably on 3 December in the sector of the 10th SS. The German leadership calculated the shift of the American operational center of gravity to the right neighbor of the 10th SS. The Allied shift came to exploit their earlier success toward the north, between Koslar in the south and Brachelen, after additional American reinforcements arrived in front of the 15th Panzer Division. A thrust against the weakly defended German sector of the Roer was not considered imminent. At 1030 hours, German forces repelled an American battalion-sized attack from the villages of Beeck and Leiffarth against the town of Würm.

When the Americans fired smoke into the areas west and south of Brachelen at 1430 hours, fighter aircraft activity and artillery fire increased. The smoke was designed to obstruct and cloak the view of German forward observers as a renewed American attack developed along the right flank against Würm. Insignificant American attacks against Brachelen were repelled easily with little effort. These attacks were considered diversionary attacks. During a raid by an assault detachment of the 22nd *SS-Panzergrenadier* Regiment, sixteen American prisoners were captured.[52]

When weather conditions deteriorated on December 4, the pressure by American forces against the 10th SS and the units of the XLVII Panzer Corps diminished further. The American posture indicated a regrouping of the U.S. Ninth Army.

Relief of portions of the 9th Panzer Division concluded in the morning on 4 December. One day earlier, rear-echelon troops of the 10th SS began improving consolidated positions along the security line east and west of the Roer River.

The XII SS Corps made available to the 10th SS one regiment of the 12th VGD, a portion of the reserve element of the LXXXI Army Corps. The new regiment was assigned to the defense of the left wing east of the Roer. The boundary of the LXXXI Army Corps remained unchanged, extending along Boslar-Flossdorf-Ederen. The 10th SS ordered scouting and assault detachment operations, combined with lively artillery fire, to disguise the division's weakened condition. While every German operation from Brachelen in the direction of Lindern was repulsed, assault detachments from the area of Rischmühle managed to temporarily infiltrate American positions along the outskirts of Linnich. Five prisoners were brought back along with numerous weapons and equipment.[53]

At 0600 hours on 5 December, the 10th SS expressly reattached and returned under the command of the XII SS Corps. The command group of the XLVII Panzer Corps detached during the night on 5 December; it was to be employed during the upcoming offensive in the Ardennes. In terms of operational combat activity, only the artillery remained active. Allied assembly areas northeast of Lindern were heavily battered. Throughout the day, and during a brief respite, the Army Group ordered the XII SS Corps to quickly relieve the 10th SS Panzer Division. The Frundsberg Division would be replaced, sector by sector, by the 340th VGD, and assemble behind the front as the army reserve in the area of Rheydt-Rhinedalen-Erkelenz-Wanlo. The change of command was to occur quickly since the division would not remain as the army reserve for long. The division was expected to be employed elsewhere and command of the sector transferred during the night on 5–6 December from the commander of the 10th SS to the 340th VGD.

Lüttwitz wrote to Harmel, in the Order of the Day, dated 5 December 1944, XLVII Panzer Corps:

> On this day the Frundsberg Division is detached from my area of operation. During its short period under my command that began on 21 November 1944, the division fought hard in the area east of Geilenkirchen and brought a stop to the superiority of enemy men and material and prevented their breakthrough. I wish to recognize and thank everyone in the division for fighting bravely. I grieve those that fell and gave their lives fighting hard for the preservation or destruction of our peoples. We lower the flags in reverence before these heroes. I wish the 10th SS Panzer Division "Frundsberg," and its cherished commander, continued success and soldier's luck in the difficult fighting that lies ahead.[54]

The divisional staff of the 10th SS relocated in the morning on 6 December to Otzenrath, 10 km east and southeast of Erkelenz. Once the troops were relieved out of the line, the march into the assembly area began. Rainy and overcast weather restricted the Allied air forces, and German units exploited the opportunity for movement to the fullest extent during daylight hours.

Elements of the division that remained in the line on 6 December reported local attacks that were repelled in the area of Lindern. From 7 to 10 December, the Allies regrouped as well. The Germans expected the Allies to launch a decisive attack against the Roer as soon as weather conditions improved. The Allies remained quiet throughout the four-day period, including their air forces, which were hampered by the weather. Thus, relief of the 10th SS proceeded according to plan without any difficulties.

Throughout 9 December and during the night on 10 December, the remaining elements of the division, including the 21st and 22nd *SS-Panzergrenadier* Regiment, were relieved by the 695th and 696th *Volksgrenadier* Regiments, of the 340th VGD. The SS regiments arrived in the divisional assembly area on 10 December.

After the 10th SS sustained heavy casualties but achieved overall success, the battle for the Roer River, on either side of Linnich, came to an end. The division reached its lowest level of men and materiel. Their combat preparedness and ability, without the possibility of or time for reinforcement, was questionable, even in the face of higher orders.

The Frundsberg Division fought both offensively and defensively for twenty-two days in the Roer River area. The division captured twenty-four prisoners and destroyed twenty-one tanks, while suffering high numbers of casualties themselves. The clever use of combined artillery, from a variety of units, enabled the division to continue to resist Allied pressure.[55]

Defensive position at a road and railroad crossing near Geilenkirchen, 1944. Source: Gemeinschaft-sarbeit des SS-Kriegsberichter-Zuges der 10.SS-Panzer-Div. "Frundsberg," *Dran Drauf und Durch! Buczacz-Caen-Nimwegen*, 1944.

A well-camouflaged Stug III of the 7th or 8th Company, 2nd Battalion, 10th SS Panzer Regiment, near Aachen, Germany, 1944. Source: Gemeinschaftsarbeit des SS-Kriegsberichter-Zuges der 10.SS-Panzer-Div. "Frundsberg," *Dran Drauf und Durch! Buczacz-Caen-Nimwegen*, 1944.

MG-42 team alongside a road near Aachen, Germany, 1944. Source: Gemeinschaftsarbeit des SS-Kriegsberichter-Zuges der 10.SS-Panzer-Div. "Frundsberg," *Dran Drauf und Durch! Buczacz-Caen-Nimwegen*, 1944.

SS-Sturmbannführer Hans Stolley, the 1st General Staff officer of the division, reviewing maps with ordnance officers. Source: Gemeinschaftsarbeit des SS-Kriegsberichter-Zuges der 10.SS-Panzer-Div. "Frundsberg," *Dran Drauf und Durch! Buczacz-Caen-Nimwegen*, 1944.

American prisoners being questioned by the 3rd General Staff officer, *SS-Hauptsturmführer* Walter Schorn, near Aachen, Germany, 1944. Source: Gemeinschaftsarbeit des SS-Kriegsberichter-Zuges der 10.SS-Panzer-Div. "Frundsberg," *Dran Drauf und Durch! Buczacz-Caen-Nimwegen*, 1944.

New *Panzerfausts* brought forward for the defense. Source: Gemeinschaftsarbeit des SS-Kriegsberichter-Zuges der 10.SS-Panzer-Div. "Frundsberg," *Dran Drauf und Durch! Buczacz-Caen-Nimwegen*, 1944.

Commitment of the 10th SS Panzer Division during Operation Wacht am Rhein and Northwind

10 December 1944–February 1945

EISENHOWER'S SUCCESSFUL broad-front strategy that began in early September showed no signs of losing momentum, despite spreading Allied forces thin in certain areas. German forces were withdrawing in all areas and Allied confidence ran high after penetrating the West Wall. The collapse of the German *Wehrmacht* appeared very near. However, while the terrain in the Ardennes offered a natural barrier, the vulnerability of the Allies in this region was acute and as early as October 1944, Hitler approved plans for a counteroffensive that would take advantage of the Allied weakness in that area. The German OKW, as well as OB West and Army Group B, had a firm grasp of the plan's operational limitations and developed an alternative, but Hitler insisted his choice would replicate the successes of the previous German attacks in 1918 and 1940.[1]

The larger German counteroffensive, code-named *Wacht am Rhine*, was aimed at severing the Allied lines of communication and breaking up the Allied coalition by concentrating three armies along an 85-mile front, crossing the Meuse River between Liege and Namur, bypassing the capital city of Brussels, and recapturing the important logistical port of Antwerp. However, these tactical and strategic plans were thwarted short of their objectives as a result of the U.S. Army's responsiveness and highly mobile armored forces. Their expedient reinforcement at St. Vith, arriving during the opening stages of the German counteroffensive, had a direct impact on the enemy's unit timetables, boundaries, logistics, and their ultimate objectives. The speedy deployment of an American armored division to the forward edge of the battle area facilitated the eventual failure of Hitler's greatest gamble in the West.

During the fighting in the Ardennes, German logistics interfered with the goal to reach the Meuse River and beyond. The speedy deployment of American armor to bolster the ad hoc American defenses around St. Vith caused unexpected delays in the German timetables, the early commitment of reserve troops to force a decisive breakthrough, traffic jams, and general confusion that prevented the most valuable supplies (fuel) from reaching the lead elements of the German attack. The spearheads of the Fifth and Sixth Panzer Armies would require continual resupply in order to maintain their advance and reach their objective. Once the first wave reached the Meuse, a second wave would resupply and reinforce the first, and collectively capture Antwerp. However, stiffened American resistance and strong counterattacks forced the German spearheads to withdraw. In some instances, the German spearheads ran out of fuel and crews abandoned their tanks, and withdrew on foot. The American delaying actions and fighting withdrawals before, in, and behind St. Vith were crucial in solidifying the failure of the German counteroffensive. General Marshall called it "the splendid stand of the 7th Armored Division at St. Vith."[2]

After especially bitter and costly fighting against the American advance in the Roer sector around Brachelen-Linnich-Erkelenz, where both sides sustained numerous casualties, the 10th SS Panzer Division withdrew out of the Roer sector and marched by night into the area Euskirchen-Münstereifel-Rhinebach. On 5 December, the 10th SS returned under the command of the XII SS Corps for employment during the upcoming counteroffensive in the Ardennes. Despite the extraction of the division from the front lines in Holland in early November, to prepare for the counteroffensive, the 10th SS continued to respond to new threats following a continued general Allied push into the Roer sector. At a time when both the Germans and the Allies were regrouping, the 10th SS finally began exiting the front lines throughout 9 and 10 December. The regiments of the division arrived in the divisional assembly area during the evening on 10 December, with only six days before the beginning of the counteroffensive. Around this time, the division accounted for the following tanks and artillery, as compared to the table of organization:

	Actual	T/O	In Transit
Pz.Kpfw.V Panther	4	60	25
Pz.Kpfw.IV	10	30	34
Assault Guns	11	21	3
Heavy Antitank	6	28	7
Light Howitzer	37	37	
Heavy Howitzer	18	18	
100mm Cannon	8	4[3]	

The losses in manpower were quickly replaced with personnel from the *Luftwaffe*. The division had already received *Luftwaffe* replacements in the early fall of 1944, after the fighting around Arnhem-Nijmegen. Both the German officers and NCOs were pushed to their limits during the training of newcomers to become capable soldiers. Those from the cadre that survived the war up to this point were still more than capable of bringing new recruits up to the basic standards. The general concern was they would not have enough time to adequately train the replacements. Many of the German replacements, especially those from *Volksgrenadier* Divisions, were originally from the *Kriegsmarine* or *Luftwaffe*. Most of the retrainees had no prior combat experience, which was a great concern to the commanders of the Panzer Armies. After the withdrawal of the German Army behind the Siegfried Line, many Allied commanders considered the Germans beaten, but as Russell F. Weigley explained:

> German divisions displayed an awesome ability to survive shattering casualties and yet rebound within weeks, as long as a reasonable remnant of the officer cadre escaped to train the replacement troops. So high were the professional attainments of the German army that a handful of German officers sufficed to accomplish apparent miracles of training and leadership. Yet so capable were German officers in transforming individual soldiers into cohesive units that in the German army the company developed a sufficient sense of comradeship and solidarity . . . that makes an army an effective fighting force.[4]

German resurgence and deception, which the Germans referred to as the "Miracle in the West" as orchestrated and credited to Field Marshal Walter Model, rested in the fact that Germany's full wartime production had not reached its peak until the fall of 1944. Moreover, additional manpower reserves remained untapped. Despite five years of war, new divisions were raised by replacing men on farms and in factories with foreign forced labor and women. Lowering the standards even further and sifting through the ranks of the sister services made available men who formed, by the end of the year, some fifty new *Volksgrenadier* divisions that fought in both the East and West with some of the most advanced weapons and equipment.[5]

The 10th SS Panzer Division was one of at least thirty-five divisions that received replacements as described above. Around 15 December, the division was brought to full strength in both personnel and materiel. Ground, administrative, airborne, and *Luftwaffe* replacement personnel were trained quickly by the older and experienced nuclei of the division, eliminating any potential deficiency in the combat strength of the division. Simultaneously, the division obtained new equipment, especially tanks and armored vehicles.

A good example of the difficulty the tank regiment faced in obtaining vehicles was experienced by Fleischer and several other men from the 6th Company, 10th SS Panzer Regiment, under the command of Erhard, all of whom headed for the German town of Linz as a panzer recovery detachment. When they arrived at the railroad station in Bocholt, Erhard received new orders and the group split in every direction. Most went home for several days, but plans were made to rendezvous in Linz on a certain day. Everyone met at Linz as agreed, except for Erhard, who arrived two days later. However, Erhard brought with him wine that everyone enjoyed and drank from glasses; Fleischer, the youngest member, had to drink from the bladder. He was told if he could not drink from the bladder, he could not have any wine.[6]

The 6th Tank Company entered quarters in a small town of Neukirchen-Irlenbusch, south of Rhinebach, and finally received their vehicles. The 6th Company also received their theoretical level in personnel, consisting of three platoons, each with three vehicles. The company command troop received two tanks, for a total of eleven tanks. The replacement personnel, mostly from the birth-year 1925, listened intently to the stories of the experienced tankers. Their experiences included the baptism of fire in Russia, the tank battles at Hills 112 and 113 in France, and the fighting against British paratroopers in Holland. Quickly the men established a degree of trust that paid off later during their training. At the conclusion of their very brief training, the commander of the division assigned the crews their vehicles after a handshake. Each vehicle

commander was expected to recite the tanker-verse: "Many enemies, and many honors. . . ."[7]

The order of battle for the 10th SS Panzer Division resembled that of a Panzer Division 1944, with the exception that the artillery regiment had an additional 100mm gun battalion.

Headquarters Staff, 10th SS Panzer Division
10th SS Divisional Escort Company
10th SS Panzer Signals Battalion
21st *SS-Panzergrenadier* Regiment; with 1 reinforced battalion
22nd *SS-Panzergrenadier* Regiment
10th SS Panzer Regiment
    1st Battalion comprised of Pz.Kpfw.V
    2nd Battalion comprised of StuG III
10th SS Antitank Battalion; comprised of approx. 45 Pz.Kpfw.IV
10th SS Reconnaissance Battalion
10th SS Pioneer Battalion
10th SS Panzer Antiaircraft Battalion
10th SS Artillery Regiment
    1st Battalion comprised of twelve 100mm on StuG III and six 150mm howitzers on Pz.Kpfw.IV (Sd.Kfz.165 or Hummel)
    2nd Battalion comprised of 3 batteries of four 105mm (*Wespen*)
    3rd Battalion comprised of 3 batteries of four 150mm (Hornissen)
    4th Battalion comprised of 3 batteries of four 100mm cannon
10th SS Panzer Repair Battalion comprised of 3 repair companies for wheeled vehicles, 1 Weapons Repair Company, and 1 Spare Parts Detachment
10th SS Subsistence Battalion; comprised of 1 Bakery Company and 1 Butcher Company
Divisional Supply Troops[8]

Upon arrival into the area of Field Marshal Model's Army Group B in Euskirchen-Münstereifel-Rhinebach, the division was subordinated as the reserves for Army Group B. Army Group B organized in the following manner:

Army Group B
Army Group Headquarters

Commanding General: Field Marshal Walter
 Model
Chief of the General Staff: General Hans Krebs

Sixth Panzer Army
 Commanding General: *SS-Oberstgruppenführer*
  Joseph Dietrich
 Chief of the General Staff: *SS-Brigadeführer*
  Fritz Krämer
 LXVII Army Corps (Lieutenant General Otto
  Hitzfeldt)
   272th Infantry Division
   326th Infantry Division
 I SS Panzer Corps (*SS-Oberstgruppenführer*
  Hermann Priess)
   12th Infantry Division
   277th Infantry Division
   3rd *Fallschirmjäger* Division
   1st SS Panzer Division
   12th SS Panzer Division
 II SS Panzer Corps (*SS-Brigadeführer* Wilhelm
  Bittrich)
   2nd SS Panzer Division
   9th SS Panzer Division
Fifth Panzer Army
 Commanding General: General Hasso von
  Manteuffel
 Chief of the General Staff: Brigadier General
  Werner Wagner
 LXVI Army Corps (General Walter Lucht)
   18th VGD
   62nd VGD
 LXVIII Panzer Corps (General Walter Krüger)
   560th Infantry Division
   116th Infantry Division
 XLVII Panzer Corps (General of Panzer Troops
  Heinrich Freiherr von Lüttwitz)
   26th Infantry Division
   2nd Panzer Division
   Panzer Lehr Division
Seventh Army
 Commanding General: General of Panzer
  Troops Erich Brandenburger
 Chief of the General Staff: Colonel Rudolf-
  Christoph Freiherr von Gersdorff
 LXXXV Army Corps (General of Infantry
  Baptist Kniess)

352nd Infantry Division
5th *Fallschirmjäger* Division
LXXX Army Corps (General of Infantry Dr.
 Franz Beyer)
  212th Infantry Division
  276th Infantry Division
LIII Army Corps (General of Cavalry Edwin
 Graf von Rothkirch und Trach)
  Security Battalions (each with six
   battalions)
  388th Volksartillery Corps
  401st Volksartillery Corps
  402nd Volksartillery Corps
  405th Volksartillery Corps
  407th Volksartillery Corps
  408th Volksartillery Corps
  766th Volksartillery Corps
  4th Projector Brigade (each with six
   battalions)
  7th Projector Brigade
  8th Launcher Brigade
  9th Projector Brigade
  15th Projector Brigade
  16th Projector Brigade
  17th Projector Brigade
  18th Launcher Brigade[9]

Army Group B ordered the division to carry out intensive training. The division was directed to prepare to march on orders within three hours. Given the fact that larger unit formations were unable to train in the field due to Allied aerial activity, divisional combat training became practically impossible.

For several weeks, the weather was very cold. Small amounts of snow lay on the ground and the ground was frozen solid. Moreover, the skies were overcast without interruption for weeks. The unprecedented concentration of units in the neighboring areas of the division suggested that something of a greater magnitude was at hand. The assumption was confirmed by the fact that the Sixth Panzer Army, in the line directly in front of the 10th SS Panzer Division, was not participating in any fighting outside the ordinary. Secrecy throughout the first two weeks in December was held at a premium.

On 12 December 1944, OB West was situated in Ziegenberg, 8 km west of Bad Nauheim.[10] Around the middle of December, a number of commanders including divisional commanders were summoned to the headquarters of OB West. The distinct pessimism that had gripped the leadership and the rank and file for months suddenly dissipated after the meeting. Many staff members were suddenly full of new life and optimism when they learned that after carefully evaluating the situation Hitler had ordered a counterattack in the West. Hitler himself sought to convince the most critical opponents of the operation.

The goal of the operation was to break through the Allied line and proceed in the general direction of Lüttich and Brussels to the sea. Panzer divisions and motorized divisions leading the attack invariably pulled with them Army troops involved in the forward assembly. Despite their late organization, *Volksgrenadier* divisions were equipped superbly, had high morale, and were tasked with guarding the flanks with the older infantry divisions. The 10th SS took its place in the third wave of the attack with the objective of pushing through to the sea from Antwerp. The goal of the operation, beyond breaking through the Allied line, was to separate the Allied forces that occupied Belgium and Holland, en masse, from the Allied forces in France. All predictions indicated that a successful execution of the operation would give the German leadership several additional months of time.

Units earmarked as the reserves for Army Group B included the 10th SS, 9th and 257th Infantry Divisions, the 3rd Panzer Grenadier Division, the 6th SS Mountain Division, and the 11th Panzer Division.[11]

According to Harmel, a plausible reason for launching the offensive was that something needed to occur since capitulation in the West was not an option. They decided to utilize the Ardennes even though its remote location and poor terrain were not suitable for major operations. The plan offered potential after the Allies arrived at the West Wall following a long victorious march against a battered German Army. The Allies did not contemplate that the German Army could launch another major attack based on the distribution of the Allied forces. The Germans expected a successful operation would have serious consequences for Allied morale and fighting strength. The German units earmarked

for the operation were among the most experienced and best available. Harmel maintained that ammunition and fuel were plentiful enough to allow the operation to be executed without problems. The assembly of armored forces in the Eifel offered the element of surprise at the onset.[12]

The weather for the selected time period of the operation was of particular importance. The sky that remained in continuous overcast throughout the period, in addition to the frozen roads, offered a certain degree of optimism. If Allied aerial activity was limited by the weather, that would be crucial to the success of the operation, as the German *Luftwaffe* was not expected to combat Allied airpower. In the end, the operation depended on continued overcast conditions as all the necessary equipment, personnel, and supply materials were brought forward to succeed. The 10th SS was supplied with at least eight units of fuel. The most glaring deficiency of the operational plan was the lack of a strong tactical air force.

The troops quietly celebrated Christmas 1944 early in anticipation of the great offensive.[13]

Around 12 December, the Army Group B ordered the 10th SS to prepare for march within one hour. That meant the attack could begin at any hour, though the Army Group did not know the exact day and hour. The most decisive factor for the success of the operation remained the poor weather.

As a component of the Army Group B reserve, the division was to push forward on Lüttich, after breaking through the Allied front and subsequent defenses. No written orders for the operation were obtained; the results of the first several days were not known. Directives and situational and orientation briefings were provided by the Army Group only verbally. Field Marshal Model and his chief of staff were optimistic the operation would succeed.[14]

Twenty-four hours before the beginning of the counteroffensive, the 10th SS received orders to release that evening their entire artillery regiment as well as the antiaircraft battalion to the Sixth Panzer Army. Both units were immediately attached to the Sixth Panzer Army. Their missions were to support artillery operations for the prelude of the attack, and then revert back to their parent commands for subsequent actions.

Army Group B intended on providing only brief preparatory artillery fire, from all available guns, to support the attacking armies. Brief artillery fire, as opposed to extended periods of fire, was essential to keep the Allies from taking early countermeasures, a result to be avoided at all costs. Neighboring units of the attacking armies were also expected to provide artillery support. The first German goal was to engage and destroy the Allied units directly at the front. At the very least, cutting the lines of communication would temporarily disable Allied units. South of the main attack, a diversionary attack was designed to help conceal the real intentions of the Army Group. Every effort was made to keep the operation secret, including the time and place of the attack.

During the evening before the attack, *Fallschirmjägers* entered the line opposite Allied positions. The employment of large numbers of *Fallschirmjägers* as light infantry within their area of operations was purely tactical, as opposed to operational. Their assignment to capture important heights and crossroads but within reasonable proximity to the front lines served to confuse the enemy during the first phase of the attack. Unexpectedly in the night a variety of troops parachuted into the former billeting areas of the 10th SS. However, because the commanders and their men knew little to nothing about the intentions of the higher leadership, these incidents caused considerable confusion among friendly troops, who could not distinguish between German and American paratroopers. Several parachutists were arrested.[15]

The same night, the commander of the 10th SS proceeded to the command post of the Sixth Panzer Army, where he remained the following day as well to maintain close and clear oversight of the latest developments.

Support fire for the attack against St. Vith came from guns from the 3rd Battalion, 10th SS Artillery Regiment, commanded by *SS-Sturmbannführer* Haas, which also included 105mm guns from the 10th Battery that established firing positions in Schönberg. The forward observer for the 10th Battery, *SS-Standartenoberjunker* Jan Sierks, directed fire onto the railroad station at St. Vith.

On the first day of the offensive, the 1st General Staff officer of the division traveled to the command post of Army Group B, situated about 5 to 8 km west of Münstereifel in a snow-covered valley. General Krebs, the chief of staff of the Army Group, personally briefed *SS-Obersturmbannführer* Stolley, the divisional 1st General Staff officer, and explained the intentions of the Army Group in general and also as it related to the 10th SS. Krebs remained unable to give orders concerning the employment of the division, as his orders would rely on the development of the events yet to unfold.

On the second day of the counteroffensive, the verbal situation briefings provided by the Army Group to the 10th SS confirmed that everything was progressing according to the plan. The enemy was taken by complete surprise and little to no resistance was met. Several armored units were advancing quickly; the 10th SS remained on the alert and prepared to march in one hour. Moreover, the Army Group informed Stolley that German troops under the command of *SS-Oberführer* Otto Skorzeny in American uniforms, taken from prisoners during the early stages of the operation, operated behind enemy lines to create confusion and hopefully could capture higher-ranking enemy officers. On the second and third day the situation did not change. The division continued to wait for operational orders. American resistance was of no relevance as no organized countermeasures were adopted. The operation appeared to be successful. As V-1 rockets flew over the heads of the divisional bivouac area, the officers and the men of the division shared a euphoric feeling that they were once again moving forward.[16]

Only the weather did not proceed according to the plan. Until the beginning of the offensive, the weather remained overcast. Once the offensive began the weather suddenly changed and the skies cleared for brilliant sunshine during the day. In the evening it was clear. Enemy aircraft exploited the opportunity during excellent flying weather. Both the attacking German units and the rear-echelon troops were attacked from the air without respite. The narrow mountainous roads through the Eifel region, which were frozen solid and easily traversed, thawed during the day. Unimaginable difficulties were encountered when tracked vehicles, prime movers, tanks, and artillery guns became stuck in the mud. There were times when nothing could move forward or backwards. The roads that snarled many vehicles also provided numerous targets for the Allied aircraft. Every town, road crossing, and smaller train station was bombed. The supply trains carrying desperately needed supplies for the attacking units were stuck. Although the supply units had everything needed to support the attack, they could not bring the supplies forward. Many trains carrying fuel for tanks fell prey to Allied aircraft.

On the fifth or sixth day after the beginning of the counteroffensive, the commander of the 10th SS Panzer Division quietly heard the first indications of failure among the Army Group. They hoped for overcast skies that would prevent Allied aircraft from disrupting the delivery of desperately needed supplies. Reserve units could only move slowly and with significant delays. In short, the enemy won time. With time on their side, the Allies were able to bring forward reserve troops deep within their lines of communication without the slightest interference by the German *Luftwaffe*. From the German perspective, the Allies experienced no shortages in men, materiel, or fuel. The Americans quickly brought forward reserve troops once the initial shock of the counteroffensive was overcome. While the German armored spearheads were not stopped altogether, the American response slowed the German advance significantly. The German lack of fuel was a key factor in the offensive coming to a halt. The slow pace of the German attack encountered more and more resistance while the German flanks grew in distance. American attacks against the flanks increased and tough defenses were encountered at the towns of Eckpfeiler, Bastogne, and St. Vith. The German spearheads that reached the Ourthe River, but did not have an opportunity to cross, were subsequently subjected to American attacks against the flanks and their fronts. The American leadership responded to the counteroffensive slowly, but they responded with greater energy and substance. A respite in German operations meant the counteroffensive had failed.[17]

By 21 December, when the attack by Army Group B petered out and the Germans were unable to dislodge American forces at Bastogne, the mounting pressure on the southern flank of the German advance from Patton's Third Army moving north required attention. An alternative plan that Hitler believed could exploit the Allies' weakened southern army group, which took the brunt of the German thrust in the Ardennes, was for a follow-up offensive in the south code-named *Unterhenhem Nordwind* or Operation Northwind. The new offensive, under the operational control of the General of Infantry Hans von Obstfelder's First Army, aimed to thrust a panzer grenadier and infantry division against the American Sarre River valley defenses, while four infantry divisions pushed off from the Bitche area to the southwest through the Vosges. In the event of success, Hitler also approved an additional attack, code-named *Zahnarzt* or Operation Dentist, south of Saarbrucken toward the Saverne Gap, in order to split the U.S. Seventh Army and clear northern Alsace. General Johannes Blaskowitz, commander of Army Group G, would provide two panzer divisions kept in reserve to exploit any breakthrough, including the 10th SS Panzer Division and the 7th Parachute Division.[18]

Meanwhile, at the beginning of January 1945, the 1st Battalion, 10th SS Panzer Regiment, which had been waiting to receive new Panther tanks since October 1943, finally obtained its vehicles at the training base at Grafenwöhr. The battalion moved to Landau and then by motorized march to the area of Stollhofen-Freistett, whereas the command post was established in Memprechtshofen.[19]

The 6th Company, 10th SS Panzer Regiment relocated by rail to the wine region of Palatinate. The company traveled to the railroad station at Limburgerhof and offloaded. The 2nd Battalion of the tank regiment bypassed Schifferstadt-Lindau, Herxheim, and stayed overnight in Hayna, but deployed the following day into a forest southwest of Kandel, and entered their assigned preparatory and bivouac positions at Forstfeld-Beinheim. The lead company, the 6th Company, 10th SS Panzer Regiment, quartered in the area around Roeschwoog and Leutenheim. The company command post, supply trains, and the 2nd and 3rd Platoons located in Roeschwoog. The 1st Platoon and company troop halted in Leutenheim. While both villages already provided quarters for troops from various branches, ample room allowed the 6th Company to find lodging.

Some men of the 6th Company, 10th SS Panzer Regiment were uneasy as they entered the Alsace region. Bernhard Westerhoff felt a certain degree of resistance from the population, despite his belief that they were on German soil and spoke the same language.[20] Nevertheless, many friendships were cultivated and each side helped one another.

The high level of Allied aerial activity required that camouflage receive the highest priority. The movement of vehicles was carefully restricted and the training emphasized weapons and functioning equipment and vehicles. The 2nd Battalion commander, *SS-Sturmbannführer* Reinhold, left the unit following the Arnhem operation. *SS-Hauptsturmführer* Kurt Wolfgang Neu took command of the battalion until Leo Franke returned to the battalion after a brief stay with the 1st Battalion.[21]

On 11 January, portions of the XXXIX Panzer Corps led an unsuccessful attack against Ritterhofen and Hatten. While the 6th Company did not participate in the operation directly, Eberhard Storch managed to capture an American Jeep. However, the continued attacks by the U.S. 12th Armored Division from the west and the 3rd French-Algerian Division from the south, against the German bridgehead at Herrlisheim-Offendorf-Gambsheim, forced the Germans to shift their center of gravity in the direction of Drusenheim.

On 14 January 1945, the order to begin marching arrived at 2200 hours. The tanks slowly moved out of their preparatory positions in a ghost-like manner and formed on the road heading toward Fort-Louis. The order of march placed the 1st Platoon at the lead, followed by the company headquarters platoon, and the 2nd and 3rd Platoons. Motorcycle messengers rode between the platoons. Notice came for radio silence. The formation of tanks passed Fort-Louis and Strattmatten heading in the direction of Drusenheim. The supply train remained behind in Roeschwoog. Traveling across the dam with only blackout lights challenged the tanks' drivers and commanders to the extreme.

In the early morning hours on 15 January, heavy blocking artillery fire covered Drusenheim. The American 232rd Infantry Regiment, of the 42nd Infantry "Rainbow" Division, cleared the town. At the break of dawn, the 6th Company, 10th SS

Panzer Regiment drove through the southern sector of Drusenheim and upon arrival immediately attacked American infantry that provided security for two armored bridges that crossed the Moder southwest of Drusenheim. The German attack surprised the Americans, who withdrew quickly and abandoned most of their gear, including American jackets, cigarettes, and rations. The 6th Company, 10th SS Panzer Regiment, also attacked around Rohrweiler-Breymühl, a village heavily contested and costly for both sides. At Breymühl the company crossed the Zorn Canal and reached their objective. They entered security positions behind a small embankment and row of bushes and trees along the heights northwest of Herrlisheim. With snow on the ground, the tank crews were very cold. The vehicles were covered with lime to conceal them from the enemy. While strictly forbidden from running their engines to conserve fuel, many crews used blowtorches inside the vehicles to stay warm.[22]

SS-Untersturmführer Helmut Stratmann received orders from *SS-Hauptsturmführer* Franke to establish contact with *SS-Obersturmführer* Frank Riedel, of the 7th Company. Together with Westerhoff's gunner, Eberhard Storch departed on foot. Unknown to the two men, the 7th Company had advanced to the bridgehead with the 22nd *SS-Panzergrenadier* Regiment and entered ready-positions in the area around Offenburg. As a result, contact with the 7th Company could not be established. Around 0600 hours, the Americans launched an attack against German positions as light snow provided the defenders distinguishable targets. The American attack ran aground amidst German mortar and machine-gun fire. Storch, as well as *SS-Untersturmführer* Stratmann, could make out a single American tank that provided security. While Stratmann returned to his company, Storch took along a *Panzerfaust* and a radio operator and closed with the tank. At 30 meters Storch fired a direct hit. Suffering significant losses, the Americans withdrew to their jump-off positions, leaving behind sixty-eight dead and one knocked out tank.[23]

On 15 January, the 13th Company of the 22nd *SS-Panzergrenadier* Regiment, a heavy infantry gun company, deployed during the day to a ferry crossing point along the Rhine at Freistett. Under fire by enemy phosphorus rounds, the gun company ferried their guns across the river on rafts. A raft carrying a single gun ran aground in shallow water and could not be offloaded; the raft had to return to the originating side before a second successful attempt offloaded the gun. Wilhelm Balbach, a forward observer with the fire direction center, recalled the air was damp and cold, and visibility was almost zero in every direction. The next day, the 13th Company pushed forward to Offendorf and entered positions with their guns on the western edge of town. Balbach and another comrade made up the observation post and directed fire for the company's two platoons of heavy infantry guns. They established contact with infantry and reconnoitered forward as far as the railroad line and the parallel road N-68 Herrlisheim-Gambsheim.[24]

Meanwhile, the first elements of the 1st Battalion, 10th SS Panzer Regiment ferried across the Rhine at Freistett during the night of 16–17 January to prevent the loss of the German bridgehead at Gambsheim. A subsequent attack from the bridgehead at Gambsheim, also known as Operation Northwind, aimed to reach Hagenau and establish communications with the 6th SS Mountain Division, to develop a defensive line stretching from the Saar to Bitsch and to the Hagenauer Forest. The 21st and 22nd *SS-Panzergrenadier* Regiments arrived alongside the dam and crest of the dike where they waited to be ferried across as well. Next to the tank ferry, the 10th SS Pioneer Battalion set up an engineer ferry and used assault boats to shuttle troops across the Rhine. Americans upstream near Strassburg floated mines down the river that frustrated the effort; measures taken to counter the threat included posting machine guns on the ferries and assault boats to shoot and detonate the mines, as well as catching the mines with fishing nets. A ferry carrying men from the 22nd *SS-Panzergrenadier* Regiment struck a mine, which forced the men to swim the remainder of the way.[25]

On 16 January, the American 12th Armored Division planned to surround Herrlisheim, in order to cut off the principal German north-south communication line within the Gambsheim bridgehead. Combat Command B (CCB) would remain engaged in the north against the town while Combat Command A (CCA), consisting of two armored infantry battalions and a reinforced tank battalion, would surround Herrlisheim from the opposite direction. According to Corporal James E. Muschell, of Company B, 43rd Tank Battalion, faulty American intelligence led him to believe that "second-rate young kids and older soldiers" were holding Herrlisheim. German artillery frustrated the efforts of CCB in the north while during the night, CCA, consisting of the 43rd Tank and the 66th Armored Infantry Battalions, south of Herrlisheim ran into strong defensive German gunfire from antitank and assault guns.[26]

General Allen's two combat commands attacked again the next morning but with two fresh companies of the 17th Armored Infantry Battalion, into the southern outskirts of Herrlisheim, while twenty-eight white-washed M4A3 Shermans from the 43rd Tank Battalion, commanded by Lieutenant Colonel Nicholas Novosel, drove east. The American frontal attack across the road and railroad line ran into two well-emplaced German 88mm antiaircraft guns camouflaged behind the railroad embankment. Here, the railroad embankment rose slightly to 2 meters high in otherwise flat terrain. In almost complete defilade the flak guns' barrels reached just above the railroad tracks, which allowed the American tanks to close within point blank range. In addition, the 3rd Company, 10th SS Panzer Regiment, launched a counterattack out from Offendorf. The commander of the 1st Panther Battalion, *SS-Sturmbannführer* Ernst Tetsch, accompanied the attack while the battalion adjutant, *SS-Untersturmführer* Erwin Bachmann, remained at the battalion combat command post.[27]

The attack stalled in front of Herrlisheim, in the face of defensive American tanks, presumably of the 43rd Tank Battalion, and antitank fire from the 17th Armored Infantry Battalion. Several German tanks were knocked out. The commander of the 3rd Company, *SS-Hauptsturmführer* Hans Penders, was wounded during the attack. Tetsch returned to the command post and reported the incident to the regiment and division. Bachmann, who listened to the conversation, took leave of Tetsch and proceeded to the 3rd Company, as they lacked a company commander during their first engagement. Previously, Bachmann served in the 3rd Company as a platoon commander.

Looking back on *SS-Untersturmführer* Bachmann's career, he volunteered for service in the SS on 28 August 1938, with the Replacement Battalion "Germania" in Hamburg. He received his first assignment with the 11th Company Germania, 5th SS Panzer Division, where he served from 1940 during the French campaign until December 1941 around Rostow. From January until June 1942, Bachmann attended the SS Officer Candidates' School at Bad Tölz. As the only remaining son after his brother was killed in action in Russia, he took a post as a platoon commander with the Replacement Company "Germania" in Arnhem. After attending Officer Preparatory Training in Ede, he volunteered for duty with the 10th SS Panzer Division.

Back at the command post, *SS-Rottenführer* Sauerwein drove Bachmann in a motorcycle sidecar to Herrlisheim. Unable to hear or see anything of the 3rd Company and the Americans, they continued into town circling around a church and then stopping at a road intersection. There remained no sign or sound of either friend or foe. Bachmann dismounted and proceeded down the road when after 30 meters he took fire from the main gun of an American Sherman tank. Bachmann immediately turned around and ran back to the motorcycle. He picked up a *Panzerfaust* and hand grenades, and told Sauerwein to return to Offenbach and bring up the two command tanks. Bachmann then reached a house from where he could see two Sherman tanks. From 30 meters he fired the *Panzerfaust* and knocked out the Sherman that fired at him earlier. Then it was quiet again.

Shortly thereafter, Bachmann could hear the sound of tanks coming from Offenbach. Two tanks from the 3rd Company arrived at the intersection. *SS-Oberscharführer* Hans Mühlbradt commanded the first tank, and *SS-Scharführer* Heinz Burger commanded the second tank. Bachmann provided both commanders a quick orientation brief:

> Sherman tank along the intersecting road. The #2 tank pushes forward on the right side of the road until reaching the bend and opens fire on my signal. The #1 tank drives on the left side of the road with the turret at 3 o'clock, as soon as the #2 tank opens fire.

> When you reach the intersecting road, immediately open fire with high explosive rounds and then turn right.

Both tanks departed according to plan. Burger opened fire and Mühlbradt closed with the intersecting road, turned to the right, and fired at the standing Sherman until a white flag emerged. Bachmann called cease fire and walked forward. The commander of Company B, 43rd Tank Battalion, offered their surrender in place of the wounded battalion commander, Lieutenant Colonel Novosel. Bachmann told the officer to tell his men to lay down their weapons. All told, sixty Americans laid down their weapons in front of Bachmann. Twenty German prisoners who had been captured earlier by the Americans also came forward. Bachmann asked the American officer, "Are those the crews from the knocked out Shermans?" The American officer pointed to a courtyard along the left side of the road and replied, "No. Those are the crews from the not-knocked out Shermans." Bachmann could see four Shermans standing facing the road. Another eight Shermans stood in two other courtyards. Without wasting time, Bachmann ordered all the American tank drivers to step forward. Each driver was assigned an armed German guard and they were told to drive to Offenbach. Bachmann radioed the battalion with news that captured Sherman tanks were approaching their position and to dispatch reinforcements to Herrlisheim and to pick up the remaining forty-eight American prisoners. For security, the two Panthers proceeded in the direction of Drusenheim to the edge of the town of Herrlisheim where an additional two Sherman tanks were knocked out. The results of the day included the capture of twelve operational Sherman tanks, and the destruction of nine Shermans. The captured Shermans operated as the 13th Company, 10th SS Panzer Regiment, until the end of the war. For his achievements, Bachmann received the Knight's Cross to the Iron Cross.[28]

Following Bachmann's ordeal, the 1st Company, 10th SS Panzer Reconnaissance Battalion, along with *Panzergrenadier* units, strengthened the bridgehead. During the very cold and especially dark night of 18 January, Balbach and his *SS-Oberscharführer* reconnoitered to the Zorn River.

As they made their way forward through the night, they encountered the silhouettes of another team also underway. They called out to determine if they were friendly, but the team scampered away without revealing their identity. During their return, they came across a knocked out Sherman tank from where they heard voices. Approaching cautiously, they determined that their own people were making off with anything they could take, such as weapons, cigarettes, clothing, or food.[29]

In the morning on the following day, the 1st Battalion, 10th SS Panzer Regiment, and the 21st *SS-Panzergrenadier* Regiment attacked westward against Gambsheim, with the mission of capturing Weyersheim, Brumath, and eventually the Zaberner Senke, a key low-level terrain feature. Batteries from the 10th SS Panzer Artillery Regiment located on the right bank of the Rhine provided fire support. The attack succeeded in capturing Kilstett and the momentum brought the attack across open terrain toward Hoerdt-Weyersheim. Outside Weyersheim, the attack ran into stiff American defensive frontal and flanking tank and antitank gunfire, not to mention intense artillery and fighter aircraft support. The attack stalled when the commander of the 1st Company, 2nd Panther Battalion, 10th SS Panzer Regiment, *SS-Hauptsturmführer* Willi Schneider, was killed when his vehicle was hit. Harmel recommended suspending the attack to higher headquarters, which resulted in the XLIX Panzer Corps issuing orders in the evening to return to the original lines.[30]

Meanwhile, the 2nd Battalion, 10th SS Panzer Regiment, along with two battalions from the 22nd *SS-Panzergrenadier* Regiment, also attacked westward but out from Offendorf.

The forward observers Balbach and *SS-Unterscharführer* Scheffler, the commander of the 2nd Heavy Infantry Gun Platoon, led their infantry across the terrain that they had reconnoitered the night before, in preparation for an attack. Again they bypassed the knocked out Sherman. The infantry groups pushed forward in deep echelon that reached from the southern forest to the Zorn; each individual gave considerable distance between the next, as sporadic incoming American artillery remained ineffective. The two forward observers situated themselves in the center of the formation. As Balbach looked back, he saw a vast formation of men carrying their weapons, advancing slowly forward and upright, despite falling enemy artillery. Shortly before the Zorn the formation reached an abandoned German position. Weapons were laying in the position, as if the occupants had surrendered or fled. Amidst enemy artillery fire, the formation crossed the Zorn with rubber rafts only to encounter even greater enemy fire. Balbach took cover next to a dead American officer. The officer still wore a set of field glasses around his neck and carried a map case. The intensity of rifle and artillery fire drastically reduced visibility so that the forward observers lost contact with the infantry and fire direction position. The forward observers dug in east of a nearby forest where they established their temporary observation post, northwest of the Zorn and west of Herrlisheim. Balbach received news that one of their units was surrounded, but he did not know if it was a platoon or a company. As best they could, the forward observers called fire missions to support the infantry, but they were unable to see well enough across the uneven terrain to provide accurate and targeted fire. With no contact with the encircled unit, the forward observers tried to orient themselves to the sound of rifle fire, and fired artillery according to the map, but without knowledge of the location of the encirclement.

To protect themselves against the bitter cold as well as falling enemy artillery rounds, Balbach used a pair of pliers to dig their observation hole deeper. Nearby, Balback recognized the commander of the 22nd *SS-Panzergrenadier* Regiment, *SS-Sturmbannführer* Kurt Walther, and his men who were also digging in. During the night, the sporadic American artillery fire intensified to destructive fire that pounded the German positions. Balbach witnessed rounds impacting directly on Walther's position. Once the fire ended, Balbach heard screams and cries for help. He ran to the positions and found Walther among the dead.[31]

On 19 January, the 1st Panther Battalion and the 21st *SS-Panzergrenadier* Regiment attacked to the west out of Gambsheim. Two supporting battalions from the 22nd *SS-Panzergrenadier* Regiment as well as the 2nd Battalion, minus the 6th Company, of the

10th SS Panzer Regiment, joined the attack. While the 6th Company remained in reserve and experienced relative quiet, the company could hear and see American tank activity. Around midday, the battalion received orders by radio to attack against an assembly of American tanks between Weyersheim and Kurtzenhouse. During an operational briefing of the enemy situation, the small woods roughly 2.5 km east of Kurtzenhouse remained free of enemy troops. The attack was planned with eleven tanks including the commander's tank. The order of march placed the 1st Platoon at the tip of the spear, followed and staggered by the 2nd and 3rd Platoons. On the outside left followed the command group. After a brief exchange of fire, the Americans fled; a few tanks were knocked out and several were smoking.

In flat terrain Quandel accidentally drove into a deep depression and got stuck. His only option to continue leading the attack was by using the radio. The 1st Platoon commanded by *SS-Untersturmführer* Stratmann consisted of three Pz.Kpfw.IV tanks; Knappe-Franke-Stratmann. They proceeded forward the furthest and crossed Point 128 at the forest ditch. Franke recalled the situation:

> Behind us we could hear the sound of fighting. We were not informed what happened to the company and we lost radio contact. Shortly behind the bridge we stopped for observation. Knappe stood on the left of me and Stratmann on the right. At 11 o'clock at a distance of roughly 600 meters, I saw a group of trees suddenly move. I opened fire with high explosive projectiles. Before I could continue firing, the vehicle commanded by Knappe received a direct hit and burst into flames. I did not fare any better and I abandoned my tank. I saw Knappe was seriously wounded. My driver Eddi Glaser did not manage to get out of the tank; he was dead. The gunner A. Scheele and loader P. Haffki, as well as the radio operator W. Klink were wounded. Stratmann, who immediately recognized the situation and fired smoke grenades, enabled us to withdraw to safety.[32]

The enemy intelligence report was faulty; when the company passed by the small woods, they were ambushed from the right flank and from behind. Stratmann returned with his vehicle and assumed command while the battalion commander, *SS-Sturmbannführer* Quandel, ran back to the 2nd Battalion command post to report the fiasco that befell the 6th Company. Stratmann gave orders to everyone who had not been wounded to proceed forward and determine the location of the tanks and then recover the wounded; Westerhoff, Stratmann, and Storch brought back Knappe by pulling him on a *Zeltbahn* through the snow. Once all the wounded were collected, they were loaded onto the platoon commander's tank and driven directly back to the river ferry. Along the way, Knappe died of his wounds.

SS-Oberscharführer Seifert commanded the 2nd Platoon and was killed during the fighting. His gunner, W. Helm, was severely wounded. The 3rd Platoon was commanded by *SS-Oberscharführer* Klein or *SS-Scharführer* Laier. The number of casualties within the 2nd and 3rd Platoons are not known, especially when considering that common practice switched personnel from different companies between vehicles on a daily basis. In some cases, tank commanders did not know their crews. At the end of the day on 19 January 1945, after the 6th Company ran into an ambush outside Kurtzenhouse, the employment of the platoon came to an end in the Alsace. The recovery platoon salvaged the commander's tank; Stratmann and the remainder of the company gathered with the company supply train back in Roeschwoog. From there the company relocated to Leimersheim near Wörth.

About two hours later, around 1400 hours, Kurt Rademacher, a driver in the 2nd Company, 10th SS Panzer Division, and the rest of the platoon went to alarm-level 2; everyone manned their posts and prepared to attack. At 1415 hours, alarm-level 1; attack in the direction of Weyersheim. Around 1500 hours they entered positions along the Zorn River. The tank commanders gave orders to traverse the tank in the direction of the woods, at a distance of 800 to 1,000 meters. As soon as Rademacher turned the vehicle, they heard a muffled bang and the inside of the vehicle got very hot. The commander ordered everyone to bail out. The radio operator and Rademacher managed to escape and ran as fast as they could into the river. Their hands, feet, and faces burned from the phosphorus projectiles. In the water they were able to shake off the phosphorus pieces. Along the banks of the river the men took cover, as American fighter aircraft attacked them as well. The two men found safety under a bridge; as soon as the aircraft departed they got on the road and headed toward Gambsheim. An ambulance picked them up along the way and brought them both to a field hospital in Baden-Baden.

The attack by the 2nd Company ended miserably with thirteen of seventeen tanks lost. The Americans fired 76mm phosphor rounds from a twin antitank gun that could melt through 200mm of plate-armored steel.[33]

Soon after the XXXIX Army Corps suspended the attack, a new main line of resistance was established from Kilstett to Herrlisheim and running eastward. Nothing of note occurred along the new line outside of typical scouting probes into the American lines. On 22 January, the German bridgehead at Gambsheim linked with units at Drusenheim coming from the north. The next day the remaining units of the 22nd *SS-Panzergrenadier* Regiment crossed the Rhine at Drusenheim. The 10th SS Panzer Division, earmarked for an attack against Hagenau by the XXXIX Panzer Corps, regrouped on 23 January and made available the 21nd *SS-Panzergrenadier* Regiment. The last regimental artillery batteries arrived by rail at Roppenheim in time for the attack; the batteries already in the area crossed the Rhine and then entered firing positions around Drusenheim-Sessenheim. The regimental artillery command post was in Schirrhofen, while the 2nd and 3rd Battalions were in Schirrheim, the 7th and 9th Batteries were just north thereof, and the forward observers were in Oberhofen and along the woods east of Hagenau.

The attack against Hagenau began on 24 January 1945 with artillery fire from the batteries of the 10th SS Panzer Artillery Regiment. The divisional command group was in Schirrheim; the divisional staff established their post in Sessenheim while the operational staff of the XXXIX Panzer Corps was in Drusenheim. The 22nd *SS-Panzergrenadier*

Regiment, supported by the 1st Battalion, 10th SS Panzer Regiment, attacked from Rohrweiler against Bischweiler. The 21st *SS-Panzergrenadier* Regiment, with tanks from the 2nd Battalion, attacked the training grounds at Hagenau. While the attack by the 1st Tank Battalion and 22nd *SS-Panzergrenadier* Regiment quickly captured Bischweiler, it ran aground before Oberhofen and the training grounds, while the 21st *SS-Panzergrenadier* Regiment dug in east of Hagenau.

The lines on both sides solidified as they dug in; the 21st *SS-Panzergrenadier* Regiment east of Hagenau was replaced by the 245th Infantry Division and 7th *Fallschirmjäger* Division. The Americans stubbornly defended Hagenau with ample artillery and aerial support. The attack in the Alsace, also known as Operation Northwind, came to an end on or around 25 January on the heels of orders for the XXXIX Panzer Corps to lead the attack, along with the 10th SS Panzer Division, in Pomerania.[34]

On 28 January 1945, the 6th Company, 10th SS Panzer Regiment received new vehicles and personnel and returned to normal duty. Between 4 and 5 February, the bulk of the divisional units moved to railheads and loaded for movement to the east. The process of movement and actual entraining was subjected to constant Allied aerial attacks during which four platoons of the 10th SS Panzer Antiaircraft Battalion lost equipment and personnel. On 10 February 1945, the 6th Company entrained at the rail station in Wörth and headed, once again, east.[35]

The main German counteroffensive in the Ardennes as well as the follow-up offensive against Hagenau both achieved local tactical successes but ultimately failed to achieve their strategic goals. The 10th SS Panzer Division that refitted to nearly full strength as a reserve for the operation in the Ardennes then suffered significant casualties and losses during the operation in upper Alsace. Remarkably, the experienced cadre of 10th SS repeatedly managed to train replacement personnel to fight another day. Despite receiving its full complement of Panther tanks, the division was no match for Allied ground forces that effectively utilized artillery and aviation assets to maintain Allied momentum.

Bernhardt Westerhoff as a POW in American captivity. Source: Westerhoff Archive.

A Pz.Kpfw.V Ausf. G with crew. Source: Westerhoff Archive.

SS-Obersturmführer Hans Quandel, commander of the 6th Company, who led the attack against Weyersheim on 19 January 1945. Source: Westerhoff Archive.

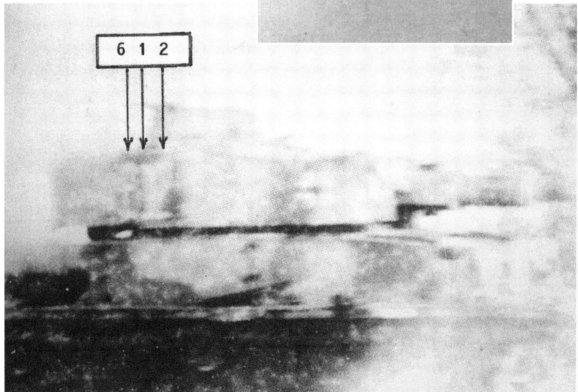

The knocked out tank of R. Knappe in Herrlisheim; 6th Company, 1st Platoon, 2nd Vehicle, Tank No. 612, January 1945. Source: Westerhoff Archive.

Gruesome images of war. Source: Westerhoff Archive.

Gruesome images of war.
Source: Westerhoff Archive.

A knocked out German Pz.Kpfw.IV west of Herrlisheim, January 1945. Source: Westerhoff Archive.

SS-Sturmbannführer Ernst
Tetsch, depicted here as a *SS-
Hauptsturmführer*, commander of the
1st (Panther) Battalion during their
first engagement on 19 January 1945
against American forces. Source:
Westerhoff Archive.

SS-Untersturmführer Erwin
Bachmann, depicted here as an *SS-
Obersturmführer*, adjutant, 1st Battalion,
10th SS Panzer Regiment, took captive
a company of functional American tanks
in Herrlisheim on 17 January 1945.
Source: Westerhoff Archive.

Knocked out German Panther Pz.Kpfw.V west of Herrlisheim. Source: Westerhoff Archive.

German grave northwest of Herrlisheim. Source: Westerhoff Archive.

CHAPTER 8

Return to the East

Demise of the 10th SS Panzer Division

ALTHOUGH THE GERMAN military situation on the Eastern Front presented far greater political and ideological concerns than in the West, both the Eastern and Western Fronts were collapsing under a general fighting withdrawal. Soviet forces raped and pillaged German villages and cities as they advanced on Berlin. In the final months of the war, the 10th SS Panzer Division relocated again from the West to the East to help stem the advance of the Soviet armies. Indeed, the shattering of the 10th SS Panzer Division did not occur overnight, but rather as an inconsequential outcome of the greater Soviet objective to capture the capital city of Berlin. The division suffered heavy casualties and gradually, through sheer attrition, became an impotent combat formation dispersed over a large region. However, the division never ceased to exist and never capitulated or surrendered as a closed unit. During the final weeks and days of the war, amidst the greatest operational chaos and confusion, the division split into three groups and operated as a stopgap measure around Finsterwalde, Spremberg, and Görlitz, where they assisted German military and civilian personnel to escape Soviet captivity.

Hitler's direct management of key operations from a map helped bring an end to the war more quickly. He frequently sacked personnel for not holding ground until the last man and ordered the relocation of personnel from one area to another, as well as units and resources. Hitler's lack of self-control over command and control inevitably reflected itself in numerous failed operations. The German counteroffensive in the Ardennes failed to achieve the goals of splitting the Allied coalitions and the Allied forces in the West and recapturing the port city of Antwerp. The scanty and in some cases inexperienced American forces in the Ardennes created enough friction to disrupt the German logistical timetables and caused the attack to run out of fuel. Well-equipped and experienced front-line German troops with high morale led the attack that penetrated 65 miles deep into Allied territory. However, American troops recuperated quickly and, aided by clearing skies and airpower, eventually brought the attack to a standstill.[1] Facing the Allies on a two-front war, the German supply of munitions required to sustain combat operations was already depleted in December 1944. Notwithstanding the fact that a stockpile of ammunition reserves existed for the Ardennes operation, the disruption of German transportation and the lack of fuel to move supplies created shortages of ammunition.[2]

The follow-up German attack *Unternehmen "Nordwind"* or Operation Northwind in the Alsace also failed to produce strategic gains after Hitler took operational control. Nevertheless, the 10th SS Panzer Division did achieve isolated tactical successes. Following the setbacks in the West and the anticipated renewal of Soviet operations in the East, the 10th SS Panzer Division relocated east on 3 February 1945 as part of the XXXIX Panzer Corps, commanded by General of Panzer Troops Karl Decker, within the new Eleventh SS Panzer Army.[3]

The Eleventh SS Panzer Army included a mix of veteran combat formations under the newly created headquarters under *SS-Oberstgruppenführer* Felix Steiner. The order of battle for the Eleventh SS Panzer Army on 5 February 1945 included the following units:

Tettau Corps
    Köslin
    Bärwalde
X SS Corps
    5th *Jäger* Division
    402nd Division
Munzel Corps
    Führer Grenadier Division
    Führer Escort Division
III SS Panzer Corps
    281st Infantry Division
    23rd *SS-Panzergrenadier* Division
    Division Voigt
    11th *SS-Panzergrenadier* Division
    27th SS Grenadier Division
XXXIX Panzer Corps
    4th *SS-Panzergrenadier* Division
    10th SS Panzer Division
    28th SS Grenadier Division
    Panzer Division Holstein
    Headquarters of Wehrkreis II
A corps-level field command
    Swinemünde Defensive Region
    Division Deneke
    9th *Fallschirmjäger* Division
Direct Army Command
    163rd Infantry Division.

Hitler's direct operational control again dictated the sequence of operations of the planned Stargard offensives. After Hitler created an independent command and diverted resources to form Army Group Vistula, under the command of the *Reichführer SS* Heinrich Himmler, a political showdown was arranged by General Heinz Guderian to take over control from Himmler, an unqualified army group commander. While not entirely successful, Hitler gave operational control to Guderian's deputy, General of Panzer Troops Walter Wenck, who preemptively committed available forces piecemeal during the night on 14 February to relieve a locally surrounded German garrison at Arnswalde. Two days later, the Eleventh SS Panzer Army launched *Unternehmen "Sonnenwende"* or Operation Solstice but blundered trying to find the best place to begin.[4]

The 10th SS Panzer Division, which marched on 15 February from Altdamm to Stargard, received orders in the morning on 16 February to attack from the area of Schlötenitz in the direction of Margaretenhof-Uslar. The XXXIX Panzer Corps attacked out of the line of the Madü-Sea and Faule Ihna with the objective of reaching the Schöning Canal. From the onset, the 10th SS Panzer Division experienced problems. The 22nd *SS-Panzergrenadier* Regiment, as well as the 1st Battalion, 10th SS Panzer Regiment, was still en route by rail. Moreover, the divisional staff did not have the opportunity to familiarize themselves with the terrain before it began offensive operations. When the attack by the 10th SS Panzer Division could not gain momentum, it shifted behind the more successful 4th *SS-Panzergrenadier* Division, which managed to break into enemy positions at Blumenberg and Brallenthin. In the afternoon on 17 February, the 2nd Battalion, 10th SS Panzer Regiment, along with the 10th SS Panzer Reconnaissance Battalion, and the 22nd *SS-Panzergrenadier* Regiment, attacked and succeeded in seizing Schöningsthal and Sallenthin. *SS-Obersturmführer* Franz Riedel, the commander of the 7th Company, destroyed thirteen Soviet T-34 medium tanks, bringing his total number of enemy tanks destroyed to forty, as well as numerous antitank guns and both light and heavy infantry weapons. For his actions, Riedel received the Knight's Cross of the Iron Cross on 28 March 1945. The 1st Battalion, 10th SS Panzer Regiment, attached to the 4th *SS-Panzergrenadier* Division and became embroiled in the fighting at Dölitz. The staff of the armored group received a direct hit and the Soviets managed to retake positions seized earlier by the staff of the armored group. Immediately, *SS-Sturmbannführer* Ernst Tetsch, the commander of the 1st Battalion, 10th SS Panzer Regiment, took control of the situation and organized a counterattack after stopping fleeing German infantry. The armored counterattack succeeded in throwing back the Soviets, and during the subsequent pursuit of the Soviets, Tetsch routed an entire Soviet brigade and destroyed their heavy weapons. For his actions, Tetsch received the Knight's Cross of the Iron Cross on 28 March 1945. *SS-Obersturmführer* Franz Scherzer, the commander of the 1st Company, 1st Battalion, 10th SS Panzer Regiment, also aided in the destruction of the Soviet brigade. For his actions, Scherzer received the Knight's Cross of the Iron Cross on 28 March 1945.[5]

In the evening on 17 February, the 10th SS Panzer Division, along with its remaining elements, gathered within the Ihna brideghead at Blumenberg and punched forward over Muscherin and Lübtow, to relieve the encircled forces at Pyritz.

The subsequent attack on 18 February by the XXXIX Panzer Corps did not develop, insofar as the Corps' main line of battle ran from the southern rim of the Madü Sea over the Linden Mountains to Sallenthin and Muscherin, and as far east as Dölitz. Unexpected stiff Soviet resistance and fresh Soviet armored forces forced Army Group Vistula to call off the operation after three days in order to save valuable forces. The war diary of Army Group Vistula noted on 20 February that their preemptive attack from the north did not disrupt the preparations of the Soviet First and Second Guard Armies when fresh Soviet forces stymied the attack. The ramifications of withdrawing Army Group Vistula resulted on 19 February in the 10th SS Panzer Division withdrawing behind the Faule Ihna. As the 10th SS Panzer Division withdrew, Soviet forces attacked in pursuit, which led to heavy fighting around Muscherin. Following the withdrawal of the 10th SS Panzer Division, the 4th *SS-Panzergrenadier* Division relocated to West Prussia. The newly vacated positions of the 4th SS

became the responsibility of the 10th SS. The main line of battle ran 5 km around the southern fringe of Stargard and the division's headquarters were in Schöneberg. On 25 Februrary, the 10th SS Panzer Division relocated to the area of Fürstenwalde along the Oder River.[6]

At 2330 hours on 3 March 1945, the battalion command post of the 3rd Battalion, 21st *SS-Panzergrenadier* Regiment was situated in a dental practice. A large number of refugees gathered in the basement, including elderly men and women and young women and children who wanted to be saved. A nurse reported that 200 additional children remained in the orphanage. The immediate priority for the commander of the 3rd Battalion, 21st *SS-Panzergrenadier* Regiment, *SS-Sturmbannführer* Friedrich Richter, was to obtain the reconnaissance report from the returning scout troops. The scout troop advanced along the road leading toward Wilhelmsfelde. After nearly 2 km, the troop detected three enemy tank turrets in defilade. The scouts veered off across a railroad line and continued their advance on Wilhelmsfelde. Along the railroad line, the scouts encountered four women fleeing from Wilhelmsfelde. When the scouts returned to the command post with the four women, the battalion commander Richter listened to their observations and personally interviewed the women who squatted closely together on the floor. It was not necessary to ask what had happened to them; one could see immediately. Their lips were bitten and bloody and their clothes were torn. One half-naked woman covered her upper body with a garment. The commander asked them, "Were there any Russian tanks in Wilhelmsfelde and did you see any German prisoners?" The women did not respond. They appeared to be completely apathetic. The dental assistant Ursula then brought them some hot coffee, which the women drank, and the doctor gave them a sip of cognac. Richter inquired again, "Please tell me if you saw any Russian tanks this evening in the village." One of the women snapped back, "What are you asking!? Here—do you want to see?" The woman yanked her blouse away and exposed her bitten and bloody breasts. Another woman commented, "Yes. There are many tanks."

Richter asked the doctor to take care of the women and evacuate them as quickly as possible to the rear areas. While the intelligence received remained minimal, the commander knew they would encounter tanks the next day.

The next day, at 0030 hours, the following individuals were at the battalion command post: the battalion commander (Richter), the adjutant *SS-Untersturmführer* Clausen, an *SS-Scharführer* as the ordnance officer, the combat clerk, an *SS-Rottenführer*, an *SS-Scharführer* as Messenger Section leader, the 10th and 12th company commanders who were both *SS-Scharführers*, and a dentist. Not present were the two commanders of the 9th and 11th Companies, who were already in action with their assigned companies.

Each company consisted of two to three platoons, although each platoon contained only two groups instead of three. The 12th Company contained one platoon of heavy mortars, half of one platoon of heavy machine guns, as well as one platoon of self-propelled 20mm antiaircraft. The medical doctor received orders to evacuate the refugees and orphans in a truck. The truck was loaded in the following order: women with small children and orphans, young girls and feeble elderly women, and any older people. The remaining civilians were told to escape on foot as soon as possible.

The 3rd Battalion command post was a secure area. Refugees or civilians in general were not authorized to enter the command post. However, at 0450 hours, a commotion broke out in the front office. *SS-Sturmbannführer* Richter could hear yelling and loud voices when suddenly a woman opened the door. Wearing a heavy fur coat, she appeared very upset and agitated. With a command voice she asked, "Are you the commander here?" Somewhat surprised, Richter responded affirmatively. She continued, "I am the wife of a colonel and I demand that you bring me to Stettin." Richter responded, "My dear lady, I have already given specific instructions concerning the evacuation of refugees. The doctor shall inform you when it is your turn. The evacuation shall precede based on order, not based on beauty." The woman yelled, "This is disgraceful! I shall file a complaint against you!" After several more minutes of her tirade, the doctor

entered the room and managed to escort the woman out. The commander and his adjutant looked at each other in disbelief.[7]

SS-Sturmbannführer Richter also received orders on 4 March 1945 to block the advance of Soviet forces across an 18 km line running from Hohenschönau to Küss to greater Sabow. However, before the line could be established, Soviet tanks and infantry reached Wilhelmsfelde, 1.5 km east of Naugard. Richter used the intelligence available to him to prepare for the anticipated fight against tanks. Richter predicted that the railroad station east of the rail line would be the first goal of the Soviets. To combat the tanks, they had to allow the tanks to enter the village, while the accompanying infantry were neutralized before they entered. The half-strength machine-gun platoon of the 12th Company entered positions along the railroad embankment, while the heavy mortars were also deployed. The reserves were made up of the two groups of the 11th Company. Richter anticipated difficulty in coordinating all the groups far apart from one another, although a thorough orientation of the messengers minimized any possible problems. The critical need for antitank weapons remained a concern to Richter, who had previously sent an urgent request to division for antitank weapons.

Shortly after 0130 hours, Richter received a young *SS-Untersturmführer* wearing a black tanker's uniform. He reported, "*SS-Sturmbannführer*! I am reporting to you with six tanks!" Without the words to respond, at first he hugged the young officer and patted him on the shoulder. Quickly, Richter gave him an overview of the situation and then personally directed him into position.

Around 0600 hours near the railroad station, morning daylight allowed for the inspection of the defensive positions. The German tanks were well camouflaged in positions between the houses along the edge of town. Several crews even managed to create firing charts with preregistered grid coordinates. Though far apart, the rifle companies were dug-in well. An eerie quiet befell the men before the storm as they anticipated the Soviet attack.

Around 0830 hours, four Soviet T-34 tanks with mounted infantry appeared at a distance of about 2,000 meters. They progressed forward confidently as if they expected to enter Naugart without encountering any resistance. When the Soviet tanks were within 800 meters, the German tanks opened fire. Each projectile hit their target; two T-34 tanks immediately erupted into flames. The third tank veered off and got away while the fourth tank attempted to follow and escape. However, as the fourth tank turned and exposed its side, a projectile stopped the tank in its tracks as smoke billowed out from the vehicle. The Russian infantry were nowhere to be seen.

Despite a respite, Richter knew the Soviets would return soon. Richter took advantage of the reprieve and visited the riflemen who, along with their *Panzerfausts*, were positioned along the sides of the houses. He gave the individual soldiers exact instructions on how to operate the *Panzerfaust*, knowing that the Russians attached wire meshing around portions of their tanks. Richter recommended they aim at the tracks of the vehicles, considering the shape charges would bounce off the wire meshing. Having left his right flank exposed, Richter accurately moved his available forces east and west of Naugard and repelled several Soviet attacks, knocking out twelve tanks with *Panzerfausts*, as well as spoiling two major Soviet advances along the main road south of Naugard. For his efforts, Richter received the Knight's Cross of the Iron Cross.[8]

In the morning around 1100 hours, a tank officer came running and reported to Richter. He cried, "*SS-Sturmbannführer*! I don't know if I should allow them to shoot. Come quickly! You must see this!" Richter followed the tank officer for about 150 meters when they stopped and together watched the events unfold. Three Soviet tanks approached in a slow methodical walking tempo. Behind the tanks followed a number of infantry. At the front of each tank two German female auxiliary helpers, easily recognized by their uniform jackets, were tied to the tanks by their legs. They hung upside down and their lower bodies were naked. A Soviet tank crew member in the first tank could be seen hitting the women with a whip from an open turret hatch, which made the women squirm. The tank officer cried, "Dear God! Living girls being used as protective tank shields!"[9]

Richter felt helpless, but never before to such a degree. As the Russian tanks came within 800

meters, the lead German tank closed the turret hatch as the remaining tanks opened fire. The tank projectiles whistled as they sailed down the street. Richter and the tank officer took cover behind a fence as the projectiles struck their targets.[10]

The frustrations of soldiers were exemplified by the lack of information, materiel, and the ever-present threat of being captured by the Soviets. On 11 March, the artillery battalions of the 10th SS Panzer Artillery Regiment relocated to the bridgehead at Altdamm. *SS-Untersturmführer* Johann Sierks, the adjutant for the 4th Battalion, commanded the battalion. Around noon, *SS-Sturmbannführer* Fritz Haas, the regimental commander, ordered Sierks to contact the 1st Battalion, in order to determine the number of guns that were ready for action. Sierks spoke to the commander, *SS-Hauptsturmführer* Behrens, who reported fifteen self-propelled guns ready for action. Sierks promptly reported fifteen guns to the regimental commander. Haas stated that Sierks had given him incorrect information, insofar as fifteen minutes ago he had personally passed the 2nd Battery on the road. Immediately, Sierks called Behrens again. Behrens reported: "Fifteen guns ready to fire; the 2nd Battery changing positions. Haas saw only two Wespen" (Sd.Kfz.124). Sierks returned to the commander and relayed the message from Behrens, but Haas ignored him and did not respond. Angered by the lack of response from Haas, Sierks again requested transfer to a battalion. Haas ignored Sierks yet again and did not respond. Frustrated, Sierks left the room and consulted with *SS-Obersturmführer* Erich Henning, the regimental adjutant, 10th SS Panzer Artillery Battalion. Neither Sierks nor Henning could make any sense of the situation with Haas.

During the next few days the Soviets were relatively inactive. During this period, Sierks spoke with Behrens about the fact that Haas had accused them of providing a false report. Sierks also mentioned that he requested a transfer to one of the battalions on two occasions. At that point Behrens asked Sierks if he would transfer to his battalion. Sierks obliged and Behrens said he would simply make the request. Behrens and Sierks were both from Schleswig-Holstein. In 1933, Behrens's father had been mayor of Kiel, and he could therefore make good use of contacts he retained in Berlin.

In the evening on 14 March, the regimental commander summoned Sierks to his command post. Haas informed Sierks that effective 15 March he would transfer to the 4th Battalion. Sierks thanked the commander, informed Henning, and also contacted the commander of the 4th Battalion, *SS-Sturmbannführer* Günter Menze and told him he would report in the morning. Sierks gave any writing materials or maps he still carried to Henning and said farewell; he also said goodbye to *SS-Hauptsturmführer* (Dr.) Will Dörr, as well as the signal officer, the map section, the motorcycle section, and his driver Peldszus. Sierks's successor would be one of the many *SS-Untersturmführers* from the regiment that were rotated in and out of various billets.[11]

Around this period, according to *SS-Obersturmführer* Dr. Hermann Kube, the adjutant of the medical section (IVb) of the divisional staff, *SS-Brigadeführer* Harmel, reported to the hospital in Berlin as a result of nerve discomfort in his extremities.[12]

Meanwhile, the combat post of the 4th Battalion relocated on 15 March to a house about 1.5 km behind Rosengarten by Stettin. Continuous fighting had taken place in the village over the previous week. Harassing artillery fire landed in the village during the previous night and the following day. Sierks paid a visit to his new driver and Volkswagen vehicle. He told the driver that he wanted at least two *Panzerfausts* at the ready, fastened behind the front seats, as well as a bag of hand grenades.

Breakfast with the commander and adjutant did not go without incident. The Signals Platoon leader reported the loss of three wire repairmen. Three days previously the three arrived as replacements. All three were busy repairing a wire about 50 meters from the combat post when a single projectile impacted near them. All three were seriously wounded, injured during their baptism of fire at the front. They were young boys at merely seventeen or eighteen years of age. Before they were transported off to the troop aid station, Sierks gave them each a bar of chocolate.[13]

Artillery projectiles continued to fall on the roads. Meanwhile, Army stragglers on foot passed by Sierks's position and told of horrific disasters; Russian tanks accompanied by infantry attacked and overran their positions. Suddenly the wire connections to the two batteries were interrupted; nothing could be done to repair the breaks as all the wire repairmen were already out in the field. Much like Sisyphus in Greek mythology, no sooner were breaks in the wire repaired than new breaks appeared. As a result, the battalion observation post lost contact with the artillery communications command post. The observation post could not be reached by radio either.

SS-Hauptsturmführer Menze ordered Sierks to re-establish contact. Immediately, Sierks and two men departed with lightweight telephone wire. Twenty minutes later they reached Rosengarten, a small village that contained many beautiful villas with about 500 inhabitants. They steered toward the observation post, which was in a single family home. Sierks entered an empty building and climbed to the attic to see across the terrain ahead of the village. A direct hit landed on the building and a large stone from a wall hit Sierks on his spine. The force of the stone forced Sierks to his knees as he fell forward face first against a wall. Sierks recovered from the impact and climbed down the attic stairs, dusting off debris from his face and clothes. On the road, *SS-Mann* Schmidt could barely contain himself and smiled without a word. Beginning from the house, the wire needed repair every 50 meters. Repairing the wire piece by piece was not worth the effort, and they decided to replace the entire length. However, the wire ran out shortly before a wooded area. Sierks connected a telephone and called the battalion to report their location. Sierks ordered the signals man into a fighting hole and went farther ahead with Schmidt. Around 1300, Sierks studied the map again to orient himself and they reached a small wooded area. While Schmidt relieved himself, Sierks continued forward alone. Sierks jumped for cover onto the ground when suddenly he heard the screaming sound of Katyusha rockets overhead. He felt the heat from the explosions on his face as earth and tree limbs landed on top of him. After the barrage he slowly stood up, luckily without a scratch.

Along the left side of the tree line stood an 88mm antiaircraft gun that belonged to the Frundsberg Division. An *SS-Untersturmführer* showed Sierks where he believed the forward-most positions of the division were located. Several hundred meters ahead, several divisional tanks were located between houses. The Russians subjected the village behind Rosengarten to heavy artillery fire and several houses caught fire.

Sierks and Schmidt came upon an Army battalion command post that suffered from great chaos as messengers came running into the post and others stumbled out. As they progressed forward, Sierks noticed the streets were completely devoid of any infantry. At one of the houses, *SS-Mann* Schmidt spotted a small red pennant flag with a white lightning bolt that indicated a radio post. They entered the home and found it empty. On a table they found a code book but no radio. Sierks looked through the code book and noticed sketches belonging to the observation post. But where did their comrades go? Under the table Sierks found a stick grenade that he stuffed in his belt. From the second floor the two men spotted Russian infantry running between a group of houses. As they departed, they heard shots coming from the same group of houses. At 150 meters they observed a German climbing out of a window who ran toward them. Several more shots rang out when the soldier dropped his rifle and collapsed. He cried out and clutched his stomach. Immediately Sierks told Schmidt, "I will retrieve him. Cover my rear! Fire on anything that moves!"

Sierks leapfrogged his way to the wounded soldier. The helmet and sleeve insignia indicated he was a *Fallschirmjäger*. He lay on his back, unconscious, and his uniform was soaked with blood. Sierks slung his American semi-automatic rifle that he had captured in St. Vith around his neck and pulled the comrade up and dragged him toward their fighting hole. Sierks could hear Schmidt yelling warnings; Sierks looked up and saw a Russian soldier running with the intent to cut him off. Sierks dropped the wounded soldier and grabbed his rifle to fire. "Jam!" The Russian fired at Sierks but took fire himself and was hit. Sierks resumed the rescue and made it back to the fighting hole. Breathing heavily, gasping for air, he asked Schmidt, "Why

didn't you shoot?!" Excitedly Schmidt replied, "I couldn't! You blocked my view the entire time!"

After the two men managed to quickly recover from their exhaustion, they pulled the *Fallschirmjäger* farther back about 200 meters when they reached a defensive position held by an Army company. An Army first lieutenant called a medic and also showed him Sierks's hand that was covered in blood. Sierks did not realize it but the Russian whom he had encountered earlier had hit him after all. Sheer adrenaline prevented Sierks from feeling any pain. Sierks gave a report to the company commander and then he and Schmidt returned to base.

At the command post, Sierks received a tetanus shot from the unit physician. The doctor bandaged Sierks, who had sustained a clean shot through the arm. The doctor stuck a wound card through the buttonhole on his uniform and brought him to an aid station. Sierks sat on the floor in a barracks-style building and waited for a short period until he was brought into the operation room. He saw two doctors operating on a comrade's half-missing head. Sierks left the room and caught a ride back to the battalion command post.[14]

The next day the Soviets attacked again. The batteries of the division engaged the attackers. Sierks heard nothing more regarding the forward observers. His commander, Behrens, visited Sierks during the evenings to ensure his recovery progressed. Behrens even made him sandwiches. On 18 March the battalion received orders to relocate back across the Oder River to Pommerensdorf. The battalion combat post moved to Stettin-Scheune. Following the demolition of the Oder bridges on 20 March, several days of quiet were enjoyed by Sierks and the 4th Battalion. During this period, the artillery guns received routine maintenance and the men were cleaned up and de-liced. The men also wrote letters and received training. The battalion adjutant, *SS-Untersturmführer* Dr. Rudolf Schwetschke, was an accomplished artilleryman. Sierks and Schwetschke got along well to the point that Schwetschke demanded Sierks call him "Rudi."[15]

The battalion commander established his quarters in a home that contained a photo studio. Everyone had their photograph taken. Sierks and

Schwetschke found quarters in a bakery. The baker was a stern party official who held the rank of *Ortsgruppenleiter* or local political group leader. On occasion the baker wore his brown uniform, though he appeared very uncomfortable when in the presence of soldiers. His wife and daughter also lived in the bakery, and they all ate together every morning and received fresh rolls for breakfast. The wife's sister cared for Sierks and the others as if she were their mother. Her husband served in Denmark. Sierks brought fresh rolls to the battalion commander every day.

On 28 March, on a warm spring day, Sierks drove to the regimental staff headquarters to receive the latest briefing. During the trip, Sierks came upon *SS-Obersturmführer* Rolf Speidel playing soccer on a field with the men from his battery. At the regimental command post Sierks obtained orders and maps, and greeted the regimental commander Haas. The artillery regiment was ordered to relocate. The next day on 29 March, Sierks loaded at the railroad station in Kolbitzow, roughly 10 km south of Scheune. The loading did not go without incident when Soviet aircraft discovered the train; however, the antiaircraft guns were able to keep the aircraft at bay. The following day on 30 March the train reached its destination at the train station at Beeskow, about 30 km southwest of Frankfurt along the Oder River. Here the artillery battalions detrained and entered quarters.

The same day, *SS-Sturmbannführer* Stolley, who frequently visited the front lines to gain a clear perspective on the situation in the trenches, received the German Cross in Gold for his contribution of the command and control of the division.

Sierks learned by happenstance on 31 March that the wife of *SS-Obersturmführer* Otto Koch, from the 1st Battalion, was visiting her husband. Sierks promptly made available to them his roomy quarters. Koch's wife remained with her husband.

On 1 April, Sierks received orders from the battalion commander to enter, as an advance party, new quarters at Heidersdorf. Sierks and several *SS-Scharführers* traveled over Görlitz and Lauban to reach their new quarters. The next day, the mayor brought Sierks a complete list of quarters that were

available because a tank unit had recently departed. Sierks gave the mayor a bottle of schnapps for his help; the mayor ran off and returned with some glasses and shared the bottle with Sierks.

The 4th Battalion arrived on 3 April 1945. The staff battalion entered quarters in a schoolhouse, whereas Sierks and Schwetschke found accommodations in a home occupied by teachers. The battalion commander found a room right next door in a small house. At the same time the division became earmarked the reserve for OKH in the area of Army Group Center, under the command of General Ferdinand Schörner. The subordination to OKH as a reserve component allowed for other tasks and requirements to be accomplished, such as training. The battalion commander declared a number of grandiose ideas and plans for refreshing and refitting. Sierks received orders to "think about political presentations you can provide." Sierks tried to conjure good ideas for presentations he could give but came up empty-handed. He consulted his colleague Schwetschke, who also could not think of any suitable presentations. Sierks placed a telephone call to Hoffmann and asked, "The commander wants us to give political presentations. Is there any way you could give a presentation for the officers?" Hoffmann knew of an NCO in his battery who spent several years at the embassy in Sweden before the war, who he believed could talk about the relationship between Germany and Sweden. *SS-Unterscharführer* von Grote called Sierks and obtained some additional information regarding the lecture and then agreed. When informed of the plan, the commander rejoiced and asked if any additional experts were among the battery.

On the evening of the presentation, von Grote visited Sierks. Von Grote appeared very nervous. All the officers were present and milled about in the room chatting quietly with one another. Upon the entrance of the commander, the senior *SS-Obersturmführer* Albert Bültmeier called the group to attention. Von Grote asked Sierks if there was anything taboo that he should not talk about. Sierks replied, "There are three Taboos in the *Waffen-SS*; God, the *Führer*, and the Mother." Menze waited for some time before he asked everyone to be seated and the presentation got underway. The interesting talk promoted many questions and lasted almost until midnight.[16]

The next day, after receiving required political training, the staff of the artillery regiment entered billeting in Geibsdorf, just 20 km east of Görlitz. The divisional staff established quarters in Pfaffendorf, roughly 7 km southwest of Görlitz. The troops received several orders and directives typical of General Schörner, such as shutting off vehicle engines when idling for more than one minute, and requiring that every soldier carry a loaded weapon, to include pistols, with a chambered cartridge and the weapon placed on safe. One rumor about General Schörner told a story about the general telling one of his officers to fire at a tree. When the officer pulled the slide back to chamber a cartridge, Schörner ordered the officer transferred to the front lines for not following orders. On 5 April 1945, Hitler promoted General Schörner to the rank of field marshal.[17]

The 4th Battalion relocated again on 5 April. *SS-Untersturmführer* Sierks remarked, "As if we had nothing better to do than change positions." The battalion moved into the dispersed settlement of Löbenslust about 1 km east of Geibsdorf, whereas both cannon batteries emplaced to the south along the heights. Camouflaging, digging in, and training allowed for the time to pass.

The next day Sierks turned twenty-one years of age and, according to his own words, "became of full age." In the morning, the daughter of the hostess from Heidersdorf, where the battalion commander quartered earlier, brought Sierks a pie baked by her mother. She congratulated Sierks and delivered an invitation to the family. The troop doctor, *Feldunterarzt* Ulrich Schwedt, assumed the coffee-making duties as a small birthday celebration took place. Every member of the staff battery who came to congratulate Sierks received a shot of schnapps. But without much time to relax, Sierks and Schwedt received permission in the afternoon to travel to Heidersdorf, about 8 km away. At their destination they were greeted with great happiness, drank coffee, ate cake with whipped cream, and shared liquor that Sierks brought along. Upon their departure they encountered the regimental commander, who commented in a very good

mood, "You found wonderful quarters for me. How did you do that?" Sierks responded, "Talent, *SS-Sturmbannführer*!" Sierks witnessed the *SS-Sturmbannführer* laugh for the first time.[18]

Seven days passed and the 4th Battalion relocated three times, of which two relocations made use of the railroad. The logistics behind moving a division required at least seventy-five railcars. The effort slowed as a result of bombing damage to railroad stations, rail lines, and cars, which further frustrated any type of railroad movement. Moreover, many divisions utilized the rail system besides the Frundsberg Division. Sierks believed that the higher leadership did not fully appreciate the fact that when full divisions were relocating and underway, thousands of men and materiel were unavailable to hold the front lines. Sierks posed a valid question: If saboteurs held many of the highest positions, and the Germans purposely withdrew fighting units holding the front lines, replacements and supplies could not make it to the front.

In the evening on 6 April 1945, *SS-Untersturmführer* Sierks dictated to the staff writer several pages for the war diary that would be approved by the commander. Afterwards, *SS-Hauptsturmführer* Menze, the adjutant Rudi Schwedtchke, the technical vehicle officer (TFK) *SS-Obersturmführer* Egon Kreis, the field doctor Uli Schwedt, and the commander of the Signals Platoon, *SS-Untersturmführer* Albert Lax, joined Sierks for an informal conversation. Schwedt drank far too much alcohol and the men placed him doubled over in a children's bed with safety bars.

The battalion commander ordered *Luftwaffe* ground troop NCOs and officer candidates who had transferred to the battalion to undergo training with the ammunition, firing tables, and twin upright telescope sections. A terrain exercise consisting of a tactical orientation march using a map and compass was undertaken to develop skills necessary for establishing observation posts, as well as firing and ammunition positions. The exercise ended with less than acceptable results: only two out of six groups were able to complete it. The *Luftwaffe* personnel lacked basic skills in the use of maps and compasses; the groups walked straight into minefields that were marked in the field. The men of the 4th

Battalion were devastated by the results of the exercise. They questioned if the soldiers lacked skill or if they lacked motivation. The poor physical stamina of the new personnel brought more and more men to the doctor's office after physical exertion. The battalion commander commented about the situation, "Our men always have the illness that our doctor read about last night."

Early the next morning, on 7 April, *SS-Hauptsturmführer* Menze personally woke up Sierks: "Get dressed immediately! You are coming along—we are leaving in five minutes!" Sierks quickly took a shower and jumped into his uniform. Unshaven he stumbled outside where he found Menze waiting in a vehicle at the wheel. Sierks asked, "What documents should I bring along?" Menze responded, "None!" They traveled together to his old Army artillery regiment, which he found operating nearby. When they arrived at the regimental command post, a great reunion and happiness ensued as everyone greeted Menze. Both Menze and Sierks received an invitation to join the regimental staff officers for lunch. Meanwhile, Sierks made use of the opportunity and gathered intelligence, maps, and situation reports from the ordnance officers. He also managed to arrange for a hot bath and a clean shave with terry cloth towels while his uniform coat and trousers were brushed and pressed, and his boots were polished. He received maps and orientation situation reports and also gave his Army counterparts a situation brief on his experiences and their mission roles. Around the lunch table the regimental commander introduced his staff to Sierks, while everyone but a few staff members knew Menze well. The atmosphere resembled a night at the casino much like during peacetime. The regimental officers acted as if they were born again. Menze provided the group a situation report, which was followed by a toast by the commander, in Menze's honor. Menze returned the toast to conclude the meal. The officers then talked and drank coffee and cognac. The Army artillery regiment remained in reserve and belonged to the Corps' artillery.[19]

The following day, Major General Werner Kampfhenkel, the 121st Higher Corps artillery commander, made a surprise visit and informed the battalion commander of the most current situation.

The Soviets were bringing forward strong forces that indicated preparations were being made for a large-scale attack in order to reach the Neisse River in the area around Lauban-Görlitz. Kampfhenkel recommended that they stock up on ammunition.

In response to the urgent situation, Sierks traveled to the village of Seidewinkel where he planned to engage with divisional supply officers to obtain ammunition and fuel rations.[20]

On 9 April Sierks returned to Löbenslust with good news, but he found the battalion commander was attending a regimental briefing. When the battalion commander (Menze) returned, he was accompanied by the commander of the 1st Battalion, *SS-Hauptsturmführer* Behrens. The latest news from the regiment included organizational changes. The 3rd Battalion reverted back to two self-propelled 150mm batteries and one 100mm cannon battery. A 4th Battalion, based on the structure of a Panzer Division 1944, was no longer required. In other words, a heavy 150mm battery from the 3rd Battalion, a 100mm cannon battery, as well as the Staff Battery along with the battalion staff needed to be disbanded or find a new mission. *SS-Hauptsturmführer* Walter Behrens offered Sierks a billet with the 1st Battalion, and then addressed the topic of Werewolves.

According to Behrens, the party chancellery had ordered the employment of Werewolves, who were ordered to undertake ambushes and sabotage operations within the occupied homeland, much like the Resistance in France. Behrens stated, "If every Werewolf destroys one enemy tank, the war will be won!" Sierks did not believe Behrens's tone of voice. After Menze departed, Sierks inquired with the commander about the details. Behrens did not know what a Werewolf was either. They pondered if Werewolves were non–service eligible former soldiers, *Pimpfs* (members of the *Jungvolk*), or women. Could it be the *Volks-wind*? Sierks believed that Germans were not inclined to be underhanded murderers, not to mention that the Soviets would be inclined to commit acts of revenge. Behrens obviously was not considering that the Party expected the secret weapon or Werewolf to also shoot down enemy aircraft as well as tanks, which German antiaircraft guns could not accomplish. Sierks remarked that Behrens was fantasizing, considering that within the sector of the 10th SS the Soviets and Americans were only 150 km apart.[21]

Most of the officers of the 4th Battalion were informed that a reorganization would take place soon. On 10 April *SS-Obersturmführer* Horst König received notice that *SS-Untersturmführer* Schwetschke had assumed command of the 11th Battery. Sierks became the battalion adjutant and the ordnance officer's billet was assigned to an enlisted man.

Meanwhile, TFK *SS-Obersturmführer* Kreis led behind him a horse with a saddle he borrowed from a farmer. Kreis brought the horse to Menze, the cavalry captain, who used it to travel from one battery to the next. Everyone enjoyed the fun.[22]

On 14 April, just north of Friedland in Bohemia, *SS-Obersturmführer* Kube, the adjutant for the medical section (IVb) of the divisional staff, was reassigned to the staff of the 10th SS Field Replacement Battalion, commanded by *SS-Sturmbannführer* Hans Lohr. Kube lived in Reichenberg, which lay roughly 25 km from the command post. Kube had not taken furlough in the last two years and had serious concerns over the safety of his wife and three children, who remained in Reichenberg. When he requested permission to travel to his home, Lohr told him that furlough restrictions remained in affect, but that as an adjutant, Kube could find some justification to travel to Reichenberg. However, Kube's self discipline prevented him from making the trip.[23]

Meanwhile, Soviet forced reconnaissance by reinforced rifle battalions appeared along the German first defensive belts. The reconnaissance began two days before the main assault on 14 April in the center and southern portions of the front. The next day, aerial attacks by two air armies complemented the advance by pounding the first defensive belts. The Soviet attack commenced at 0500 hours on 16 April 1945 with several thousand cannon. The fire mission lasted thirty minutes.[24]

Throughout the first months of 1945, the Soviets had begun their preparations for the final assault on Berlin. The strategic plans of the Soviet high command included the destruction of the German forces defending along the Berlin axis, seizing the capital, and then linking with the Allies along the Elbe River.[25]

In the north, Rokossovsky's 2nd Belorussian Front consisted of five armies and five separate mobile corps that planned attacks several days after the initial assault by the center and southern armies. The objective of the northern prong included attacking in the Stetting-Schwedt area, destroying German troops around Stettin, sealing off the Third Panzer Army and preventing the reinforcement of troops to Berlin, pushing forward to occupy northern Brandenburg, and finally linking with the British along the Elbe River.

Zhukov's 1st Belorussian Front, situated in the center at the Kustrin Bridgehead, consisting of seven Soviet and one Polish armies, two tank armies, and four separate mobile corps, planned to launch the main attack against strong German defenses on the Seelow Heights and two secondary attacks on either side of the Kustrin Bridgehead. Zhukov expected to reach Berlin within six days

Konev's southern 1st Ukrainian Front was made up of five Soviet armies and one Polish army, two tank armies, and four mobile corps. The main attack in the south focused on crossing the Neisse River and seizing Cottbus. Additional objectives included Brandenburg, Dessau, and southern portions of Berlin. A secondary attack to cover the right flanks aimed at Dresden and served as a jump-off point for latter operations into Czechoslovakia.[26]

To counter the threat, three belts of German forces defended Berlin, including in the north, Army Group Vistula, commanded by General Gottard Heinrici, consisting of the Third Panzer Army, Ninth Army, the Fourth Panzer Army of Army Group Center, and the Berlin garrison. All told, the Germans mustered about 800,000 men. Three Soviet Fronts were planned for the attack, including the 2nd Belorussian in the north, the 1st Belorussian in the center, and the 1st Ukrainian in the south. The Soviets massed 2.5 million troops against the Germans.

The German general public living in areas still under German control continued to receive optimistic propaganda reports from Berlin that all was not lost. The German High Command in Berlin desperately clung to the idea that German *Wunderwaffen* or Wonder Weapons would save Germany just in time. These weapons included, for example, the V-2 rockets, high-speed jets, helicopters, and the atomic bomb. However, the wonder weapons did not appear soon enough to make a strategic difference. In the Berlin *Morgenpost* newspaper, dated 2 January 1945, General Heinz Guderian admitted that Soviet victories had brought the fighting to the borders of Germany. Nevertheless, he continued to believe that with good weapons and unshakeable confidence in Hitler, somehow, Germany would emerge triumphant. In Hitler's New Year address to the Nation, he assured Germans: "like a Phoenix out of the ashes, the German Will has risen anew from the rubble of our cities . . . , and thousands of People's Assault battalions have been established." [27]

In stark contrast to the remnants of German military units still operating in the field, the German *Heimwehr* or Home Defense Forces, which were raised from the remaining population still available, consisted primarily of elderly men, soldiers no longer fit for combat duty, and children. Conscription was broadened to the ages between sixteen and sixty. Their training consisted merely of how to fire a bolt-action rifle and a *Panzerfaust*.[28]

Undeniably, the end loomed only days or even hours away in earshot of those remaining free from Soviet control. Evacuation plans were implemented hastily in many towns where the threat appeared imminent. However, the mass exodus of refugees streaming westward in search of safety made it clear that many municipal officials were unprepared for a humanitarian crisis that required large quantities of food and shelter. Any remaining stores of food were quickly depleted.[29] Reports from survivors who managed to escape to the West described the Soviet takeover as "sheer hell." In the book, *When Titans Clash*, David Glantz and Jonathan House asserted:

> Only the most fanatical adherents of National Socialism retained any hope of ultimate victory, but the brutality of the Red Army in the eastern provinces of the Reich boded ill for the safety of anyone, civilian or soldier, who fell into Soviet hands. Indeed, German accounts of the final Soviet campaigns have given the Red Army a justified reputation for atrocities.[30]

On 1 March, despite continued Soviet gains, Joseph Goebbels proclaimed, "Our situation has become especially precarious, however, it not without the slightest prospects." Along the outskirts of towns, ad hoc units consisting of the Home Guard, RAD, and Hitler Youth members were thrown into the line to stem the tide. Most hoped that the Soviets could either be stopped or, if nothing else, war would simply pass them by. Many of the inhabitants asked themselves if they should remain or flee. However, where could they go to escape the imminent situation?[31]

While the majority of the regimental staff of the panzer regiment had already evacuated, *SS-Obersturmführer* Konrad Lenhardt, the logistics officer (Ib), remained at the regimental combat command post on 16 March. Several regimental tanks remained engaged at Hökendorf. In the ground floor of an apartment building in the southern section of Altdamm, enemy tank and artillery fire landed around the command post when *SS-Obersturmbannführer* Paetsch summoned Lenhardt. Upon Lenhardt's arrival, he saw Paetsch standing upright despite incoming artillery fire and speaking on the telephone with someone at division. Paetsch ordered Lenhardt to drive his command tank to the divisional command post to obtain continuing orders. He would follow in his own *Kübelwagen*. The divisional command post was in the basement of a house in Finkenwalde at the edge of the airport. Lenhardt and *SS-Unterscharführer* Sefan Gorski, the driver, were heading toward Finkenwalde when they came to a road intersection. The road leading straight forward along a railroad embankment came under rocket fire, and Lenhardt ordered Gorski to turn right, following a road that passed the airport. From the commander's cupola, Lenhardt observed Paetsch's *Kübelwagen* hurtling past them at full speed but traveling down the road under fire. As the *Kübelwagen* passed them on the left, Lenhardt also recognized *SS-Untersturmführer* Robert Zottel, the ordnance officer, who was also in the vehicle. At the divisional command post in Finkenwalde, the dying regimental commander Paetsch was brought in after his vehicle took a direct hit. Zottel was also killed. On 20 March, Paetsch was buried during a Soviet bombing attack that killed the nineteen-year-old *SS-Oberjunker* Müncheberg.

After having left Pomerania and the Oder River behind them, portions of the panzer regiment were recuperating in Stettin. At the same time, the staff of the panzer regiment, as well as the staff and maintenance company, were in the area around Pomellen. A large number of the Shermans captured by *SS-Obersturmführer* Bachmann were being kept on a farming estate. None of the vehicles had a single round of ammunition. *SS-Obersturmführer* Lenhardt, competent with weapons and equipment as the logistics officer, experimented with captured Soviet 76mm ammunition from a T-34 tank; the Sherman tanks were made operational with Soviet ammunition.[32]

At the onset of the Soviet offensive on 16 April 1945, the 4th Battalion, 10th SS Panzer Artillery Battalion began their march toward Cottbus. Between Spremberg and Cottbus, the 10th and 11th Batteries were halted and ordered to return to positions east of Spremberg. The firing positions were situated along the heights, east of Spremberg, near the Slamen brickworks. When multiple reports were received of quickly approaching Soviet troops, the 10th Battery fired upon reported enemy movements directly on and next to the road Wadelsdorf-Hornow. The 11th Battery fired upon reported movements on the road Graustein-Wolfshain-Schönheide-Tschernitz.

On the same day, the 10th SS Panzer Division was attached to the Fourth Panzer Army, which also included the 344th Infantry Division, the LVII Panzer Corps consisting of the 408th Division, 8th Panzer Division, 103rd Panzer Brigade, and the Führer Escort Division, and the Panzer Corps "Gross Deutschland" that consisted of three *Kampfgruppen, Panzergrenadier* Division "Brandenburg," the 1st Parachute Panzer Division "Hermann Göring," and the 20th *Panzergrenadier* Division—and finally the bulk of the 21st Panzer Division. The situation report for the Fourth Panzer Army, dated 16 April, indicated that after two hours of preparatory artillery fire, Soviet tank formations supported attacks southeast of Rothenburg and between Muskau and Forst. Southeast of Rothenburg the Soviets managed to cross the Neisse River with tank-supported infantry and penetrated 6 km across a broad front of 10 km. The *Kampfgruppe* "Hermann Göring" counterattacked and remained engaged defensively by

the late afternoon in the north around Görlitz. The Soviet attack center of gravity struck between Forst and Muskau where the *Kampfgruppen* of the 545th and 342nd Infantry Divisions were overrun, which resulted in a 10-km-deep penetration but was finally halted along the eastern rail line of Weisswasser-Forst. While individual *Kampfgruppen* defended their strongpoints, the 21st Panzer Division and Führer Escort Division counterattacked the Soviet forces moving west. An immediate counterattack stopped a Soviet armored thrust as far forward as southeastern Forst when five tanks were destroyed; however, the bridgehead at Forst was cut off when Soviet tanks attacked north along the Neisse.

The next day on 17 April, the 4th Battalion, 10th SS Panzer Artillery Battalion, fired its first rounds at a distance of approximately 14 km. The following day, the distance was reduced from 8 to 3 km, directly in front of the firing positions. The speedy Soviet armored advance across the Neisse River did not allow their artillery to keep pace. While the enemy artillery remained distant and out of German battery range, Soviet armored penetrations were expected. The positions of the 10th and 11th Batteries were in earshot of the battalion command post as they prepared for close combat. The batteries and panzer grenadiers formed defensive strongholds. Wire communications were often shot to pieces and the wire repairmen were unable to repair the connections. For targets in wooded areas, the batteries fired projectiles with fuses with contact detonators and fifteen-second time delays. An identical configuration was applied for direct ricochet fire with zero deflection.

German blocking fire along Soviet armored routes of advance aimed to stop both tanks and mounted infantry and support weapons, such as the truck-mounted Katyusha rocket launchers. Smoke projectiles were mixed in between missions. Soviet tank engine cooling systems sucked in the smoke and forced the crews to use their gas masks, thereby stopping the assault. The batteries fired at targets as close as 1,000 meters in front of the firing position. Blocking fire was suspended 200 meters before friendly lines. The blocking fire was in waves of two-minute intervals and each battery fired sixty rounds.

Between 18 and 19 April, *SS-Hauptsturmführer* Karl Dietrich, the divisional liaison officer for the 10th SS assigned to the General Staff of the Fourth Panzer Army, continued to receive orders from the Fourth Panzer Army. Under the greatest confusion, and in an attempt to carry out orders received on 17 April, to cut off and isolate the armored spearheads of the Soviet attacks south of Cottbus, Dietrich departed in the early afternoon in a Fiesler-Storch reconnaissance aircraft to observe the closing pocket at Spremberg. Dietrich hoped to gain a better perspective on the overall situation for continued operations of the 10th SS Panzer Division. As they approached the airstrip at Welzow at tree-top level, the aircraft was shot down and landed in a kale dump. The pilot was severely wounded and Dietrich sustained burns on both feet and legs. Both men were transferred into a transport aircraft and evacuated to Dresden.[33]

On 19 April, the guns of the 4th Batteries fired smoke to cover their withdrawal. The same day, Marshal Konev launched the great Soviet offensive with the 1st Ukrainian Front against Berlin and central Germany. The offensive thrust cut across the Lusatian Neisse River between Forst and Bad Muskau as well as both sides of Rothenburg. With over 300 Russian artillery pieces available for every 1 kilometer along the front, the Soviet attack smashed even the strongest and most spirited defense of decimated German units. The massed artillery flattened many of the German defensive positions. The following attacks with tanks supported by fighter-bomber aircraft were unstoppable.

The Führer Escort Division, commanded by Major General Otto Ernst Remer, held the forward positions of Spremberg. The 344th Infantry Division, commanded by Brigadier General Erwin Jolasse, provided support to the Führer Escort Division. The 344th Infantry Division suffered heavy casualties during the fighting in Silesia and refitted with very young and old replacements. Among them were defenders who stood fast at the bridgehead at Baranow, which the Soviets overran.

When a gap developed between Cottbus and Spremberg, through which the Soviets sent their tanks in the direction of the Elbe River and Berlin, the 10th SS Panzer Division was alerted and rushed forward from the area of Görlitz to close the gap,

attacking the Soviet forces in the flank, and encircling. During the approach march, the division began experiencing difficulties. The supply troops separated from the combat troops during an attack on Bautzen. Portions of the 10th Field Replacement Battalion were encircled at Pulsnitz. In desperation and with very few options, *SS-Sturmbannführer* Hans Lohr, commander of the 1st Battalion, 21st *SS-Panzergrenadier* Regiment, shot himself on 22 April. The 10th SS Panzer Reconnaissance Battalion and portions of the 21st *SS-Panzergrenadier* Regiment were cut off after they launched their attack against Cottbus and ended up encircled in the pocket at Halbe. The remaining units were threatened with encirclement at Spremberg.[34]

The Germans attempted to break out at Kausche and Neupetershain. Only half of approximately 20,000 men made it to safety, whereas the others either were killed or entered captivity. According to eyewitnesses at Greifenhain, some 200 German prisoners were made to undress down to their trousers and then beaten to death with steel rods and wood clubs.[35] During the breakout from Kausche, a collection point for the wounded was established in a farmhouse courtyard. These men could not be transported to safety due to the severity of their wounds. *SS-Obersturmführer* Franz Erlmann, the doctor assigned to them, decided to stay with the men; a young lady from the village assisted him.

The Soviets that occupied the village spared none of the wounded or the doctor. The young woman, knocked unconscious after a blow to the head, was thought dead. Max Belka from Gosda witnessed the terror against helpless prisoners and wounded German soldiers:

> My neighbor took care of a wounded, who lay on the couch in our living room. When the Russians discovered him, he was shot in the house. All the wounded in Grosda were murdered in a gruesome manner. A German officer was literally butchered into pieces at the estate of Wulf-Bogott. Several women that were hiding in the gatehouse witnessed the slaughtering. A Russian Commissar at the estate of Melo, in the village sector of Old Buden, shot ten wounded German

soldiers found hiding in a cellar. Six soldiers that were drowned were recovered from the water reservoir. Altogether we buried eighty soldiers that were murdered.[36]

During the breakout from Kausche, *SS-Hauptsturmführer* Walter Behrens of the 10th SS Panzer Artillery Regiment commanded the rear guard. His command tank carried his wife and two-year-old daughter.

Having heard the type of brutal treatment women could expect at the hands of the Soviets or Czechs, Behrens's wife fled the garrison at Prague where she lived and managed to reach the outskirts of Dresden. She recognized and followed the tactical signs for the Frundsberg Division in order to find her husband. When the Behrens family reunited in the field, they had no options but to stay together.

The armored group, consisting of the last three remaining 150mm self-propelled *Hummeln* and 105mm *Wespen* from the 1st Battalion, a half-track from the Führer Escort Division, as well as several command Pz.Kpfw.IIIs, penetrated forward as far as Geisendorf and established a defensive position. *SS-Rottenführer* Erwin Fischer operated the radio in the command tank of the 1st Battery commander, *SS-Obersturmführer* Otto Koch. The westerly sound of heavy weapons and fighting coming from Grossräschen suggested that German units were conducting a fighting withdrawal. Behrens decided to fight in the same direction in hope of linking with German troops. Leading the breakout in his command tank, Behrens's attempt to cross open terrain resulted in the loss of all the tracked vehicles, knocked out by antitank fire between Geisendorf and Alt Petershain. The command tank also took a hit on the left side. The tank radio operator, *SS-Unterscharführer* Rudi Gnade, and the driver, Erwin König, were both slightly wounded but managed to escape the burning vehicle with Behrens's wife and child.

Despite the direct hit and subsequent fire, the wife and child sustained only minor injuries. After exiting the burning vehicle, the tank crew and civilians crossed the open terrain on their stomachs. Soviet troops remained entrenched along the left flank and fired at the survivors. The mother with

child under her arm crawled first. When she nearly reached the tree line she stood up, but too early. An antitank projectile hit the mother's upper body, killing her instantly. Shortly behind the mother, Rudi Gnade grabbed the crying child and ducked into the nearby forest for safety. With pistols drawn the young SS soldiers made their way past older Army soldiers, who wanted the screaming child shot.[37]

During their escape, the child was given to an elder-teacher couple in Obhut. When Rudi Gnade arrived with Erwin König at his hometown in Aspenstedt, he was arrested shortly thereafter by British military police. König tried to continue his escape, but went missing.[38]

The 10th SS Panzer Pioneer Battalion led the attack against Kausche. *SS-Hauptsturmführer* Albert Brand, the commander of the pioneer battalion, lost his eyesight when an antitank projectile hit the machine-gun shield on the half-track. He was transferred to the division commander's half-track.

Meanwhile, the radio operator, *SS-Mann* Albrecht Henning, originally from Bremerhaven, succeeded in breaking out across the fields of carnage with several other comrades and managed to reach Lindthal near Finsterwalde. Henning managed to locate a guesthouse he knew existed in Lindthal, which was owned by a wheel maker. The guesthouse had a cellar full of schnapps. Many women that were bombed out of their homes were living at the guesthouse. Henning met several women he knew from Bremerhaven. The women were preparing to flee when the Russians arrived in Lindthal. Albert Henning and three other Frundsbergers, along with a Russian Vlasov soldier were shot in the village. A thirteen-year-old boy was forced to bury the soldiers. The first communist mayor of the village ordered the soldiers' pay books destroyed.[39]

The attempt to break out at Kausche succeeded for *SS-Unterführer* Walter Kohlschmidt of the 1st Company, 10th SS Panzer Signal Battalion, who accompanied the spearhead-group, which centered on *SS-Brigadeführer* Harmel. Kohlschmidt lost several documents along the way, which prolonged the delivery of three death notices from Kausch to the parents until the following summer. After the breakout, Kohlschmidt ran into one of his comrades from the 2nd Company, *SS-Rottenführer* Ernst Kuhnert, who was from the neighboring village.

Harmel most often traveled in communications or radio half-tracks from the 2nd Company. The Swedish *SS-Scharführer* Sven Erik Olsson belonged to the radio half-track crew. The company commander, Friedhelm Lohbeck, was well admired by his men and not left behind after he suffered a severe stomach wound during the breakout. Harmel broke out of the pocket through the forest at Reddern, located between Grossräschen and Altbödern. At the village of Barzig the group made use of the highway. Between Saalhausen and Dollenchen the Frundsberger group overran a Russian supply unit. The tanks and half-tracks that were wired and prepared for demolition were gassed up and placed back into action. The small group attacked a Russian defensive antitank line in the direction of Meuro around Annahütte. After eliminating the Russian defense, the group remained in Annahütte for the night.[40]

The Breakout Group Harmel, 10th SS Panzer Division, marched over Kostebau across the Ochsen Mountains until they reached the Upper Forestry Grünhaus, south of Finsterwalde. A short commanders meeting took place at the forestry, attended by *SS-Sturmbannführer* Stolley and Lieutenant Colonel Georg Schnappauf, of the 1st Panzer Regiment of the Führer Escort Division.

Gernot Traupel, assigned commander of the 2nd Panzer Battalion at Spremberg, commanded the remaining tanks. The German breakout was directed to advance parallel to the attacking Soviet troops. However, the direction changed in order to reach the lead elements of the Parachute Panzer Corps "Hermann Göring."

From Grünhaus the group marched in the direction of Gorden-Hohenleipisch, in order to arrive at Plessa after traversing the summit of the Black Elster. When the snaking military convoy arrived at Gorden, the young boy Wolf Walther witnessed the arrival of the German soldiers. However, he was unaware that several kilometers away his father and soldiers of the 2nd Parachute *Panzergrenadier* Division were holding open an escape route for the breakout group. In Hohenleipisch the group became

embroiled in combat with Russian troops, which spilled over into the neighboring town of Plessa. *SS-Unterführer* Edmund Erhardt, 7th Company, 10th SS Panzer Regiment, was wounded by shrapnel from a Russian tank projectile while looking out of the cupola of a Pz.Kpfw.IV as it departed the town limits of Hohenleipisch. At the same time, *SS-Rottenführer* Ernst Kuhnert provided security for the radio half-track of the 2nd Company, 10th SS Panzer Signals Battalion, when an Army officer appeared carrying the identification papers belonging to Friedhelm Lobeck. He explained to the soldiers in the half-track that their company commander had committed suicide.

After crossing the Elster Bridge in Plessa, a brief pause was made in Hirschfeld. At this location, Harmel spoke to his remaining soldiers and the numerous refugees that joined the Frundsbergers. Shortly thereafter, a Fieseler-Storch reconnaissance aircraft landed in Hirschfeld, to bring Harmel and Stolley to the command post of General Gräser, the commander of the Fourth Panzer Army.

Between 19 and 21 April, the Fourth Panzer Army ordered counterattack after counterattack to seal off Soviet penetrations along their lines. The 10th SS Panzer Division, Führer Escort Division, and the 344th Infantry Division formed the *Kampfgruppe* Jolasse, and were subordinated under Army Group Center. On 20 April, *Kampfgruppe* Jolasse, which was squeezed into a narrow corridor west of Spremberg, received orders to hold the line and counterattack toward Spreewitz. On 21 April, the *Kampfgruppe* received orders to close the gap at Görlitz and Spremberg and cut off the spearheads of Soviet attacks in northwest Spremberg. Indeed, the reports by the Fourth Panzer Army of 211 Soviet tanks destroyed may have contributed to the resurgence of hope as orders to counterattack continued. However, Army Group Vistula reported on the same day that their defensive lines were overrun by enemy units that also reached the outer defenses of Berlin, not to mention the report of 300 Soviet tanks and 500 motorized vehicles moving northwest. When the Fourth Panzer Army was attached to Army Group Vistula during the night 20–21 April, all units were ordered to hold their ground while the *Volkssturm* approached to secure the southern flank near the Spree Forest. To make a bad situation worse, Hitler's orders made the following demands:

> The current situation on the Eastern Front is not in our favor due to the imbalance of forces, materiel, and ammunition. Nevertheless, and for that very reason, the highest activity must be carried out with utmost decorum. Only the attack against the enemy's flanks and rear, and the disruption and cutting of lines of communications shall ensure success. The total sum of the ever-present opportunities to counterattack against the rear areas of the enemy, together with limited war, shall make possible total victory.[41]

SS-Untersturmführer Jan Sierks, the battalion adjutant for 4th Battalion, 10th SS Panzer Artillery Regiment, assumed command of the rear guard for the breakout group from Kausche. In the past, Sierks had participated in similar honeymoon operations. According to Sierks, all the units in and around Kausch were part of an inexplicable mess. From the late afternoon on 21 April 1945 into the night, units worked their way closer to the encirclement and then again broke out in two directions. During the breakout, Sierks received orders to defend the eastern rim of Kausch against the pursuing Russians with 100 men. On 22 April, around 1400 hours, Sierks carried out the order. By 1600 hours, as the last German soldier, he departed the village. In continual close combat, the group fought a path to Geisendorf, which remained free of Russian forces that were penetrating forward from Steinitz.

In the morning hours on 22 April 1945, Sierks attended a situation brief, and learned of the rally point for the division in the area around Grossräschen. The Führer Escort Division and 344th Infantry Division were also ordered to assemble in the same area. The orders were distributed by Lieutenant Colonel Wulf, the 1st General Staff officer of the Führer Escort Division.

SS-Rottenführer Alexander Grenda also participated in the last rear-guard action. Grenda arrived to join the division in 1943 at the Troop Training facility Labracon, near Angoulême in France, and received assignment to the antitank battalion.

After the breakout from Kausche, Grenda lost contact with his comrades during the fighting within the forest. Near Geisendorf, he came upon a fighting hole, in which he found a dead Russian. The Russian was roughly fifty years old, big and strong like a bear with black hair and a wild moustache. The Russian had been shot in the head and sat in the hole as if he slept. In the town, Grenda entered captivity. The Russians shot about twenty of his comrades along a building wall. The Russians spared Grenda's life after they determined he spoke Russian. He originated from the area around Suwalki and had been employed as a translator since 1944. The Russians delivered Grenda to a commissar, who wore a cap with a blue band. The commissar approached Grenda and said, "Now then Comrade. You now ten years work in Russian and then go back home." Meanwhile, Grenda heard his comrades being shot and plundered all around him. Grenda thought only of escape.

When the captured prisoners were marched off in the direction of Neupetershain, the Soviets discovered an officer from the Führer Escort Division hiding in the bushes. The Soviets screamed wildly, "Hey! A spy! A spy!" They pulled him out of the bushes and the officer cried out, "Comrades! Please help me! I am not a spy! All I want to do is go home!" No one would intervene on his behalf. He was shot and his belongings plundered and left alongside the road.[42]

Between Neu-Petershain and Geisendorf, *SS-Obersturmführer* Erich Hennig, the adjutant for the regimental artillery, sustained severe wounds that left his arm half torn off. *SS-Hauptsturmführer* Dr. Dörr, the 1st Battalion dentist, 10th SS Panzer Artillery Regiment, attended to Hennig and amputated the arm with a pocket knife. Hennig was picked up by the breakout group with Harmel, and received brandy to help with the pain. Other officers severely wounded during the breakout included *SS-Sturmbannführer* Waldemar Rösch, from the divisional Logistics Section, who lost a leg, and *SS-Hauptsturmführer* Albert Brandt, who lost his eyesight.

During the breakout, several vehicles were lost to enemy fire, but also to mechanical failure and the lack of fuel, including several half-tracks. Outside the village of Lubuchow, a vehicle malfunctioned that carried members of the divisional staff, including the adjutant, *SS-Sturmbannführer* Rudolf Reinicke, *SS-Obersturmführer* Hans-Walter Wehler, the ordnance officer, as well as the divisional commander's personal driver, *SS-Oberscharführer* Sepp Hinterhölzel, Jupp Kolf, and Willy Gertz. While they managed to make their way to the west on foot, they lost contact with the remainder of the division near the Castle Moritzburg.[43]

SS-Untersturmführer Sierks joined the last few men belonging to the group of *SS-Hauptsturmführer* Behrens. Sierks sustained a wound to the leg in Kausch, and rode for a short period on the command tank of Behrens. Sierks was nearby when the wife of Behrens was fatally struck. As the men around their commander entered captivity, Sierks hid in the shallow waters of the Tschugga Lake.

With several other men, Sierks managed to escape over Lindchen. The group grew in size within the forest as additional stragglers joined the ranks. The group marched through the woods north of Grossräschen until they reached Wormlage. The group spent the night in the estate house, while Polish foreign workers celebrated in the basement. Despite carrying weapons, the Frundsbergers did not venture upstairs. The group traveled farther through the forest toward Schacksdorf over Dollenchen and Sallgast. The railroad tracks of the Schippkau-Finsterwalder Railroad afforded some form of directional orientation for the group. In the village of Bergheide, the group of soldiers stopped at a house. A German woman came out of the house and became frightened when she noticed the soldiers. She brought them food and told the group that Russian soldiers were in the house. The group bypassed the house and continued farther to the brick factory at Schacksdorf. Another group of thirteen men were not as lucky; between Sallgast and Poley they were captured and shot by Soviets. Among them was the seventeen-year-old *SS-Panzergrenadier* Hans-Joachim Wenck, from Meissen.[44]

An additional group consisting of twenty-three men, including a French volunteer of the *Waffen-SS*, attempted to break out after acquiring a vehicle from a municipal fire department in Grossräschen and managed to get as far as western Lauchhammer. After some 300 meters, they took the wrong path in the direction of Plessa and drove straight into the arms of the Russians. Not one of the twenty-three survived. The Russians did not permit the bodies to be buried; instead they tried dumping a cart full of manure on the bodies. In the end, local farmers managed to bury the bodies.[45]

SS-Untersturmführer Sierks and several other followers separated from the group at the brick factory in Schacksdorf. A portion of the soldiers attempted to reach Fischwasser.[46] The Austrian Josef Oberlasser fell into Soviet hands on 26 April. However, Jan Sierks and another fellow soldier remained behind in Schacksdorf where a young boy about ten years old brought them food. The following night they departed for Nehesdorf after traversing around the outskirts of the airport at Schacksdorf, where a Soviet aircraft already stood.

Their whereabouts were betrayed and the Russians captured them in a barnyard. The Soviets brought them to a schoolyard in Lauchhammer where they joined other prisoners. The first local trials or tribunals took place. They were marched farther to a prison camp in Senftenberg. Along the way, twenty-three soldiers who collapsed from exhaustion were shot. The bodies were left along the road. Within the prison camp, twenty to thirty soldiers were murdered and buried in a water shaft within a mine, north of the cemetery in Lauchhammer. The bodies of the soldiers were left exposed out in the open for about one week, which many civilians witnessed. Sierks managed to escape to his hometown in Holstein.[47]

Meanwhile, Lieutenant Herbert Kübler, of the 2nd Company, 1st Parachute *Panzergrenadier*, found himself in a similar situation as most German soldiers: conducting a fighting withdrawal. Kübler was born in Ulm on 16 August 1924 and entered military service on 10 July 1942. He entered officer training in the *Luftwaffe* as a maritime patrol scout. In 1943, Kübler attended the 1st Air War College in Dresden-Klotzsche and by August 1944, Kübler had undertaken training at the 101st Long-Range Reconnaissance Squadron in Grossenhain that ended abruptly when he received orders to report to the ground troops with the Division

"Hermann Göring." On 19 September 1944, he reported to the barracks near his hometown at Berlin-Reinickendorf. Promoted to lieutenant on 1 November 1944, he commanded the 2nd Company, 1st Parachute *Panzergrenadier* Regiment.

In the morning on 30 April 1945, Kübler was relieved and exited the main line of battle north of Bautzen and conducted a motorized march with the battalion by way of Göda-Bischofswerda-Radeberg-Dresden-Klotzsche-Moritzburg-Rödern. In the evening they bypassed Moritzburg and made their way to attack positions in the north. They rested for several hours at an estate from where they observed the flash of battle on the horizon and heard the thunder of artillery. Early the next morning at 0400 hours, Kübler and the company left their vehicles behind and entered the areas of the preparatory positions in an old quarry, about 1 to 2 kilometers north of Rödern. The attack was planned to commence at 0500 hours after preparatory artillery fire. To the left and right of Kübler, the 1st and 3rd Companies of the battalion entered the forest. The preparatory artillery fire did not materialize and the attack was postponed to 0700 hours. By 1100 hours the company had reached Schönfeld by way of the cemetery, and continued toward Lampertswalde after passing the castle Schönfeld. Around noon they reached the railroad station at Lampertswalde and encountered Soviet resistance. Forward progress halted before the rail station, but after regrouping the attack pushed the Soviets back. Mop-up operations along the main road followed and the village inhabitants greeted them with flowers alongside the road. Past the church the attack took a different direction toward Schönborn. At the windmill at Schönborn the company encountered the battalion commander, Captain Weitzig. Weitzig admonished Kübler for arriving late with the company. The battalion prepared for a new attack in the direction of Raschützwald. Suddenly, a turret hatch on one of the tanks opened. The commander appeared and greeted Kübler as a former school comrade from the high school at Ehingen. The two exchanged greetings and wished each other well and best of luck to survive the nearing end of the war.

At 1400–1500 hours, a dispute arose between Kübler and the battalion commander Weitzig,

concerning the tactical plan. The attack was intended to begin across open terrain. Weitzig, an artilleryman, had no experience in infantry tactics. At the conclusion of the argument, Kübler's company remained in reserve along the railroad embankment. As expected, the attack across open terrain resulted in high casualties and was easily repelled by the Soviets. Two German tanks were destroyed in the process. Kübler received orders to join the attack. Kübler gave orders to the remaining tank to fire on the Russians occupying the railroad tower. Kübler and his company attacked the enemy under cover of the railroad line and penetrated forward through the woods. The Russians withdrew.

Around 1700 hours the company reached the edge of the woods before Blochwitz and established contact with the battalion's 1st and 3rd Companies. Contact with the battalion commander was impossible. The companies received heavy enemy fire from Blochwitz, including rocket fire from Katyushas, also known as "Stalin's Organs." With binoculars the Germans determined Blochwitz was heavily occupied by Soviet troops. The Soviets brought forward artillery and constructed a new main line of battle before the village. Without the support of heavy weapons, an attack against Blochwitz spelled disaster. The three company commanders discussed the potential for a successful attack. Kübler, the junior commander, objected to an attack despite orders to capture the village. He justified his objections by noting the lack of tactical necessity and the anticipated cost of life nearing the end of the war. Considering the village inhabitants had already fled, the commander of the 3rd Company agreed with Kübler. However, the commander of the 1st Company, First Lieutenant Nilson, fresh from Norway without any front-line experience, wanted to follow orders and capture Blochwitz. Although Kübler opposed the attack, he offered covering company machine-gun fire along the tree line in Raschütz before Blochwitz. The 1st Company attacked but heavy enemy defensive fire stopped the attack in the open terrain. The company withdrew with their wounded to their start positions; however, the dead wcrc left on the battlefield. The casualties included nineteen dead, mostly between the ages of seventeen and eighteen.

In the evening, Kübler and his company occupied a new main line of battle along the edge of the woods. Shortly thereafter, the platoon commander reported that all the men in the line were asleep with their weapons. The earlier success of pushing back the Russians 15 kilometers now showed in the aftermath; the men were exhausted and too tired to keep going. Kübler decided to withdraw the entire company back 150 meters and consolidate around a thicket. Every man paired with another man closely together covering themselves with *Zeltbahns* or shelter-quarters, their weapons next to them at the ready. Kübler established a watch schedule and stood the first shift himself, setting a good example. However, the guards fell asleep, including Kübler. At 0500 hours Kübler woke up, half frozen, laying without any covering on the forest floor. With his submachine gun at his side, Kübler jumped up and woke the entire company, which remained in a deep sleep. Now they were rested and able to enter the defensive positions.[48]

Meanwhile, the 10th SS Medical Battalion broke out with the second group in the direction of Welzow and Proschim. In Proschim, a collection point for the wounded was established. *SS-Untersturmführer* Adolf Adam led a medical ambulance convoy several times into the encirclement to recover the wounded. The wounded were driven from Proschim to Senftenberg, where a hospital train continued to operate on 22 April and departed the city in the direction of Bischofswerda and Bad Schandau.

Several breakout groups that traveled along the southern route managed to reach the forward-most units of the Parachute Panzer Corps, which were some 30 to 40 kilometers away. The seventeen-year-old Werner Kunze, a member of the 6th Company, 2nd Parachute Grenadier Regiment, of the 2nd Parachute Division, commanded by Major General Erich Walter, recalled:

We were positioned in the Zeissholz along the north end of the troop training place at Königsbrück. One of our group was in a forward position at the Neitscher mill. This group included *SS-Untersturmführer* Günter Seybold, a member of the Frundsberg Division, who made his way out of the

encirclement and fought through to us, where he was employed as a machine-gun platoon leader. We repelled several Russian attacks originating from Lipsa and captured an American half-track. Several of our snipers silenced an enemy antitank gun, which fired on us repeatedly and killed the twenty-one-year-old woman Dora Böhme. We also captured the gun.[49]

According to Kunze, the Soviets attacked the village on 3 May 1945 with infantry and T-34 tanks. With only *Panzerfausts* and machine guns to mount a defense, Captain Lohrmann was injured and the troops pulled back to the troop training location where they gathered in a bunker. The machine-gun troop and *SS-Untersturmführer* Seybold fell into Soviet hands and were shot. All told, twelve men were captured; their eyes were poked out and they were bound with barbed wire and buried up to their necks.[50]

Burchard Willenbrock, a member of the 55th Panzer Reconnaissance Battalion, Panzer Group Stegemann, was employed as a reserve in a defensive position at Neisse and located in Gross Luja. The 55th Panzer Reconnaissance Battalion was from Hirschberg in Schlesien. Following the Russian breakthrough at the Neisse, the 55th withdrew on Spremberg. Willenbrock's recollections capture the chaotic nature of operations and the desperation of German troops as they did everything possible to elude Soviet troops:

At the city outskirts, the soldiers were integrated with the tanks of the Frundsberg Division. Within the city, the soldiers barely eluded a Russian bombing attack on Spremberg. A group of soldiers from the battalion was formed, which included the company commander, First Lieutenant Powelske, and approximately fifty men. Our orders were to reach the 2nd Company at Senftberg.

The Russians bypassed the group on the right and left. At the town exit of Spremberg, Willenbrock and the others rode with several self-propelled Hummels belonging to the Frundsberg Division. Willenbrock recalled:

I sat on the side and fell asleep. We passed through a tank barricade when the sling of my submachine gun caught on a tree that pulled me from the tank. I tumbled to the side to avoid being hit by the following tank.

When the Frundsberg Division entered positions to the left of the 55th Panzer Reconnaissance Battalion, the scouting battalion continued marching on foot through the forest toward Senftenberg. The 2nd Company, consisting of only forty men, became engaged in heavy fighting within the forest. In an effort to disengage and escape encirclement, the 2nd Company turned northward. However, thirty Russian T-34 tanks with mounted infantry overran the company. With the aid of a compass, a small group marched through the Kiefern Forest in the direction of Finsterwald. The group linked up with the remainder of the 55th Reconnaissance Battalion in the village of Freienhufen. Numbering about 150 men, the group received orders to block the road. The group had one 88mm antitank gun with fifteen rounds, and a few machine guns. Willenbrock recalled:

We entered positions at the village entrance. With one machine gun and First Lieutenant Powelske, we took up positions on the right side of the road. The Russians approached with three JS Stalin tanks followed by fifteen T-34. The antitank fired on the first Stalin, which turned its turret and returned fire; the antitank gun and its crew were knocked out. We fired on the infantry that jumped off the tanks, but the T-34s attacked the village across a broad front.

Lacking antitank weapons, their only option was to flee into the forest. Within the woods they counted Lieutenant Powelske, four sergeants, and eighteen men. They did not know what had happened to the 120 men on the other side of the road. The group continued to march through the woods toward Finsterwald when they observed Russian units on the roads heading west. Eluding detection as they passed Finsterwald, they linked up with a pioneer unit in Fischwasser. The men received their first meal in several days from an artillery unit that had no ammunition. The following day a major on a motorcycle came upon the group and ordered them to take up positions. The group also heard a rumor that the Americans had declared war against the Soviets and were approaching their location. Willenbrock recalled:

We had fourteen men, one submachine gun, eight rifles, but no contact to our left and right. We marched through Liebenverda on to Mühlberg in order to cross the Elbe River. Ten men reached Mühlberg with no time to spare; Russian cavalry pressed on our tails. However, four men could not swim and they did not want us to pull them. They ended up falling into Russian hands. We entered the water and began swimming, as the Russians conducted target practice. Only Sergeant Holzhauser and I made it across. Lieutenant Powelske, the NCO Nierobisch, Sergeant Bämel and a corporal were killed in the river. We reached the other side and entered American captivity.[51]

The Parachute Panzer Corps "Herman Göring" absorbed individual breakout-groups and integrated them into the ranks. Major Ebel withdrew the 1st Parachute Panzer Division via Auer into preparatory positions at Rödern, after successfully recapturing Bautzen. On 1 May 1945, the Corps planned to launch a counterattack, supported by the 20th Panzer Division, in a northerly direction against the line Grossen-Kamenz. Additional support for the Parachute Panzer Division in Grosshain came from four Pz.Kpfw.IV tanks commanded by *SS-Obersturmführer* Hans Quandel, of the 6th Company, 10th SS Panzer Regiment. Quandel's tanks reached the airport but withdrew lacking infantry support. Eddi Zalewski, a member of the 10th SS Panzer Signals Battalion, located at Kupferberg, reported the following:

After the Frundsberg Division returned from employment in the areas of Stettin-Altdamm-Rosengarten-Podejuch, we reported to the divisional field combat post in Stettin-Brunn.

Our command half-track was repaired by the first squadron. During the fighting, several bolts broke and the bogie wheels were damaged from a hit by an antitank gun.

In Brunn they received a few days off duty. Once the vehicles were repaired, they conducted a motorized march to Pfaffendorf. Zalewski recalled:

We headed back and forth. The division was split into three groups; Finsterwalde, Spremberg, and Görlitz. We were in the latter group in near proximity to Lauban. We heard artillery fire in the distance. We buried the half-track and then time passed cleaning weapons. We wrote letters to loved ones and sent packages; the normal things associated with being a Landser.[52]

On the same day, 1 May 1945, Zalewski reported to the company commander of the 10th SS Panzer Signals Battalion, *SS-Hauptsturmführer* Helmut Speck. Zalewski received orders to proceed to an alarm unit in Görlitz, which was assigned to the Field Replacement Battalion. The reason for the transfer was to provide Zalewski operational experience.

In Görlitz, Zalewski took command of a group of grenadiers about sixteen to seventeen years of age, who came from the *Luftwaffe* and members of the rehabilitation platoon. The group traveled through Hoyerswerda to Bärwalde, the location of a divisional combat post. A cohesive unit did not exist. At this location, Zalewski heard that Hitler had been killed in action fighting in and around Berlin, and that their divisional commander, Heinz Harmel, was replaced by the new commander, *SS-Obersturmbannführer* Franz Roestel. The older experienced men of the division were shocked to hear the news and found it hard to believe that their fatherly commander was forced to relinquish command to a junior officer.

Needless to say, Zalewski and his men were needed yet elsewhere to continue fighting. The alarm unit, elevated to *Kampfgruppe* and manning positions in Kupferberg, participated in a counterattack on 4 May 1945, which led them against Grossenhain. Zalewski recalled:

After we took over the new positions along the main line of battle, the Soviets probed our lines with scouting and reconnaissance troops. Soon we were engulfed by enemy artillery fire, which allowed us only to seek cover on the ground. My group managed to enter the basement of a house that offered protection against incoming projectiles.

In the late afternoon Zalewski received orders from a *SS-Untersturmführer* to establish contact with an 88mm antitank position belonging to the HG Division. Shortly before departing, Zalewski continued:

Two of the men in my group were seriously wounded by artillery fire. Quickly, as best we could, we cared for our wounded fellow soldiers without the help of a medic. Suddenly I was alone, and upon reaching the antitank gun, the gunner (NCO) advised me that only two rounds were left and contact with his company commander was broken. I planned to return to my own position in order to report to the *SS-Untersturmführer* what I heard and witnessed.

Caught in the open, artillery fire from all calibers landed all around him. Zalewski came across a hole in which he took cover. From there he observed the antitank gun crew hooking the gun onto a prime mover. He jumped out of his hole and managed to catch up with the gun, which was already underway. Suddenly, three T-34 tanks appeared before them when another five tanks approached from the left side. The gunner ordered the prime mover to stop, swung the barrel around 180 degrees, and fired the last two available rounds. Zalewski and two other crew members found *Panzerfausts* on the prime mover that they fired at the tanks. Zalewski continued:

I do not know if we hit anything, but the enemy tanks responded with a deluge of machine-gun fire. A steel splinter hit my shin, but it did not bother me the least. Despite the continued enemy tank and machine-gun fire, we were able to extricate ourselves from the danger zone several minutes later.

The group met other grenadiers who had already received the order to withdraw. Zalewski also met with the *SS-Untersturmführer* who gave him the previous order. The *SS-Untersturmführer* explained the position was not tenable, despite the greatest resistance. There were significant casualties and several men killed. The *SS-Untersturmführer* received orders to withdraw southwest of Dresden, along with the remainder of the *Kampfgruppe*. Renewed fighting with Soviet troops broke out when they arrived outside Dresden, but Zalewski managed to catch a ride on a Pz.Kpfw.IV belonging to the 10th SS Panzer Regiment. However, during a local counterattack, an enemy antitank gun disabled the tank by hitting the tracks on one side, and Zalewski was forced to dismount. After jumping off the tank, he then woke up in an ambulance, among other wounded, and headed for a field aid station.[53]

Hans Oebel, born on 21 August 1925, belonged to the category of young men who volunteered for service but were unable to participate in the fighting soon enough. He changed the 5 to a 3 on his birthdate during in-processing and entered service with the 4th SS Police Division at the age of fifteen. He transferred to the Frundsberg Division when the division first became organized and joined the SS Panzer Recovery Platoon, 1st Battalion, 10th SS Panzer Regiment. Regardless of whether he was on the Eastern or Western Front, Oebel responded when the tanks of the division were either knocked out or stuck in the mud. Often the platoon recovered vehicles behind enemy lines that were separated by many kilometers from the maintenance post. Without being detected by the enemy, the vehicles were towed back to friendly lines. Oebel displayed great courage in recovering vehicles, but even more so when his wounded fellow soldiers were left behind in their knocked out vehicles. Oebel and his recovery crew, known as the jacks-of-all-trades, were always successful and brought many fellow soldiers home to safety. Hans Oebel always had a trick up his sleeve. In April 1945, when the *Feldgendarmerie* was overly active, the commander of the Panzer Recovery Platoon, *SS-Obersturmführer* Hans Bauer, ended up in the Görlitz prison, despite having valid marching orders to the tank regiment. Hans Oebel and his comrades used an engineer tank with a

shovel to drive through the prison gate and knocked down the cell door to free their commander.[54]

Between the end of April and the beginning of May 1945, the remnants of the 10th SS Panzer Divison escaped the encirclement between Spremberg and Spreewald. The greater portions of the 10th SS Panzer Reconnaissance Battalion, portions of the 10th SS Panzer Antiaircraft Battalion, remnants of panzer grenadier units as well as supplies, and various headquarters staff made their way west in small individual groups. The remainder of the division that was conducting a fighting withdrawal gathered in the area around Dresden, while individual *Kampfgruppen* from the 10th SS Panzer Division held out against the Soviets within the Upper Lausitz triangle of Bautzen-Kamenz-Bischofswerda. *SS-Brigadeführer* Heinz Harmel, who received orders to counterattack with his armored group between Spremberg and Cottbus to cut off the Soviet armored spearheads from their supply, chose instead to move his small armored group westward. Field Marshal Schörner relieved Harmel of his command and replaced him with the senior ranking officer, *SS-Obersturmbannführer* Roestel.

Erwin Roestel, a reserve officer and a ministerial director by profession, gained the attention of Heinrich Himmler when Roestel received the German Cross in Gold as the commander of an Army assault gun battalion. Himmler arranged for the transfer of Roestel as an instructor to the SS Assault Gun School, until Roestel received orders to command the 10th SS Tank Destroyer Battalion.

Together with the commander of the 10th SS Panzer Regiment, *SS-Sturmbannführer* Ernst Tetsch, and other willing members of the division, Roestel followed the orders that, in the beginning of May, relocated the division marching south in the direction of Prague. What remained of the division assembled around Dresden. *SS-Sturmbannführer* Tetsch was to lead the convoy eastward and then southward along the only road along the Elbe River toward Prague over Pirna-Bad Schandau-Teschen-Aussig-Leitmeritz-Prague. Under the Fourth Panzer Army, Roestel received orders on 4 May to withdraw to the south into the Ore Mountains and establish a defensive line. However, the same order did not reach everyone. By 8 May, Roestel and those units with him reached Zinnwald in the Ore Mountains. Upon his arrival in Bohemia, Roestel reported to Field Marshal Ferdinand Schörner, the commander of Army Group Center, who awarded Roestel with the Knight's Cross of the Iron Cross.

SS-Obersturmbannführer Roestel released those around him from their oath of service and dissolved the 10th SS Panzer Division. The divisional members underway along the Elbe who remained embroiled in the fighting never received the order and were left to their own fate.[55]

The German defeat in Europe rested on the strategic genius of the Allied coalition that began in the early spring 1944, on the Eastern Front, when the Soviets opened their spring offensive against Army Group South. When German forces were shifted away from the western European coast, in order to deal with the Soviet offensive, the airborne and amphibious landings at Normandy succeeded in securing a beachhead in Western Europe that marked the beginning of the end of the war against

Germany. Following the Soviet thrust against Army Group South, the 10th SS Panzer Division rushed to the Ukraine and participated in the relief of the encircled First Panzer Army at Kamenez-Podolsk. The 10th SS returned to the West after the Allies landed at Normandy, and participated in numerous key battles only to return back to the East, and fight up to the last day of the war. The demise of the 10th SS Panzer Division occured by sheer attrition during the Soviet attack on Berlin. Amidst the fog of war, including confusion, the breakdown of communications, and general operational chaos, the division fragmented into separate groups, operating as stopgap measures at various locations to assist German military and civilian personnel to escape Soviet captivity.

The German armed forces faced overwhelming odds in trying to stop the momentum of numerous Soviet armies containing tanks, artillery, and aircraft, which swallowed everything in their path until they reached Berlin.

Heinz Harmel in the divisional Fieseler Fi 156 "Storch" (Stork) liaison aircraft. Source: Sieberhagen Archive.

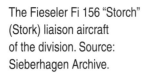

The Fieseler Fi 156 "Storch" (Stork) liaison aircraft of the division. Source: Sieberhagen Archive.

Members missing in action, 10th SS Panzer Division. Source: Sieberhagen Archive.

Georg Aulig, Signals Troop, 22nd *SS-Panzergrenadier* Regiment. Source: Sieberhagen Archive.

Georg Aulig and his sister Gerda (killed 1945), and his parents. At the bottom, Georg's best friend, Eddi Ammann. Source: Sieberhagen Archive.

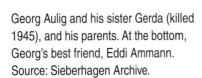

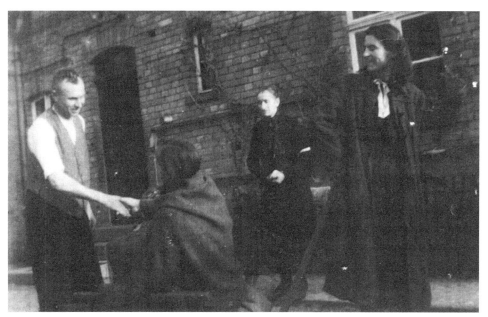

The schoolteacher Gerda Schmidt bringing the wounded *SS-Unterscharführer* Erich Reichert from Wormloge to the field hospital in Altdöbern, May 1945. Source: Sieberhagen Archive.

The forester's greenhouse near Finsterwalde where the 10th SS Panzer Division established radio contact with the headquarters of the Fourth Panzer Army, 25 April 1945. Source: Sieberhagen Archive.

Karl Godau, 10th SS Panzer Artillery Regiment, who entered Soviet captivity with his battalion in Bülow. Source: Sieberhagen Archive.

SS-Unterscharführer Sven-Eric Olson, commander of the Half-Track Detachment, 2nd Company, 10th SS Panzer Signals Battalion. Source: Sieberhagen Archive.

SS-Funker (Radio Operator) Albrecht Henning in the Half-Track Detachment, 10th SS Panzer Pioneer Battalion. Source: Sieberhagen Archive.

Depicted as an *SS-Unterscharführer* while serving with a *Totenkopf* regiment, Günther Rahn attained the rank of *SS-Untersturmführer*, serving with the 22nd *SS-Panzergrenadier* Regiment, who went missing at Halbe. Source: Sieberhagen Archive.

Depicted as an *SS-Sturmscharführer*, Otto Morgenstern attained the rank of *SS-Obersturmführer* and was killed in action in April 1945 at Grünewald, with the 10th SS Panzer Reconnaissance Battalion. Source: Sieberhagen Archive.

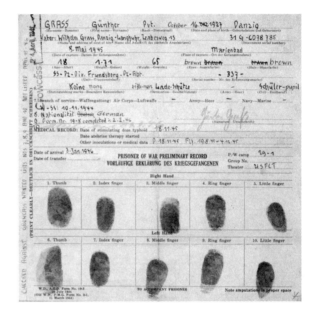

The prisoner of war record of Günther Grass. Source: Stenger Archive.

A Pz.Kpfw.V Ausf. G in ready position. Source: Westerhoff Archive.

A member of the tank crew
Laier, 19 April 1945. Source:
Westerhoff Archive.

Stop along open road during employment in Pommern, 1945.
Source: Westerhoff Archive.

A knocked out Soviet T-34 medium tank, March 1945. Source: Westerhoff Archive.

On the right, Stratmann recovering in a hospital after being wounded in the legs when his tank was hit by a Soviet T-34 medium tank. Source: Westerhoff Archive.

Tank crew Laier on 19 April 1945, one of only five tanks remaining. Source: Westerhoff Archive.

SS-Obersturmführer Franz Riedel, the senior company commander and frequent acting commander for the 2nd Battalion. Source: Westerhoff Archive.

Epilogue

IN 1977, HEINZ HARMEL was depicted fictitiously as *SS-Brigadeführer* Karl Ludwig, by the German film actor Hardy Krüger in the movie, *A Bridge Too Far*, based on the 1974 book by Cornelius Ryan. Despite historical accuracy, the movie received little attention in the United States and did not do well at the box office, though it earned a better reception in Europe. Whether featured in a film or not, the 10th SS Panzer Division never received the kind of attention as other *Waffen-SS* divisions have. Divisions such as the 1st SS Panzer Division at Malmedy, the 2nd SS Panzer Division at Oradour-sur-Glane, and the 3rd SS Panzer Division at Le Paradis, to name the most disreputable, are better known for the war crimes they committed, while the 10th SS Panzer Division has remained rather obscure to this day. Nevertheless, the division shall forever remain associated with a criminal organization and a verdict that has been validated by professional historians since the end of World War II.

The *Schutzstaffel* (SS) or protective squad became an enormous, multifaceted empire, which under Heinrich Himmler gained unequivocal power within Nazi Germany. The SS penetrated every sphere of German life, including education, personal privacy, health care, and industry. The most notable mark the SS left behind was the planned execution of ruthless wars against countries and populations, in violation of the rules and customs of war. The SS was responsible for wholesale murder, wrongful treatment of civilians, and the deportation of civilian populations for slave labor. It also participated in the murder and improper treatment of prisoners of war, the taking and killing of hostages, the plunder of public and private property, the wanton destruction of cities, towns, and villages, and devastation not justified by military necessity. The common plan, which became typical and systematic, came to embrace crimes against humanity, both within Germany and within occupied territories. Before and during the war the plan was executed against civilian populations, who were persecuted on political, racial, or religious grounds. A question that immediately comes to mind, given the verdict of the Nuremberg trials, is where did the 10th SS Panzer Division fit against this legacy?

Throughout the less than two and a half years the 10th SS Panzer Division existed, the German members of the division usually followed a common path from adolescent political indoctrination, which began before grammar school, to compulsory labor service, basic military training, and from combat specialty training directly to combat units in the front lines.[1] Non-German or ethnic German members were often conscripted against their will directly into training battalions followed by assignments to combat units. The officer corps and NCOs brought to the cadre extensive combat experience, as well as formal military education and inter-service training. Heinz Harmel, for example, took command of the division shortly after attending the divisional commanders course. At the same time, many individuals who formed the cadre of the division fit neatly within Heinrich Himmler's concept of a racially pure and elite political soldier.[2] These members of the cadre belonged to units that participated in the earliest reign of terror that spread across Germany, into Austria, Czechoslovakia, and Poland. For example, *SS-Obersturmbannführer* Michael Lippert, a member of the 10th SS Panzer Division in 1943, participated in 1934 in the purge of the *Sturmabteilung* or SA and may have been responsible for murdering the leader of the SA Ernst Röhm.[3]

The combat chronology of the division ran its course contrary to the very principle of Hitler's ideological war: the continuation of politics by other means. Carl von Clausewitz, a military philosopher who helped reform the Prussian military after their defeats at Jena in 1806, theorized that war was not a pastime, but rather a serious means to a serious end. Clausewitz wrote:

When whole communities go to war—whole peoples, and especially *civilized* peoples—the reason always lies in some political situation, and the occasion is always due to some political object. War, therefore, is an act of policy. Policy, then, will permeate all the military operations, and, in so far as their violent nature will admit, it will have a continuous influence on them.[4]

Hitler's political plan to wage war was no mystery. Under the cover of military operations, the killing of innocent civilians intentionally saw no limit. Hitler deliberately escalated terror as a means for complete conquest. The obliteration by mass killing of scholars, politicians, and social elites that formed the intelligentsia by SS *Einsatzgruppen* or Special Purpose Units followed combat and noncombat operations into Austria, Czechoslovakia, and Poland that set the example for future operations into every occupied country.[5]

By the time the 10th SS entered combat operations in 1944, the strategic and tactical initiatives enjoyed early by the German armed forces had transferred to the Allies and forced German combat formations into a state of perpetual withdrawal, characterized by limited stopgap operations and desperate measures. In this regard, the chronological survey of the division's operational life reveals the true nature of combat when fighting

against a coalition of opponents who enjoyed far greater numbers in manpower and materiel. From its combat debut in April 1944 until the last day of the war, the surviving cadre repeatedly transformed the division into a capable fighting formation. The employment of the divisional artillery regiment stands out as a crucial factor in contributing to operational success on the battlefield, as well as the basic continued survival of the division to the end of the war. A potential area for more informative study are the theories and effectiveness of combined artillery that utilized guns at every level of command, put to use in particular by the division in September 1944, which became standardized around the same time at the Corps-levels and above, but too late to make a difference. Replacements for the division came from all the service branches as well as paramilitary organizations including the Army, *Luftwaffe*, *Kriegsmarine*, and RAD. From one battle to the next, manpower levels reached the absolute bare minimum, to the point that personnel within supporting units were pressed into the front lines. Despite the shortages, the 10th SS Panzer Division repeatedly managed to reconstitute itself as a viable fighting formation that some historians have rated as among the best. According to Charles Whiting, the author of *The Other Battle of the Bulge: Operation Northwind*:

The 10th SS had fought brilliantly in Russia, had been shattered in Normandy, and had then taken part with the 9th SS Panzer Division in the slaughter of the British 1st Airborne Division in Arnhem in September, 1944. In fact, it can be said that the 10th SS Panzer gained Germany's only real victory on the Western Front in 1944.[6]

George H. Stein, the author of *The Waffen-SS: Hitler's Elite Guard at War 1939–1945*, wrote that during the Stargard offensive only a handful of formations bearing the name SS were top notch, including the 10th SS Panzer Division.[7]

There is no doubt the 10th SS Panzer Division made a significant contribution during the last two years of World War II, at a time when the German armed forces experienced irreversible operational setbacks, based on poor strategy, which ultimately created an untenable situation in every theater. While the combat chronology presented herein contains a blend of operational history and the human drama associated with the personnel of the division, its purpose shall be to gain a different perspective on the war and a better appreciation of how the *Waffen-SS* operated in the field. At the same time, the exploits of career SS soldiers and eyewitness accounts from all ranks give a good indication why this particular *Waffen-SS* division earned a reputation for combat competence.

Georg von Frundsberg
10th SS Panzer Division

GEORG VON FRUNDSBERG was born on 24 September 1473, in the castle of Mindelheim near Memmingen, into an old line of southern Tyrolean knights that settled in Upper Swabia. At the age of nineteen, Frundsberg fought on behalf of the Reich to suppress regional forces that forced Duke Albrecht of Bavaria to relinquish the city of Regensburg. In 1504, Frundsberg fought against the Pfalz-Counts Philipp and Ruprecht. He distinguished himself during the Battle of Regensburg to such a degree that shortly thereafter, King Maximilian I personally bestowed him with knighthood.

One year later, Frundsberg became the commander of the *Landsknecht* (mercenaries) in the lower countries. Thereafter, Frundsberg lived an uninterrupted life of war, campaigning for the king and Reich. In 1509, Frundsberg became the "Highest Field Captain" of the *Landsknecht* Regiment (occupation force) and defended the city of Verona against numerous attacks. During the fighting against the Republic of Venice in 1513, Frundsberg's calm and collected demeanor carried his forces to victory during the Battle of Vicenz, despite the numerical superiority of the enemy that encircled the Reich's army.

In 1521, when the German king Karl V fought Franz I of France, Frundsberg helped lead the army into Picardie. When Franz I appeared on the battlefield with a force of approximately 40,000 men, the clever withdrawal of the German

Georg von Frundsberg. Source: Stenger Archive.

king's army saved its existence. Frundsberg considered the withdrawal on Valenciennes as both the luckiest and the most appropriate measure during the war.

After the French campaign in 1522 ended and Frundsberg resigned from the leadership of the *Landesknechts*, he returned to lead the march on upper Italy. Within a short period, 6,000 men followed the beat of his campaign drum and the magic in his name. A difficult alpine crossing through deep snow led to the Battle of Biccocca near Mailand. Swiss nationals on foot fought alongside Frundsberg, who led and fought from the front, together with the Swiss knight Arnold Winkelried. The Kaiser's victory at Biccocca allowed for the return of the old Kingdom's Parliamentary Cabinet Lands of Genua and Mailand.

In 1525, after a brief stop in Mindelheim as the "Highest Field Captain" of the entire German nation (consisting of 12,000 men and twenty-nine flag bearers), Frundsberg moved again toward upper Italy to relieve Pavia and to save the Reich's Duchy of Mailand. With an additional 6,000 men (some of whom were Spanish) in battle against an enemy that was twice as strong, Frundsberg won his most famous victory at Pavia by capturing the French king.

Only one year later, in 1526, Frundsberg received a call for help from the Kaiser's army in Lombardei, to help decide the war. Albeit an insufficient amount,

he obtained 36,000 German Taler to organize the new army. During his occupation of Mindelheim, Frundsberg borrowed money and sold off his silver table-settings and his wife's jewelry to acquire the remaining funds to raise the army. In less than three weeks, Frundsberg organized over 12,000 men and crossed the Alps during the middle of November. However, order and discipline broke in 1527, when no decisive battle developed after months of campaigning in Italy. Payment for the mercenaries remained overdue and, in the end, even Frundsberg was unable to rally the *Landsknechts* and restore order. The matter shook the old commander to such an extent that he suffered a stroke. Unable to regain his physical strength, Frundsberg was moved to Germany after a long struggle in Italian hospitals. Tormented by great anxiety over the situation with his mercenaries, the loss of his personal estate, as well as the death of a son, Georg von Frundsberg died on 20 August 1528, in his castle in Mindelheim.

Source: 10.SS-Pz.Div. "Frundsberg," Abt.VI/Az.37g/Lt./Dr; Div.St.Qu., dtd 6.11.43, NA/RG242/T354/R150/F791940-791948.

Theoretical Table of Organization

SS Panzer Division 1943

Divisional Headquarters Staff (2 LMG)
- Divisional Mapping Office (motorized) (2 LMG)
- Military Police Detachment (motorized) (2 LMG)
- Music Corps
- Escort Company (4 LMG and 7 heavy MG)
  - Motorcycle Messenger Platoon (6 motorcycles; 6 LMG)
  - Light Infantry Gun Platoon (two 75mm light infantry guns/18)
  - Light Antiaircraft Platoon (4 self-propelled 1-ton 20mm Flak guns [Sd.Kfz. 10/4])
  - Towed Heavy Antitank Platoon (three 75mm Pak 39L/48; 3 LMG)
  - War Correspondent Platoon
- Panzer Regiment with Regimental Staff
  - Staff Company (20 LMG) (unknown number of tanks)
  - Panzer Battalion (20 LMG)
    - Battalion Staff and Battalion Staff Company (12 LMG and 3 Pz.Kpfw.III)
    - 1st Battalion (8 command Pz.Kpfw.V)
      - 1st Company (22 Pz.Kpfw.V)
      - 2nd Company (22 Pz.Kpfw.V)
      - 3rd Company (22 Pz.Kpfw.V)
      - 4th Company (22 Pz.Kpfw.V)
    - 2nd Battalion (8 command Pz.Kpfw.III)
      - Flamethrower Tank Platoon (7 Pz.Kpfw.III [flamethrower])
      - 5th Company (22 Pz.Kpfw.IV or StuG III)
      - 6th Company (22 Pz.Kpfw.IV or StuG III)
      - 7th Company (22 Pz.Kpfw.IV or StuG III)
      - 8th Company (22 Pz.Kpfw.IV or StuG III)
      - Panzer Maintenance Company (4 LMG)
- Panzer Grenadier Regiment (armored)
  - Staff and PzGrenRgt Staff Company
    - Motorcycle Messenger Platoon (6 motorcycles; 6 LMG)
    - Signals Platoon (7 LMG)
    - Pioneer Platoon (6 LMG and 6 flamethrowers)
    - Heavy Antitank Platoon (three 75mm Pak 39L/48 and 3 LMG)

1st Battalion (armored) with Staff

    1st Panzer Grenadier Company (39 LMG, 4 heavy MG, 2 medium mortars, three 37mm combat vehicle cannon L/45, two 75mm combat vehicle cannon L/43 or 48)

    2nd Panzer Grenadier Company (39 LMG, 4 heavy MG, 2 medium mortars, three 37mm combat vehicle cannon L/45, two 75mm combat vehicle cannon L/43 or 48)

    3rd Panzer Grenadier Company (39 LMG, 4 heavy MG, 2 medium mortars, three 37mm combat vehicle cannon L/45, two 75mm combat vehicle cannon L/43 or 48)

    4th Heavy Panzer Grenadier Company (12 LMG and 9 heavy MG, three 75mm Pak 40 L/46, two 75mm light infantry gun18, six 75mm combat vehicle cannon L/43 or 48)

2nd Battalion (motorized) with Staff

    1st Panzer Grenadier Company (18 LMG, 4 heavy MG, 2 medium mortars)

    2nd Panzer Grenadier Company (18 LMG, 4 heavy MG, 2 medium mortars)

    3rd Panzer Grenadier Company (18 LMG, 4 heavy MG, 2 medium mortars)

    4th Heavy Panzer Grenadier Company (4 LMG, four medium mortars, three 75mm Pak)

    Antiaircraft Company (12 SP 20mm, 4 LMG)

    Heavy Infantry Gun Company (6 SP 105mm, 7 LMG)

    Panzer Grenadier Pioneer Company

        Panzer Pioneer Platoon (13 LMG, one 20mm combat vehicle cannon, 6 flamethrowers)

        Panzer Pioneer Platoon (motorized) (8 LMG and 12 flamethrowers)

Panzer Grenadier Regiment (motorized)

  Staff and PzGrenRgt Staff Company

    Motorcycle Messenger Platoon (6 motorcycles; 6 LMG)

    Signals Platoon (7 LMG)

    Heavy Antitank Platoon (three 75mm Pak 39L/48 and 3 LMG)

  1st Battalion (motorized) with Staff

    1st Panzer Grenadier Company (39 LMG, 4 heavy MG, 2 medium mortars, three 37mm combat vehicle cannon L/45, two 75mm combat vehicle cannon L/43 or 48)

    2nd Panzer Grenadier Company (39 LMG, 4 heavy MG, 2 medium mortars, three 37mm combat vehicle cannon L/45, two 75mm combat vehicle cannon L/43 or 48)

    3rd Panzer Grenadier Company (39 LMG, 4 heavy MG, 2 medium mortars, three 37mm combat vehicle cannon L/45, two 75mm combat vehicle cannon L/43 or 48)

    4th Heavy Panzer Grenadier Company (12 LMG and 9 heavy MG, three 75mm Pak 40 L/46, two 75mm light infantry gun18, six 75mm combat vehicle cannon L/43 or 48)

  2nd Battalion (motorized) with Staff

    1st Panzer Grenadier Company (18 LMG, 4 heavy MG, 2 medium mortars)

    2nd Panzer Grenadier Company (18 LMG, 4 heavy MG, 2 medium mortars)

    3rd Panzer Grenadier Company (18 LMG, 4 heavy MG, 2 medium mortars)

    4th Heavy Panzer Grenadier Company (4 LMG, 4 medium mortars, three 75mm Pak)

    Antiaircraft Company (12 SP 20mm, 4 LMG)

    Heavy Infantry Gun Company (6 SP 105mm, 7 LMG)

        Panzer Grenadier Pioneer Company (motorized) (12 LMG 18 flamethrowers)

  Panzer Reconnaissance Battalion

    Staff and Signal Platoon (motorized) (3 LMG)

    Heavy Cannon Platoon (heavy armored scout car with six 75mm combat vehicle cannon [Sd.Kfz.234/3] and 6 LMG) (applied only on special orders)

    Light Armored Scout Company (18 light armored scout cars [Sd.Kfz.234/1] with 20mm and 24 LMG)

    Light Armored Scout Company (16 light armored scout cars [Sd.Kfz.250/9] with 20mm combat vehicle cannon 38 L/55 and 25 LMG)

    Panzer Reconnaissance Company (Sd.Kfz.251) (56 LMG, 4 heavy MG, 3 Pak 37mm, 2 medium mortars)

    Reconnaissance Company (motorcycle, Kettenrad, or VW) (18 LMG, 4 heavy MG, two 81mm mortars)

    Heavy Reconnaissance Company (Sd.Kfz.251)

1st Heavy Reconnaissance Platoon (3 combat vehicle cannon 37mm and 4 LMG)
2nd Heavy Reconnaissance Platoon (3 combat vehicle cannon 37mm and 4 LMG)
Infantry Gun Platoon (two 75mm light infantry gun/18 and 4 LMG)
Heavy Antitank Platoon (three 75mm Pak 40 and 9 LMG)
Pioneer Platoon (13 LE.MG, one 20mm combat vehicle cannon 38 L/55, and 6 flamethrowers)
Light Panzer Reconnaissance Convoy Battalion (3 LMG)
Panzer Antitank Battalion (self-propelled)
Staff (6 LMG) and Staff Platoon (self-propelled 75mm Pak 40)
1st Panzer Antitank Company (self-propelled) (fourteen 75mm Sd.Kfz.142/1 [StuG III Ausf G] and 14 LMG)
2nd Panzer Antitank Company (self-propelled) (fourteen 75mm Sd.Kfz.142/1 [StuG III Ausf G] and 14 LMG)
3rd Panzer Antitank Company (self-propelled) (fourteen 75mm Sd.Kfz.142/1 [StuG III Ausf G] and 14 LMG)
Panzer Artillery Regiment
Staff and Staff Battery (2 LMG)
1st Battalion (self-propelled)
Staff and Staff Battery (2 LMG)
1st Battery (six 105mm le.F.H.18/2 [Sd.Kfz.124] and 5 LMG)
2nd Battery (six 105mm le.F.H.18/2 [Sd.Kfz.124] and 5 LMG)
3rd Battery (six 105mm le.F.H.18/2 [Sd.Kfz.124] and 5 LMG)
2nd Battalion (towed)
Staff and Staff Battery (2 LE.MG)
1st Battery (four 105mm le.F.H.18 M L/28 or 18/40 and 2 LMG)
2nd Battery (four 105mm le.F.H.18 M L/28 or 18/40 and 2 LMG)
3rd Battery (four 105mm le.F.H.18 M L/28 or 18/40 and 2 LMG)
3rd Battalion (towed)
Staff and Staff Battery (2 LE.MG)
1st Battery (four 150mm heavy field howitzers/18 L/29,6 and 5 LMG)
2nd Battery (four 150mm heavy field howitzers/18 L/29,6 and 5 LMG)
3rd Battery (four 100mm heavy Cannon/18 L/52 and 5 LMG)
Army Antiaircraft Artillery Battalion (motorized)
Staff and Staff Battery (2 LMG)
1st Heavy Flak Battery (four 88mm Flak 36, three 20mm Flak 38 and 2 LMG)
2nd Heavy Flak Battery (four 88mm Flak 36, three 20mm Flak 38 and 2 LMG)
Light Flak Battery (twelve 20mm Flak 38, 4 LMG, and 4 spotlights 600mm)
Light Flak Convoy (motorized 20-ton) (2 LMG)
Panzer Pioneer Battalion
Staff (2 LE.MG) and Staff Company
Armored Reconnoiter Platoon (12 LMG)
Staff Signals Platoon/Squadron
1st Panzer Pioneer Company (motorized) (18 LMG, 2 medium mortars, 6 flamethrowers)
2nd Panzer Pioneer Company (armored) (43 LMG, 3 light antitank rocket launchers, 2 medium mortars, 6 flamethrowers)
Panzer Bridging Convoy J (3 LMG)
Panzer Signals Battalion
Staff
Telephone Company (motorized) (21 LMG)
Wireless Radio Company (35 LMG)
Light Signals Convoy (motorized) (4 LMG)
Panzer Field-Replacement Battalion (4 units) (weapons T/E unknown)
Panzer Division Supply Battalion
Staff (2 LMG)
1st Truck Company (120-ton and 8 LMG)

2nd Truck Company (120-ton and 8 LMG)
3rd Truck Company (120-ton and 8 LMG)
4th Truck Company (120-ton and 8 LMG)
5th Truck Company (120-ton and 8 LMG)
6th Truck Company (120-ton and 8 LMG)
7th Truck Company (120-ton and 8 LMG)
Supply Company (motorized) (8 LMG)
Motorized Vehicle Troops
    1st Workshop Company (motorized) (4 LMG)
    2nd Workshop Company (motorized) (4 LMG)
    3rd Workshop Company (motorized) (4 LMG)
Medical Troops
    1st Medical Company (motorized) (4 LMG)
    2nd Medical Company (motorized) (4 LMG)
    Ambulance Company (2 LMG)
Administrative Troops
    Bakery Company (motorized) (6 LMG)
    Butcher Company (motorized) (4 LMG)
    Administration Company (motorized) (DVA)(2 LMG)
Field Post Office (motorized) (1 LMG)

Total Weapons (w/o Replacement Battalion)

96 light machine guns	2 combat vehicle cannon 20mm
65 heavy machine guns	18 combat vehicle cannon 37mm
48 medium 81mm mortars	18 combat vehicle cannon 75mm
6 light infantry guns	12 towed light field howitzers
12 heavy infantry guns	18 self-propelled light field howitzers
46 Flak 20mm	8 heavy field howitzers/towed
8 Flak 88mm	4 cannon 100mm towed cannon
3 light antitank guns	34 armored scout cars
3 medium antitank guns	51 Pz.Kpfw.V
64 heavy antitank guns	68 Pz.Kpfw.IV
66 flamethrowers	

Source: OKH/Gen.St.d.H./Org.Abt./Nr.I/4500/43 gKdos v.4.10.43. Also consulted Dr. F. M. v.Senger u. Etterlin, *Die Panzer-Grenadiere: Geschichte u. Gestalt der mechanisierten Infanterie 1930–1960* (München: J. F. Lehmanns Verlag, 1961), 203, and Dr. F. M. v.Senger u. Etterlin, *Die deutschen Geschütze 1939–1945* (München: J. F. Lehmanns Verlag, 1961).

Panzer Regiment Organization

10th SS Panzer Regiment

Command Section:
Regimental Commander
Adjutant
Ordnance Officer
Intelligence Officer
Administrative Officer
Regimental Doctor
Technical Officer for Vehicles
Technical Officer for Weapons
Commander, Headquarters Staff
Commander, Supply Company

1st Battalion
Battalion Commander
Adjutant
Ordnance Officer
Intelligence Officer
Administrative Officer
Regimental Doctor
Technical Officer for Vehicles
Technical Officer for Weapons
Commander, Headquarters Staff
Commander, 1st Company
Commander, 2nd Company
Commander, 3rd Company
Commander, 4th Company
Commander, Supply Detachment

2nd Battalion
Battalion Commander
Adjutant
Ordnance Officer
Intelligence Officer

Administrative Officer
Regimental Doctor
Technical Officer for Vehicles
Technical Officer for Weapons
Commander, Headquarters Staff
Commander, 1st Company
Commander, 2nd Company
Commander, 3rd Company
Commander, 4th Company
Commander, Supply Detachment

Detailed Command Section:
Regimental Commander

Ia   Leading the Troops   (Adjutant)
      Tactical Orders
      Tactical Measures
      Combat Correspondent
      Organization
      Training
      Instruction (individual classes)
Ia/ Maps
      Survey
      Directives

Ordnance Officer I

      Commanders Aid
      Combat Reports
      War Diary
      Routing Orders
      Messenger Squadron
      Trails
      Biological Defense

Ic Enemy Intelligence Service
Enemy Situation Maps
Enemy Reconnaissance (air and ground)
Enemy Information Acquisition through special
methods
Intelligence (sabotage, espionage, counterintelligence)
Special Occasions
Inspection of Secret-Material (under lock)

Supply:
Ib Ammunition
Fuel
Weapons and Equipment
Evaluation of BAV for troops

Adjutant:
IIa Matters concerning officer
Promotions, Transfers
Assignments
Grooming
Personal matters concerning the commander
Registrar; central office for written correspondence
and daily orders

IIb Matters concerning NCOs
Matters concerning the troops
Promotions, Transfers
Questions concerning Recruiting/Replacement
Supplementation
Supply

Legal:
III Disciplinary Punishments and Matters concerning
complaints
Military Courts-Martial
Case Reports

Administration:
IVa Economy and Planning
Fiscal
Studies/Testing Organization
Requirements for Troops
Market Analysis/Changes

Medical:
IVb Regimental Doctor
Medical Service for the Troops
Epidemic Prevention
Medical Training
Guarding Troop Hygiene

Motor Vehicles:
V Motor Vehicle Maintenance
Equipping
Repair
Quality Control/Testing
Motor Vehicle Advisor for officers
Motor Vehicle Training
Recruiting/Replacements

Ideological Training/Propaganda:
VI Preparation for Propaganda Training
Welfare
Books
Burial Concerns

Communications Officer:
Ia/N Communications Service
Radio
Radio Operator Training

Ordnance Officer II:
Supply of Troops in Combat (in conjunction with Ib)
Determination of Fortified Positions
Regimental Situational Liaison

In combat, the tank command vehicles provided the following functions:

Regimental Commander's Tank
Leading the Troops
Tactical Orders
Tactical Directives
Communication with superior and subordinate
commands

Regimental Adjutant's Tank
The same responsibilities as the commander's but
also
Supply of ammunition and fuel
Repair service

Ordnance Officer's Tank
Supply of ammunition and fuel
Repair service
Air liaison

Source: 10.SS Panzer Division "Frundsberg," SS-Pz.Rgt, Rgt.Gef.Std., 13.7.1944, Dienstanweisung für den Stab SS-Panzer-Regiment 10, NA/RG242/T354/R152/F3795129-3795132.

Panzer Division Staff

10th SS Panzer Division

Division Commander

Command Staff Section (Ia)
1st General Staff Officer

1st Ordnance Officer (01)
3rd General Staff Officer (Ic)
3rd Ordnance Officer (03)
Division Maps
Chief of Intelligence
Division Escort Company
Military Police Company

Section VI Propaganda and Troop Welfare

Adjutant:
Section IIa: Division Adjutant
Section IIb: Personnel Chief for NCO and Troops

Section III: Division Courts (Legal)
                    Defense Council
                    Judges
Commandant's Staff Quarters
Graves Registration

Supply Section (Ib)
2nd General Staff Officer
2nd Ordnance Officer (02)
Ammunition

Section IVa: Division Director
Section IVb: Division Doctor
                    Division Dentist

Section V: Division Engineer

Details:
Ia   Leading the Troops (1st General Staff Officer)
        Tactical Orders
        Tactical Measures
Combat Correspondent:
        Organization
        Training
        Instruction (individual classes)
Ia/   Maps
        Survey
        Directives

Ordnance Officer I

        Commanders Aid
        Combat Reports
        War Diary
        Routing Orders
        Messenger Squadron
        Trails
        Biological Defense

Ic   Enemy Intelligence Service
        Enemy Situation Maps
        Enemy Reconnaissance (air and ground)
        Enemy Information Acquisition through special
            methods
        Intelligence (sabotage, espionage, counter-
            intelligence)
        Special Occasions
        Inspection of Secret-Material (under lock)

Supply:

Ib   Ammunition
     Fuel
     Weapons and Equipment
     Evaluation of BAV for Troops

Adjutant:

IIa   Matters concerning officer
     Promotions, Transfers
     Assignments
     Grooming
     Personal matters concerning the commander
     Registrar; central office for written correspondence
       and daily orders

IIb   Matters concerning NCOs
     Matters concerning the troops
     Promotions, Transfers
     Questions concerning Recruiting/Replacement
     Supplementation
     Supply

Legal:

III   Disciplinary Punishments and Matters concerning
      complaints
     Military Courts-Martial
     Case Reports

Administration:

IVa Economy and Planning
     Fiscal
     Studies/Testing Organization
     Requirements for Troops
     Market Analysis/Changes

Medical:

IVb Regimental Doctor
        Medical Service for the Troops
        Epidemic Prevention
        Medical Training
        Guarding Troop Hygiene

Motor Vehicles:

V   Motor Vehicle Maintenance
     Equipping
     Repair
     Quality Control/Testing
     Motor Vehicle Advisor for officers
     Motor Vehicle Training
     Recruiting/Replacements

Ideological Training/Propaganda:

VI   Preparation for Propaganda Training
     Welfare
     Books
     Burial Concerns

Communications Officer:

Ia/N Communications Service
     Radio
     Radio Operator Training

Ordnance Officer II:

     Supply of Troops in Combat (in conjunction with Ib)
     Determination of Fortified Positions
     Regimental Situational Liaison

Source: 10.SS Panzer Division "Frundsberg," SS-Pz.Rgt, Rgt.Gef.Std., 13.7.1944, Dienstanweisung für den Stab SS-Panzer-Regiment 10, NA/RG242/T354/R152/F3795129-3795132.

Training Plan, Staff Company

10th SS Panzer Assault Gun Battalion

Time	Type of Training	Instructor
	Monday 4 October 1943	
0630	Reveille	Duty NCO
0730	Formation	
0740–0830	Drill (each 10 minutes)	SS-Uscha.Eisentraut
	a) basic formation without rifle	
	b) practice forming a formation	
	c) facing movements	
	d) saluting	
	e) change formation as a group	
0845–1200	Vehicle Maintenance/Servicing	SS-Rttf.Altfel
1400–1445	Classroom Curriculum: Soldier Conduct During and Off Duty	SS-Uscha.Eisentraut
1500–1700	<u>Combat Training</u>:	SS-Uscha.Eisentraut
	Target Identification, distance estimation, messenger evaluation of the terrain via situation brief	
1715–1815	Weapons cleaning	SS-Uscha.Steinkogler
	Tuesday 5 October 1943	
0630	Reveille	Duty NCO 0730
0730	Formation	
0740–0830	Drill	SS-Uscha.Eisentraut
	a) basic formation with rifle	
	b) practice forming a formation	
	c) marksmanship training: combat and terrain firing	
0845–1200	Vehicle Maintenance/Servicing	SS-Rttf.Altfel

(*continued*)

Time	Type of Training	Instructor
1400–1515	Classroom Curriculum: Sketching	Adjutant
1530–1700	<u>Messenger Training</u>:	
	a) Conduct at the battalion combat command post	
	b) Obtaining messages	
	c) Drawing sketches	
1715–1815	Weapons cleaning	SS-Uscha.Steinkogler

Wednesday 6 October 1943

0630	Reveille	Duty NCO
0730	Formation	
0740–0830	Drill	SS-Uscha.Eisentraut
	a) changing formations	
	b) stacking rifles	
	c) combat and terrain impacts	
0845–1200	Vehicle Maintenance/Servicing	SS-Rttf.Altfel
1400–1445	Correspondence	SS-Uscha.Eisentraut
1500–1700	<u>Messenger Training</u>: same as previous	SS-Uscha.Eisentraut
1715–1815	Weapons cleaning/organizing things	SS-Uscha.Steinkogler
1930–2030	Hour of Work: writing biography	

Thursday 7 October 1943

0630	Reveille	Duty NCO
0730	Formation	
0740–0830	Drill	SS-Uscha.Eisentraut
	a) basic formation and turning	
	b) rifle training	
	c) firing from the prone position	
0845–1200	Vehicle Maintenance/Servicing	SS-Rttf.Altfel
1400–1515	Classroom Curriculum:	SS-Uscha.Eisentraut
	The Purity of Man	
	Clean Barracks	
1500–1600	Gas Warfare: practical applications	
	a) application of the gas cape	
	b) application of decontamination substances for skin and	
	weapons, as well as other decontamination techniques	
	c) gas mask training	
	d) cleaning gas protective equipment	
1600–1700	Antiaircraft defense: practical applications with machine gun	
	and rifle	
1715–1815	Weapons and gas mask cleaning	SS-Uscha.Steinkogler

Friday 8 October 1943

0630	Reveille	Duty NCO 0730
0730	Formation	
0740–0830	<u>Marksmanship Training</u>:	SS-Uscha.Eisentraut
	a) loading and placing on safe in every situation	
	b) target practice	
	c) firing mechanism	

(continued)

Time	Type of Training	Instructor
0845–1200	Vehicle Maintenance/Servicing	SS-Rttf.Altfel
1400–1500	Classroom Curriculum: messenger service	SS-Uscha.Eisentraut Adjutant
1515–1700	Close Combat Training a) quick fire b) firing from the hip c) aiming d) hand grenade distance throwing e) confidence training in the field	
1930–2030	Singing	SS-Uscha.Steinkogler SS-Rttf.Altfel

Saturday 9 October 1943

Time	Type of Training	Instructor
0630	Reveille	Duty NCO
0730	Formation	
0740–0830	<u>Marksmanship Training</u>: a) rifle 5 shots on targets in terrain b) machine gun 5 shot-bursts on targets in terrain	Adjutant
1400–1500	Global Perspective Training a) the week in review, political and military	SS-Ustuf.Schmidt
1500–1600	Weapons cleaning	SS-Uscha.Steinkogler
1600–1700	Organizing cleaning things	
1700–1800	Prepare for Inspection	Adjutant
1800	Inspection	

Sunday 10 October 1943

Time	Type of Training	Instructor
0800	Reveille Off duty	Duty NCO

Source: 10.SS-Division (Panzer-Grenadier-Division), Sturmgeschütz-Abteilung, "Wochen-Dienstplan für den Stab SS-Stu.Gesch. Abt.10, für die Zeit vom 4.-11.10.1943," O.U. den 2.10.43, NA/RG242/T354/R150/F3792683-3792684.

Theoretical Table of Organization

SS Panzer Division 1944 (free organization)

Divisional Headquarters Staff
    Divisional Mapping Office (motorized)
    Military Police Detachment (motorized) (5 LMG)
    Escort Company
        Motorcycle Messenger Platoon (6 LMG)
        Grenadier Platoon (6 LMG, 2 heavy MG, 2 medium mortars)
        Flak Platoon (SP w 4 Flak 20mm)
    Panzer Regiment
        Staff and Staff Company (5 Pz.Kpfw.IV and 3 Pz.Kpfw.V [command vehicles])
        Pz. Flak Platoon with 8 Flak Pz.IV (35mm)
        Panzer Battalion "Panther"
            Staff and staff company (9 LMG, 4 Flak 20mm [SP], 5 Pz.Kpfw.V and 3 Pz.Kpfw.V [command vehicles], and 5 medium half-tracks).
            1st Company (17 Pz.Kpfw.V)
            2nd Company (17 Pz.Kpfw.V)
            3rd Company (17 Pz.Kpfw.V)
            4th Company (17 Pz.Kpfw.V)
            Pz. V Supply Company (4 LMG)
        Panzer Battalion IV
            Staff and Staff Company (9 LMG, 3 Flak 20mm [SP], 5 Pz.Kpfw.IV and 3 Pz.Kpfw.IV [command vehicles], 5 medium half-tracks).
            1st Company (17 Pz.Kpfw.IV)
            2nd Company (17 Pz.Kpfw.IV)
            3rd Company (17 Pz.Kpfw.IV)
            4th Company (17 Pz.Kpfw.IV)
            Pz.IV Supply Company (4 LMG)

Panzer Maintenance Company Pz.IV/V (4 LMG, 2 recovery tanks III)

Panzergrenadier Regiment (armored)
- Staff and Staff Company
  - Motorcycle Messenger Platoon
  - Signals Platoon (5 LMG, 9 medium half-tracks.)
- 1st Panzergrenadier Battalion (armored) with staff
  - 1st Panzergrenadier Company (18 LMG, 3 heavy MG, 2 medium mortars, 7 Flak 20mm, 23 half-tracks)
  - 2nd Panzergrenadier Company (18 LMG, 3 heavy MG, 2 medium mortars, 7 Flak 20mm, 23 half-tracks)
  - 3rd Panzergrenadier Company (18 LMG, 3 heavy MG, 2 medium mortars, 7 Flak 20mm, 23 half-tracks)
  - 4th Heavy Panzergrenadier Company (partially armored)
    - Officer Group (2 half-tracks)
    - Heavy Mortar Platoon (4 heavy mortars and 7 half-tracks)
    - Heavy Cannon Platoon (75mm armored w six 75mm K-37 aircraft guns and 8 half-tracks)
  - Supply Company (armored) (4 LMG)
- 2nd Panzergrenadier Battalion (motorized) with staff
  - 1st Panzergrenadier Company (motorized) (18 LMG, 4 heavy MG, 2 medium mortars)
  - 2nd Panzergrenadier Company (motorized) (18 LMG, 4 heavy MG, 2 medium mortars)
  - 3rd Panzergrenadier Company (motorized) (18 LMG, 4 heavy MG, 2 medium mortars)
  - 4th Heavy Panzergrenadier Company (motorized)
    - Flak Platoon (6 Flak 20mm motorized)
    - Heavy Mortar Platoon (4 heavy mortars w 2 LMG)
  - Supply Company (armored) (4 LMG)
  - Panzergrenadier Pioneer Company (14 LMG, 2 heavy MG, 2 medium mortars, 1 Flak 20mm aircraft guns, 14 half-tracks)
  - Heavy Gun Company (motorized-SP) (3 LMG and 6 heavy infantry guns, and 5 medium half-tracks)

Panzergrenadier Regiment (motorized)
- Staff and Staff Company
  - Motorcycle Messenger Platoon (6 LMG)
  - Signals Platoon (6 LMG)
  - Heavy Antitank Platoon (motorized) (three 75mm Pak 40 and 3 LMG)
- 1st Panzergrenadier Battalion (motorized) with staff
  - 1st Panzergrenadier Company (18 LMG, 3 heavy MG, 2 medium mortars, 7 Flak 20mm, 23 half-tracks)
  - 2nd Panzergrenadier Company (18 LMG, 3 heavy MG, 2 medium mortars, 7 Flak 20mm, 23 half-tracks)
  - 3rd Panzergrenadier Company (18 LMG, 3 heavy MG, 2 medium mortars, 7 Flak 20mm, 23 half-tracks)
  - 4th Heavy Panzergrenadier Company (partially armored)
  - Officer Group (2 half-tracks)
    - Heavy Gr.W. Platoon (4 heavy mortars and 7 half-tracks)
    - Heavy Cannon Platoon (75mm armored w six 75mm K-37 aircraft guns and 8 half-tracks)
  - Supply Company (motorized) (4 LMG)
- 2nd Panzergrenadier Battalion (motorized) with staff
  - 1st Panzergrenadier Company (motorized) (18 LMG, 4 heavy MG, 2 medium mortars)
  - 2nd Panzergrenadier Company (motorized) (18 LMG, 4 heavy MG, 2 medium mortars)
  - 3rd Panzergrenadier Company (motorized) (18 LMG, 4 heavy MG, 2 medium mortars)
  - 4th Heavy Panzergrenadier Company (motorized)
    - Flak Platoon (6 Flak 20mm motorized)
    - Heavy Mortar Platoon (4 heavy mortars w 2 LMG)
  - Supply Company (motorized) (4 LMG)
  - Panzergrenadier Pioneer Company (12 LMG, 2 heavy MG, 2 medium mortars)
  - Heavy Gun Company (motorized) (2 LMG and 4 heavy infantry guns)
- Panzer Reconnaissance Battalion
  - Staff and Signal Platoon (armored) (13 75mm K-37-aircraft guns and 75mm combat vehicle cannon 40 aircraft guns, 10 medium half-tracks, 16/19 armored scout cars)

Armored Scout Company (16 75mm K-37 aircraft guns, 25 Sd.Kfz.250/9 with 20mm and 24 LMG)

Light Armored Reconnaissance Company (2 medium mortars, two 75mm combat vehicle cannon 40 aircraft guns, 30 light half-tracks)

Panzer Reconnaissance Company (armored) (Sd.Kfz.251) (56 LMG, 4 heavy MG, 3 Pak 37mm, 2 medium mortars)

Heavy Reconnaissance Company (Sd.Kfz.251)

Command Group (2 medium half-tracks)

Heavy Mortar Platoon (4 heavy mortars. and 7 medium half-tracks)

Heavy Cannon Platoon (six 75mm K-37 aircraft guns and 8 medium half-tracks)

Pioneer Platoon (armored) (6 LMG, 7 medium half-tracks)

Panzer Supply Reconnaissance Battalion (4 LMG)

Mixed Panzer Antitank Battalion (self-propelled)

Staff and staff company (1 LMG, two 75mm Pak 39, 1 medium half-tracks, 3 light Tank Destroyers IV)

1st Antitank (StuG) Company (10 75mm Pak 39 aircraft guns and 14 light Tank Destroyers IV)

2nd Heavy Antitank Company (motorized) (12 LMG and 12 75mm Pak 40)

3rd Heavy Antitank Company (motorized) (12 LMG and 12 75mm Pak 40)

4th Supply Company Mixed Antitank Company (3 LMG, 2 recovery tanks III)

Panzer Artillery Regiment

Staff and Staff Battery (motorized w 2 LMG)

1st Panzer Howitzer Battalion

Staff and staff battery (21 LMG, 3 Geb.Flak 20mm, and 1 medium half-tracks)

1st Light Panzer Howitzer Battery (2 LMG, 6 light field howitzers 18/2 SP., 1 medium half-tracks)

2nd Light Panzer Howitzer Battery (2 LMG, 6 light field howitzers 18/2 SP., 1 medium half-tracks)

3rd Heavy Panzer Howitzer Battery (2 LMG, 6 heavy field howitzers/18/1 SP., 1 medium half-tracks)

2nd Panzer Artillery Battalion (motorized)

Staff and staff battery (2 LMG, 3 Geb.Flak 20mm)

1st Battery (two light field howitzers [motorized] w 4 LMG and 4 light field howitzers [motorized])

2nd Battery (two light field howitzers [motorized] w 4 LMG and 4 light field howitzers [motorized])

3rd Panzer Artillery Battalion (motorized)

Staff and staff battery (2 LMG, 3 Geb.Flak 20mm)

1st Battery (two heavy field howitzers [motorized] w 4 LMG and 4 heavy field howitzers [motorized])

2nd Battery (two heavy field howitzers [motorized] w 4 LMG and 4 heavy field howitzers [motorized])

3rd Battery 100mm Cannon (motorized) w 4 LMG and 4 100mm Cannon

Army Antiaircraft Artillery Battalion (motorized)

Staff and staff battery (2 LMG)

1st Heavy Flak Battery (3 LMG, three 20mm Flak, 4–6 88mm Flak)

2nd Heavy Flak Battery (3 LMG, three 20mm Flak, 4–6 88mm Flak)

Light Flak Battery (4 LMG, 3 Flakvierling 20mm, 9 Flak 37mm, and 4 spotlights 600mm)

Light Flak Convoy (motorized 20-ton) (2 LMG)

Panzer Pioneer Battalion

Staff (2 LMG) and supply company (8 LMG and 6 medium half-tracks)

1st Pioneer Company (motorized) (18 LMG, 2 heavy MG, 2 medium mortars)

2nd Pioneer Company (motorized) (18 LMG, 2 heavy MG, 2 medium mortars)

2nd Panzer Pioneer Company (18 LMG, 2 heavy MG, 2m.Gr.W, 3 Geb.Flak. 20mm, 25 medium half-tracks)

Light Panzer Bridging Convoy (3 LMG)

Panzer Signals Battalion

Staff

Telephone Company (Pz.Div.) (5 LMG)

Wireless Radio Company (Pz.Div.) (5 LMG)

Supply Detachment (2 LMG)

Panzer Field-Replacement Battalion (Pz.Div.) (for 800-man replacement detachment within 4 units) (50 LMG, 12 heavy MG, 6 medium mortars, 2 heavy mortars, 1 Flak 20mm, 1 Pak 40 75mm , 1 light field howitzer)
Panzer Division Supply Battalion
    Staff and Staff Company (10 LMG)
        1st Truck Company (120-ton and 4 LMG)
        2nd Truck Company (120-ton and 4 LMG)
        3rd Truck Company (120-ton and 4 LMG)
        4th Truck Company (120-ton and 4 LMG)
        5th Truck Company (120-ton and 4 LMG)
        6th Weapons Maintenance Platoon (2 LMG)
        7th Weapons Maintenance Platoon (2 LMG)
    Motorized Vehicle Troops
        1st Workshop Company (4 LMG)
        2nd Workshop Company (4 LMG)
        3rd Workshop Company (one light and one heavy platoon) (4 LMG)
        4th Mobile Supply Detachment for Replacement Troops (75-T)(2 LMG)
    Administrative Troops
        Bakery Company (motorized) (4 LMG)
        Butcher Company (motorized) (4 LMG)
        Administration Company (motorized) (2 LMG)
    Medical Troops
        1st Medical Company (motorized) (4 LMG)
        2nd Medical Company (motorized) (4 LMG)
        Ambulance Company (4 LMG)
    Field Post Office (motorized) (1 LMG)

Theoretical strength, weapons, and equipment for a Panzer Division 1944:

Officers	408
Clerks	84
NCO	3,044
Enlisted men	9,585
Helpers	712
Total	13,833

Total Weapons (w/o Replacement Battalion)

3,254 pistols	9,115 rifles	1,070 submachine guns	561 SMG (mounted)
631 light machine guns	610 LMG (mounted)	72 heavy machine guns	
52 medium mortars	18 heavy mortars	10 heavy infantry guns	
25 Flak 20mm (motorized)	4 Flak 20mm SP	9 Flak Vierlinge 20mm SP	
12 Geb.Flak 20mm	29 Flak 20mm (aircraft guns)	9 Flak 37mm towed	
8 Flak 37mm SP	8–12 Flak 88mm	4 Flak 60mm spotlights	
22 PAK 75mm 39 (aircraft guns)	16 PAK 40 75mm towed		
41 75mm K-37 (aircraft guns)	86 75mm combat vehicle cannon 40 (aircraft guns)		
79 75mm combat vehicle cannon 42 (aircraft guns)			
13 light field howitzers (mechanized)		12 le light field howitzers 18/2 SP	
8 heavy field howitzers (mechanized)		6 heavy field howitzers 18/1 SP	
4 Cannon 100mm (mechanized)			
86 Pz.Kpfw.IV	73 Pz.Kpfw.V	3 Pz.Kpfw.IV (command)	
6 Pz.Kpfw.V (command)			
55 light half-tracks	232 med half-tracks	16/19 Armored Scout Cars	
24 SP for Hummeln, Wespen, heavy infantry guns			
31 light Pz.Jg.IV	2 Recovery Pz.Kpfw.III		
311 Kettenräder	68 motorcycles with sidecars		95 motorcycles
55 automobiles (o)	590 automobiles (gl)	620 trucks (o)	850 trucks (gl)
137 Maultiere	60 Kr.Kw.	210 KOM	144 Kfz.Anh.
7 Sd.Kfz.100			
25 prime mover 1t	29 prime mover 3t	40 prime mover 8t	13 prime mover 12t
10 prime mover 1t	13 prime mover 35t	6 misc prime mover	

Source: Gen.Insp.d.Pz.Tr./Abt.Org./Kartei Nr. 2500/44 gKdos v.15.8.44. See Dr. F. M. v.Senger u. Etterlin, *Die Panzer-Grenadiere: Geschichte u. Gestalt der mechanisierten Infanterie 1930–1960* (München: J. F. Lehmanns Verlag, 1961), 218–20.

Table of Organization

10th SS Panzer Pioneer Battalion, 1 April 1944

Billet	Name	Rank	Remarks
Commander	Tröbinger, Leopold	*SS-Hauptsturmführer*	wounded early July 1944
	Benger, Hugo	*SS-Hauptsturmführer*	as of early July 1944
Adjutant	Schlee, Wolf	*SS-Obersturmführer*	until July 1944
Doctor	Awender, Dr. Josef	*SS-Hauptsturmführer*	
Administration	Kroll, Herbert	*SS-Obersturmführer*	
TKW	Podzuweit, Otto	*SS-Hauptsturmführer*	
Staff Company	Munsky, Oskar	*SS-Obersturmführer*	
Recon Platoon	Ohlhoff, Otto	*SS-Obersturmführer*	wounded/died July 1944
Brücko B	Schaz, Otto	*SS-Obersturmführer*	
Staff NCO	Nawa, Hubert	*SS-Hauptscharführer*	
Supply	Rupprecht, Alois	*SS-Hauptscharführer*	
1st Company			
Co Commander	Schättiger, Gerd	*SS-Obersturmführer*	
Plt Commander	Lessner, Erich	*SS-Oberscharführer*	
	Arloth		
2nd Company			
Co Commander	Brandt, Albert	*SS-Hauptsturmführer*	
Plt Commander	Meierhoff	*SS-Untersturmführer*	KIA Medwedowce 17.4.44
Staff NCO	Lindau, Heinz	*SS-Oberscharführer*	
Supply Chief	Stotz		

(continued)

Billet	Name	Rank	Remarks
3rd Company			
Co Commander	Schneider, Horst	*SS-Obersturmführer*	KIA Hill 112 17.7.44
Plt Commander	Flügge	*SS-Untersturmführer*	
	Ringe		
16th Company, 21st SS Pz.Gren.Rgt.			
Co Commander	Keck, Karl	*SS-Hauptsturmführer*	KIA 11.7.44
	Markus, Willi	*SS-Hauptsturmführer*	as of 11.7.44
Plt Commander	Wunderlich	*SS-Untersturmführer*	
	Grünschel	*SS-Sturmscharführer*	
	Hummel	*SS-Sturmscharführer*	
Staff NCO	Schoppmeyer		
Kitchen	Grumbach	*SS-Rottenführer*	
16th Company, 22st SS Pz.Gren.Rgt.			
Co Commander	Bauch, Heinrich	*SS-Hauptsturmführer*	until 4.44
	Munsky, Oskar	*SS-Obersturmführer*	as of 4.44
Plt Commander	Wille, Wilhelm	*SS-Untersturmführer*	transferred 4.44
	Weiss, Adolf	*SS-Oberscharführer*	
Pioneer Plt, 10th SS Reconnaissance Btl.			
Plt Commander	Hartmann	*SS-Hauptscharführer*	
NCO	Schulz, Gerhard	*SS-Oberscharführer*	
	Ebner	*SS-Unterscharführer*	
	Boneß	*SS-Unterscharführer*	
	Krug	*SS-Unterscharführer*	
Supply Chief	Kaiser	*SS-Oberscharführer*	
Pioneer Plts, 10th SS Pz. Rgt.			
1st Battalion			
Plt Commander	Himstedt	*SS-Oberscharführer*	until Fall 44
	Niederbichler, Reinhold	*SS-Oberscharführer*	as of Fall 44

Source: Pionier Kameradschaft "Dresden." *10.SS-Panzer-Div. "Frundsberg": Chronik der Pioniereinheiten der 10.SS-PzDiv "Frundsberg,"* Unpublished association manuscript, 1990.

Table of Organization
Soviet Divisional Strengths

Soviet Rifle Division July 1943

3 Rifle Regiments with four 76mm and twelve 45mm guns
1 Artillery Regiment with twelve 122mm and twenty 76mm guns
1 Antitank Battalion with twelve 45mm guns
1 Sapper Battalion
1 Signal Company
1 Reconnaissance Company

Strength: 9,380 men
10,670 in guards division
44 guns
160 mortars
48 antitank guns

Soviet Cavalry Division 1943

3 Cavalry Regiments with six 76mm and six 45mm guns
1 Artillery Regiment with sixteen 76mm and eight 122mm guns
1 Reconnaissance Battalion
1 Antiaircraft Squadron
1 Engineer Squadron
1 Signal Squadron

Strength: 4,700 men
42 guns
18 antitank guns
6 antiaircraft guns

Soviet Tank Corps December 1943

3 Tank Brigades (65 tanks each)
1 Motorized Rifle Brigade
1 Mortar Regiment
1 Antiaircraft Regiment
1 Self-propelled Artillery Regiment (SU-76)
1 Self-propelled Artillery Regiment (SU-85)
1 Guards Mortar Battalion
1 Motorcycle Battalion
1 Sapper Battalion
1 Signal Battalion
1 Transport Company
2 Repair Companies
1 Chemical Defense Company
1 Aviation Company

Strength: 10,997 men
              208 tanks
              49 SP guns
              152 guns/mortars
              8 multiple rocket launchers

Soviet Mechanized Corps December 1943

3 Mechanized Brigades
1 Tank Brigade (65 tanks)
1–2 Self-propelled Artillery Regiments (SU-76, SU-85)
1 Mortar Regiment
1 Antiaircraft Regiment
1 Tank Destroyer Regiment
1 Guards Mortar Battalion
1 Motorcycle Battalion
1 Sapper Battalion
1 Signal Battalion
1 Medical Battalion
1 Transport Company
1 Repair, Reconstruction Company

Strength: 16,369 men
              197 tanks
              49 SP guns
              252 guns/mortars
              8 multiple rocket launchers

Source: David M. Glantz, *Soviet Military Operational Art: In Pursuit of Deep Battle* (London: Frank Cass and Company Limited, 1991), 140–42.

Theoretical Table of Organization

SS Panzer Division 1945

Divisional Headquarters Staff with Mapping Office (motorized) (2 LMG)
    Military Police Detachment (motorized) (5 LMG)
    Escort Company (motorized) (4 LMG and 7 heavy MG)
        Grenadier Platoon (6 LMG, 2 heavy MG, and 2 medium mortars)
        Motorcycle Messenger Platoon (6 LMG)
        Light Antiaircraft Platoon (4 self-propelled 1-ton 20mm)
    Mixed Panzer Regiment with staff (2 Pak 75mm, and 6 LMG on half-tracks)
        Staff Company (motorized)
            Staff Platoon
            Signals Platoon (20 LMG) (8 command Pz.Kpfw.V)
        First Panzer Battalion with staff (1 LMG)
            Staff Company (w Staff Company, 4 LMG)
                Antitank Platoon (6 Pak 75mm and 1 LMG)
                Panzer Pioneer Platoon
            1st Company (10 Pz.Kpfw.)
            2nd Company (10 Pz.Kpfw.)
            3rd Company (10 Pz.Kpfw.)
            4th Company (10 Pz.Kpfw.)
        Second Half-Track Battalion with Staff (1 LMG)
            Staff Company (half-tracks) (Staff Company, 4 LMG)
            5th Panzergrenadier Company (SPW) (21 LMG and 3 Flak 20mm)
            6th Panzergrenadier Company (SPW) (21 LMG and 3 Flak 20mm)
            7th Panzergrenadier Company (SPW) (21 LMG and 3 Flak 20mm)
            8th Panzergrenadier Supply Company (motorized) (3 heavy antitank gun and 1 LMG)
        Panzer Maintenance Company (4 LMG)
    1st Panzergrenadier Regiment (motorized) w staff (3 heavy antitank guns)
        Staff Company (4 LMG)
            Motorcycle Messenger Platoon
            Signals Platoon
            Combat Supply (motorized) and Combat Convoy (3 LMG)

1st Panzergrenadier Battalion (motorized) with staff (3 heavy antitank guns)
   1st Panzergrenadier Company (no vehicles) (12 LMG and 3 heavy antitank guns)
      Assault Platoon (w StG44)
   2nd Panzergrenadier Company (no vehicles) (12 LMG and 3 heavy antitank guns)
      Assault Platoon (w StG44)
   3rd Panzergrenadier Company (no vehicles) (12 LMG and 3 heavy antitank guns)
      Assault Platoon (w StG44)
   4th Heavy MG Company (motorized)
      1st Heavy MG Platoon (4 heavy MG)
      2nd Heavy MG Platoon (4 heavy MG)
      3rd Light Flak Platoon (6 Flak 20mm and 1 LMG)
      4th Supply Platoon (motorized) (3 heavy antitank guns and 2 LMG)
   5th Pioneer Company (motorized) (9 heavy antitank guns and 9 LMG)
2nd Panzergrenadier Regiment (motorized) w staff (3 heavy antitank guns)
   Staff Company (4 LMG)
      Motorcycle Messenger Platoon
      Signals Platoon
      Combat Supply (motorized) and Combat Convoy (3 LMG)
   1st Panzergrenadier Battalion (motorized) with staff (3 heavy antitank guns)
      1st Panzergrenadier Company (no vehicles) (12 LMG and 3 heavy antitank guns)
         Assault Platoon (w StG44)
      2nd Panzergrenadier Company (no vehicles) (12 LMG and 3 heavy antitank guns)
         Assault Platoon (w StG44)
      3rd Panzergrenadier Company (no vehicles) (12 LMG and 3 heavy antitank guns)
         Assault Platoon (w StG44)
      4th Heavy MG Company (motorized)
         1st Heavy MG Platoon (4 heavy MG)
         2nd Heavy MG Platoon (4 heavy MG)
         3rd Light Flak Platoon (6 Flak 20mm and 1 LMG)
         4th Supply Platoon (motorized) (3 heavy antitank guns and 2 LMG)
      5th Pioneer Company (motorized) (9 heavy antitank guns and 9 LMG)
   Panzer Reconnaissance Battalion w staff (1 heavy antitank gun and 1 LMG)
      Mixed Panzer Reconnaissance Company (half-tracks) (10 combat vehicle cannon 75mm, 3 Flak Vierlinge 20mm, 8 Pak 20mm, and 8 LMG)
      1st Reconnaissance Company (motorized) (9 LMG, 2 heavy MG, and 2 medium mortars)
      2nd Reconnaissance Company (motorized) (9 LMG, 2 heavy MG, and 2 medium mortars)
      3rd Supply Company (motorized) (1 LMG)
   Tank Destroyer Battalion with staff (1 LMG)
      Staff Company (2 Pak SP.)
      1st Tank Destroyer Company (10 Jgd.Pz.)
         Tank Destroyer Escort Platoon (10 LMG)
      2nd Tank Destroyer Company (10 Jgd.Pz.)
         Tank Destroyer Escort Platoon (10 LMG)
      3rd Antitank Company (half-tracks) (9 Pak 75mm and 1 LMG)
      4th Supply Company (motorized) (4 LMG)
Panzer Artillery Regiment with Staff
   Staff Battery (motorized) (2 LMG)
   1st Battalion (self-propelled) w staff
      Staff Battery (self-propelled) (3 Flak 20mm and 2 LMG)
      1st Battery (6 light field howitzers and 4 LMG)
      2nd Battery (6 light field howitzers and 4 LMG)
      3rd Battery (6 light field howitzers and 4 LMG)

2nd Battalion (towed)
    Staff Battery (motorized) (3 Flak 20mm and 2 LMG)
    1st Battery (6 light field howitzers [towed] and 4 LMG)
    2nd Battery (6 light field howitzers [towed] and 4 LMG)
3rd Battalion (mixed towed heavy)
    Staff Battery (motorized) (3 Flak 20mm and 2 LMG)
    1st Battery (four 100mm cannon [towed] and 4 LMG)
    2nd Battery (4 heavy field howitzers and 4 LMG)
    3rd Battery (4 heavy field howitzers and 4 LMG)
Army Antiaircraft Artillery Battalion (towed)(with staff)
    Staff Battery (motorized) (2 LMG)
    1st Heavy Flak Battery (6 Flak 88mm, 3 Flak 20mm, and 2 LMG)
    2nd Heavy Flak Battery (6 Flak 88mm, 3 Flak 20mm, and 2 LMG)
    3rd Light Flak Battery (3 Flak Vierling 20mm SP and 3 LMG)
        1st Flak Platoon (3 Flak 37mm and 2 LMG)
        2nd Flak Platoon (3 Flak 37mm and 2 LMG)
        3rd Flak Platoon (3 Flak 37mm and 2 LMG)
    Light Flak Convoy (motorized 20-ton) (2 LMG)
Panzer Pioneer Battalion with Staff (9 LMG)
    Staff and Supply Company (4 LMG)
        Staff Platoon
        Supply Platoon
        Bridging Convoy
    1st Panzer Pioneer Company (motorized) (18 LMG, 2 heavy MG, and 2 medium mortars)
    2nd Panzer Pioneer Company (motorized) (18 LMG, 2 heavy MG, and 2 medium mortars)
    3rd Panzer Pioneer Company (armored) (half-tracks) (19 LMG, 2 heavy MG)
Panzer Signals Battalion with staff
    Supply Platoon (2 LMG)
    Panzer Telephone Company (11 LMG)
    Panzer Wireless Radio Company (19 LMG)
Panzer Field-Replacement Battalion with Staff and Supply Company (50 LMG, 1 heavy MG, 6 medium mortars,
    2 heavy mortars, 1 Flak 20mm, 2 flamethrowers, and 1 light field howitzer)
Commander of the Panzer Supply Troops
    Staff Company (motorized) (2 LMG)
    1st Truck Company (120-ton and 4 LMG)
    2nd Truck Company (120-ton and 4 LMG)
    3rd Light Truck Convoy (30-ton and 2 LMG)
    4th Light Truck Convoy (30-ton and 2 LMG)
    5th Light Truck Convoy (30-ton and 2 LMG)
    6th Truck Maintenance Platoon (motorized)
Vehicle Maintenance Troops
    1st Panzer Maintenance Company (motorized) (2 LMG)
    2nd Panzer Maintenance Company (motorized) (2 LMG)
    3rd Replacement Parts Detachment (motorized) (75-ton)
Medical Troops
    1st Medical Company (motorized) (2 LMG)
    2nd Ambulance Company (1 LMG)
Veterinarian Troops
    Veterinarian Platoon
Administrative Troops (3 LMG)
    Administration Platoon
    Bakery Platoon
    Butcher Platoon
Field Post Office (motorized)

Distribution of the half-tracks (Sd.Kfz.251)

	Group 251/1	Ambul. 251/8	Flame. 251/16	20mm Trip. 251/21	75mm Pak 251/22	Total
Div Staff	2					2
Pz.Gren.Btl. (SPW)	24	8		9	6	47
Pz.Rgt.		2				2
Pz.Art.Rgt.		4				4
Pz.Art.Rgt.		4				4
Pz.Jgr.Abt.		1			9	10
Pz.Pi.Kp.	6	1	5			12
	32	20	5	9	15	81

Panzer Reconnaissance Battalion (type not indicated)   13

Source: Gen.Insp.d.Pz.Tr./OKH/Gen.Std.H./Org.Abt./Nr.I/1600/45 gKdos v.25.3.45. See Dr. F. M. v.Senger u. Etterlin, *Die Panzer-Grenadiere: Geschichte u. Gestalt der mechanisierten Infanterie 1930–1960* (München: J. F. Lehmanns Verlag, 1961), 226–27.

World War II Rank Equivalents

Waffen SS	Wehrmacht and Luftwaffe	U.S. Army
	Reischmarschall	
SS-Reichsführer	Generalfeldmarschall	General of the Army
SS-Oberstgruppenführer	Generaloberst	General
SS-Obergruppenführer	General der Infanterie General der Artillerie General der Kavallerie General der Flieger General der Panzer Truppen	Lieutenant General
SS-Gruppenführer	Generalleutnant	Major General
SS-Brigadeführer	Generalmajor	Brigadier General
SS-Oberführer. Entitled to wear the gray lapel facings on the greatcoat as worn by generals, and to wear a general's silver braid.		
SS-Standartenführer	Oberst	Colonel
SS-Obersturmbannführer	Oberstleutnant	Lieutenant Colonel
SS-Sturmbannführer	Major	Major
SS-Hauptsturmführer	Hauptmann	Captain
SS-Obersturmführer	Oberleutnant	1st Lieutenant
SS-Untersturmführer	Leutnant	2nd Lieutenant
SS-Sturmscharführer	Stabsfeldwebel	Sergeant Major
SS-Oberjunker. Officer Candidate with substantive rank of SS-Hauptscharführer.		

(*continued*)

Waffen SS	Wehrmacht and Luftwaffe	U.S. Army
SS-Hauptscharführer	Oberfeldwebel	First Sergeant Master Sergeant
SS-Oberscharführer	Feldwebel Wachmeister	Technical Sergeant
SS-Scharführer	Unterfeldwebel	Sergeant
SS-Junker. Officer Candidate with substantive rank of SS-Unterscharführer.		
SS-Stabsscharführer. Senior NCO of a unit. Appointment rather than rank, denoted by two braided rings on lower portion of sleeve of the tunic. Could go to any rank from SS-Unterscharführer and higher. Also known as the Spiess.		
SS-Unterscharführer	Unteroffizier	Senior Corporal
SS-Rottenführer	Obergrefreiter	Corporal
SS-Unterführeranwärter. Soldier nominated as NCO Candidate with contract for 12 years service.		
SS-Sturmmann	Gefreiter	Private First Class
SS-Oberschütze. Senior Private after six months service.	Obersoldat	
SS-Schütze or Mann. Includes specialty rank, such as Pionier, Grenadier, Panzerschütze, etc.	Soldat	Private

Combat Vehicles

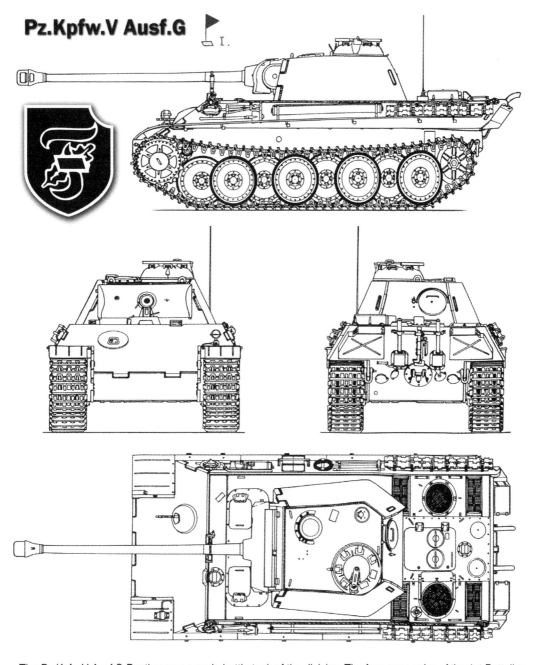

Pz.Kpfw.V Ausf.G

The Pz.Kpfw.V Ausf.G Panther was a main battle tank of the division. The four companies of the 1st Battalion were made up exclusively of the Pz.Kpfw.V Ausf. G.

Pz.Kpfw.IV Ausf.G

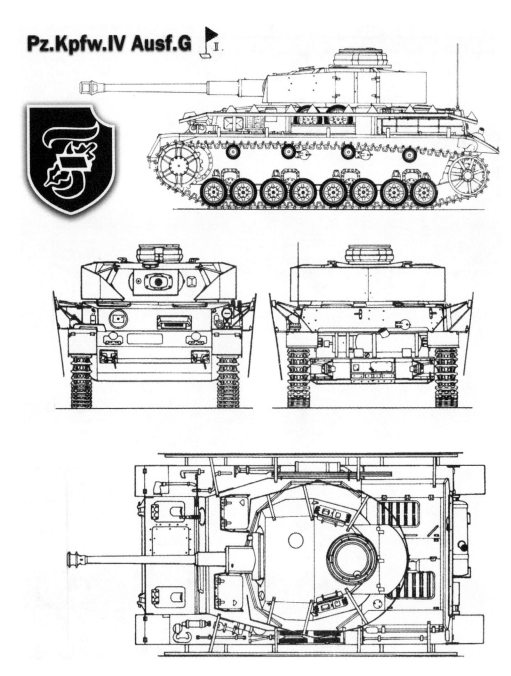

The Pz.Kpfw.IV Ausf. H was a main battle tank of the division. The 5th and 6th Companies of the 2nd Battalion were made up exclusively of the Pz.Kpfw.IV Ausf. H.

StuG III Ausf.G

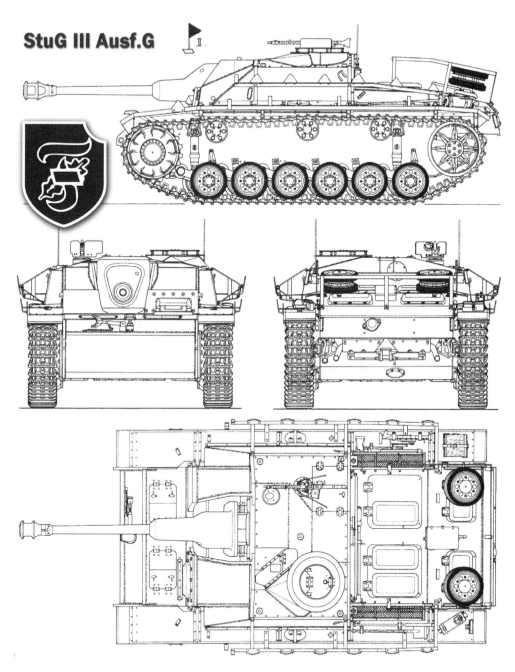

The StuG III or assault gun was a self-propelled artillery gun but also served as a primary combat vehicle of the division to make up shortages of the Pz.Kpfw.IV Ausf. H. The 7th and 8th Companies of the 2nd Battalion were made up of StuG IIIs.

Endnotes

CHAPTER 1

1. Helmuth Greiner and Percy E. Schramm, *Kriegstage-buch des Oberkommandos der Wehrmacht (Wehrmacht-führungsstab): 1940–1945* (cited hereafter as *KTB-OKW*) (München: Bernard & Graefe Verlag, 1982), 2:1158, 5:20, and 5:74; and Wilhelm Tieke, *In the Firestorm of the Last Years of the War: II.SS-Panzerkorps with the 9. and 10.SS-Divisions "Hohenstaufen" and "Frundsberg,"* Frederick Steinhardt, trans. (Winnipeg: J.J. Fedorowicz Publishing, 1999), 1–3. In Tieke's book, the numbers of men mustered from the volunteer drive reflects the projected total by OKW. Gottlob Berger would lead readers to believe that the RAD could not supply enough men for the SS when, in fact, it was the primary source. The RAD refers to the auxiliary, quasi-military organization that constituted one of the steps along the path to military service. Mandatory service in the RAD began on 26 June 1935, and during the war, the term of duty in the RAD was cut to three months. Principally, everybody recruited by the *Waffen-SS* came by way of the RAD, although there were exceptions of volunteers who entered directly into the *Waffen-SS*, avoiding the RAD. In 1935, German law required every nineteen-year-old male to serve in the RAD for six months prior to beginning service in the armed forces. For information concerning the RAD, see Klaus Ewald of Weil im Schönbach, interviewed by author, 6 April 2004; and Dr. Helmut Meschenmoser, "Reiseerlebnisse von Alfred Meschenmoser: Eisenbahnfahrten von 1941 bis in die 50er Jahre," *Landesbildstelle Berlin*, 2000, www .bics.be.schule.de/son/verkehr/eisenbah/augen/amesch/rad.htm. *Aktion Rü 43 Tausch* refers to the exchange of service-eligible German or ethnic German workers for forced laborers from outside Germany.

2. Lothar Debes, service record dossier, National Archives (cited hereafter as NA), Record Group (cited hereafter RG) 242, Berlin Document Center (cited hereafter as BDC), Microfilm Publication (cited hereafter as MP) A3343, Series SSO-074, Frames 1423–1472. For more information regarding his military career, see Appendix A. For information regarding officer retention in the *Waffen-SS*, see General Major Doerffler-Schuband, *Officer Procurement in the Waffen-SS: Reception, Processing, and Training*, 1–9, NA/RG549/MPM1035, Foreign Military Studies (cited hereafter as FMS), D-178.

3. *Reichsdeutsche* were natural German-born citizens within the immediate borders of the German Reich, whereas *Volksdeutsche* were ethnic German citizens living outside the Reich. In this case, *Volksdeutsche* referred to people in occupied foreign areas, such as Poland, Yugoslavia, Rumania, and Russia. The *Jungvolk* (young nation) was the junior NSDAP organization of the *Hitler Jugend* (Hitler Youth). Young boys between the ages of ten and fourteen learned how to drill and camp, and paramilitary training was emphasized. Members of the Hitler Youth usually graduated into military service between the ages of seventeen and eighteen. The *Sturmabteilung* (Storm Troopers or brown shirts) refers to the earliest organization of the NSDAP that was responsible for guarding the beer halls where Hitler spoke in public. An *Abteilung* refers to a section, branch, detachment, or battalion. For combat arms units such as tanks, antitank, artillery, and reconnaissance, it refers to battalion-sized formations. For more information about the intricacies of German unit designations, see Nicholas Zetterling, *Normandy 1944: German Military Organization, Combat Power and Organizational Effectiveness* (Winnipeg: J.J. Fedorowicz Publishing, 2000), 15. The *Allgemeine SS* (general SS) refers to the earliest ranks of the *Schutzstaffel* that provided personal bodyguards for Hitler. Consulted was David Littlejohn, *The Hitler Youth* (Columbia, SC: Agincourt Publishers, 1988), 1–13; Craig W. H. Luther, *Blood and Honor: The History of the 12th SS Panzer Division "Hitler Youth," 1943–1945* (San Jose: R. James Bender Publishing, 1987), 12–14; and the Gemeinschaftsarbeit des SS-Kriegsberichter-Zuges der 10.SS-Panzer-Div. "Frundsberg," *Dran Drauf und Durch! Buczacz-Caen-Nimwegen* (Division Propaganda Branch IV: 1944), 11.

4. Operation Gisela was the planned German counterstroke in northern Spain against an Allied occupation of the Iberian Peninsula. This measure involved five German divisions, to include the 9th SS "Hohenstaufen." See Greiner and Schramm, *KTB-OKW*, 5:25, and Herbert Fürbringer, *9.SS-Panzer-Division "Hohenstaufen" 1944: Normandie-Tarnopol-Arnhem* (Heimdal: Editions Heimdal, 1984), 54.

5. The locations of individual Training and Replacement Battalions were based on an analysis of soldiers' pay books collected from members of the division in captivity. See Ewald Klapdor, *Die Entscheidung: Invasion 1944* (Siek: privately printed, 1984), 16. It should be noted that each battalion for each branch of service provided replacements for all units and therefore not solely for the Frundsberg Division.

6. The organizing detachment consisted of staff officers and technical maintenance specialists in various service branches, including motor transport, artillery, tanks, weapons, etc. The *Feldpostnummer* (field postal number) for the 10th SS Organizing Battalion was 26218/A. Kameradschafts-Vereinigung und Suchdienst Frundsberg e.V. Hannover (cited hereafter as Suchdienst Frundsberg e.V. Hannover), *Die Hellebarde: Nachrichten der Kameradschaftsvereinigung Suchdienst Frundsberg*, No. 5 (Hannover: Kameradschafts-Vereinigung und Suchdienst Frundsberg e.V. Hannover, 1980), 4. The reference to Buchenwald refers to the greater SS facility that incorporated SS barracks, SS training facilities, as well as the concentration camp. The platoon leaders' course, a second level officer's training requirement that followed officer candidates' school, was held at the Buchenwald facility, home to one of three death's head regiments, the SS Death's Head Regiment "Thüringen." See Bernd Wegner, *The Waffen-SS, Organization, Ideology and Function*, Ronald Webster, trans. (Paderborn: Ferdinand Schoningh, 1982), English translation copy (Oxford: Basil Blackwell Ltd., 1990), 91.

7. Bernhard Westerhoff, *Weg einer Panzer-Kompanie 1943–1945: 6.Kompanie SS-Panzer-Regiment 10 "Frundsberg,"* 1986, 2–3. Reference to the older and experienced divisions of the *Waffen-SS* refers to the first five divisions that included the 1st SS Panzer Division "*Leibstandarte* Adolf Hitler," 2nd SS Panzer Division "Das Reich," 3rd SS Panzer Division "Totenkopf," 4th SS Panzer Division "Polizei," and 5th SS Panzer Division "Wiking."

8. Leo Franke, service record dossier, 14.SS-Pz.Jgr.Kp. "Der Führer," O.U., 17.3.1941, RG242/A3343/SSO-0218/F1015, 10.SS Panzer Division, Rgt.Gef.Std., 25.5.1944, F996-97, and SS-Pz.Ers.Rgt., Bitsch/Lager, 26.2.1943, F1002-03.

9. Alexander Grenda of Wolfsburg, interviewed by author, March 2004. Jozef Pilsudski was the dictator of Poland from 1926 to 1935. Rydz-Smigly, who served under Pilsudski in the Polish Legions, assumed power as dictator until September 1939, when he fled to Rumania after both Germany and Russia invaded Poland. See Federal Research Division and Glenn E. Curtis (ed.). *Poland: A Country Study*, 3rd ed., Library of Congress (Washington, DC: Government Printing Office [hereafter abbreviated GPO], 1994), 28–33.

10. Westerhoff, *Weg einer Panzer-Kompanie*, 1–2.

11. The *SS-Verfügungstruppe* or SS-VT (dispositional troops) organized into two regiments, next to the *Leibstandarte* (life standard) and served to protect Hitler at his disposal. Both the *Leibstandarte* and the SS Dispositional Troops formed the foundation for the latter *Waffen-SS*. Rick D. Joshua, "Tarnished Warriors: The Waffen-SS and Popular Misconception" (thesis, Brunel University, 1994), 9.

12. Suchdienst Frundsberg (hereafter cited as Suchdienst Frundsberg e.V. Köln), *Die Hellebarde: Nachrichten der Kameradschaftsvereinigunng Suchdienst Frundsberg*, No. 19 (Köln: Suchdienst Frundsberg e.V., 1997), 32–33. In 1943, the training and replacement facility for the 1st SS Antitank Training and Replacement Battalion was located in Rastenburg, Germany. See Klapdor, *Die Entscheidung*, 16. Klapdor was an *SS-Untersturmführer* in the reconnaissance battalion.

13. Suchdienst Frundsberg e.V. Köln, *Die Hellebarde*, No. 19 (1997): 33.

14. Based on correspondence between the author and Otto Jacob, August 2001.

15. Based on a report by Erich Lessner, an NCO in the 1st Company, 10th SS Pioneer Battalion, in the Pionier Kameradschaft "Dresden," *10.SS-Panzer-Div. "Frundsberg": Chronik der Pioniereinheiten der 10.SS-PzDiv "Frundsberg"* (hereafter cited as "*Chronik der Pioniereinheiten*") (Archive Westerhoff, 1990), 4.

16. Ibid., 4–5. The term "pioneer" refers to the equivalent of Engineers in the US Army. The US Marines also referred to engineers as pioneers during World War II.

17. Ibid., 5–6. The locations for the training and lodging of pioneers included Pikowitz, Hradischko, and Dawle.

18. Karl Keck, service record dossier, NA/RG242/A3343/SSO-0159A.

19. *Kriegstagebuch* (war diary)(cited hereafter as KTB), 1st Battalion, 21st *SS-Panzergrenadier* Regiment, Abt.Ia., Mar-Dez 1943, NA/RG242/T354/R150/F3792087.

20. Ibid., F3792087-88.

21. Greiner and Schramm, *KTB-OKW*, 5:159-60. In comparison, the organization of the 12th SS Panzer Division *Hitler Jugend*, considered part of the German program for "total war" after the loss of 91,000 men at Stalingrad, ran a less difficult course by recruiting from the birth year 1926, i.e., directly from the 30,000-strong Hitler Youth. Less than one year after Hitler directed its organization in June 1943, the 12th SS Panzer Division mustered 20,540 men. See: Hubert Meyer, *Kriegsgeschichte der 12.SS-Panzerdivision "Hitlerjugend,"* vol. 1, 4th ed. (Coburg: Nation Europa Verlag GmbH, 1999), 11–17.

22. KTB, 1st Battalion, 21st *SS-Panzergrenadier* Regiment, NA/RG242/T354/R150/F3792088; and *SS-Panzergrenadier* Division "Karl der Grosse," Div.St.Qu., 3.3.43,

Betr.: Schweigepflicht-Verschlußsachen, NA/RG242/
T354/R150/F3792063-64. For more information re-
garding *Jagdkommandos*, or search parties refer to the
secret battalion order, I./SS-Pz.Gren.Rgt.1, "Karl der
Grosse," Ia./Tgb.Nr. 14/43, 10.5.1943, NA/RG242/T354/
R150/F3792129.

23. In report by Erich Lessner, a platoon commander in the 1st
Company, Pionier Kameradschaft "Dresden," *Chronik der
Pioniereinheiten*, 6, 9–10.

24. For more information concerning Army disciplinary
measures on the Eastern Front, see Omer Bartov, *Hitler's
Army: Soldiers, Nazis, and War in the Third Reich* (New
York: Oxford University Press, 1991), 93–98; and Pz.Jg.
Abt., Kp.Gef.St., 2.6.44, Strafliste von Mannschaften, NA/
RG242/T354/R152/F3795716. Nine men were sentenced
to some form of arrest.

25. *SS-Obersturmführer* Leonid Ehrenburg sold a vaccine
to the SS that proved ineffective. Himmler demanded
the return of 160,000 Reichsmarks. Unable to repay the
large sum of money, Ehrenburg was forced to resign his
commission and banished from the SS. See the personal
dossier of Leonid Ehrenburg, NA/RG242/BDC/A3343/
SSO-176/F984-98.

26. KTB, 1st Battalion, 21st *SS-Panzergrenadier* Regiment,
NA/RG242/T354/R150/F3792088.

27. Karl Bastian, service record dossier, NA/RG242/BDC/
A3343/SSO-0038. The Sudetenland was the mountainous
rim of north and northeastern Czechoslovakia that was
inhabited by an overwhelmingly German population.
Hitler annexed this area into the Greater German Reich
in October 1938 under the Munich agreement. On 15
March 1939, the Protectorates of Bohemia and Moravia
were proclaimed. For more information, see Gerhard L.
Weinberg, *A World at Arms: A Global History of World
War II* (New York: Cambridge University Press, 2004),
27–28.

28. Pionier Kameradschaft "Dresden," *Chronik der Pioniereinheiten*, 7.

29. Westerhoff, *Weg einer Panzer-Kompanie*, 5 and 11.

30. Ibid., 14–15.

31. KTB, 1st Battalion, 21st *SS-Panzergrenadier* Regiment,
NA/RG242/T354/R150/F3792089. On 7 May, Debes
promoted the commander of the 1st Battalion, *SS-
Hauptsturmführer* Laubscheer, to the rank of *SS-
Sturmbannführer*.

32. 10.SS-Division, Abt.VI, Div.St.Qu. 1.6.43, Grundgesetze
der SS, NA/RG242/T354/R150/F3791856-59, Aufgaben
der SS and Gliederung und Aufbau der SS, 29.5.43,
F3791860-66. For an evaluation of *Waffen-SS* soldiers by
a contemporary American historian in a political context,
as opposed to an evaluation of soldierly virtues, see
Weinberg, *A World at Arms*, 458.

33. 10.SS-Division, Abt.VI, Div.St.Qu. 12.5.43, Weltanschauliche Führung, NA/RG242/T354/R150/F379882;
and 22.6.43, Betriff: Schulungsthema "SS-Mann und
Blutsfrage," F3791952.

34. KTB, 1st Battalion, 21st *SS-Panzergrenadier* Regiment,
NA/RG242/T354/R150/F3792089; and Pionier Kameradschaft "Dresden," *Chronik der Pioniereinheiten*, 9.

35. Westerhoff, *Weg einer Panzer-Kompanie*, 15. A thorough
cleaning was required before the men could occupy the
barracks because the French soldiers were black.

36. KTB, 1st Battalion, 21st *SS-Panzergrenadier* Regiment,
NA/RG242/T354/R150/F3792089.

37. Westerhoff, *Weg einer Panzer-Kompanie*, 16–17.

38. Memo from the commander of the division, *SS-
Brigadeführer* Lothar Debes, 10.SS-Pz.Gren.Div., Abt.
VI., Div.St.Qu., 27.7.43, Betr.: Weltanschauliche Führung,
NA/RG242/T354/R150/F3791880-81. It is unclear if
twelve hours was the total training requirement for each
month.

39. Pionier Kameradschaft "Dresden," *Chronik der Pioniereinheiten*, 8–9.

40. A report by *SS-Oberschütze* Adolf Körner, 5./SS-
Panzer-Regiment 10., O.U., 13.8.1943, concerning the
deployment of the 5th Company from 7 August 1943 to
11 August 1943. See NA/RG242/T354/R152/F3794721-
23.

41. KTB, 1st Battalion, 21st *SS-Panzergrenadier* Regiment,
NA/RG242/T354/R150/F3792093.

42. The *Panzerkampfwagen* III (Pz.Kpfw.) or *Sonder-
kraftfahrzeug* 141 (Sd.Kfz.) originally served as a tank-
to-tank combat vehicle and provided infantry support
alongside the infantry support Panzer IV. By 1942 the
Pz.Kpfw.III became obsolete in its role and production
ended in 1943. By 1944, the Pz.Kpfw.III was used strictly
as a training vehicle.

43. Westerhoff, *Weg einer Panzer-Kompanie*, 19–21. As a
result of partisan activity, portions of the company were
distributed to guard bridges and key points along the
railroad. No incidents with partisans were reported.

44. A report by Erich Werkmeister, Pionier Kameradschaft
"Dresden," *Chronik der Pioniereinheiten*, 10.

45. KTB, 1st Battalion, 21st *SS-Panzergrenadier* Regiment,
NA/RG242/T354/R150/F3792093.

46. Based on a report by Gerhard Schulz, an NCO in the pioneer
platoon, 5th Company, 10th SS Panzer Reconnaissance
Battalion, in the Pionier Kameradschaft "Dresden,"
Chronik der Pioniereinheiten, 9. The deployment of the
division to southern France resulted from the capitulation
of Italy and fear of Allied landings along the south coast
of France; see Klapdor, *Die Entscheidung*, 17.

47. KTB, 1st Battalion, 21st *SS-Panzergrenadier* Regiment,
F3792091, and F3792093, and John R. Angolia, *For
Führer and Fatherland: Military Awards of the Third
Reich* (San Jose: R. James Bender Publishing, 1976), 299.
The War Merit Cross without Swords was awarded to
civilians.

48. Officers assigned to the regimental staff were not
General Staff qualified. In the case of Sumper, he
was not responsible for armaments or equipment, but
rather provided aid to the commander, prepared combat

reports and the war diary, routed orders, commanded the messenger squadron, and oversaw the biological defense.

49. *SS-Untersturmführer* Hans-Dieter Sauter, "Querschuesse und Intrigen?" *Die Hellebarde*, no. 21 (2001): 35–36.

50. KTB, 1st Battalion, 21st *SS-Panzergrenadier* Regiment, F3792091, and F3792093. In terms of the praise Laubscheer received from General Sodenstern, conflicting reports exist concerning who led the exercise. The KTB entry for 20 September 1943, which follows sequentially 23 September 1943, reports Laubscheer leaving the battalion to command the 2nd (later redesignated 22nd) *SS-Panzergrenadier* Regiment from 20 September to 10 October 1943. *SS-Hauptsturmführer* Gropp assumed command of the battalion just days before the exercise began.

51. Tieke, *In the Firestorm of the Last Years of the War*, 9–10.

52. From 9 October to 15 October, records identify units with a single numeral, to include the I./SS-Pz.Gren.Rgt.1, or II./SS-Pz.Rgt.1. In both cases, provisional organizational numbers were used until the units received their final designation. KTB, 1st Battalion, 21st *SS-Panzergrenadier* Regiment, NA/RG242/T354/R150/F3792092; and Tieke, *In the Firestorm of the Last Years of the War*, 10.

53. SS-FHA, Amt II, Org.Abt.Ia/II, Tgb.Nr.16432/43 g.Kdos, dated 26 October 1943, Pionier Kameradschaft "Dresden," *Chronik der Pioniereinheiten*, 11; and U.S. War Department, *Handbook on German Military Forces*, with introduction by Stephen Ambrose (Baton Rouge, LA: 1990), 156 and 507.

54. See OKH/Gen.St.d.H./Org.Abt./Nr.I/4500/43 gKdos v.4.10.43., as in Dr. F.M. v. Senger u. Etterlin, *Die Panzer-Grenadiere: Geschichte u. Gestalt der mechanisierten Infanterie 1930–1960* (München: J.F. Lehmans Verlag, 1961), 203–4 and 218–20.

55. See 5./10th SS Panzer Regiment, 1.3.1944, Übergabe-Verhandlung, NA/RG242/T354/R152/F3794742 and 3794751; and Westerhoff, *Weg einer Panzer-Kompanie*, 26. Also consulted v. Senger u. Etterlin, *Die Panzer-Grenadiere*, 203–4 and 218–20. For more information concerning the assault gun, see Walter J. Spielberger, *Sturmgeschütz & Its Variants*, James C. Cable, trans. (Atglen: Schiffer Publishing Ltd., 1993), 247. Only the 5th, 9th, and 10th SS Panzer Divisions received forty-four Assault Guns (StuGs) to be distributed between two companies.

56. For more details concerning various German tanks, see Peter Chamberlain and Hilary Doyle, *Encyclopedia of German Tanks of World War Two: A Complete Illustrated Directory of German Battle Tanks, Armoured Cars, Self-Propelled Guns and Semi-Tracked Vehicles, 1933–1945*, revised ed. (London: Arms and Armour Press, 1993), 98, and 244–56.

57. While Lingner attended the Army General Staff Academy, it does not appear he completed the course. In an appraisal by his divisional commander, dated 21 November 1942, Lingner was recalled from the academy to support the new

organization of the SS Panzer Corps and reorganization of the 2nd SS Division to an *SS-Panzergrenadier* Division. See Beurteilung über *SS-Hauptsturmführer* Lingner, Div.St.Qu., 21.11.1942, SS-Division "Das Reich," Kommandeur, NA/RG242/A3343/SSO-0266A. On 21 December 1940, the *SS-Verfügungs-Division* was renamed to SS Division "Reich" and organized as a motorized division. In May 1942, the division was renamed to SS-Division "Das Reich," and on 9 November converted to *Panzergrenadier* division with the name *SS-Panzergrenadier* Division "Das Reich." On 22 October 1943, the division converted to a panzer division named 2nd SS Panzer Division "Das Reich." The individual regiments were as follows:

1940
SS Regiment Der Führer
SS Regiment Deutschland
11th SS Infantry Regiment

1942
SS-Panzergrenadier Regiment Deutschland
SS-Panzergrenadier Regiment Der Führer
SS-Panzergrenadier Regiment Langemark

1943
2nd SS Panzer Regiment "Das Reich"
3rd *SS-Panzergrenadier* Regiment "Deutschland"
4th *SS-Panzergrenadier* Regiment "Der Führer"
SS Infantry Regiment "Langemarck"

See James Lucas, *Das Reich: The Military Role of the 2nd SS Division* (London: Arms and Armour Press, 1991), 15–26, and *Lexikon der Wehrmacht*, www.lexikon -der-wehrmacht.de/Gliederungen/PanzerdivisionenSS/ Gliederung.htm.

58. Fürbringer, *9.SS-Panzer-Division*, 552–53, and the 10.SS Panzer Division "Frundsberg," SS-Pz.Rgt, Rgt.Gef.Std., 13.7.1944, Dienstanweisung für den Stab SS-Panzer-Regiment 10, NA/RG242/T354/R152/F3795129-3795132. It should be noted that German ordnance officers were not similar to American ordnance officers, who were responsible for weapons, armored vehicles, and artillery.

59. 10.SS-Division (Panzer-Grenadier-Division), Sturmgeschütz-Abteilung, "Wochen-Dienstplan für den Stab SS-Stu. Gesch.Abt.10, für die Zeit vom 4.-11.10.1943," O.U. den 2.10.43, NA/RG242/T354/R150/F3792683-3792684; and 10.SS Panzer Division "Frundsberg" 2./Sturmgeschütz-Abt., "Dienstplan für die Zeit 22.11-28.11.1943," O.U. den 19.11.43, F3792687-3792692.

60. 10.SS Panzer Division "Frundsberg," Abt.VI/Az.37g/ Lt./Dr; Div.St.Qu., dtd 6.11.43, NA/RG242/T354/R150/ F3791940-791948.

61. Westerhoff, *Weg einer Panzer-Kompanie*, 20–22, and Pionier Kameradschaft "Dresden," *Chronik der Pioniereinheiten*, 8–9.

62. The training regiment number 1 was officially redesignated to Regiment 21 on 6 November 1943. KTB, 1st Battalion, 21st *SS-Panzergrenadier* Regiment, NA/RG242/T354/R150/F3792090. The 711th Infantry Division, commanded by Generalleutnant Josef Reichert, was one of three divisions that formed the LXXXI Army Corps, commanded by General of Panzer Troops Adolf Kuntzen. The other two divisions included the 245th Infantry Division and the 17th *Luftwaffe* Field Division.

63. Ibid., F3792090 and 792094.

64. Pionier Kameradschaft "Dresden," *Chronik der Pioniereinheiten*, 8–9. This came as a direct result of Allied air attacks.

65. 10.SS-Panzer-Division "Frundsberg," 25.11.1943, Betrifft: Politische-weltanschauliche Führung, NA/RG242/T354/R150/F3791876-3791877; and a memo from the Chief of the Abt.VI, 7.12.1943, Betrifft: Weltanschauliche Führung und Truppenbetreuung, F3791874-3791875. No other correspondence was found that would suggest Debes did not take political indoctrination very seriously.

66. Based on interviews conducted on 30 and 31 Jan 2005, with Bernhard Westerhoff, Werner Pietzka, and Otto Jacob, regarding the frequency and content of indoctrination training. The phrase "soldier just like others too" was coined by Paul Hausser and used in 1966 for the title of his book.

67. Tieke, *In the Firestorm of the Last Years of the War*, 1. Paul Hausser was a professional soldier and veteran of World War I. He gained the respect and admiration of all the German soldiers. After the war, he defended the *Waffen-SS* against accusations of war crimes during the Nuremberg Trials. For a summary concerning the life and times of Paul Hausser, see E. G. Krätschmer, *Die Ritterkreuzträger der Waffen-SS*, 4. ergänzte Auflage (fourth revised ed.) (Coburg: Nation Europa Verlag GmbH, 1999), 158–81.

68. Karl v. Treuenfeld, service record dossier, NA/RG242/A3343/SSO-0189B/F908-909. No information is available that indicates where Treuenfeld resided between 5 July 1941 and January 1942.

69. Pionier Kameradschaft "Dresden," *Chronik der Pioniereinheiten*, 8–9. Standard 1-ton armored half-tracks (s.Kfz.232) were equipped with pairs of bridging sections and stored on the tops of vehicles. Every group received two half-group vehicles, each with pioneer equipment and two MG-42 machine guns. When dismounted, the assistant driver operated one MG-42 that remained on the vehicle for security.

70. Hermann Max Gerhard, *My Life in the Middle of the 20th Century*, unpublished manuscript, 1997, 1, 12–13, and 21–30. The MG-42 machine gun was a crew-served weapon and the best in its class. Its cyclic rate of fire was more than 2,500 rounds per minute. In February 1944, SS Officer Candidate Gerhard returned to the 2nd Battalion, 22nd *SS-Panzergrenadier* Regiment, as the signal troop commander.

71. Westerhoff, *Weg einer Panzer-Kompanie*, 26.

72. Information provided to the author by Klaus Ewald of Siek, transcript Stenger Archive, 7 July 2005. Klaus Ewald was a motorcycle messenger in the Hitler Youth Division.

73. Westerhoff, *Weg einer Panzer-Kompanie*, 32.

74. See the article by Patrick Agte, "Scharfschützenabzeichen der 10.SS-Panzerdivision "Frundsberg," *Der Freiwillige*, no. 4 (2005): 6–7. In the event that a sniper did not successfully complete individual segments of the shooting requirement during the first attempt, a second attempt was authorized. However, the German Army generally frowned upon locally created badges and awards. The *Scharfschützenabzeichen* was an official *Wehrmacht*-level award. The Frundsberg-award, more than likely, involved the soldiers of the division who qualified for the *Wehrmacht* award.

75. The main purpose of disbanding the assault gun battalion was to fill the gaps in the regimental tank battalions. The 1st "Panther" Battalion did not yet exist, and the 2nd Battalion only had two companies of Pz.Kpfw.IVs. The assault guns filled the ranks of the 7th and 8th Companies. See SS-Pz.Rgt.10, Abt.V, Kfz.Sb. 1/44, Uebernahme der Sturm-Geschütz-Abteilung, 1.7.44, NA/RG242/T354/R152/F3796020-3796023; and Westerhoff, *Weg einer Panzer-Kompanie*, 32. Officers and NCOs from the disbanded 10th SS Assault Gun Battalion were distributed throughout the companies of the 2nd Battalion, 10th SS Panzer Regiment. Westerhoff reported that four men joined the 6th Company. However, the 2nd Battalion directive 7/44, dated 8 January 1944, ordered that forty-four officers and NCOs transfer to the 6th Company.

76. *SS-Untersturmführer* Hans-Dietrich Sauter, "Querschuesse und Intrigen?", *Die Hellebarde*, No. 21 (2001): 35–36.

77. Westerhoff, *Weg einer Panzer-Kompanie*, 34.

78. Ibid., 35.

79. Westerhoff, *Weg einer Panzer-Kompanie*, 35–39; and Pz.Rgt.10, Ib., Personal-Befehl 19/44, 14.2.44, NA/RG242/T354/R152/F3795958-3795961. Twenty-two additional men from the 2nd Battalion transferred to the 17th *SS-Panzergrenadier* Division "Götz von Berlichingen."

80. 5./SS-Pz.Rgt.10, 1.3.1944, Übergabe-Verhandlung, NA/RG242/T354/R152/F3794742 and 3794751. Prime movers were vehicles that pulled artillery guns.

81. A report by Erich Werkmeister in the Pionier Kameradschaft "Dresden," *Chronik der Pioniereinheiten*, 10; and Westerhoff, *Weg einer Panzer-Kompanie*, 39. Also see Tieke, *In the Firestorm of the Last Years of the War*, 11.

82. Franz Holtrichter, *Die Hellebarde*, No. 14, 1991, 102. Holtrichter believed de Paris to have been in contact with the French Resistance and therefore responsible for the attack.

CHAPTER 2

1. SS-Kriegsberichter-Zuges der 10.SS-Panzer-Div. "Frundsberg," *Dran Drauf und Durch!* 12. Details on the history

and splitting of Poland between Russia and Germany in 1939 were derived from Herbert Fürbringer, *9.SS-Panzer-Division "Hohenstaufen,"* 172–76, and Glenn E. Curtis, *Poland: A Country Study*, 35–38. With Poland under Soviet control from 1939 to 1941, over 1.5 million Poles were moved to labor camps throughout the Soviet Union. The most notorious incident during the Soviet reign of terror included the murder of 4,000 Polish officers, discovered in 1943 by the Germans in the Katyn Forest. After the Germans invaded, Poland became the predominant killing ground of the Holocaust with three major death camps in Auschwitz, Majdanek, and Treblinka. Nearly all of the three million Polish Jews died.

2. For more information regarding the general strategic situation on the Eastern Front and the development of the pocket at Kamenez-Podolsk, see Paul Carell, *Verbrannte Erde: Schlacht zwischen Wolga und Weichsel* (Frankfurt/M-Berlin: Verlag Ullstein GmbH, 1966), 387–404; and Erich von Manstein, *Verlorene Siege* (Bonn: Athenäum-Verlag Junker und Dünnhaupt KG, 1955, reprint Bonn: Athenäum-Verlag 1957), 582–619.

3. Six and a half divisions, surrounded at Tscherkassy at the beginning of February 1944, were able to avoid the earlier fate of the Sixth Army. While the majority of the units survived, most of the heavy equipment did not come out of the pocket because of the weather. The divisions then came out of the line for rest. For more details on Tscherkassy, see Erich von Manstein, *Verlorene Siege,* 582–84. For the disposition of Russian forces, see David M. Glantz and Jonathan House, *When Titans Clash: How the Red Army Stopped Hitler* (Lawrence: University Press of Kansas, 1995), 188–89.

4. David M. Glantz, *Soviet Military Operational Art: In Pursuit of Deep Battle* (London: Frank Cass and Company Limited, 1991), 134–36.

5. Carell, *Verbrannte Erde*, 397. See also Percy Schramm, *KTB: OKW; 1944–45*, Book 7, Part 1, 12. Actually, several assault gun battalions and one infantry division transferred to the East before Hitler stripped the reserve from OB West. Surviving *Kampfgruppen* from decimated panzer divisions, earmarked for raising new divisions in the West, were never released from the Russian Front and delayed the reinforcement of the West.

6. By 17 April, Army Group North Ukraine was commanded by Model, not Manstein. See Glantz, *When Titans Clash*, 189–90.

7. Carell, *Verbrannte Erde*, 399.

8. The *Panzerarmeebefehl* or Panzer Army Order Nr. 63 required that supply elements of both divisions of the II SS Panzer Corps were available. As a result, the 10th SS provided their support personnel and twenty field stoves for three days. For a complete review of the order, see Klapdor, *Die Entscheidung*, 21–23. See also Tieke, *In the Firestorm of the Last Years of the War*, 19.

9. Westerhoff, *Weg einer Panzer Kompanie*, 40–41.

10. SS-Kriegsberichter-Zuges, *Dran Drauf Durch!* 15, Kriegstagebuch (KTB) der 6./SS-Panzer-Regiment 10 "Frundsberg," compiled by *SS-Obersturmführer* Quandel, NA/RG352/R152/F3794563; and Westerhoff, *Weg einer Panzer Kompanie*, 42.

11. Suchdienst Frundsberg e.V. Köln, "Divisiongeschichte 'Frundsberg'," *Die Hellebarde*, No. 14, 1991, 93–94.

12. The *Kommandant des rückwärtigen Armeegebiets* 585 (Korück 585) or Commandant of the Rearward Army Area 585 organized on 10 September 1939 in the 10th Armed Forces District. The staff directly supported the Sixth Army in the West and stationed in Belgium and France. In April 1941, the staff transferred along with the Sixth Army to the East. Following the destruction of the Sixth Army at Stalingrad, the staff was renamed in January 1943 to Commanding General of Security Troops and Commandant in Army Area Don. On 25 April 1943, Korück 585 was reorganized. The new staff consisted of the disbanded Staff Gericke, the former Korück 585, assigned to Army Group South. In this case, the staff supported Korück 593, of the Fourth Panzer Army, employed first in southern Russia. In the spring of 1944, the staff was employed in northern Ukraine. See *Lexikon der Wehrmacht*, www.lexikon-der-wehrmacht.de/Gliederungen/Korueck/Korueck585-R.htm.

13. SS-Kriegsberichter-Zuges, *Dran Drauf Durch!* 14-15, KTB, 6./SS-Panzer-Regiment 10, F3794563; and Westerhoff, *Weg einer Panzer Kompanie*, 41–42.

14. Klapdor, *Die Entscheidung*, 24–25.

15. There were almost no shortages of fuel and ammunition thanks to the efforts of Major General Friedrich-Wilhelm Morzik's 2nd Transport who delivered supplies night after night. Comparatively, the Soviets were incapable of conducting after-dark operations, whereas the Germans capitalized on their ability to move materiel in this way. For a detailed report on the air operations in the pocket, see Major General Friedrich-Wilhelm Morzik, *German Air Force Airlift Operations*, USAF Historical Studies: No. 167 (USAF Historical Division, Research Studies Institute, June 1961). See also Will-Feodor von Neumann von Schmiedeberg von Winckler and Dieter Stenger, *Fahnenjunker Frontbewährung: The Eyewitness Account of a German Officer Candidate on the Eastern Front 1943–1944* (Spotsylvania, VA: Stenger Historica Publishing, 2000), 59; and Klapdor, *Die Entscheidung*, 24–25.

16. According to Klapdor, the KTB of the Pz.AOK 4 reported the 10th SS Panzer Division having only 32 Pz.Kpfw.IV and 38 StuG.III on 4 April. See Klapdor, *Die Entscheidung*, 26; Tieke, *In the Firestorm of the Last Years of the War*, 24–25; SS-Kriegsberichter-Zuges, *Dran Drauf Durch!* 15, KTB, 6./SS-Panzer-Regiment 10, NA/RG352/R152/F3794563; and Westerhoff, *Weg einer Panzer Kompanie*, 42.

17. Tieke, *In the Firestorm of the Last Years of the War*, 27–28. Also consulted the personnel dossier of *SS-*

Obersturmführer Gerhard Hinze, SS-Pz.Aufkl.Abt.10, Abt.Gef.St., 5 Aug 1944, Vorschlag für die Verleihung des Deutschen Kreuz in Gold, NA/RG242/A3343/SSO-100A/F189-195.

18. SS-Kriegsberichter-Zuges, *Dran Drauf Durch!* 15; KTB, 6./SS-Panzer-Regiment 10, F3794563; and Westerhoff, *Weg einer Panzer Kompanie*, 42. The dates of the first encounter between Russian antitank guns and the 6./SS-Pz.Rgt.10, in the KTB 6./SS-Pz.Rgt.10, conflict with those of Tieke and Klapdor, but the latter is the most reliable.

19. Suchdienst Frundsberg e.V. Köln, *Die Hellebarde*, No. 21, 13–16. According to Sauter, the loss of German materiel would have been far greater if Russian pilots were more skilled.

20. Tieke, *In the Firestorm of the Last Years of the War*, 28.

21. Letter from Heinz Harmel to the adjutant, Reichsführer SS, Div.Gef.St. dated 13.12.1944, "Vorschlag zur Verleihung des D.K.i.G. an SS-Stubaf. Laubscheer, Kdr.21st *SS-Panzergrenadier* Regiment." See the personnel dossier of Heinz Laubscheer, NA/RG242/A3343/SSO-245A/F399-523. According to Harmel, the commanding general of the XXVII Army Corps, General Ostfelder, wrote a letter to Himmler recognizing Laubscheer's actions. Cross-referenced with the profile on Heinrich Schuldt found in Krätschmer, *Die Ritterkreuzträger der Waffen-SS*, 276–77.

22. Westerhoff, *Weg einer Panzer Kompanie*, 42–43; and KTB, 6./SS-Panzer-Regiment 10, NA/RG242/T354/R150/F3794563.

23. Westerhoff, *Weg einer Panzer Kompanie*, 44.

24. Ibid., 44–45.

25. Capturing the village of Monasterzyska was the regimental objective for the following day. Elements of the reconnaissance battalion provided flank security in the northeast. See SS-Kriegsberichter-Zuges, *Dran Drauf Durch!* 16; and Suchdienst Frundsberg e.V. Köln, *Die Hellebarde*, No. 21, 16. The Dive Bomber Squadron 77 organized on 18 October 1943 from elements of the 1st Group in Brieg and was renamed the 77th Combat Squadron. Commanded by Major Helmut Bruck, from its inception until 15 February 1945, the squadron consisted of a staff and ten squadrons divided into three groups, operating Ju 87D and G "Stuka" models and Fw 190F and G models, from a variety of airfields including Lemberg and Kamenez-Podolsk. The 5th, 6th, and 10th Squadrons organized from the 2nd Stuka Squadron "Immelmann." On 1 May 1939, Major Bruck took command of the 1st Squadron of the 77th Stuka Squadron. After participating in Poland, France, and England, Bruck commanded the I Group on 20 August 1940. By 1 April 1941, after promotion to Hauptmann, he deployed with the group to the Balkans. Bruck flew missions over Crete and subsequently over Russia when he received the Knight's Cross of the Iron Cross on 4 September 1941. A standard practice for Stuka pilots was to rescue aircraft crews by landing and quickly taking back off, while another Stuka fought off the Russians with their aircraft guns. On 28

February 1942, Bruck flew his 300th mission. One year later, he received the Oak Leaves to the Knight's Cross of the Iron Cross on 19 February 1943 and, the following day, command of 77th Stuka Squadron. By the end of the war, Bruck had flown more than 800 missions. See Holger Nauroth, *Stukageschwader 2 Immelmann: Eine Dokumentation über das erfolgreichste deutsche Stukageschwader* (Preußisch Oldendorf: Verlag K.W. Schütz, 1988), 247–49.

26. Eduard Deisenhofer personnel dossier, NA/RG242/A3343/SSO-140, F1283, and Krätschmer, *Die Ritterkreuzträger der Waffen-SS*, 314–17.

27. SS-Kriegsberichter-Zuges, *Dran Drauf Durch!* 19.

28. *SS-Obersturmführer* Hans-Dietrich Sauter, "GFM-Model und der Maultierklau," in Suchdienst Frundsberg e.V. Köln *Die Hellebarde*, No. 21, 2001, 24.

29. Will-Feodor v. Neumann, *Fahnenjunker Frontbewährung*, 60; and Suchdienst Frundsberg e.V. Köln e.V. Köln, *Die Hellebarde*, No. 21, 16–17.

30. Suchdienst Frundsberg e.V. Köln e.V. Köln, *Die Hellebarde*, No. 21, 18. Franz Kleffner disobeyed the order given by Treuenfeld to attack Buczacz. To what extent Kleffner was relieved is not known. Later, Kleffner assumed command of a grenadier regiment when its commander was wounded.

31. Franz Kleffner, service record dossier, NA/RG242/A3343/SSO-176A/F1174-1246.

32. Ibid. Of interest is the fact that Kleffner first worked for the NSDAP as a cell ward.

33. Ibid.

34. OB 1.Panzerarmee, A.H.Qu., 9.4.44, Armeetagesbefehl, NA/RG242/T354/R152/F3795087-88.

35. Ibid., 25–27.

36. Abt.Gef.St., 5. August 1944, SS-Pz.Aufkl.Abt.10, Vorschlag für die Verleihung des Deutschen Kreuzes in Gold, Gerhard Hinze, NA/RG242/A3343/SSO-100A/F189-195. The reconnaissance battalion was credited with shooting down three Russian fighter aircraft with small arms fire. Also consulted Tieke, *In the Firestorm of the Last Years of the War*, 31–32.

37. Later, Ohlig was evacuated by aircraft back to Germany. His right arm was broken in half and two pieces of shrapnel remained stuck in his legs. Ohlig died on 1 Oct 1998. A report by *SS-Unterscharführer* Werner Ohlig in Suchdienst Frundsberg e.V. Köln, *Die Hellebarde*, No. 21, 22–23.

38. Tieke, *In the Firestorm of the Last Years of the War*, 33.

39. Westerhoff, *Weg einer Panzer-Kompanie*, 45–46; and KTB, 6./SS-Panzer-Regiment 10, NA/RG242/T354/R150/F3794563.

40. A report submitted by the company staff NCO, 5./SS-Pz. Rgt.10, Kp.Gef.St. 7.4.1944, Tagesmeldung, NA/RG242/T354/R150/F3794814-15.

41. Abt.Gef.St., 2 September 1944, SS-Pz.Aufkl.Abt.10, Vorschlag für die Verleihung des Deutschen Kreuzes in Gold, Rudolf Harmstorf, NA/RG242/A3343/SSO-064A/

F1259-1260; and Tieke, *In the Firestorm of the Last Years of the War*, 33.

42. A report submitted by the company commander, *SS-Untersturmführer* Schmidt, 5./SS-Pz.Rgt.10, Kp.Gef.St., 15.4.1944, Totalausfallmeldung NA/RG242/T354/R150/F3794808 and 813; also see Tieke, *In the Firestorm of the Last Years of the War*, 34.

43. Suchdienst Frundsberg e.V. Köln, *Die Hellebarde*, No. 5, 95–96.

44. In the report by *SS-Untersturmführer* Sauter, the adjutant, I./SS-Pz.Art.Rgt.10. Suchdienst Frundsberg e.V. Köln, *Die Hellebarde*, No. 21, 19.

45. Tieke, *In the Firestorm of the Last Years of the War*, 34–38.

46. Tieke, *In the Firestorm of the Last Years of the War*, 38; and SS-Kriegsberichter-Zuges, *Dran Drauf Durch!* 20.

47. See the report by *SS-Sturmbannführer* Hans Löffler, Suchdienst Frundsberg e.V. Köln, *Die Hellebarde*, No. 16, 14–20. Stalin's Organ was the nickname given to the Soviet 82mm BM-8 and 132mm BM-13 Katyusha rocket launchers.

48. Tieke, *In the Firestorm of the Last Years of the War*, 39.

49. Based on the SS personnel dossier of Hermann Friedrichs, NA/RG242/A3343/SSO-224/F226-398, and the evaluation from his commanding officer, 3rd SS Death's Head Regiment "Thüringen," dated 25.10.1938, F398.

50. II./13.SS-Totenkopfstandarte, Wien, 6.8.1940, "Personalbericht des *SS-Obersturmführer* Hermann Friedrichs," SS personnel dossier, Hermann Friedrichs, NA/RG242/A3343/SSO-224/F226.

51. Ibid., F295-97.

52. The Chief of the Armed Forces (OKW) released over 2,080 reports between 1 Sep 1939 and 9 May 1945. The reports were prepared by the department group for the Armed Forces propaganda (OKW/WPr) from reports submitted by the Chief of the Army and Navy, the Chief of the *Luftwaffe* and Armed Forces High Command (WFSt). The Chief of the WFSt (General Jodl) submitted the reports to Adolf Hitler for approval. The *Waffen-SS* fell under the command of the Army. The guidelines, established on 18 June 1941, dictated that reports be truthful and released after confirmation. Questionable reports were released only after enemy or foreign sources made confirmation. Reports that divulged enemy intelligence based on the use of weapons, tactics, and operations were not authorized. The German OKW reports, prepared for the world and German people, were truthful accounts of factual events on the battlefield. See Karl Cerff, *Die Waffen-SS im Wehrmachtbericht* (Osnabrück: Munin Verlag GmbH, 1971), 66–67.

53. The personnel dossier of Gerhard Hinze, SS-Pz.Aufkl. Abt.10, Abt.Gef.St., 5 Aug 1944, "Vorschlag für die Verleihung des Deutschen Kreuzes in Gold," NA/RG242/A3343/SSO-100A/F189-195; and Egon Kleine and Volkmar Kühn, *Tiger: Die Geschichte einer legendären Waffe 1942–45*, 2nd ed. (Stuttgart: Motorbuch Verlag, 1976), 151.

54. Suchdienst Frundsberg e.V. Köln, *Die Hellebarde*, No. 16, 17.

55. As many as fifty Russian tanks were reported in the KTB, 6./SS-Panzer-Regiment 10. *SS-Untersturmführer* Stark assumed command of the 6th Company on 12 April. The next day, a report of Russian T-34 tanks put the company back on the alert. See Bernhard Westerhoff, *Weg einer Panzer-Kompanie*, 47; and KTB, 6./SS-Panzer-Regiment 10, NA/RG242/T354/R150/F3794564. Schmidt prepared the vehicle casualty reports, 5./SS-Pz.Rgt.10, Kp.Gef. St. 15.4.1944, "Totalausfallmeldung," NA/RG242/T354/R150/F3794810 and F3794812. Also see SS-Kriegsberichter-Zuges, *Dran Drauf Durch!* 19.

56. Panzer-Artillerie Regiment, 10.SS-Pz.Div. Frundsberg, Rgt.Gef.St., 30 July 1944, "Vorschlag für die Verleihung des Deutschen Kreuz in Gold," in service record dossier Harry Jobst, NA/RG242/A3343/SSO-138A/F1455-1499.

57. *SS-Untersturmführer* Jan Sierks, "Kampfsatz," Suchdienst Frundsberg e.V. Köln, *Die Hellebarde*, No. 21, 2001, 53–55.

58. See SS-Kriegsberichter-Zuges, *Dran Drauf Durch!*, 20–21. The entire story, originally entitled "Four Men—Four Tanks (The Achievement of Younger Frundsberger)," is disputed in the *Hellebarde* No. 16, 44–45. Apparently, members of the pioneer platoon that were employed at Pilawa did not recall such an event ever taking place. The story was written by the *SS-Kriegsberichter* (war correspondent) Kurt Fervers, which also appeared in the account by the pioneer battalion association, Pionier-Kameradschaft "Dresden." *10.SS-Panzer-Div. "Frundsberg": Chronik der Pioniereinheiten der 10.SS-PzDiv "Frundsberg."* If the event did occur, the four men should have individually received the Tank Destruction Badge for the single-handed destruction of a tank.

59. 10.SS-Pz.Div. "Frundsberg," Flak-Abteilung, 31 July 1944, "Vorschlag für die Verleihung des Deutschen Kreuz in Gold," Gottlob Ellwanger personnel dossier, NA/RG242/A3343/SSO-184, F512-515; and Kradmelder Kurt Tews, SS-Pz.Gren.Rgt.22, Suchdienst Frundsberg e.V. Köln, *Die Hellebarde*, No. 5, 96.

60. Alois Pühringer service record dossier, NA/RG242/A3343/SSO-369A/F194-198.

61. Suchdienst Frundsberg e.V. Köln, *Die Hellebarde*, No. 5, 90–91. The Soviet attempt to blow up the Strypa bridges was confirmed by the messenger Kurt Tews, of the regimental staff, 22nd *SS-Panzergrenadier* Regiment, see p. 96.

62. Suchdienst Frundsberg e.V. Köln, *Die Hellebarde*, No. 16, 18; and the personnel dossier of Heinz Laubscheer, NA/RG242/A3343/SSO-245A, F521, Div.Gef.St. dated 13.12.1944, "Vorschlag zur Verleihung des D.K.i.G. an SS-Stubaf. Laubscheer, Kdr.21st *SS-Panzergrenadier* Regiment."

63. In accordance with the regimental personnel order 2/44, Zi.1, the 5th Company, 10th SS-Panzer Regiment, reported a strength of 159 men, of which two officers,

twenty-five NCOs, and ninety-nine men were fit for duty. The company casualties during the reporting period included three dead and ten wounded. By 17 April, the 5th Company suffered four additional losses: two wounded and two dead. See 5./SS-Pz.Rgt.10, 13.4.1944, "Stärkemeldung," NA/RG242/T354/R152/F3794598-99. For the details on the awards, see II./SS-Pz.Gren.Rgt.22, Btl.Gef.St., 16.4.44, "Verleihung des Eisernen Kreuzes II. Klasse," NA/RG242/T354/R152/F3795565-68.

64. Bernhard Westerhoff, *Weg einer Panzer-Kompanie*, 47.

65. A report by *SS-Untersturmführer* Schmidt, 5./SS-Pz. Rgt.10, Kp.Gef.St. 15.4.1944, "Totalausfallmeldung," NA/RG242/T354/R152/F3794809.

66. According to the award citation for the German Cross in Gold for Hinze, the 2nd Company, 10th SS Panzer Reconnaissance Battalion evacuated the village of Bobulince on 13 April. See the personnel dossier of Gerhard Hinze, SS-Pz.Aufkl.Abt.10, Abt.Gef.St., 5 August 1944, "Vorschlag für die Verleihung des Deutschen Kreuz in Gold," NA/RG242/A3343/SSO-100A/F189-195. See also Tieke, *In the Firestorm of the Last Years of the War*, 40–41.

67. Two reports by Hans Löffler including the newspaper article dated 2 June 1944, by *SS-Kriegsberichter* Georg Wilhelm Pfeiffer, "Kommandeur Knackt den ersten Feindpanzer," in the Suchdienst Frundsberg e.V. Köln, *Die Hellebarde*, No. 16, 19–21.

68. Suchdienst Frundsberg e.V. Köln, *Die Hellebarde*, No. 16, 22 and Btl.Gef.St., II./SS-Pz.Gren.Rgt.22, 2.5.1944, "Verleihung des Eisernen Kreuzes II.Klasse," NA/RG242/T354/R152/F3795543-45; Abt.Gef.St., 2 September 1944, SS-Pz.Aufkl.Abt.10, "Vorschlag für die Verleihung des Deutschen Kreuzes in Gold," Rudolf Harmstorf, NA/RG242/A3343/SSO-064A/F1259-1260; and 5./SS-Pz. Gren.Rgt.22, IIb, "Verleihung v. Kriegsauszeichnungen," 8.4.44, NA/RG242/T354/R152/F3795551. See also Tieke, *In the Firestorm of the Last Years of the War*, 42–43.

69. Suchdienst Frundsberg e.V. Köln, *Die Hellebarde*, No. 16, 23–24.

70. KTB, 6./SS-Panzer-Regiment 10, NA/RG242/T354/R150/F3794564. The *Panzerkampfabzeichen* (Tank Assault Badge) was instituted 20 December 1939 and awarded in silver to officers, NCOs, troops, and crews of the *Panzertruppen*. The badge was awarded after three combat actions on three separate days. See Kommissions-Verlag Friederichsen, *Lohn der Tat: Die Auszeichnungen des Heeres*, new abbreviated reprint (Nürnberg: Verlag-Kienseberger, 2000, reprint Hamburg: Verlag C. Pahl & Co., n.d.); and KTB, 6./SS-Panzer-Regiment 10, NA/RG242/T354/R150/F3794564.

71. Suchdienst Frundsberg e.V. Köln, *Die Hellebarde*, No. 5, 93–95.

72. Suchdienst Frundsberg e.V. Köln, *Die Hellebarde*, No. 16, 23–24.

73. Tieke, *In the Firestorm of the Last Years of the War*, 62–63.

74. Regarding Treuenfeld's transfer, see Hausser's letter to the division, 10.SS-Pz.Div. Frundsberg, IIa, Div.Gef. St., 22.4.44, T354, R150, F3792399. For information concerning Treuenfeld's award, see Karl v. Treuenfeld, service record dossier, NA/RG242/A3343/SSO-0189B/ F902-04. For items related to Harmel, see service record dossier, Heinz Harmel, NA/RG242/A3343/SSO-64A/ F346.

75. See SS-Rgt. "Der Führer," Abt.Ia Pe, Rgts.St.Qu., 20 February 1941, "Beurteilung über den *SS-Hauptsturmführer* Harmel, Heinz, II./SS 'DF'." Harmel's evaluation in the personnel dossier of Heinz Harmel, NA/RG242/A3343/ SSO-64A, *SS-Obersturmbannführer* Otto Kumm, the regimental commander's four-page "Kurze Begründung und Stellungnahme der Zwischenvorgesetzten"; as well as the four-page recommendation by Walter Krüger for the Oak Leaves to the Knight's Cross of the Iron Cross, SS-Pz.Gren.Div. "Das Reich," 20.8.1943.

76. The Rossbach Group or *Sturmabteilung* Rossbach refers to a post–World War I formation of the *Freikorps* (Free Corps), whose purpose was to liberate Germany of traitors and weaklings. The leader, Gerhard Rossbach, was an open homosexual. A staff member of the group, Lieutenant Edmund Heines, became the lover of Ernst Röhm, the leader of the SA. Also among the ranks was Rudolf Franz Hoess, who became the commander of the death camp Auschwitz. When necessary, the Rossbach Group resorted to murder. According to G. S. Graber, the Rossbach Group consisted of men with no real political ideology who sought out brutality and violence. See G. S. Graber, *The History of the SS* (New York: David McKay Company, Inc., 1978), 30–31. The *Frontbann* (Front Union) was an illegal organization organized after the abolition of the *Sturmabteilung* (SA). It continued to operate after the 1923 Beer-Hall Putsch. See Dr. Louis L. Snyder, *Encyclopedia of the Third Reich*, paperback ed. 1989, Paragon House Publishers (New York: McGraw-Hill, Inc., 1976), 301. The *Stahlhelm* (Steel Helmet) was a Nationalist World War I veterans' organization of the older conservative political faction that opposed the German revolution and called for the restoration of the Hohenzollern monarchy. After Hitler rose to power in 1933, the *Stahlhelm* was absorbed into the SA and SA-reserves. Heinrich Bruening, a captain of a machine-gun company and recipient of the Iron Cross during World War I, was the parliamentary leader of the Catholic Center Party. His political conservatism attracted the Army and distinguished veterans, such as General Kurt von Schleicher. See William L. Shirer, *The Rise and Fall of the Third Reich: A History of Nazi Germany*, reprint (New York: Simon and Schuster Inc., 1960), 137 and 154. See the biography written by Heinz Harmel while in the East as the commander of the 2nd Battalion "Der Führer," dated 7.10.1941, in the personnel dossier of Heinz Harmel, NA/RG242/A3343/SSO-64A; the two-page informational spreadsheet for officers of the *Waffen-SS*; the regimental

commander *SS-Obersturmnbannführer* Otto Kumm's four-page "Kurze Begründung und Stellungsnahme der Zwischenvorgesetzten"; and Krätschmer, *Die Ritterkreuzträger der Waffen-SS*, 427.

77. Krätschmer, *Die Ritterkreuzträger der Waffen-SS*, 428–29.

78. See "Kurze Begründung und Stellungsnahme der Zwischenvorgesetzten," in the personnel dossier of Heinz Harmel, NA/RG242/A3443/SSO-64A, the four-page recommendation by Walter Krüger for the Oak Leaves to the Knight's Cross of the Iron Cross, SS-Pz.Gren.Div. "Das Reich," 20.8.1943.

79. See *SS-Untersturmführer* Hans-Dietrich Sauter, "Die unsichtbare Flagge!" in the Suchdienst Frundsberg e.V. Köln, *Die Hellebarde*, No. 21, 2001, 28. Dr. Willi Dörr remained the battalion troop doctor until the last day of the war. Under machine-gun and antitank fire on the deadly fields at Neupetershain, in the pocket at Spremberg, Dr. Dörr used a pocket knife to amputate the upper arm of the severely wounded regimental artillery adjutant, *SS-Obersturmführer* Erich Hennig. Dörr then carried the unconscious Hennig through enemy lines and delivered him to friendly forces. Hennig survived the war into the year 2000.

80. Tieke, *In the Firestorm of the Last Years of the War*, 66–68. For further reading on the Soviet deception plan see Lieutenant Colonel Richard N. Armstrong, *Soviet Operational Deception: The Red Cloak* (Fort Leavenworth, KS: Combat Studies Institute, 1988). David Glantz erroneously cites the completion of the second phase of the Russian offensive, to clear the Ukraine and Crimea, from early March through mid-May 1944. See Glantz, *When Titans Clash*, 189.

81. 10.SS-Pz.Div. "Frundsberg," Ia, Tgb.Nr.1498/44, Div. Gef.St. 25.6.44, Betr.: Flugabwehr mit Handwaffen auf Eisenbahnzügen, NA//RG242/T354/R150/F3792998.

82. II./SS-Pz.Rgt.10, Abt.Gef.Std, 2 June 1944, "Neuaufstellung des Panzer-Flammzuges," NA/RG242/T354/R150/F3795711; and "Personal Befehel" F3795712-14.

83. KTB, II./SS-Pz.Rgt.10, NA/RG242/T354/R150/F3792259.

84. See Pionier-Kameradschaft Dresden, *10.SS-Panzer-Div. "Frundsberg,"* 18.

85. The letter of recognition by General Model was copied into the daily secret order 240/44, 10.SS-Pz.Div. "Frundsberg," IIa, dated 22.6.44, NA/RG242/T354/R150/F3793005. For train assignments, see KTB, II./SS-Pz. Rgt.10, F3792260.

86. Archer Jones, *The Art of War in the Western World* (Chicago: University of Illinois Press, 1987), 658.

87. Ibid., 542–43.

88. Glantz, *Soviet Military Operational Art*, 140–42.

89. Ibid., 140.

90. Ibid., 146.

91. Ibid, 146–47, 149.

92. Based on a questionnaire regarding the capabilities of German and Russian tanks, Werner Pietzka, 2004.

93. Tieke, *In the Firestorm of the Last Years of the War*, 44–61. The 10th SS Panzer Pioneer participated in the relief effort of Tarnopol. See Hugo Benger's report in Pionier-Kameradschaft Dresden, *10.SS-Panzer-Div. "Frundsberg,"* 17.

94. For a discussion of Soviet and Allied strategies, see both Condoleezza Rice, "The Making of Soviet Strategy," 673, and Maurice Matloff, "Allied Strategy in Europe, 1939–1945," in Philip A. Crowl and Peter Paret, eds., *Makers of Modern Strategy: From Machiavelli to the Nuclear Age* (Princeton: Princeton University Press, 1986), 686–89.

95. Glantz, *When Titans Clash*, 186, 298, and 307. "The Right Bank of Ukraine Offensive" was the first phase of the Soviet offensive to clear the right flank of the Ukraine.

CHAPTER 3

1. Heinz Harmel, *Die 10.SS Panzer-Division "Frundsberg" im Einsatz vom Juni bis November 1944*, Foreign Military Studies, NA/RG549/MPM1035/P-163 (cited hereafter as "P-163"), 2.

2. Harmel, P-163, 1–2; Zetterling, *Normandy 1944*, 15; and Fürbringer, *9.SS-Panzer-Division*, 16 and 259. The 9th SS Panzer Division "Hohenstaufen" received its complement of *Jagdpanzer* IV (Sd.Kfz.162), armed with the 7.5 cm PaK42 (L/70), around 10 June. Three companies formed the battalion; the first two were equipped with 15 *Jadgpanzer*, and the third with 28 towed 7.5 cm PaK. A fourth company formed using captured Soviet T-34 tanks, nicknamed "Moon Light Battalion," which was located exclusively in Rastenburg and operated primarily at night as an alarm unit.

3. KTB, II./10th SS Panzer Regiment, NA/RG242/T354/R150/F3792259-60; Harmel, P-163, 5; Pionier-Kameradschaft Dresden, *10.SS-Panzer-Div. "Frundsberg,"* 18; and Bernhard Westerhoff, *Weg einer Panzer-Kompanie 1943–1945*, 68.

4. See 10.SS-Pz.Div. Frundsberg, Divisions-Befehl Nr.1, Ia/Tgb.Nr. West 1/44, Div.Gef.Std., 16.6.1944, NA/RG242/T354/R150/F3793007-09.

5. Pionier-Kameradschaft Dresden, *10.SS-Panzer-Div. "Frundsberg,"* 18.

6. Westerhoff, *Weg einer Panzer-Kompanie 1943–1945*, 68. On 22 June, *SS-Obersturmführer* Heggemann assumed command of the 6th Company. Quandel reverted back to command the 1st Platoon.

7. See Fürbringer, *9.SS-Panzer-Division*, 17–18 and 271. The subsequent 200-kilometer road march placed tremendous stress on the new vehicles.

8. Captain Helmut Ebersprächer, of the 1st Squadron, 10th Fast Attack Squadron, 51st Combat Squadron, 3rd Group, was located along the Loire in Tours, France. After the new year in 1944, the unit anticipated an Allied landing along the French coast; their daily conversations

revolved around this topic. The *Luftwaffe* neared complete impotency after the Allies bombed almost every airfield in northern France and Belgium. Crews and aircraft were operationally ready, but they could no longer take off. Ebersprächer's unit was one of the few exceptions. Even after the U.S. Army Air Force (USAAF) destroyed the airfield in Tours, a pair of planes were salvaged and operated from a meadow along the banks of the Loire River; despite the fact that the Americans could claim complete air superiority. Missions to southern England were flown only at night and the aircraft were camouflaged in a forest before sunrise to avoid detection by U.S. reconnaissance planes that controlled the skies across the entire northwest of France. For the most part, the Allies could operate freely in the skies and they never faced a threat of substance. While Ebersprächer claims the provisional airfield was known to everyone in France, the French Resistance did not report the German presence to the Allies. Ebersprächer never noticed any activity from the active resistance. Nevertheless, German aircraft took off and landed without interruption until American tanks approached from the south and eventually captured Tours. In the night on 5–6 June 1944, Ebersprächer shot down three Allied four-engine bombers for which he received the German Cross in Gold. Based on correspondence between Ebersprächer and the author dated 2004. Also see Harmel, P-163, 161.

9. The assembly area of the 10th SS Panzer Division, in the Briouze-Falaise-Gace triangle, was not a major center of resistance activity. However, in the northern city of Caen and just southwest thereof were major centers of activity. The partisans that supported the Normandy landings were trained by Allied tripartite Special Operations and Special Operations Executive SO/SOE and Jedburgh Teams. Operation Jedburgh began before the Normandy landings that placed three-man Allied teams behind German lines, consisting of either an American or British officer, a French officer, and an enlisted radio operator. Their objective was to organize, train, and later lead the Maquis into battle. For details on the Jedburgh Teams, see Major General John K. Singlaub, U.S. Army (Ret.), and Malcolm McConnell, *Hazardous Duty: An American Soldier in the Twentieth Century* (New York: Summit Books, 1991), 38.

10. Martin Blumenson, *United States Army in World War II: The European Theater of Operations, Breakout and Pursuit* (Washington, DC: GPO, 1989), 14–15; Carlo D'Este, *Decision in Normandy* (New York: HarperCollins, 1994), 195–99; and Harmel, P-163, 7.

11. The city of Caen is centered 14 km from the English Channel, 51 km southwest of Le Havre, 101 km east-southeast of Cherbourg, 96 km west-southwest of Rouen, and 236 km west-northwest of Paris. Norsemen invaded the northwestern region of France during the ninth and tenth centuries whereby the city became important under the tenet of Norman dukes. Under the rule of William the Conqueror, Caen was the capital of lower Normandy.

During the French and English Hundred Years' War, the English captured the city in 1346 and occupied it from 1417 to 1450. Following the revocation of the Edict of Nantes in 1685, the Protestant city's prosperity eroded with the emigration of its populace. During the French Revolution from 1789 to 1799, Caen was the center for the anti-Revolutionary Girondist movement. See J. H. Robinson, ed., *Readings in European History,* 2 vols. (Boston: Ginn, 1906), 2:287–91; and John A. English, *The Canadian Army and the Normandy Campaign: A Study of Failure in High Command* (New York: Praeger, 1991), 204–6.

12. D'Este, *Decision in Normandy*, 235.

13. Ibid., 239–40.

14. Harmel, P-163, 7; and J. J. How, *Hill 112: Cornerstone of the Normandy Campaign* (Winnipeg: J.J. Fedorowicz Publishing, 2004), 87. It should be noted that Joe How, himself a veteran of the Normandy battles, accurately identifies the addition of ninety Panther tanks to the II SS Panzer Corps. The Panthers belonged to the 9th SS Panzer Division. *SS-Obergruppenführer* Bittrich, the former commander of the 9th SS, gave his former division priority over the 10th SS that followed a natural order of sequence. However, the 10th SS was committed to more complex combat action throughout the life of the corps.

15. On 28 June, 1700 hours, Panzer Group West, commanded by General Geyr von Schweppenburg, which remained temporarily attached to the Seventh Army, assumed command over the I and II SS Panzer Corps as well as the XLVII Panzer Corps. See Harmel, P-163, 7–8. For an excellent German account of Operation Epsom, see Meyer, *Kriegsgeschichte der 12.SS-Panzerdivision "Hitlerjugend,"* vol. I, 178–224.

16. Harmel, P-163, 8.

17. Suchdienst Frundsberg e.V. Hannover, *Die Hellebarde*, No. 5, 56.

18. The exchange of information by neighboring German units and the impact thereof was evident by the report of the British prisoners of war. Later, the 1st General Staff officer for the 10th SS issued directives that made individual soldiers accountable for escaped prisoners. For details on the report, see 10th SS Panzer Division Frundsberg, Ia/Ic, Div.Gef.Std., 6.7.44, Ic-Sonder-Befehl, Betr.: Fluchterleichterung von engl.Kriegsgefangenen, NA/RG242/RG354/R151/F3793241.

19. The commander of the II SS Panzer Corps, *SS-Oberst-gruppenführer* Paul Hausser, assumed command of the Seventh Army after the death of General Dollmann. *SS-Standartenführer* Thomas Müller, the commander of the 20th SS Grenadier Regiment, assumed command of the 9th SS Panzer Division. See Fürbringer, *9.SS-Panzer-Division "Hohenstaufen,"* 278–79; and Harmel, P-163, 8–9.

20. A report by the company commander of the 7th Company, 10th SS Panzer Regiment, *SS-Obersturmführer* Franz Riedel, Suchdienst Frundsberg e.V. Hannover, *Die Helle-barde*, No. 5, 53.

21. In this case, the bulk refers to a *Kampfgruppe* that remained engaged in combat during the rail transportation of the division from the east to the west. The *Kampfgruppe* was slowed during a forced detrainment as early as Saarbrücken and again during the approach-march due to a lack of fuel. See Harmel, P-163, 9; and Meyer, *12.SS-Panzerdivision*, 224.

22. See Harmel, P-163, 9–11; and Pionier-Kameradschaft Dresden, *10.SS-Panzer-Div. "Frundsberg,"* 18. Horst Schneider was killed on 17 July 1944 on Hill 112.

23. No specific information was found regarding the death of the crew of vehicle 634, including Junker Bier, his driver Sturmmann Voith, and one other crewmember. Westerhoff, *Weg einer Panzer-Kompanie 1943–1945*, 77.

24. Harmel, P-163, 9–11; and Meyer, *12.SS-Panzerdivision*, 224.

25. Widmann, *Mit "Totenkof" und "Frundsberg" und Ost- und Westfront: Kriegserlebnisse eines Kradmelders* (Riesa: Nation and Wissen, 2011), 157–59.

26. Fürbringer does not cite the capture of an officer. See Fürbringer, *9.SS-Panzer-Division*, 282; and How, *Hill 112*, 95–97.

27. Fürbringer, *9.SS-Panzer-Division*, 282; Meyer, *12.SS-Panzerdivision*, 225–26; How, *Hill 112*, 97; D'Este, *Decision in Normandy*, 242; and Schramm, KTB, OKW, No. 7, Part I, 322. Contrary to D'Este's evaluation of "beating off the counterattack," it is debatable if the German losses in equipment qualify as "a rout."

28. With regard to the achievements of Menzel, see SS-Pz. Rgt.10, Rgt.Gef.Std., 28.7.1944, NA/RG242/T354/R150; Harmel, P-163, 11–13, and Westerhoff, *Weg einer Panzer-Kompanie, 1943–1945*, 68–70.

29. During the night on 10–11 July, *SS-Hauptsturmführer* Keck was wounded in action during a counterattack against British forces that broke through the German lines on Hill 112. Keck later died of his wounds. On 23 August 1944, Keck was posthumously awarded the Knight's Cross to the Iron Cross (Nr. 3473). See Karl Keck, service record dossier, NA/RG242/A3343/SSO-0159A.

30. For the attack, the 1st Battalion, 22nd *SS-Panzergrenadier* Regiment reported one NCO killed, one NCO and three men wounded. See I./22nd *SS-Panzergrenadier* Regiment, "Gefechtsbericht," Ia, Btl.Gef.Std., 2.7.1944, NA/RG242/T354/R151/F3795422; and Harmel, P-163, 13.

31. A report by Erich Werkmeister, 2./SS-Pi.Btl.10, in the Pionier-Kameradschaft Dresden, *10.SS-Panzer-Div. "Frundsberg,"* 19.

32. Harmel, P-163, 15.

33. 5./22nd *SS-Panzergrenadier* Regiment, "Vorschlagsliste Nr.1 für die Verleihung des E.K.II," 7.7.1944, NA/RG242/T354/R151/F3795528, and II./22nd *SS-Panzergrenadier* Regiment, Ia, "Vorschlagsliste für die Verleihung des Eisernen Kreuzes II. Klasse," Btl.Gef.St., 8.7.1944, F3795525-27.

34. I./22nd *SS-Panzergrenadier* Regiment, "Verluste," Ia, Btl. Gef.Std., 9.7.1944, NA/RG242/T354/R151/F3795127; Pionier-Kameradschaft Dresden, *10.SS-Panzer-Div. "Frundsberg,"* 18; and Harmel, P-163, 15. During the first few days of July, the command post of the pioneer battalion was located in Avenay. See How, *Hill 112*, 97, for the report by Bittrich to Hausser.

35. See D'Este, *Decision in Normandy*, 242–44.

36. Suchdienst Frundsberg e.V. Hannover, *Die Hellebarde*, No. 5, 54. Dr. Moeferdt began his westward journey from east Poland on 8 June 1944, and traveled by rail from Lemberg to Nonancourt near Versailles. After offloading on 18 June, his march continued on 27 June onto Evrecy where Moeferdt arrived on 29 July and established the first field hospital. The next day, the battalion relocated to Esquay.

37. I./22nd *SS-Panzergrenadier* Regiment, "Gefechtsbericht," Ia, Btl.Gef.Std., 2.7.1944, NA/RG242/T354/R151/F3795422-23; and I./22nd *SS-Panzergrenadier* Regiment, "Verluste," Ia, Btl.Gef.Std., 9.7.1944, F3795127.

38. This assault tactic became characteristic of the fighting for Hill 112. Harmel, P-163, 15–16. For the achievements of Bindl, see II./22nd *SS-Panzergrenadier* Regiment, Ia., "Vorschlagsliste für die Verleihung des Eiserne Kreuzes II. Klasse," Btl.Gef.St., 8.7.1944, NA/RG242/T354/R151/F3795525-28.

39. Harmel, P-163, Appendix 1, item 5, 2; and I./22nd *SS-Panzergrenadier* Regiment, "Verluste," Ia, Btl.Gef.Std., 9.7.1944, NA/RG242/T354/R151/F3795127.

40. Suchdienst Frundsberg e.V. Hannover, *Die Hellebarde*, No. 5, 57.

41. According to the commander of the 10th SS Panzer Division, the change of command resulted in the disruption of ammunition and fuel re-supply for the troops. See Harmel, P-163, 16, and Schramm, KTB, OKW, No. 7, 1944–1945, Part I, 324.

42. Harmel, P-163, 16; and I./22nd *SS-Panzergrenadier* Regiment, "Verluste," Ia, Btl.Gef.Std., 9.7.1944, NA/RG242/T354/R151/F3795127.

43. Details of the battle are in the report prepared by *SS-Brigadeführer* Sylvester Stadler, the commander of the 9th SS Panzer Division, on 30 March 1947; the combat experience of the 9th SS Panzer Division equalled that of the 10th SS Panzer Division An excellent source for detailed information about the 9th SS is the seminal work by Fürbringer, *9.SS-Panzer-Division "Hohenstaufen" 1944*. See also Harmel, P-163, 17–18.

44. In 1943, a so-called Tiger organization and working-staff was established that complemented the 500th Panzer Replacement and Training Detachment at Paderborn. The staff was responsible for organizing or replenishing Tiger battalions that were withdrawn from action. At the onset, Major Otto led the staff at the training barracks at Mailly-le-Camp, France. Major Jürgens assumed command when the staff transferred to the Training Barracks Wezep, Zwolle. The accommodations at Wezep had to be abandoned as a result of enemy activity, and Major Jürgens and his staff were transferred to the Training Barracks Ohrdruf, Thüringen. For more information on Tiger tank battalions, see Kleine and Kühn, *Tiger*, 196–98.

45. Harmel, P-163, 18–19; and I./22nd *SS-Panzergrenadier* Regiment, "Verluste," Ia, Btl.Gef.Std., 9.7.1944, NA/RG242/T354/R151/F3795127.

46. Blumenson, *Breakout and Pursuit*, 120; and D'Este, *Decision in Normandy*, 305 and 325. The American First Army outnumbered the Germans three to two in infantry and eight to one in tanks.

47. See the intelligence special order, SS-Pz.Div.10 "Frundsberg," Abt.IC, Div.Gef.Std., 4.7.44, Betr.: Haltung von Angehörigen der Division gegenüber Kriegsgefangenen, NA/RG242/T354/R151/F3793243.

48. To complete the task, personnel from supply and rear-echelon units able to fight were reassigned to combat units.

49. According to Stadler, the 9th SS Panzer Division assumed control of the sector Hill 112-Odon River on 8 July. This was not the case as Hill 112 remained under the exclusive control of the 10th SS Panzer Division. The 9th SS did occupy Hill 113 north of Evrecy; the western spur of the mountain represented the dividing boundary between the two divisions. See Stadler, *Die 9.SS-Pz.Div.*, MS # B-740, 5.

50. Blumenson, *Breakout and Pursuit*, 120–22; and D'Este, *Decision in Normandy*, 331–32.

51. D'Este, *Decision in Normandy*, 318; I./22nd *SS-Panzergrenadier* Regiment, "Verluste," Ia, Btl.Gef.Std., 9.7.1944, NA/RG242/T354/R151/F3795127; and Wesley Frank Craven, James Lea Cate, eds, and the USAF Historical Division, *The Army Air Forces in World War II. Volume Three Europe: Argument to V-E Day January 1944 to May 1945* (Chicago: University of Chicago Press, 1951), 208. Outside a few operations, heavy Allied bombing in support of ground operations remained unproven. In the case of Caen, aerial fratricide was a major concern. The rubble and cratering caused by the bombing hampered the movement of Allied tanks and slowed the general advance.

52. Gerhard, *My Life in the Middle of the 20th Century*, 57.

53. KTB, 5./II./10th SS Panzer Regiment, dated 25 July 44, regarding special achievements of personnel, and 5./II., regarding the tally of destroyed Allied tanks by 5./10th SS Panzer Regiment, dated 25 July 44, NA/RG242/T354/R152. On 10 July 44, the 5./II./10th SS Panzer Regiment accounted for the destruction of eleven Sherman tanks and three antitank guns. The number of men killed in action was found in a company letter dated 23 July 1944, NA/RG242/T354/R152.

54. Harmel reported each prong of the Allied attack consisted of fifty to sixty tanks. The special ammunition had a more limited "killing zone" with a greater effect on troop morale. The attacker could pass near the point of impact without fear of injury. Harmel, P-163, 19–21.

55. Harmel, P-163, 23; and Westerhoff, *Weg einer Panzer-Kompanie, 1943–1945*, 70.

56. *SS-Hauptsturmführer* Handrick was killed in action on 12 July 1944. 10th SS Panzer Regiment, Rgt.Gef.Std., 28.7.1944, NA/RG242/T354/R150.

57. During the advance of the 1st Platoon on the right, vehicle 221, commanded by *SS-Hauptsturmführer* Endemann, moved forward through the depression and remained missing thereafter. See Kleine and Kühn, *Tiger*, 196–97. Also see the narrative by Will Fey, based on the war diary accounts of Ernst Streng and Heinz Trautmann in Will Fey, *Panzer im Brennpunkt der Fronten* (Munich: J. F. Lehmanns Verlag, 1960), 73.

58. After approximately eight days, Dr. Horst Moeferdt and his two assistants were shipped to Hampton, Great Britain, where they were separated. In April 1948, Moeferdt was released. For more information concerning his captivity, see Suchdienst Frundsberg e.V. Hannover, *Die Hellebarde*, No. 5, 54–55.

59. See 5./10th SS Panzer Regiment, Betr. Abschußergebnisse der Kompanie, 25.7.1944, NA/RG242/T354/R152; and Westerhoff, *Weg einer Panzer-Kompanie 1943–1945*, 84.

60. Kleine and Kühn, *Tiger*, 196–97; Fey, *Panzer im Brennpunkt der Fronten*, 74–75; and Harmel, P-163, 24.

61. CO ltr, 5./II., destroyed Allied tanks by 5./10th SS Panzer Regiment, dtd 25 Jul 44, NA/RG242/T354/R152; and 10th SS Panzer Regiment, Rgt.Gef.Std., 28.7.1944, NA/RG242/T354/R150.

62. Harmel, P-163, 23.

63. Neither the Germans nor the Allies recaptured the castle, as it became a forward-lying bastion. However, both sides utilized reconnaissance troops to watch over it. Harmel, P-163, 24. For information concerning the pioneer battalion, consulted the report by Hugo Benger, Helmut Vogelmann, 16./21st *SS-Panzergrenadier* Regiment, and Georg Scheffel, 16./22nd *SS-Panzergrenadier* Regiment, in Pionier-Kameradschaft Dresden, *10.SS-Panzer-Div. "Frundsberg,"* 18.

64. D'Este, *Decision in Normandy*, 342–43; and Craven and Cate, *The Army Air Forces in World War II*, 208.

65. The boundary between both corps: Mutrécy (I.)-Vieux (II.)-Verson (II.). See Harmel, P-163, 24–25.

66. Ibid., Appendix A, number 7, 2.

67. Harmel, P-163, 25; and Westerhoff, *Weg einer Panzer-Kompanie 1943–1945*, 70.

68. Harmel, P-163, 26.

69. The account is based on official award documentation for the Knight's Cross to the Iron Cross, provided by Paul Egger to the author in written correspondence dated 15 July 2001. Egger was also decorated with the German Cross in Gold. Trained as a *Luftwaffe* pilot, Egger flew one hundred missions until he was shot down over the English Channel. Due to severe head wounds, he could not continue to fly.

70. Harmel, P-163, Appendix A, number 8, 3; and SS-Kriegsberichter-Zuges, *Dran Drauf Durch!*, 47.

71. The remaining elements of the reconnaissance battalion returned on 14 July from their assignment as the reserves for the Army Group, east of the Orne River. The 2nd Battalion, 272nd Infantry Division, arrived for action and moved into the line west of Maltot on the night of 16 July. Harmel, P-163, 26.

72. See SS-Pz.Rgt.10, Rgt.Gef.Std., 28.7.1944, NA/RG242/ T354/R150; and Westerhoff, *Weg einer Panzer-Kompanie 1943–1945*, 70.

73. Westerhoff, *Weg einer Panzer-Kompanie 1943–1945*, 72–73.

74. See Hans Reiter personnel dossier, NA/RG242/A3343/ SSO-0022B.

75. See Harmel, P-163, 26–28; and Fürbringer, *9.SS-Panzer-Division "Hohenstaufen,"* 326–31; and Karl Cerff, *Die Waffen-SS im Wehrmachtbericht*, 69.

76. Craven and Cate, *The Army Air Forces in World War II*, 208; and Harmel, P-163, 28–29.

77. Harmel, P-163, 29.

78. D'Este, *Decision in Normandy*, 287. Over 200 Allied tanks were lost.

79. Harmel, P-163, 31.

80. Harmel, P-163, 31; and Appendix A, number 9, 3.

81. Pionier-Kameradschaft Dresden, *10.SS-Panzer-Div. "Frundsberg,"* 23–24.

82. Pionier-Kameradschaft Dresden, *10.SS-Panzer-Div. "Frundsberg,"* 19. For more information concerning the failed attempt to assassinate Hitler on 20 July 1944, see Philipp Freiherr von Boeselager, "Der Widerstand in der Heeresgruppe Mitte," No. 40, *Beiträge zum Widerstand 1933–1945, Gedenkstätte Deutscher Widerstand Berlin*. Felgentreff & Goebel GmbH (Berlin: 1990). Baron Philipp Freiherr von Boeselager belonged to the small group of individuals involved in the failed coup against Hitler on 20 July 1944. As a major, von Boeselager commanded the 1st Battalion, 31st Cavalry Regiment, 3rd Cavalry Brigade. Under the command of his brother, Colonel Georg Baron von Boeselager, commander of the 3rd Cavalry Brigade, Philipp was directed to assemble 1,200 men (six squadrons), and move them to the airfield in German-occupied Poland. They were to arrive at the Tempelhof airfield in Berlin once Hitler was assassinated to help with the insurrection. As planned, Major Boeselager moved his troops on 15 July to Brest where they arrived in the afternoon of 20 July. Ready to be transported to the airfield in trucks, they never received the call. After the uprising failed, they returned to the front.

83. Consulted Westerhoff, *Weg einer Panzer-Kompanie 1943–1945*, 70.

84. Details concerning Karl Bastian were obtained from NA/ RG242/A3343/SSO-0038.

85. Westerhoff, *Weg einer Panzer-Kompanie 1943–1945*, 84.

86. Harmel, P-163, 32.

87. Harmel, P-163, Appendix A, number 10, 3–4; and 10.SS-Pz.Div, "Abschrift PS Kommandierender General II.SS-Pz.Korps vom 22.7.1944," IIa, Div.Gef.Std, 25.7.1944, NA/RG242/T354/R150/F3795133.

88. Harmel, P-163, Appendix A, number 11, 4.

89. Westerhoff, *Weg einer Panzer-Kompanie 1943–1945*, 73.

90. Harmel, P-163, 32–33.

91. See the KTB 1944, *SS-Werfer-Abteilung 102, Kriegstagebuch Nr. 2*, from hereon in referred to as KTB SS-Werfer.Abt.102, 59–60. For information concerning the theoretical table of organization, consult the U.S. War Department, *Handbook on German Military Forces* (Baton Rouge: Louisiana State University Press, 1990), 158–59. Artillery Kommandeur or ARKO was the abbreviation for the name given to a defined group of artillery officers of the rank of colonel and above. Consulted the interrogation of Karl Tholohe, "A German Reflects Upon Artillery," *The Field Artillery Journal* (December 1945), 710–11.

92. Harmel, P-163, 33. The west wing of Panzer Group West was formed by the LXXXIV Army Corps that shortly before had assumed command from the XLVII Panzer Corps. Throughout several days, Panzer Group West was redesignated as Fifth Panzer Army.

93. Ibid., 35.

94. KTB, SS-Werfer.Abt.102, 60. The left neighbor of the SS projector battalion received an additional training projector battalion from the 1st Army Projector Training Regiment. Around 1930 hours, orders arrived to relocate, along with the 8th Projector Brigade, as part of the II SS Panzer Corps, in opposition to an Allied breakthrough along the left sector.

95. Otto Paetsch married Ruth Scharfe on 29 December 1934, and fathered one daughter and three sons. Despite his family, on 4 June 1940, Paetsch wrote an emotional letter to his commanding officer, requesting transfer to a combat unit. Paetsch felt unlucky not to be honored with the opportunity to fight at the front. See Otto Paetsch, service record dossier, NA/RG242/A3343/SSO-363A; and Westerhoff, *Weg einer Panzer-Kompanie*, 73–74.

96. For information related to the rocket battalion, see KTB, SS-Werfer.Abt.102, 60. For information concerning the *Kampfgruppe*, see Otto Paetsch, service record dossier, NA/RG242/A3343/SSO-363A. The command post was first located in La Chevalerie, 800 km south of St. Jean, and later 1.5 km north of La Huan.

97. The approach of the division was presumably delayed as a result of difficulties experienced during the relief of the division within the sector along the front. Moreover, larger movements were restricted by Allied aircraft and could only take place under the cover of darkness. See Harmel, P-163, 36–40.

98. The 22nd *SS-Panzergrenadier* Regiment, constituting strength of merely a battalion, appeared to have been the divisional reserve southwest of Aunay; it is not known if the battalion was engaged during the course of the day.

99. The Knight's Cross of the Iron Cross award citation for Paetsch varies significantly from the report by Harmel. The citation indicates that the *Kampfgruppe* was comprised of the 10th SS Panzer Regiment, elements of the 1st Battalion, 21st *SS-Panzergrenadier* Regiment, 1st Battalion, 10th SS Panzer Artillery Regiment, and 1st Company, 10th SS Panzer Pioneer Battalion. The citation suggests that the *Kampfgruppe* was responsible for recapturing Hill 188, whereas Harmel suggests it was the reinforced 21st *SS-Panzergrenadier* Regiment. Otto Paetsch, service

record dossier, 10.SS-Pz.Div. "Frundsberg," Div.Gef.St., 5.8.1944, "Vorschlag der Verleihung des Ritterkreuzes des Eisernen Kreuzes," NA/RG242/A3343/SSO-363A.

100. Erich Rech, service record dossier, 10.SS-Pz.Div. "Frundsberg," Div.Gef.St., 23.8.1944, "Vorschlag der Verleihung des Ritterkreuzes des Eisernen Kreuzes." The actions of Rech were incorrectly cited at a later date, around 31 August, in Tieke's book, *In the Firestorm of the Last Years of the War*, 213–14.

101. The personnel dossier of Gerhard Hinze, SS-Pz.Aufkl. Abt.10, Abt.Gef.St., 5 August 1944, "Vorschlag für die Verleihung des Deutschen Kreuz in Gold," NA/RG242/A3343/SSO-100A/F189-195.

102. Documents concerning the strength and organization of the Divisional Reserve do not exist. Harmel, P-163, 40–42.

103. The new boundary between the Fifth Panzer Army and Seventh Army ran along the line Flers-Presles. Both villages were occupied by the Seventh Army. During this period, the 6th Company, 10th SS Panzer Regiment, was forced to blow up one tank with plate mines. See both Westerhoff, *Weg einer Panzer-Kompanie 1943–1945*, 74; and Harmel, P-163, 43–47.

104. Harmel, P-163, 45–47.

105. The 1st Battalion was to be returned to the regiment. Ibid., 47–48.

106. Ibid., 48.

107. Ibid., 48–49.

108. Ibid., 49–50. The numbers for the combat strength of the 21st *SS-Panzergrenadier* Regiment and the 10th SS Panzer Pioneer Battalion do not include staff and supply units, but the staff and supply units are included for the 10th SS Panzer Reconnaissance Battalion. The fact that the Allies blew up the Ergenne Bridge at Verdrie did not support such intentions.

109. Ibid., 50–51.

110. According to the KTB, OB West, the intent was to attach the 10th SS Panzer Division to Panzer Group Eberbach that was being formed at the Foret d'Ecouves (forest) for a tactical mobile role in the southern flank of the Seventh Army. Ibid., 51–53.

111. Ibid., 53–54.

112. Suchdienst Frundsberg e.V. Hannover, *Die Hellebarde*, No. 5, 63.

113. Harmel, P-163, 53–54; and Suchdienst Frundsberg, *Die Hellebarde*, No. 5, 63.

114. A report by Hugo Benger, in the Pionier-Kameradschaft Dresden, *10.SS-Panzer-Div. "Frundsberg,"* 20.

115. Harmel, P-163, 54–56.

116. Ibid.

117. Suchdienst Frundsberg e.V. Hannover, *Die Hellebarde*, No. 5, 63.

118. Harmel, P-163, 56. The devastating effects in the pocket battle of Falaise-Argentan are covered in detail in the report by Rudolf-Christoph Freiherr von Gersdorff, *The Campaign in Northern France, Vol. VI: Falais–Argentan Pocket 12–21 August*, Foreign Military Studies, MS # B-727, 1946.

119. No other official records or documents outside the memory of the commanding officer are available; see Harmel, P-163, 56.

120. See the after-action report prepared by Otto Paetsch for the award of the Knight's Cross to the Iron Cross with Swords for Heinz Harmel. SS-Panzer-Regiment 10, Ia, Rgt.Gef.St., 24.10.1944, "Gefechtsbericht für den 20. u. 21. August 1944," NA/RG242/A3343/SSO-363A; and Westerhoff, *Weg einer Panzer-Kompanie 1943–1945*, 74.

121. SS-Panzer-Regiment 10, Ia, Rgt.Gef.St., 24.10.1944, "Gefechtsbericht für den 20. u. 21. August 1944," NA/RG242/A3343/SSO-363A, 1–5.

122. SS-Panzer-Regiment 10, Ia, Rgt.Gef.St., 24.10.1944, "Gefechtsbericht für den 20. u. 21. August 1944," NA/RG242/A3343/SSO-363A, 1–5; and Suchdienst Frundsberg e.V. Hannover, *Die Hellebarde*, No. 5, 64–65.

123. Suchdienst Frundsberg e.V. Hannover, *Die Hellebarde*, No. 5, 69.

124. Ibid., 67.

125. Suchdienst Frundsberg e.V. Hannover, *Die Hellebarde*, No. 5, 67; and Abt.Gef.St., 2 September 1944, SS-Pz.Aufkl.Abt.10, "Vorschlag für die Verleihung des Deutschen Kreuzes in Gold," Rudolf Harmstorf, NA/RG242/A3343/SSO-064A/F1259-1260.

126. Suchdienst Frundsberg e.V. Hannover, *Die Hellebarde*, No. 5, 69–70.

127. SS-Panzer-Regiment 10, Ia, Rgt.Gef.St., 24.10.1944, "Gefechtsbericht für den 20. u. 21. August 1944," NA/RG242/A3343/SSO-363A, 1–5.

128. SS-Panzer-Regiment 10, Ia, Rgt.Gef.St., 24.10.1944, "Gefechtsbericht für den 20. u. 21. August 1944," NA/RG242/A3343/SSO-363A, 1–5; 10th SS Panzer Regiment, Kommandeur, Regt.St.Qu. 11 November 1944, 1–2, Heinz Harmel, personnel dossier, NA/RG242/A3343/SSO-066A; and the personal letter from Otto Paetsch to *SS-Obersturmbannführer* Werner Kment, NA/RG242/A3343/SSO-363A, presumably a member in Himmler's adjutants office in Berlin. General Lüttwitz was awarded Oak Leaves to the Knight's Cross of the Iron Cross, which he received several days later. Paetsch's letter to Kment pointed out that Harmel had not received his award as late as 11 November, and asked that he personally look into the matter. Also consulted was Krätschmer, *Die Ritterkreuzträger der Waffen-SS*, 190–94. Theodor Wisch was severely wounded on both legs. On 28 August, Wisch received Oak Leaves to the Knight's Cross of the Iron Cross, as the 94th recipient. Despite the reported strength of the 1st SS Panzer Division of 19,691 on 20 June 1944, the actual number of combat-effective troops was far less. Only the 1st Panzer Regiment, led by *SS-Obersturmbannführer* Joachim Peiper, had its full complement of tanks and equipment. Over the first few days of fighting at Normandy, Peiper's regiment accounted for over one hundred destroyed Allied tanks.

129. On Wednesday, 22 August, the Allies delivered Reimers to a prisoner collection point. For Reimers, the war ended as he entered captivity and traveled to Great Britain, the United States, and eventually back to France. On 10 August 1948, almost four years later, he was released from captivity and returned home. Suchdienst Frundsberg e.V. Hannover, *Die Hellebarde*, No. 5, 68.

130. Ibid., 65–66.

131. Ibid., 71–72.

132. Harmel, P-163, 59; and Westerhoff, *Weg einer Panzer-Kompanie 1943–1945*, 75.

133. Blumenson, *Breakout and Pursuit*, 576–77.

134. Westerhoff claims the 6th Company lost all of their tanks. See Westerhoff, *Weg einer Panzer-Kompanie 1943–1945*, 85.

CHAPTER 4

1. Russell F. Weigley, *Eisenhower's Lieutenants: The Campaign of France and Germany, 1944–45* (Bloomington: Indiana University Press, 1981), 213–15.

2. Gersdorff, *Falaise-Argentan*, 62; and Weigley, *Eisenhower's Lieutenants*, 215.

3. Schramm, *KTB OKW*, 357. The diary goes on to say it was the second American opportunity squandered when the Allies were unable to cut off an entire army. German optimism that followed the loss of great quantities of materiel and manpower gives more credence to the theory that many in the German leadership at every level suffered from severe denial and would not accept defeat.

4. Harmel, P-163, 61–63.

5. Ibid., 63.

6. The General Staff of the I SS Panzer Army Corps was relieved by the II SS Panzer Corps and received orders to form a task force south of Dreux in order to provide security along the southern flank of the Fifth Panzer Army and the Seventh Army. Ibid., 63–65.

7. The message of 24 August 1944, in the KTB, OB West, "Extraction of the 10.SS-Pz.Div. underway (angelaufen)," refers to the crossing of the 10th SS Panzer Reconnaissance Battalion. Harmel, P-163, 66–68.

8. Bericht von *SS-Obersturmfuehrer* Gottlob Ellwanger, 4.Bttr. (3,7cm), SS-Flak-Abt.10, Suchdienst Frundsberg, e.V. Köln, *Die Hellebarde*, No. 18, 1996, 45.

9. The 13th Company, 21st *SS-Panzergrenadier* Regiment, crossed the Seine River 4 km north of Elbeuf at Gd.Couronne. See Harmel, P-163, 66–68.

10. Harmel, P-163, 68–69.

11. Ibid., 69–70. Other units included the 13th Company of the 21st *SS-Panzergrenadier* Regiment, which crossed 4 km north of Elbeuf at Gd. Couronne.

12. The following extract was taken from the staff directive "Klosterkemper," dated 31 August 1944. The staff was responsible for administrating movements behind the front.

I. List of Reception Centers (Meldekopfliste):
After 1 September, the following reception centers shall be organized:
Bapaume, Arras, Cambrai, Farmers (2 km south of Valenciennes), Cinly (2 km south of Mons), Mignault, Genappe, Givet.

II. New areas west of the Maas River are assigned to supply and logistics troops for the following divisions:
10.SS-Pz.Div.: area 30 km south of Brussels, Reception Center Chastre (12 km south of Wavre).
Combat capable units are not authorized to march to the specified locations, but rather bound to the orders of their commanding officer or the division.

13. Harmel, P-163, 70.

14. Harmel, P-163, 70; and "Bericht Ewald Klapdor SS-Hstuf/01 Div.Stab. 10.SS-Pz.Div.Frundsberg," Suchdienst Frundsberg e.V. Köln, *Die Hellebarde*, No. 18, 1996, 17.

15. Harmel, P-163, 70–72.

16. According to the KTB, OB West, dated 1 September 1944, the 10th SS Panzer Division attached to the LXXXVI Army Corps on 31 August. Heinz Harmel did not report this development; presumably he never received the order. Harmel, P-163, 72–75; and *SS-Untersturmführer* Hans-Dietrich Sauter, "Erbeutete Geschuetze," in the Suchdienst Frundsberg e.V. Köln, *Die Hellebarde*, No. 21, 2001, 38–39.

17. Bericht Friedrich Richter, *SS-Hauptsturmfuhrer*, SS-Pz. Gren.Rgt.22/"KG-Richter," Suchdienst Frundsberg e.V. Köln, *Die Hellebarde*, No. 18, 1996, 50.

18. Johannes Juhl, *Als Pionier an der Westfront 1944/1945: Mein Kriegseinsatz als junger Soldat. Johannes Juhl, Jahrgang 1926*, unpublished manuscript, 243–44. Juhl's memoirs are an outstanding survey of German combat pioneer practices in combat during the Battle of the Bulge. However, his opinions are from the perspective of an enscripted and often bitter *Volksgrenadier* who fought against his will. Moreover, Juhl ran into the Field Police on several occasions. According to Juhl, forming such expedient combat task forces was ineffective, considering that no one knew each other and no one knew if they could depend on the other person in combat. This measure for establishing new combat formations, according to Juhl, did not prove effective. The weapons available and experience of the men was not sufficient to offer the enemy a worthwhile opposition. The men either immediately entered captivity or they abandoned their posts in order to again set forth their escape. Juhl believed that according to the strategists or leadership, the soldier was merely cannon fodder.

19. Bericht Friedrich Richter, *SS-Hauptsturmfuhrer*, SS-Pz. Gren.Rgt.22/"KG-Richter," Suchdienst Frundsberg, *Die Hellebarde*, No. 18, 1996, 50.

20. Bericht Ewald Klapdor, SS-Hstuf/01 Div.Stab.10.SS-Pz. Div.Frundsberg, Suchdienst Frundsberg e.V. Köln, *Die Hellebarde*, No. 18, 1996, 28.

21. Personnel dossier Rudolf Dannetschek, NA/RG242/ A3343/SSO-136/F121-122.

22. Bericht Gerhardt Franzky, *SS-Rottenfuehrer*, Funktrupp, Rgt.Stab SS-Pz.Gren.Rgt.22, Suchdienst Frundsberg e.V. Köln, *Die Hellebarde*, No. 18, 1996, 24.

23. Ibid.

24. Franzky, in Frundsberg e.V. Köln, *Die Hellebarde*, No. 18, 1996, 25. Franzky's luck ran out on 4 September when the Free French captured the men. Held in a barn, other wounded members of the regiment explained that the regimental commander Schultze, nicknamed "the old Prussian," elected "free death" on 1 or 2 September. Franzky never saw the old Prussian again.

25. Bericht Erwin Markowski, *SS-Rottenfuehrer*, 3.Kp./I. (SPW-Btl.) 21st *SS-Panzergrenadier* Regiment, Suchdienst Frundsberg e.V. Köln, *Die Hellebarde*, No. 18, 1996, 26.

26. Ibid., 27.

27. Blumenson, *Breakout and Pursuit*, 682–84. The official U.S. Army history confirms the breakout of the LVIII Panzer and II SS Panzer Corps as the only headquarters units actively willing to fight. See also Wilhelm Bittrich: "Ausbruch aus dem Kessel von Mons 2-3.9.1944," in the Suchdienst Frundsberg e.V. Köln, *Die Hellebarde*, No. 18, 1996, 21.

28. See report by Walter Harzer, *9th Panzer Division (SS) "Hohenstaufen," July 25–November 1944, on the Western Front*, Foreign Military Studies, MS # P-162, 1954; and Harmel, P-163, 76.

29. Montgomery considered the Americans to be equals with the Italians, and continuously expected to command all ground forces in Europe. He insisted on a single-thrust strategy directed in the north through the Ruhr and onto Berlin. Eisenhower was more than tolerant of Montgomery and did, in fact, give priority to the attack in the north. See Schramm, *Kriegstagebuch OKW 1944–1945*, Vol. I, 364; Thomas E. Griess, ed., *The Great War* (Wayne, NJ: Avery Publishing Group Inc., 1986), 174–75; Blumenson, *Breakout and Pursuit*, 686; and Weigley, *Eisenhower's Lieutenants*, 9 and 348–50.

30. The order was to be communicated, in part, by radio and the ordnance officers. Harmel, P-163, 75.

31. *SS-Hauptsturmführer* Karl Godau, "Erbeutete Geschuetze" (aber aus Wehrmachtseigenen Beständen), in the Suchdienst Frundsberg e.V. Köln, *Die Hellebarde*, No. 21, 2001, 39–41.

32. *SS-Untersturmführer* Hans-Dietrich Sauter, "Erbeutete Geschuetze," in the Suchdienst Frundsberg e.V. Köln, *Die Hellebarde*, No. 21, 2001, 38–39.

33. Harmel, P-163, 78.

34. Consulted the report by Harzer, *9th Panzer Division (SS) "Hohenstaufen," July 25–November 1944*; and Harmel, P-163, 76.

35. Harmel, P-163, 78.

36. During the night of the breakout, the command post of the II SS Panzer Corps was located in Manage, approximately 20 km east-northeast of Mons. The commanding general of the LXXXI Army Corps and his aide met the staff of the II SS Panzer Corps in Manage. During the breakout, the chief of the General Staff, II SS Panzer Corps, *SS-Sturmbannführer* Pipkorn, was wounded. See Bittrich, "Ausbruch aus dem Kessel von Mons 2-3.9.1944," in the Suchdienst Frundsberg e.V. Köln,, *Die Hellebarde*, No. 18, 1996, 22.

37. Harmel, P-163, 78.

CHAPTER 5

1. Harmel, P-163, 79. At the end of August, a general directive to consolidate all combat elements stripped units of all unnecessary troops. The report by Bittrich, "The II.SS-Pz.A.K. in September until November 1944," makes reference to this measure on page 1.

2. Report by *SS-Obersturmführer* Gottlob Ellwanger, 4.Bttr. (3.7cm) SS-Flak-Abt.10, in the Suchdienst Frundsberg e.V. Köln, *Die Hellebarde*, No. 18, 1996, 45.

3. On 12 October 1944, Ellwanger sent a letter to the parents of Alfred Wolter, informing them of their missing son. Ellwanger explained that Alfred went missing but was presumed captured or in a field hospital. Ibid., 46–47.

4. Harmel, P-163, 79–81. Harmel does not clarify if the organization of the 10th SS included the material from the 9th SS, which included a single panzer grenadier and artillery battalion. See Tieke, *In the Firestorm of the Last Years of the War*, 222–23.

5. The First Parachute Army was organized as a training staff in March 1944 from the General Staff of the Eleventh Flyers' Corps. On 4 September 1944, under the command of *Generaloberst* Karl Student, the staff was employed under *Herresgruppe* B at Oberrhein as the Command General of the Army. The table of organization consisted of corps troops, consisting of Higher Artillery, a signal regiment, and supply troops. Subordinated units included on 16 September 1944, the LXXXVI Army Corps, II Parachute Army Corps, II SS Corps, XII SS Corps, and the 526th Infantry Division. For more information see *Lexikon der Wehrmacht*, www.lexikon-der-wehrmacht.de/ Gliederungen/ArmeenLW/1FallArmee.htm.

6. Harmel, P-163, 81.

7. After eleven days and no sign of Edmund Zalewski, his company commander reported him missing on 20 September 1944. Suchdienst Frundsberg e.V. Köln, *Die Hellebarde*, No. 5, 78–81. As part of the 275th Infantry Division, the 275th Füsilier Battalion organized on 11 January 1944 in western France after the renaming of the Reserve Grenadier Battalion 190. See *Lexikon der Wehrmacht*, http://www.lexikon-der-wehrmacht.de/Gliederungen/ Infanteriedivisionen/275ID.htm.

8. Bericht Matthias Hutwagner, *SS-Sturmmann*, 4.Battr. (3.7 cm), 10th SS Antiaircraft Battalion, in the Suchdienst Frundsberg e.V. Köln, *Die Hellebarde*, No. 18, 1996, 48.

9. Chamberlain and Doyle, *Encyclopedia of German Tanks of World War Two*, 183–84; F.M. von Senger u. Etterlin, *Die Deutschen Geschütze 1939–1945*, (München: J. F. Lehmanns Verlag, 1961), 210.

10. Hutwagner, Suchdienst Frundsberg e.V. Köln, *Die Hellebarde*, No. 18, 1996, 48.

11. Ibid., 49.

12. Karl Godau, "Bearbeitung von Karl Godau über Sperrverband Heinke und seine artilleristische Ausstattung, vom 25.09.1982," Suchdienst Frundsberg e.V. Köln, *Die Hellebarde*, No. 21, 2001, 44–45.

13. Generalfeldmarschall Gerd v. Rundsedt, "Lagebeurteilung des OB West vom 7.9.1944, 18.00, Ia. Nr. 805/44, geh.Kdos.Ch., Suchdienst Frundsberg e.V. Köln, *Die Hellebarde*, No. 18, 1996, 33.

14. Ibid., 34.

15. Harmel, P-163, 82, and Appendix C, number 1 and 2.

16. Bericht Friedrich Richter, *SS-Hauptsturmfuhrer*, SS-Pz. Gren.Rgt.22/"KG-Richter," Suchdienst Frundsberg e.V. Köln, *Die Hellebarde*, No. 18, 1996, 51.

17. Daily order prepared by the divisional 1st General Staff officer, *SS-Sturmbannführer* Buethe, Ia/Tgb.Nr.:II/22/44 geh., Div.Gef.St., 8.9.1944, Suchdienst Frundsberg e.V. Köln, *Die Hellebarde*, No. 18, 1996, 39.

18. Westerhoff, *Weg einer Panzer Kompanie*, 85.

19. The pejorative term "Golden Pheasants" referred to Nazi Party political leaders who wore golden-brown uniforms. However, this term may not be appropriate for Dutch Front Workers who generally wore black uniforms. Dutch Front Workers were members of the Nationaal-Socialistische Beweging in Nederland (NSB) or National Socialist Movement in the Netherlands, a Dutch fascist and later national socialist political party. J. A. Tesebelt, a member of the NSB and Dutch collaborator, was the mayor of Zupften in September 1944. During the night of 8 September between Arnhem and Oosterbeek, German soldiers with armored cars who were separated from their units received lodging at a home for retired Catholic priests. The Germans left the next day and gave the hosts bottles of wine for their hospitality. See Martin Middlebrook, *Arnhem 1944: The Airborne Battle* (Boulder, CO: Westview Press, 1994), 53 and 91.

20. Westerhoff, *Weg einer Panzer Kompanie*, 85–86.

21. Ibid., 86–87.

22. Fürbringer, *9.SS-Panzer Division Hohenstaufen*, 417. Fürbringer maintains the 9th SS provided an entire battalion of artillery, to include two 105mm batteries and one heavy 100mm battery. Erroneously, Fürbringer reported the 10th SS received on 10 September their entire 1st Battalion allotment of Panthers and 27 *Jagdpanthers* for the 10th SS Tank Destroyer Battalion in Arnhem. According to Walter Harzer, of the 9th SS, only a single battery from the artillery regiment was transferred to the 10th SS. See Harzer, *9th Panzer Division (SS) "Hohenstaufen."* At this

juncture, Tieke maintains the organization of the 10th SS included the material from the 9th SS. See Tieke, *In the Firestorm of the Last Years of the War*, 222–23.

23. See personnel dossier, Karl-Heinz Euling, NA/RG242/A3343/SSO-192.

24. Harmel, P-163, 82, and Appendix C, number 3. The 10th SS Tank Destroyer Battalion, commanded by *SS-Sturmbannführer* Roestel, was not allotted to its division, but rather the divisional *Kampfgruppe* Walther at Neerpelt. In terms of the 1st Battalion, 10th SS Panzer Regiment, the battalion was located in St. Wendel and Winterbach, near the Black Forest. Lacking tanks, the battalion was employed as infantry to conduct security operations. During the middle of September, the Panther battalion was scheduled to relocate to the training base at Grafenwöhr.

25. Chamberlain and Doyle, *Encyclopedia of German Tanks of World War Two*, 128.

26. Harmel, P-163, 82–83.

27. According to General Sixt, the editor of Harmel's manuscript, the main SS office located in Bad Saarow, which was responsible for providing personnel and supplies for the *Waffen SS*, may have been informed about the OKW directive to refresh the 9th and 10th SS Panzer Divisions. The 10th SS was located near the front lines, whereas the 9th SS was located in Germany. The main SS office ordered personnel replacements for the 9th SS to the area of Siegen/Westfalen. See Harmel, P-163, Appendix C, number 1 and 2. Christian Lindemans, a Dutch underground leader forced to work for the Gestapo after they captured his brother, provided information to the Germans on or about 15 September about the Allied operation. Harmel claims the information was available as early as 8 September, whereas the account by Robert Urquhart, the commander of the British 1st Airborne Division, appears to be more plausible. See Robert Elliott Urquhart, *Arnhem: Britain's Infamous Airborne Assault of WWII* (Los Angeles: Royal Publishing Company, 1995), 190–91.

28. *SS-Obersturmführer* Karl-Godau, "Südholland 1944," in Suchdienst Frundsberg e.V. Köln, *Die Hellebarde*, No. 21, 2001, 42–43. Only two artillery batteries were available to the II SS Panzer Corps.

29. Ibid.

30. Report by *SS-Obersturmführer* Ellwanger, 4.Bttr.(3.7cm) SS-Flak-Abt.10, in Suchdienst Frundsberg e.V. Köln, *Die Hellebarde*, 46–47.

31. Charles B. MacDonald, *United States Army in World War II: The European Theater of Operations, The Siegfried Line Campaign,* first printed in 1963 (Washington, DC: GPO, 1990), 119–20; and Urquhart, *Arnhem*, 1. Urquhart specifically mentions the additional objective of eliminating the escape routes of those responsible for V-2 attacks.

32. Karl Schneider, "Frundsberg-Grenadiere," Suchdienst Frundsberg e.V. Köln, *Die Hellebarde,* No. 14, 1991, 16.

33. Ibid., 17.

34. Ibid., 13.

35. The 9th SS Panzer Reconnaissance Battalion released portions of the section to the 10th SS Panzer Reconnaissance Battalion, but other portions had already departed for Siegen-Westfalen. See Harmel, P-163, Appendix C, number 4.

36. Ibid., 84, and pages 1 and 2 of Appendix C, number 4. Friedrich Sixt, the general editor for the study by Harmel, favored Bittrich's account. However, the final analysis is not clear.

37. Ibid., 86. Based on statements of Ziehbrecht, the commander of the 1st Company, 10th SS Panzer Reconnaissance Battalion.

38. Taken from the combat after-action report by Oskar Schwappacher, Ia., V./SS-Art.Ausb.u.Ers.Regt., Gef.St., 29.9.44, Betr.: Einsatz der Abteilung bei den Kämpfen un Nijmegen, NA/RG242/A3343/SSO-121B.

39. The German Cross in Gold was instituted in 1941 and awarded for outstanding achievement in combat that did not warrant an award for the Knight's Cross of the Iron Cross. As in the case of Reinhold, the decoration was often awarded to commanders for the success of their men in battle. Approximately 30,000 were awarded to all branches of the German Armed Forces, including 894 members of the *Waffen-SS*. See the officer's dossier for Leo Reinhold, NA/RG242/A3343/SSO-020B.

40. The *Landesschützen-Kampfgruppe* Hartung was employed in the village of Lent. See Harmel, P-163, 87.

41. Trapp, "Der Kampf in *Arnhem*," in Suchdienst Frundsberg e.V. Köln, *Die Hellebarde*, No. 14, 1991, 13.

42. The fact that the 9th SS Panzer Reconnaissance Battalion returned north provides further evidence that the battalion was not attached to the 10th SS on 17 September, which is consistent with the report by General Bittrich. Harmel, P-163, 87–88. For the breakdown of *Kampfgruppe* Henke, see George Nafziger, "German Forces, Battle of Arnhem, 13–29 September 1944," *The Nafziger Orders of Battle Collection*, 944GIAD, 260, United States Army Combined Arms Center, Fort Leavenworth, KS, http://usacac.army.mil/cac2/CGSC/CARL/nafziger/944GIAD.pdf. For the breakdown of the Herman Göring Company Runge or *Kampfgruppe* Runge, see Frank van Lunteren, *The Battle of the Bridges: The 504 Parachute Infantry Regiment in Operation Market Garden* (Havertown, PA: Casemate Publishers, 2014), 108.

43. Ibid., 88. Specific objectives for the attack from the bridgehead at Nijmegen to the south resulted from this arrangement.

44. Harmel incorrectly identified the supporting heavy tanks belonging to 502nd Heavy Panzer Battalion, consisting of three King Tiger tanks. Around September 1944, the s.Pz.Abt.502 fought in the Kurland supporting Army Group Nord. For details, see Klein and Kühn, *Tiger*, 280. In relation to the 502nd Heavy Panzer Battalion, see 222–23.

45. Gen.Insp.d.Pz.Tr./Abt.Org./Kartei Nr. 2500/44 g.K.v.15.8.1944., as in v. Senger u. Etterlin, *Die Panzer-Grenadiere*, 218–20, and Klein and Kühn, *Tiger*, 279.

46. Harmel, P-163, 89.

47. Ibid., 63 and 90.

48. Ibid., 14.

49. Trapp, "Der Kampf in Arnhem," Suchdienst Frundsberg e.V. Köln *Die Hellebarde,* 14–15.

50. Schwappacher, Ia., V./SS-Art.Ausb.u.Ers.Regt., Gef.St., 29.9.44, Betr.: Einsatz der Abteilung bei den Kämpfen un Nijmegen, NA/RG242/A3343/SSO-121B. The Hermann Göring Company Runge belonged to those forces already present at Nijmegen, as part of *Kampfgruppe* Henke, consisting of the Staff Henke, *Fallschirmjäger* Training Regiment, three companies of the 6th Replacement Battalion, Herman Göring Company Runge, the NCO School Company, two companies of the Railway Guards/Police Reservists, and a Flak Battery consisting of 88mm and 20mm guns.

51. Harmel, P-163, 91.

52. Schwappacher, Ia., V./SS-Art.Ausb.u.Ers.Regt., Gef.St., 29.9.44, Betr.: Einsatz der Abteilung bei den Kämpfen un Nijmegen, NA/RG242/A3343/SSO-121B.

53. Karl Godau, "Bearbeitung von Karl Godau über Sperrverband Heinke und seine artilleristische Ausstattung, vom 25.09.1982," in Suchdienst Frundsberg e.V. Köln, *Die Hellebarde*, No. 21, 2001, 45.

54. Harmel, P-163, 91. The German assumption that Allied armor linked with the 82nd Airborne Division was correct. In fact, the Guards reached south of Grave by 0830 on Tuesday morning, after traveling 55 kilometers beyond Zon. For more details from the American perspective, see Weigley, *Eisenhower's Lieutenants*, 310.

55. Westerhoff, *Weg einer Panzer Kompanie*, 86–87.

56. Schwappacher, Ia., V./SS-Art.Ausb.u.Ers.Regt., Gef.St., 29.9.44, Betr.: Einsatz der Abteilung bei den Kämpfen un Nijmegen, NA/RG242/A3343/SSO-121B.

57. See Schwappacher, Ia., V./SS-Art.Ausb.u.Ers.Regt., Gef. St., 29.9.44, Betr.: Einsatz der Abteilung bei den Kämpfen un Nijmegen, NA/RG242/A3343/SSO-121B. For details on the 82nd Airborne Division, see Weigley, *Eisenhower's Lieutenants*, 314–15. Cross-referenced with Wilhelm Bittrich, "Das II.SS-Pz.A.K. Sept/Okt 1944," Foreign Military Studies, MS # P-155, 1954, 16. The description of the Allied advance varies somewhat from the report of Bittrich, "Das II.SS-Pz.A.K. Sept/Okt 1944." However, Harmel was an eyewitness of the event, and stands by his version as being correct. Also consulted Dieter Stenger, "Courage Under Fire: Crossing the Waal River, Battle of Nijmegen, Market Garden, September 1944," *Army History,* U.S. Army Center of Military History, Fall 2014, PB 20-14-4, No. 93, 28.

58. Schwappacher, Ia., V./SS-Art.Ausb.u.Ers.Regt., Gef.St., 29.9.44, Betr.: Einsatz der Abteilung bei den Kämpfen un Nijmegen, NA/RG242/A3343/SSO-121B.

59. Harmel, P-163, 95; Karl Godau, "Gefunden im Harmel-Nachlaß-2001," in Suchdienst Frundsberg e.V. Köln, *Die Hellebarde*, No. 21, 2001, 44; and "Vorschlag für die Verleihung des Ritterkreuz des Eisernen Kreuz," Div.Gef. St. dated 17.10.1944, for *SS-Hauptsturmführer* Karl Heinz Euling, in the officer dossier file for Karl Heinz Euling, NA/RG242/A3343/SSO-192. See also Schwappacher, Ia., V./SS-Art.Ausb.u.Ers.Regt., Gef.St., 29.9.44, Betr.: Einsatz der Abteilung bei den Kämpfen un Nijmegen, NA/RG242/A3343/SSO-121B.

60. It is not known if Krüger survived the war, although Schwappacher claims he was shot by Americans in the first aid bunker. See Schwappacher, Ia., V./SS-Art.Ausb.u.Ers. Regt., Gef.St., 29.9.44, Betr.: Einsatz der Abteilung bei den Kämpfen un Nijmegen, NA/RG242/A3343/SSO-121B.

61. Lieutenant General Hans von Tettau was a veteran of the campaigns into Poland, France, and Russia. Von Tettau was decorated with the Knight's Cross to the Iron Cross for the achievements of the 24th Infantry Division following the capture of the fortress at Sevastopol. After transferring to the Führer-Reserve of the OKH, he then became on 1 September 1943 the training chief and commander of the Training Staff in the Netherlands. As commander of the Divisional *Kampfgruppe* von Tettau, the division consisted of the following units:

SS Infantry Battalion Krafft
6/14 Naval Manning Battalion
184th Artillery Regiment, consisting of one battalion with no guns
3rd SS Wach Battalion Helle (6 companies)
SS Lippert NCO Training School "Arnhem" Regiment
SS Schulz Battalion
SS Mattusch Battalion (Waal line, later reinforced with some elements of 10th and 14th SS Manning Bns)
SS Oelkers Battalion (Waal line)

See George Nafziger, *The Nafziger Orders of Battle Collection*, "German Forces, Battle of Arnhem, 13–29 September 1944," 944GIAD, 260, United States Army Combined Arms Center, Fort Leavenworth, KS, http://usacac.army.mil/cac2/CGSC/CARL/nafziger/944GIAD .pdf; as well as Schwappacher, Ia., V./SS-Art.Ausb.u.Ers. Regt., Gef.St., 29.9.44, Betr.: Einsatz der Abteilung bei den Kämpfen un Nijmegen, NA/RG242/A3343/SSO-121B.

62. Harmel, P-163, 95; Schwappacher, Ia., V./SS-Art. Ausb.u.Ers.Regt., Gef.St., 29.9.44, Betr.: Einsatz der Abteilung bei den Kämpfen un Nijmegen, NA/RG242/ A3343/SSO-121B; and Weigley, *Eisenhower's Lieutenants*, 315.

63. Harmel, P-163, 95.

64. Kommandeur, 10.SS-Pz.Div."Frundsberg," Div.Gef.St., den 14 February 1945, "Vorschlag Nr. 646, für die Verleihung des Deutsches Kreuzes in Gold," as in the dossier for Hans Stolley, NA/RG242/A3343/SSO-163B.

65. Harmel, P-163, 95.

66. Personalverfügung, SS-Sturmbannführer Haas, Fritz, SS-Führungshauptamt, Amt V/Abt.IIa/Ref.1, dated 27.9.1944; and Beurteilung für den SS-Sturmbannführer Haas, Fritz, geb. 19.7.1912, Artillerie-Schule II, dated 21.10.1944, in the officer dossier of Fritz Haas, NA/ RG242/A3343/SSO-046A. The performance appraisal of Haas indicates he transferred to the 10th SS on 22.9.44, whereas the orders from the SS Central Headquarters Office directed the transfer effective 20 September. Harmel, P-163, 95; Harmel refers to the regimental artillery under the command of Sanders, Sonnenstuhl, and Haas on 20 September.

67. Harmel, P-163, 95–97, and Appendix C item 5. Allied reinforcements flowed across the two bridges and over a pontoon ferry service west of the city on the northern bank of the Waal. The crossing points were subjected to German battery fire from the 4th Company, 10th SS Panzer Artillery Battalion, equipped with 100mm cannon.

68. Ibid., 97. Soldiers of the 9th SS Panzer Reconnaissance Battalion, ordered to return to Arnhem, assisted in clearing the wreckage after arriving in Arnhem from the refitting area of Siegen.

69. Harmel, P-163, 97; and Bittrich, "Das II.SS-Pz.A.K. Sept/ Okt 1944," 18. Harmel's version of the countermeasure against the Polish airborne forces varies from the report by Bittrich. The report by Bittrich reported the Corps could only allocate limited forces to counter the threat at Driel. Blocking Unit Harzer, a regimental-sized force relocated 2 km west of Driel along the railroad embankment, attached to the Regimental Staff *SS-Standartenführer* Gerhardt. Bittrich did not report the relocation of the 10th SS Panzer Reconnaissance Battalion to Driel.

70. Harmel, P-163, 97–99.

71. *SS-Obersturmbannführer* Hans-Georg Sonnenstuhl, "Not macht Erfinderisch," Suchdienst Frundsberg e.V. Köln, *Die Hellebarde*, No. 21, 2001, 70–72. Comments on the effectiveness of Sonnenstuhl's tactics were taken from an account by *SS-Obersturmbannführer* Horst König, 78–79. It is completely plausible that such larger quantities of artillery fire could be massed at any point in the vicinity of Arnhem. Fürbringer, *9.SS-Panzer Division Hohenstaufen*, 458, noted that on 25 September, the 9th SS Hohenstaufen also worked together with the 191st Artillery Regiment and could bring 110 artillery guns into action in and around Arnhem including:

4 heavy field howitzers 18 (150mm)
30 light field howitzers 18 (105mm)
2 heavy cannon K 18 (100mm)
12 heavy infantry guns 33 (150mm)
12 light infantry guns 42 (75mm)
10 heavy rocket launchers 41 (210m)
20 heavy antiaircraft guns 41 (88mm)
20 heavy antiaircraft guns 38 (105mm)
10 heavy mortars (120mm)

72. See the service dossier for Leo Reinhold, NA/RG242/A3343/SSO-020B.

73. Karl Godau, "Bearbeitung von Karl Godau über Sperrverband Heinke und seine artilleristische Ausstattung, vom 25.09.1982," Suchdienst Frundsberg e.V. Köln, *Die Hellebarde*, No. 21, 2001, 45.

74. Harmel, P-163, 99.

75. Ibid., 102.

76. See Harmel, P-163, Appendix C, number 10.

77. Harmel, P-163, 102; and Klein and Kühn, *Tiger*, 279.

78. Chamberlain, *Encyclopedia of German Tanks*, 142–43, 244–45, and 254–55.

79. Harmel, P-163, 103; and the personnel dossier, Euling, NA/RG242/A3343/SSO-192.

80. Harmel, P-163, 103; and Bittrich, "Das II.SS-Pz.A.K. Sept./Nov.1944," 21 and 22. On 2 August 1914, Curt von Gottberg volunteered at the age of eighteen for service with the Cuirassiers Regiment "Graf Wrangel" in Königsberg. He transferred to the 1st Guard Foot Regiment in Potsdam and was severely wounded in 1917. After a thirteen-year hiatus as a farmer, he joined the *Waffen-SS* in 1933 and commanded a battalion in Ellwangen. In 1936, Gottberg lost his lower left leg as a result of an accident. For details on Gottberg, see Krätschmer, *Die Ritterkreuzträger der Waffen-SS*, 722–23.

81. Harmel, P-163, 104.

82. Ibid., 104–5.

83. Kurt Gätzschmann, *Sieg und Niederlage: Zeitzeuge der Panzertruppe 1935–1945*, (Fredericksburg, VA: Stenger Historica Publishing, 2001), 1, 66–67.

84. Harmel, P-163, 105.

85. Harmel, P-163, 106; Donald L. Caldwell, *JG26: Top Guns of the Luftwaffe* (New York: Orion Books, 2001), 294–95; and Phil Nordyke, *All American All the Way: The Combat History of the 82nd Airborne Division in World War II* (St. Paul: Zenith Press, 2005), 568–73. According to Bittrich, the German High Command hoped to recapture the bridge at Nijmegen, which contradicted the directives of Army Group B, to destroy the bridges over the lower Rhine. According to Friedrich Sixt, the editor for the report P-163 authored by Harmel, German aircraft carried flying bombs under their bellies on 27 September to destroy the bridges across the Waal. Soldiers referred to the aircraft "Father and Son." According to Caldwell, the third group of JG26 flew a rare ground attack mission to Nijmegen on 25 September.

86. Karl Godau, "Bearbeitung von Karl Godau über Sperrverband Heinke und seine artilleristische Ausstattung, vom 25.09.1982," in Suchdienst Frundsberg e.V. Köln, *Die Hellebarde*, No. 21, 2001, 44–45.

87. During an evening recovery of an Allied airborne supply canister, which landed in a garden in Heveadorp on 22 September, British soldiers captured Schneider and locked him in a basement. Schneider escaped two days later at the same time a truce was arranged for the British to collect their wounded. He headed north toward friendly lines when shortly thereafter members of the 9th SS Panzer Division "Hohenstaufen" absorbed him into their unit. After the conclusion of the fighting around Arnhem on 26 September, the *Kampfgruppe* Bruhns of the 9th SS withdrew and returned to Germany. Karl Schneider, "Frundsberg-Grenadiere," in Suchdienst Frundsberg e.V. Köln, *Die Hellebarde*, No. 14, 1991, 17–18.

88. Harmel, P-163, Appendix C, number 13. The description of events by Harmel differs from that of Major General Erwin Jollasse, author of the Foreign Military Study, P-161 "Einsatz der 9.Pz. Div. im Okt./Nov.1944." Jollasse reported the divisional boundary between the 9th Panzer Division and the 10th SS Panzer Division as Angeren–Bemmel–Ressen (villages occupied by the 10th SS), whereas Harmel and Bittrich identify a more northerly line Angeren–Huis de Karburg–Vergert–Merm. According to Jollasse, a battalion of the 9th Panzer Division captured Heuvel on 1 October. A lack of documentation prevented the differences of opinion from being clarified. However, the diversionary attack by the 10th SS Panzer Division, over the southern rim of Heuvel in the direction of Vergert, was in both reports by Jollasse and Bittrich.

89. Harmel, P-163, 106–8.

90. 10.SS-Pz.Div., Div.Gef.St., "Vorschlag für die Verleihung des Ritterkreuz des Eisernen Kreuzes," dated 17.10.1944, Euling, A/RG242/A3343/SSO-192; and Harmel, P-163, 109.

91. In response to anticipated enemy airborne landings, the 10th SS redesignated the 10th SS Field Replacement Battalion to the 10th Field SS Training Battalion, thereby making the unit available as the ready reserve. The battalion could thereby also be equipped with light and heavy infantry weapons. The battalion was motorized and reinforced with the 1st Training Battery, consisting of four light field howitzers, of the 10th SS Artillery Regiment. The battalion commander was required to remain at the divisional combat command post at all times. Newly arriving replacements from the homeland were consolidated within the 10th SS Field Replacement Battalion. The separation between the Field Replacement and Field Training battalions was maintained and paid off later; replacements that arrived from the *Luftwaffe* required infantry training. As a result of anticipated enemy airborne operations, the 10th SS Panzer Division received responsibility to prepare to defend against enemy airborne landings in the rearward areas, along the left boundary Rees–Ijsselburg, and the right boundary Pannerden–

Doetichem. See Harmel, P-163, 109, and Appendix C, number 14.

92. Harmel, P-163, 109.

93. 10.SS-Pz.Div., Div.Gef.St., "Vorschlag für die Verleihung des Ritterkreuz des Eisernen Kreuz," dated 17.10.1944, Euling, A/RG242/A3343/SSO-192; and Harmel, P-163, 109–11.

94. Harmel, P-163, 111.

95. Ibid., 111–12. During the fighting, the II SS Panzer Corps referred to the 10th SS Panzer Division as *Kampfgruppe* Harmel, due to its reduction of force. The attack across the overall front of the II SS Panzer Corps was not suspended completely until 7 October. The higher command ordered attacks, for 6 October, in the direction of Driel and Elst, in conjunction with attacks by the 12th SS Panzer Division from Orpheusden to the east and from the bridgehead south of Doorwerth to the east.

96. Ibid., 112.

97. Ibid., 112–14.

98. Ibid., 114–15.

99. General Model ordered flooding the terrain between the Lower Rhine and the Waal by demolition of the dam south of Arnhem. SS Major Albert Brandt, the commander of the 10th SS Panzer Pioneer Battalion, received the task and nearly completed the preparations when Army Group B, for no apparent reason, abandoned the plan. See Harmel, P-163, 115, and Appendix C, number 17.

100. Harmel, P-163, 115.

101. Heinz Winzbeck, "Eine Werkstatt blieb zurück," in Suchdienst Frundsberg e.V. Köln, *Die Hellebarde*, No. 14, 1991, 84.

102. Harmel, P-163, 115.

103. Ibid., 116, and Appendix C, number 18.

104. Harmel, P-163, Appendix C, number 19.

105. Ibid., 116–17.

106. Information is not available about the combat strength of the individual units belonging to the *Kampfgruppe* Roestel, at the time of its arrival at the division.

107. Harmel, P-163, 117.

108. The commander of the tank regiment returned to Germany to acquire Panthers and Pz.Kpfw.IVs. Harmel, P-163, 119, and Appendix C, number 20.

109. Ibid., 119.

110. Ibid.

111. Ibid., 119–20.

112. Karl Schneider, "Frundsberg-Grenadiere," in Suchdienst Frundsberg e.V. Köln, *Die Hellebarde*, No. 14, 1991, 19. No documentation exists to support Schneider's claim that the commander of the *Kampfgruppe* in Doornenburg brought the II SS Panzer Corps to intervene or investigate the matter.

113. Ibid., 19–20.

114. Ibid.

115. Harmel, P-163, 120.

116. Ibid., 119–20, and Appendix C, number 21.

117. Hans-Georg Sonnenstuhl, "Not macht erfinderisch," dated 25.10.1987 in a letter to Harmel, reproduced by Willi Weber, *Frundsberg Nachrichten Extra*, June 2005, 20–22; *SS-Unterstuermführer* Hans-Dietrich Sauter, "Erbeutete Geschuetze," in Suchdienst Frundsberg e.V. Köln, *Die Hellebarde*, No. 21, 2001, 38–39; and Walther-Peer Fellgiebel, *Die Träger des Ritterkreuzes des Eisernen Kreuzes 1939–1945: Die Inhaber der höchsten Auszeichnung des Zweiten Weltkrieges aller Wehrmachtteile* (Friedberg: Podzun-Pallas, 2000), 254.

CHAPTER 6

1. MacDonald, *The Siegfried Line Campaign*, 390–91.

2. Günther Blumentritt, *XII SS Corps (October 20, 1944– January 31, 1945)*, Foreign Military Studies, B-290, NA/RG549/MPM1035. The war diary of OB West did not report that the 10th SS relocated west of Erkelenz. See also Harmel, P-163, 121, and Appendix D, number 1.

3. Harmel, P-163, 121–23; and Karl Schneider, "Frundsberg-Grenadiere," in Suchdienst Frundsberg e.V. Köln, *Die Hellebarde*, No. 14, 1991, 20.

4. The original text, as it relates to the shots that killed the number 1 gunner and wounded Schneider, referred to *Explosivgeschoss*, or explosive projectiles. This type of cartridge is commonly referred to in English as hollow-point ammunition, and was banned by the Geneva Convention in 1889. It is highly unlikely that the American forces used hollow-point ammunition. Standard American airborne infantry during World War II used the .30 caliber M1 Garand rifle. Troopers of crew-served weapons and staff noncommissioned officers used the M1 and M1A1 carbine that fired a .30 caliber carbine cartridge, which was known to be underpowered. Paratrooper snipers used the M1D Garand rifle with an M84 Weaver telescope. The M1 Garand rifle fired the .30 caliber ball M1906 cartridge, which was a copy of the German "Spitzer" round with a pointed tip. When the M1906 ball bullet passes through the human body and hits bone, it will ricochet and tumble, thereby causing a large exit wound. It would be fair to say that standard .30 caliber ball ammunition would, indeed, cause an exit wound after hitting a rib, which was reported broken on Schneider. However, the accusation that Americans used hollow-point ammunition is unfounded. Karl Schneider transferred on 22 November to the field hospital in Rhineladen. After several blood transfusions, the doctors performed medical operations on his chest cavity. Having been wounded a third time, the *ObersStabarzt* (senior staff doctor) awarded Schneider with the Wound Badge in Silver. On 20 December 1944, Schneider and several other wounded men boarded a train

for southern Germany. Due to a fever and short periods of not breathing, Schneider was removed from the train at Neuss and admitted to a hospital, where he remained until 5 January 1945. During his relocation by rail to the hospital in Heidelberg, Allied fighter aircraft attacked the hospital train and caused additional casualties. By April 1945, and after further layovers at various facilities, American troops were approaching the Reserve Hospital in Heidenheim. Schneider relocated to a small hospital in Schorndorf, which lay near a family relative. As an outpatient, number 974, he was authorized to reside with his aunt, but when fighting neared the house, Schneider decided to return to Schorndorf. While crossing the street, with barely a hundred meters to the hospital, American troops captured Schneider. The Americans led Schneider away for interrogation and subsequently to a factory where POWs were assembled. Wearing his *Waffen SS* coat and all his decorations, he was transported by truck on the following day to a facility at Backnang, at which time he stuffed his pay book and decorations into his pockets and discarded his coat. From that point on, Schneider was always considered a regular Army soldier. After numerous transfers to various facilities, Schneider was released on 8 June 1946 and went home. See Schneider, "Frundsberg-Grenadiere," in Suchdienst Frundsberg e.V. Köln, *Die Hellebarde*, No. 14, 1991, 20.

5. Harmel, P-163, 123. On 22 November, the Headquarters, Fifth Panzer Army was employed and retained the designation Group Manteuffel.

6. Harmel, P-163, 123–24. The 7th Panzer Division was formed within Wehrkreis IX, consisting of the Wehrersatzbezirk Kassel, Frankfurt am Main, and Weimar Er that incorporated Wehrbezirke Kassel I–II, Korbach, Marburg, Hersfeld, Siegen, Wetzlar, Fulda, Gießen, Frankfurt / Main I–II, Offenbach, Aschaffenburg, Friedberg, Hanau, Weimar, Sangerhausen, Gera, Rudolfstadt, Mülhausen / Thüringen, Erfurt, Eisenach, Gotha and Meiningen. See *Lexikon der Wehrmacht*, www.lexikon-der-wehrmacht.de/Gliederungen/Panzerdivisionen/7PD.htm. The 548th Grenadier Division organized on 11 July 1944 as a "Sperr-Division" of the 29th Wave via Wehrkeis IV. Wehrkreis IV incorporated the regions of the provinces in Saxony with the headquarters located in Dresden. On 9 October 1944 the division reorganized as the 548th Volks-Grenadier-Division. See *Lexikon der Wehrmacht*, www.lexikon-der-wehrmacht.de/Gliederungen/Grenadier divisionen/548GD.htm.

7. Harmel, P-163, 124, and Appendix D, number 2.

8. Harmel, P-163, 125.

9. Harmel, P-163, 126–27, and Appendix D, Number 3.

10. The 9th Panzer Division and the 10th SS Panzer Division experienced the same tactical dilemma between the Lower Rhine and Waal Rivers. The divisions were well-attuned to one another. In fact, the commander of the 9th Panzer Division, Lieutenant General Harald Freiherr von Elverfeldt, taught Harmel tactics at the Divisional Commanders' Course in Hirschberg, Silesia. See Harmel, P-163, and Appendix D, number 4.

11. See Harmel, P-163, 128, and Appendix D, number 5.

12. See Harmel, P-163, 128, and Appendix D, number 6.

13. See Harmel, P-163, Appendix D, number 6.

14. See Harmel, P-163, 129, and Appendix D, number 7; as well as the account by Euling in Hans Kramp, *Rurfront 1944/45: Zweite Schlacht am Hubertuskreuz zwischen Wurm, Rur, und Inde*, 2nd ed. (Geilenkirchen: Verlag Fred Gatzen, 1981), 305.

15. Harmel, P-163, 131.

16. *Dran Drauf und Durch!*, 95; and Harmel, P-163, Appendix D, number 8.

17. Orders from OB West directed the division to operate as a closed or complete division. The commander of the division also advocated maintaining all the battalions under his control. However, the objective of the division remained only to occupy the heights west of Linnich. Harmel, P-163, and Appendix D, number 9.

18. Harmel, P-163, 131, and Appendix D, number 6.

19. Harmel's scope of study did not take into consideration psychological processes and how they were experienced by enlisted men and officers on a daily basis. However, in his judgment, such considerations should not be omitted when evaluating the situation. If they were omitted, readers would consider many points as unbelievable or against regulations. Harmel also wrote in a letter to Sixt, dated 23 January 1955, regarding the command structure within the sector of Beeck-Linnich, of the 9th Panzer Division, which was being relieved out of the line during the gradual arrival of the 10th SS Panzer Division. Harmel claimed that at the higher levels of command, it appeared that theoretically the sectors of the two divisions were commanded by the 9th Panzer Division. Moreover, Harmel noted that perhaps this arrangement had been ordered; however, he was not aware of the situation. Both commanders commanded with the same degree of success. See Harmel, P-163, 132–33, and Appendix D, number 12.

20. Ibid.

21. The portions of the artillery located west of the Roer in the area around Brachelen were not employed into action for the same reasons as cited previously. See Harmel, P-163, 133, and Appendix D, number 10.

22. Harmel misidentified the heavy Tigers to be from the 874th Heavy Panzer Battalion. While the incorrect number has been repeated within the book by Hans Kramp, *Rurfront 1944/45,* as well as in Wilhelm Tieke, *In the Firestorm of the Last Years of War*, there is no evidence this battalion existed. See Kleine and Kühn, *Tiger*, 279–80; and Harmel, P-163, 134.

23. Harmel, P-163, 134–35.

24. Harmel, P-163, 135, and Appendix D, number 11.

25. See Harmel, P-163, 135. The right wing of the 340th Volks-Grenadier Division intended to occupy the cliffs on Hill 97.6 east of Ederen. The division did, in fact, occupy

the area for a brief period. On several occasions due to heavy Allied artillery fire, the division pulled back to the cliffs 1 km east and 1.5 km northeast of Ederen.

26. Harmel, P-163, 135–37, and Appendix D, number 13.

27. Inconsistencies exist regarding the time the 10th SS arrived in the sector of the 9th Panzer Division and the time of relief, as in the report by Harmel (P-163) and that of Erwin Jolasse, "Employment of the 9th Panzer Division in October/November 1944," Foreign Military Studies, MS # P-161, 1954. On page 53, it states, "Before noon (on 24 November), the first portions of the division, including the 11th Panzergrenadier Regiment, were finally relieved by the 10th SS and placed in march, into the area of Hückelhofen-Baal, for an accelerated refreshing." Harmel maintains his report is accurate. He added, "The relief of the 9th Panzer Division, as well as the transfer of command for the former sector of the division, began in the evening on 22 November 44, and continued throughout the night on 23 November and into the following day; at the same time the 10th SS deployed into action; units of the 9th Panzer Division already began their withdrawal."

After the relief of the last portions of the 11th *Panzergrenadier* Regiment by the 10th SS Panzer Reconnaissance Battalion, in the sector of Roerdorf on 24 November, the 10th SS Panzer Division received orders to relieve portions of the 9th Panzer Division engaged at Beeck and to assume command of the entire sector stretching from the railroad line at Erkelenz-Geilenkirchen to Roerdorf. This took place on 25 November. In retrospect, the interpretation of relief by the 10th SS as in the report P-161 is in harmony with this report. See Harmel, P-163, 137, and Appendix D, number 14.

28. Harmel, P-163, 137–38.

29. Harmel, P-163, 139. Volks Artillery Corps were organized to combine heavy artillery. In September 1944, Army Artillery Brigades were organized and renamed in November to Volks-Artillery Corps. The Corps were actually reinforced artillery regiments with five or six battalions, about half of a light or heavy battalion. For more information related to Volks Artillery Corps, see www.lexikon-der-wehrmacht.de.

30. See Harmel, P-163, 139–41.

31. Ibid., p. 141–43

32. See Harmel, P-163, 143–44, and Appendix D, number 15.

33. See Harmel, P-163, 144, and Appendix D, number 16.

34. Harmel, P-163, 144–45.

35. Ibid., 145–46.

36. Ibid., 146.

37. Ibid., 148.

38. Ibid., 149.

39. Harmel, P-163, 150; and Kramp, *Rurfront 1944/45*, 382.

40. Harmel, P-163, 150.

41. Ibid., 150–54.

42. Ibid., 156. Harmel assumed the Allied objective was to re-establish contact with elements that managed to break into Lindern.

43. Ibid., 158–59, and Appendix D, number 17.

44. Ibid., 159. Heinz Fischer was listed incorrectly as being KIA on 11 Nov 1944.

45. Harmel, P-163, 159, and Appendix D, number 18.

46. Harmcl, P-163, 160–61.

47. See Harmel, P-163, 161–63, and Appendix D, number 19.

48. See Harmel, P-163, 163, and Appendix D, number 20.

49. Harmel, P-163, 164, and Appendix D, number 21.

50. Harmel, P-163, 165.

51. Precise information does not exist as to the amount of terrain the 10th SS Panzer Division assumed responsibility for holding when relieving elements of the 9th Panzer Division. Additional elements of the 10th SS Panzer Division did not arrive on 2 December, as suggested by Gustav von Zangen, *Die 15.Armee im Abwehrkampf an Roer und Rhine, 22.11.44 bis 9.3.45*, Foreign Military Studies, MS # B-811, 1947, 17.

52. Harmel, P-163, 165–67.

53. Ibid., 167.

54. Ibid., 168.

55. Ibid., 168–69, and Appendix D, number 22.

CHAPTER 7

1. David T. Zabecki, "Germany's Strategic Crapshoot," *Military History*, Battle of the Bulge 70th Anniversary Special Issue, Winter 2015, 17–18.

2. Dieter Stenger, *Saint Vith: The U.S. Army Tank Doctrine—Tactical Mobility and Strategic Victory*, thesis, American Military University, 1997, 1–2.

3. T/O is the abbreviation for Table of Organization. Harmel, P-163, 168–69; and Tieke, *In the Firestorm of the Last Year of the War*, 337. Tieke identified the area as Blatzheim-Kerpen-Euskirchen. Tieke's source for the breakout of equipment was the Bundesarchiv-Abt. Militärarchiv (BAMA), Freiburg/Br.

4. Weigley, *Eisenhower's Lieutenants*, 53.

5. MacDonald, *The Siegfried Line Campaign*, 393–94.

6. Heinz Harmel, *Fragen zur Ardennen-Offensive*, Foreign Military Studies, NA/RG549/MPM1035/P-109f (cited hereafter as "P-109f"), 1.

7. Bernhard Westerhoff and Karl Schneider, *Geschichte Einer Panzer-Kompanie im Elsaß: 6 Kompanie SS Pz.-Rgt. 10, Frundsberg, Winter 1944–1945*, unpublished manuscript, not dated, 9.

8. Harmel, P-109f, 2–3.

9. Tieke, *In the Firestorm of the Last Years of the War*, 310.

10. Harmel, P-109f, 3.

11. Harmel, P-109f, 4; and Tieke, *In the Firestorm of the Last Years of the War*, 311.

12. Harmel, P-109f, 5.

13. Ibid., 5–6.

14. Ibid., 6–8.

15. Ibid., 8.

16. Harmel, P-109f, 8–9; and Tieke, *In the Firestorm of the Last Years of the War*, 314.

17. Harmel, P-109f, 9.

18. Harmel, P-109f, 9; Zabecki, "Germany's Strategic Crapshoot," 24; and Jeffrey J. Clarke and Robert Ross Smith, *United States Army in World War II: The European Theater of Operations, Riviera to the Rhine* (Washington, DC: GPO, 1993), 497–98.

19. Tieke, *In the Firestorm of the Last Years of the War*, 337. The actual number of Panther tanks received by the 1st Battalion is not known. Tieke maintains they received their full complement of tanks, suggesting they only received a total of twenty-nine, which is well below the authorized strength of no less than sixty-eight vehicles in 1944.

20. Westerhoff and Schneider, *Geschichte Einer Panzer-Kompanie im Elsaß*, 9. At the time, Westerhoff could not understand why the locals opposed the Germans, especially when many men from the Elsass fought for Germany. What he did not know was that the men were forced to serve.

21. Ibid.

22. Ibid., 10.

23. See the eyewitness account of U.S. Army captain Arthur Gottlieb in Westerhoff and Schneider, *Geschichte Einer Panzer-Kompanie im Elsaß*, 11; and David T. Zabecki and Keith Wooster, "Death of an American Combat Command," *World War II* (Leesburg, VA: Weider History Group, 1999), 28.

24. An eyewitness account of Wilhelm Balbach, in Westerhoff and Schneider, *Geschichte Einer Panzer-Kompanie im Elsaß*, 25.

25. Balbach, *Geschichte Einer Panzer-Kompanie im Elsaß*, 25; and Zabecki and Wooster, "Death of an American Combat Command," 49.

26. Clarke and Smith, *Riviera to the Rhine*, 524; and James E. Muschell, *From Bloody Herrlisheim to a Slave Labor Camp* (Cheboygan, MI: United Associates, 2005), 22.

27. Balbach, *Geschichte Einer Panzer-Kompanie im Elsaß*, 25; Zabecki and Wooster, "Death of an American Combat Command," 49; and Clarke and Smith, *Riviera to the Rhine*, 525.

28. Based on an eyewitness account and report prepared by Ernst Bachmann, contained in Westerhoff and Schneider, *Geschichte Einer Panzer-Kompanie im* Elsaß, 20b, 25–26; as well as Krätschmer, *Die Ritterkreuzträger der Waffen-SS*, 822–23; Tieke, *In the Firestorm of the Last Years of the War*, 339; and Zabecki and Wooster, "Death of an American Combat Command," 49. Zabecki mentions the loss of only four tanks as opposed to twelve claimed by Bachmann. The latter number appears more accurate, considering surviving photographs of the captured Shermans from Herrlisheim that were used later on the Russian front that made up the 13th Company, 2nd Battalion, 10th SS Panzer Regiment. The official U.S. Army history stated,

an American artillery observer flying over Herrlisheim on the 18th reported several destroyed tanks in the eastern section of Herrlisheim and, flying east of the town, spotted 4 or 5 more and then 12 to 15 others, dug in and deployed in a circle for allaround defense, some painted white and others burned black. That evening German radio broadcasts boasted that an American lieutenant colonel and 300 of his men had been taken prisoner at Herrlisheim and 50 American tanks captured or destroyed.

See Clarke and Smith, *Riviera to the Rhine*, 525. The veteran from the 43rd Tank Battalion, James E. Muschell, *From Bloody Herrlisheim to a Slave Labor Camp*, 37, claims the battalion lost a total of sixty-two tanks either destroyed or disabled in two days.

29. Tieke, *In the Firestorm of the Last Years of the War*, 340; and Balbach, in Westerhoff and Schneider, *Geschichte Einer Panzer-Kompanie im Elsaß*, 26.

30. Tieke, *In the Firestorm of the Last Years of the War*, 340.

31. The death of *SS-Sturmbannführer* Kurt Walther occurred on 21 January 1945. See Balbach, in Westerhoff and Schneider, *Geschichte Einer Panzer-Kompanie im Elsaß*, 26.

32. An eyewitness account of *SS-Hauptsturmführer* Leo Franke, in Westerhoff and Schneider, *Geschichte Einer Panzer-Kompanie im Elsaß*, 11–12.

33. An eyewitness account by Kurt Rademacher, 2nd Company, 10th SS Panzer Regiment, in Westerhoff and Schneider, *Geschichte Einer Panzer-Kompanie im Elsaß*, 21.

34. Tieke, *In the Firestorm of the Last Years of the War*, 341–42.

35. Franke, in Westerhoff and Schneider, *Geschichte Einer Panzer-Kompanie im Elsaß*, 13; and Tieke, *In the Firestorm of the Last Years of the War*, 342.

CHAPTER 8

1. Harmel, P-109f, 2–5.

2. Hugh M. Cole, *United States Army in World War II: The European Theater of Operations: The Ardennes, Battle of the Bulge* (Washington, DC: GPO, 1965), 663–64. The U.S. Army's official history cited many examples that support the theory that the lack of ammunition should be charged to transport failure rather than to paucity of artillery shells at the Rhine dumps. For example, the Panzer Lehr Division first reported running out of and then reported a shortage of ammunition.

3. Karl Decker was born on 30 November 1897, in Borntin, Pommern. In 1914 Decker volunteered for service with the 54th Infantry Regiment. Commissioned and promoted to lieutenant and platoon commander, he served in 1923 in the Reichswehr with the 6th Cavalry Regiment. On 1

October 1930 he was promoted to cavalry captain. In 1935 he attained the rank of major and assignment to the staff of the 15th Cavalry Regiment. One year later he received assignment as commander of the 38th Antitank Battalion and on 1 April 1939 was promoted to first lieutenant. After the Polish campaign, he assumed on 10 April 1940 command of the 1st Battalion, 3rd Panzer Regiment. For his decisive actions during the Battle Thermopile he received on 13 June 1941 the Knight's Cross. On 13 May 1941 he assumed command of the 3rd Panzer Regiment, which he led as of October 1941 into Russia. On 1 February 1942 Decker attained the rank of colonel and on 1 August 1942 received the German Cross in Gold. On 7 September 1943, Decker commanded the 5th Panzer Division and was promoted on 1 December 1943 to brigadier general. For the achievements of the division, Decker received on 4 May 1944 the Oak Leaves to the Knight's Cross of the Iron Cross. On 1 June 1944 Decker was promoted to lieutenant general. On 15 October 1944 he became the commanding general of the XXXIX Army Corps and on 1 January 1945 was promoted to General of the Panzer Troops. After heavy defensive fighting, the corps relocated to the West in April. Recognizing the hopelessness of the general German situation, Decker committed suicide near Grossbrunsrode in Braunschweig. Posthumously he received on 26 April 1945 the Swords of the Knight's Cross of the Iron Cross. See Peter Stockert, *Die Eichenlaubträger 1940–1945*, 4 vols. (Bad Friedrichshall: Friedrichshaller Rundblick, 1996).

4. Earl F. Ziemke, *Stalingrad to Berlin: The German Defeat in the East*, first printed 1968, CMH Pub 30-5 (Washington, DC: GPO, 1987), 445–47.

5. Krätschmer, *Die Ritterkreuzträger der Waffen-SS*, 873–74.

6. Felix Steiner, *Die Freiwilligen Der Waffen-SS: Idee und Opferung*, first published in 1958 by Verlag K.W. Schültz KG, Preussen Oldenburg (New York: Ishi Press, 2011), 318–21. Steiner refers to the Führer Escort Brigade, which by 26 January 1945 had been renamed to Führer Escort Division. See www.lexikon-der-wehrmacht.de.

7. "Naugart/Pommern," Suchdienst Frundsberg e.V. Köln, *Die Hellebarde*, vol. 2, 1980, 31–32.

8. "Naugart/Pommern," Suchdienst Frundsberg e.V. Köln, *Die Hellebarde*, 32. Richter also sent a messenger to the command post to enquire if the 11th Company made enemy contact. See also Krätschmer, *Die Ritterkreuzträger der Waffen-SS*, 874–75.

9. "Naugart/Pommern," Suchdienst Frundsberg e.V. Köln, *Die Hellebarde*, 33.

10. Ibid.

11. Based on the personal daily journal of Johann Sierks, "SS-Panzer-Art.Rgt.10 'Frundsberg'," Suchdienst Frundsberg e.V. Köln, *Die Hellebarde*, No. 17, 1995, 66–67.

12. Suchdienst Frundsberg e.V. Köln, *Die Hellebarde*, No. 20, 1999, 33, 53, and 59. Kube claims that Roestel replaced Harmel later in March due to Harmel's hospitalization, although *SS-Obersturmführer* Gernot Traupel, the adjutant

of the 2nd Battalion, 10th SS Panzer Regiment, claims Field Marshal Schörner wanted Roestel's skills as a tank destroyer commander under his control.

13. Sierks, "SS-Panzer-Art.Rgt.10 'Frundsberg'," Suchdienst Frundsberg e.V. Köln, *Die Hellebarde*, 67.

14. Ibid., 67–69.

15. Ibid., 70.

16. Ibid., 70–71.

17. Ibid. Much like Field Marshal Model, General Schörner also punished cowardice, or anyone found behind the front lines without orders, aggressively with immediate sentencing by hanging, for which he was criticized by German veterans. A loyal and devoted Nazi, he was exceptionally brutal and one of Hitler's favorites.

18. Ibid., 72.

19. Ibid., 73.

20. Ibid.

21. Ibid., 74.

22. Ibid.

23. Hermann Kube, "Der Anfang vom Ende," in the Suchdienst Frundsberg e.V. Köln, *Die Hellebarde*, No. 20, 1999, 33–34. *SS-Obersturmführer* Kube's wife and three children planned to relocate to Bavaria to avoid the threat of Czechoslovakians returning to the area, but she became complacent after the death of her twenty-year-old brother. Kube claims his two-year-old son, Rüdiger, was tortured to death in a hospital occupied by Poles.

24. Glantz and House, *When Titans Clash*, 263.

25. Ibid., 258–59.

26. Ibid., 260–61.

27. Christian Lucia, *Von Kausche bis Ressen: Wege eines Ausbruchs im April 1945* (Digital Druck, Welzow, Germany: 2000), 14; and Dieter Stenger, "To the Bitter End: The German MP44/StG44 Assault Rifle," *Army History*, PB 20-15-3 No. 96, Summer 2015, 22.

28. Lucia, *Von Kausche bis Ressen*, 13–16; and Glantz and House, *When Titans Clash*, 257.

29. Lucia, *Von Kausche bis Ressen*, 16.

30. Glantz and House, *When Titans Clash*, 256. Historians have also considered the near four-year conflict between Germany and the Soviets as an ideological war characterized by ruthless brutality and scorched earth. Regardless of the motives, when entire nations are mobilized for war, the civilian populations usually suffer the most with little to no protection against crimes committed by military forces.

31. Lucia, *Von Kausche bis Ressen*, 19.

32. Eyewitness account of *SS-Obersturmführer* Konrad Lenhardt, "Bericht, wie unser Kdr.SS-Ostubaf. Otto Paetsch gefallen ist," Suchdienst Frundsberg e.V. Köln, *Die Hellebarde*, No. 20, 1999, 28.

33. *SS-Untersturmführer* Jan Sierks, "Artilleristischer Einsatz IV.Abt/SS-Pz.Art.Abt.10 vom 17–19 April 1945," Suchdienst Frundsberg e.V. Köln, *Die Hellebarde*, No. 21, 2001, 93–94; and Suchdienst Frundsberg e.V. Köln, *Die Hellebarde*, No. 17, 1995, 57–58.

34. Maik Sieberhagen, "Soldatenschicksale in der Nie-derlausitz 1945," *Der Freiwillige*, Nr. 5, 2000, 19.

35. Ibid. The discovery of skeletal remains in the area of Greifenhain that exhibited injuries consistent with the claims of the eyewitness confirm the accounts.

36. Ibid.

37. Maik Sieberhagen, "Soldatenschicksale in der Nie-derlausitz 1945," "Schwerpunkt bei 10.SS-Pz.Div." "Frundsberg" und "Führerbegleitdivision," part 2, *Der Freiwillige*, Nr. 6, 2000, 9; and Suchdienst Frundsberg e.V. Köln, *Die Hellebarde*, No. 16, 1994, 86–87; and Erwin Fischer, "Der Untergang der I.Abt./SS-pZ.Art.Rgt.10 'Frundsberg' bei Geisendorf," Suchdienst Frundsberg e.V. Köln, *Die Hellebarde*, No. 21, 2001, 94–95. It is not clear what happened to *SS-Hauptsturmführer* Behrens; however, he entered Russian captivity on 22 April 1945 for ten years until 26 June 1955.

38. Sieberhagen, "Soldatenschicksale in der Niederlausitz 1945," Schwerpunkt bei 10.SS-Pz.Div. "Frundsberg" und "Führerbegleitdivision," 9. The British brought Rudi Gnade to the prison in Wernigrode. He transferred in the winter 1945/46 to a prisoner camp in Belgium, and from there to England. Gnade met his former commander from the 1st Battalion, 10th SS Panzer Artillery Regiment, Hans Dietrich Sauter. After his release from captivity, Rudi Gnade contacted Behrens's father, the former mayor of Kiel. Walter Behrens himself entered Russian captivity in April 1945. The grandfather asked Rudi to find the child. In 1949, Rudi returned to the combat area and looked for the now six-year-old child. The elderly couple had passed away and the child was found living in an orphanage. The records indicated that an unknown soldier dropped off the child, which cried for days and called out repeatedly, "Gugelhupf" and "blood is in the shoe." This allowed Rudi to make a positive identification and it allowed him to bring the child to its grandparents in Kiel. Moreover, it reunited Walter Behrens with his daughter after he left his dead wife behind and after ten years of captivity in Russia.

39. Ibid, 10. Russian Vlasov soldiers were Russian volunteers who enlisted in the German Army. The Russian Liberation Army or POA (Cyrillic) or ROA (Latin), was also referred to as the Vlasov army (Wlassow in German). The Vlasov Army, organized by the former Red Army general Andrey Vlasov, who tried to unite anticommunist Russians opposed to the communist regime in the Soviet Union, consisted of volunteers who were mostly Soviet POWs but also included White Russian émigrés or veterans of the anticommunist White Army during the Russian Civil War. After the war, the brother of Albert Henning searched for his brother's grave. He was not able to actively search for the grave until after the transition from Soviet communist rule to East German communist rule, by which time the grave was covered over. In 1997, after many verbal differences of opinion with the officials of the Department at Massen and a malicious campaign by

the local television station, the grave was relocated and re-established with the help of a priest from Massen.

40. Ibid.

41. Suchdienst Frundsberg e.V. Köln, *Die Hellebarde*, No. 17, 1995, 59–61.

42. Eventually Grenda was sold to the Poles and survived several internment camps. Grenda attempted no fewer than ten escapes, which led him through Poland and eastern portions of occupied Germany. See Sieberhagen, "Soldatenschicksale in der Niederlausitz 1945," 20, 22.

43. Suchdienst Frundsberg e.V. Köln, *Die Hellebarde*, No. 17, 1995, 63–65.

44. The graves of the thirteen men and seventeen-year-old boy are in the community cemetery of Sallgast, which has been cared for by the women of the village since the end of the war.

45. In 1994, the Citizen's Group of Lauchhammer exhumed the bodies and gave them a proper burial. The group planned to relocate the bodies to the Soldier's Cemetery Lauchhammer East. However, during a "Night and Fog Operation," the soldiers were relocated to Halbe, without informing the Citizen's Group Lauchhammer, and reburied as "Unknown." Among the items found at the graves were seven identification discs, personal belongings, and wedding bands.

46. No one knows if anyone made it. However, ten graves were in the woods at Schacksdorf, well into the 1960s. Sieberhagen, "Soldatenschicksale in der Niederlausitz 1945," Part 4, 2000, 17.

47. Sierks was eventually arrested by the Allies and placed on trial in Holstein but he was released in 1947. He was released by a German civilian court handling the denazification of former soldiers.

48. Sieberhagen, "Soldatenschicksale in der Niederlausitz 1945: Schilderungen aus dem Bereich der 10.SS-Pz. Div. 'Frundsberg,' 'Führer-Begleitdivision,' Fallschirm-panzerkorps 'Hermann Göring,'" part 6, *Der Freiwillige*, Nr. 10, 2000, 20–21.

49. Sieberhagen, "Soldatenschicksale in der Nieder-lausitz 1945: Schilderungen aus dem Bereich der 10.SS-Pz.Div.'Frundsberg,''Führer-Begleitdivision,' Fallschirmpanzerkorps 'Hermann Göring,'" part 5, *Der Freiwillige*, Nr. 6, 2000, 19.

50. Ibid. *SS-Untersturmführer* Günther Seybold belonged to the 10th SS Panzer Regiment. Several kilometers before, *SS-Obersturmführer* Otto Morgenstern was buried as an "unknown." Morgenstern belonged to the 10th SS Panzer Reconnaissance Battalion. A scouting troop of the 10th SS Panzer Reconnaissance Battalion with two scouting vehicles operated as far as the area around Riesa-Oschatz.

51. Ibid.

52. Ibid.

53. Ibid., 20. The 55th Panzer Reconnaissance Battalion, out of Görlitz/Hirschberg, the motorized 30th Grenadier Replacement Battalion, 116/54th Light Howitzer Training Battery out of Oppeln, as well as tank units from Sagan/

Kamenz, antitank platoons and antiaircraft combat troops of the 48th Army Antiaircraft Replacement and Training Battalion from Liegnitz made up the short-lived Panzer Unit Stegemann. After the beginning of February 1945, Panzer Unit Stegemann held positions along the Oder River and responded to one critical spot after another and assisted with the organization of a blocking unit for Army Group Center during the new creation of a defensive front in Silesia. The Panzer Unit Stegemann fought at Ohlau, at the Zobten, Görlitz, and finally in the defense of the county of Glatz. See *Lexikon der Wehrmacht*, www.lexikon-der -wehrmacht.de.

54. Hans Oebel, in Suchdienst Frundsberg e.V. Hannover, *Die Hellebarde*, No. 2, 1980, 46. At some point in 1945, Hans Oebel also disguised himself as a Russian truck convoy officer and enabled refugees who were stuck in a truck to reach safety within Germany.

55. "8.Mai 1945 Frundsberg-Ende," Suchdienst Frundsberg e.V. Köln, *Die Hellebarde*, No. 17, 1995, 142–43; Krätschmer, *Die Ritterkreuzträger der Waffen-SS*, 876.

EPILOGUE

1. The common steps along the path to military service included membership in the *Jungvolk*, Hitler Youth, and *Reichsarbeitsdienst* (RAD) or compulsory labor service, all auxiliary, quasi-military organizations. See Meschenmoser, *Landesbildstelle*.

2. The SS achieved societal supremacy by blending ideological functions within national institutions including law enforcement, politics, and military service branches, to create the ideal SS man or political soldier, based on his social conduct rather than stature while adhering to the social code of the SS. Wegner, *The Waffen-SS*, 32–33.

3. Besides Theodore Eicke, there were no other witnesses to the killing of Röhm. After the war, Lippert was tried in Germany for the murder of Röhm, but there was no proof that Lippert actually killed Röhm. See Heinze Höhne, *The Order of the Death's Head: The Story of Hitler's SS*, translated from the German by Richard Barry (New York: Ballantine Books, New York: 1971), p. 144; and Charles Messenger, *Hitler's Gladiator: The Life and Wars of Panzer Army Commander Sepp Dietrich* (Conway, England: Maritime Press, 2005), 204–5.

4. Carl von Clausewitz, *On War*, Michael Howard and Peter Paret, eds., indexed ed. (Princeton: Princeton University Press, 1984), 87.

5. Gerhard L. Weinberg, "Total War; The Global Dimensions of Conflict," in Roger Chickering, Stig Förster, and Bernd Greiner, eds., *A World at Total War: Global Conflict and the Politics of Destruction, 1937–1945* (Cambridge: Cambridge University Press, 2005), 20. Hitler outlined his plan in his book *Mein Kampf*, which he wrote in prison after the failed Putsch in 1923 in Munich.

6. Charles Whiting, *The Other Battle of the Bulge: Operation Northwind* (New York: Avon Books, 1990), 125.

7. George H. Stein, *The Waffen-SS: Hitler's Elite Guard at War 1939–1945* (Ithaca, NY: Cornell University Press: 1984), 238.

Selected Bibliography

ARCHIVES

National Archives Collection of Foreign Records Seized, Record Group 242, SS Officer Service Record Files, Microfilm Publication A3343, Series SSO, 909 rolls.

———. German Military Situation Maps, Oberkommando der Wehrmacht, 1933–1945.

———. Nazi Party and SS Records, Miscellaneous SS Records: Einwandererzentralstelle, Waffen-SS, SS-Oberabschnitte, Microfilm Publication T354, 799 rolls.

———. Records of German Field Commands: Army Groups, Microfilm Publication T311, 305 rolls.

———. Records of German Field Commands: Corps, Microfilm Publication T314, 1,670 rolls.

———. Records of German Field Commands: Divisions, Microfilm Publication T315, 2,379 rolls.

———. Records of Headquarters, German Army High Command (Oberkommando des Heeres/OKH), Microfilm Publication T78, 993 rolls.

———. Records of U.S. Army, Europe, Record Group 549, Foreign Military Studies, 1945–1954, Microfiche Publication M1035.

———. SS Enlisted Men Personnel Files, Microfilm Publication A3343, Series SM, 1,738 rolls.

The National Archives, Kew, Richmond, Surrey, TW9 4DU, Great Britain, WO 171/844 11 Hussars (Prince Albert's Own) 1944 June–December.

———. WO 171/4690 11 Hussars (Prince Albert's Own) 1945 January–December.

BOOKS

Von Ahlfen, Hans. *Der Kampf um Schlesien: Ein authentischer Dokumentarbericht*. Munich: Gräfe und Unzer Verlag, 1961.

Ambrose, Stephen E. *Band of Brothers: E Company, 506th Regiment, 101st Airborne from Normandy to Hitler's Eagle's Nest*. New York: Simon and Schuster, 1992.

Angolia, John R. *For Führer and Fatherland: Military Awards of the Third Reich*, 3rd ed. San Jose, CA: R. James Bender Publishing, 1976.

Armstrong, Richard N. *Soviet Operational Deception: The Red Cloak*. Fort Leavenworth, KS: Combat Studies Institute, 1988.

Bartov, Omer. *Hitler's Army: Soldiers, Nazis, and War in the Third Reich*. New York: Oxford University Press, 1991.

Berndt, Eberhard. *Die Kämpfe um Weißenberg und Bautzen im April 1945*. Eggolsheim: Dörfler Verlag, 2012.

Blumenson, Martin. *United States Army in World War II: The European Theater of Operations, Breakout and Pursuit*. Washington, DC: Government Printing Office, 1989.

Brunnegger, Herbert. *Saat in den Sturm: Ein Soldat der Waffen SS berichtet*. Graz, Austria: Leopold Stocker Verlag, 2000.

Caldwell, Donald L. *JG26: Top Guns of the Luftwaffe*. New York: Orion Books, 2001.

Carell, Paul. *Verbrannte Erde: Schlacht zwischen Wolga und Weichsel*. Frankfurt/M-Berlin: Verlag Ullstein GmbH, 1966.

Cerff, Karl. *Die Waffen-SS im Wehrmachtbericht*. Osnabrück: Munin Verlag, 1971.

Chamberlain, Peter, and Hilary Doyle. *Encyclopedia of German Tanks of World War Two: A Complete Illustrated Directory of German Battle Tanks, Armoured Cars, Self-Propelled Guns and Semi-Tracked Vehicles, 1933–1945*, revised ed. London: Arms and Armour Press, 1993.

Chickering, Roger, Stig Förster, and Bernd Greiner, eds. *A World at Total War: Global Conflict and the Politics of Destruction, 1937–1945*. Cambridge: Cambridge University Press, 2005.

Clarke, Jeffrey J., and Robert Ross Smith. *United States Army in World War II: The European Theater of Operations, Riviera to the Rhine*. Washington, DC: Government Printing Office, 1993.

Clausewitz, Carl von. *On War*. Michael Howard and Peter Paret, eds., indexed ed. Princeton: Princeton University Press, 1984.

Cole, Hugh M. *United States Army in World War II: The European Theater of Operations: The Ardennes, Battle of the Bulge*. Washington, DC: Government Printing Office, 1965.

Craven, Wesley Frank, James Lea Cate, eds., and the USAF Historical Division. *The Army Air Forces in World War II. Volume Three Europe: Argument to V-E Day January 1944 to May 1945*. Chicago: University of Chicago Press, 1951.

Crowl, Philip A., and Peter Paret, eds. *Makers of Modern Strategy: From Machiavelli to the Nuclear Age*. Princeton: Princeton University Press, 1986.

D'Este, Carlo. *Decision in Normandy*, fiftieth anniversary ed. New York: HarperCollins Publishers, 1994.

Federal Research Division and Glenn E. Curtis (ed.). *Poland: A Country Study*, 3rd ed., Library of Congress. Washington, DC: Government Printing Office, 1994.

Fellgiebel, Walther-Peer. *Die Träger des Ritterkreuzes des Eisernen Kreuzes 1939–1945: Die Inhaber der höchsten Auszeichnung des Zweiten Weltkrieges aller Wehrmachtteile*. Friedberg: Podzun-Pallas, 2000.

Fey, Will. *Panzer im Brennpunkt der Fronten*. Munich: J. F. Lehmanns Verlag, 1960.

Fürbringer, Herbert. *9.SS-Panzer-Division "Hohenstaufen" 1944: Normandie-Tarnopol-Arnheim*. Heimdal: Editions Heimdal, 1984.

Gätzschmann, Kurt. *Sieg und Niederlage: Zeitzeuge der Panzertruppe 1935–1945*. Fredericksburg, VA: Stenger Historica Publishing, 2001.

Gemeinschaftsarbeit des SS-Kriegsberichter-Zuges der 10.SS-Panzer-Div. "Frundsberg," *Dran Drauf und Durch! Buczacz-Caen-Nimwegen*, 1944.

Gill, H. A., III. *Soldier Under Three Flags: The Exploits of Special Forces Captain Larry A. Thorne*. Ventura: Pathfinder Publishing of California, 1998.

Glantz, David M. *Soviet Military Operational Art: In Pursuit of Deep Battle*. London: Frank Cass and Company Limited, 1991.

Glantz, David M., and Jonathan House. *When Titans Clash: How the Red Army Stopped Hitler*. Lawrence: University Press of Kansas, 1995.

Goldensohn, Leon. *The Nuremberg Interviews*. Robert Gellately, ed. New York: Alfred A. Knopf, 2004.

Graber, G. S. *The History of the SS*. New York: David McKay Company, Inc., 1978.

Grass, Günter. *Die Blechtrommel*, 6th ed. Munich: Deutscher Taschenbuch Verlag, 1997.

Greiner, Helmuth, and Percy Ernst Schramm. *Kriegstagebuch des Oberkommandos der Wehrmacht (Wehrmachtführungsstab): 1940–1945*. Vols. 1–8. München: Bernard & Graefe Verlag, 1982.

Hausser, Paul. *Soldaten Wie Andere Auch*. Osnabrück: Munin Verlag, 1966.

Höhne, Heinz. *The Order of the Death's Head: The Story of Hitler's SS*, translated from the German by Richard Barry, New York: Ballantine Books, 1971.

How, Major J. J. *Hill 112: Cornerstone of the Normandy Campaign*. Winnipeg: J. J. Fedorowicz Publishing, 2004.

Hughes, Daniel J., ed. *Moltke: On the Art of War. Selected Writings*, translated by Harry Bell and Daniel J. Hughes. Novato, CA: Presidio Press, 1993.

Jones, Archer. *The Art of War in the Western World.* Chicago: University of Illinois Press, 1987.

Klapdor, Ewald. *Die Entscheidung: Invasion 1944.* Siek: privately printed, 1984.

Kleine, Egon, and Volkmar Kühn. *Tiger: Die Geschichte einer legendären Waffe 1942–45*, 2nd ed. Stuttgart: Motorbuch Verlag, 1976.

Kommissions-Verlag Friederichsen. *Lohn der Tat: Die Auszeichnungen des Heeres.* Hamburg: Verlag C. Pahl & Co.; new and rev. reprint, Nürnberg: Verlag-Kienseberger, 2000.

Konev, I. *Year of Victory.* David Mishne, transl., second printing. USSR: Progress Publishers, 1984.

Krätschmer, Ernst-Günther. *Die Ritterkreuzträger der Waffen-SS*, 4. ergänzte Auflage (fourth revised ed.). Coburg: Nation Europa Verlag GmbH, 1999.

Kramp, Hans. *Rurfront 1944/45: Zweite Schlacht am Hubertuskreuz zwischen Wurm, Rur, und Inde*, 2nd ed. Geilenkirchen: Verlag Fred Gatzen, 1981.

Langdon, Allen. *"Ready": The History of the 505th Parachute Infantry Regiment, 82nd Airborne Division, World War II.* Indianapolis: Western Newspaper Publishing Co., Inc., 1986.

Littlejohn, David. *The Hitler Youth.* Columbia, SC: Agincourt Publishers, 1988.

Lucas, James. *Das Reich: The Military Role of the 2nd SS Division.* London: Arms and Armour Press, 1991.

Lucia, Christian. *Von Kausche bis Ressen: Wege eines Ausbruchs im April 1945*, digital print. Welzow: 2000.

van Lunteren, Frank. *The Battle of the Bridges: The 504 Parachute Infantry Regiment in Operation Market Garden.* Havertown, PA: Casemate Publishers, 2014.

Luther, Craig W. H. *Blood and Honor: The History of the 12th SS Panzer Division "Hitler Youth," 1943–1945.* San Jose, CA: R. James Bender Publishing, 1987.

MacDonald, Charles B. *United States Army in World War II: The European Theater of Operations, The Siegfried Line Campaign.* Washington, DC: Government Printing Office, 1963.

———. *United States Army in World War II: The European Theater of Operations, The Last Offensive.* Washington, DC: Government Printing Office, 1993.

von Manstein, Erich. *Verlorene Siege.* Bonn: Athenäum-Verlag Junker und Dünnhaupt KG, 1955; reprint, Bonn: Athenäum-Verlag, 1957.

Messenger, Charles. *Hitler's Gladiator: The Life and Wars of Panzer Army Commander Sepp Dietrich.* Conway, England: Maritime Press, 2005.

Meyer, Hubert. *Kriegsgeschichte der 12.SS-Panzerdivision "Hitlerjugend,"* vol. 1, 4th ed. Coburg: Nation Europa Verlag GmbH, 1999.

Middlebrook, Martin. *Arnhem 1944: The Airborne Battle.* Boulder, CO: Westview Press, 1994.

Muschell, James E. *From Bloody Herrlisheim to a Slave Labor Camp.* Cheboygan, MI: United Associates, 2005.

Nauroth, Holger. *Stukageschwader 2 Immelmann: Eine Dokumentation über das erfolgreichste deutsche Stukageschwader.* Preußisch Oldendorf: Verlag K. W. Schütz, 1988.

von Neumann von Schmiedeberg von Winckler, Will-Feodor, and Dieter Stenger. *Fahnenjunker Frontbewährung: The Eyewitness Account of a German Officer Candidate on the Eastern Front 1943–1944.* Spotsylvania, VA: Stenger Historica Publishing, 2000.

Nordyke, Phil. *All American All the Way: The Combat History of the 82nd Airborne Division in World War II.* St. Paul, MN: Zenith Press, 2005.

Rigg, Bryan Mark. *Hitler's Jewish Soldiers: The Untold Story of Nazi Racial Laws and Men of Jewish Descent in the German Military,.* Lawrence: University Press of Kansas, 2002.

Robinson, J. H., ed. *Readings in European History*, 2 vols. Boston: Ginn, 1906.

Scherzer, Veit. *Die Ritterkreuzträger: 1939–1945 Die Inhaber des Ritterkreuzes des Eisernen Kreuzes 1939 von Heer, Luftwaffe, Kriegsmarine, Waffen-SS, Volkssturm sowie mit Deutschland verbündeter Streitkräfte nach den Unterlagen des Bundesarchives.* Jena: Scherzers Militaer-Verlag, 2007.

von Senger u. Etterlin, Dr. F. M. *Die Panzer-Grenadiere: Geschichte u. Gestalt der mechanisierten Infanterie 1930–1960*. München: J. F. Lehmanns Verlag, 1961.

———. *Die deutschen Geschütze 1939–1945*. München: J. F. Lehmanns Verlag, 1961.

———. *German Tanks of World War II: The Complete Illustrated History of German Armoured Vehicles 1926–1945*. New York: Galahad Books, 1969.

Shirer, William L. *The Rise and Fall of the Third Reich: A History of Nazi Germany*, reprint. New York: Simon and Schuster Inc., 1960.

Singlaub, Major General John K., and Malcolm McConnell. *Hazardous Duty: An American Soldier in the Twentieth Century*. New York: Summit Books, 1991.

Snyder, Louis L. *Encyclopedia of the Third Reich*, paperback ed. New York: Paragon House Publishers, 1989 (orig. New York: McGraw-Hill, Inc., 1976).

Spielberger, Walter J. *Sturmgeschütz & Its Variants*. James C. Cable, trans. Atglen: Schiffer Publishing Ltd., 1993.

Stein, George H. *The Waffen-SS: Hitler's Elite Guard at War 1939–1945*, paperback ed. Ithaca: Cornell University Press, 1984.

Steiner, Felix. *Die Freiwilligen Der Waffen-SS: Idee und Opferung*. Oldenburg: Verlag K.W. Schültz KG; reprint with introduction by Sam Sloan, New York: Ishi Press, 2011.

———. *Die Armee der Geächteten*. First published in 1963. Reprint with introduction by Sam Sloan. New York: Ishi Press, 2011.

Stockert, Peter. *Die Eichenlaubträger 1940–1945*, 4 vols. Bad Friedrichshall: Friedrichshaller Rundblick, 1996.

Tieke, Wilhelm. *In the Firestorm of the Last Years of War: II.SS-Panzerkorps wih the 9. and 10.SS-Divisions "Hohenstaufen" and "Frundsberg,"* Frederick Steinhardt, trans. Winnipeg: J.J. Fedorowicz Publishing, 1999.

———. *Das Ende Zwischen Oder und Elbe: Der Kampf um Berlin 1945*, second printing. Stuttgart: Motor Buch Verlag, 1992.

Urquhart, Robert Elliott. *Arnhem: Britain's Infamous Airborne Assault of WWII*. Los Angeles: Royal Publishing Company, 1995.

U.S. War Department. *Handbook on German Military Forces*, with an introduction by Stephen E. Ambrose. Baton Rouge: Louisiana State University Press, 1990.

Walker, Marianne G. *A Burning Desire to Be Free*. Danbury, CT: Rutledge Books Inc., 1998.

Webster, David Kenyon. *Parachute Infantry: An American Paratrooper's Memoir of D-Day and the Fall of the Third Reich*. New York: Random House, Inc. 1994.

Wegner, Bernd. *The Waffen-SS: Organization, Ideology and Function*, Ronald Webster, trans. (Paderborn: Ferdinand Schoningh, 1982), English translation copy, Oxford: Basil Blackwell, Ltd., 1990.

Weigley, Russell F. *Eisenhower's Lieutenants: The Campaign of France and Germany, 1944–1945*. Bloomington: Indiana University Press, 1981.

Weinberg, Gerhard L. *A World at Arms: A Global History of World War II*. New York: Cambridge University Press, 2004.

Whiting, Charles. *The Other Battle of the Bulge: Operation Northwind*. New York: Avon Books, 1990.

Widmann, Franz. *Mit "Totenkopf" und "Frundsberg" und Ost-und Westfront: Kriegserlebnisse eines Kradmelders*. Riesa: Nation und Wissen, 2011.

Williamson, Gordon. *Loyalty Is My Honor: Personal Accounts from the Waffen-SS*. Osceola, WI: Motorbooks International Publishers and Wholesalers, 1995.

Zabecki, David T. *Steel Wind: Colonel Georg Bruchmüller and the Birth of Modern Artillery*. Westport, CT: Praeger Publishers, 1994.

Zetterling, Nicholas. *Normandy 1944: German Military Organization, Combat Power and Organizational Effectiveness*. Winnipeg: J.J. Fedorowicz Publishing, 2000.

Ziemke, Earl F. *Stalingrad to Berlin: The German Defeat in the East*, first printed 1968, CMH Pub 30-5. Washington, DC: Government Printing Office, 1987.

INTERNET SOURCES

Lexikon der Wehrmacht, www.lexikon-der-wehrmacht.de.

Meschenmoser, Dr. Helmut. "Reiseerlebnisse von Alfred Meschenmoser: Eisenbahnfahrten von 1941 bis in die 50er Jahre," Landesbildstelle Berlin, 2000, www.bics.be.schule.de/son/verkehr/eisenbah/augen/amesch/index.htm.

INTERVIEWS AND CORRESPONDENCE

von Boeselager, Philipp, Freiherr. Correspondence dated 28 March 2000.

Ebersprächer, Helmut. 10th Fast Attack Squadron, correspondence dated 2004.

Egger, Paul. 501st SS Heavy Panzer Battalion, correspondence dated 15 July 2001.

Ewald, Klaus. 12th SS Panzer Division, correspondence dated 7 July 2005.

Fransky, Gerhard. 10th SS Panzer Signal Battalion, correspondence dated 2004.

Grenda, Alexander. Interview by Dieter Stenger, March 2004, interview transcript. Stenger Interview Archive, Spotsylvania, VA.

Heck, Erwin. 10th SS Panzer Regiment, correspondence dated 7 May 2000.

Jacob, Otto. 10th SS Panzer Artillery Regiment, correspondence dated 2001. Interviews dated 30 and 31 January 2005.

Meyer, Hubert. 1st General Staff Officer, 12th SS Panzer Division, correspondence dated 28 March 2001.

Pietzka, Werner. 6th Company, 10th SS Panzer Regiment, correspondence dated 2001 and 2004. Interviews dated 30 and 31 January 2005.

Westerhoff, Bernhard. 6th Company, 10th SS Panzer Regiment, correspondence dated 2001. Interviews dated 30 and 31 January 2005.

PERIODICALS

Boeselager, Philipp, Freiherr von. "Der Widerstand in der Heeresgruppe Mitte." No. 40, *Beiträge zum Widerstand 1933–1945, Gedenkstätte Deutscher Widerstand Berlin*, 1990.

Center for Military Studies. *Normandy: The U.S. Army Campaigns of World War II.* CMH Publication 720-18, Washington, DC: Government Printing Office, 1995.

Munin Verlag GmbH. *Der Freiwillige.* 51st Year, 4th ed., 2005.

Stenger, Dieter. "To the Bitter End: The German MP44/StG44 Assault Rifle." *Army History.* PB 20-15-3, Summer, No. 96, 2015.

Suchdienst Frundsberg eV. *Die Hellebarde: Nachrichten der Kameradschaftsverein Suchdienst Frundsberg* (various issues).

Tholte, Karl. "A German Reflects Upon Artillery." *The Field Artillery Journal.* 709–15, December 1945.

Zabecki, David T. "Germany's Strategic Crapshoot." *Military History.* Battle of the Bulge 70th Anniversary Special Issue, Winter, 2015.

Zabecki, David T., and Keith Wooster. "Death of an American Combat Command," in *World War II.* Leesburg, VA: Weider History Group, 1999.

UNPUBLISHED MANUSCRIPTS

Bittrich, Wilhelm. *The II.SS-Pz.A.K. in September until November 1944.* Foreign Military Studies, MS # P-155, 1954.

Doerffler-Schuband, General Major. *Officer Procurement in the Waffen-SS: Reception, Processing, and Training.* Foreign Military Studies, MS # D-178, 1954.

Gerhard, Hermann Max. *My Life in the Middle of the 20th Century,* 1997.

von Gersdorff, Rudolf-Christoph Freiherr. *The Campaign in Northern France, Vol. VI: Falaise–Argentan Pocket 12–21 August.* Foreign Military Studies, MS # B-727, 1946.

Harmel, Heinz. *Die 10.SS Panzer-Division "Frundsberg" im Einsatz vom Juni bis November 1944.* Foreign Military Studies, MS # P-163, 1954.

———. *Fragen zur Ardennen-Offensive.* Foreign Military Studies, MS # P-109f, 1951.

Harzer, Walter. *9th Panzer Division (SS) "Hohenstaufen," July 25–November 1944, on the Western Front.* Foreign Military Studies, MS # P-162, 1954.

Jolasse, Erwin. *Employment of the 9th Panzer Division in October/November 1944*, Foreign Military Studies, MS #P-161, 1954.

Joshua, Rick D. "Tarnished Warriors: The Waffen-SS And Popular Misconception." Thesis, Brunel University, 1994.

Juhl, Johannes. *Als Pionier an der Westfront 1944/1945: Mein Kriegseinsatz als junger Soldat. Johannes Juhl, Jahrgang 1926.*

Kriegstagebuch 1944 *SS-Werfer-Abteilung 102: Kriegstagebuch Nr.2.* Bernhardt Westerhoff Archive. Not Dated.

Kriegstagebuch SS-Panzer-Grenadier-Regiment 21 "Frundsberg." Welzow: Private Archive Daniel Popielas, 2010.

Müller-Hillebrand, Burkhart. *1. Fallschirmarmee: August bis September 1944.* Foreign Military Studies, MS # P-154, 1954.

Pionier Kameradschaft "Dresden." *10.SS-Panzer-Div. "Frundsberg": Chronik der Pioniereinheiten der 10.SS-PzDiv "Frundsberg,"* 1990.

Westerhoff, Bernhard. *Weg einer Panzer-Kompanie 1943–1945: 6.Kompanie SS-Panzer-Regiment 10 "Frundsberg,"* 1986.

Westerhoff, Bernhard, and Karl Schneider. *Geschichte einer Panzer-Kompanie im Elsaß: 6 Kompanie SS Pz.-Rgt. 10 "Frundsberg" Winter 1944–1945.* Not Dated.

von Zangen, Gustav. *Die 15.Armee im Abwehrkampf an Roer und Rhein, 22.11.44 bis 9.3.45*, Foreign Military Studies, MS # B-811, 1947.

Index

About the Author

Dieter Stenger completed his undergraduate degree at Framingham State College in Massachusetts. After the U.S.-led Coalition Forces liberated Kuwait in January 1991, Stenger enlisted in the U.S. Marine Corps. After deploying with the I Marine Expeditionary Force and serving as an instructor at the Amphibious Assault School, he left the Marine Corps after six years with an honorable discharge. Continuing to serve as a civil servant in the historical museum field for the next eighteen years, Stenger has written and published extensively on material culture for the U.S. Marine Corps and Army. For almost two decades Stenger has provided research services for archival material and German to English translation services, servicing all archival holdings in the DC Metro area. Having served the federal government for more than twenty-five years, Stenger is considered a subject matter expert in German military history and currently is the Chief of Arms and Ordnance, U.S. Army Museum Enterprise, U.S. Army Center of Military History.